YBM
실전토익
LC1000

3

YBM
실전토익
LC 1000 3

발행인 권오찬
발행처 YBM

문항 개발 Marilyn Hook
편집 이혜진
디자인 이현숙
마케팅 전경진, 정연철, 박천산, 고영노, 박찬경, 김동진, 김윤하

초판 발행 2021년 1월 4일
2쇄 발행 2021년 2월 5일

신고일자 1964년 3월 28일
신고번호 제 300-1964-3호
주소 서울시 종로구 종로 104
전화 (02) 2000-0515 [구입문의] / (02) 2000-0436 [내용문의]
팩스 (02) 2285-1523
홈페이지 www.ybmbooks.com

ISBN 978-89-17-23816-7

저작권자 © 2021 YBM
이 책의 저작권, 책의 제호 및 디자인에 대한 모든 권리는 출판사인 YBM에게 있습니다.
서면에 의한 저자와 출판사의 허락 없이 내용의 일부 혹은 전부를 인용 및 복제하거나 발췌하는 것을 금합니다.

낙장 및 파본은 교환해 드립니다.
구입철회는 구매처 규정에 따라 교환 및 환불처리 됩니다.

토익 주관사가 제시하는 진짜 토익
YBM 실전토익 LC 1000 3을 발행하며

지난 30여 년간 우리나라에서 토익 시험을 주관하면서 토익 시장을 이끌고, 꾸준히 베스트셀러를 출간해 온 YBM에서 〈YBM 실전토익 LC 1000 3〉을 출간하게 되었습니다.

YBM 토익은 이렇게 다릅니다!

YBM의 명성에 자부심을 가지고 개발했습니다!

YBM은 지난 1982년부터 우리나라의 토익 시험을 주관해온 토익 주관사로서, 지난 30여 년간 400여 권의 토익 베스트셀러를 출판해왔습니다. 그 오랜 시간 토익 문제를 분석하고 교재를 출판하면서 쌓아온 전문성과 실력으로 이번에 〈YBM 실전토익 LC 1000 3〉을 선보이게 되었습니다.

토익 주관사로서의 사명감을 가지고 개발했습니다!

토익 주관사로서 사명감을 갖고 최신 경향을 철저히 분석하여 〈YBM 실전토익 LC 1000 3〉을 개발하였습니다. 실제 시험과 가장 유사한 고난도 문제를 다수 수록하였고, 핵심 출제 포인트를 해설집에 상세히 담았습니다.

ETS 교재를 출간한 노하우를 가지고 개발했습니다!

출제기관 ETS의 토익 교재를 독점 출간하는 YBM은 그동안 쌓아온 노하우를 바탕으로 〈YBM 실전토익 LC 1000 3〉을 개발하였습니다. 본 책에 실린 1000개의 문항은 출제자의 의도를 정확히 반영하였기 때문에 타사의 어떤 토익 교재와도 비교할 수 없는 퀄리티를 자랑합니다.

YBM의 모든 노하우가 집대성된 〈YBM 실전토익 LC 1000 3〉은 최단 시간에 최고의 점수를 수험자 여러분께 약속 드립니다.

YBM 토익연구소

토익의 구성과 수험 정보

TOEIC은 어떤 시험인가요?

Test of English for International Communication(국제적 의사소통을 위한 영어 시험)의 약자로서, 영어가 모국어가 아닌 사람들이 일상생활 또는 비즈니스 현장에서 꼭 필요한 실용적 영어 구사 능력을 갖추었는가를 평가하는 시험이다.

시험 구성

구성	Part	내용		문항수	시간	배점
듣기 (L/C)	1	사진 묘사		6	45분	495점
	2	질의 & 응답		25		
	3	짧은 대화		39		
	4	짧은 담화		30		
읽기 (R/C)	5	단문 빈칸 채우기(문법/어휘)		30	75분	495점
	6	장문 빈칸 채우기		16		
	7	독해	단일 지문	29		
			이중 지문	10		
			삼중 지문	15		
Total		7 Parts		200문항	120분	990점

TOEIC 접수는 어떻게 하나요?

TOEIC 접수는 한국 토익 위원회 사이트(www.toeic.co.kr)에서 온라인 상으로만 접수가 가능하다. 사이트에서 매월 자세한 접수 일정과 시험 일정 등의 구체적 정보 확인이 가능하니, 미리 일정을 확인하여 접수하도록 한다.

시험장에 반드시 가져가야 할 준비물은요?

신분증 규정 신분증만 가능
(주민등록증, 운전면허증, 기간 만료 전의 여권, 공무원증 등)

필기구 연필, 지우개 (볼펜이나 사인펜은 사용 금지)

시험은 어떻게 진행되나요?

09:20	입실 (09:50 이후는 입실 불가)
09:30 – 09:45	답안지 작성에 관한 오리엔테이션
09:45 – 09:50	휴식
09:50 – 10:05	신분증 확인
10:05 – 10:10	문제지 배부 및 파본 확인
10:10 – 10:55	듣기 평가 (Listening Test)
10:55 – 12:10	독해 평가 (Reading Test)

TOEIC 성적 확인은 어떻게 하죠?

시험일로부터 12일 후 인터넷과 ARS(060-800-0515)로 성적을 확인할 수 있다. TOEIC 성적표는 우편이나 온라인으로 발급 받을 수 있다(시험 접수시, 양자 택일). 우편으로 발급 받을 경우는 성적 발표 후 대략 일주일이 소요되며, 온라인 발급을 선택하면 유효기간 내에 홈페이지에서 본인이 직접 1회에 한해 무료 출력할 수 있다. TOEIC 성적은 시험일로부터 2년간 유효하다.

TOEIC은 몇 점 만점인가요?

TOEIC 점수는 듣기 영역(LC) 점수, 읽기 영역(RC) 점수, 그리고 이 두 영역을 합계한 전체 점수 세 부분으로 구성된다. 각 부분의 점수는 5점 단위이며, 5점에서 495점에 걸쳐 주어지고, 전체 점수는 10점에서 990점까지이며, 만점은 990점이다. TOEIC 성적은 각 문제 유형의 난이도에 따른 점수 환산표에 의해 결정된다.

토익 경향 분석

PART 1 사진 묘사 Photographs

총 6문제

사람 또는
사물 중심 사진
33%

1인
등장 사진
33%

**PART 1
최신 출제 경향**

사물/
배경 사진
17%

2인 이상
등장 사진
17%

1인 등장 사진
주어는 He/She, A man/woman 등이며 주로
앞부분에 나온다.

2인 이상 등장 사진
주어는 They, Some men/women/people,
One of the men/women 등이며 주로
중간 부분에 나온다.

사물/배경 사진
주어는 A car, some chairs 등이며 주로 뒷부분에
나온다.

사람 또는 사물 중심 사진
주어가 일부는 사람, 일부는 사물이며 주로 뒷부분에
나온다.

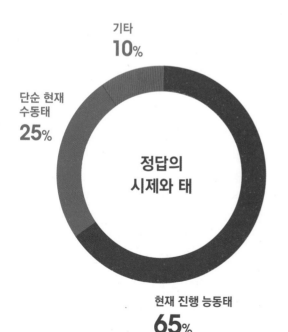

기타
10%

단순 현재
수동태
25%

**정답의
시제와 태**

현재 진행 능동태
65%

현재 진행 능동태
〈is/are + 현재분사〉 형태이며 주로 사람이 주어이다.

단순 현재 수동태
〈is/are + 과거분사〉 형태이며 주로 사물이 주어이다.

기타
〈is/are + being + 과거분사〉 형태의 현재 진행 수동
태, 〈has/have + been + 과거 분사〉 형태의 현재 완
료 수동태, '타동사 + 목적어' 형태의 단순 현재 능동태,
There is/are와 같은 단순 현재도 나온다.

PART 2 질의 & 응답 Question-Response

평서문
질문이 아니라 객관적인 사실이나 화자의 의견 등을 나타내는 문장이다.

명령문
동사원형이나 Please 등으로 시작한다.

의문사 의문문
각 의문사마다 1~2개씩 나온다. 의문사가 단독으로 나오기도 하지만 What time ~?, How long ~?, Which room ~? 등에서처럼 다른 명사나 형용사와 같이 나오기도 한다.

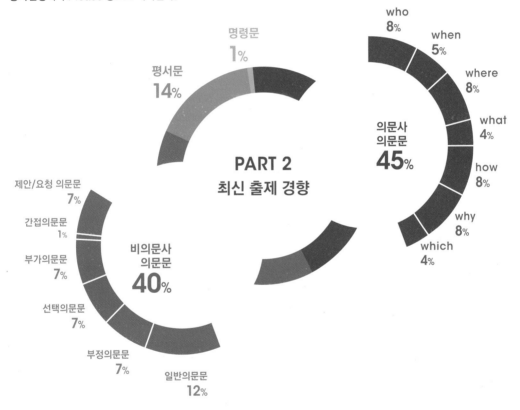

PART 2
최신 출제 경향

명령문 **1**%
평서문 **14**%
who **8**%
when **5**%
where **8**%
what **4**%
의문사 의문문 **45**%
how **8**%
why **8**%
which **4**%
비의문사 의문문 **40**%
제안/요청 의문문 **7**%
간접의문문 **1**%
부가의문문 **7**%
선택의문문 **7**%
부정의문문 **7**%
일반의문문 **12**%

비의문사 의문문
일반(Yes/No) 의문문 적게 나올 때는 한두 개, 많이 나올 때는 서너 개씩 나오는 편이다.
부정의문문 Don't you ~?, Isn't he ~? 등으로 시작하는 문장이며 일반 긍정 의문문보다는 약간 더 적게 나온다.
선택의문문 A or B 형태로 나오며 A와 B의 형태가 단어, 구, 절일 수 있다. 구나 절일 경우 문장이 길어져서 어려워진다.
부가의문문 ~ don't you?, ~ isn't he? 등으로 끝나는 문장이며, 일반 부정 의문문과 비슷하다고 볼 수 있다.
간접의문문 의문사가 문장 처음 부분이 아니라 문장 중간에 들어 있다.
제안/요청 의문문 정보를 얻기보다는 상대방의 도움이나 동의 등을 얻기 위한 목적이 일반적이다.

PART 3 짧은 대화 Short Conversations

총 13대화문 39문제 (지문당 3문제)

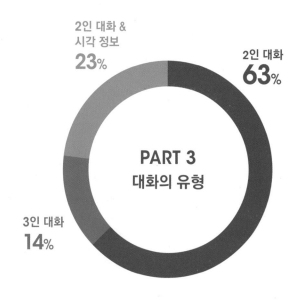

PART 3
대화의 유형

2인 대화 & 시각 정보 **23**%

2인 대화 **63**%

3인 대화 **14**%

- 3인 대화의 경우 남자 화자 두 명과 여자 화자 한 명 또는 남자 화자 한 명과 여자 화자 두 명이 나온다. 따라서 문제에서는 2인 대화에서와 달리 the man이나 the woman이 아니라 the men이나 the women 또는 특정한 이름이 언급될 수 있다.

- 대화 & 시각 정보는 항상 파트의 뒷부분에 나온다.

- 시각 정보의 유형으로 chart, map, floor plan, schedule, table, weather forecast, directory, list, invoice, receipt, sign, packing slip 등 다양한 자료가 골고루 나온다.

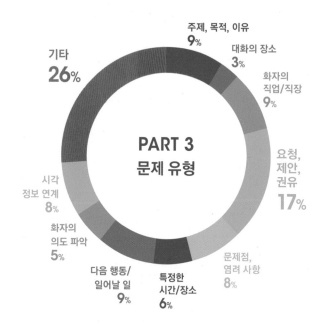

PART 3
문제 유형

주제, 목적, 이유 **9**%

대화의 장소 **3**%

화자의 직업/직장 **9**%

요청, 제안, 권유 **17**%

문제점, 염려 사항 **8**%

특정한 시간/장소 **6**%

다음 행동/일어날 일 **9**%

화자의 의도 파악 **5**%

시각 정보 연계 **8**%

기타 **26**%

- 주제, 목적, 이유, 대화의 장소, 화자의 직업/직장 등과 관련된 문제는 주로 대화의 첫 번째 문제로 나오며 다음 행동/일어날 일 등과 관련된 문제는 주로 대화의 세 번째 문제로 나온다.

- 화자의 의도 파악 문제는 주로 2인 대화에 나오지만, 가끔 3인 대화에 나오기도 한다. 시각 정보 연계 대화에는 나오지 않고 있다.

- Part 3 안에서 화자의 의도 파악 문제는 2개 나오고 시각 정보 연계 문제는 3개 나온다.

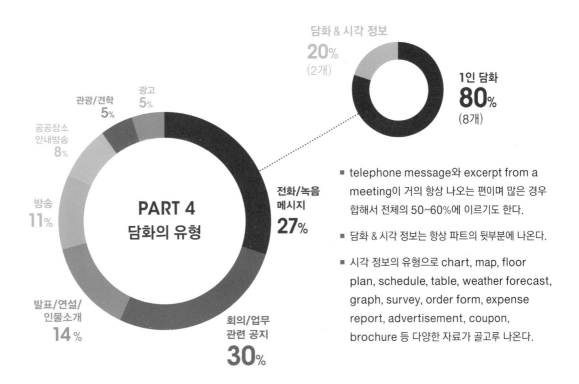

- telephone message와 excerpt from a meeting이 거의 항상 나오는 편이며 많은 경우 합해서 전체의 50~60%에 이르기도 한다.
- 담화 & 시각 정보는 항상 파트의 뒷부분에 나온다.
- 시각 정보의 유형으로 chart, map, floor plan, schedule, table, weather forecast, graph, survey, order form, expense report, advertisement, coupon, brochure 등 다양한 자료가 골고루 나온다.

- 문제 유형은 기본적으로 Part 3과 거의 비슷하다.
- 주제, 목적, 이유, 담화의 장소, 화자나 청자의 직업/직장 등과 관련된 문제는 주로 담화의 첫 번째 문제로 나오며 다음 행동/일어날 일 등과 관련된 문제는 주로 담화의 세 번째 문제로 나온다.
- Part 4 안에서 화자의 의도 파악 문제는 3개 나오고 시각 정보 연계 문제는 2개 나온다.

토익 경향 분석

PART 5 단문 빈칸 채우기 Incomplete Sentences

문법 문제

시제와 대명사와 관련된 문법 문제가 2개씩, 한정사와 분사와 관련된 문법 문제가 1개씩 나온다. 시제 문제의 경우 능동태/수동태나 수의 일치와 연계되기도 한다. 그 밖에 한정사, 능동태/수동태, 부정사, 동명사 등과 관련된 문법 문제가 나온다.

어휘 문제

동사, 명사, 형용사, 부사와 관련된 어휘 문제가 각각 2~3개씩 골고루 나온다. 전치사 어휘 문제는 3개씩 꾸준히 나오지만, 접속사나 어구와 관련된 어휘 문제는 나오지 않을 때도 있고 3개가 나올 때도 있다.

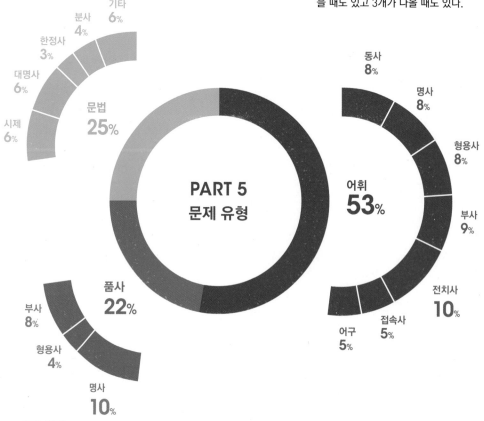

품사 문제

명사와 부사와 관련된 품사 문제가 2~3개씩 나오며, 형용사와 관련된 품사 문제가 상대적으로 적은 편이다.

PART 6 장문 빈칸 채우기 Text Completion

한 지문에 4문제가 나오며 평균적으로 어휘 문제가 2개, 품사나 문법 문제가 1개, 문맥에 맞는 문장 고르기 문제가 1개 들어간다. 문맥에 맞는 문장 고르기 문제를 제외하면 문제 유형은 기본적으로 파트 5와 거의 비슷하다.

어휘 문제
동사, 명사, 부사, 어구와 관련된 어휘 문제는 매번 1~2개씩 나온다. 부사 어휘 문제의 경우 therefore(그러므로)나 however(하지만)처럼 문맥의 흐름을 자연스럽게 연결해 주는 부사가 자주 나온다.

문맥에 맞는 문장 고르기
문맥에 맞는 문장 고르기 문제는 지문당 한 문제씩 나오는데, 나오는 위치의 확률은 4문제 중 두 번째 문제, 세 번째 문제, 네 번째 문제, 첫 번째 문제 순으로 높다.

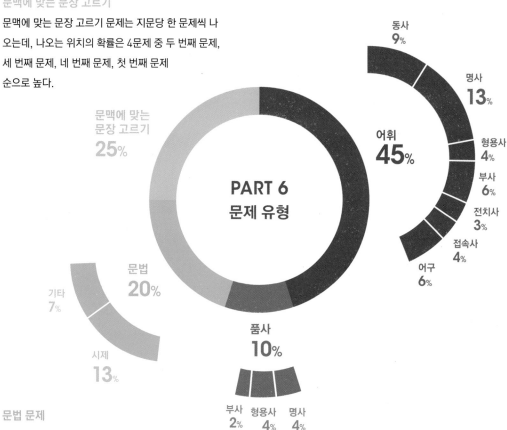

PART 6
문제 유형

동사 9%
명사 13%
형용사 4%
부사 6%
전치사 3%
접속사 4%
어구 6%
어휘 45%

문맥에 맞는 문장 고르기 25%

기타 7%
시제 13%
문법 20%

품사 10%
부사 2% 형용사 4% 명사 4%

문법 문제
문맥의 흐름과 밀접하게 관련이 있는 시제 문제가 2개 정도 나오며, 능동태/수동태나 수의 일치와 연계되기도 한다. 그 밖에 대명사, 능동태/수동태, 부정사, 접속사/전치사 등과 관련된 문법 문제가 나온다.

품사 문제
명사나 형용사 문제가 부사 문제보다 좀 더 자주 나온다.

토익 경향 분석

PART 7 독해 Reading Comprehension

총 15지문 54문제 (지문당 2~5문제)

지문 유형	지문당 문제 수	지문 개수	비중 %
단일 지문	2문항	4개	약 15%
	3문항	3개	약 16%
	4문항	3개	약 22%
이중 지문	5문항	2개	약 19%
삼중 지문	5문항	3개	약 28%

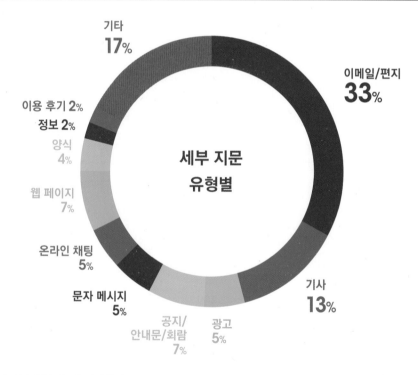

세부 지문
유형별

- 기타 **17%**
- 이메일/편지 **33%**
- 이용 후기 2%
- 정보 2%
- 양식 4%
- 웹 페이지 7%
- 온라인 채팅 5%
- 문자 메시지 5%
- 공지/안내문/회람 7%
- 광고 5%
- 기사 **13%**

■ 이메일/편지, 기사 유형 지문은 거의 항상 나오는 편이며 많은 경우 합해서 전체의 50~60%에 이르기도 한다.

■ 기타 지문 유형으로 agenda, brochure, comment card, coupon, flyer, instructions, invitation, invoice, list, menu, page from a catalog, policy statement, report, schedule, survey, voucher 등 다양한 자료가 골고루 나온다.

(이중 지문과 삼중 지문 속의 지문들을 모두 낱개로 계산함 – 총 23지문)

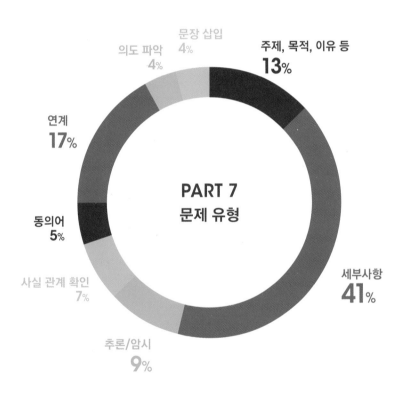

문장 삽입
4%

의도 파악
4%

주제, 목적, 이유 등
13%

연계
17%

PART 7
문제 유형

동의어
5%

세부사항
41%

사실 관계 확인
7%

추론/암시
9%

- 동의어 문제는 주로 이중 지문이나 삼중 지문에 나온다.
- 연계 문제는 일반적으로 이중 지문에서 한 문제, 삼중 지문에서 두 문제가 나온다.
- 의도 파악 문제는 문자 메시지(text-message chain)나 온라인 채팅(online chat discussion) 지문에서 출제되며 두 문제가 나온다.
- 문장 삽입 문제는 주로 기사, 이메일, 편지, 회람 지문에서 출제되며 두 문제가 나온다.

점수 환산표

LISTENING Raw Score (맞은 개수)	LISTENING Scaled Score (환산 점수)
96-100	480-495
91-95	435-490
86-90	395-450
81-85	355-415
76-80	325-375
71-75	295-340
66-70	265-315
61-65	240-285
56-60	215-260
51-55	190-235
46-50	160-210
41-45	135-180
36-40	110-155
31-35	85-130
26-30	70-105
21-25	50-90
16-20	35-70
11-15	20-55
6-10	15-40
1-5	5-20
0	5

READING Raw Score (맞은 개수)	READING Scaled Score (환산 점수)
96-100	460-495
91-95	410-475
86-90	380-430
81-85	355-400
76-80	325-375
71-75	295-345
66-70	265-315
61-65	235-285
56-60	205-255
51-55	175-225
46-50	150-195
41-45	120-170
36-40	100-140
31-35	75-120
26-30	55-100
21-25	40-80
16-20	30-65
11-15	20-50
6-10	15-35
1-5	5-20
0	5

* 이 환산표는 본 교재에 수록된 Test용으로 개발된 것이다. 이 표를 사용하여 자신의 실제 점수를 환산 점수로 전환하도록 한다. 즉, 예를 들어 Listening Test의 실제 정답 수가 61~65개이면 환산 점수는 240점에서 285점 사이가 된다. 여기서 실제 정답 수가 61개이면 환산 점수가 240점이고, 65개이면 환산 점수가 285점임을 의미하는 것은 아니다. 본 책의 Test를 위해 작성된 이 점수 환산표가 자신의 영어 실력이 어느 정도인지 대략적으로 파악하는 데 도움이 되긴 하지만, 이 표가 실제 TOEIC 성적 산출에 그대로 사용된 적은 없다는 사실을 밝혀 둔다.

CONTENTS

TEST 1

LISTENING TEST

In the Listening test, you will be asked to demonstrate how well you understand spoken English. The entire Listening test will last approximately 45 minutes. There are four parts, and directions are given for each part. You must mark your answers on the separate answer sheet. Do not write your answers in your test book.

PART 1

Directions: For each question in this part, you will hear four statements about a picture in your test book. When you hear the statements, you must select the one statement that best describes what you see in the picture. Then find the number of the question on your answer sheet and mark your answer. The statements will not be printed in your test book and will be spoken only one time.

Statement (C), "They're sitting at a table," is the best description of the picture, so you should select answer (C) and mark it on your answer sheet.

1.

2.

GO ON TO THE NEXT PAGE

3.

4.

5.

6.

GO ON TO THE NEXT PAGE ➡

PART 2

Directions: You will hear a question or statement and three responses spoken in English. They will not be printed in your test book and will be spoken only one time. Select the best response to the question or statement and mark the letter (A), (B), or (C) on your answer sheet.

7. Mark your answer on your answer sheet.

8. Mark your answer on your answer sheet.

9. Mark your answer on your answer sheet.

10. Mark your answer on your answer sheet.

11. Mark your answer on your answer sheet.

12. Mark your answer on your answer sheet.

13. Mark your answer on your answer sheet.

14. Mark your answer on your answer sheet.

15. Mark your answer on your answer sheet.

16. Mark your answer on your answer sheet.

17. Mark your answer on your answer sheet.

18. Mark your answer on your answer sheet.

19. Mark your answer on your answer sheet.

20. Mark your answer on your answer sheet.

21. Mark your answer on your answer sheet.

22. Mark your answer on your answer sheet.

23. Mark your answer on your answer sheet.

24. Mark your answer on your answer sheet.

25. Mark your answer on your answer sheet.

26. Mark your answer on your answer sheet.

27. Mark your answer on your answer sheet.

28. Mark your answer on your answer sheet.

29. Mark your answer on your answer sheet.

30. Mark your answer on your answer sheet.

31. Mark your answer on your answer sheet.

PART 3

Directions: You will hear some conversations between two or more people. You will be asked to answer three questions about what the speakers say in each conversation. Select the best response to each question and mark the letter (A), (B), (C), or (D) on your answer sheet. The conversations will not be printed in your test book and will be spoken only one time.

32. Where most likely does the man work?

(A) At an interior design firm
(B) At an apartment management office
(C) At a moving company
(D) At a hotel

33. What problem does the woman describe?

(A) An appliance is not working.
(B) A wall has been damaged.
(C) Some loud noises can be heard.
(D) Some furniture is uncomfortable.

34. What does the man ask the woman to do?

(A) Take some measurements
(B) Wait for a company representative
(C) Send him some pictures
(D) Read a set of instructions

35. Where most likely are the speakers?

(A) At a train terminal
(B) On an airplane
(C) At a restaurant
(D) At a park

36. What does the woman say has caused a problem?

(A) Some meals were not cooked properly.
(B) Some boxes have not been unpacked.
(C) A tour has too many participants.
(D) A form was filled out incorrectly.

37. What does the man ask for?

(A) A partial refund
(B) Some extra food
(C) Directions to a store
(D) A different seat assignment

38. What kind of service does the men's company provide?

(A) Advertising
(B) Catering
(C) Accounting
(D) Web design

39. Why has the woman hired the men's company?

(A) To grow her business
(B) To save money
(C) To follow a regulation
(D) To give herself more free time

40. What does the woman say about a suggestion?

(A) It has been tried before.
(B) It may not be effective.
(C) It would be expensive.
(D) It is complicated.

41. Which department does the woman most likely work in?

(A) Public Relations
(B) Human Resources
(C) Information Technology
(D) Sales and Marketing

42. What problem are the speakers discussing?

(A) A slow response time
(B) A scheduling conflict
(C) A customer complaint
(D) A missing detail

43. What does the woman recommend the man do first?

(A) Speak with his manager
(B) Check some software settings
(C) Post a correction notice
(D) Restart a machine

GO ON TO THE NEXT PAGE

44. What is the man about to do?

(A) Clean some clothing
(B) Use a sewing machine
(C) Arrange a window display
(D) Test some product samples

45. What does the woman point out about a fabric?

(A) Its color is due to special chemicals.
(B) It has been decorated with beads.
(C) Its cost has recently risen.
(D) It is lightweight.

46. What does the woman agree to do?

(A) Increase some lighting
(B) Hold a hand tool
(C) Postpone a photo session
(D) Provide some training

47. Why does the man say he comes to the bakery frequently?

(A) It is near his home.
(B) It has a pleasant atmosphere.
(C) It sells a special type of baked goods.
(D) It has convenient operating hours.

48. Why does the woman say, "these chocolate cupcakes have marshmallow frosting"?

(A) To point out a mistake on a label
(B) To propose an alternative purchase
(C) To express surprise at a suggestion
(D) To explain a pricing decision

49. What does the woman offer the man?

(A) A onetime discount
(B) A list of the ingredients in a recipe
(C) A chance to attend a tasting session
(D) A takeout container

50. Where do the speakers most likely work?

(A) At a construction company
(B) At a warehouse
(C) At a farm
(D) At a car repair shop

51. What has caused a problem?

(A) Some packages have been misplaced.
(B) Some roads are closed.
(C) A staff member is out sick.
(D) A vehicle has broken down.

52. What does the woman say she will do?

(A) Work overtime today
(B) Put up a warning sign
(C) Conduct a safety inspection
(D) Contact another company

53. Who most likely is Ms. Lee?

(A) A journalist
(B) A city official
(C) A travel agent
(D) A researcher

54. What does the man say about the construction of a train line?

(A) It caused him to be late.
(B) It will take many years to complete.
(C) It will relieve crowding in other lines.
(D) It has shortened his commute.

55. What does Ms. Lee ask the man to do next?

(A) Show her a ticket
(B) Watch a video clip
(C) Sit down at a table
(D) Sign a document

56. What most likely is the mission of the speakers' organization?

(A) To educate children
(B) To take care of animals
(C) To protect the environment
(D) To support the arts

57. What does the man say he will do soon?

(A) Earn a degree
(B) Move away
(C) Take a vacation
(D) Donate some supplies

58. What does the woman mean when she says, "You've been an excellent volunteer"?

(A) She is happy to fulfill the man's request.
(B) She is sorry that the man is quitting.
(C) She is surprised by the man's mistake.
(D) She is pleased that the man will become more involved.

59. What are the speakers discussing?

(A) A promotion
(B) A career fair
(C) An interview
(D) A transfer

60. What does the woman say she has been doing?

(A) Collecting some records
(B) Processing some applications
(C) Communicating with some recruiters
(D) Replacing some equipment

61. What does the man give the woman?

(A) A job advertisement
(B) An applicant's résumé
(C) An employment agreement
(D) An orientation schedule

Bus Departures

Destination	Boarding Area	Time
Grammett	D	DEPARTED
Cookville	E	7:20 A.M.
Owenton	B	7:53 A.M.
Grammett	D	8:04 A.M.
Cookville	E	8:10 A.M.

62. What are the speakers going to do?

(A) Visit a factory
(B) Oversee a building project
(C) Participate in a conference
(D) Attend an awards ceremony

63. What did the woman initially forget to bring?

(A) A set of gifts
(B) A travel document
(C) Some special clothing
(D) Some presentation materials

64. Look at the graphic. When does the man suggest departing?

(A) At 7:20 A.M.
(B) At 7:53 A.M.
(C) At 8:04 A.M.
(D) At 8:10 A.M.

GO ON TO THE NEXT PAGE

Brooks Gym

Buy a class package and save!

	Total	Savings per class
5 classes	$90	$2
10 classes	$160	$4
15 classes	$210	$6
20 classes	$240	$8

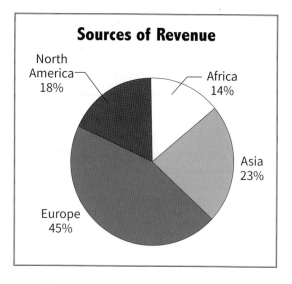

Sources of Revenue

North America 18%
Africa 14%
Asia 23%
Europe 45%

65. Where most likely did the man get the coupon?

(A) At a gym class
(B) On the street
(C) In the mail
(D) On a Web site

66. Look at the graphic. How much will the man save per class?

(A) $2
(B) $4
(C) $6
(D) $8

67. What does the woman say about the class packages?

(A) They were recently introduced.
(B) They are valid for a limited time.
(C) They are not eligible for refunds.
(D) They allow entry to any type of class.

68. Look at the graphic. Which figure does the woman say is larger than before?

(A) 14%
(B) 18%
(C) 23%
(D) 45%

69. According to the man, what does the company plan to do?

(A) Enter an additional industry
(B) Replace its chief executive
(C) Relocate its headquarters
(D) Expand into a new region

70. What does the man recommend reading?

(A) A section of a report
(B) An article on a Web page
(C) A summary of some laws
(D) An invitation to a celebration

PART 4

Directions: You will hear some talks given by a single speaker. You will be asked to answer three questions about what the speaker says in each talk. Select the best response to each question and mark the letter (A), (B), (C), or (D) on your answer sheet. The talks will not be printed in your test book and will be spoken only one time.

71. What is the message mainly about?

(A) A prescription medication
(B) An appointment time
(C) A doctor's specialty
(D) A hospital bill

72. What does the speaker say he has received?

(A) An electronic payment
(B) An insurance authorization
(C) Some promotional brochures
(D) Some past medical records

73. What does the speaker say will happen tomorrow?

(A) He will update a database.
(B) He will call the listener again.
(C) A business will be closed.
(D) A delivery will arrive.

74. What have some employees complained about?

(A) The quality of a workplace amenity
(B) The temperature of their office
(C) The distribution of a workload
(D) The behavior of their coworkers

75. What does the speaker say about Human Resources?

(A) It is currently understaffed.
(B) It follows specific procedures.
(C) It handles only significant matters.
(D) It has made an announcement.

76. What does the speaker ask the listeners to do?

(A) Review part of the employee handbook
(B) Participate in a team-building activity
(C) Brainstorm some possible solutions
(D) View an online training film

77. What field does Ms. Datta most likely work in?

(A) Politics
(B) Medicine
(C) Engineering
(D) Publishing

78. What will Ms. Datta talk about?

(A) A book about her experiences
(B) A documentary about a journey
(C) An organization she founded
(D) A prize she received

79. What does the speaker imply when she says, "there are a hundred other people here"?

(A) Some of the listeners do not usually attend lectures.
(B) It will be easy to reach a fund-raising goal.
(C) There are not enough seats for the whole audience.
(D) The listeners should not take too long with their questions.

80. Where most likely is the announcement being made?

(A) At a public library
(B) At a shopping mall
(C) At an amusement park
(D) At a conference center

81. What does the speaker say about Mr. Adams?

(A) He is searching for an acquaintance.
(B) One of his possessions has been found.
(C) He is about to act as the host of an event.
(D) Information about him has been put on display.

82. What does the speaker say is newly available?

(A) A dining facility
(B) A mobile app
(C) A job opportunity
(D) A transportation service

GO ON TO THE NEXT PAGE

83. Who most likely are the listeners?

(A) Bank tellers
(B) Store clerks
(C) Factory workers
(D) Real estate agents

84. What does the speaker list?

(A) Pieces of equipment
(B) Marketing strategies
(C) Employee rest areas
(D) Customer complaints

85. Why does the speaker say, "There are some pencils on that table"?

(A) To show disappointment that a facility is messy
(B) To suggest that the listeners have lost some belongings
(C) To recommend using the pencils to take notes
(D) To offer the pencils to the listeners as gifts to take home

86. What type of service does the speaker's company provide?

(A) Security
(B) Shipping
(C) Landscaping
(D) Telecommunications

87. What is the speaker calling about?

(A) A review posted on a Web site
(B) An account password
(C) A reward for certain customers
(D) A malfunctioning electronic device

88. Why should the listener return the phone call?

(A) To schedule a home visit
(B) To learn more about a discount
(C) To receive installation instructions
(D) To find out where to send an item

89. Where is the tour taking place?

(A) On a mountain
(B) In a forest
(C) By a lake
(D) In a desert

90. What does the speaker imply when he says, "the van will be close behind us"?

(A) Listeners do not have to worry about getting lost.
(B) Listeners can ride in the van during the tour.
(C) Listeners should be careful around a vehicle.
(D) Listeners can access their baggage at any time.

91. What are the listeners asked to do next?

(A) Look at a route map
(B) Fill out some paperwork
(C) Put on some safety gear
(D) Throw away some trash

92. What does the speaker thank the listeners for?

(A) Taking part in the meeting
(B) Reporting some problems
(C) Working additional hours
(D) Going to an exposition

93. According to the speaker, what will happen in June?

(A) A competition will be held.
(B) An executive will retire.
(C) A new branch will open.
(D) A holiday will be celebrated.

94. What does the speaker clarify?

(A) The names included on a guest list
(B) The availability of some hotel rooms
(C) The requirements for a submission
(D) The responsibilities of a position

Project Schedule

Planning	July 1–19
Data collection	July 22–August 30
Data analysis	September 2–6
Report preparation	September 9–20
Presentation of results	September 23

Festival Floor Plan

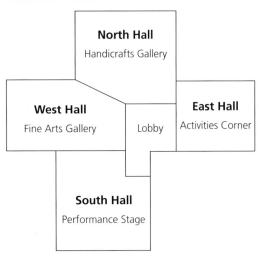

95. Look at the graphic. On which date is the speaker calling?

(A) July 1
(B) July 22
(C) September 2
(D) September 9

96. What has the speaker just finished doing?

(A) Calculating an expense
(B) Arranging some interviews
(C) Running some software
(D) Meeting with team members

97. What does the speaker want to discuss with the listener?

(A) The size of the research team
(B) The due date of the report
(C) The format of the questionnaire
(D) The strategy for attracting participants

98. What kind of organization is holding the festival?

(A) An art school
(B) A museum
(C) A student-run association
(D) A city government department

99. When did the festival begin?

(A) Three weeks ago
(B) Last week
(C) Yesterday
(D) This morning

100. Look at the graphic. In which hall will a special event take place?

(A) The North Hall
(B) The West Hall
(C) The East Hall
(D) The South Hall

This is the end of the Listening test.

TEST 2

LISTENING TEST

In the Listening test, you will be asked to demonstrate how well you understand spoken English. The entire Listening test will last approximately 45 minutes. There are four parts, and directions are given for each part. You must mark your answers on the separate answer sheet. Do not write your answers in your test book.

PART 1

Directions: For each question in this part, you will hear four statements about a picture in your test book. When you hear the statements, you must select the one statement that best describes what you see in the picture. Then find the number of the question on your answer sheet and mark your answer. The statements will not be printed in your test book and will be spoken only one time.

Statement (C), "They're sitting at a table," is the best description of the picture, so you should select answer (C) and mark it on your answer sheet.

1.

2.

GO ON TO THE NEXT PAGE

3.

4.

5.

6.

GO ON TO THE NEXT PAGE

PART 2

Directions: You will hear a question or statement and three responses spoken in English. They will not be printed in your test book and will be spoken only one time. Select the best response to the question or statement and mark the letter (A), (B), or (C) on your answer sheet.

7. Mark your answer on your answer sheet.

8. Mark your answer on your answer sheet.

9. Mark your answer on your answer sheet.

10. Mark your answer on your answer sheet.

11. Mark your answer on your answer sheet.

12. Mark your answer on your answer sheet.

13. Mark your answer on your answer sheet.

14. Mark your answer on your answer sheet.

15. Mark your answer on your answer sheet.

16. Mark your answer on your answer sheet.

17. Mark your answer on your answer sheet.

18. Mark your answer on your answer sheet.

19. Mark your answer on your answer sheet.

20. Mark your answer on your answer sheet.

21. Mark your answer on your answer sheet.

22. Mark your answer on your answer sheet.

23. Mark your answer on your answer sheet.

24. Mark your answer on your answer sheet.

25. Mark your answer on your answer sheet.

26. Mark your answer on your answer sheet.

27. Mark your answer on your answer sheet.

28. Mark your answer on your answer sheet.

29. Mark your answer on your answer sheet.

30. Mark your answer on your answer sheet.

31. Mark your answer on your answer sheet.

Directions: You will hear some conversations between two or more people. You will be asked to answer three questions about what the speakers say in each conversation. Select the best response to each question and mark the letter (A), (B), (C), or (D) on your answer sheet. The conversations will not be printed in your test book and will be spoken only one time.

32. Where most likely are the speakers?

(A) At an airport
(B) At a hotel
(C) On a bus
(D) In a taxi

33. What is the purpose of the man's trip?

(A) To evaluate a facility
(B) To attend a social event
(C) To receive some training
(D) To promote a business

34. What does the woman recommend doing?

(A) Trying a local dish
(B) Visiting a tourist attraction
(C) Storing some baggage temporarily
(D) Taking a certain route to a destination

35. What has the man agreed to do?

(A) Proofread some writing
(B) Participate in an interview
(C) Analyze an industry
(D) Produce some graphics

36. Why is the woman calling?

(A) To determine a fee
(B) To check some statistics
(C) To introduce a journalist
(D) To change a schedule

37. What will the man receive today?

(A) An electronic payment
(B) A draft of an article
(C) Some guidelines
(D) Some contact information

38. What are the speakers mainly discussing?

(A) A power outage
(B) Some poor weather
(C) An employee absence
(D) Some roadwork

39. What does the woman suggest doing?

(A) Closing down for the day
(B) Notifying a neighboring business
(C) Teaching a skill to some workers
(D) Buying a special machine

40. What does the woman mean when she says, "Shaun is posting on social media right now"?

(A) Shaun is neglecting his duties.
(B) Shaun is making an announcement.
(C) Shaun is seeking more detailed information.
(D) Shaun is more familiar with a marketing method.

41. What problem does the man mention?

(A) He has not received his paycheck.
(B) His paycheck is not itemized clearly.
(C) His pay amount is different from before.
(D) His pay was issued using an inconvenient method.

42. According to the woman, what caused the problem?

(A) An address is incorrect.
(B) A tax law has been revised.
(C) A software program is not working properly.
(D) A form was misplaced.

43. What does the man say he is currently doing?

(A) Setting aside some money
(B) Taking overtime shifts
(C) Applying for a departmental transfer
(D) Renting an apartment

GO ON TO THE NEXT PAGE

TEST 2   **23**

44. What does Edith want to do?

(A) Take on more responsibility
(B) Relieve some physical discomfort
(C) Improve a workplace relationship
(D) Increase her efficiency

45. What does the man recommend asking Jackie for?

(A) An opinion
(B) An apology
(C) Some paperwork
(D) Some equipment

46. What does Jackie offer to do?

(A) Help with an installation procedure
(B) Look in the company handbook
(C) Show Edith a computer accessory
(D) Connect Edith with another coworker

47. What does the woman say she just did?

(A) Spoken with a patron
(B) Read a publication
(C) Attended a lecture
(D) Posted a notice

48. What does the woman suggest offering?

(A) Private meeting facilities
(B) Classes on library resources
(C) A mobile book collection
(D) A longer borrowing period

49. What does the woman agree to do?

(A) Clean out a space
(B) Create a document
(C) Gather some colleagues
(D) Review a budget

50. What is the main topic of the conversation?

(A) A shipping service
(B) A building process
(C) A rental contract
(D) A vehicle repair

51. Why is Mr. Swanson surprised?

(A) A request has been denied.
(B) A cost estimate has risen.
(C) A task has not been completed.
(D) A project manager has been replaced.

52. What does Pete explain?

(A) The reason for a change
(B) The steps of a procedure
(C) The features of some software
(D) The options of a choice

53. What has the man become interested in?

(A) Fishing
(B) Cooking
(C) Playing an instrument
(D) Learning a new language

54. What is the man planning to do this weekend?

(A) Purchase some supplies
(B) Join a hobby club
(C) Go on a group trip
(D) Stream some videos

55. What kind of event does the woman mention?

(A) A dinner party
(B) A television show shoot
(C) A skills demonstration
(D) A competition

56. What kind of business does the woman work for?

(A) An information technology consulting firm
(B) An employment agency
(C) A research laboratory
(D) An educational institute

57. What does the man ask about?

(A) A number of people
(B) A source of funding
(C) A required qualification
(D) A usual start time

58. Why does the woman say, "information security would be a difficult area"?

(A) To indicate that she is impressed
(B) To recommend an additional service
(C) To justify a heavy workload
(D) To give the man a warning

59. How did the man learn about the woman's business?

(A) From an industry magazine
(B) From an outdoor advertisement
(C) From a local newspaper
(D) From a Web site

60. What does the man say about his store?

(A) Some of its merchandise is out of stock.
(B) It does not have many customers.
(C) Part of it is being remodeled.
(D) A parking area is being added.

61. What does the woman propose doing first?

(A) Inspecting a manufacturing plant
(B) Discussing the terms of an agreement
(C) Distributing some product samples
(D) Reviewing some sales figures

Directory	
Floor	**Products**
1	Cosmetics & Jewelry
2	Women's Clothing
3	Men's Clothing
4	Home Goods

62. Look at the graphic. Which floor are the speakers on?

(A) The first floor
(B) The second floor
(C) The third floor
(D) The fourth floor

63. Why is the woman uncertain about buying an item?

(A) It may be the wrong size.
(B) It would be easy to damage.
(C) It has an unusual design.
(D) It is expensive.

64. What does the man suggest doing?

(A) Trying on an item
(B) Paying in installments
(C) Going to online stores
(D) Looking for a salesperson

GO ON TO THE NEXT PAGE

References

Timothy Ward   555-0145
(Manager at Slangal)

Maureen Jacobs   555-0182
(Supervisor at Zubina Consultants)

Anita Bajwa   555-0176
(Director at Soares Engineering)

Frank Oliver   555-0109
(Manager at Soares Engineering)

Crabtree Deli

Order Form

Item	Quantity
Ham sandwich	3
Tuna sandwich	4
Potato salad (container)	1
House salad	2

65. Who most likely is the woman?

(A) A job applicant
(B) A hiring manager
(C) A department head
(D) A corporate recruiter

66. Look at the graphic. Which phone number is the man having trouble with?

(A) 555-0145
(B) 555-0182
(C) 555-0176
(D) 555-0109

67. What does the woman say caused a problem?

(A) A technological issue
(B) A typing error
(C) A company policy
(D) A personnel change

68. What is taking place at the woman's company?

(A) A board meeting
(B) A client visit
(C) A sales workshop
(D) An orientation session

69. Look at the graphic. What is the woman missing?

(A) A ham sandwich
(B) A tuna sandwich
(C) A container of potato salad
(D) A house salad

70. What does the man say he will do next?

(A) Send a scanned copy of a form
(B) Refund the cost of the order
(C) Contact a delivery person
(D) Make some more food

PART 4

Directions: You will hear some talks given by a single speaker. You will be asked to answer three questions about what the speaker says in each talk. Select the best response to each question and mark the letter (A), (B), (C), or (D) on your answer sheet. The talks will not be printed in your test book and will be spoken only one time.

71. What is the purpose of the meeting?
    (A) To describe a tourism campaign
    (B) To announce an office relocation
    (C) To report on a construction process
    (D) To recommend a company outing

72. What does the speaker say about Valtside?
    (A) It hosts an annual festival.
    (B) It is beautiful in spring.
    (C) It is the oldest part of the city.
    (D) It is accessible by public transportation.

73. What does the speaker show the listeners?
    (A) A neighborhood map
    (B) A train schedule
    (C) A floor plan
    (D) An organization chart

74. What type of product is being advertised?
    (A) Furniture
    (B) Electronics
    (C) Luggage
    (D) Footwear

75. According to the speaker, what has the company done?
    (A) Invented a production technique
    (B) Conducted market research
    (C) Begun exporting to other countries
    (D) Collaborated with a famous designer

76. What will happen on December 4 ?
    (A) A new store branch will open.
    (B) A sales promotion will begin.
    (C) New products will be launched.
    (D) The winner of a contest will be chosen.

77. What will the listener hold a party to celebrate?
    (A) A marriage anniversary
    (B) A retirement
    (C) A promotion
    (D) A birthday

78. What does the speaker confirm a change to?
    (A) The menu for a celebration
    (B) The theme of some decorations
    (C) The time of a reservation
    (D) The size of a group

79. What does the speaker imply when she says, "we just booked a band for that night"?
    (A) A preference has been accommodated.
    (B) An additional charge will be imposed.
    (C) A seating arrangement must be modified.
    (D) Some noise at a venue is inevitable.

80. What will the survey results be used for?
    (A) Making an expansion decision
    (B) Developing new programs
    (C) Attracting advertisers
    (D) Planning in-person events

81. What does the speaker say about the survey?
    (A) It is targeted toward listeners of a certain age.
    (B) It only has multiple choice questions.
    (C) There are two ways to access it.
    (D) The station has conducted it before.

82. What will survey participants have the chance to win?
    (A) A cash prize
    (B) Concert tickets
    (C) Branded merchandise
    (D) A station tour

GO ON TO THE NEXT PAGE

83. Where most likely is the workshop taking place?

(A) At a bank
(B) At a law firm
(C) At a government office
(D) At an accounting company

84. What does the speaker mean when she says, "you'd be surprised"?

(A) Some problems happen frequently.
(B) Some conflicts have already been resolved.
(C) Some mistakes have serious consequences.
(D) Some errors are easy to prevent.

85. What does the speaker say she will do next?

(A) Tell a true story
(B) Give a short quiz
(C) Pass out an agenda
(D) Begin a slide show

86. What is the purpose of the message?

(A) To offer a referral
(B) To ask for approval
(C) To apologize for a delay
(D) To answer a question

87. What does the speaker say about a landscaping project?

(A) It will lead to other work opportunities.
(B) It involves special materials.
(C) It has been postponed.
(D) It requires several permits.

88. What does the speaker say will happen if the listener does not act quickly?

(A) Seasonal weather will become a problem.
(B) Discounted prices will no longer be available.
(C) A potential customer will hire a competitor.
(D) A property may fail an inspection.

89. What industry will be featured at the trade show?

(A) Pharmaceuticals
(B) Construction
(C) Energy
(D) Agriculture

90. What does the speaker imply when she says, "Hall C in particular gets a lot of foot traffic"?

(A) Hall C exhibitors paid the highest registration fee.
(B) Hall C staff should take extra care not to block the aisles.
(C) Hall C would be a good place to hand out a resource.
(D) Hall C must be cleaned more often than other halls.

91. Why should listeners speak to Mr. Hayashi?

(A) To have their working hours recorded
(B) To obtain a communication device
(C) To report problems on the trade show floor
(D) To be reimbursed for a travel expense

92. What do the listeners most likely have in common?

(A) They studied at the same university.
(B) They hold the same type of job.
(C) They work for the same employer.
(D) They support the same sports team.

93. What does the speaker encourage listeners to do?

(A) Stop by a photo booth
(B) Make a financial donation
(C) Join a regional association
(D) Cast a vote

94. What will take place next?

(A) A keynote speech
(B) An award ceremony
(C) A dance performance
(D) A buffet meal

	Width x Length
Table 1	4 ft. x 6 ft.
Table 2	4 ft. x 7 ft.
Table 3	6 ft. x 6 ft.
Table 4	7 ft. x 7 ft.

95. Where will a new table be placed?

(A) In a patio
(B) In a lobby
(C) In a dining room
(D) In a conference room

96. Look at the graphic. Which table does the speaker prefer?

(A) Table 1
(B) Table 2
(C) Table 3
(D) Table 4

97. What does the speaker ask the listener to do?

(A) Place a purchase order
(B) Read a reply e-mail
(C) Arrange a furniture removal
(D) Verify the space's measurements

Yowek, Inc.

LONG-TERM PARKING PASS

#011923

Issued: January 1
Valid until: December 31

98. Who most likely are the listeners?

(A) Delivery drivers
(B) Graphic designers
(C) Parking attendants
(D) Senior executives

99. Look at the graphic. Which piece of information looked different before?

(A) The company name
(B) The pass type
(C) The pass number
(D) The expiration date

100. What does the speaker mention about an earlier design?

(A) It featured an image.
(B) It was a darker color.
(C) It included additional text.
(D) It made use of a heavier material.

This is the end of the Listening test.

TEST 3

LISTENING TEST

In the Listening test, you will be asked to demonstrate how well you understand spoken English. The entire Listening test will last approximately 45 minutes. There are four parts, and directions are given for each part. You must mark your answers on the separate answer sheet. Do not write your answers in your test book.

PART 1

Directions: For each question in this part, you will hear four statements about a picture in your test book. When you hear the statements, you must select the one statement that best describes what you see in the picture. Then find the number of the question on your answer sheet and mark your answer. The statements will not be printed in your test book and will be spoken only one time.

Statement (C), "They're sitting at a table," is the best description of the picture, so you should select answer (C) and mark it on your answer sheet.

1.

2.

GO ON TO THE NEXT PAGE

Test 3

3.

4.

5.

6.

GO ON TO THE NEXT PAGE

PART 2

Directions: You will hear a question or statement and three responses spoken in English. They will not be printed in your test book and will be spoken only one time. Select the best response to the question or statement and mark the letter (A), (B), or (C) on your answer sheet.

7. Mark your answer on your answer sheet.

8. Mark your answer on your answer sheet.

9. Mark your answer on your answer sheet.

10. Mark your answer on your answer sheet.

11. Mark your answer on your answer sheet.

12. Mark your answer on your answer sheet.

13. Mark your answer on your answer sheet.

14. Mark your answer on your answer sheet.

15. Mark your answer on your answer sheet.

16. Mark your answer on your answer sheet.

17. Mark your answer on your answer sheet.

18. Mark your answer on your answer sheet.

19. Mark your answer on your answer sheet.

20. Mark your answer on your answer sheet.

21. Mark your answer on your answer sheet.

22. Mark your answer on your answer sheet.

23. Mark your answer on your answer sheet.

24. Mark your answer on your answer sheet.

25. Mark your answer on your answer sheet.

26. Mark your answer on your answer sheet.

27. Mark your answer on your answer sheet.

28. Mark your answer on your answer sheet.

29. Mark your answer on your answer sheet.

30. Mark your answer on your answer sheet.

31. Mark your answer on your answer sheet.

PART 3

Directions: You will hear some conversations between two or more people. You will be asked to answer three questions about what the speakers say in each conversation. Select the best response to each question and mark the letter (A), (B), (C), or (D) on your answer sheet. The conversations will not be printed in your test book and will be spoken only one time.

32. Where do the speakers work?
- (A) At a factory
- (B) At an airport
- (C) At a restaurant
- (D) At a movie theater

33. What does the man suggest?
- (A) Putting up a sign
- (B) Hiring more staff
- (C) Widening an entrance
- (D) Automating a process

34. What does the woman say the man's suggested action might cause?
- (A) Service delays
- (B) A shortage of space
- (C) An unpleasant atmosphere
- (D) A budget problem

35. What does the man plan to do?
- (A) Move to a different residence
- (B) Purchase a new appliance
- (C) Put his belongings in storage
- (D) Renovate an apartment

36. Why does the man say he is concerned?
- (A) A job must be completed quickly.
- (B) An activity will be noisy.
- (C) An item may be damaged.
- (D) A room may be too small.

37. What does the woman offer to give the man?
- (A) Referrals to other companies
- (B) An informal cost estimate
- (C) A legal document
- (D) Packaging supplies

38. What is the topic of the conversation?
- (A) Keeping a current client account
- (B) Attracting internship applicants
- (C) Meeting shareholders' expectations
- (D) Maintaining employee satisfaction

39. What does the man propose?
- (A) Making use of a local resource
- (B) Reducing time spent commuting
- (C) Starting a volunteer program
- (D) Expanding an orientation session

40. What do the speakers agree to do?
- (A) Develop the man's suggestion
- (B) Seek alternative options
- (C) Announce a decision
- (D) Ask for workers' opinions

41. Who most likely is the man?
- (A) A trade show exhibitor
- (B) A tour guide
- (C) A workshop leader
- (D) An airline representative

42. What does the man tell the group about?
- (A) A building entrance
- (B) A form of transportation
- (C) An instruction manual
- (D) A storage facility

43. What does the man say is causing a problem?
- (A) He is not used to dealing with large groups.
- (B) His audio equipment is malfunctioning.
- (C) Some demonstration machinery is very loud.
- (D) The usual venue for a talk is unavailable.

GO ON TO THE NEXT PAGE

44. Where are the speakers?

(A) At a law firm
(B) At a hair salon
(C) At a doctor's office
(D) At an auto repair shop

45. Why did the woman schedule her appointment for today?

(A) She completed some preparations yesterday.
(B) She does not have to work this afternoon.
(C) She will attend a banquet this evening.
(D) She will leave for a trip tomorrow.

46. What does the man suggest doing?

(A) Updating some records
(B) Postponing a service
(C) Talking to a manager
(D) Saving a copy of a form

---

47. What has the speakers' organization received?

(A) A grant from a government agency
(B) A prize from a national contest
(C) Additional funds from its headquarters
(D) A donation from a businessperson

48. What does the woman suggest doing with the money?

(A) Producing some brochures
(B) Giving bonuses to employees
(C) Holding a speaker series
(D) Offering a school scholarship

49. What does Jonas decide to do?

(A) Plan a gathering
(B) Issue a questionnaire
(C) Call a consultant
(D) Draft an article

---

50. Why is the man calling the woman?

(A) To get some feedback
(B) To notify her of a problem
(C) To confirm some instructions
(D) To volunteer for an assignment

51. What does the woman imply when she says, "our main priority is our visitors' comfort"?

(A) She is not concerned about cost.
(B) She does not mind extending a deadline.
(C) A room should have more open space.
(D) Some seating looks uncomfortable.

52. What does the woman agree to do?

(A) Pay a deposit
(B) Visit a store
(C) Approve a design
(D) Wait for a shipment

---

53. Who most likely is the woman?

(A) A bookstore clerk
(B) A repair technician
(C) A pharmacist
(D) A librarian

54. What does the woman offer to do?

(A) Provide a refund
(B) Assist with a search
(C) Restart a computer system
(D) Recommend an alternative

55. What does the man say will happen next month?

(A) A registration period will begin.
(B) A product will be removed from the market.
(C) A certification exam will be held.
(D) A return policy will become invalid.

---

56. What did the woman post on social media?

(A) Some images
(B) Some statistics
(C) Some questions
(D) Some advice

57. Why does the man say, "this got a lot of people talking"?

(A) To reject the woman's request
(B) To point out an unintended benefit of an action
(C) To express concern about some criticism
(D) To admit that he was wrong about a strategy

58. What does the man ask the woman to do?

(A) Edit a sentence
(B) Write another post
(C) Monitor a discussion
(D) Respond to some comments

---

59. What type of event is about to take place?

(A) An arts festival
(B) A career fair
(C) A store opening
(D) An advertising seminar

60. Why is the woman pleased?

(A) Some marketing materials are attractive.
(B) A piece of furniture is larger than expected.
(C) The man has agreed to her proposal.
(D) A space is in a busy area.

61. What did the man forget to do?

(A) Clean some decorations
(B) Seal a box tightly
(C) Bring some refreshments
(D) Put fuel in a vehicle

	Wednesday	Thursday
Morning shift	Christina	Christina
Afternoon shift	Neil	Ruby
Night shift	Alton	Hakeem

62. What is causing a scheduling conflict for the man?

(A) A family gathering
(B) Some planned travel
(C) A medical appointment
(D) A university course

63. Look at the graphic. Who will the man next ask to take his shift?

(A) Christina
(B) Alton
(C) Ruby
(D) Hakeem

64. What does the woman suggest doing when a manager arrives?

(A) Making a reminder note
(B) Getting some contact details
(C) Referring a friend for employment
(D) Reporting the status of a task

GO ON TO THE NEXT PAGE

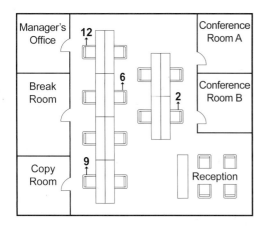

65. What does the woman ask about?

(A) Computer sizes
(B) Privacy measures
(C) Meeting frequencies
(D) Temperature conditions

66. Look at the graphic. Which desk does the woman choose?

(A) 2
(B) 6
(C) 9
(D) 12

67. What will the speakers do next?

(A) Fill out paperwork
(B) Greet a department head
(C) Shop online for supplies
(D) Go to a workstation

Portable Sound Systems	
Model	**Sound coverage** *(square feet)*
The Boom	2,000
Amplifire	8,000
Silver Tone	15,000
PowerVox	25,000

68. What does the woman plan to do?

(A) Perform some music
(B) Organize some lectures
(C) Host a sports event
(D) Hold a party

69. Look at the graphic. Which model does the man recommend?

(A) The Boom
(B) Amplifire
(C) Silver Tone
(D) PowerVox

70. What does the man say about the store's portable sound systems?

(A) They are kept behind the counter.
(B) They can be paid for in installments.
(C) A new model will be released this month.
(D) Some of them may be rented.

PART 4

Directions: You will hear some talks given by a single speaker. You will be asked to answer three questions about what the speaker says in each talk. Select the best response to each question and mark the letter (A), (B), (C), or (D) on your answer sheet. The talks will not be printed in your test book and will be spoken only one time.

71. What does the speaker say EMC Furniture received recognition for?

    (A) Their excellent customer service
    (B) Their innovative loyalty program
    (C) Their large inventory
    (D) Their reasonable prices

72. According to the speaker, what can shoppers do in the store?

    (A) Access the Internet
    (B) Watch a repair process
    (C) Sit down to take a break
    (D) Receive personalized advice

73. What is currently on sale?

    (A) A disposal method
    (B) A club membership
    (C) Furniture customization
    (D) A product guarantee

74. What is the main purpose of the talk?

    (A) To promote some cleaning products
    (B) To outline the schedule of a tour
    (C) To give assignments to a work crew
    (D) To introduce some safety videos

75. What does the speaker say about Ranvex Spray?

    (A) It smells good.
    (B) It is powerful.
    (C) It is a window cleaner.
    (D) It comes in a small bottle.

76. According to the speaker, what has each listener received?

    (A) A communication device
    (B) Some protective clothing
    (C) Some brochures
    (D) A floor plan

77. What news from the city does the speaker mention?

    (A) An inspector will visit local businesses.
    (B) An area's power will be turned off.
    (C) A construction project will begin.
    (D) A major road will be closed.

78. What does the speaker mean when he says, "That'll be the only change"?

    (A) Employees should use the same login information.
    (B) Employees should not submit extra reports.
    (C) Employees should work their usual hours.
    (D) Employees should not prepare for an evaluation.

79. What type of project are the listeners working on?

    (A) Doing market research
    (B) Designing an automobile
    (C) Remodeling an office
    (D) Building a Web site

80. What is the speaker most likely talking about?

    (A) Rearranging a work space
    (B) Preparing for a workshop
    (C) Setting up some interviews
    (D) Handling some vacation requests

81. What problem does the speaker mention?

    (A) Some equipment cannot be located.
    (B) Some furniture is very heavy.
    (C) A conference room is unavailable.
    (D) A software program is slow.

82. What does the speaker mean when she says, "Ms. Kwak's flight arrives at 4 P.M., right"?

    (A) She is offering assistance to the listener.
    (B) She recommends postponing a decision.
    (C) She thinks a message contains incorrect information.
    (D) She is grateful for the listener's support.

GO ON TO THE NEXT PAGE

83. What does Patton Enterprises sell?

(A) Power tools
(B) Floor coverings
(C) Home appliances
(D) Safety gear

84. What does the speaker mention about the business's merchandise?

(A) It is energy-efficient.
(B) It is made from recycled materials.
(C) Its ratings are consistently positive.
(D) Its availability changes regularly.

85. What does the speaker offer to do for the listener?

(A) Send a catalog
(B) Deliver items for free
(C) Give a demonstration
(D) Provide a consultation

86. What kind of event is taking place?

(A) A sports competition
(B) A groundbreaking ceremony
(C) An outdoor fund-raiser
(D) A street parade

87. Why does the speaker say, "I got here at 6 A.M."?

(A) To make a recommendation about future events
(B) To emphasize how popular the event is
(C) To explain how she got an advantage
(D) To indicate frustration with a delay

88. What is available on a Web site?

(A) A route map
(B) Game highlights
(C) Athlete biographies
(D) A public discussion

89. Where most likely is the announcement being made?

(A) At a television studio
(B) At a shopping mall
(C) At a sports stadium
(D) At a manufacturing plant

90. What does the speaker say about a television show episode?

(A) It will include an action scene.
(B) It will be broadcast next week.
(C) It will feature a guest star.
(D) It will be one hour long.

91. What are the listeners asked to do?

(A) Distribute costumes to employees
(B) Conduct an inspection of a facility
(C) Avoid certain parts of a workplace
(D) Review the contents of a document

92. What does the speaker say she recently did?

(A) She went to an industry conference.
(B) She contacted a start-up company.
(C) She spoke with an acquaintance.
(D) She read a retail trade magazine.

93. How does the speaker propose increasing sales?

(A) By making a deal to buy some goods in bulk
(B) By expanding into new areas of the country
(C) By selling discount vouchers through an online platform
(D) By raising the commission paid to salespeople

94. What does the speaker ask the listeners to discuss?

(A) Their departments' achievements
(B) The creation of a project team
(C) A possible launch date
(D) Disadvantages of her idea

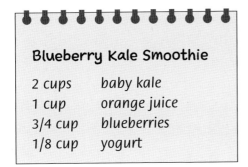

Blueberry Kale Smoothie

2 cups   baby kale
1 cup   orange juice
3/4 cup   blueberries
1/8 cup   yogurt

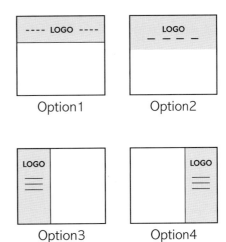

---- LOGO ----
Option1

LOGO
Option2

LOGO
Option3

LOGO
Option4

95. Who most likely are the listeners?

(A) Viewers of an online video
(B) Visitors to a supermarket
(C) Students at a cooking school
(D) The audience of a radio show

96. Look at the graphic. Which amount does the speaker say can be adjusted?

(A) 2 cups
(B) 1 cup
(C) 3/4 cup
(D) 1/8 cup

97. What does the speaker recommend doing?

(A) Consuming the smoothie immediately
(B) Refrigerating the ingredients beforehand
(C) Serving small amounts as appetizers
(D) Using a special setting on the blender

98. Look at the graphic. Which option does the speaker prefer?

(A) Option 1
(B) Option 2
(C) Option 3
(D) Option 4

99. Where most likely does the speaker work?

(A) At a real estate firm
(B) At a photography studio
(C) At a hotel chain
(D) A tour agency

100. What does the speaker suggest doing over the phone?

(A) Discussing layout styles
(B) Apologizing to a client
(C) Carrying out an interview
(D) Giving some driving directions

This is the end of the Listening test.

TEST 4

LISTENING TEST

In the Listening test, you will be asked to demonstrate how well you understand spoken English. The entire Listening test will last approximately 45 minutes. There are four parts, and directions are given for each part. You must mark your answers on the separate answer sheet. Do not write your answers in your test book.

PART 1

Directions: For each question in this part, you will hear four statements about a picture in your test book. When you hear the statements, you must select the one statement that best describes what you see in the picture. Then find the number of the question on your answer sheet and mark your answer. The statements will not be printed in your test book and will be spoken only one time.

Statement (C), "They're sitting at a table," is the best description of the picture, so you should select answer (C) and mark it on your answer sheet.

1.

2.

GO ON TO THE NEXT PAGE

3.

4.

5.

6.

GO ON TO THE NEXT PAGE

Test 4

PART 2

Directions: You will hear a question or statement and three responses spoken in English. They will not be printed in your test book and will be spoken only one time. Select the best response to the question or statement and mark the letter (A), (B), or (C) on your answer sheet.

7. Mark your answer on your answer sheet.

8. Mark your answer on your answer sheet.

9. Mark your answer on your answer sheet.

10. Mark your answer on your answer sheet.

11. Mark your answer on your answer sheet.

12. Mark your answer on your answer sheet.

13. Mark your answer on your answer sheet.

14. Mark your answer on your answer sheet.

15. Mark your answer on your answer sheet.

16. Mark your answer on your answer sheet.

17. Mark your answer on your answer sheet.

18. Mark your answer on your answer sheet.

19. Mark your answer on your answer sheet.

20. Mark your answer on your answer sheet.

21. Mark your answer on your answer sheet.

22. Mark your answer on your answer sheet.

23. Mark your answer on your answer sheet.

24. Mark your answer on your answer sheet.

25. Mark your answer on your answer sheet.

26. Mark your answer on your answer sheet.

27. Mark your answer on your answer sheet.

28. Mark your answer on your answer sheet.

29. Mark your answer on your answer sheet.

30. Mark your answer on your answer sheet.

31. Mark your answer on your answer sheet.

PART 3

Directions: You will hear some conversations between two or more people. You will be asked to answer three questions about what the speakers say in each conversation. Select the best response to each question and mark the letter (A), (B), (C), or (D) on your answer sheet. The conversations will not be printed in your test book and will be spoken only one time.

32. What are the speakers most likely doing?
    (A) Delivering some groceries
    (B) Giving a cooking demonstration
    (C) Catering a celebration
    (D) Holding a bake sale

33. According to the woman, what is causing a problem?
    (A) An inefficient process
    (B) A large number of people
    (C) Damage to an appliance
    (D) Bad weather

34. Where will the woman most likely go next?
    (A) To an automobile
    (B) To a front entrance
    (C) To a storage area
    (D) To a kitchen

35. What are the women doing?
    (A) Touring an office space
    (B) Shopping for electronics
    (C) Checking in at a conference
    (D) Learning to use a software program

36. Why is Theresa concerned?
    (A) A retail price is high.
    (B) A piece of equipment is large.
    (C) An opportunity might be missed.
    (D) A conflict might occur.

37. What does the man emphasize the availability of?
    (A) A special transportation service
    (B) A form of commercial insurance
    (C) A short-term commitment option
    (D) A free training resource

38. Why has the woman come to the gallery?
    (A) To see a new piece of artwork
    (B) To inquire about exhibiting
    (C) To finalize a purchase
    (D) To listen to a talk

39. What does the man ask the woman to provide?
    (A) Proof of a membership
    (B) The name of her friend
    (C) The title of a painting
    (D) A credit card

40. Why will the woman be unable to enter Garrett Hall?
    (A) Its contents have been loaned out.
    (B) It is being renovated.
    (C) Business hours are over.
    (D) A pass has some restrictions.

41. What service does the woman plan to receive?
    (A) Pet care
    (B) Vehicle washing
    (C) Interior decorating
    (D) Plumbing repair

42. What mistake did the woman make?
    (A) She gave the wrong address.
    (B) She failed to provide an important detail.
    (C) She chose an inconvenient appointment time.
    (D) She did not realize that a deal had ended.

43. What does the man say about his business?
    (A) It uses advanced technology.
    (B) It charges a fee to fulfill certain requests.
    (C) It encourages staff to receive certifications.
    (D) It tries to accommodate customers.

GO ON TO THE NEXT PAGE

44. Why is the man calling the woman?

(A) To arrange an interview with her
(B) To ask for a document
(C) To offer her a job
(D) To assess her professional qualifications

45. What does the woman say is attractive about a position?

(A) The salary for it is high.
(B) The work involved seems enjoyable.
(C) It is with a famous company.
(D) Its hours are flexible.

46. What does the woman agree to do?

(A) Send some paperwork
(B) Visit a workplace
(C) Make a phone call
(D) Prepare a presentation

47. Who most likely is the woman?

(A) An auto mechanic
(B) A fitness instructor
(C) A medical clinic receptionist
(D) A real estate agent

48. What do the men want to know about?

(A) A customized service
(B) A routine inspection
(C) Some test results
(D) Some safety rules

49. Why does the woman ask the men to wait?

(A) A supervisor must approve a request.
(B) A budget has not been finalized yet.
(C) She must rearrange some furniture.
(D) She needs to check a schedule.

50. Why is the man in the conference room?

(A) To have a quick snack
(B) To prepare for a seminar
(C) To lead a videoconference
(D) To work in a quiet place

51. What does the woman say she recently did?

(A) She calculated some costs.
(B) She complained to a manager.
(C) She made plans to travel abroad.
(D) She went to another floor of the building.

52. What might the speakers' company buy for employees?

(A) Some audio equipment
(B) Some special seating
(C) A cooling appliance
(D) A beverage machine

53. What are the speakers mainly discussing?

(A) An activity group
(B) A business trip
(C) A promotional event
(D) An employee newsletter

54. What does the man say about a book?

(A) He has not started reading it.
(B) He owns several copies.
(C) It is very popular.
(D) It gives investment tips.

55. What does the woman imply when she says, "that's a really big book"?

(A) The book will not fit in a display.
(B) It will take a long time to read the book.
(C) The book probably contains certain information.
(D) It will be uncomfortable to carry the book.

56. What is the purpose of the call?

(A) To order some office supplies
(B) To complain about the quality of some goods
(C) To ask about a charge on an invoice
(D) To check the status of a shipment

57. Why does the man mention his coworkers?

(A) To describe how a mistake was noticed
(B) To explain the need for some items
(C) To clarify whom the woman should contact
(D) To highlight an advantage of a proposal

58. What does the woman offer the man?

(A) A discount coupon
(B) A tracking number
(C) A branded gift
(D) A return authorization

59. Where is the conversation taking place?

(A) At a flower shop
(B) At a clothing retailer
(C) At an art supply store
(D) At a supermarket

60. What does the man say about some merchandise?

(A) It should be added to a display.
(B) It is in the stockroom.
(C) It has sold out.
(D) It needs to be organized.

61. What does the man imply when he says, "It's lucky that Chae-Young was here"?

(A) A task required two people.
(B) He was very busy today.
(C) Chae-Young has a special skill.
(D) Chae-Young provided useful information.

Framing Assignments

Area	Crew Leader
Stairs	Whitney
Roof	Grant
Walls	Santos
Windows	Jim

62. What most likely is being built?

(A) An apartment complex
(B) A store
(C) A hotel
(D) A school building

63. What does the woman suggest doing?

(A) Hiring some subcontractors
(B) Postponing an opening day
(C) Installing a protective covering
(D) Contacting other suppliers

64. Look at the graphic. Whom are the speakers going to see?

(A) Whitney
(B) Grant
(C) Santos
(D) Jim

GO ON TO THE NEXT PAGE

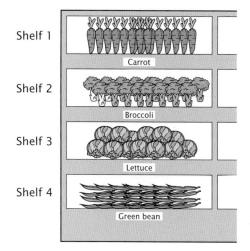

Shelf 1 — Carrot
Shelf 2 — Broccoli
Shelf 3 — Lettuce
Shelf 4 — Green bean

Beginners' Classes

Class	Current Registrants/Capacity
Rumba	7 / 22
Salsa	16 / 16 (FULL)
Swing	11 / 18
Waltz	19 / 20

65. Look at the graphic. Which shelf's vegetables is the woman concerned about?

(A) Shelf 1
(B) Shelf 2
(C) Shelf 3
(D) Shelf 4

66. What does the woman say she will make a list of?

(A) Types of produce
(B) Staff members
(C) Cleaning tasks
(D) Purchase dates

67. What will the man most likely do next to some vegetables?

(A) Carry them to another area
(B) Spray water on them
(C) Examine them for defects
(D) Rearrange them into piles

68. What does the woman ask about?

(A) How long each session lasts
(B) Whether she can attend alone
(C) How much experience an instructor has
(D) What kind of dance the man recommends

69. Look at the graphic. Which class does the woman want to sign up for?

(A) Rumba
(B) Salsa
(C) Swing
(D) Waltz

70. What does the woman agree to do online?

(A) Order some merchandise
(B) Get driving directions
(C) Register for a class
(D) Read some advice

PART 4

Directions: You will hear some talks given by a single speaker. You will be asked to answer three questions about what the speaker says in each talk. Select the best response to each question and mark the letter (A), (B), (C), or (D) on your answer sheet. The talks will not be printed in your test book and will be spoken only one time.

71. Where do the listeners work?

    (A) At a moving company
    (B) At a manufacturing plant
    (C) At a storage facility
    (D) At a construction firm

72. What does the speaker remind the listeners to do first?

    (A) Put on some safety gear
    (B) Refer to a floor plan
    (C) Study a warning label
    (D) Inspect the parts of a machine

73. According to the speaker, where can listeners find additional information?

    (A) On a handout
    (B) In a user manual
    (C) On a Web site
    (D) In a break room

74. Whom did the speaker meet with today?

    (A) Potential investors
    (B) Current clients
    (C) Business consultants
    (D) Government regulators

75. What does the speaker mean when she says, "my flight just started boarding"?

    (A) Her trip is behind schedule.
    (B) She has to end the call.
    (C) It is too late to make a change.
    (D) She will be unable to get a message.

76. What does the speaker ask the listener to do?

    (A) Reply to an e-mail
    (B) Pick her up from the airport
    (C) Set up a morning meeting
    (D) Eat a meal with her

77. Where is the tour taking place?

    (A) A city street
    (B) A nature reserve
    (C) An aircraft factory
    (D) A movie studio

78. What are the listeners asked to do?

    (A) Remain seated in a vehicle
    (B) Save questions until the end
    (C) Watch an introductory video
    (D) Turn off personal electronics

79. What will the speaker talk about next?

    (A) A company's expansion plans
    (B) The course of the tour
    (C) The history of a site
    (D) An upcoming celebration

80. According to the broadcast, what type of event will occur on Saturday?

    (A) An athletic competition
    (B) A career fair
    (C) An exhibition opening
    (D) A trade show

81. Why does the speaker say attendees should arrive to the event early?

    (A) To ensure entrance
    (B) To meet a local celebrity
    (C) To gain discounted admission
    (D) To find parking nearby

82. What will listeners most likely hear next?

    (A) An interview
    (B) A weather report
    (C) A sports update
    (D) An advertisement

GO ON TO THE NEXT PAGE

83. What does the speaker congratulate the listeners on?

(A) Finishing a team-building program
(B) Launching a new product
(C) Breaking a sales record
(D) Receiving promotions

84. Who is the speaker?

(A) A previous customer
(B) A business researcher
(C) A current supervisor
(D) A city official

85. Why does the speaker say, "Now, I know we need to do this again"?

(A) An activity was effective.
(B) Some results were unexpected.
(C) Participants performed poorly.
(D) Other people should observe an activity.

86. What is the topic of the talk?

(A) Carpet cleaning
(B) House painting
(C) Light fixture repair
(D) Window installation

87. What does the speaker say about a product?

(A) It is durable.
(B) It comes with instructions.
(C) It is sold in a variety of colors.
(D) It is affordable.

88. What does the speaker say she did before the talk?

(A) Cleared out a room
(B) Mixed some chemicals
(C) Covered some surfaces
(D) Measured an object

89. What is the announcement mainly about?

(A) A project for a client
(B) A corporate merger
(C) An office relocation
(D) An annual budget

90. Why does the speaker say, "Have you seen the amenities they offer"?

(A) To inquire about some facilities
(B) To suggest a policy change
(C) To criticize a venue's management
(D) To emphasize some benefits

91. What does the speaker ask listeners to do?

(A) Download some computer software
(B) Pack up their personal items
(C) Register for a meeting time
(D) Look at an employee handbook

92. What is taking place?

(A) A charity dinner
(B) A music festival
(C) A groundbreaking ceremony
(D) An industry conference

93. What does the speaker say the listeners can do?

(A) Purchase event merchandise
(B) Meet a company executive
(C) Network with others
(D) Sample some refreshments

94. What does the speaker say has changed?

(A) The focus of an organization
(B) The location of an event
(C) The date of a launch
(D) The cost of a ticket

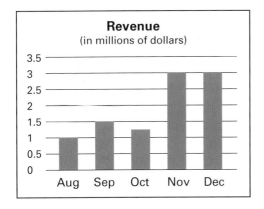

Revenue
(in millions of dollars)

95. Who most likely are the listeners?

    (A) Snack food developers
    (B) Financial analysts
    (C) Grocery store managers
    (D) Advertising professionals

96. Look at the graphic. In which month was a product line released?

    (A) September
    (B) October
    (C) November
    (D) December

97. What will Takuya most likely do?

    (A) Assign some responsibilities to the listeners
    (B) Address the listeners' concerns about a policy
    (C) Teach the listeners some promotional techniques
    (D) Present an award to one of the listeners

Rewards for Fund-raiser Participants

Level	Minimum amount raised	Prize(s)
1	$10	Certificate
2	$50	Certificate + bag
3	$100	Certificate + bag + T-shirt
4	$200	Certificate + bag + T-shirt + movie tickets

98. What did some fund-raiser participants do?

    (A) They completed a sports challenge.
    (B) They gave a musical performance.
    (C) They donated some homemade food.
    (D) They decorated an outdoor space.

99. Look at the graphic. Which level did the participating listeners most likely reach?

    (A) Level 1
    (B) Level 2
    (C) Level 3
    (D) Level 4

100. What will the funds be used for?

    (A) Medical research
    (B) Improvements to a park
    (C) The renovation of a community center
    (D) An educational program

This is the end of the Listening test.

Test 4

TEST 5

LISTENING TEST

In the Listening test, you will be asked to demonstrate how well you understand spoken English. The entire Listening test will last approximately 45 minutes. There are four parts, and directions are given for each part. You must mark your answers on the separate answer sheet. Do not write your answers in your test book.

PART 1

Directions: For each question in this part, you will hear four statements about a picture in your test book. When you hear the statements, you must select the one statement that best describes what you see in the picture. Then find the number of the question on your answer sheet and mark your answer. The statements will not be printed in your test book and will be spoken only one time.

Statement (C), "They're sitting at a table," is the best description of the picture, so you should select answer (C) and mark it on your answer sheet.

1.

2.

GO ON TO THE NEXT PAGE

Test 5

3.

4.

5.

6.

GO ON TO THE NEXT PAGE

PART 2

Directions: You will hear a question or statement and three responses spoken in English. They will not be printed in your test book and will be spoken only one time. Select the best response to the question or statement and mark the letter (A), (B), or (C) on your answer sheet.

7. Mark your answer on your answer sheet.

8. Mark your answer on your answer sheet.

9. Mark your answer on your answer sheet.

10. Mark your answer on your answer sheet.

11. Mark your answer on your answer sheet.

12. Mark your answer on your answer sheet.

13. Mark your answer on your answer sheet.

14. Mark your answer on your answer sheet.

15. Mark your answer on your answer sheet.

16. Mark your answer on your answer sheet.

17. Mark your answer on your answer sheet.

18. Mark your answer on your answer sheet.

19. Mark your answer on your answer sheet.

20. Mark your answer on your answer sheet.

21. Mark your answer on your answer sheet.

22. Mark your answer on your answer sheet.

23. Mark your answer on your answer sheet.

24. Mark your answer on your answer sheet.

25. Mark your answer on your answer sheet.

26. Mark your answer on your answer sheet.

27. Mark your answer on your answer sheet.

28. Mark your answer on your answer sheet.

29. Mark your answer on your answer sheet.

30. Mark your answer on your answer sheet.

31. Mark your answer on your answer sheet.

Directions: You will hear some conversations between two or more people. You will be asked to answer three questions about what the speakers say in each conversation. Select the best response to each question and mark the letter (A), (B), (C), or (D) on your answer sheet. The conversations will not be printed in your test book and will be spoken only one time.

32. What kind of business do the speakers most likely work for?
    (A) A hardware store
    (B) A construction firm
    (C) A building equipment manufacturer
    (D) A landscaping company

33. What has the woman recently done?
    (A) Rearranged a storage area
    (B) Met with potential investors
    (C) Attended a live demonstration
    (D) Replaced one of her belongings

34. What does the woman say has changed about the Wenton X Series?
    (A) It now has additional features.
    (B) It is now made of a different metal.
    (C) It has become less expensive.
    (D) It has become safer to use.

35. What are the speakers mainly discussing?
    (A) A video shoot
    (B) A department supervisor
    (C) A training program
    (D) An upcoming presentation

36. Why does the woman say, "I don't think anyone thought that"?
    (A) To decline an offer
    (B) To justify a decision
    (C) To agree with the man
    (D) To correct a misunderstanding

37. What does the man say he will do tomorrow?
    (A) Arrive to work late
    (B) Wear attractive clothes
    (C) Watch a television broadcast
    (D) Bring in his camera

38. What does the woman ask about?
    (A) A size limit
    (B) A bulk price
    (C) A minimum quantity
    (D) A likely completion date

39. What does Demetri recommend that the woman do?
    (A) Inquire at other print shops
    (B) Wait until new stock is delivered
    (C) Look at some samples online
    (D) Choose a different material

40. What does the woman say about Demetri's recommendation?
    (A) She will consider it.
    (B) She will implement it.
    (C) She wants to hear more about it.
    (D) She does not believe it is suitable.

41. Where most likely does the conversation take place?
    (A) At a real estate agency
    (B) At a medical clinic
    (C) At a post office
    (D) At a law firm

42. What problem does the woman describe?
    (A) She did not receive a piece of mail.
    (B) She did not understand some instructions.
    (C) She misplaced a document.
    (D) She is uncertain about a proposal.

43. What does the man ask the woman to choose?
    (A) When an appointment will be rescheduled for
    (B) Whether she will authorize a transaction
    (C) How she will fill out some forms
    (D) Where a shipment will be sent

GO ON TO THE NEXT PAGE

44. What is the main topic of the conversation?

(A) An employee's performance evaluation
(B) A technical difficulty with some software
(C) A system for issuing scheduling reminders
(D) A convenience facility in a building

45. What does the woman want to do?

(A) Administer a companywide survey
(B) Lower some maintenance spending
(C) Learn about upgrade options
(D) Clarify some guidelines

46. What does the woman ask the man to do?

(A) Set up a meeting
(B) Draft a notice
(C) Clean out a room
(D) Search a database

47. Why is the man at the store?

(A) To have some footwear repaired
(B) To buy a gift for a family member
(C) To return some unwanted goods
(D) To place an advance order

48. What does the woman request that the man do?

(A) Estimate a person's shoe size
(B) Complete some paperwork
(C) Provide proof of a purchase
(D) Show her the problem with an item

49. What does the woman apologize for?

(A) A long shipping duration
(B) An unfavorable store policy
(C) The small selection of merchandise
(D) A malfunctioning payment system

50. What do the women hope to do?

(A) Reserve an earlier train
(B) Use a self-service machine
(C) Take advantage of a promotion
(D) Change their seating assignments

51. What problem does the man describe?

(A) Some tickets have sold out.
(B) Some departures will be delayed.
(C) A computer server is down.
(D) A voucher has expired.

52. What will the women most likely do next?

(A) Notify a coworker
(B) Reevaluate a budget
(C) Divide up some work tasks
(D) Consider other travel methods

53. What most likely is the man's job?

(A) A journalist
(B) A graphic designer
(C) A newspaper editor
(D) A receptionist

54. According to the woman, what is the problem with an article?

(A) Some details are missing.
(B) There are some errors.
(C) The meaning of its title is unclear.
(D) It was placed in the wrong section.

55. What does the man ask the woman to do?

(A) Verify her professional qualifications
(B) Check the online version of the article
(C) Wait for him to locate a colleague
(D) File her complaint electronically

56. What is the man calling about?

(A) A sales event
(B) A repair service
(C) A new business
(D) A product order

57. What does the woman mean when she says, "I'm at work right now"?

(A) She does not have access to an item.
(B) She forgot about an appointment.
(C) She does not have time to talk.
(D) She is unaware of an issue that has arisen.

58. What will the woman most likely do next?

(A) Write down some contact information
(B) Stand near the entrance to a building
(C) Make a drawing of a space
(D) Take a bus to her house

---

59. What does the man thank the woman for?

(A) Lending him a resource
(B) Introducing him to an acquaintance
(C) Allowing him to use a workstation
(D) Looking over his writing

60. What does the man say happened last week?

(A) A publishing decision was announced.
(B) A research interview took place.
(C) A university institution was closed.
(D) A submission was made.

61. What does the man ask the woman about?

(A) Her experience with a process
(B) Her favorite coffee drink
(C) Her opinions on a book
(D) Her availability in the near future

Order Form	
Item	**No.**
File organizers	3
Paper clips boxes	5
Pen sets	2
Staplers	1
Sticky notes pads	4

62. Who most likely is Mr. Han?

(A) A government inspector
(B) A board member
(C) A new hire
(D) A vendor

63. What does the man say he is currently doing?

(A) Organizing some files
(B) Making a schedule
(C) Reviewing an agreement
(D) Collecting some supplies

64. Look at the graphic. Which number does the woman recommend changing?

(A) 3
(B) 5
(C) 2
(D) 4

GO ON TO THE NEXT PAGE

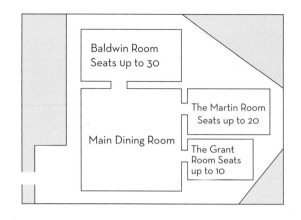

http://gold-star-employers.com
Average ratings for Custas Associates
Career Opportunities ★ ★ ★ ☆ ☆
Management ★ ★ ★ ★ ☆
Pay and Benefits ★ ★ ☆ ☆ ☆
Work-Life Balance ★ ★ ☆ ☆ ☆

65. What is the woman organizing?

(A) A fund-raiser
(B) An office dinner
(C) An awards ceremony
(D) A retirement party

66. Look at the graphic. What room will the woman's group use?

(A) The Main Dining Room
(B) The Baldwin Room
(C) The Martin Room
(D) The Grant Room

67. What does the man say the woman will have to do?

(A) Make a partial payment beforehand
(B) Approve a fixed menu of dishes
(C) Vacate the room by a certain time
(D) Read some guidelines for patrons

68. What problem does the man mention?

(A) A news report criticized the company.
(B) It is difficult to attract new staff.
(C) A client did not renew a contract.
(D) Several employees have quit their jobs.

69. Look at the graphic. Which category does the woman want to know more about?

(A) Career Opportunities
(B) Management
(C) Pay and Benefits
(D) Work-Life Balance

70. What will the man do today?

(A) Share a Web link with the woman
(B) Alert other supervisors about a discovery
(C) Create a summary of some content
(D) Post a review on the Web site

PART 4

Directions: You will hear some talks given by a single speaker. You will be asked to answer three questions about what the speaker says in each talk. Select the best response to each question and mark the letter (A), (B), (C), or (D) on your answer sheet. The talks will not be printed in your test book and will be spoken only one time.

71. What is the purpose of the hotline?

(A) To give updates
(B) To provide advice
(C) To accept donations
(D) To take reports on community problems

72. What does the speaker mention about potential call recipients?

(A) They follow strict rules.
(B) They are currently busy.
(C) They are given regular training.
(D) They are not paid workers.

73. What does the speaker ask listeners to do during their call?

(A) Be brief
(B) Take notes
(C) Speak clearly
(D) Remain polite

74. What is Edge Thinking?

(A) A company that promotes healthy workplaces
(B) A government campaign targeting an industry
(C) An annual human resources conference
(D) A Web site operated by a research organization

75. What did the speaker arrange?

(A) A tour of a factory
(B) A team-building outing
(C) An assessment of an office
(D) A seminar on well-being

76. What does the speaker show the listeners?

(A) Some revisions to a floor plan
(B) Images of furniture
(C) A list of job benefits
(D) A potential itinerary

77. What kind of event is the speaker most likely attending?

(A) A cosmetics convention
(B) An arts and crafts festival
(C) A food and beverage exposition
(D) A pharmaceutical trade show

78. What does the speaker imply when she says, "I have about twenty sample bottles left"?

(A) More giveaway stock is urgently needed.
(B) Her return journey will not be difficult.
(C) A prediction about a product was correct.
(D) A display should be removed from a booth.

79. What does the speaker say she will do?

(A) Have lunch with a possible distributor
(B) Check the details of a contract
(C) Take an overnight flight
(D) Send the listener an e-mail

80. What does the speaker emphasize about the Cessna Institute?

(A) Its long history
(B) Its convenient location
(C) Its high admission requirements
(D) Its variable entrance costs

81. What does the speaker say about Mr. Duncan?

(A) He opened a new restaurant.
(B) His classroom is well-equipped.
(C) He studied at the Cessna Institute.
(D) His business received an award.

82. Why are the listeners encouraged to register soon?

(A) Classes are filling up quickly.
(B) A special offer is about to end.
(C) The deadline is approaching.
(D) A new policy will be adopted shortly.

GO ON TO THE NEXT PAGE

83. Who is the announcement most likely for?

(A) Theater patrons
(B) Shoppers
(C) Gym users
(D) Travelers

84. What does the speaker announce?

(A) A correction to an advertisement
(B) An issue with some plumbing
(C) A shortage of inventory
(D) A change in venue

85. What does the speaker say some staff members will do?

(A) Arrange a form of compensation
(B) Oversee the sharing of a resource
(C) Make further announcements
(D) Help listeners leave the area

86. Where does the speaker work?

(A) At a research facility
(B) At a manufacturing plant
(C) At a city government agency
(D) At a shipping center

87. What does the speaker mean when he says, "there's a reason we put that sign up"?

(A) An activity can be dangerous.
(B) Storage spaces must be kept secure.
(C) Visitors need special assistance.
(D) Some old equipment is fragile.

88. What does the speaker apologize for?

(A) Not noticing a mistake earlier
(B) Not explaining a procedure
(C) Addressing all of the listeners
(D) Limiting access to an amenity

89. What event are the listeners attending?

(A) A guest lecture
(B) A welcome reception
(C) An exhibition opening
(D) A tour of an artist's workshop

90. Who most likely is Ms. Carlson?

(A) An art scholar
(B) A painter
(C) A gallery owner
(D) A museum donor

91. According to the speaker, what will happen after Ms. Carlson speaks?

(A) Some refreshments will be served.
(B) Some photographs will be taken.
(C) The listeners will ask questions.
(D) The listeners will walk around.

92. What is the main topic of the broadcast?

(A) A special status for a residence
(B) The activities of a citizens' organization
(C) The possible purchase of a structure
(D) A publication on a city's history

93. Why does the speaker say, "the building is in bad condition"?

(A) To express disapproval of a proposal
(B) To report the result of an official inspection
(C) To suggest that a project will be harder than expected
(D) To explain an assumption she has made

94. What does the speaker encourage some listeners to do?

(A) Apply for membership in a group
(B) Provide financial support for a cause
(C) Make a public comment on a matter
(D) See a property in person

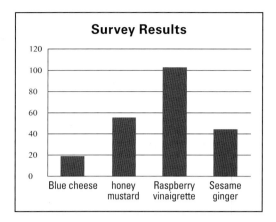

Survey Results

95. Who most likely are the listeners?

    (A) Restaurant staff
    (B) Lunch customers
    (C) Product developers
    (D) Marketing specialists

96. Look at the graphic. Which type of salad dressing does the speaker point out?

    (A) Blue cheese
    (B) Honey mustard
    (C) Raspberry vinaigrette
    (D) Sesame ginger

97. What has the speaker decided to do?

    (A) Contact an outside consultant
    (B) Offer a promotional discount
    (C) Discontinue two types of dressing
    (D) Increase a regular supply order

BOHEIM HORSE SHOW

Ticket pricing (per person)

1–3 people	£30
4–10 people	£27
11+ people	£24

98. Who will the speaker attend the show with?

    (A) Work colleagues
    (B) Relatives
    (C) Potential clients
    (D) Fellow members of a club

99. Look at the graphic. How much would the speaker like to pay per person?

    (A) £33
    (B) £30
    (C) £27
    (D) £24

100. What is the speaker concerned about?

    (A) Rules may prohibit bringing certain items.
    (B) The tickets may not be refundable.
    (C) Part of the show may be canceled.
    (D) A sale period may have ended.

This is the end of the Listening test.

TEST 6

LISTENING TEST

In the Listening test, you will be asked to demonstrate how well you understand spoken English. The entire Listening test will last approximately 45 minutes. There are four parts, and directions are given for each part. You must mark your answers on the separate answer sheet. Do not write your answers in your test book.

PART 1

Directions: For each question in this part, you will hear four statements about a picture in your test book. When you hear the statements, you must select the one statement that best describes what you see in the picture. Then find the number of the question on your answer sheet and mark your answer. The statements will not be printed in your test book and will be spoken only one time.

Statement (C), "They're sitting at a table," is the best description of the picture, so you should select answer (C) and mark it on your answer sheet.

1.

2.

GO ON TO THE NEXT PAGE ➡

Test 6

3.

4.

5.

6.

GO ON TO THE NEXT PAGE ➡

PART 2

Directions: You will hear a question or statement and three responses spoken in English. They will not be printed in your test book and will be spoken only one time. Select the best response to the question or statement and mark the letter (A), (B), or (C) on your answer sheet.

7. Mark your answer on your answer sheet.

8. Mark your answer on your answer sheet.

9. Mark your answer on your answer sheet.

10. Mark your answer on your answer sheet.

11. Mark your answer on your answer sheet.

12. Mark your answer on your answer sheet.

13. Mark your answer on your answer sheet.

14. Mark your answer on your answer sheet.

15. Mark your answer on your answer sheet.

16. Mark your answer on your answer sheet.

17. Mark your answer on your answer sheet.

18. Mark your answer on your answer sheet.

19. Mark your answer on your answer sheet.

20. Mark your answer on your answer sheet.

21. Mark your answer on your answer sheet.

22. Mark your answer on your answer sheet.

23. Mark your answer on your answer sheet.

24. Mark your answer on your answer sheet.

25. Mark your answer on your answer sheet.

26. Mark your answer on your answer sheet.

27. Mark your answer on your answer sheet.

28. Mark your answer on your answer sheet.

29. Mark your answer on your answer sheet.

30. Mark your answer on your answer sheet.

31. Mark your answer on your answer sheet.

PART 3

Directions: You will hear some conversations between two or more people. You will be asked to answer three questions about what the speakers say in each conversation. Select the best response to each question and mark the letter (A), (B), (C), or (D) on your answer sheet. The conversations will not be printed in your test book and will be spoken only one time.

32. Where are the speakers?

(A) At a restaurant
(B) At a vacation resort
(C) At a conference center
(D) At a car rental agency

33. What problem does the woman mention?

(A) She has misplaced a set of keys.
(B) She does not know how long a trip will take.
(C) She did not receive an e-mail.
(D) She is unsure about operating a device.

34. What does the woman say she will do?

(A) Check some instructions
(B) Use a storage compartment
(C) Make an initial payment
(D) Watch a video

35. What does the man mean when he says, "the delivery was this morning"?

(A) He needs to put away some stock.
(B) He is available to have a discussion.
(C) He does not require the woman's help.
(D) He is confused about a work schedule.

36. According to the woman, what does the CEO want to do?

(A) Open a new branch
(B) Hire more servers
(C) Expand a menu
(D) Offer a discount

37. What does the woman decide to do?

(A) Share an idea with an executive
(B) Visit a competitor
(C) Conduct online research
(D) Make an official announcement

38. Who most likely is the woman?

(A) An office receptionist
(B) A human resources manager
(C) An information technology technician
(D) A maintenance supervisor

39. What problem does the man have?

(A) He forgot a password.
(B) He missed an orientation.
(C) He cannot get into his office.
(D) His computer is malfunctioning.

40. What will the woman probably do next?

(A) Go to pick up a machine
(B) Search for a publication
(C) Assign a task to a worker
(D) Approve a spending request

41. What most likely is the man's job?

(A) Vehicle mechanic
(B) Parking attendant
(C) Car salesperson
(D) Delivery driver

42. What does the man say he dislikes about his job?

(A) The lack of promotion opportunities
(B) The competitive colleagues
(C) The irregular finish time
(D) The long commute

43. What does the woman suggest that the man do?

(A) Submit an application form
(B) Accompany her to an event
(C) Speak to their mutual friend
(D) Read a job advertisement

GO ON TO THE NEXT PAGE

Test 6

44. Who most likely are the men?

    (A) City officials
    (B) Real estate agents
    (C) Interior decorators
    (D) Event planners

45. What does the woman mention about the property?

    (A) It is currently unfurnished.
    (B) It will also be used for business.
    (C) It is located downtown.
    (D) It is in need of repairs.

46. What will the men probably do next?

    (A) Show the woman some paperwork
    (B) Unload some equipment
    (C) Interview the woman
    (D) Tour the residence

47. Why does the woman say she is unable to accept an assignment?

    (A) Her workload is too heavy.
    (B) She does not have a necessary skill.
    (C) It would violate a company policy.
    (D) She is going out of town soon.

48. What does the woman suggest asking Angelina to do?

    (A) Provide some training
    (B) Contact new clients
    (C) Update a database
    (D) Postpone a vacation

49. What does the man say he will check?

    (A) A building directory
    (B) A work calendar
    (C) A staff handbook
    (D) A survey report

50. What is the man concerned about?

    (A) The price of a service
    (B) The quality of an image
    (C) The color of a logo
    (D) The size of an order

51. What does the woman say her assistant will do this afternoon?

    (A) Prepare a revised invoice
    (B) Print additional copies
    (C) Send a design electronically
    (D) Pack up some posters

52. Why does the man want to change an appointment time?

    (A) He has to attend a business gathering.
    (B) His coworker is using a company car.
    (C) He needs to pick up some clients.
    (D) His office is scheduled to close early.

53. What type of business do the speakers most likely work for?

    (A) A movie theater
    (B) A hotel
    (C) A museum
    (D) A travel agency

54. What does the woman mention about the surrounding neighborhood?

    (A) It has a new leisure facility.
    (B) It has an interesting history.
    (C) It has a confusing layout.
    (D) It lacks parking.

55. What does the woman imply when she says, "Michael knows the area pretty well"?

    (A) It is surprising that Michael made a mistake.
    (B) Michael might be able to answer a question.
    (C) The man should not be concerned about a delay.
    (D) She thinks Michael is suitable for a role.

56. What types of products does Harumi want to review?

(A) Security systems
(B) Digital cameras
(C) Game consoles
(D) Audio equipment

57. What does the man ask Harumi about?

(A) Determining some standards
(B) Encouraging readers to leave comments
(C) Clearing out a space for shipments
(D) Negotiating a deal with manufacturers

58. What does the man request that Janelle do?

(A) Monitor an online discussion
(B) Locate a project file
(C) Meet with a coworker
(D) Edit some articles

---

59. What does the man ask for the woman's advice on?

(A) Evaluating suppliers
(B) Recruiting volunteers
(C) Participating in conferences
(D) Attracting customers

60. What does the woman recommend?

(A) Relaxing some communication rules
(B) Analyzing posts on a Web platform
(C) Subscribing to a news source
(D) Increasing marketing activities

61. Why is the man uncertain about the woman's suggestion?

(A) A venue may not be available.
(B) A budget may not be large enough.
(C) A timeline cannot be extended.
(D) A law may not allow a change.

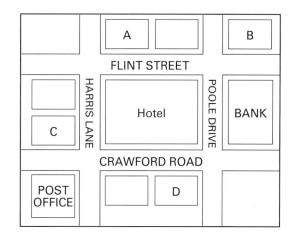

62. Who most likely is the man?

(A) A painter
(B) A gardener
(C) A caterer
(D) A repair person

63. Look at the graphic. Where does the woman live?

(A) At Location A
(B) At Location B
(C) At Location C
(D) At Location D

64. What is the problem?

(A) A service has been canceled.
(B) The man had the wrong address.
(C) A road has been closed to traffic.
(D) The woman's house has been renovated.

GO ON TO THE NEXT PAGE

Northside Home Goods

Sale on Shanter brand

❧ floral dinnerware sets! ❧

sets for 2 people: $5 off	sets for 4 people: $10 off	sets for 8+ people: $15 off

Destination	Scheduled Departure	Status
Detroit	07:35	Delayed (30 minutes)
Indianapolis	07:55	On Time
Toledo	08:15	Delayed (45 minutes)
Milwaukee	08:25	Delayed (2 hours)

65. What does the man want to know about the dinnerware sets?

(A) Why they are on sale
(B) How they should be washed
(C) How many pieces they include
(D) Whether they can be heated

66. Look at the graphic. How much money will the man save?

(A) $5
(B) $10
(C) $15
(D) $20

67. What does the woman say about Shanter's products?

(A) They are easy to return.
(B) They are designed to be long-lasting.
(C) They are not offered by many retailers.
(D) They are not discontinued often.

68. What does the woman say she has brought?

(A) A computer accessory
(B) Some refreshments
(C) Some gifts
(D) A printout

69. Look at the graphic. What is the speakers' destination?

(A) Detroit
(B) Indianapolis
(C) Toledo
(D) Milwaukee

70. What does the woman suggest doing?

(A) Making a phone call
(B) Reviewing some plans
(C) Going to a departure platform
(D) Reserving some accommodations

PART 4

Directions: You will hear some talks given by a single speaker. You will be asked to answer three questions about what the speaker says in each talk. Select the best response to each question and mark the letter (A), (B), (C), or (D) on your answer sheet. The talks will not be printed in your test book and will be spoken only one time.

71. Who most likely is the listener?

(A) A job applicant
(B) A reference provider
(C) An external recruiter
(D) A career coach

72. What does the speaker say the listener has?

(A) Relevant experience
(B) A large number of contacts
(C) A sample legal agreement
(D) Generous funding

73. What does the speaker ask the listener to do?

(A) Submit a document
(B) Return his call
(C) Visit a Web site
(D) Confirm some data

74. What product does the speaker's company sell?

(A) Automobiles
(B) Electronics
(C) Furniture
(D) Luggage

75. What does the company's target market want?

(A) Better durability
(B) Increased comfort
(C) Improved safety
(D) Reduced cost

76. What does the speaker say she has done?

(A) Employed a consultant
(B) Ordered some materials
(C) Talked to a facility manager
(D) Made a list of features

77. What event will the listener attend on Thursday?

(A) A trade exposition
(B) A recruitment fair
(C) A training workshop
(D) A grand opening

78. What does the speaker say about a form?

(A) It is incomplete.
(B) It was submitted relatively late.
(C) It includes an unusual request.
(D) It has been misplaced.

79. Why does the speaker say, "West Coast Air flies direct to San Francisco"?

(A) To point out a mistake that he discovered
(B) To answer a question the listener about an itinerary
(C) To suggest an alternative travel option
(D) To explain why he made a decision

80. What type of event is the speaker advertising?

(A) An outdoor concert
(B) A movie festival
(C) A street parade
(D) A sports tournament

81. What are listeners encouraged to do?

(A) Try a special kind of food
(B) Wear warm clothing
(C) Bring their own seating
(D) Use public transportation

82. Why should listeners visit a Web site?

(A) To become a volunteer worker
(B) To download a map of a venue
(C) To see an entertainment lineup
(D) To purchase tickets in advance

GO ON TO THE NEXT PAGE

Test 6

83. What is being discussed?

(A) A park restoration
(B) A building expansion
(C) An educational program
(D) An election campaign

84. What does the speaker imply when she says, "we're still waiting for Joslyn Associates"?

(A) She is worried that a deadline will not be met.
(B) She is unable to grant a request at this time.
(C) Joslyn Associates will contribute to an initiative.
(D) Joslyn Associates has a lot of influence in the city.

85. What was the speaker concerned about before?

(A) Expensive permit fees
(B) A shortage of personnel
(C) Negative public opinion
(D) Poor seasonal weather

86. What is the topic of the podcast?

(A) Writing advice
(B) Book reviews
(C) Famous authors
(D) Publishing trends

87. What does the speaker apologize for?

(A) Pronouncing a name incorrectly
(B) Misunderstanding a listener question
(C) Including a segment with bad sound quality
(D) Interrupting the show for an advertisement

88. What does the speaker encourage listeners to do?

(A) Report any errors she makes
(B) Recommend ideas for future episodes
(C) Support the podcast's sponsor
(D) Follow her social media account

89. According to the speaker, what will happen soon?

(A) A project team will be formed.
(B) A leadership position will be filled.
(C) A product will be announced.
(D) A mobile app will be released.

90. What does the speaker want the listeners to do?

(A) Provide some feedback
(B) Create a recording
(C) Gather some supplies
(D) Revise some sales figures

91. What does the speaker ask Barbara to hand out?

(A) Entrance passes
(B) A set of prototypes
(C) A draft of a script
(D) Notepads

92. Where most likely is the talk taking place?

(A) At a fitness center
(B) At a construction site
(C) In a hospital
(D) In a factory

93. What does the speaker ask the listeners to do?

(A) Wear safety gear
(B) Watch a demonstration
(C) Clean some machines
(D) Pack some boxes

94. What does the speaker mean when he says "Just look around at the other workers"?

(A) A requirement applies to everyone at a workplace.
(B) The listeners can learn a task by observing others.
(C) The listeners' negative feelings are common.
(D) There is serious competition for an opportunity.

Requested Quantities of Wireless Keyboards

Branch	Quantity
Bristol	25
Manchester	35
Norwich	40
Liverpool	45

Exeter Science Museum

Family fun Day Demonstrations

9:00 A.M.	Invisible Ink
11:00 A.M.	Homemade Slime
1:00 P.M.	Glitter Volcano
3:00 P.M.	Miniature Windmill
5:00 P.M.	Rocket Balloon Car

95. Who most likely will use the keyboards?

(A) Customer service representatives
(B) Data entry specialists
(C) Software designers
(D) Newspaper staff

96. Look at the graphic. Which branch does the speaker work for?

(A) Bristol
(B) Manchester
(C) Norwich
(D) Liverpool

97. What does the speaker ask about?

(A) When a shipment will arrive
(B) How to start a return process
(C) Whom to notify about an issue
(D) Whether an order has been finalized

98. Look at the graphic. Which demonstration does the speaker say will take place twice?

(A) Invisible Ink
(B) Homemade Slime
(C) Glitter Volcano
(D) Rocket Balloon Car

99. What does the speaker say he will do?

(A) Post an announcement
(B) Lead visitors on a tour
(C) Set up a temporary exhibit
(D) Hand out some badges

100. Why will Mr. Dixon observe some of the listeners?

(A) To prepare to write an article
(B) To give performance evaluations
(C) To carry out scientific research
(D) To receive training for his job

This is the end of the Listening test.

TEST 7

LISTENING TEST

In the Listening test, you will be asked to demonstrate how well you understand spoken English. The entire Listening test will last approximately 45 minutes. There are four parts, and directions are given for each part. You must mark your answers on the separate answer sheet. Do not write your answers in your test book.

PART 1

Directions: For each question in this part, you will hear four statements about a picture in your test book. When you hear the statements, you must select the one statement that best describes what you see in the picture. Then find the number of the question on your answer sheet and mark your answer. The statements will not be printed in your test book and will be spoken only one time.

Statement (C), "They're sitting at a table," is the best description of the picture, so you should select answer (C) and mark it on your answer sheet.

1.

2.

GO ON TO THE NEXT PAGE

3.

4.

5.

6.

GO ON TO THE NEXT PAGE

PART 2

Directions: You will hear a question or statement and three responses spoken in English. They will not be printed in your test book and will be spoken only one time. Select the best response to the question or statement and mark the letter (A), (B), or (C) on your answer sheet.

7. Mark your answer on your answer sheet.

8. Mark your answer on your answer sheet.

9. Mark your answer on your answer sheet.

10. Mark your answer on your answer sheet.

11. Mark your answer on your answer sheet.

12. Mark your answer on your answer sheet.

13. Mark your answer on your answer sheet.

14. Mark your answer on your answer sheet.

15. Mark your answer on your answer sheet.

16. Mark your answer on your answer sheet.

17. Mark your answer on your answer sheet.

18. Mark your answer on your answer sheet.

19. Mark your answer on your answer sheet.

20. Mark your answer on your answer sheet.

21. Mark your answer on your answer sheet.

22. Mark your answer on your answer sheet.

23. Mark your answer on your answer sheet.

24. Mark your answer on your answer sheet.

25. Mark your answer on your answer sheet.

26. Mark your answer on your answer sheet.

27. Mark your answer on your answer sheet.

28. Mark your answer on your answer sheet.

29. Mark your answer on your answer sheet.

30. Mark your answer on your answer sheet.

31. Mark your answer on your answer sheet.

Directions: You will hear some conversations between two or more people. You will be asked to answer three questions about what the speakers say in each conversation. Select the best response to each question and mark the letter (A), (B), (C), or (D) on your answer sheet. The conversations will not be printed in your test book and will be spoken only one time.

32. Where most likely is the woman going?

    (A) To a shopping mall
    (B) To a city park
    (C) To a conference center
    (D) To a railway terminal

33. What is mentioned about Bryson Rotary?

    (A) It usually has heavy traffic.
    (B) It is the site of a city festival.
    (C) It has a subway stop.
    (D) It is partially under construction.

34. What does the man recommend doing?

    (A) Parking in a garage
    (B) Walking along a pedestrian street
    (C) Returning via a different bus route
    (D) Postponing a trip for a few hours

35. Where most likely do the speakers work?

    (A) At a fitness center
    (B) At a home furnishings store
    (C) At a coffee shop
    (D) At a clothing store

36. What is scheduled to take place Saturday?

    (A) A grand opening celebration
    (B) A safety inspection
    (C) A closure for inventory
    (D) A recycling collection event

37. What does the man say he will do next?

    (A) Prepare some discount vouchers
    (B) Place some boxes in storage
    (C) Update a planning spreadsheet
    (D) Process a customer refund

38. Why does the man want to purchase an electric bike?

    (A) To add to a city's bike-share program
    (B) To replace an older sport bike
    (C) To transport building materials
    (D) To shorten his daily commute

39. According to the woman, what is a disadvantage of the Y10 bike?

    (A) Its size
    (B) Its appearance
    (C) Its battery life
    (D) Its cost

40. What does the woman say the store is offering that week?

    (A) Trial use of a charging station
    (B) Extended warranties on bikes
    (C) Reduced prices for repair services
    (D) Free installation of accessories

41. Who most likely is the man?

    (A) A customer service manager
    (B) A software designer
    (C) A shipping clerk
    (D) An event planner

42. Why most likely does the woman say, "I've done that before"?

    (A) To argue that a task must be possible
    (B) To acknowledge a mistake she made
    (C) To explain why she is working alone
    (D) To show understanding of a problem

43. What does the woman suggest doing?

    (A) Asking a team leader for additional help
    (B) Referring to an instruction book during a process
    (C) Sending a product back to its manufacturer
    (D) Keeping a record of some actions

GO ON TO THE NEXT PAGE

Test 7

44. What did Mr. Taylor just finish doing?

    (A) Cleaning a power tool
    (B) Unloading a truck
    (C) Landscaping a yard
    (D) Repairing a sink

45. What does the woman say she will do?

    (A) Organize a neighborhood event
    (B) Refer others to Mr. Taylor's business
    (C) Pay for services with a credit card
    (D) Move a parked vehicle

46. What does Tom ask Mr. Taylor for?

    (A) A cost estimate
    (B) A regular client discount
    (C) A printed receipt
    (D) A copy of a contract

47. What does the man say he is looking for?

    (A) A souvenir T-shirt
    (B) A camera carrying bag
    (C) An illustrated guidebook
    (D) A set of drawing tools

48. According to the woman, why is the museum special?

    (A) It has free admission.
    (B) It is the city's oldest museum.
    (C) It has exhibits on sporting history.
    (D) It allows visitors to take photographs.

49. What will the woman ask a manager for?

    (A) A product code
    (B) A key to a cabinet
    (C) Some gift wrapping
    (D) Some business cards

50. What does the speakers' company most likely manufacture?

    (A) Soft drinks
    (B) Skin care products
    (C) Eating utensils
    (D) Food seasonings

51. What will the woman help the man do?

    (A) Place products into shipping boxes
    (B) Adjust a machine's operating speed
    (C) Change the design of a logo
    (D) Order additional equipment

52. What will the man most likely do next?

    (A) Phone a company technician
    (B) Search for an instruction manual
    (C) Inform a team of a work interruption
    (D) Choose an alternative type of packaging

53. According to the man, what needs improvement?

    (A) A promotional flyer
    (B) Some guidance signs
    (C) Some outdoor gardens
    (D) A restaurant in a food court

54. Who most likely will participate in next week's focus group?

    (A) Maintenance workers
    (B) Mall shoppers
    (C) Store owners
    (D) Real estate developers

55. What does Susan offer to do?

    (A) Contact a consultant
    (B) Post notices in a building
    (C) Lead a training session
    (D) Redesign a questionnaire

56. What are the speakers mainly discussing?

(A) A new work-from-home policy
(B) The layout of a workplace
(C) An upcoming video shoot
(D) New procedures for collecting data

57. What problem does the woman report?

(A) Some documents are hard to access.
(B) Some employees have long commutes to work.
(C) Some storage areas have no more space.
(D) Some hallways are often noisy.

58. What will the woman ask Mr. Kim to do?

(A) Move to a smaller office
(B) Purchase a piece of furniture
(C) Revise a research report
(D) Extend a submission deadline

---

59. What did the speakers' business do recently?

(A) Expanded its range of products
(B) Held an anniversary celebration
(C) Joined an industry association
(D) Renovated a shopping area

60. Why most likely does the man say, "other organic grocery stores have hands-on cooking classes"?

(A) To show surprise at a local trend
(B) To suggest offering in-store activities
(C) To highlight the health benefits of organic foods
(D) To express doubt about the effectiveness of a promotion

61. What will the man probably do next?

(A) Water some plants
(B) Visit a nearby farm
(C) Clear off a display shelf
(D) Request a catalog

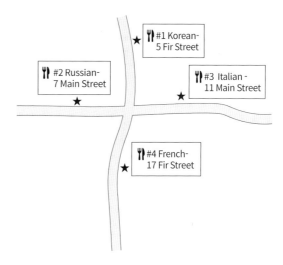

62. What does the man say he put on the business's Web site?

(A) A link
(B) An apology
(C) Some praise
(D) Some prices

63. What does the woman say she will do next week?

(A) Arrange a staff appreciation party
(B) Speak with a local business owner
(C) Purchase a navigation device
(D) View some vacant apartments

64. Look at the graphic. Which location number is no longer accurate?

(A) #1
(B) #2
(C) #3
(D) #4

GO ON TO THE NEXT PAGE

Test 7

Interview Schedule
Conference Room

David Meyer	10:00 A.M.
Erica Yang	11:00 A.M.
LUNCH BREAK	12:00 P.M.–1:00 P.M.
Lance Dedham	1:30 P.M.
Joy Nelson	3:00 P.M.

General Goods Section

Aisle 1	Garden supplies
Aisle 2	Carpet and flooring
Aisle 3	Sports equipment
Aisle 4	Office stationery

65. What does the woman say the magazine will start doing next month?

(A) Reducing rates for advertisements
(B) Publishing letters from subscribers
(C) Giving tours of its headquarters complex
(D) Releasing special issues regularly

66. What does the man plan to do?

(A) Take photos for a Web site
(B) Proofread some writing
(C) Set up audiovisual equipment
(D) Send out text messages

67. Look at the graphic. Which candidate will be interviewed in a different room?

(A) David Meyer
(B) Erica Yang
(C) Lance Dedham
(D) Joy Nelson

68. What problem do the speakers mention?

(A) A missing form
(B) A delayed delivery
(C) A shortage of employees
(D) An out-of-date training manual

69. Look at the graphic. Which aisle will the speakers work in that afternoon?

(A) Aisle 1
(B) Aisle 2
(C) Aisle 3
(D) Aisle 4

70. According to the woman, what happened last week?

(A) A staff recruiting event
(B) A district managers' meeting
(C) A building renovation
(D) A seasonal sale

PART 4

Directions: You will hear some talks given by a single speaker. You will be asked to answer three questions about what the speaker says in each talk. Select the best response to each question and mark the letter (A), (B), (C), or (D) on your answer sheet. The talks will not be printed in your test book and will be spoken only one time.

71. Where is the announcement being given?
    (A) On a high-speed train
    (B) On an airport shuttle bus
    (C) In a baggage claim area
    (D) At an airport departure lounge

72. What does the speaker mention about Delray Airport?
    (A) It is one of two airports in the city.
    (B) It mainly handles cargo planes.
    (C) It offers international flights.
    (D) It was recently expanded.

73. What does the speaker encourage listeners to do?
    (A) Observe airport operations
    (B) Make use of luggage racks
    (C) Request additional station stops
    (D) Register for a notification service

74. What is the main purpose of the meeting?
    (A) To address listeners' feedback on a plan
    (B) To brainstorm names for a product
    (C) To familiarize attendees with a software program
    (D) To review a consultant's report

75. According to the speaker, what is the problem with a mobile phone app?
    (A) High user fees
    (B) Slow loading speed
    (C) Unclear illustrations
    (D) Complex navigation

76. What will the speaker probably do next?
    (A) Evaluate design proposals
    (B) Welcome a guest speaker
    (C) Pass out sample items
    (D) Discuss a presentation slide

77. What does the speaker mention about Lorna's Market?
    (A) It was recently remodeled.
    (B) It has a seafood department.
    (C) It has a loyalty card program.
    (D) Its management has changed.

78. What is the main purpose of the announcement?
    (A) To remind shoppers about extended hours
    (B) To publicize current job openings
    (C) To encourage use of self-checkout machines
    (D) To share the results of a survey

79. According to the announcement, what will start on June 1?
    (A) A series of cooking demonstrations
    (B) The construction of a new location
    (C) A home delivery service
    (D) A prize giveaway contest

80. Where most likely does the speaker work?
    (A) At a transportation service
    (B) At an architecture firm
    (C) At an educational institution
    (D) At a dining establishment

81. What does the speaker mean when she says, "remember that people do live here"?
    (A) Listeners should be respectful toward residents.
    (B) Older homes are more attractive to buyers.
    (C) Residents depend on tourism revenue.
    (D) It is unusual for a historic district to be occupied.

82. What does the speaker say the listeners will see next?
    (A) A live performance
    (B) Some architectural drawings
    (C) Some classic vehicles
    (D) A body of water

GO ON TO THE NEXT PAGE

83. What is the main topic of the news report?

(A) A profile of a local politician
(B) An upcoming community activity
(C) Driving conditions on area roadways
(D) Problems with an environmental project

84. What are listeners invited to do?

(A) Participate in an opinion poll
(B) Attend an outdoor event
(C) Join a volunteer organization
(D) View an online catalog

85. What most likely will be heard next?

(A) A list of business closures
(B) A paid advertisement
(C) A call from a radio listener
(D) An explanation of a competition

86. Who most likely is the speaker?

(A) An interior designer
(B) A convention organizer
(C) A hotel manager
(D) A real estate agent

87. Why most likely does the speaker say, "the wallpaper and lamps are quite old"?

(A) To indicate that she is impressed by some materials' durability
(B) To justify the decision to change a venue
(C) To emphasize the need to make updates
(D) To compliment a structure's vintage decorations

88. What does the speaker say she will do later that day?

(A) Recruit additional workers
(B) Introduce the listener to a colleague
(C) Provide a written proposal
(D) Issue a partial refund

89. Where most likely is the introduction taking place?

(A) At a university student center
(B) At an art museum
(C) At a formal garden
(D) At a photo studio

90. What will the speaker give the listeners?

(A) An audio device
(B) A gift shop coupon
(C) A guide map to a facility
(D) A link to a mobile phone app

91. What does the speaker suggest doing?

(A) Watching an introductory film
(B) Ordering a meal in advance
(C) Starting a tour in a less crowded area
(D) Filling out a feedback survey

92. Why most likely does the speaker congratulate the listener?

(A) He gave a successful presentation.
(B) He recently purchased a new house.
(C) His transfer request was granted.
(D) His sales team won an award.

93. What does the speaker imply when she says, "there are a lot of moving companies in this area"?

(A) She needs more details about a project.
(B) The region has many new residents.
(C) It will not be difficult to hire a mover.
(D) A new company might struggle at first.

94. What does the speaker say will be helpful for the listener?

(A) Browsing a Web site
(B) Modifying a travel itinerary
(C) Completing an electronic form
(D) Holding a special staff meeting

Name of Trainer	Room number
Gregor	305
Jim	307
Becky	309
Yuko	311

Sign

1	**Delivery Drivers Must Sign in at Office**
2	**Visitors Must Wear ID Badges**
3	**Area Monitored by Security Camera**
4	**Parking for Delivery Vehicles Only**

95. What kind of business does the speaker most likely work for?

(A) At a merchandise display distributor
(B) At a software development firm
(C) At a footwear manufacturer
(D) At a package shipping company

96. According to the speaker, what will interns be required to do?

(A) Oversee an online messaging board
(B) Create posts for a social media account
(C) Test a feature of a computer program
(D) Compile statistics about clients

97. Look at the graphic. Which room will most likely NOT be used for training?

(A) 305
(B) 307
(C) 309
(D) 311

98. What does the speaker first announce a change to?

(A) A work schedule
(B) The staff dress code
(C) A stocking system
(D) A floor plan

99. According to the speaker, what will happen in the summer?

(A) A new product will be launched.
(B) A busy period will begin.
(C) A facility will close temporarily.
(D) A sales contest will take place.

100. Look at the graphic. Which sign did the speaker install yesterday?

(A) Sign #1
(B) Sign #2
(C) Sign #3
(D) Sign #4

This is the end of the Listening test.

TEST 8

LISTENING TEST

In the Listening test, you will be asked to demonstrate how well you understand spoken English. The entire Listening test will last approximately 45 minutes. There are four parts, and directions are given for each part. You must mark your answers on the separate answer sheet. Do not write your answers in your test book.

PART 1

Directions: For each question in this part, you will hear four statements about a picture in your test book. When you hear the statements, you must select the one statement that best describes what you see in the picture. Then find the number of the question on your answer sheet and mark your answer. The statements will not be printed in your test book and will be spoken only one time.

Statement (C), "They're sitting at a table," is the best description of the picture, so you should select answer (C) and mark it on your answer sheet.

1.

2.

GO ON TO THE NEXT PAGE

3.

4.

5.

6.

GO ON TO THE NEXT PAGE ➤

PART 2

Directions: You will hear a question or statement and three responses spoken in English. They will not be printed in your test book and will be spoken only one time. Select the best response to the question or statement and mark the letter (A), (B), or (C) on your answer sheet.

7. Mark your answer on your answer sheet.

8. Mark your answer on your answer sheet.

9. Mark your answer on your answer sheet.

10. Mark your answer on your answer sheet.

11. Mark your answer on your answer sheet.

12. Mark your answer on your answer sheet.

13. Mark your answer on your answer sheet.

14. Mark your answer on your answer sheet.

15. Mark your answer on your answer sheet.

16. Mark your answer on your answer sheet.

17. Mark your answer on your answer sheet.

18. Mark your answer on your answer sheet.

19. Mark your answer on your answer sheet.

20. Mark your answer on your answer sheet.

21. Mark your answer on your answer sheet.

22. Mark your answer on your answer sheet.

23. Mark your answer on your answer sheet.

24. Mark your answer on your answer sheet.

25. Mark your answer on your answer sheet.

26. Mark your answer on your answer sheet.

27. Mark your answer on your answer sheet.

28. Mark your answer on your answer sheet.

29. Mark your answer on your answer sheet.

30. Mark your answer on your answer sheet.

31. Mark your answer on your answer sheet.

Directions: You will hear some conversations between two or more people. You will be asked to answer three questions about what the speakers say in each conversation. Select the best response to each question and mark the letter (A), (B), (C), or (D) on your answer sheet. The conversations will not be printed in your test book and will be spoken only one time.

32. What does the woman say she is pleased with?

(A) A larger work area
(B) An extended vacation
(C) Some budget decisions
(D) Some recent sales results

33. What kind of business most likely is B & R Services?

(A) An event planning firm
(B) A temporary staffing agency
(C) An interior decorating provider
(D) A carpet cleaning company

34. What will the speakers probably do next?

(A) Review information on a Web site
(B) Prepare a presentation
(C) Rearrange some devices
(D) Ask for approval from a manager

35. According to the woman, what has changed about a trip itinerary?

(A) The operator of a flight
(B) The departure point
(C) The duration
(D) The number of connecting flights

36. What does the man say happened on Friday?

(A) He received a notification message.
(B) He canceled a previous booking.
(C) He changed the date of a trip.
(D) He was given a ticket discount.

37. What does the man want to know about?

(A) Choosing a seating option
(B) Checking in large baggage
(C) Requesting special meals
(D) Using an airport lounge

38. What was the man previously instructed to do?

(A) Bring his old dental records
(B) Enter through a side door
(C) Arrive early for an appointment
(D) Refer acquaintances to a clinic

39. What does the woman say about some paperwork?

(A) It had already been filled out electronically.
(B) It has marked sections for completion.
(C) It contains some printing errors.
(D) It was recently revised.

40. What does the woman give the man?

(A) Some tooth care tools
(B) Some customized stationery
(C) Some coupons for future visits
(D) Some bottled water

41. Who most likely is Nancy Batra?

(A) A visiting professor
(B) An in-house translator
(C) A departmental intern
(D) A newspaper journalist

42. Why does the man say, "many students are learning from home"?

(A) To decline an assignment
(B) To suggest delaying a product release
(C) To express agreement with the woman
(D) To admit that he is concerned about market competition

43. What will the woman probably do next?

(A) Contact a consultant
(B) Make a delivery
(C) Proofread a report
(D) Set up some equipment

GO ON TO THE NEXT PAGE

44. What has caused a problem?

(A) An outdated software program
(B) A malfunctioning monitor
(C) A loose cable connection
(D) A faulty electrical outlet

45. What does Stan mention about himself?

(A) He supervises an intern.
(B) He has a project due soon.
(C) He previously tried to fix a computer.
(D) He referred Ms. Jacobs to a service.

46. What is the woman asked to do?

(A) Distribute his business card
(B) Provide online feedback
(C) Present a warranty document
(D) Review an installation procedure

47. According to the woman, what did the man do recently?

(A) Took a knowledge test
(B) Opened a souvenir shop
(C) Published a guidebook
(D) Trained a tour leader

48. Why does the woman say the city's history museum is important?

(A) It is the city's oldest tourist attraction.
(B) It is larger than other museums.
(C) It has new interactive exhibits.
(D) It is the starting point for walking tours.

49. What does the man ask the woman about?

(A) Taking special transportation to a venue
(B) Introducing himself to a group of people
(C) Earning a professional qualification
(D) Keeping a record of a conversation

50. Where most likely is the conversation taking place?

(A) At a city park
(B) At a garden supply shop
(C) At an organic farm
(D) At a natural history museum

51. What does the man suggest doing for a project?

(A) Placing some plants in an indoor area
(B) Checking a local weather forecast daily
(C) Choosing plants that normally grow in a region
(D) Starting it during a warmer season

52. What does the man show the woman?

(A) A directional sign
(B) An informational Web site
(C) An artificial body of water
(D) A price list for services

53. What kind of products does the man's company sell?

(A) Adjustable desks
(B) Instructional books
(C) Business software
(D) Motivational posters

54. What do the women say they like about the man's company?

(A) It provides a fast delivery service.
(B) It uses environmentally-friendly materials.
(C) It participates in community fundraisers.
(D) It has a wide selection of products.

55. What does Sandra say about her department?

(A) It will sponsor a running race.
(B) It will be given a different name.
(C) It will have team-building day.
(D) It will merge with another department.

56. What kind of event is the woman planning?

    (A) An awards banquet
    (B) A birthday party
    (C) An anniversary celebration
    (D) A cooking contest

57. What does the man say to reassure the woman about a catering service?

    (A) It has won recognition from publications.
    (B) It is used by the area's biggest companies.
    (C) It can be provided in a range of venues.
    (D) It is available outside of regular business hours.

58. What does the man suggest doing?

    (A) Requesting a discount for a large group
    (B) Reserving a particular banquet room
    (C) Phoning a business proprietor directly
    (D) Ordering meals from an online menu

59. What does the woman say she did?

    (A) Uploaded some images to the Internet
    (B) Repaired some harvesting equipment
    (C) Packed a box of produce for pick-up
    (D) Submitted an order form to a manufacturer

60. Why most likely does the man say, "I grew up on a farm"?

    (A) To support an opinion
    (B) To explain a misunderstanding
    (C) To offer assistance
    (D) To show curiosity

61. What does the woman suggest the man do?

    (A) Feed some farm animals
    (B) Park closer to an entrance
    (C) Read over a promotional flyer
    (D) Look at some flower arrangements

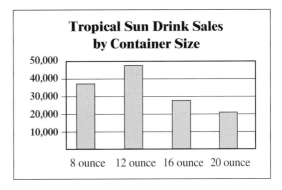

62. According to the speakers, what has the company done?

    (A) Relocated its head office
    (B) Expanded its sales territory
    (C) Created a new corporate logo
    (D) Replaced a celebrity spokesperson

63. What is mentioned about the Tropical Sun drink?

    (A) It is stocked mostly in restaurants.
    (B) It has a combination of flavors.
    (C) It will soon be sold at discounts.
    (D) It comes in glass bottles.

64. Look at the graphic. Which size of drink's sales data will the speakers focus on?

    (A) 8 ounce
    (B) 12 ounce
    (C) 16 ounce
    (D) 20 ounce

GO ON TO THE NEXT PAGE

Enzio's Cafe—Daily Specials

Monday	Chicken curry $13
Tuesday	Vegetable pasta $10
Wednesday	Cheese pizza $12
Thursday	Grilled salmon $14

Return code	Reason for return
01	Damaged in shipping
02	Defective—does not work properly
03	Wrong item shipped
04	Changed mind—do not want

65. What does the man say about some employees?

(A) They have been telecommuting.
(B) They will transfer to overseas offices.
(C) Their workloads have been reduced.
(D) They are attending a product launch.

66. According to the woman, what has Enzio's Café recently done?

(A) Raised its food prices
(B) Renovated its dining room
(C) Opened an additional location
(D) Simplified an ordering process

67. Look at the graphic. What special will the speakers probably order for delivery?

(A) Chicken curry
(B) Vegetable pasta
(C) Cheese pizza
(D) Grilled salmon

68. What does the man mention about the woman?

(A) She is working overtime.
(B) She is a new employee.
(C) She will soon go on vacation.
(D) She is handling a colleague's responsibilities.

69. Look at the graphic. Which return code will most likely be entered?

(A) Code 01
(B) Code 02
(C) Code 03
(D) Code 04

70. What will the man probably do next?

(A) Go to a different part of a building
(B) Use a loudspeaker to ask for assistance
(C) Write down some questions
(D) Restart a handheld device

Directions: You will hear some talks given by a single speaker. You will be asked to answer three questions about what the speaker says in each talk. Select the best response to each question and mark the letter (A), (B), (C), or (D) on your answer sheet. The talks will not be printed in your test book and will be spoken only one time.

71. What kind of business most likely is Caldarr Center?
    (A) A home furnishings retailer
    (B) An electronics store
    (C) A telecommunications service
    (D) A maker of office supplies

72. According to the advertisement, what has Caldarr Center done recently?
    (A) Added a new way to shop
    (B) Launched a loyalty program
    (C) Expanded its range of products
    (D) Hired new staff members

73. What does the speaker encourage listeners to do?
    (A) Browse a customer feedback page
    (B) Upgrade some warranty coverage
    (C) Purchase special gift cards
    (D) Vote on a potential improvement

74. What is mentioned about the Northern Express Train?
    (A) It costs more than ordinary trains.
    (B) It operates several times each day.
    (C) It makes no stops en route to its destination.
    (D) It is divided into two seating classes.

75. What are passengers in Car Four of the train asked to do?
    (A) Present photo identification
    (B) Store luggage between cars
    (C) Avoid mobile phone conversations
    (D) Move forward to the next car

76. According to the announcement, what will happen shortly?
    (A) Tickets will be inspected.
    (B) A video will be shown.
    (C) Boarding will be completed.
    (D) Refreshments will be available.

77. What kind of business recorded the message?
    (A) A real estate firm
    (B) A travel agency
    (C) A medical clinic
    (D) A mobile app developer

78. What does the speaker apologize for?
    (A) A recent price increase
    (B) An upcoming holiday closure
    (C) Extended holding times
    (D) Possible audio problems

79. What is the listener encouraged to do?
    (A) Meet a representative in person
    (B) Prepare some documentation
    (C) Use a business's other locations
    (D) Try calling on another day

80. Who most likely is the listener?
    (A) A neighbor
    (B) A plumber
    (C) A house painter
    (D) A delivery person

81. What most likely does the speaker mean when she says, "there are a lot of white houses in the area"?
    (A) A maintenance service could become popular.
    (B) A neighborhood has few nearby businesses.
    (C) Some renovations will make a home stand out.
    (D) Some instructions may have been unclear.

82. What does the speaker say she will do next?
    (A) Add her signature to an agreement
    (B) Make a space available for parking
    (C) Take some letters to a post office
    (D) Put up some signs outside a structure

GO ON TO THE NEXT PAGE

83. According to the report, what delayed the mall's completion?

(A) Changes to its floor plan
(B) Difficulty receiving some permits
(C) A shortage of construction workers
(D) The hiring of a new contractor

84. What does the speaker say is a feature of the mall?

(A) A performance space
(B) An indoor garden
(C) A large entrance hall
(D) A public transportation stop

85. What are listeners invited to do?

(A) Stream footage of an opening-day event
(B) Submit feedback surveys to mall management
(C) Register for an e-mail update program
(D) Participate in a phone-in talk show

86. What kind of business most likely is Revdecc Plus?

(A) A publishing company
(B) A real estate developer
(C) A fitness center
(D) An advertising agency

87. Why most likely does the speaker say, "we've had design challenges before"?

(A) To suggest buying new design software
(B) To emphasize the need to recruit more staff
(C) To reassure the listeners about a task
(D) To praise the listeners for an accomplishment

88. What does the speaker recommend doing in the afternoon?

(A) Distributing some brochures
(B) Holding a team meeting
(C) Working past the end of a shift
(D) Visiting a client together

89. What most likely is being taught in the workshop?

(A) Hiking for fitness
(B) Growing plants
(C) Writing journals
(D) Painting pictures

90. According to the speaker, what is special about the workshop?

(A) It has a high enrollment.
(B) It is being held outdoors.
(C) It is taught by two instructors.
(D) It takes place over multiple days.

91. What are listeners advised to do?

(A) Obtain parking permits
(B) Carry minimal belongings
(C) Avoid picking flowers
(D) Walk carefully

92. What will the speaker's company do soon?

(A) Relocate to a different office
(B) Host a visit from potential clients
(C) Rearrange its current workspace
(D) Undergo a safety inspection

93. What does the speaker imply when he says, "it's Thursday afternoon"?

(A) An executive is probably busy.
(B) A deadline is approaching.
(C) A previously stated date is incorrect.
(D) A meeting will be postponed.

94. What does the speaker say he will do next?

(A) Clean a work station
(B) Wait next to an external door
(C) Organize a supply closet
(D) Set up a waste container

Imported Items

Top

Third

Second

Bottom

95. According to the speaker, what is being sold at reduced prices?

(A) Health foods
(B) Cooking tools
(C) Products sold in bulk
(D) Discontinued merchandise

96. Look at the graphic. Which shelf did the speaker remove items from?

(A) The top shelf
(B) The third shelf
(C) The second shelf
(D) The bottom shelf

97. What are listeners asked to emphasize about a sale?

(A) It applies mostly to high priced items.
(B) It involves a mobile app.
(C) It will last for only one day.
(D) It does not require coupons.

Day 2 training
1:00 P.M. to 5:00 P.M.

Module 1	Company policies
Module 2	Making presentations
Module 3	Software training
Module 4	Customer relations

98. Where most likely is the introduction taking place?

(A) At a luggage manufacturer
(B) At a graphic design firm
(C) At a jewelry seller
(D) At a software developer

99. Look at the graphic. Which module most likely will be shortened?

(A) Module 1
(B) Module 2
(C) Module 3
(D) Module 4

100. What does the speaker tell the listeners to do?

(A) Look at some product samples
(B) Share materials with a partner
(C) Ensure that a booklet is complete
(D) Turn off any personal electronics

This is the end of the Listening test.

TEST 9

LISTENING TEST

In the Listening test, you will be asked to demonstrate how well you understand spoken English. The entire Listening test will last approximately 45 minutes. There are four parts, and directions are given for each part. You must mark your answers on the separate answer sheet. Do not write your answers in your test book.

PART 1

Directions: For each question in this part, you will hear four statements about a picture in your test book. When you hear the statements, you must select the one statement that best describes what you see in the picture. Then find the number of the question on your answer sheet and mark your answer. The statements will not be printed in your test book and will be spoken only one time.

Statement (C), "They're sitting at a table," is the best description of the picture, so you should select answer (C) and mark it on your answer sheet.

1.

2.

GO ON TO THE NEXT PAGE

Test 9

3.

4.

5.

6.

GO ON TO THE NEXT PAGE ➡

Test 9

PART 2

Directions: You will hear a question or statement and three responses spoken in English. They will not be printed in your test book and will be spoken only one time. Select the best response to the question or statement and mark the letter (A), (B), or (C) on your answer sheet.

7. Mark your answer on your answer sheet.

8. Mark your answer on your answer sheet.

9. Mark your answer on your answer sheet.

10. Mark your answer on your answer sheet.

11. Mark your answer on your answer sheet.

12. Mark your answer on your answer sheet.

13. Mark your answer on your answer sheet.

14. Mark your answer on your answer sheet.

15. Mark your answer on your answer sheet.

16. Mark your answer on your answer sheet.

17. Mark your answer on your answer sheet.

18. Mark your answer on your answer sheet.

19. Mark your answer on your answer sheet.

20. Mark your answer on your answer sheet.

21. Mark your answer on your answer sheet.

22. Mark your answer on your answer sheet.

23. Mark your answer on your answer sheet.

24. Mark your answer on your answer sheet.

25. Mark your answer on your answer sheet.

26. Mark your answer on your answer sheet.

27. Mark your answer on your answer sheet.

28. Mark your answer on your answer sheet.

29. Mark your answer on your answer sheet.

30. Mark your answer on your answer sheet.

31. Mark your answer on your answer sheet.

Directions: You will hear some conversations between two or more people. You will be asked to answer three questions about what the speakers say in each conversation. Select the best response to each question and mark the letter (A), (B), (C), or (D) on your answer sheet. The conversations will not be printed in your test book and will be spoken only one time.

32. What does the man say will happen next month?

(A) A conference will take place.
(B) A new law will go into effect.
(C) A tour will be given.
(D) A staff member will retire.

33. What does the woman say she did?

(A) Picked up some materials
(B) Made some reservations
(C) Had lunch with a client
(D) Posted a job listing

34. What does the man ask the woman to do immediately?

(A) Listen to a telephone message
(B) Make copies of a file
(C) Correct a mistake
(D) Send a notification

35. What does the woman ask for?

(A) A take-away cup
(B) A sales receipt
(C) A gift certificate
(D) An ingredient replacement

36. What does Bill correct Carl about?

(A) The name of a drink
(B) The operating hours of a café
(C) The availability of an item
(D) The cost of a change

37. How does the woman want to pay for her order?

(A) With cash
(B) With a voucher
(C) With a credit card
(D) With a mobile app

38. What are the speakers most likely choosing cast members for?

(A) A television program
(B) A feature film
(C) A stage show
(D) An online advertisement

39. What does the man say about Mr. Witherspoon?

(A) He does not have a necessary skill.
(B) He should play another character.
(C) He will have to audition again.
(D) He has a scheduling conflict.

40. What does the man decide to do?

(A) Speak with an investor
(B) Rewatch a performance
(C) Postpone a discussion
(D) Move a location

41. Where most likely is the conversation taking place?

(A) In a parking garage
(B) In a banquet hall
(C) In a seminar room
(D) In a hotel lobby

42. What does the woman imply when she says, "I arrived yesterday morning"?

(A) She was not present for a talk.
(B) There is an error on an invoice.
(C) She did not have time for a social activity.
(D) There was strong competition for an opportunity.

43. What will the woman most likely do next?

(A) Look over a timetable
(B) Make a call to a colleague
(C) Search through her handbag
(D) E-mail the man from a device

GO ON TO THE NEXT PAGE

Test 9

44. Who most likely is the woman?

(A) An assembly line manager
(B) A truck driver
(C) A warehouse worker
(D) A sales clerk

45. What is the man concerned about?

(A) The status of a shipment
(B) The woman's health
(C) The opinion of an executive
(D) The woman's job satisfaction

46. What does the man offer the woman?

(A) Help from another staff member
(B) Use of a special piece of equipment
(C) A career development opportunity
(D) A referral to a service provider

47. What does the man hope to do?

(A) Release some music
(B) Rent some machinery
(C) Sell a piece of property
(D) Relocate a retail store

48. What problem does the woman mention?

(A) A contract's terms are unfavorable.
(B) A space has some security issues.
(C) A local regulation is complicated.
(D) A certification has expired.

49. What does the woman ask the man about?

(A) His familiarity with a process
(B) His willingness to negotiate
(C) His ability to prove a claim
(D) His access to a resource

50. What does the man mention about the meeting?

(A) It was not originally scheduled for today.
(B) It includes a remote participant.
(C) It is being recorded.
(D) It might last past closing time.

51. What kind of project are the speakers working on?

(A) Recruiting for staff openings
(B) Developing a questionnaire
(C) Organizing a training program
(D) Rewriting a set of policies

52. What will the speakers do next?

(A) Give individual progress updates
(B) Read the minutes of a previous meeting
(C) Choose their preferred assignments
(D) Wait for an additional attendee

53. What does the man say about his trip?

(A) He plans to visit a friend.
(B) It will be one week long.
(C) It has been enjoyable.
(D) He is traveling for work.

54. How does the woman assist the man?

(A) By giving him an extra cushion
(B) By agreeing to talk to another passenger
(C) By accepting a container for disposal
(D) By lending him a writing tool

55. According to the woman, what can the man do?

(A) Lean his seat back
(B) Access a storage area
(C) Leave part of a form blank
(D) Turn off an overhead light

56. Where do the speakers most likely work?

    (A) At a public relations agency
    (B) At an architectural firm
    (C) At a recording studio
    (D) At an art museum

57. What does the man say will happen soon?

    (A) A computer program will be upgraded.
    (B) A building will be remodeled.
    (C) Some interns will be selected.
    (D) Business hours will change temporarily.

58. What does the woman agree to do?

    (A) Calculate a budgetary requirement
    (B) Telecommute for a short period
    (C) Deliver a speech to a group
    (D) Conduct some phone interviews

59. What does the man say he is currently doing?

    (A) Repairing some electronics
    (B) Assembling some furniture
    (C) Packing a moving crate
    (D) Installing an appliance

60. What is the problem with a nearby building?

    (A) It is blocking some light.
    (B) It is increasing noise levels.
    (C) It is reflecting some heat.
    (D) It is causing higher winds.

61. What does the man mean when he says, "I left my blue screwdriver on my desk"?

    (A) He is willing to lend his belongings to the woman.
    (B) He will not be able to complete his task right away.
    (C) He does not mind returning to his work station.
    (D) He would like the woman to bring a tool to him.

18°C / 24°C	15°C / 21°C	16°C / 21°C	17°C / 26°C
Tuesday	Wednesday	Thursday	Friday

62. What industry do the speakers most likely work in?

    (A) Energy utilities
    (B) Rail transportation
    (C) Road construction
    (D) Groundskeeping

63. Look at the graphic. Which day does the woman suggest scheduling extra workers for?

    (A) Tuesday
    (B) Wednesday
    (C) Thursday
    (D) Friday

64. What does the man recommend doing first?

    (A) Asking a supervisor for approval
    (B) Giving workers a chance to volunteer
    (C) Determining some crews' responsibilities
    (D) Checking some different forecasts

GO ON TO THE NEXT PAGE

GWC002   GWC014

GSC001   GSC009

"Amita Mittal" June 23	40 minutes
"Mateo Lozano" June 16	39 minutes
"Josh Dennis" June 9	42 minutes
"Verna Armstrong" June 2	44 minutes

65. Look at the graphic. Which gate does the man choose?

(A) GWC002
(B) GWC014
(C) GSC001
(D) GSC009

66. What does the man say about his yard?

(A) He will keep a pet there.
(B) He will grow produce there.
(C) He plans to have parties there.
(D) He will put in a swimming pool there.

67. Who will the woman most likely call next?

(A) A supplier
(B) An employee
(C) Another client
(D) An inspector

68. What most likely has the man just finished doing?

(A) Buying food at a roadside store
(B) Putting fuel in a vehicle
(C) Arranging some baggage
(D) Receiving advice about a route

69. What is mentioned about the people featured on the podcast?

(A) They founded their own businesses.
(B) They have spoken at a famous event.
(C) They are in the same industry.
(D) They conducted interesting research.

70. Look at the graphic. Which episode will the man play first?

(A) "Amita Mittal"
(B) "Mateo Lozano"
(C) "Josh Dennis"
(D) "Verna Armstrong"

PART 4

Directions: You will hear some talks given by a single speaker. You will be asked to answer three questions about what the speaker says in each talk. Select the best response to each question and mark the letter (A), (B), (C), or (D) on your answer sheet. The talks will not be printed in your test book and will be spoken only one time.

---

71. What kind of business is the speaker calling?

(A) A fitness center
(B) A hardware store
(C) An employment agency
(D) A shipping company

72. What is the purpose of the call?

(A) To confirm an address
(B) To make an appointment
(C) To ask about parking options
(D) To learn about a pricing system

73. What is the speaker concerned about?

(A) An additional fee
(B) A limited amount of time
(C) An identification requirement
(D) A large number of customers

---

74. What has caused traffic problems?

(A) Bad weather
(B) A street closure
(C) Holiday travel
(D) A major event

75. According to the speaker, what has a government department done?

(A) Issued a mass text message
(B) Sent personnel to an area
(C) Posted a statement online
(D) Suspended a transportation service

76. What are the listeners asked to do?

(A) Visit a city Web site
(B) Avoid a neighborhood
(C) Drive more slowly than usual
(D) Await a second radio announcement

---

77. What does the speaker thank Jeremy for?

(A) Creating some visual aids
(B) Leading a discussion group
(C) Organizing the current meeting
(D) Preparing some lotion samples

78. Why does the speaker say, "the 'scent' category received the highest approval rating, at 74%"?

(A) To show disappointment with all of the results
(B) To indicate a new direction for a marketing campaign
(C) To congratulate some of the listeners on an achievement
(D) To request that the listeners ignore some design flaws

79. What does the speaker ask for the listeners' opinions on?

(A) Performing more market research
(B) Contacting a manufacturer
(C) Forming a special team
(D) Extending a deadline

---

80. What type of service is being advertised?

(A) Sign printing
(B) Clothes cleaning
(C) Automobile repair
(D) Air conditioner maintenance

81. What does the speaker say is available for free?

(A) A care product
(B) Delivery service
(C) An initial inspection
(D) An extended warranty

82. How can listeners receive the offer?

(A) By installing a mobile app
(B) By mentioning the advertisement to a clerk
(C) By spending a certain amount of money
(D) By joining a mailing list

GO ON TO THE NEXT PAGE

Test 9

83. What did the speaker interview Mr. Young about?

(A) An award he won
(B) A structure he built
(C) His personal Web site
(D) His new book

84. What does the speaker encourage listeners to do?

(A) Attend a celebration
(B) Phone the radio station
(C) Make an online purchase
(D) Write down some information

85. What does the speaker imply when she says, "he's a full-time parent to three kids"?

(A) Mr. Young does not have much time to talk.
(B) Mr. Young's productivity is impressive.
(C) Mr. Young is an expert on a topic.
(D) Mr. Young often engages in an activity.

86. What does Londa help users do?

(A) Learn a foreign language
(B) Improve their physical fitness
(C) Manage their finances
(D) Follow current affairs

87. Why does the speaker say, "Londa is designed to be simple"?

(A) To provide reassurance about user-friendliness
(B) To justify a lack of sophisticated features
(C) To explain why an optional service is not necessary
(D) To express confusion about some advertising claims

88. According to the speaker, what is an advantage of Londa?

(A) It can be downloaded for free.
(B) It offers excellent customer support.
(C) It can retrieve data from many sources.
(D) It does not require much storage space.

89. Why is the speaker interested in buying a car?

(A) She often has to move large items.
(B) She wants to go on unplanned trips out of town.
(C) She lives in an area with unreliable public transportation.
(D) She likes to have privacy when going on journeys.

90. What feature does the speaker ask about?

(A) Electronic door locks
(B) Power seats
(C) Darkened windows
(D) Temperature control systems

91. What does the speaker say she will do in the evening?

(A) Go for a test drive
(B) Attend a job interview
(C) Have dinner with friends
(D) Suggest a sale price

92. What does the speaker mention about his appointment to CEO?

(A) It has not been officially announced.
(B) It has caused controversy.
(C) It will be temporary.
(D) It was unexpected.

93. What does the speaker say he will try to do?

(A) Expand a training initiative
(B) Improve internal communication
(C) Upgrade the safety of a facility
(D) Increase employee benefits

94. What most likely will take place next?

(A) A question-and-answer session
(B) A welcome reception
(C) A slide presentation
(D) A photo shoot

Vallond Video Hosting Packages

Package	Features	Monthly Cost
Package A	20 videos	Free
Package B	100 videos	$25
Package C	500 videos + viewing statistics	$100
Package D	Unlimited videos + viewing statistics	$300

Appointment Confirmation

Line 2 ---------- Steele Salon
Line 3 ---------- Stylist Greg Byrd
Line 4 ---------- Saturday, October 17
Line 5 ---------- 1:30 P.M.

Text "Yes" to confirm or call 555-0148 to change.

95. Where most likely do the listeners work?

(A) At a commercial farm
(B) At a plant shop
(C) At a public park
(D) At a landscaping firm

96. What does the speaker say all packages allow customers to do?

(A) Customize the video player's appearance
(B) Place regional restrictions on videos
(C) Enable viewers to share videos
(D) Display a Web link in a video

97. Look at the graphic. Which package does the speaker recommend?

(A) Package A
(B) Package B
(C) Package C
(D) Package D

98. What does the speaker say he was doing when the text message arrived?

(A) Playing a sport
(B) Making a call
(C) Seeing a movie
(D) Boarding a flight

99. Look at the graphic. Which line includes information that the speaker would like to change?

(A) Line 2
(B) Line 3
(C) Line 4
(D) Line 5

100. What does the speaker want to know about the salon?

(A) Whether its shampoos contain certain chemicals
(B) Whether it offers a product for purchase
(C) How much it charges for a hair treatment
(D) How long the effects of one of its services will last

This is the end of the Listening test.

Test 9

TEST 10

LISTENING TEST

In the Listening test, you will be asked to demonstrate how well you understand spoken English. The entire Listening test will last approximately 45 minutes. There are four parts, and directions are given for each part. You must mark your answers on the separate answer sheet. Do not write your answers in your test book.

PART 1

Directions: For each question in this part, you will hear four statements about a picture in your test book. When you hear the statements, you must select the one statement that best describes what you see in the picture. Then find the number of the question on your answer sheet and mark your answer. The statements will not be printed in your test book and will be spoken only one time.

Statement (C), "They're sitting at a table," is the best description of the picture, so you should select answer (C) and mark it on your answer sheet.

1.

2.

GO ON TO THE NEXT PAGE

Test 10

3.

4.

5.

6.

GO ON TO THE NEXT PAGE

Test 10

PART 2

Directions: You will hear a question or statement and three responses spoken in English. They will not be printed in your test book and will be spoken only one time. Select the best response to the question or statement and mark the letter (A), (B), or (C) on your answer sheet.

7. Mark your answer on your answer sheet.

8. Mark your answer on your answer sheet.

9. Mark your answer on your answer sheet.

10. Mark your answer on your answer sheet.

11. Mark your answer on your answer sheet.

12. Mark your answer on your answer sheet.

13. Mark your answer on your answer sheet.

14. Mark your answer on your answer sheet.

15. Mark your answer on your answer sheet.

16. Mark your answer on your answer sheet.

17. Mark your answer on your answer sheet.

18. Mark your answer on your answer sheet.

19. Mark your answer on your answer sheet.

20. Mark your answer on your answer sheet.

21. Mark your answer on your answer sheet.

22. Mark your answer on your answer sheet.

23. Mark your answer on your answer sheet.

24. Mark your answer on your answer sheet.

25. Mark your answer on your answer sheet.

26. Mark your answer on your answer sheet.

27. Mark your answer on your answer sheet.

28. Mark your answer on your answer sheet.

29. Mark your answer on your answer sheet.

30. Mark your answer on your answer sheet.

31. Mark your answer on your answer sheet.

PART 3

Directions: You will hear some conversations between two or more people. You will be asked to answer three questions about what the speakers say in each conversation. Select the best response to each question and mark the letter (A), (B), (C), or (D) on your answer sheet. The conversations will not be printed in your test book and will be spoken only one time.

32. What is the purpose of the man's visit?

(A) To inquire about a bill
(B) To pick up an order
(C) To renew a prescription
(D) To request a fit adjustment

33. What does the woman say is available?

(A) Some publications
(B) Some beverages
(C) Internet access
(D) Charging stations

34. What problem does the man mention?

(A) He did not bring a required item.
(B) He is unable to use an amenity.
(C) He can only wait a short duration.
(D) His contact information has changed.

35. Where does the woman work?

(A) At a city department
(B) At a financial institution
(C) At a news outlet
(D) At a law office

36. What does the man plan to do?

(A) Donate money to a charity
(B) Bid for a government contract
(C) Organize a community activity
(D) Launch a retail business

37. Why does the woman ask the man to visit her office?

(A) To discuss an idea
(B) To submit a payment
(C) To review some paperwork
(D) To meet a manager

38. According to the man, what took place in the morning?

(A) A training workshop
(B) A laboratory meeting
(C) A university class
(D) An inventory check

39. Why does the man say, "I took detailed notes"?

(A) To explain why he could not be contacted
(B) To emphasize the value of some information
(C) To show willingness to share a resource with the woman
(D) To decline the woman's offer of assistance

40. What is the woman nervous about?

(A) Leading a research project
(B) Interviewing for a job opening
(C) Learning the result of an application
(D) Giving a conference presentation

41. What has the woman's crew come to do?

(A) Connect power wiring
(B) Modify an outdoor space
(C) Install some interior surfaces
(D) Set up temperature control systems

42. What problem does Eric report?

(A) A budget limit has been reached.
(B) Some design plans have been revised.
(C) Some construction materials have flaws.
(D) The weather has been unfavorable.

43. What does Eric say to reassure the woman?

(A) Her company's expertise will still be necessary.
(B) Her company can probably complete a job swiftly.
(C) Her company will not be blamed for an issue.
(D) Her company will receive a cancelation fee.

GO ON TO THE NEXT PAGE

44. What has the woman decided to do?

(A) Ask for a pay raise
(B) Suspend a subscription
(C) Obtain an academic degree
(D) Resign from her position

45. What problem does the woman mention?

(A) Her compensation is unusually small.
(B) The market for a service is shrinking.
(C) A required task is unpleasant.
(D) Her workload has increased.

46. What does the man promise to do?

(A) Consider a request
(B) Supervise a transition
(C) Deliver some feedback
(D) Make an introduction

---

47. Who is the man?

(A) An author
(B) A musician
(C) An entrepreneur
(D) A politician

48. What does Tracy ask the man about?

(A) Challenges he faced
(B) His advice for youth
(C) His hopes for the future
(D) People who influenced him

49. What does the man recommend doing?

(A) Seeking a mentor relationship
(B) Reading a certain book
(C) Traveling to other countries
(D) Choosing a small university

---

50. What does the woman tell the man about?

(A) A negative review
(B) A broken Web link
(C) A scheduling error
(D) A security risk

51. Why will the man speak to Ashley?

(A) To ask for her help
(B) To give her some news
(C) To express his gratitude
(D) To provide some guidance

52. According to the woman, what must the speakers' company do?

(A) Issue a partial refund
(B) Save copies of some images
(C) Replace a software program
(D) Make an official announcement

---

53. What does the man's store mainly sell?

(A) Cosmetics
(B) Health food
(C) Housewares
(D) Stationery

54. What does the woman mention about the Cantling product?

(A) It was recently released.
(B) It is imported from abroad.
(C) It is not often sold at a discount.
(D) It has been discontinued.

55. What does the woman most likely mean when she says, "I'll be back soon"?

(A) She expects to use up a purchase quickly.
(B) She hopes that the man will do a favor for her.
(C) She parked close to the store's entrance.
(D) She intends to become a regular customer.

---

56. What does the woman say about a company executive?

(A) He does not speak a local language.
(B) He will bring a lot of luggage.
(C) He has a minor injury.
(D) He will not have much time.

57. According to the woman, what will not be necessary?

(A) Arranging ground transportation
(B) Giving a special greeting
(C) Reserving a private rest space
(D) Sending electronic flight updates

58. What will the woman most likely do after the conversation?

(A) Forward a confirmation e-mail
(B) Make another phone call
(C) Begin a car journey
(D) Visit a travel Web site

59. What service does the man say he has scheduled?

(A) Plant care
(B) Appliance repair
(C) Window cleaning
(D) Furniture removal

60. According to the man, what is special about the service?

(A) It is done outside of business hours.
(B) It does not involve hazardous chemicals.
(C) It is not available in all seasons.
(D) It is performed by machines.

61. What does the woman say she will do?

(A) Watch a demonstration
(B) Inform some colleagues
(C) Permit an inconvenience
(D) Take the rest of the day off

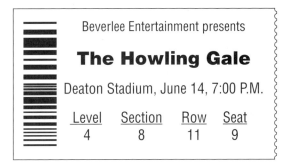

Beverlee Entertainment presents

The Howling Gale

Deaton Stadium, June 14, 7:00 P.M.

Level	Section	Row	Seat
4	8	11	9

62. Why is the woman late?

(A) It took her a long time to find parking.
(B) She was unaware of an admission policy.
(C) She misunderstood a spoken invitation.
(D) There was traffic around the stadium.

63. Look at the graphic. What section did the woman go to by mistake?

(A) 4
(B) 8
(C) 11
(D) 9

64. What does the man ask the woman to do?

(A) Bring him some refreshments
(B) Send him a photograph
(C) Look for concert staff
(D) Wait by a landmark

GO ON TO THE NEXT PAGE

Test 10

**2nd Annual Jasper
Environmental Awards Winners**

Conservation
Jamie Wright

Waste Management
Taylor Bowers

Technology
Hyun-Jin Wi

Communications
Cameron Kennedy

Operating Expenses	
520	Business Supplies
530	Utilities
540	Telecommunications
550	Repair and Maintenance

65. Who most likely is the woman?

(A) A city official
(B) A reporter
(C) A nonprofit executive
(D) A marketing consultant

66. What does the woman say about the awards program?

(A) It deserves more publicity.
(B) It selects surprising winners.
(C) It added a new category this year.
(D) Its ceremony can be viewed online.

67. Look at the graphic. Whom will the woman most likely contact?

(A) Jamie Wright
(B) Taylor Bowers
(C) Hyun-Jin Wi
(D) Cameron Kennedy

68. Look at the graphic. Which code will the expense most likely be entered under?

(A) 520
(B) 530
(C) 540
(D) 550

69. Why is the man concerned about the invoice?

(A) Its due date has already passed.
(B) It does not include some details.
(C) It is from an unfamiliar company.
(D) It requests an unusual amount of money.

70. What did the woman most likely do recently?

(A) Watched a television news show
(B) Cleared out a storage area
(C) Attended an industry event
(D) Delegated a task to an employee

Directions: You will hear some talks given by a single speaker. You will be asked to answer three questions about what the speaker says in each talk. Select the best response to each question and mark the letter (A), (B), (C), or (D) on your answer sheet. The talks will not be printed in your test book and will be spoken only one time.

71. What did the company recently adopt a policy on?

(A) How meeting notifications are sent out
(B) How many people must attend a meeting
(C) How meeting spaces can be used
(D) How long meetings can last

72. What does the speaker ask the listeners to do first?

(A) Put away some snacks
(B) Examine an agenda
(C) Prepare to take notes
(D) Write their names on a form

73. What is the purpose of the meeting?

(A) To discuss a safety issue
(B) To choose a new employee
(C) To evaluate a training program
(D) To plan an annual gathering

74. What did the speaker do in the morning?

(A) Finalized a digital drawing
(B) Browsed a furniture catalog
(C) Checked a sample item
(D) Received a sales proposal

75. What does the speaker imply when she says, "I guess it's not native to your area"?

(A) She knows why a cost might be high.
(B) She understands how a mistake happened.
(C) She is suggesting entering a new market.
(D) She is doubtful about a product's authenticity.

76. What does the speaker ask the listener to do?

(A) Give his opinion
(B) Expedite an order
(C) Update some machinery
(D) Search for an alternative

77. Where most likely are the listeners?

(A) On a bus
(B) On a boat
(C) On a footpath
(D) On an aircraft

78. What does the speaker point out to the listeners?

(A) Some wild animals
(B) Some rare plants
(C) A famous building
(D) A large body of water

79. What does the speaker encourage listeners to do later?

(A) Return some rental gear
(B) Purchase a video souvenir
(C) Post their photographs online
(D) Recommend the tour to others

80. What is the speaker announcing?

(A) The revision of a document
(B) The relocation of a workplace
(C) The reorganization of a company
(D) The retirement of an executive

81. What does the speaker imply when he says, "this will be a major change"?

(A) The listeners might be feeling concerned.
(B) A process will take place over a long period.
(C) He is optimistic about an outcome.
(D) A previous project had a limited impact.

82. What are the listeners asked to do?

(A) Schedule regular planning sessions
(B) Conserve some office supplies
(C) Monitor the results of a transition
(D) Avoid disclosing some information

Test 10

GO ON TO THE NEXT PAGE

83. Where does the speaker work?

(A) At a hotel
(B) At a travel agency
(C) At an architectural firm
(D) At a cleaning company

84. What does the speaker indicate about the listener?

(A) He has recently been hired.
(B) He has won a competition.
(C) He is a member of a rewards club.
(D) He is a professional public speaker.

85. What does the speaker say the listener can do?

(A) Try out a new offering
(B) Submit a form electronically
(C) Enjoy upgraded accommodations
(D) Participate in a celebration remotely

86. Who most likely are the listeners?

(A) Company shareholders
(B) Potential clients
(C) Volunteer workers
(D) Safety inspectors

87. What does the speaker mention about the convention center?

(A) It is the largest venue in the region.
(B) It will be renovated soon.
(C) It is affordable to rent.
(D) It uses modern technology.

88. What type of company is A Perfect Night?

(A) A prepared-meal delivery provider
(B) A chauffeur service
(C) An event organizer
(D) An employment agency

89. What does the speaker show on a screen?

(A) A list of actions
(B) A customer profile
(C) A set of statistics
(D) A Web page

90. Why does the speaker say, "Would you like to hear that"?

(A) To confirm that she should set up some audio equipment
(B) To express surprise at the listeners' interest in a story
(C) To make the listeners consider another person's perspective
(D) To indicate that a certain part of the workshop is unpopular

91. What will the listeners most likely do next?

(A) Take a short break
(B) Vote on a suggestion
(C) Open some packages
(D) Engage in role plays

92. What is the news report mainly about?

(A) A forthcoming mode of transportation
(B) The banning of automobiles from a street
(C) Some work to improve the quality of a road
(D) The creation of additional parking facilities

93. What does the speaker indicate about a project?

(A) It is intended to reduce environmental damage.
(B) It is opposed by a merchants' association.
(C) Its scope might expand in the future.
(D) It was carried out successfully in other cities.

94. What did the city government do for citizens in the past month?

(A) Notified them of an upcoming change
(B) Surveyed them about a proposal
(C) Relaxed a local regulation
(D) Held a special public event

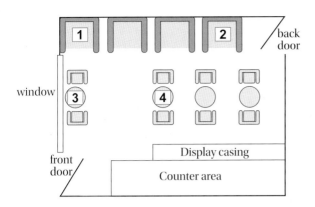

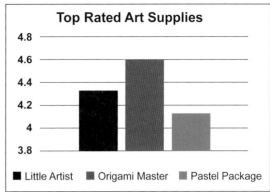

Top Rated Art Supplies

■ Little Artist ■ Origami Master ■ Pastel Package

95. What was the speaker mainly doing at the café?

(A) Engaging in a leisure activity
(B) Completing some freelance work
(C) Speaking with a business associate
(D) Studying for a professional exam

96. Look at the graphic. At which location was the speaker sitting?

(A) 1
(B) 2
(C) 3
(D) 4

97. What does the speaker say about the umbrella?

(A) It was expensive.
(B) It was a gift.
(C) Its design is unique.
(D) It belongs to a relative.

98. Look at the graphic. What Web site is the chart for?

(A) Hall's Market
(B) Success Arts
(C) Delta Mall Online
(D) Creative Ideas

99. What does the speaker propose doing?

(A) Hiring a consulting firm
(B) Expanding a product line
(C) Renegotiating a contract
(D) Increasing a promotional effort

100. What does the speaker ask Jenny about?

(A) Some financial resources
(B) Some employees' availability
(C) A manufacturing process
(D) A competitor's practices

This is the end of the Listening test.

ANSWER SHEET

YBM 실전토익 LC 1000

수험번호

응시일자 : 20 년 월 일

성명
한글
한자
영자

Test 01 (Part 1~4)

1	21	41	61	81
2	22	42	62	82
3	23	43	63	83
4	24	44	64	84
5	25	45	65	85
6	26	46	66	86
7	27	47	67	87
8	28	48	68	88
9	29	49	69	89
10	30	50	70	90
11	31	51	71	91
12	32	52	72	92
13	33	53	73	93
14	34	54	74	94
15	35	55	75	95
16	36	56	76	96
17	37	57	77	97
18	38	58	78	98
19	39	59	79	99
20	40	60	80	100

Test 02 (Part 1~4)

1	21	41	61	81
2	22	42	62	82
3	23	43	63	83
4	24	44	64	84
5	25	45	65	85
6	26	46	66	86
7	27	47	67	87
8	28	48	68	88
9	29	49	69	89
10	30	50	70	90
11	31	51	71	91
12	32	52	72	92
13	33	53	73	93
14	34	54	74	94
15	35	55	75	95
16	36	56	76	96
17	37	57	77	97
18	38	58	78	98
19	39	59	79	99
20	40	60	80	100

ANSWER SHEET

YBM 실전토익 LC 1000

수험번호

응시일자 : 20   년   월   일

성 명	한글
	한자
	영자

Test 03 (Part 1~4)

Test 04 (Part 1~4)

ANSWER SHEET

YBM 실전토익 LC 1000

수험번호

응시일자 : 20   년   월   일

성명: 한글 / 한자 / 영자

Test 05 (Part 1~4)

1	21	41	61	81
2	22	42	62	82
3	23	43	63	83
4	24	44	64	84
5	25	45	65	85
6	26	46	66	86
7	27	47	67	87
8	28	48	68	88
9	29	49	69	89
10	30	50	70	90
11	31	51	71	91
12	32	52	72	92
13	33	53	73	93
14	34	54	74	94
15	35	55	75	95
16	36	56	76	96
17	37	57	77	97
18	38	58	78	98
19	39	59	79	99
20	40	60	80	100

Test 06 (Part 1~4)

1	21	41	61	81
2	22	42	62	82
3	23	43	63	83
4	24	44	64	84
5	25	45	65	85
6	26	46	66	86
7	27	47	67	87
8	28	48	68	88
9	29	49	69	89
10	30	50	70	90
11	31	51	71	91
12	32	52	72	92
13	33	53	73	93
14	34	54	74	94
15	35	55	75	95
16	36	56	76	96
17	37	57	77	97
18	38	58	78	98
19	39	59	79	99
20	40	60	80	100

ANSWER SHEET

YBM 실전토익 LC 1000

수험번호						

응시일자 : 20 년 월 일

성명		
	한 글	
	한 자	
	영 자	

Test 07 (Part 1~4)

1	ⓐ ⓑ ⓒ ⓓ	21	ⓐ ⓑ ⓒ	41	ⓐ ⓑ ⓒ ⓓ	61	ⓐ ⓑ ⓒ ⓓ	81	ⓐ ⓑ ⓒ ⓓ
2	ⓐ ⓑ ⓒ ⓓ	22	ⓐ ⓑ ⓒ	42	ⓐ ⓑ ⓒ ⓓ	62	ⓐ ⓑ ⓒ ⓓ	82	ⓐ ⓑ ⓒ ⓓ
3	ⓐ ⓑ ⓒ ⓓ	23	ⓐ ⓑ ⓒ	43	ⓐ ⓑ ⓒ ⓓ	63	ⓐ ⓑ ⓒ ⓓ	83	ⓐ ⓑ ⓒ ⓓ
4	ⓐ ⓑ ⓒ ⓓ	24	ⓐ ⓑ ⓒ	44	ⓐ ⓑ ⓒ ⓓ	64	ⓐ ⓑ ⓒ ⓓ	84	ⓐ ⓑ ⓒ ⓓ
5	ⓐ ⓑ ⓒ ⓓ	25	ⓐ ⓑ ⓒ	45	ⓐ ⓑ ⓒ ⓓ	65	ⓐ ⓑ ⓒ ⓓ	85	ⓐ ⓑ ⓒ ⓓ
6	ⓐ ⓑ ⓒ ⓓ	26	ⓐ ⓑ ⓒ	46	ⓐ ⓑ ⓒ ⓓ	66	ⓐ ⓑ ⓒ ⓓ	86	ⓐ ⓑ ⓒ ⓓ
7	ⓐ ⓑ ⓒ	27	ⓐ ⓑ ⓒ	47	ⓐ ⓑ ⓒ ⓓ	67	ⓐ ⓑ ⓒ ⓓ	87	ⓐ ⓑ ⓒ ⓓ
8	ⓐ ⓑ ⓒ	28	ⓐ ⓑ ⓒ	48	ⓐ ⓑ ⓒ ⓓ	68	ⓐ ⓑ ⓒ ⓓ	88	ⓐ ⓑ ⓒ ⓓ
9	ⓐ ⓑ ⓒ	29	ⓐ ⓑ ⓒ	49	ⓐ ⓑ ⓒ ⓓ	69	ⓐ ⓑ ⓒ ⓓ	89	ⓐ ⓑ ⓒ ⓓ
10	ⓐ ⓑ ⓒ	30	ⓐ ⓑ ⓒ	50	ⓐ ⓑ ⓒ ⓓ	70	ⓐ ⓑ ⓒ ⓓ	90	ⓐ ⓑ ⓒ ⓓ
11	ⓐ ⓑ ⓒ	31	ⓐ ⓑ ⓒ	51	ⓐ ⓑ ⓒ ⓓ	71	ⓐ ⓑ ⓒ ⓓ	91	ⓐ ⓑ ⓒ ⓓ
12	ⓐ ⓑ ⓒ	32	ⓐ ⓑ ⓒ ⓓ	52	ⓐ ⓑ ⓒ ⓓ	72	ⓐ ⓑ ⓒ ⓓ	92	ⓐ ⓑ ⓒ ⓓ
13	ⓐ ⓑ ⓒ	33	ⓐ ⓑ ⓒ ⓓ	53	ⓐ ⓑ ⓒ ⓓ	73	ⓐ ⓑ ⓒ ⓓ	93	ⓐ ⓑ ⓒ ⓓ
14	ⓐ ⓑ ⓒ	34	ⓐ ⓑ ⓒ ⓓ	54	ⓐ ⓑ ⓒ ⓓ	74	ⓐ ⓑ ⓒ ⓓ	94	ⓐ ⓑ ⓒ ⓓ
15	ⓐ ⓑ ⓒ	35	ⓐ ⓑ ⓒ ⓓ	55	ⓐ ⓑ ⓒ ⓓ	75	ⓐ ⓑ ⓒ ⓓ	95	ⓐ ⓑ ⓒ ⓓ
16	ⓐ ⓑ ⓒ	36	ⓐ ⓑ ⓒ ⓓ	56	ⓐ ⓑ ⓒ ⓓ	76	ⓐ ⓑ ⓒ ⓓ	96	ⓐ ⓑ ⓒ ⓓ
17	ⓐ ⓑ ⓒ	37	ⓐ ⓑ ⓒ ⓓ	57	ⓐ ⓑ ⓒ ⓓ	77	ⓐ ⓑ ⓒ ⓓ	97	ⓐ ⓑ ⓒ ⓓ
18	ⓐ ⓑ ⓒ	38	ⓐ ⓑ ⓒ ⓓ	58	ⓐ ⓑ ⓒ ⓓ	78	ⓐ ⓑ ⓒ ⓓ	98	ⓐ ⓑ ⓒ ⓓ
19	ⓐ ⓑ ⓒ	39	ⓐ ⓑ ⓒ ⓓ	59	ⓐ ⓑ ⓒ ⓓ	79	ⓐ ⓑ ⓒ ⓓ	99	ⓐ ⓑ ⓒ ⓓ
20	ⓐ ⓑ ⓒ	40	ⓐ ⓑ ⓒ ⓓ	60	ⓐ ⓑ ⓒ ⓓ	80	ⓐ ⓑ ⓒ ⓓ	100	ⓐ ⓑ ⓒ ⓓ

Test 08 (Part 1~4)

1	ⓐ ⓑ ⓒ ⓓ	21	ⓐ ⓑ ⓒ	41	ⓐ ⓑ ⓒ ⓓ	61	ⓐ ⓑ ⓒ ⓓ	81	ⓐ ⓑ ⓒ ⓓ
2	ⓐ ⓑ ⓒ ⓓ	22	ⓐ ⓑ ⓒ	42	ⓐ ⓑ ⓒ ⓓ	62	ⓐ ⓑ ⓒ ⓓ	82	ⓐ ⓑ ⓒ ⓓ
3	ⓐ ⓑ ⓒ ⓓ	23	ⓐ ⓑ ⓒ	43	ⓐ ⓑ ⓒ ⓓ	63	ⓐ ⓑ ⓒ ⓓ	83	ⓐ ⓑ ⓒ ⓓ
4	ⓐ ⓑ ⓒ ⓓ	24	ⓐ ⓑ ⓒ	44	ⓐ ⓑ ⓒ ⓓ	64	ⓐ ⓑ ⓒ ⓓ	84	ⓐ ⓑ ⓒ ⓓ
5	ⓐ ⓑ ⓒ ⓓ	25	ⓐ ⓑ ⓒ	45	ⓐ ⓑ ⓒ ⓓ	65	ⓐ ⓑ ⓒ ⓓ	85	ⓐ ⓑ ⓒ ⓓ
6	ⓐ ⓑ ⓒ ⓓ	26	ⓐ ⓑ ⓒ	46	ⓐ ⓑ ⓒ ⓓ	66	ⓐ ⓑ ⓒ ⓓ	86	ⓐ ⓑ ⓒ ⓓ
7	ⓐ ⓑ ⓒ	27	ⓐ ⓑ ⓒ	47	ⓐ ⓑ ⓒ ⓓ	67	ⓐ ⓑ ⓒ ⓓ	87	ⓐ ⓑ ⓒ ⓓ
8	ⓐ ⓑ ⓒ	28	ⓐ ⓑ ⓒ	48	ⓐ ⓑ ⓒ ⓓ	68	ⓐ ⓑ ⓒ ⓓ	88	ⓐ ⓑ ⓒ ⓓ
9	ⓐ ⓑ ⓒ	29	ⓐ ⓑ ⓒ	49	ⓐ ⓑ ⓒ ⓓ	69	ⓐ ⓑ ⓒ ⓓ	89	ⓐ ⓑ ⓒ ⓓ
10	ⓐ ⓑ ⓒ	30	ⓐ ⓑ ⓒ	50	ⓐ ⓑ ⓒ ⓓ	70	ⓐ ⓑ ⓒ ⓓ	90	ⓐ ⓑ ⓒ ⓓ
11	ⓐ ⓑ ⓒ	31	ⓐ ⓑ ⓒ	51	ⓐ ⓑ ⓒ ⓓ	71	ⓐ ⓑ ⓒ ⓓ	91	ⓐ ⓑ ⓒ ⓓ
12	ⓐ ⓑ ⓒ	32	ⓐ ⓑ ⓒ ⓓ	52	ⓐ ⓑ ⓒ ⓓ	72	ⓐ ⓑ ⓒ ⓓ	92	ⓐ ⓑ ⓒ ⓓ
13	ⓐ ⓑ ⓒ	33	ⓐ ⓑ ⓒ ⓓ	53	ⓐ ⓑ ⓒ ⓓ	73	ⓐ ⓑ ⓒ ⓓ	93	ⓐ ⓑ ⓒ ⓓ
14	ⓐ ⓑ ⓒ	34	ⓐ ⓑ ⓒ ⓓ	54	ⓐ ⓑ ⓒ ⓓ	74	ⓐ ⓑ ⓒ ⓓ	94	ⓐ ⓑ ⓒ ⓓ
15	ⓐ ⓑ ⓒ	35	ⓐ ⓑ ⓒ ⓓ	55	ⓐ ⓑ ⓒ ⓓ	75	ⓐ ⓑ ⓒ ⓓ	95	ⓐ ⓑ ⓒ ⓓ
16	ⓐ ⓑ ⓒ	36	ⓐ ⓑ ⓒ ⓓ	56	ⓐ ⓑ ⓒ ⓓ	76	ⓐ ⓑ ⓒ ⓓ	96	ⓐ ⓑ ⓒ ⓓ
17	ⓐ ⓑ ⓒ	37	ⓐ ⓑ ⓒ ⓓ	57	ⓐ ⓑ ⓒ ⓓ	77	ⓐ ⓑ ⓒ ⓓ	97	ⓐ ⓑ ⓒ ⓓ
18	ⓐ ⓑ ⓒ	38	ⓐ ⓑ ⓒ ⓓ	58	ⓐ ⓑ ⓒ ⓓ	78	ⓐ ⓑ ⓒ ⓓ	98	ⓐ ⓑ ⓒ ⓓ
19	ⓐ ⓑ ⓒ	39	ⓐ ⓑ ⓒ ⓓ	59	ⓐ ⓑ ⓒ ⓓ	79	ⓐ ⓑ ⓒ ⓓ	99	ⓐ ⓑ ⓒ ⓓ
20	ⓐ ⓑ ⓒ	40	ⓐ ⓑ ⓒ ⓓ	60	ⓐ ⓑ ⓒ ⓓ	80	ⓐ ⓑ ⓒ ⓓ	100	ⓐ ⓑ ⓒ ⓓ

ANSWER SHEET

YBM 실전토익 LC 1000

수험번호						

응시일자 : 20 년 월 일

성명	한글	
	한자	
	영자	

Test 09 (Part 1~4)

1	ⓐ ⓑ ⓒ ⓓ	21	ⓐ ⓑ ⓒ	41	ⓐ ⓑ ⓒ ⓓ	61	ⓐ ⓑ ⓒ ⓓ	81	ⓐ ⓑ ⓒ ⓓ
2	ⓐ ⓑ ⓒ ⓓ	22	ⓐ ⓑ ⓒ	42	ⓐ ⓑ ⓒ ⓓ	62	ⓐ ⓑ ⓒ ⓓ	82	ⓐ ⓑ ⓒ ⓓ
3	ⓐ ⓑ ⓒ ⓓ	23	ⓐ ⓑ ⓒ	43	ⓐ ⓑ ⓒ ⓓ	63	ⓐ ⓑ ⓒ ⓓ	83	ⓐ ⓑ ⓒ ⓓ
4	ⓐ ⓑ ⓒ ⓓ	24	ⓐ ⓑ ⓒ	44	ⓐ ⓑ ⓒ ⓓ	64	ⓐ ⓑ ⓒ ⓓ	84	ⓐ ⓑ ⓒ ⓓ
5	ⓐ ⓑ ⓒ ⓓ	25	ⓐ ⓑ ⓒ	45	ⓐ ⓑ ⓒ ⓓ	65	ⓐ ⓑ ⓒ ⓓ	85	ⓐ ⓑ ⓒ ⓓ
6	ⓐ ⓑ ⓒ ⓓ	26	ⓐ ⓑ ⓒ	46	ⓐ ⓑ ⓒ ⓓ	66	ⓐ ⓑ ⓒ ⓓ	86	ⓐ ⓑ ⓒ ⓓ
7	ⓐ ⓑ ⓒ	27	ⓐ ⓑ ⓒ	47	ⓐ ⓑ ⓒ ⓓ	67	ⓐ ⓑ ⓒ ⓓ	87	ⓐ ⓑ ⓒ ⓓ
8	ⓐ ⓑ ⓒ	28	ⓐ ⓑ ⓒ	48	ⓐ ⓑ ⓒ ⓓ	68	ⓐ ⓑ ⓒ ⓓ	88	ⓐ ⓑ ⓒ ⓓ
9	ⓐ ⓑ ⓒ	29	ⓐ ⓑ ⓒ	49	ⓐ ⓑ ⓒ ⓓ	69	ⓐ ⓑ ⓒ ⓓ	89	ⓐ ⓑ ⓒ ⓓ
10	ⓐ ⓑ ⓒ	30	ⓐ ⓑ ⓒ	50	ⓐ ⓑ ⓒ ⓓ	70	ⓐ ⓑ ⓒ ⓓ	90	ⓐ ⓑ ⓒ ⓓ
11	ⓐ ⓑ ⓒ	31	ⓐ ⓑ ⓒ	51	ⓐ ⓑ ⓒ ⓓ	71	ⓐ ⓑ ⓒ ⓓ	91	ⓐ ⓑ ⓒ ⓓ
12	ⓐ ⓑ ⓒ	32	ⓐ ⓑ ⓒ ⓓ	52	ⓐ ⓑ ⓒ ⓓ	72	ⓐ ⓑ ⓒ ⓓ	92	ⓐ ⓑ ⓒ ⓓ
13	ⓐ ⓑ ⓒ	33	ⓐ ⓑ ⓒ ⓓ	53	ⓐ ⓑ ⓒ ⓓ	73	ⓐ ⓑ ⓒ ⓓ	93	ⓐ ⓑ ⓒ ⓓ
14	ⓐ ⓑ ⓒ	34	ⓐ ⓑ ⓒ ⓓ	54	ⓐ ⓑ ⓒ ⓓ	74	ⓐ ⓑ ⓒ ⓓ	94	ⓐ ⓑ ⓒ ⓓ
15	ⓐ ⓑ ⓒ	35	ⓐ ⓑ ⓒ ⓓ	55	ⓐ ⓑ ⓒ ⓓ	75	ⓐ ⓑ ⓒ ⓓ	95	ⓐ ⓑ ⓒ ⓓ
16	ⓐ ⓑ ⓒ	36	ⓐ ⓑ ⓒ ⓓ	56	ⓐ ⓑ ⓒ ⓓ	76	ⓐ ⓑ ⓒ ⓓ	96	ⓐ ⓑ ⓒ ⓓ
17	ⓐ ⓑ ⓒ	37	ⓐ ⓑ ⓒ ⓓ	57	ⓐ ⓑ ⓒ ⓓ	77	ⓐ ⓑ ⓒ ⓓ	97	ⓐ ⓑ ⓒ ⓓ
18	ⓐ ⓑ ⓒ	38	ⓐ ⓑ ⓒ ⓓ	58	ⓐ ⓑ ⓒ ⓓ	78	ⓐ ⓑ ⓒ ⓓ	98	ⓐ ⓑ ⓒ ⓓ
19	ⓐ ⓑ ⓒ	39	ⓐ ⓑ ⓒ ⓓ	59	ⓐ ⓑ ⓒ ⓓ	79	ⓐ ⓑ ⓒ ⓓ	99	ⓐ ⓑ ⓒ ⓓ
20	ⓐ ⓑ ⓒ	40	ⓐ ⓑ ⓒ ⓓ	60	ⓐ ⓑ ⓒ ⓓ	80	ⓐ ⓑ ⓒ ⓓ	100	ⓐ ⓑ ⓒ ⓓ

Test 10 (Part 1~4)

1	ⓐ ⓑ ⓒ ⓓ	21	ⓐ ⓑ ⓒ	41	ⓐ ⓑ ⓒ ⓓ	61	ⓐ ⓑ ⓒ ⓓ	81	ⓐ ⓑ ⓒ ⓓ
2	ⓐ ⓑ ⓒ ⓓ	22	ⓐ ⓑ ⓒ	42	ⓐ ⓑ ⓒ ⓓ	62	ⓐ ⓑ ⓒ ⓓ	82	ⓐ ⓑ ⓒ ⓓ
3	ⓐ ⓑ ⓒ ⓓ	23	ⓐ ⓑ ⓒ	43	ⓐ ⓑ ⓒ ⓓ	63	ⓐ ⓑ ⓒ ⓓ	83	ⓐ ⓑ ⓒ ⓓ
4	ⓐ ⓑ ⓒ ⓓ	24	ⓐ ⓑ ⓒ	44	ⓐ ⓑ ⓒ ⓓ	64	ⓐ ⓑ ⓒ ⓓ	84	ⓐ ⓑ ⓒ ⓓ
5	ⓐ ⓑ ⓒ ⓓ	25	ⓐ ⓑ ⓒ	45	ⓐ ⓑ ⓒ ⓓ	65	ⓐ ⓑ ⓒ ⓓ	85	ⓐ ⓑ ⓒ ⓓ
6	ⓐ ⓑ ⓒ ⓓ	26	ⓐ ⓑ ⓒ	46	ⓐ ⓑ ⓒ ⓓ	66	ⓐ ⓑ ⓒ ⓓ	86	ⓐ ⓑ ⓒ ⓓ
7	ⓐ ⓑ ⓒ	27	ⓐ ⓑ ⓒ	47	ⓐ ⓑ ⓒ ⓓ	67	ⓐ ⓑ ⓒ ⓓ	87	ⓐ ⓑ ⓒ ⓓ
8	ⓐ ⓑ ⓒ	28	ⓐ ⓑ ⓒ	48	ⓐ ⓑ ⓒ ⓓ	68	ⓐ ⓑ ⓒ ⓓ	88	ⓐ ⓑ ⓒ ⓓ
9	ⓐ ⓑ ⓒ	29	ⓐ ⓑ ⓒ	49	ⓐ ⓑ ⓒ ⓓ	69	ⓐ ⓑ ⓒ ⓓ	89	ⓐ ⓑ ⓒ ⓓ
10	ⓐ ⓑ ⓒ	30	ⓐ ⓑ ⓒ	50	ⓐ ⓑ ⓒ ⓓ	70	ⓐ ⓑ ⓒ ⓓ	90	ⓐ ⓑ ⓒ ⓓ
11	ⓐ ⓑ ⓒ	31	ⓐ ⓑ ⓒ	51	ⓐ ⓑ ⓒ ⓓ	71	ⓐ ⓑ ⓒ ⓓ	91	ⓐ ⓑ ⓒ ⓓ
12	ⓐ ⓑ ⓒ	32	ⓐ ⓑ ⓒ ⓓ	52	ⓐ ⓑ ⓒ ⓓ	72	ⓐ ⓑ ⓒ ⓓ	92	ⓐ ⓑ ⓒ ⓓ
13	ⓐ ⓑ ⓒ	33	ⓐ ⓑ ⓒ ⓓ	53	ⓐ ⓑ ⓒ ⓓ	73	ⓐ ⓑ ⓒ ⓓ	93	ⓐ ⓑ ⓒ ⓓ
14	ⓐ ⓑ ⓒ	34	ⓐ ⓑ ⓒ ⓓ	54	ⓐ ⓑ ⓒ ⓓ	74	ⓐ ⓑ ⓒ ⓓ	94	ⓐ ⓑ ⓒ ⓓ
15	ⓐ ⓑ ⓒ	35	ⓐ ⓑ ⓒ ⓓ	55	ⓐ ⓑ ⓒ ⓓ	75	ⓐ ⓑ ⓒ ⓓ	95	ⓐ ⓑ ⓒ ⓓ
16	ⓐ ⓑ ⓒ	36	ⓐ ⓑ ⓒ ⓓ	56	ⓐ ⓑ ⓒ ⓓ	76	ⓐ ⓑ ⓒ ⓓ	96	ⓐ ⓑ ⓒ ⓓ
17	ⓐ ⓑ ⓒ	37	ⓐ ⓑ ⓒ ⓓ	57	ⓐ ⓑ ⓒ ⓓ	77	ⓐ ⓑ ⓒ ⓓ	97	ⓐ ⓑ ⓒ ⓓ
18	ⓐ ⓑ ⓒ	38	ⓐ ⓑ ⓒ ⓓ	58	ⓐ ⓑ ⓒ ⓓ	78	ⓐ ⓑ ⓒ ⓓ	98	ⓐ ⓑ ⓒ ⓓ
19	ⓐ ⓑ ⓒ	39	ⓐ ⓑ ⓒ ⓓ	59	ⓐ ⓑ ⓒ ⓓ	79	ⓐ ⓑ ⓒ ⓓ	99	ⓐ ⓑ ⓒ ⓓ
20	ⓐ ⓑ ⓒ	40	ⓐ ⓑ ⓒ ⓓ	60	ⓐ ⓑ ⓒ ⓓ	80	ⓐ ⓑ ⓒ ⓓ	100	ⓐ ⓑ ⓒ ⓓ

ANSWER SHEET

YBM 실전토익 LC 1000

수험번호

응시일자 : 20 년 월 일

성명
- 한글
- 한자
- 영자

Part 1~4

(answer bubbles for questions 1–100)

Part 1~4

(answer bubbles for questions 1–100)

YBM
실전토익
LC1000
3

YBM

1 (D)	2 (C)	3 (A)	4 (C)	5 (B)
6 (C)	7 (C)	8 (B)	9 (B)	10 (C)
11 (A)	12 (B)	13 (C)	14 (A)	15 (A)
16 (B)	17 (C)	18 (A)	19 (C)	20 (B)
21 (B)	22 (C)	23 (A)	24 (B)	25 (B)
26 (A)	27 (A)	28 (C)	29 (B)	30 (B)
31 (A)	32 (A)	33 (B)	34 (C)	35 (D)
36 (D)	37 (B)	38 (D)	39 (A)	40 (B)
41 (C)	42 (D)	43 (B)	44 (A)	45 (B)
46 (D)	47 (C)	48 (B)	49 (A)	50 (B)
51 (C)	52 (D)	53 (A)	54 (C)	55 (D)
56 (B)	57 (A)	58 (A)	59 (D)	60 (A)
61 (C)	62 (C)	63 (D)	64 (D)	65 (B)
66 (D)	67 (D)	68 (A)	69 (D)	70 (A)
71 (A)	72 (B)	73 (C)	74 (C)	75 (C)
76 (A)	77 (C)	78 (A)	79 (D)	80 (B)
81 (C)	82 (B)	83 (B)	84 (A)	85 (C)
86 (D)	87 (C)	88 (A)	89 (A)	90 (B)
91 (C)	92 (B)	93 (A)	94 (D)	95 (B)
96 (D)	97 (C)	98 (D)	99 (B)	100 (C)

PART 1

1 M-Cn

(A) She's drinking coffee in a café.
(B) She's arranging books on a windowsill.
(C) She's plugging in a notebook computer.
(D) She's talking on a mobile phone.

(A) 여자는 카페에서 커피를 마시고 있다.
(B) 여자는 창턱에 책을 배열하고 있다.
(C) 여자는 노트북 컴퓨터를 전원에 연결하고 있다.
(D) 여자는 휴대폰으로 통화하고 있다.

어휘 arrange 정리하다, 배열하다 windowsill 창턱 plug in 전원을 연결하다

해설 1인 등장 사진 – 인물의 동작 묘사
(A) 동사 오답. 여자가 카페에서 커피를 마시고 있는(is drinking coffee in a café) 모습이 아니므로 오답.
(B) 동사 오답. 여자가 창턱에 책을 배열하고 있는(is arranging books on a windowsill) 모습이 아니므로 오답.
(C) 동사 오답. 여자가 노트북 컴퓨터를 전원에 연결하고 있는(is plugging in a notebook computer) 모습이 아니므로 오답.
(D) 정답. 여자가 휴대폰으로 통화하고 있는(is talking on a mobile phone) 모습이므로 정답.

2 W-Br

(A) He's pulling a string to close some blinds.
(B) He's painting the outside of a house.
(C) He's cleaning a window with a cloth.
(D) He's using a tool to repair a roof.

(A) 남자는 블라인드를 치기 위해 끈을 당기고 있다.
(B) 남자는 집 외관을 페인트칠하고 있다.
(C) 남자는 천으로 창문을 닦고 있다.
(D) 남자는 지붕을 수리하기 위해 도구를 사용하고 있다.

어휘 string 줄, 끈 blind 블라인드 cloth 천, 헝겊 repair 수리하다

해설 1인 등장 사진 – 인물의 동작 묘사
(A) 동사 오답. 남자가 블라인드를 치기 위해 끈을 당기고 있는(is pulling a string to close some blinds) 모습이 아니므로 오답.
(B) 동사 오답. 남자가 집 외관을 페인트칠하고 있는(is painting the outside of a house) 모습이 아니므로 오답.
(C) 정답. 남자가 천으로 창문을 닦고 있는(is cleaning a window with a cloth) 모습이므로 정답.
(D) 사진에 없는 명사를 이용한 오답. 사진에 지붕(roof)의 모습이 보이지 않으므로 오답.

3 M-Au

(A) Some passengers are seated in an airplane.
(B) Some food has been placed on a tray.
(C) Some suitcases are standing in an aisle.
(D) Some storage compartments have been left open.

(A) 승객들 몇 명이 기내에 앉아 있다.
(B) 음식이 쟁반에 놓여 있다.
(C) 여행 가방 몇 개가 통로에 놓여 있다.
(D) 짐칸 몇 개가 열려 있다.

어휘 passenger 승객 tray 쟁반 suitcase 여행 가방 aisle 통로 storage compartment 짐칸

해설 혼합 사진 – 사람 또는 사물 묘사
(A) 정답. 승객들 몇 명(some passengers)이 기내에 앉아 있는(are seated in an airplane) 모습이므로 정답.
(B) 사진에 없는 명사를 이용한 오답. 사진에 음식(food)의 모습이 보이지 않으므로 오답.
(C) 사진에 없는 명사를 이용한 오답. 사진에 여행 가방(suitcases)의 모습이 보이지 않으므로 오답.
(D) 동사 오답. 짐칸 몇 개(some storage compartments)가 열려 있는(have been left open) 모습이 아니므로 오답.

4 W-Am 고난도

(A) Railings are being installed on a platform.
(B) There is a row of signs inside a warehouse.
(C) A set of stairs leads to a doorway.
(D) A truck is parked near an intersection.

(A) 승강장에 난간이 설치되고 있다.
(B) 창고 안에 표지판이 줄지어 있다.
(C) 계단이 출입구 쪽으로 이어진다.
(D) 트럭 한 대가 교차로 근처에 주차되어 있다.

어휘 railing 난간 install 설치하다 platform 승강장 row 열[줄]
sign 표지판 warehouse 창고 lead to ~로 이어지다 doorway
출입구 intersection 교차로

해설 배경 사진 – 실외 사물의 상태 묘사
(A) 동사 오답. 난간이(railings)이 승강장에 설치되고 있는(are being installed on a platform) 모습이 아니므로 오답.
(B) 위치 오답. 창고 안(inside a warehouse)에 표지판이 줄지어 있는(there is a row of signs) 모습이 아니므로 오답.
(C) 정답. 계단(a set of stairs)이 출입구 쪽으로 이어지는(leads to a doorway) 모습이므로 정답.
(D) 동사 오답. 트럭 한 대(a truck)가 교차로 근처에 주차되어 있는(is parked near an intersection) 모습이 아니므로 오답.

5 M-Cn

(A) Some charts are being projected onto a screen.
(B) A group of people are looking at some papers.
(C) A woman is writing on a whiteboard.
(D) Some cups are being stacked on a table.

(A) 차트 몇 개가 스크린에 비춰지고 있다.
(B) 여러 사람들이 서류를 보고 있다.
(C) 여자 한 명이 화이트보드에 글을 쓰고 있다.
(D) 탁자 위에 컵 몇 개가 쌓이고 있다.

어휘 project (영상 등을) 비추다 stack 쌓다; 무더기

해설 혼합 사진 – 사람 또는 사물 묘사
(A) 사진에 없는 명사를 이용한 오답. 사진에 스크린(a screen)의 모습이 보이지 않으므로 오답.
(B) 정답. 여러 사람들(a group of people)이 서류를 보고 있는(are looking at some papers) 모습이므로 정답.

(C) 사진에 없는 명사를 이용한 오답. 사진에 화이트보드(a whiteboard)의 모습이 보이지 않으므로 오답.
(D) 동사 오답. 컵 몇 개(some cups)가 탁자 위에 쌓이고 있는(are being stacked on a table) 모습이 아니므로 오답.

6 W-Br 고난도

(A) Some bushes are being planted.
(B) There are chairs next to a swimming pool.
(C) A fence has been built around a grassy area.
(D) A small lawn is being mowed.

(A) 관목들이 심어지고 있다.
(B) 수영장 옆에 의자들이 있다.
(C) 풀로 덮인 땅 주변에 울타리가 세워졌다.
(D) 작은 잔디밭이 깎이고 있다.

어휘 bush 관목 plant (나무 등을) 심다; 식물 fence 울타리 grassy
풀로 덮인 lawn 잔디 mow 깎다

해설 배경 사진 – 실외 사물의 상태 묘사
(A) 동사 오답. 관목들(some bushes)이 심어지고 있는(are being planted) 모습이 아니므로 오답.
(B) 사진에 없는 명사를 이용한 오답. 사진에 수영장(a swimming pool)의 모습이 보이지 않으므로 오답.
(C) 정답. 울타리(a fence)가 풀로 덮인 땅 주변에 세워져 있는(has been built around a grassy area) 모습이므로 정답.
(D) 동사 오답. 작은 잔디밭(a small lawn)이 깎이고 있는(is being mowed) 모습이 아니므로 오답.

PART 2

7

M-Cn Where's the shopping mall you're going to?
W-Br (A) Let's use the company credit card.
(B) Mostly clothing and electronics stores.
(C) Over on the north side of town.

당신이 가려는 쇼핑몰이 어디에 있나요?
(A) 법인 카드를 씁시다.
(B) 주로 의류와 전자제품 매장이요.
(C) 시내 북쪽에요.

어휘 mostly 주로 electronics 전자 기기

해설 쇼핑몰의 위치를 묻는 Where 의문문
(A) 연상 단어 오답. 질문의 shopping에서 연상 가능한 credit card를 이용한 오답.
(B) 연상 단어 오답. 질문의 shopping mall에서 연상 가능한 stores를 이용한 오답.
(C) 정답. 쇼핑몰의 위치를 묻는 질문에 시내 북쪽에 있다고 구체적으로 응답하고 있으므로 정답.

8

W-Am When did Bernard join this study group?

M-Cn (A) For conversation practice.

(B) Last semester.

(C) Twice a week.

버나드는 언제 이 연구 모임에 합류했나요?
(A) 대화 연습을 위해서요.
(B) 지난 학기요.
(C) 일주일에 두 번요.

어휘 semester 학기

해설 버나드가 모임에 합류한 시점을 묻는 When 의문문
(A) 질문과 상관없는 오답. Why 의문문에 대한 응답이므로 오답.
(B) 정답. 버나드가 연구 모임에 합류한 시점을 묻는 질문에 지난 학기라고 시점을 알려주고 있으므로 정답.
(C) 질문과 상관없는 오답. How often 의문문에 대한 응답이므로 오답.

9

M-Au Why is Ms. Hill leaving the conference early?

W-Am (A) On the express train.

(B) To attend an important meeting.

(C) Yes, the session on marketing.

힐 씨는 왜 학회를 일찍 떠나죠?
(A) 급행열차로요.
(B) 중요한 회의에 참석하려고요.
(C) 네, 마케팅에 관한 회의입니다.

어휘 conference 학회, 회의 express train 급행 열차 session 회의
(특정 활동을 위한) 시간

해설 힐 씨가 학회를 일찍 떠나는 이유를 묻는 Why 의문문
(A) 연상 단어 오답. 질문의 leave에서 연상 가능한 train을 이용한 오답.
(B) 정답. 힐 씨가 학회를 일찍 떠나는 이유를 묻는 질문에 중요한 회의에 참석하기 위해서라고 구체적으로 응답하고 있으므로 정답.
(C) Yes/No 불가 오답. Why 의문문에는 Yes/No 응답이 불가능하므로 오답.

10

고난도

W-Br Who had the idea of labeling these drawers?

M-Au (A) Only the locked ones.

(B) Use green labels for current clients.

(C) It has certainly helped, hasn't it?

누가 이 서랍들에 라벨을 붙일 생각을 한 거죠?
(A) 잠긴 것들만요.
(B) 기존 고객들에게는 녹색 라벨을 사용하세요.
(C) 확실히 도움이 됐어요, 그렇죠?

어휘 label 상표[이름표]를 붙이다; 표[라벨] drawer 서랍 locked 잠긴
current 현재의

해설 상표를 붙일 아이디어를 낸 사람을 묻는 Who 의문문
(A) 연상 단어 오답. 질문의 drawer에서 연상 가능한 locked를 이용한 오답.
(B) 파생어 오답. 질문의 labeling과 파생어 관계인 labels를 이용한 오답.
(C) 정답. 서랍에 라벨을 붙일 생각을 한 사람이 누구인지 묻는 질문의 의도를 아이디어를 칭찬하기 위한 질문으로 받아들여 해당 아이디어가 도움이 되었다고 동의를 표하고 있으므로 정답.

11

고난도

W-Br How often should we change the batteries?

M-Cn (A) This light will flash when they start to run out.

(B) You don't like the way it looks now?

(C) It's our latest energy bill.

얼마나 자주 건전지를 교체해야 하나요?
(A) 닳기 시작하면 불빛이 깜박거릴 거예요.
(B) 지금 모습이 마음에 들지 않으세요?
(C) 그것은 가장 최근 에너지 요금이에요.

어휘 run out 다 떨어지다 latest 최근의 bill 청구서

해설 건전지 교체 주기를 묻는 How often 의문문
(A) 정답. 건전지를 얼마나 자주 교체해야 하는지를 묻는 질문에 깜박이는 불빛으로 교체 시기를 확인할 수 있다고 알려주므로 정답.
(B) 연상 단어 오답. 질문의 change에서 연상 가능한 don't like를 이용한 오답.
(C) 연상 단어 오답. 질문의 batteries에서 연상 가능한 energy를 이용한 오답.

12

W-Am Can I borrow your pen to fill out this questionnaire?

M-Cn (A) Just answer as honestly as possible.

(B) Sure, as soon as I'm finished with it.

(C) Sorry, it's already full.

이 설문지를 작성하게 펜 좀 빌릴 수 있을까요?
(A) 가능한 솔직히 답변해주세요.
(B) 그럼요, 제가 다 쓰고 나면 바로 쓰세요.
(C) 죄송합니다, 이미 꽉 찼어요.

어휘 fill out 작성하다 questionnaire 설문지 honestly 솔직히

해설 부탁/요청의 의문문
(A) 연상 단어 오답. 질문의 questionnaire에서 연상 가능한 answer를 이용한 오답.
(B) 정답. 설문지를 작성하기 위해 펜을 빌릴 수 있는지 부탁하는 질문에 그럼요(Sure)라고 수락한 뒤, 자신이 다 쓰고 나면 바로 쓰라며 긍정 답변과 일관된 내용을 덧붙이고 있으므로 정답.
(C) 연상 단어 오답. 질문의 fill(채우다)에서 연상 가능한 full(꽉 찬)을 이용한 오답.

13

W-Am Has the printer been repaired yet?

M-Au (A) Yes, a faster model.

(B) They charge ten cents per page.

(C) I haven't tried using it.

프린터는 이미 수리되었나요?

(A) 네, 더 빠른 모델이요.

(B) 페이지당 10센트씩 받던데요.

(C) 아직 사용해보지 않았어요.

어휘 repair 수리하다   charge 청구하다; 요금   per ~당

해설 프린터 수리 여부를 확인하는 조동사(Has) 의문문

(A) 연상 단어 오답. 질문의 printer에서 연상 가능한 model을 이용한 오답.

(B) 연상 단어 오답. 질문의 printer에서 연상 가능한 page를 이용한 오답.

(C) 정답. 인쇄기가 수리되었는지를 묻는 질문에 아직 사용해보지 않았다며 답변을 줄 수 없다는 점을 우회적으로 응답하고 있으므로 정답.

14

M-Cn What did the doctor recommend?

M-Au (A) My appointment was cancelled.

(B) Just a minor cold.

(C) I like the clinic on Morton Street.

의사가 무엇을 권했나요?

(A) 제 예약이 취소되었어요.

(B) 그냥 가벼운 감기예요.

(C) 저는 모튼 가에 있는 병원이 좋아요.

어휘 recommend 권하다   appointment 예약   cancel 취소하다   minor 가벼운, 작은

해설 의사의 권고 사항을 묻는 What 의문문

(A) 정답. 의사의 권고 사항을 묻는 질문에 진료가 취소되었다며 답변을 줄 수 없음을 우회적으로 응답하고 있으므로 정답.

(B) 연상 단어 오답. 질문의 doctor에서 연상 가능한 cold를 이용한 오답.

(C) 연상 단어 오답. 질문의 doctor에서 연상 가능한 clinic을 이용한 오답.

15

M-Cn Wasn't Craig looking for this book?

W-Br (A) Yes—we should take it to him.

(B) Try page eighty-two.

(C) No, it was already booked.

크레이그가 이 책을 찾고 있지 않았나요?

(A) 네, 그에게 가져다줘야겠어요.

(B) 82쪽을 보세요.

(C) 아니요, 이미 예약이 됐어요.

해설 크레이그가 책을 찾고 있었는지 여부를 확인하는 부정의문문

(A) 정답. 크레이그가 책을 찾고 있었는지 여부를 묻는 질문에 네(Yes)라고 대답한 뒤, 그에게 가져다줘야겠다며 긍정 답변과 일관된 내용을 덧붙이고 있으므로 정답.

(B) 연상 단어 오답. 질문의 book에서 연상 가능한 page를 이용한 오답.

(C) 유사 발음 오답. 질문의 book과 발음이 유사한 booked를 이용한 오답.

16

W-Am Why don't you ask Nick Reynolds to interview for the position?

M-Au (A) I don't have the required experience.

(B) Well, he seems happy with his current job.

(C) In an e-mail to all of the candidates.

닉 레이놀즈에게 그 직책에 면접을 보라고 하는 게 어때요?

(A) 저는 필수 경력이 없어요.

(B) 글쎄요, 그는 지금 직업에 만족하는 것 같아요.

(C) 지원자 모두에게 보낸 이메일에서요.

어휘 position 자리   required 필수의   current 현재의   candidate 지원자

해설 제안/권유의 의문문

(A) 연상 단어 오답. 질문의 interview와 position에서 연상 가능한 required experience를 이용한 오답.

(B) 정답. 닉에게 면접을 볼 것을 권하라고 제안하는 질문에 그는 지금 직업에 만족하는 것 같다며 거절의 뜻을 우회적으로 밝히고 있으므로 정답.

(C) 연상 단어 오답. 질문의 interview와 position에서 연상 가능한 candidates를 이용한 오답.

17

M-Cn How are we getting to the factory for the inspection?

W-Am (A) The household appliances it makes.

(B) Sure, that would be fine.

(C) Don't worry, I brought my car today.

점검하러 공장에 어떻게 갈까요?

(A) 거기서 만드는 가전제품들이요.

(B) 물론이죠, 그러면 좋겠네요.

(C) 걱정 마요, 오늘은 제 차를 가져왔어요.

어휘 inspection 검사, 점검   household appliances 가전제품

해설 공장에 가는 방법을 묻는 How 의문문

(A) 연상 단어 오답. 질문의 factory에서 연상 가능한 appliances를 이용한 오답.

(B) Yes/No 불가 오답. How 의문문에는 Yes/No 응답이 불가능한데, Sure도 일종의 Yes 응답이라고 볼 수 있으므로 오답.

(C) 정답. 공장에 가는 방법을 묻는 질문에 차를 가져왔다고 우회적으로 응답하고 있으므로 정답.

18

M-Au Do you want to order lunch from Haley's Diner again, or try somewhere new?

W-Br (A) Haley's sounds good.

(B) Yes, I cooked it myself.

(C) In front of the restaurant.

헤일리즈 식당에서 또 점심을 주문할까요 아니면 새로운 곳을 시도해 볼까요?

(A) 헤일리즈 식당이 좋을 것 같아요.

(B) 네, 제가 직접 요리했어요.

(C) 식당 앞에서요.

어휘 order 주문하다 diner 작은 식당 somewhere 어딘가에

해설 식사 주문을 어느 식당에서 할지 묻는 선택의문문

(A) 정답. 점심식사를 어느 식당에서 주문할지를 묻는 선택의문문에 헤일리즈 식당이 좋을 것 같다며 두 선택안 중 하나를 택해 응답하고 있으므로 정답.

(B) 연상 단어 오답. 질문의 lunch에서 연상 가능한 cooked를 이용한 오답.

(C) 연상 단어 오답. 질문의 lunch에서 연상 가능한 restaurant을 이용한 오답.

19

M-Cn Isn't the new office furniture arriving this afternoon?

W-Am (A) The address is written here.

(B) I've found it very comfortable.

(C) There's been a shipping delay.

새 사무실 가구가 오늘 오후에 도착하지 않나요?

(A) 주소가 여기에 쓰여 있네요.

(B) 그거 정말 편하더군요.

(C) 배송이 지연됐어요.

어휘 furniture 가구 address 주소 comfortable 편한 shipping 배송 delay 지연

해설 새 가구의 도착 시점을 확인하는 부정의문문

(A) 연상 단어 오답. 질문의 arrive에서 연상 가능한 address를 이용한 오답.

(B) 연상 단어 오답. 질문의 furniture에서 연상 가능한 comfortable을 이용한 오답.

(C) 정답. 새 사무실 가구가 오후에 도착하는지 여부를 묻는 질문에 배송이 지연되었다며 오후에 배송되지 않을 것임을 우회적으로 응답하고 있으므로 정답.

20 고난도

W-Br It looks like there are two open seats in that row.

W-Am (A) The five P.M. showing.

(B) But isn't Sung-Won coming, too?

(C) They're supposed to be that low.

저 열에 빈 좌석이 두 개 있는 것 같아요.

(A) 오후 5시 상영이요.

(B) 그런데 성원 씨도 오시지 않나요?

(C) 원래 그렇게 낮아야 돼요.

어휘 row 열[줄] showing 상영 be supposed to ~하기로 되어 있다

해설 정보 전달의 평서문

(A) 연상 단어 오답. 평서문의 seats, row에서 연상 가능한 showing을 이용한 오답.

(B) 정답. 저쪽 열에 빈 좌석이 두 개 있는 것 같다는 평서문에 한 명이 더 오지 않는지 물으며, 좌석 수가 부족함을 우회적으로 나타내고 있으므로 정답.

(C) 유사 발음 오답. 질문의 row와 발음이 유사한 low를 이용한 오답.

21 고난도

M-Au When will the accounting interns start work?

W-Br (A) The London branch.

(B) They're not hiring any this year.

(C) We'll count them again.

회계 인턴 사원들은 언제 근무를 시작하나요?

(A) 런던 지사요.

(B) 올해는 안 뽑아요.

(C) 다시 세어 볼게요.

어휘 accounting 회계 intern 인턴 사원 branch 지사 count 세다

해설 인턴 사원의 근무 시작 시점을 묻는 When 의문문

(A) 질문과 상관없는 오답. Where 또는 Which 의문문에 대한 응답이므로 오답.

(B) 정답. 회계 인턴 사원들이 근무를 시작하는 시점을 묻는 질문에 올해는 뽑지 않는다며 해당 사항이 없음을 밝히고 있으므로 정답.

(C) 유사 발음 오답. 질문의 accounting과 부분적으로 발음이 유사한 count를 이용한 오답.

22

W-Am Did you figure out how to operate the camera?

M-Au (A) This silver one here, please.

(B) The figures have been updated.

(C) I'm reading the manual right now.

카메라 작동법을 알아냈나요?

(A) 여기 이 은색 제품으로 부탁합니다.

(B) 수치가 수정되었습니다.

(C) 지금 설명서를 읽고 있어요.

어휘 figure out 알아내다 operate 작동하다 figure 수치 manual 설명서

해설 카메라 작동법을 알아냈는지 여부를 확인하는 조동사(Did) 의문문

(A) 연상 단어 오답. 질문의 camera에서 제품 색상을 연상하게 하는 silver one을 이용한 오답.

(B) 단어 반복 오답. 질문의 figure를 반복 이용한 오답.

(C) 정답. 카메라 작동법을 알아냈는지 여부를 묻는 질문에 설명서를 읽고 있다며 확인 중임을 알리고 있으므로 정답.

23 고난도

W-Br Have you seen the expected cost of that project?

M-Cn (A) That's why we're considering other options.

(B) It was put in storage after the inspection.

(C) I'm not sure what he looks like.

그 프로젝트의 예상 비용을 보셨나요?

(A) 그래서 지금 다른 선택 사항들을 고려 중이에요.

(B) 검사 후에 그것을 창고에 두었어요.

(C) 그 사람이 어떻게 생겼는지 확실하지 않아요.

어휘 cost 비용 option 선택(권) storage 보관소 inspection 검사

해설 프로젝트 예상 비용 확인 여부를 확인하는 조동사(Have) 의문문

(A) 정답. 프로젝트의 예상 비용을 확인했는지 여부를 묻는 질문에 그래서 지금 다른 선택 사항들을 고려 중이라며 이미 비용을 확인했음을 우회적으로 응답하고 있으므로 정답.

(B) 질문과 상관없는 오답.

(C) 연상 단어 오답. 질문의 seen에서 연상 가능한 looks를 이용한 오답.

24

W-Am Where's the office of the payroll department?

M-Cn (A) No, it's always free for employees.

(B) Ayuka would probably know that.

(C) The first business day of every month.

경리과 사무실이 어디죠?

(A) 아니요, 직원들은 항상 무료예요.

(B) 아유카가 아마도 알 거예요.

(C) 매달 첫 평일이요.

어휘 payroll department 경리과

해설 경리과의 위치를 묻는 Where 의문문

(A) Yes/No 불가 오답. Where 의문문에는 Yes/No 응답이 불가능하므로 오답.

(B) 정답. 경리과의 위치를 묻는 질문에 아유카가 알 거라며 본인이 알지 못함을 우회적으로 밝히고 있으므로 정답.

(C) 질문과 상관없는 오답. When 의문문에 대한 응답이므로 오답.

25

M-Au Weren't you going to change the window display?

W-Am (A) Would you like to try them on?

(B) I'll do it after we close tonight.

(C) I don't know how to play.

쇼윈도 상품 진열을 바꾸려고 하지 않았나요?

(A) 한번 입어보시겠어요?

(B) 오늘 밤 마감 후에 할 거예요.

(C) 어떻게 연주하는지를 모르겠어요.

어휘 display 전시[진열] try on ~을 입어보다

해설 상품 진열을 바꾸려 했었는지 여부를 확인하는 부정의문문

(A) 연상 단어 오답. 질문의 window display에서 옷가게에서의 상황을 연상하게 하는 try on을 이용한 오답.

(B) 정답. 쇼윈도 상품 진열을 바꾸려고 하지 않았는지 확인하는 질문에 대해 Yes/No를 생략하고 오늘 밤 마감 후에 할 거라며 긍정의 의사를 전달하고 있으므로 정답.

(C) 유사 발음 오답. 질문의 display와 부분적으로 발음이 유사한 play를 이용한 오답.

26

W-Br I'm here to deliver a package to Catrina Ortiz.

M-Au (A) Her desk is over there.

(B) A box and a roll of tape.

(C) Yes, she has some baggage.

카트리나 오리츠 씨께 소포를 배달하러 왔어요.

(A) 그녀의 책상은 저쪽이에요.

(B) 상자 하나와 테이프 하나요.

(C) 네, 그녀는 짐이 좀 있어요.

어휘 package 상자 baggage 짐

해설 정보 전달의 평서문

(A) 정답. 카트리나 오리츠 씨에게 소포를 배달하러 왔다는 정보를 알려주는 평서문에 그녀의 책상은 저쪽이라며 정보를 알려주고 있으므로 정답.

(B) 연상 단어 오답. 평서문의 package에서 연상 가능한 box와 tape를 이용한 오답.

(C) 유사 발음 오답. 질문의 package와 부분적으로 발음이 유사한 baggage를 이용한 오답.

27

M-Cn You went to Matthew's birthday party, didn't you?

W-Br (A) I had an urgent deadline at work.

(B) Twenty-nine years old.

(C) Birthday cards are in Aisle Four.

매튜의 생일 파티에 갔죠, 그렇지 않나요?

(A) 회사에서 급한 마감이 있었어요.

(B) 29살이에요.

(C) 생일 카드는 4번 통로에 있어요.

어휘 urgent 긴급한 aisle 통로

해설 매튜의 생일 파티에 갔었는지 여부를 확인하는 부가의문문

(A) 정답. 매튜의 생일 파티에 갔었는지 여부를 확인하는 질문에 회사에 급한 마감이 있었다며 가지 못했음을 우회적으로 밝히고 있으므로 정답.

(B) 연상 단어 오답. 질문의 birthday에서 연상 가능한 나이를 이용한 오답.

(C) 단어 반복 오답. 질문의 birthday를 반복 이용한 오답.

28

W-Am Where can we get those vests and helmets?

M-Cn (A) To keep you safe during your visit.

(B) Here's a list of our investment activities.

(C) They're provided at the construction site.

저 조끼와 헬멧은 어디에서 구할 수 있나요?

(A) 방문하시는 동안 당신의 안전을 위해서요.

(B) 여기 우리 투자 활동 목록이 있어요.

(C) 공사장에서 제공됩니다.

어휘 vest 조끼 investment 투자 activity 활동 construction site 공사장

해설 안전 장비의 출처를 묻는 Where 의문문

(A) 연상 단어 오답. 질문의 vests와 helmets에서 연상 가능한 safe를 이용한 오답.

(B) 유사 발음 오답. 질문의 vests와 부분적으로 발음이 유사한 investment를 이용한 오답.

(C) 정답. 조끼와 헬멧을 구할 수 있는 장소를 묻는 질문에 공사장에서 제공된다며 구체적인 장소를 알려주고 있으므로 정답.

29

W-Am Are we hanging these flyers up or handing them out?

M-Au (A) Because we're having a sale.

(B) The plan is to do both.

(C) I think Peter agreed to.

이 전단들을 걸어 둘까요, 아니면 배포할까요?

(A) 할인을 하고 있어서요.

(B) 둘 다 할 계획이에요.

(C) 피터가 하기로 했던 것 같아요.

어휘 flyer 전단 hand out 나눠주다

해설 전단을 처리할 방법을 묻는 선택의문문

(A) 질문과 상관없는 오답. Why 의문문에 대한 응답이므로 오답.

(B) 정답. 전단을 처리할 방법을 묻는 선택의문문에서 둘 다 할 계획이라고 응답하고 있으므로 정답.

(C) 질문과 상관없는 오답. Who 의문문에 대한 응답이므로 오답.

30

고난도

W-Br The lights in the gallery were left on again last night.

M-Au (A) Some of the paintings are quite heavy.

(B) You'd better remind Sylvia to be careful.

(C) Thanks—the interior designer chose them.

어젯밤에 미술관 조명이 또 켜져 있었어요.

(A) 그림 몇 점은 꽤 무거워요.

(B) 실비아에게 주의하라고 말하는 게 좋겠어요.

(C) 고맙습니다, 인테리어 디자이너가 그것들을 선택했어요.

어휘 gallery 미술관 quite 꽤 remind 상기시키다

해설 정보 전달의 평서문

(A) 연상 단어 오답. 평서문의 gallery에서 연상 가능한 paintings를 이용한 오답.

(B) 정답. 어젯밤에 미술관 조명이 또 켜져 있었다는 평서문에 실비아에게 주의하라고 말하는 게 좋겠다며 문제 해결책을 제시하고 있으므로 정답.

(C) 연상 단어 오답. 평서문의 lights에서 연상 가능한 interior를 이용한 오답.

31

고난도

M-Cn Should we send out a paper memo about the new policy?

W-Br (A) Staff don't often check their inboxes.

(B) The expense reimbursement process.

(C) I'll show you how to use the shredder.

새 정책에 대해 지면으로 회람을 보내야 할까요?

(A) 직원들이 우편함을 자주 확인하지 않아요.

(B) 비용 환급 절차입니다.

(C) 파쇄기 사용법을 보여드릴게요.

어휘 policy 정책 inbox 우편함 expense 비용 reimbursement 환급 process 절차 shredder 파쇄기

해설 제안/권유의 의문문

(A) 정답. 새 정책에 대해 지면으로 쪽지를 보낼지 제안하는 질문에 직원들이 우편함을 자주 확인하지 않는다며 거절의 의사를 우회적으로 밝히고 있으므로 정답.

(B) 연상 단어 오답. 질문의 policy에서 연상 가능한 reimbursement process를 이용한 오답.

(C) 연상 단어 오답. 질문의 paper에서 연상 가능한 shredder를 이용한 오답.

PART 3

32-34

W-Am Hi, this is Kim Solomon. ³²**Your firm renovated my apartment last month.**

M-Au Hello, Ms. Solomon. What can we do for you today?

W-Am ³³**Well, I was just moving around some furniture while vacuuming my living room, and I noticed large scratches on the wall behind the sofa.** I'm sure I didn't cause them, so...

M-Au Oh, I'm sorry to hear that. We'll take care of it. ³⁴**Could you take a few clear photographs of the problem and e-mail them to me?** We need to know how serious it is.

여 여보세요, 김 솔로몬입니다. 그쪽 회사가 지난달에 제 아파트 보수 공사를 해주셨어요.

남 안녕하세요, 솔로몬 씨. 오늘은 어떻게 도와드릴까요?

여 그게, 제가 거실에서 진공 청소기로 청소를 하면서 가구를 좀 옮기던 중에, 소파 뒤의 벽에 커다랗게 긁힌 자국을 발견했어요. 제가 그런 건 확실히 아니라서….

남 오, 최송합니다. 저희가 처리하겠습니다. 그 부분을 사진으로 선명하게 몇 장 찍으셔서 저에게 이메일로 보내주시겠어요? 얼마나 심각한지 봐야 해서요.

어휘 firm 회사 renovate 보수하다, 개조하다 vacuum 진공청소기로 청소하다 scratch 긁힌 자국, 긁다 take a photograph 사진을 찍다

32

Where most likely does the man work?

(A) At an interior design firm

(B) At an apartment management office

(C) At a moving company

(D) At a hotel

남자는 어디에서 일하는 것 같는가?

(A) 인테리어 디자인 회사

(B) 아파트 관리 사무소

(C) 이삿짐 센터

(D) 호텔

해설 **전체 내용 관련 – 남자의 근무지**

여자가 첫 대사에서 남자의 회사에서 지난달에 자신의 아파트 보수 공사를 해 줬다(Your firm renovated my apartment last month)고 한 것으로 보아 정답은 (A)이다.

33

What problem does the woman describe?

(A) An appliance is not working.
(B) A wall has been damaged.
(C) Some loud noises can be heard.
(D) Some furniture is uncomfortable.

여자는 무슨 문제를 언급하는가?
(A) 가전제품이 작동하지 않는다.
(B) **벽이 손상되었다.**
(C) 큰 소음이 들린다.
(D) 몇몇 가구가 불편하다.

어휘 appliance 가전제품 damaged 손상된 uncomfortable 불편한

해설 **세부 사항 관련 – 여자가 언급한 문제점**

여자가 두 번째 대사에서 거실에서 청소를 하면서 가구를 옮기던 중에 소파 뒤의 벽에 커다랗게 긁힌 자국을 발견했다(I was just moving around some furniture ~ I noticed large scratches on the wall behind the sofa)고 문제점을 언급했으므로 정답은 (B)이다.

34

What does the man ask the woman to do?

(A) Take some measurements
(B) Wait for a company representative
(C) Send him some pictures
(D) Read a set of instructions

남자는 여자에게 무엇을 하라고 요청하는가?
(A) 치수 재기
(B) 회사 직원 기다리기
(C) **사진 몇 장 보내기**
(D) 설명서 읽기

어휘 measurement 측정, 치수 representative 대표, 직원 instruction 설명, 지시

해설 **세부 사항 관련 – 남자가 여자에게 요청한 일**

남자가 마지막 대사에서 그 부분을 사진으로 선명하게 찍어서 이메일로 보내 달라(Could you take a few clear photographs of the problem and e-mail them to me)고 요청했으므로 정답은 (C)이다.

▸▸ **Paraphrasing** 대화의 photographs → 정답의 pictures

35-37

W-Am All right, everyone. ³⁵ **Now that we've handed out your packed lunches, you'll have half an hour to eat before we**

continue our tour of Fannon Park.

M-Cn Ms. Sasaki, can I talk to you? The sandwich in my meal has ham in it, but I'm a vegetarian.

W-Am I'm sorry, Mr. Johnson, but I looked over the tour registration forms very carefully. ³⁶ **You must have forgotten to check the "vegetarian" box in the meal preference section.** We do have some extra lunches, but they're all non-vegetarian.

M-Cn ³⁷ **Well, could I have some of the fruit and snacks from those meals?** I'm really hungry from all this walking.

여 좋습니다, 여러분. 점심 도시락을 나눠드렸으니까, 30분 동안 점심을 드시고 나서 패논 공원 투어를 계속하겠습니다.
남 사사키 씨, 얘기 좀 할 수 있을까요? 제 샌드위치에 햄이 들어가 있는데, 저는 채식주의자이거든요.
여 죄송합니다, 존슨 씨. 그런데 제가 투어 신청서를 아주 꼼꼼하게 살펴보는데요. 선호하는 식사 부분에 "채식주의자"라고 표기하시는 걸 깜박하신 것 같아요. 도시락 여분이 좀 있긴 한데, 전부 비채식주의자용이에요.
남 그럼, 그 도시락에서 과일과 스낵만 좀 먹을 수 있을까요? 많이 걸어서 그런지 정말 허기지거든요.

어휘 hand out 나눠주다 continue 계속하다 vegetarian 채식주의자 registration form 신청서 meal preference 선호하는 식사 section 부분

35

Where most likely are the speakers?

(A) At a train terminal
(B) On an airplane
(C) At a restaurant
(D) At a park

화자들은 어디에 있을 것 같은가?
(A) 기차역
(B) 비행기
(C) 식당
(D) **공원**

해설 **전체 내용 관련 – 대화의 장소**

여자가 첫 대사에서 점심 도시락을 나눠드렸으니까 30분 동안 점심을 드시고 나서 패논 공원 투어를 계속하겠다(Now that we've handed out ~ before we continue our tour of Fannon Park)고 한 것으로 보아 정답은 (D)이다.

36

What does the woman say has caused a problem?

(A) Some meals were not cooked properly.
(B) Some boxes have not been unpacked.
(C) A tour has too many participants.
(D) A form was filled out incorrectly.

여자는 무엇이 문제의 원인이라고 말하는가?

(A) 일부 식사가 제대로 요리되지 않았다.
(B) 몇몇 상자가 개봉되지 않았다.
(C) 투어에 너무 많은 인원이 참가했다.
(D) 서류가 제대로 작성되지 않았다.

어휘 properly 제대로 unpack 꺼내다 participant 참가자 fill out 작성하다 incorrectly 부정확하게

해설 세부 사항 관련 – 여자가 말하는 문제의 원인

여자가 두 번째 대사에서 남자에게 선호하는 식사 부분에 "채식주의자"라고 표기하는 걸 깜박한 것 같다(You must have forgotten to check the "vegetarian" box in the meal preference section)고 한 것으로 보아 서류가 제대로 작성되지 않았음을 알 수 있다. 따라서 정답은 (D)이다.

37

What does the man ask for?

(A) A partial refund
(B) Some extra food
(C) Directions to a store
(D) A different seat assignment

남자는 무엇을 요청하는가?

(A) 부분적인 환불
(B) 여분의 음식
(C) 가게로 가는 길 안내
(D) 다른 좌석의 배정

어휘 partial 부분적인 refund 환불 direction 길 안내 assignment 배정, 임무

해설 세부 사항 관련 – 남자의 요청 사항

남자가 마지막 대사에서 도시락에서 과일과 스낵만 좀 먹을 수 있을지(could I have some of the fruit and snacks from those meals?)를 묻고 있으므로 정답은 (B)이다.

▸▸ Paraphrasing 대화의 some of the fruit and snacks
→ 정답의 some extra food

38-40 3인 대화

M-Cn **38 Ms. Ortega, thank you again for choosing us to create your Web site.** Now, tell us more about your wedding planning business.

W-Br I started the company a year ago, and it's been going well. **39 I'm hoping that the Web site can attract even more clients.**

M-Au Sure. What sets you apart from your competitors?

W-Br We focus on what clients want, not on following trends. It means we've planned some really unusual ceremonies!

M-Cn That's interesting! Would you like to feature photos of them on the Web site?

W-Br Actually... I'm not sure. **40 That might make some potential clients less likely to choose us.**

M-Au OK. We'll put that idea aside for now.

남1 오테가 씨, 귀사의 웹사이트 제작에 저희를 선택해주셔서 다시 한번 감사드립니다. 그럼 이제, 당신의 결혼식 준비 업체에 대해 좀 더 말씀해주세요.

여 저는 일 년 전에 창업했고, 사업은 잘되고 있어요. 웹사이트로 훨씬 많은 고객을 끌어들일 수 있길 바라고요.

남2 물론이죠. 귀사가 경쟁 업체와 차별화된 점은 무엇인가요?

여 우리는 트렌드를 따르기보다는 고객들이 원하는 것에 초점을 맞춰요. 그 말은 즉, 우리가 정말 색다른 기념식을 준비한다는 거고요!

남1 흥미롭네요! 웹사이트에 그 기념식 사진들을 특별히 포함시키길 원하시나요?

여 사실… 모르겠어요. 일부 잠재 고객들은 그 때문에 우리를 선택하지 않을 수도 있을 것 같아서요.

남2 좋습니다. 당분간은 그 아이디어는 제외하기로 하죠.

어휘 attract 끌어들이다 set apart 구별하다 competitor 경쟁 상대 ceremony 의식 feature 포함하다, 특징으로 삼다 potential 잠재적인 put aside ~을 따로 남겨두다 for now 당분간

38

What kind of service does the men's company provide?

(A) Advertising
(B) Catering
(C) Accounting
(D) Web design

남자들의 회사는 어떤 종류의 서비스를 제공하는가?

(A) 광고
(B) 음식 조달
(C) 회계
(D) 웹 디자인

해설 전체 내용 관련 – 남자들의 회사가 제공하는 서비스의 종류

첫 번째 남자가 첫 대사에서 귀사의 웹사이트 제작에 저희를 선택해주셔서 다시 한번 감사드린다(Ms. Ortega, thank you again for choosing us to create your Web site)고 했으므로 남자들의 회사는 웹사이트를 만드는 일을 한다는 것을 알 수 있다. 따라서 정답은 (D)이다.

39

Why has the woman hired the men's company?

(A) To grow her business
(B) To save money
(C) To follow a regulation
(D) To give herself more free time

여자는 왜 남자들의 회사를 고용했는가?

(A) 사업을 키우기 위해
(B) 돈을 아끼기 위해
(C) 규정을 따르기 위해
(D) 자유 시간을 좀 더 갖기 위해

어휘 regulation 규정

해설 세부 사항 관련 – 여자가 남자들의 회사를 고용한 이유

여자가 첫 대사에서 웹사이트로 훨씬 많은 고객을 끌어들일 수 있길 바란다(I'm hoping that the Web site can attract even more clients)고 했으므로 정답은 (A)이다.

▸▸ Paraphrasing 대화의 **attract even more clients**
→ 정답의 **grow her business**

40 고난도

What does the woman say about a suggestion?

(A) It has been tried before.
(B) It may not be effective.
(C) It would be expensive.
(D) It is complicated.

여자는 제안에 대해 뭐라고 말하는가?

(A) 전에 시도했었다.
(B) 효과적이지 않을 수도 있다.
(C) 비용이 많이 들 것이다.
(D) 복잡하다.

어휘 effective 효과적인 complicated 복잡한

해설 세부 사항 관련 – 여자가 제안에 대해 말하는 것

여자가 마지막 대사에서 일부 잠재 고객들은 그 때문에 우리를 선택하지 않을 수도 있을 것 같다(That might make some potential clients less likely to choose us)고 한 것으로 보아 정답은 (B)이다.

41-43

M-Au	Hi, Monica? This is Paul in Sales. **⁴¹I need some technical help with the new vacation scheduling system. ⁴²I'm not seeing the submission date on my team members' electronic request forms.**
W-Br	Are you looking at the bottom right-hand side of the forms?
M-Au	Yes—there's no information there. I think there must be a problem with the software.
W-Br	Maybe. **⁴³But let's start by making sure your display settings are correct.** You can find that information in the "Options" menu. I'll wait.

남	여보세요, 모니카? 영업팀의 폴이에요. 새 휴가 일정 관리 시스템에 기술적인 도움이 좀 필요해요. 제 팀원들의 전자 신청서에 제출 날짜가 보이지 않아요.
여	서류의 오른쪽 아래를 보고 계신가요?
남	네, 거기에 정보가 없어요. 소프트웨어에 문제가 있는 것 같아요.
여	아마도요. 그래도 화면 설정이 올바른지부터 확인해봅시다. 해당 정보는 '선택 사항' 메뉴에서 찾을 수 있어요. 기다릴게요.

어휘 vacation 휴가 scheduling 일정 관리 submission 제출 electronic 전자의 request form 신청서 right-hand side 오른쪽 option 선택(권)

41

Which department does the woman most likely work in?

(A) Public Relations
(B) Human Resources
(C) Information Technology
(D) Sales and Marketing

여자는 어느 부서에서 일할 것 같은가?

(A) 홍보부
(B) 인사부
(C) 정보 통신부
(D) 영업 마케팅부

해설 전체 내용 관련 – 여자의 근무 부서

남자가 첫 대사에서 여자에게 새 휴가 일정 관리 시스템에 기술적인 도움이 좀 필요하다(I need some technical help with the new vacation scheduling system)며 시스템과 관련해 도움을 요청한 것으로 보아 정답은 (C)이다.

42 고난도

What problem are the speakers discussing?

(A) A slow response time
(B) A scheduling conflict
(C) A customer complaint
(D) A missing detail

화자들은 무슨 문제를 논의하고 있는가?

(A) 느린 응답 시간
(B) 겹치는 일정
(C) 고객 불만
(D) 정보 누락

어휘 response 응답 conflict 충돌 complaint 불만 missing 빠진

해설 세부 사항 관련 – 화자들의 논의 중인 문제

남자가 첫 대사에서 팀원들의 전자 신청서에 제출 날짜가 보이지 않는다(I'm not seeing the submission date on my team members' electronic request forms)고 한 것으로 보아 정답은 (D)이다.

43

What does the woman recommend the man do first?

(A) Speak with his manager
(B) Check some software settings
(C) Post a correction notice
(D) Restart a machine

여자는 남자에게 무엇부터 하라고 권하는가?

(A) 관리자와 대화할 것
(B) 소프트웨어 설정을 확인할 것
(C) 정정 공고문을 게시할 것
(D) 기계를 다시 시작할 것

어휘 post 게시[공고]하다 notice 공고문

해설 세부 사항 관련 – 여자가 남자에게 먼저 하라고 권하는 것

여자가 마지막 대사에서 그래도 화면 설정이 올바른지부터 확인해보자(But let's start by making sure your display settings are correct)고 했으므로 정답은 (B)이다.

어휘 be about to 막 ~하려던 참이다 sewing machine 재봉틀

해설 세부 사항 관련 – 남자가 하려던 일

남자가 두 번째 대사에서 상표에는 특정 화학 약품만 드레스에 사용될 수 있다고 나와 있는데, 드라이 클리닝 기계에 집어넣기 전에 왜 그런지 알고 싶다(The label says that only certain chemicals can be used on it, and I want to know why before I put it into the dry-cleaning machine)고 한 것으로 보아 정답은 (A)이다.

44-46

M-Cn	Shanice, could I ask you about this dress that a customer just brought in?
W-Am	Sure, Brandon.
M-Cn	**44 The label says that only certain chemicals can be used on it, and I want to know why before I put it into the dry-cleaning machine.**
W-Am	**45 Oh, it's because of all of these plastic beads that have been sewn onto the fabric.** Some dry-cleaning chemicals can damage them.
M-Cn	Got it. You know, I'd like to learn more of this kind of background information. **46 Could we hold informal training sessions every now and then?**
W-Am	I'd be happy to do that. How about starting next Monday before work?

남	샤니스, 고객 한 분이 방금 가지고 오신 이 드레스에 대해 물어봐도 될까요?
여	물론이죠, 브랜든.
남	상표에는 특정 화학 약품만 드레스에 사용될 수 있다고 나와 있는데, 드라이 클리닝 기계에 집어넣기 전에 왜 그런지 알고 싶어요.
여	오, 그건 옷감 위에 바느질 된 플라스틱 구슬 장식들 때문이에요. 일부 드라이 클리닝 약품 때문에 그것들이 손상될 수 있거든요.
남	그렇군요. 있잖아요, 이런 배경 정보에 대해 좀 더 배웠으면 해요. 가끔 약식으로 교육 시간을 가질 수 있을까요?
여	기꺼이요. 다음 주 월요일 근무 전에 시작하는 게 어떨까요?

어휘	label 상표[라벨] chemicals 화학 약품 bead 비드[구슬] sewn sew(바느질하다)의 과거분사 background 배경 informal 비공식의 every now and then 가끔

44

What is the man about to do?

(A) Clean some clothing
(B) Use a sewing machine
(C) Arrange a window display
(D) Test some product samples

남자는 무엇을 하려던 참인가?

(A) 의류 세탁
(B) 재봉틀 사용
(C) 쇼윈도의 상품 진열
(D) 제품 샘플 테스트

45

What does the woman point out about a fabric?

(A) Its color is due to special chemicals.
(B) It has been decorated with beads.
(C) Its cost has recently risen.
(D) It is lightweight.

여자는 옷감에 대해 무엇을 언급하는가?

(A) 색깔이 특별한 화학 약품으로 인한 것이다.
(B) 구슬로 장식되었다.
(C) 최근에 가격이 올랐다.
(D) 가볍다.

어휘 decorate 장식하다 lightweight 가벼운

해설 세부 사항 관련 – 여자가 옷감에 대해 언급한 것

여자가 두 번째 대사에서 그건 옷감 위에 바느질 된 플라스틱 구슬 장식들 때문이다(it's because of all of these plastic beads that have been sewn onto the fabric)라고 했으므로 정답은 (B)이다.

46

What does the woman agree to do?

(A) Increase some lighting
(B) Hold a hand tool
(C) Postpone a photo session
(D) Provide some training

여자는 무엇을 하는 것에 동의하는가?

(A) 조명을 늘리는 것
(B) 연장을 잡고 있는 것
(C) 사진 촬영을 미루는 것
(D) 교육을 제공하는 것

어휘 lighting 조명 hand tool 수공구 postpone 미루다

해설 세부 사항 관련 – 여자가 하기로 동의한 것

남자가 마지막 대사에서 가끔 약식으로 교육 시간을 가질 수 있을지(Could we hold informal training sessions every now and then?)를 물었고, 여자가 기꺼이요(I'd be happy to do that)라고 대답했으므로 정답은 (D)이다.

47-49

M-Cn	Excuse me. This is the third time that I've come in to find that you don't have any strawberry cupcakes with marshmallow

frosting. May I speak to a manager about that?

W-Am Absolutely, sir. I'm the manager today.

M-Cn Oh. ⁴⁷ **Well, I come to this bakery every week just to get those cupcakes, even though I don't live nearby. You know, they're not sold anywhere else.** What's going on?

W-Am ⁴⁸ **I'm sorry, but those cupcakes have actually been discontinued.** But these chocolate cupcakes have marshmallow frosting.

M-Cn Hmm... I don't know. They're more expensive.

W-Am ⁴⁹ **Well, I could lower the price just this once.** Consider it our apology for getting rid of the strawberry flavor option.

남 실례합니다. 제가 여기 방문해서 마시멜로가 올라간 딸기 컵케이크가 없다고 들은 게 이번이 세 번째입니다. 관리자 분과 그 점에 대해 얘기할 수 있을까요?

여 물론입니다, 손님. 제가 오늘 담당자입니다.

남 오. 저는 가까이에 살지도 않는데, 단지 그 컵케이크들을 사러 매주 이 빵집에 옵니다. 아시다시피, 다른 곳에서는 그것들을 팔지 않거든요. 대체 무슨 상황인 겁니까?

여 죄송하지만, 그 컵케이크들은 사실 단종되었습니다. 하지만 이 초콜릿 컵케이크들에도 마시멜로가 올라가 있어요.

남 흠… 잘 모르겠어요. 더 비싸네요.

여 그럼, 제가 이번 한 번은 가격을 낮춰드리겠습니다. 딸기 맛 케이크를 중단한 것에 대한 사과로 받아주세요.

어휘 frosting 프로스팅(설탕을 입힘)   nearby 가까이에
anywhere else 다른 어느 곳에서도   discontinue 중단하다
lower 낮추다   apology 사과   get rid of ~을 없애다
flavor 맛   option 선택(권)

47

고난도

Why does the man say he comes to the bakery frequently?

(A) It is near his home.
(B) It has a pleasant atmosphere.
(C) It sells a special type of baked goods.
(D) It has convenient operating hours.

남자는 왜 그 빵집에 자주 온다고 말하는가?

(A) 집에서 가깝다.
(B) 분위기가 쾌적하다.
(C) 특별한 제과 제품을 판매한다.
(D) 영업시간이 편리하다.

어휘 frequently 자주   pleasant 쾌적한   atmosphere 분위기
goods 제품   convenient 편리한   operating hours 영업시간

해설 세부 사항 관련 – 남자가 빵집에 자주 온다고 말한 이유

남자가 두 번째 대사에서 가까이에 살지도 않는데 단지 그 컵케이크들을 사러 매주 이 빵집에 온다(I come to this bakery every week just to get

those cupcakes, even though I don't live nearby)라며, 아시다시피 다른 곳에서는 그것들을 팔지 않는다(You know, they're not sold anywhere else)라고 한 것으로 보아 정답은 (C)이다.

> **▸▸ Paraphrasing**   대화의 **not sold anywhere else**
> → 정답의 **sells a special type**

48

고난도

Why does the woman say, "these chocolate cupcakes have marshmallow frosting"?

(A) To point out a mistake on a label
(B) To propose an alternative purchase
(C) To express surprise at a suggestion
(D) To explain a pricing decision

여자가 "이 초콜릿 컵케이크들에도 마시멜로가 올라가 있어요"라고 말한 이유는 무엇인가?

(A) 상표의 오류를 지적하기 위해
(B) 대체품을 제안하기 위해
(C) 제안에 대해 놀라움을 나타내기 위해
(D) 가격 결정에 대해 설명하기 위해

어휘 label 상표[라벨]   propose 제안하다   alternative 대안이 되는; 대안   express 나타내다   pricing decision 가격 결정

해설 화자의 의도 파악 – 이 초콜릿 컵케이크들에도 마시멜로가 올라가 있다는 말의 의도

앞에서 여자가 죄송하지만, 그 컵케이크들은 사실 단종되었다(I'm sorry, but those cupcakes have actually been discontinued)라며 더 이상 남자가 찾는 제품을 살 수 없음을 설명한 뒤, 인용문에서 단종된 제품과 비슷한 다른 제품을 소개한 것으로 보아 정답은 (B)이다.

49

What does the woman offer the man?

(A) A onetime discount
(B) A list of the ingredients in a recipe
(C) A chance to attend a tasting session
(D) A takeout container

여자는 남자에게 무엇을 제안하는가?

(A) 일회성 할인
(B) 조리법의 재료 목록
(C) 시식회에 참석할 기회
(D) 포장 음식 용기

어휘 ingredient 재료   recipe 조리법   tasting session 시식[시음]회   takeout 포장 음식   container 용기

해설 세부 사항 관련 – 여자가 남자에게 제안한 것

여자가 마지막 대사에서 이번 한 번은 가격을 낮춰드리겠다(I could lower the price just this once)라고 했으므로 정답은 (A)이다.

> **▸▸ Paraphrasing**   대화의 **lower the price just this once**
> → 정답의 **onetime discount**

W-Br ⁵⁰**Adam, why haven't those boxes been moved to their storage shelves?** I thought they were unloaded from the trucks an hour ago.

M-Au ⁵¹**Oh, one of the regular forklift operators wasn't feeling well enough to come in today.** The backup driver isn't as skilled, so we're a little behind.

W-Br Hmm. Will the shipment to Prentell Industries go out by two P.M. as scheduled?

M-Au That might be a little difficult. It'll more likely be ready at around two-thirty or three.

W-Br Well, that doesn't sound too bad. ⁵²**But just to be safe, I'm going to call Prentell.** They like to be warned about potential problems.

여 아담, 어째서 저 상자들이 보관 선반으로 옮겨지지 않은 거죠? 한 시간 전에 트럭에서 내려진 것 같은데요.

남 오, 지게차 기사 중 한 명이 오늘 몸이 좋지 않아서 출근을 못 했어요. 대체 기사는 그만큼 노련하질 않아서 일정이 조금 뒤처졌네요.

여 흠. 프렌텔 인더스트리즈에 보낼 배송품은 예정대로 오후 2시까지 나갈 건가요?

남 조금 힘들 수도 있어요. 2시 반이나 3시쯤이면 준비될 것 같아요.

여 그렇게 나쁘지 않네요. 혹시 모르니까, 제가 프렌텔에 전화해둘게요. 잠재적인 문제에 대해 통지받고 싶어 하거든요.

어휘 storage 보관(소) shelf 선반 unload (짐을) 내리다 forklift 지게차 operator 조작[운전]하는 사람 backup 예비[대체] skilled 노련한 shipment 배송(품) potential 잠재적인

50

Where do the speakers most likely work?

(A) At a construction company

(B) At a warehouse

(C) At a farm

(D) At a car repair shop

화자들은 어디에서 일할 것 같은가?

(A) 건설 회사

(B) 물류 창고

(C) 농장

(D) 자동차 정비소

해설 전체 내용 관련 - 화자들의 근무지

여자가 첫 대사에서 어째서 저 상자들이 보관 선반으로 옮겨지지 않은 거죠(why haven't those boxes been moved to their storage shelves?)라며 묻고 있는 것으로 보아 화자들은 물품을 보관하는 곳에서 일하는 것임을 알 수 있다. 따라서 정답은 (B)이다.

51

What has caused a problem?

(A) Some packages have been misplaced.

(B) Some roads are closed.

(C) A staff member is out sick.

(D) A vehicle has broken down.

무엇 때문에 문제가 발생했는가?

(A) 일부 상자들이 분실되었다.

(B) 일부 도로가 폐쇄되었다.

(C) **직원 한 명이 병가를 냈다.**

(D) 차량 한 대가 고장 났다.

어휘 misplace 제자리에 두지 않다, 분실하다 vehicle 차량 break down 고장 나다

해설 세부 사항 관련 - 문제의 발생 원인

남자가 첫 대사에서 지게차 기사 중 한 명이 오늘 몸이 좋지 않아서 출근을 못 했다(one of the regular forklift operators wasn't feeling well enough to come in today)고 했으므로 정답은 (C)이다.

▸▸ Paraphrasing 대화의 **wasn't feeling well enough to come in** → 정답의 **is out sick**

52

What does the woman say she will do?

(A) Work overtime today

(B) Put up a warning sign

(C) Conduct a safety inspection

(D) Contact another company

여자는 무엇을 하겠다고 말하는가?

(A) 오늘 초과 근무하기

(B) 경고판 세워 두기

(C) 안전 점검 실시하기

(D) **다른 회사에 연락하기**

어휘 conduct 실시[수행]하다 inspection 점검

해설 세부 사항 관련 - 여자가 하겠다고 말한 것

여자가 마지막 대사에서 혹시 모르니까 프렌텔에 전화해두겠다(But just to be safe, I'm going to call Prentell)고 했으므로 정답은 (D)이다.

53-55 3인 대화

W-Am Excuse me, sir. ⁵³**My name is Min-Sun Lee, and I'm a reporter with Channel Six News.** Would you be willing to be interviewed on camera about the new metro train line the city plans to construct?

M-Au Sure. Uh, right now?

W-Am Yes, just stand right there. So, what do you think about the new line?

M-Au It's a good idea. **⁵⁴I've been commuting on the Norman line for years, and it's become packed with people. The new line will help with that.**

W-Am Great. That was perfect. **⁵⁵Now I just need your signature on the consent form my producer is holding.**

W-Br It gives us permission to broadcast the clip we just made. Here's a pen, too.

여1 실례합니다, 선생님. 제 이름은 이민선이고, 채널 6 뉴스의 기자입니다. 시에서 건설 계획 중인 새 지하철 노선에 대한 카메라 인터뷰에 응해주실 수 있을까요?

남 물론이죠. 어, 지금 당장이요?

여1 네, 딱 거기에 서 계시면 됩니다. 새로운 노선에 대해 어떻게 생각하시나요?

남 좋은 생각이라고 생각해요. **수년째 노만 노선으로 출퇴근 중인데, 사람들로 꽉 차 버렸어요. 새 노선이 도움이 될 겁니다.**

여1 훌륭해요. 완벽합니다. **이제 저희 프로듀서가 들고 있는 동의서에 서명만 좀 해 주시면 돼요.**

여2 방금 찍은 영상을 방송할 수 있도록 허락하신다는 서류예요. 펜도 여기 있습니다.

어휘 metro train 지하철 commute 통근하다; 통근 be packed with ~로 꽉 차다 signature 서명 consent form 동의서 permission 허락 broadcast 방송하다 clip (TV의) 짧은 뉴스

53

Who most likely is Ms. Lee?

(A) A journalist
(B) A city official
(C) A travel agent
(D) A researcher

이 씨는 누구일 것 같은가?

(A) 기자
(B) 시 공무원
(C) 여행사 직원
(D) 연구원

해설 세부 사항 관련 – 이 씨의 직업

첫 번째 여자가 첫 대사에서 제 이름은 이민선이고 채널 6 뉴스의 기자입니다(My name is Min-Sun Lee, and I'm a reporter with Channel Six News)라고 했으므로 정답은 (A)이다.

54

고난도

What does the man say about the construction of a train line?

(A) It caused him to be late.
(B) It will take many years to complete.
(C) It will relieve crowding in other lines.
(D) It has shortened his commute.

남자는 지하철 건설에 대해 무엇을 말하는가?

(A) 그로 인해 지각하게 되었다.
(B) 완공하는 데 수년이 걸릴 것이다.
(C) 다른 노선의 과밀 문제가 완화될 것이다.
(D) 통근 시간이 짧아질 것이다.

어휘 relieve 완화하다 crowding 과밀 shorten 단축하다

해설 세부 사항 관련 – 남자가 지하철 건설에 대해 말하는 것

남자가 두 번째 대사에서 수년째 노만 노선으로 출퇴근 중인데 사람들로 꽉 차 버렸다(I've been commuting on the Norman line for years, and it's become packed with people)면서, 새 노선이 도움이 될 것이다(The new line will help with that)라고 한 것으로 보아 정답은 (C)이다.

▸▸ Paraphrasing	대화의 packed with people → 정답의 crowding
	대화의 help with → 정답의 relieve

55

What does Ms. Lee ask the man to do next?

(A) Show her a ticket
(B) Watch a video clip
(C) Sit down at a table
(D) Sign a document

이 씨는 남자에게 다음에 무엇을 해달라고 요청하는가?

(A) 표를 보여줄 것
(B) 동영상을 볼 것
(C) 탁자에 앉을 것
(D) 서류에 서명할 것

해설 세부 사항 관련 – 이 씨가 남자에게 다음에 해달라고 요청한 것

첫 번째 여자가 마지막 대사에서 이제 저희 프로듀서가 들고 있는 동의서에 서명만 좀 해주면 된다(Now I just need your signature on the consent form my producer is holding)고 했으므로 정답은 (D)이다.

56-58

W-Am Oh, hi Martin. **⁵⁶Did you finish walking the dogs and cleaning their cages?**

M-Cn Hi, Ms. Cruz. Yes, I did. Uh, do you have a minute? I wanted to talk to you about something.

W-Am Sure. Have a seat.

M-Cn Thanks. **⁵⁷As you know, I'm about to graduate from university, so I'm starting to look for jobs.** I already listed my work with this organization on my résumé. **⁵⁸Could I give your name as a reference as well?**

W-Am **⁵⁸Absolutely.** You've been an excellent volunteer. Do you already know my official job title and contact details?

M-Cn I do. Thank you so much!

여	오, 안녕하세요 마틴 씨. 개 산책과 우리 청소는 끝내셨나요?
남	안녕하세요. 크루즈 씨. 네, 다 했어요. 잠깐 시간 좀 있으세요? 말씀드릴 게 좀 있어서요.
여	그럼요. 앉으세요.
남	고맙습니다. 아시다시피, 제가 곧 대학교 졸업을 앞두고 있어서 직장을 구해보려고요. 제 이력서에 이 단체에서 제가 했던 일을 이미 열거해 놓았어요. 크루즈 씨 성함을 추천인으로 기입해도 될까요?
여	물론이죠. 당신은 훌륭한 자원봉사자였습니다. 제 공식 직함과 연락처는 알고 있나요?
남	네, 정말 감사합니다!

어휘	cage 우리, 새장 graduate 졸업하다 organization 단체 résumé 이력서 reference 추천인[서] volunteer 자원봉사자 official 공식적인 contact 연락

56

고난도

What most likely is the mission of the speakers' organization?

(A) To educate children
(B) To take care of animals
(C) To protect the environment
(D) To support the arts

화자들이 소속한 단체의 임무는 무엇일 것 같은가?
(A) 어린이들을 교육시키는 일
(B) 동물들을 돌보는 일
(C) 환경을 보호하는 일
(D) 예술을 후원하는 일

어휘 mission 임무 educate 교육하다 environment 환경 support 지원하다

해설 세부 사항 관련 – 화자들이 소속한 단체의 임무
여자가 첫 대사에서 개 산책과 우리 청소는 끝내셨나요(Did you finish walking the dogs and cleaning their cages?)라고 남자에게 묻고 있는 것으로 보아 정답은 (B)이다.

57

What does the man say he will do soon?

(A) Earn a degree
(B) Move away
(C) Take a vacation
(D) Donate some supplies

남자는 곧 무엇을 할 것이라고 말하는가?
(A) 학위 취득
(B) 이사
(C) 휴가
(D) 물품 기부

해설 세부 사항 관련 – 남자가 곧 할 것이라고 말한 일
남자가 두 번째 대사에서 아시다시피 곧 대학교 졸업을 앞두고 있어서 직장을 구하려 한다(As you know, I'm about to graduate from university, so I'm starting to look for jobs)고 말했으므로 정답은 (A)이다.

> ▸▸ Paraphrasing 대화의 graduate from university
> → 정답의 earn a degree

58

고난도

What does the woman mean when she says, "You've been an excellent volunteer"?

(A) She is happy to fulfill the man's request.
(B) She is sorry that the man is quitting.
(C) She is surprised by the man's mistake.
(D) She is pleased that the man will become more involved.

여자가 "당신은 훌륭한 자원봉사자였습니다"라고 말한 의도는 무엇인가?
(A) 남자의 요청을 기꺼이 들어주겠다.
(B) 남자가 그만두게 되어 유감이다.
(C) 남자의 실수에 놀랐다.
(D) 남자가 좀 더 일에 관여하게 되어 기쁘다.

어휘 fulfill 이행하다 request 요청 quit 그만두다 involved 관여하는

해설 화자의 의도 파악 – 당신은 훌륭한 자원봉사자였다는 말의 의도
남자가 두 번째 대사에서 당신의 성함을 추천인으로 기입해도 되겠는지(Could I give your name as a reference as well?)를 묻자 여자가 물론(Absolutely)이라며 흔쾌히 수락한 뒤 인용문을 언급했으므로 남자의 부탁을 기꺼이 들어주겠다는 것을 표현하기 위한 의도임을 알 수 있다. 따라서 정답은 (A)이다.

59-61

M-Cn	Sandy, thanks for coming in. 59I have some news—the move you requested came through. You'll be able to start working at the Lambert office on August first.
W-Br	Wow, that's soon! 60It's a good thing that I've already started gathering documentation on my work processes to give to my replacement.
M-Cn	Oh, have you? That's excellent. 61Now, here's a draft of your new job contract. It's very similar to your current one, but there are a few differences. Take a look at it and let me know if you have any questions.

남	샌디, 와줘서 고마워요. 전할 말이 있어요. 전근 신청하신 게 승인됐어요. 8월 1일부터 램버트 사무실에서 일을 시작할 수 있을 거예요.
여	와우, 얼마 안 남았네요! 후임자에게 건네줄 제 업무 절차에 대해 미리 서류를 취합하기 시작하길 잘했네요.
남	오, 그랬나요? 훌륭하네요. 새로운 근무 계약서 초안이 여기 있어요. 기존 것과 아주 비슷하지만 다른 점들도 약간 있어요. 한번 보시고 궁금한 게 있으면 알려주세요.

어휘	come through 승인되다 documentation 서류 process 절차 replacement 후임자 draft 초안

59

What are the speakers discussing?

(A) A promotion
(B) A career fair
(C) An interview
(D) A transfer

화자들은 무엇을 논의하고 있는가?
(A) 승진
(B) 취업 박람회
(C) 면접
(D) 전근

해설 **전체 내용 관련 – 대화의 주제**
남자가 첫 대사에서 전할 말이 있다(I have some news)며 전근 신청이 승인되었다(the move you requested came through)고 여자에게 전근 관련 소식을 전하며 대화를 시작한 것으로 보아 정답은 (D)이다.

60
고난도

What does the woman say she has been doing?

(A) Collecting some records
(B) Processing some applications
(C) Communicating with some recruiters
(D) Replacing some equipment

여자는 무엇을 해왔다고 말하는가?
(A) 문서를 모으는 일
(B) 지원서를 처리하는 일
(C) 몇몇 모집자들과 소통하는 일
(D) 일부 장비를 교체하는 일

어휘 process 처리하다: 절차 application 지원서 recruiter 모집자 replace 교체하다 equipment 장비

해설 **세부 사항 관련 – 여자가 해왔다고 말한 것**
여자가 첫 대사에서 후임자에게 건네줄 업무 절차에 대해 미리 서류를 취합하기 시작하길 잘했다(It's a good thing that I've already started gathering documentation on my work processes to give to my replacement)고 말했으므로 정답은 (A)이다.

▸▸ **Paraphrasing** 대화의 gathering documentation
→ 정답의 collecting some records

61

What does the man give the woman?

(A) A job advertisement
(B) An applicant's résumé
(C) An employment agreement
(D) An orientation schedule

남자는 여자에게 무엇을 주는가?
(A) 구인 광고
(B) 지원자의 이력서
(C) 고용 계약서
(D) 예비 교육 일정표

어휘 applicant 지원자 employment 고용 orientation 예비 교육

해설 **세부 사항 관련 – 남자가 여자에게 준 것**
남자가 마지막 대사에서 새로운 근무 계약서 초안이 여기 있다(here's a draft of your new job contract)며 여자에게 계약서를 건네고 있으므로 정답은 (C)이다.

▸▸ **Paraphrasing** 대화의 job contract
→ 정답의 employment agreement

62-64 대화 + 출발 안내 전광판

M-Au	Vera, where are you? Our bus is leaving in five minutes. **62 It's going to make a bad impression on the other industry attendees if we miss the beginning of the conference.**
W-Br	I'm so sorry, Nathan. **63 I was halfway to the bus terminal this morning before I realized that I'd left two of my structural models at home. I wouldn't be able to lead my session without them.** Anyway, I won't arrive at the departure area for another twenty minutes, so you should go ahead without me.
M-Au	No, that's all right. **64 I think you'll be able to make the bus to Cookville that leaves after eight.** I'll try to get us tickets for that one.

남	베라, 어디예요? 5분 뒤에 버스가 출발할 거예요. 회의 초반부를 놓치게 되면 다른 업계 참석자들에게 안 좋은 인상을 줄 거예요.
여	미안해요, 나단. 오늘 아침 버스 정류장로 가던 도중에 구조 모형 두 개를 집에 두고 온 걸 깨달았어요. 그것들이 없으면 발표를 할 수가 없거든요. 어쨌든, 20분 이내로 출발 구역에 도착하지 못할 것 같으니 먼저 출발하세요.
남	아니요, 괜찮아요. 8시 이후에 출발하는 쿡빌행 버스는 탈 수 있을 것 같아요. 그 버스로 표를 사 놓을게요.

어휘 impression 인상 industry 산업 attendee 참석자 conference 학회[회의] halfway 중간에 realize 깨닫다 structural 구조상의 ahead 미리, 앞에

Bus Departures

Destination	Boarding Area	Time
Grammett	D	DEPARTED
Cookville	E	7:20 A.M.
Owenton	B	7:53 A.M.
Grammett	D	8:04 A.M.
64 Cookville	E	8:10 A.M.

버스 출발

목적지	탑승 구역	시간
그래멧	D	출발 완료
쿡빌	E	오전 7:20
오웬턴	B	오전 7:53
그래멧	D	오전 8:04
64 쿡빌	E	오전 8:10

62

What are the speakers going to do?

(A) Visit a factory
(B) Oversee a building project
(C) Participate in a conference
(D) Attend an awards ceremony

화자들은 무엇을 할 것인가?
(A) 공장 방문
(B) 건설 프로젝트 감독
(C) 회의 참석
(D) 시상식 참석

어휘 oversee 감독하다 participate in ~에 참석하다

해설 세부 사항 관련 – 화자들이 하려는 일
남자가 첫 대사에서 회의 초반부를 놓치게 되면 다른 업계 참석자들에게 안 좋은 인상을 줄 것이다(It's going to make a bad impression on the other industry attendees if we miss the beginning of the conference)라고 말한 것으로 보아 화자들은 회의에 참석하려는 중임을 알 수 있다. 따라서 정답은 (C)이다.

63 [고난도]

What did the woman forget to bring?

(A) A set of gifts
(B) A travel document
(C) Some special clothing
(D) Some presentation materials

여자는 무엇을 가져오는 것을 잊었는가?
(A) 선물 세트
(B) 여행 서류
(C) 특수 의류
(D) 발표 자료

어휘 document 서류 material 자료, 재료

해설 세부 사항 관련 – 여자가 잊고 안 가져온 물건
여자가 첫 대사에서 오늘 아침 버스 정류장로 가던 도중에 구조 모형 두 개를 집에 두고 온 걸 깨달았다(I was halfway to the bus terminal this morning before I realized that I'd left two of my structural models at home)며 그것들이 없으면 발표를 할 수가 없다(I wouldn't be able to lead my session without them)고 한 것으로 보아 발표에 필요한 물건을 두고 왔음을 알 수 있다. 따라서 정답은 (D)이다.

64

Look at the graphic. When does the man suggest departing?

(A) At 7:20 A.M.
(B) At 7:53 A.M.
(C) At 8:04 A.M.
(D) At 8:10 A.M.

시각 정보에 의하면, 남자는 언제 출발하자고 제안하는가?
(A) 오전 7시 20분
(B) 오전 7시 53분
(C) 오전 8시 4분
(D) 오전 8시 10분

해설 시각 정보 연계 – 남자가 제안한 출발 시각
남자가 마지막 대사에서 8시 이후에 출발하는 쿡빌행 버스는 탈 수 있을 것 같다(I think you'll be able to make the bus to Cookville that leaves after eight)고 했고, 버스 출발 시간이 표시된 시각 자료에 의하면 8시 이후 쿡빌행 버스는 8시 10분에 출발하므로 정답은 (D)이다.

65-67 대화 + 쿠폰

W-Am	Welcome to Brooks Gym. How can I help you today?
M-Au	**65I was just handed this coupon as I was passing by outside, so I wanted to come in and see what kind of classes you offer.**
W-Am	Sure. Here's a list.
M-Au	Oh, kickboxing! I'd like to try that.
W-Am	Great. Which class package would you like?
M-Au	Let's see… **66I don't want to make a big commitment before I know if I like it, so I'll go with the ten-class package.**
W-Am	Great choice. **67And you should know— these packages don't have any limits on the kind of class.** If you decide that kickboxing isn't for you, you can try another activity.

여 브룩스 체육관에 오신 것을 환영합니다. 오늘 무엇을 도와드릴까요?
남 밖을 지나다 이 쿠폰을 받았는데 들어와서 어떤 종류의 강좌들을 제공하는지 보고 싶었어요.
여 그렇군요. 여기 목록이 있습니다.
남 오, 킥복싱이 있네요! 그걸 한번 해 보고 싶은데요.
여 좋아요. 어떤 강좌 패키지를 원하세요?
남 어디 봅시다… 마음에 드는지 알기 전에 큰 부담을 지고 싶지는 않으니까 10강좌 패키지로 할게요.
여 탁월한 선택이십니다. 한 가지 아셔야 할 점이 이 패키지는 강좌 종류에 전혀 제한이 없습니다. 킥복싱이 맞지 않다고 생각하시면, 다른 운동을 해보셔도 됩니다.

어휘 hand 건네주다 pass by 지나가다 commitment 약속, 전념, (돈·시간·인력의) 투입 limit 제한

Brooks Gym
Buy a class package and save!

	Total	Savings per class
5 classes	$90	$2
66 **10 classes**	**$160**	**$4**
15 classes	$210	$6
20 classes	$240	$8

브룩스 체육관
강좌 패키지에 등록하시고 절약하세요!

	총액	강좌당 총 절약 금액
5강좌	90달러	2달러
66 10강좌	160달러	4달러
15강좌	210달러	6달러
20강좌	240달러	8달러

65
고난도

Where most likely did the man get the coupon?

(A) At a gym class
(B) On the street
(C) In the mail
(D) On a Web site

남자는 어디에서 쿠폰을 받았을 것 같은가?
(A) 체육관 강좌에서
(B) 길거리에서
(C) 우편으로
(D) 웹사이트에서

해설 세부 사항 관련 – 남자가 쿠폰을 받았을 것 같은 장소
남자가 첫 대사에서 밖을 지나다 쿠폰을 받았는데 들어와서 어떤 종류의 강좌들을 제공하는지 보고 싶었다(I was just handed this coupon as I was passing by outside, so I wanted to come in and see what kind of classes you offer)고 말한 것으로 보아 정답은 (B)이다.

66

Look at the graphic. How much will the man save per class?

(A) $2
(B) $4
(C) $6
(D) $8

시각 정보에 의하면, 남자는 강좌당 얼마를 아낄 수 있는가?
(A) 2달러
(B) 4달러
(C) 6달러
(D) 8달러

해설 시각 정보 연계 – 남자가 강좌당 아낄 수 있는 금액
남자가 세 번째 대사에서 마음에 드는지 알기 전에 큰 부담을 지고 싶지는 않으니까 10강좌 패키지로 하겠다(I don't want to make a big commitment before I know if I like it, so I'll go with the ten-class package)고 했고, 시각 정보에 의하면 10강좌 패키지는 강좌당 4달러를 절약할 수 있으므로 정답은 (B)이다.

67
고난도

What does the woman say about the class packages?

(A) They were recently introduced.
(B) They are valid for a limited time.
(C) They are not eligible for refunds.
(D) They allow entry to any type of class.

여자는 강좌 패키지에 대해 무엇을 말하는가?
(A) 최근에 도입되었다.
(B) 한정된 시간 동안 유효하다.
(C) 환불을 받을 수 없다.
(D) 아무 강좌에나 들어갈 수 있다.

어휘 introduce 소개하다 valid 유효한 limited 한정된 eligible ~을 할[가질] 수 있는 entry 입장

해설 세부 사항 관련 – 여자가 강좌 패키지에 대해 말한 것
여자가 마지막 대사에서 한 가지 알아야 할 점은 이 패키지는 강좌 종류에 전혀 제한이 없는 것(And you should know—these packages don't have any limits on the kind of class)이라고 한 것으로 보아 정답은 (D)이다.

▶▶ Paraphrasing 대화의 **don't have any limits on the kind of class** → 정답의 **allow entry to any type of class**

68-70 대화 + 원 그래프

M-Cn Sabrina, have you read the company's annual report yet?

W-Br I'm doing that right now, actually. This "Sources of Revenue" chart is surprising. 68 **You know, it's been less than five years since we started doing business in Africa, and look how much it's grown as a source of revenue.**

M-Cn It's impressive, isn't it? 69 **I think that's why the company is planning to enter the South American market.** The CEO is predicting similar success there.

W-Br Oh really?

M-Cn 70 **Yes, the last few pages are about that. You'll definitely want to read that part.**

TEST 1 **19**

남	사브리나, 회사 연례 보고서 읽어봤어요?
여	실은, 지금 읽는 중이에요. 이 '수입원' 차트가 놀랍네요. **아프리카에서 사업을 시작한 지 5년도 안 되었는데, 수입원으로서 얼마나 성장했는지 보세요.**
남	인상적이에요, 그렇죠? 그래서 회사에서 남미 시장에 진출하려고 계획하고 있는 것 같아요. 최고 경영자가 그곳에서도 비슷한 성공을 예측하고 있어요.
여	오, 정말이요?
남	네, 마지막 몇 장은 그것에 관한 이야기예요. 그 부분을 꼭 읽어보세요.

어휘	annual 연례의 source 원천 revenue 수입[수익] impressive 인상적인 predict 예측하나 definitely 분명히

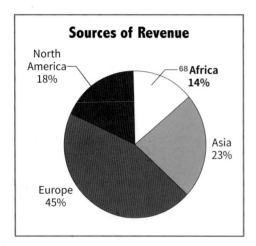

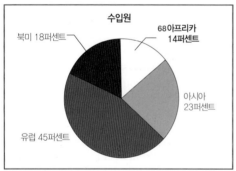

68

Look at the graphic. Which figure does the woman say is larger than before?

(A) 14%
(B) 18%
(C) 23%
(D) 45%

시각 정보에 의하면, 여자는 어떤 수치가 전보다 커졌다고 말하는가?

(A) 14퍼센트
(B) 18퍼센트
(C) 23퍼센트
(D) 45퍼센트

어휘 figure 수치

해설 시각 정보 연계 – 여자가 전보다 커졌다고 말한 수치

여자가 첫 대사에서 아프리카에서 사업을 시작한 지 5년도 안 되었는데, 수입원으로서 얼마나 성장했는지 보라(You know, it's been less than five years since we started doing business in Africa, and look how much it's grown as a source of revenue)고 했고, 시각 정보에 의하면 여자가 언급한 아프리카 지역의 수치는 14%이므로 정답은 (A)이다.

69

According to the man, what does the company plan to do?

(A) Enter an additional industry
(B) Replace its chief executive
(C) Relocate its headquarters
(D) Expand into a new region

남자에 따르면, 회사는 무엇을 계획하는가?

(A) 추가 산업으로의 진입
(B) 최고 책임자의 교체
(C) 본사의 이전
(D) 새로운 지역으로의 확장

어휘 industry 산업 chief executive 최고 책임자 relocate 이전하다 headquarters 본사 expand 확장하다 region 지역

해설 세부 사항 관련 – 남자가 말하는 회사의 계획

남자가 두 번째 대사에서 그래서 회사에서 남미 시장에 진출하려고 계획하고 있는 것 같다(I think that's why the company is planning to enter the South American market)고 말한 것으로 보아 정답은 (D)이다.

▸▸ **Paraphrasing** 대화의 enter the South American market
→ 정답의 expand into a new region

70

What does the man recommend reading?

(A) A section of a report
(B) An article on a Web page
(C) A summary of some laws
(D) An invitation to a celebration

남자는 무엇을 읽으라고 권하는가?

(A) 보고서의 한 부분
(B) 웹페이지의 기사
(C) 일부 법률의 요약
(D) 기념식의 초대장

어휘 section 부분 summary 요약 celebration 기념 (행사)

해설 세부 사항 관련 – 남자가 읽으라고 권한 것

남자가 마지막 대사에서 보고서의 마지막 몇 장은 그것에 관한 이야기(the last few pages are about that)라며, 그 부분을 꼭 읽어보라(You'll definitely want to read that part)고 했으므로 정답은 (A)이다.

PART 4

71-73 전화 메시지

> M-Au Hi, Ms. Gibson. This is Kwang-Ho at Pelston Pharmacy. **71The medicine that Doctor Walsh prescribed for your eye condition is ready.** I apologize for the delay. **72It took some time to get your insurance provider's approval. But we finally did, so you won't have to pay anything out-of-pocket for the medicine.** You can come by and pick it up during our business hours, which are from eight to six. **73Oh, but we have to close down tomorrow for maintenance reasons, so don't come then.** Call us if you have any questions. Thanks.
>
> 여보세요, 깁슨 씨. 펠스턴 약국의 광호입니다. 월시 선생님께서 깁슨 씨의 눈 상태에 대해 처방하신 약이 준비되었습니다. 늦어져서 죄송합니다. 깁슨 씨의 보험업체에서 승인을 받는 데 시간이 좀 걸렸습니다. 하지만 결국 승인을 받아서 약에 대해 사후 정산되는 금액은 전혀 없습니다. 약국 영업시간인 8시부터 6시 사이에 들르셔서 약을 받아 가시면 됩니다. 오, 그런데 내일은 관리상의 이유로 약국이 문을 닫아야 하니까 내일은 오지 마십시오. 질문 있으시면 전화 주세요. 감사합니다.
>
> 어휘 pharmacy 약국 prescribe 처방하다 insurance 보험 approval 승인 out-of-pocket 사후 정산되는 maintenance 유지

71

What is the message mainly about?

(A) A prescription medication
(B) An appointment time
(C) A doctor's specialty
(D) A hospital bill

메시지는 주로 무엇에 관한 내용인가?

(A) 처방약
(B) 예약 시간
(C) 의사의 전문 분야
(D) 병원 청구서

어휘 prescription 처방 medication 약 specialty 전문, 전공

해설 전체 내용 관련 – 메시지의 주제

화자가 초반부에 월시 선생님께서 깁슨 씨의 눈 상태에 대해 처방하신 약이 준비되었다(The medicine that Doctor Walsh prescribed for your eye condition is ready)며 처방약에 관한 이야기로 메시지를 시작한 것으로 보아 정답은 (A)이다.

72

What does the speaker say he has received?

(A) An electronic payment
(B) An insurance authorization
(C) Some promotional brochures
(D) Some past medical records

화자는 무엇을 받았다고 말하는가?

(A) 온라인 결제
(B) 보험 승인
(C) 홍보용 책자
(D) 과거 진료 기록

어휘 electronic 전자의 authorization 인가 promotional 홍보의 brochure 안내책자

해설 세부 사항 관련 – 화자가 받았다고 말한 것

화자가 중반부에 깁슨 씨의 보험업체에서 승인을 받는 데 시간이 좀 걸렸다(It took some time to get your insurance provider's approval)면서 하지만 결국 승인을 받아서 약에 대해 사후 정산되는 금액은 전혀 필요 없다(But we finally did, so you won't have to pay anything out-of-pocket for the medicine)고 한 것으로 보아 정답은 (B)이다.

> ▸▸ Paraphrasing 담화의 insurance provider's approval
> → 정답의 insurance authorization

73

What does the speaker say will happen tomorrow?

(A) He will update a database.
(B) He will call the listener again.
(C) A business will be closed.
(D) A delivery will arrive.

화자는 내일 무슨 일이 일어날 것이라고 말하는가?

(A) 데이터베이스를 업데이트할 것이다.
(B) 청자에게 다시 전화할 것이다.
(C) 업체가 문을 닫을 것이다.
(D) 배송물이 도착할 것이다.

해설 세부 사항 관련 – 화자가 내일 일어날 것이라고 말한 일

화자가 후반부에 내일은 관리상의 이유로 약국이 문을 닫아야 하므로 내일은 오지 마라(but we have to close down tomorrow for maintenance reasons, so don't come then)고 했으므로 정답은 (C)이다.

74-76 회의 발췌

> M-Cn Before we finish up this office-wide meeting, I'd like to address a problem that's come to my attention. **74It seems that several of you have complained to Human Resources about your coworkers taking calls from family and friends at their workstations.** I know that it can be difficult to concentrate when you can hear others' personal conversations, but this is not the kind of matter that should be brought to HR. **75Human Resources deals with major workplace issues. 76Its functions are clearly laid out in the staff handbook, which you should all have a copy of. When you return to your desks today, please take a minute to look over that section.** Thank you.

사무실 전체 회의를 마무리하기 전에, 제 주목을 끈 문제를 다루고자 합니다. 여러분 중 몇몇이 인사부에 사무실에서 가족 및 친구의 전화를 받는 동료 직원들에 대해 불평을 한 것 같습니다. 다른 사람의 사적인 대화를 듣는 것이 집중을 어렵게 할 수 있다는 것을 잘 압니다만, 이는 인사부에 제기될 수 있는 종류의 문제가 아닙니다. 인사부는 중요한 직장 문제들을 처리합니다. 인사부의 역할은 직원 편람에 명백히 제시되어 있으며 여러분 모두 사본을 가지고 있을 겁니다. 오늘 자리로 돌아가시면 시간 내어 해당 부분을 살펴보시기 바랍니다. 감사합니다.

어휘 office-wide 전사무실의 attention 주의, 관심 complain 불평하다 Human Resources 인사부 concentrate 집중하다 deal with ~을 다루다 lay something out (계획·주장 등을 잘 정리하여) 제시하다 staff handbook 직원 편람 section 부분

74

What have some employees complained about?

(A) The quality of a workplace amenity
(B) The temperature of their office
(C) The distribution of a workload
(D) The behavior of their coworkers

일부 직원들은 무엇에 대해 불평했는가?

(A) 직장 편의시설의 질
(B) 사무실의 온도
(C) 업무 분배
(D) 동료의 품행

어휘 amenity 편의시설 temperature 온도 distribution 분배 workload 업무량 behavior 행동, 품행

해설 세부 사항 관련 – 직원들의 불만 사항
화자가 초반부에 일부 직원들이 사무실에서 가족 및 친구의 전화를 받는 동료 직원들에 대해 불평을 한 것 같다(It seems that several of you have complained to Human Resources ~ taking calls from family and friends at their workstations)고 했으므로 정답은 (D)이다.

75

What does the speaker say about Human Resources?

(A) It is currently understaffed.
(B) It follows specific procedures.
(C) It handles only significant matters.
(D) It has made an announcement.

화자는 인사부에 대해 무엇을 말하는가?

(A) 현재 직원이 부족하다.
(B) 구체적인 절차를 따른다.
(C) 중요한 문제만 다룬다.
(D) 발표를 했다.

어휘 understaffed 인원이 부족한 specific 구체적인 procedure 절차 handle 다루다 significant 중요한 announcement 발표

해설 세부 사항 관련 – 화자가 인사부에 대해 말하는 것
화자가 중반부에 인사부는 중요한 직장 문제들을 처리한다(Human Resources deals with major workplace issues)고 했으므로 정답은 (C)이다.

▸▸ Paraphrasing 담화의 deals with major workplace issues → 정답의 handles significant matters

76

What does the speaker ask the listeners to do?

(A) Review part of the employee handbook
(B) Participate in a team-building activity
(C) Brainstorm some possible solutions
(D) View an online training film

화자는 청자들에게 무엇을 하라고 요청하는가?

(A) 직원 편람의 일부를 검토한다.
(B) 단합 대회에 참가한다.
(C) 가능한 해결책들을 구상한다.
(D) 온라인 교육 영상을 본다.

어휘 review 검토하다 activity 활동 brainstorm 아이디어를 짜내다

해설 세부 사항 관련 – 화자가 청자들에게 요청하는 것
화자가 후반부에 인사부의 역할이 직원 편람에 명백히 제시되어 있으며 자리로 돌아가서 해당 부분을 시간 내서 살펴보라(Its functions are clearly laid out in the staff handbook, ~ please take a minute to look over that section)고 했으므로 정답은 (A)이다.

▸▸ Paraphrasing 담화의 look over that section → 정답의 review part of ~

77-79 소개

W-Am Welcome to this evening's lecture. I'm pleased to introduce our speaker, Gurleen Datta. [77]Over her thirty-year career, Ms. Datta has been involved in the design and construction of dams all over the country, including one on the enormous Cataldo River. [78]To share some of the wisdom she has acquired, she has written an autobiography detailing her successes and failures, and she's going to tell us all about it today. Ms. Datta will speak for one hour and then take questions from the audience. [79]One note about the Q and A—the time will be limited, so if you decide to participate, please remember that there are a hundred other people here. All right. Please welcome Gurleen Datta!

오늘 저녁 강연에 오신 것을 환영합니다. 우리의 연설자인 걸린 다타 씨를 소개하게 되어 기쁩니다. 30년의 경력 동안, 다타 씨는 거대한 카탈도 강에 있는 댐을 포함해 전국 각지의 댐 설계 및 건설에 몸담아 왔습니다. 그녀는 습득한 지혜의 일부를 공유하기 위해 자신의 성공과 실패를 상세히 기술한 자서전을 썼고, 오늘 그에 관한 모든 것을 우리에게 이야기할 것입니다. 다타 씨는 한 시간 동안 연설한 뒤 청중들로부터 질문을 받을 예정입니다. 질의응답 시간에 대해 한 가지 주

의하실 점은 시간이 한정적이므로 참여하게 되실 경우 **여기 백 명의 다른 사람들이 있다는 걸** 기억해주세요. 자 그럼, 걸린 다타 씨를 환영해주세요!

> 어휘 lecture 강의 involved in ~에 종사하는 enormous 거대한 wisdom 지혜 acquire 습득하다 autobiography 자서전 detail 상세히 기술하다; 세부 사항 audience 청중 limited 한정된 participate 참여하다

77 고난도

What field does Ms. Datta most likely work in?
(A) Politics
(B) Medicine
(C) Engineering
(D) Publishing

다타 씨는 어떤 분야에서 일할 것 같은가?
(A) 정치
(B) 의학
(C) **공학 기술**
(D) 출판

해설 세부 사항 관련 – 다타 씨의 업무 분야
화자가 초반부에 30년의 경력 동안 다타 씨는 거대한 카탈도 강에 있는 댐을 포함해 전국 각지의 댐 설계 및 건설에 몸담아 왔다(Over her thirty-year career, Ms. Datta has been involved in the design and construction of dams all over the country, including one on the enormous Cataldo River)고 했으므로 정답은 (C)이다.

78 고난도

What will Ms. Datta talk about?
(A) A book about her experiences
(B) A documentary about a journey
(C) An organization she founded
(D) A prize she received

다타 씨는 무엇에 대해 이야기할 것인가?
(A) **자신의 경험에 대한 책**
(B) 여행에 대한 다큐멘터리
(C) 자신이 설립한 단체
(D) 자신이 받은 상

> 어휘 documentary 다큐멘터리 organization 단체 found 설립하다

해설 세부 사항 관련 – 다타 씨의 연설 주제
화자가 중반부에 그녀(다타 씨)는 습득한 지혜의 일부를 공유하기 위해 자신의 성공과 실패를 상세히 기술한 자서전을 썼고 오늘 그에 관한 모든 것을 우리에게 이야기할 것이다(To share some of the wisdom she has acquired, she has written an autobiography detailing her successes and failures, and she's going to tell us all about it today)라고 했으므로 정답은 (A)이다.

▸▸ Paraphrasing 담화의 **autobiography detailing her successes and failures** → 정답의 **book about her experiences**

79 고난도

What does the speaker imply when she says, "there are a hundred other people here"?
(A) Some of the listeners do not usually attend lectures.
(B) It will be easy to reach a fund-raising goal.
(C) There are not enough seats for the whole audience.
(D) The listeners should not take too long with their questions.

화자가 "여기 백 명의 다른 사람들이 있다"라고 말한 의미는 무엇인가?
(A) 일부 청자들은 평소 강연에 참석하지 않는다.
(B) 모금 목표에 도달하기가 쉬울 것이다.
(C) 전체 청중을 위한 좌석이 충분하지 않다.
(D) **청자들은 질문을 너무 오래 해서는 안 된다.**

> 어휘 fund-raising 모금

해설 화자의 의도 파악 – 여기 백 명의 다른 사람들이 있다는 말의 의도
앞에서 질의응답 시간에 대해 한 가지 주의할 점은 시간이 한정적이므로 참여하려면 기억해달라(One note about the Q and A—the time will be limited, so if you decide to participate, please remember)고 하면서 인용문을 언급한 것이므로 사람이 많으니 질문을 오래 하지 말라는 의도로 한 말임을 알 수 있다. 따라서 정답은 (D)이다.

80-82 안내 방송

> W-Br **80 Good afternoon, Prensfield Plaza shoppers.** We have some brief announcements to make. **81 First, the youth talent show, presided over by local news anchor Dean Adams, is starting in ten minutes.** Join Mr. Adams in the central atrium for a wonderful display of singing, dancing, and more. **82 Also, we encourage our shoppers to download Prensfield Plus, our new application for smartphones and other mobile devices.** It features detailed information on our shops and restaurants, alerts about sales and entertainment events, and exclusive coupons. That's Prensfield Plus, available through all major app stores. Thank you, and enjoy your visit to Prensfield Plaza.

안녕하세요, 프렌스필드 플라자 쇼핑객 여러분. 간단한 전달 사항이 있습니다. 먼저, 지역 뉴스 앵커 딘 아담스가 진행하는 청소년 장기 쇼가 10분 후에 시작됩니다. 중앙 아트리움으로 오셔서 아담스와 함께 노래, 춤, 그리고 그 밖의 것들을 즐기세요. 또한, 모든 쇼핑객 여러분께 저희의 새로운 스마트폰 및 기타 휴대 장치용 애플리케이션인 프렌스필드 플러스의 다운로드를 권해드립니다. 앱에는 저희 매장과 식당에 관한 상세한 정보, 할인 및 공연 행사 관련 알림 기능과 전용 쿠폰 등이 포함되어 있습니다. 프렌스필드 플러스는 모든 주요 앱 스토어에서 다운로드 받으실 수 있습니다. 감사합니다. 프렌스필드 플라자에서 즐거운 시간 보내시기 바랍니다.

어휘 brief 짧은, 간단한 preside over ~의 사회를 보다 atrium 아트리움, 건물의 중앙홀 encourage 권장하다 device 장치 feature 특별히 포함하다 detailed 상세한 alert 알림, 알리다 exclusive 전용의, 독점적인 available 이용할 수 있는

80

Where most likely is the announcement being made?

(A) At a public library
(B) At a shopping mall
(C) At an amusement park
(D) At a conference center

공지가 나온 장소는 어디일 것 같은가?
(A) 공공 도서관
(B) 쇼핑몰
(C) 놀이공원
(D) 컨퍼런스 센터

해설 전체 내용 관련 – 공지의 장소
화자가 도입부에 안녕하세요, 프렌스필드 플라자 쇼핑객 여러분(Good afternoon, Prensfield Plaza shoppers)이라고 했으므로 정답은 (B)이다.

81

What does the speaker say about Mr. Adams?

(A) He is searching for an acquaintance.
(B) One of his possessions has been found.
(C) He is about to act as the host of an event.
(D) Information about him has been put on display.

화자는 아담스 씨에 대해 무엇을 말하는가?
(A) 지인을 찾고 있다.
(B) 그의 소지품 중 하나가 발견되었다.
(C) 행사 사회자 역할을 하려고 한다.
(D) 그에 대한 정보가 전시되었다.

어휘 search for ~을 찾다 acquaintance 아는 사람 possession 소지품 be about to 막 ~하려고 하다 host 주최측

해설 세부 사항 관련 – 화자가 아담스 씨에 대해 말하는 것
화자가 초반부에 지역 뉴스 앵커인 딘 아담스가 진행하는 청소년 장기 쇼가 10분 후에 시작된다(the youth talent show, presided over by local news anchor Dean Adams, is starting in ten minutes)고 했으므로 정답은 (C)이다.

82

What does the speaker say is newly available?

(A) A dining facility
(B) A mobile app
(C) A job opportunity
(D) A transportation service

화자는 무엇이 새롭게 이용 가능하다고 말하는가?
(A) 식당
(B) 모바일 앱
(C) 구직 기회
(D) 교통 서비스

어휘 dining 식사 facility 시설 transportation 운송

해설 세부 사항 관련 – 화자가 새롭게 이용 가능하다고 말한 것
화자가 중반부에 쇼핑객 여러분께 저희의 새로운 스마트폰 및 기타 휴대 장치용 애플리케이션인 프렌스필드 플러스의 다운로드를 권한다(we encourage our shoppers to download Prensfield Plus, our new application for smartphones and other mobile devices)고 했으므로 정답은 (B)이다.

83-85 설명

M-Au Thank you all for coming in to learn about our new point-of-sale system. **83 Once you've all been fully trained on it, you'll find that you can check out customers twice as fast as you did with the old cash registers. 84 Now, the system includes a touch screen, a barcode scanner, a credit card reader, a receipt printer, and a cash drawer—and today you'll find out how to use all of them.** To help, I've made these copies of the directions provided by the manufacturer. **85 Still, as I demonstrate how to use the system, you'll want to write down some extra details or clarifications.** There are some pencils on that table. All right. Ready?

저희의 새로운 판매관리 시스템에 대해 배우고자 이렇게 와주신 데 대해 여러분 모두에게 감사드립니다. 교육이 완전히 끝나고 나면, 기존 금전 등록기를 이용한 것보다 2배는 빠르게 고객들의 계산을 처리하실 수 있을 겁니다. 자, 이 시스템은 터치 스크린과 바코드 스캐너, 신용카드 판독기, 영수증 출력기, 현금 보관 서랍으로 구성되어 있습니다. 오늘 이 모든 것에 대한 사용법을 알게 되실 거예요. 도움이 되고자, 제가 제조업체에서 제공한 설명서를 복사해 뒀습니다. 그래도 제가 시스템 사용법을 보여드리는 동안, 추가 정보나 설명을 필기하실 필요가 있을 거예요. 탁자에 연필들이 있습니다. 자 그럼, 준비되셨나요?

어휘 point-of-sale system 판매관리 시스템 cash register 금전 등록기 cash drawer 현금 보관 서랍 direction 지시, 방향 manufacturer 제조업체 demonstrate 시연하다 detail 세부 사항 clarification 설명

83

Who most likely are the listeners?

(A) Bank tellers
(B) Store clerks
(C) Factory workers
(D) Real estate agents

청자들은 누구일 것 같은가?
(A) 은행 직원
(B) 매장 점원
(C) 공장 직원
(D) 부동산 중개인

해설 전체 내용 관련 – 청자들의 직업

화자가 초반부에 교육이 완전히 끝나고 나면 기존 금전 등록기를 이용한 것보다 2배는 빠르게 고객들의 계산을 처리할 수 있을 것(Once you've all been fully trained on it, you'll find that you can check out customers twice as fast as you did with the old cash registers)이라고 한 것으로 보아 정답은 (B)이다.

84

What does the speaker list?

(A) Pieces of equipment
(B) Marketing strategies
(C) Employee rest areas
(D) Customer complaints

화자는 무엇을 열거하는가?

(A) 장비 구성품
(B) 마케팅 전략
(C) 직원 휴게실
(D) 고객 불만

해설 세부 사항 관련 – 화자가 열거한 것

화자가 중반부에 이 시스템은 터치 스크린과 바코드 스캐너, 신용카드 판독기, 영수증 출력기, 현금 보관 서랍으로 구성되어 있고, 오늘 이 모든 것에 대한 사용법을 알게 될 것(Now, the system includes a touch screen, a barcode scanner, a credit card reader, a receipt printer, and a cash drawer—and today you'll find out how to use all of them)이라고 했으므로 정답은 (A)이다.

85

고난도

Why does the speaker say, "There are some pencils on that table"?

(A) To show disappointment that a facility is messy
(B) To suggest that the listeners have lost some belongings
(C) To recommend using the pencils to take notes
(D) To offer the pencils to the listeners as gifts to take home

화자가 왜 "탁자에 연필들이 있습니다"라고 말하는 이유는 무엇인가?

(A) 설비가 지저분해 실망이라는 점을 보여주려고
(B) 청자들이 몇몇 소지품을 잃어버렸다는 점을 알리려고
(C) 연필을 사용해 필기를 하도록 권하려고
(D) 청자들에게 집에 가져가는 선물로 연필을 제공하려고

어휘 messy 지저분한 belongings 소지품

해설 화자의 의도 파악 – 탁자에 연필들이 있다는 말의 의도

화자가 시스템 사용법을 보여드리는 동안 추가 정보나 설명을 필기할 필요가 있을 것(Still, as I demonstrate how to use the system, you'll want to write down some extra details or clarifications)이라고 한 뒤, 인용문을 언급하며 필기 도구가 어디 있는지를 알려준 것으로 보아 정답은 (C)이다.

▸▸ Paraphrasing   담화의 **write down some extra details** → 정답의 **take notes**

86-88 전화 메시지

W-Am Hello, Mr. Odiatu. This is Alyssa at Nealon Global. **86We've just reviewed your account and noticed that you've been using our Internet, phone, and cable services for five years.** **87It's Nealon Global's policy to show our appreciation to loyal customers like you, so we'd like to give you a digital home assistant made by our partner company—for free.** This voice-activated device, which retails for one hundred dollars, can play music, search the Internet, issue reminders, and much more. **88If you're interested, call me back at 1-800-555-0156, extension 85, and let me know when to send a technician to your house to install the device.** And again, thank you for being a Nealon Global customer.

여보세요, 오디아투 씨, 저는 닐론 글로벌의 엘리사입니다. 고객님의 계정을 살펴봤는데 저희 인터넷과 전화, 케이블 서비스를 5년 동안 사용하고 계시더라고요. 고객님과 같은 단골 고객분들께 감사의 뜻을 보여드리는 것이 닐론 글로벌의 방침이라서, 저희 협력사에서 만든 디지털 홈 도우미를 무료로 보내드리고자 합니다. 이 음성 인식 장치는 소매가 100달러에 판매되고 있으며, 음악 재생, 인터넷 검색, 알림 발송과 기타 더욱 많은 기능이 가능합니다. 관심 있으시면 1-800-555-0156, 내선번호 85로 저에게 전화 주셔서, 언제 기사를 보내 장치를 댁에 설치하면 될지를 알려주시기 바랍니다. 닐론 글로벌을 이용해주셔서 감사합니다.

어휘 review 검토하다 account 계정 notice ~을 알다; 알아챔 policy 방침 loyal 충실한 voice-activated 음성 기동의 device 장치 retail (특정 가격에) 팔리다; 소매 reminder 상기시키는 것 extension 내선번호 technician 기술자 install 설치하다

86

What type of service does the speaker's company provide?

(A) Security
(B) Shipping
(C) Landscaping
(D) Telecommunications

화자의 회사는 어떤 종류의 서비스를 제공하는가?

(A) 보안
(B) 배송
(C) 조경
(D) 이동 통신

해설 세부 사항 관련 – 화자의 회사가 제공하는 서비스

화자가 초반부에 고객의 계정을 살펴봤는데 자사 인터넷과 전화, 케이블 서비스를 5년 동안 사용하고 있더라(We've just reviewed your account and noticed that you've been using our Internet, phone, and cable services for five years)라고 한 것으로 보아 정답은 (D)이다.

87

What is the speaker calling about?

(A) A review posted on a Web site
(B) An account password
(C) A reward for certain customers
(D) A malfunctioning electronic device

화자는 무엇에 대해 전화하는가?

(A) 웹사이트에 게시된 후기
(B) 계정 비밀번호
(C) **특정 고객들을 위한 보상**
(D) 고장난 전자 기기

어휘 post 게시하다   malfunctioning 제대로 작동하지 않는
electronic 전자의

해설 전체 내용 관련 – 전화 메시지의 주제
화자가 중반부에 고객님과 같은 단골 고객분들께 감사의 뜻을 보여드리는 것이 닐론 글로벌의 방침이라서, 협력사에서 만든 디지털 홈 도우미를 무료로 보내드리고자 한다(It's Nealon Global's policy to show our appreciation to loyal customers like you, so we'd like to give you a digital home assistant made by our partner company—for free)고 했으므로 정답은 (C)이다.

> ▸▸ Paraphrasing   담화의 show our appreciation to loyal
> customers
> → 정답의 reward for certain customers

88

Why should the listener return the phone call?

(A) To schedule a home visit
(B) To learn more about a discount
(C) To receive installation instructions
(D) To find out where to send an item

청자는 왜 전화 회신을 해야 하는가?

(A) **가정 방문 일정을 잡기 위해**
(B) 할인에 대해 더 알기 위해
(C) 설치 안내를 받기 위해
(D) 어디로 제품을 보내야 할지 알아내기 위해

해설 세부 사항 관련 – 청자가 전화 회신을 해야 하는 이유
화자가 후반부에 관심이 있으면 1-800-555-0156, 내선번호 85로 전화해서 언제 기사를 보내 장치를 댁에 설치하면 될지를 알려주기 바란다(If you're interested, call me back at 1-800-555-0156, extension 85, and let me know when to send a technician to your house to install the device)고 했으므로 정답은 (A)이다.

89-91 여행 정보

> M-Cn Wow, isn't that a beautiful sky? OK, now that the sun has risen fully, it's time to begin the second part of our tour. ⁸⁹**Luke has gotten our bikes out of the tour van so that we can cycle**

back down the mountain. As you know, this is expected to take four hours. ⁹⁰**We will stop twice for breaks, but if you still start to feel too tired to keep riding,** the van will be close behind us. You can see the same beautiful views from the van, so don't hesitate to speak to me if you need it. ⁹¹**OK, please get your bike helmets on.** They're in this box here.

와우, 하늘이 정말 아름답지 않나요? 좋습니다. 이제 해가 완전히 떴으니, 우리 여행의 두 번째 일정을 시작할 때가 되었네요. **자전거를 타고 산을 내려갈 수 있도록 루크가 관광 버스에서 자전거를 꺼내 놓았어요.** 아시다시피, 자전거 여행은 4시간이 소요될 예정입니다. **두 번 정도 멈춰서 쉴 예정인데, 너무 피곤해서 계속 자전거를 타기 힘드시면 버스가 우리 뒤에 가까이 있을 겁니다.** 버스에서도 똑같이 아름다운 풍경을 감상하실 수 있으니, 필요하시면 망설이지 말고 말씀해 주세요. 자, 그럼 **자전거용 헬멧을 착용해주세요.** 여기 이 상자 안에 있습니다.

어휘 van 승합차   cycle 자전거를 타다   break 휴식   hesitate
망설이다

89

Where is the tour taking place?

(A) On a mountain
(B) In a forest
(C) By a lake
(D) In a desert

관광 중인 장소는 어디인가?

(A) **산 위**
(B) 숲 속
(C) 호숫가
(D) 사막

해설 전체 내용 관련 – 관광 중인 장소
화자가 초반부에 자전거를 타고 산을 내려갈 수 있도록 루크가 관광 버스에서 자전거를 꺼내 놓았다(Luke has gotten our bikes out of the tour van so that we can cycle back down the mountain)고 한 것으로 보아 정답은 (A)이다.

90   고난도

What does the speaker imply when he says, "the van will be close behind us"?

(A) Listeners do not have to worry about getting lost.
(B) Listeners can ride in the van during the tour.
(C) Listeners should be careful around a vehicle.
(D) Listeners can access their baggage at any time.

화자가 "버스가 우리 뒤에 가까이 있을 겁니다"라고 말한 의미는 무엇인가?

(A) 청자들은 길을 잃을까 걱정할 필요가 없다.
(B) **청자들은 여행 동안 버스에 탈 수 있다.**
(C) 청자들은 차량 주변에서 조심해야 한다.
(D) 청자들은 어느 때나 짐에 접근할 수 있다.

어휘 get lost 길을 잃다 vehicle 차량 access 접근하다 baggage 짐, 수하물

해설 화자의 의도 파악 – 버스가 우리 뒤에 가까이 있을 것이라는 말의 의도 앞에서 화자가 두 번 정도 멈춰서 쉴 예정인데 너무 피곤해서 계속 자전거를 타기 힘들면(We will stop twice for breaks, but if you still start to feel too tired to keep riding)이라고 한 뒤, 인용문을 언급했으므로 버스가 가까이 있으니 힘들 경우 버스에 바로 탈 수 있다는 의도로 한 말임을 알 수 있다. 따라서 정답은 (B)이다.

91

What are the listeners asked to do next?

(A) Look at a route map
(B) Fill out some paperwork
(C) Put on some safety gear
(D) Throw away some trash

청자들은 다음에 무엇을 하라고 요청되는가?
(A) 노선도를 볼 것
(B) 서류를 작성할 것
(C) 안전 장비를 착용할 것
(D) 쓰레기를 버릴 것

어휘 route map 노선도 fill out 작성하다 safety gear 안전 장비 trash 쓰레기

해설 세부 사항 관련 – 청자들이 다음에 하라고 요청받은 것
화자가 후반부에 자전거용 헬멧을 착용해달라(please get your bike helmets on)고 했으므로 정답은 (C)이다.

▸▸ Paraphrasing   담화의 get your bike helmets on
                   → 정답의 put on some safety gear

92-94 회의 발췌

W-Br Let's get started. ⁹²**First, I want to express my gratitude to all of you for taking on extra shifts while the business exposition was in town.** Our hotel handled the increase in guests without any major problems. ⁹³**That said, we have another busy week coming up in June during the annual Waltsville Marathon.** So in today's meeting, we'll discuss the issues we did have and how to avoid them in the future. For example, we sometimes had long check-in lines because front desk staff were answering tourism-related questions. ⁹⁴**But I want to make it clear that that's not actually part of their job.** Instead, guests with such inquiries should be directed to use the concierge desk.

시작합시다. 먼저, 기업 박람회가 시내에서 열리는 동안 추가 근무를 해주신 여러분 모두에게 감사를 전하고 싶습니다. 우리 호텔은 별 주요한 문제 없이 투숙객 증가에 대처했습니다. 그렇긴 하지만 6월에 연례 왈츠빌 마라톤이 열리는 동안 우리는 또 바쁜 한 주를 맞이하게 됩니다. 오늘 회의에서, 우리는 발생했던 문제들과 향후 문제들을 피할 방법에 대해 논의할 예정입니다. 일례를 들면, 안내 데스크 직원들이 관광 관련 질문에 답하느라 체크인 줄이 때때로 길어졌습니다. 하지만 이는 사실 그들의 업무가 아님을 분명히 말하고 싶습니다. 대신에, 그런 질문이 있는 투숙객들은 서비스 데스크를 이용하도록 안내되어야 합니다.

어휘 gratitude 감사 shift 근무 시간 exposition 박람회 handle 다루다 major 주요한 that said 그렇긴 하지만 annual 연례의 avoid 피하다 related 관련된 instead 대신에 inquiry 문의 direct 보내다 concierge (호텔의) 안내원

92

What does the speaker thank the listeners for?

(A) Taking part in the meeting
(B) Reporting some problems
(C) Working additional hours
(D) Going to an exposition

화자는 청자들에게 무엇을 감사하는가?
(A) 회의 참석
(B) 문제 보고
(C) 연장 근무
(D) 박람회 참석

어휘 take part in ~에 참가하다

해설 세부 사항 관련 – 화자가 청자들에게 감사한 일
화자가 초반부에 기업 박람회가 시내에서 열리는 동안 추가 근무를 해주신 여러분 모두에게 감사를 전하고 싶다(I want to express my gratitude to all of you for taking on extra shifts while the business exposition was in town)고 했으므로 정답은 (C)이다.

▸▸ Paraphrasing   담화의 **taking on extra shifts**
                   → 정답의 **working additional hours**

93

According to the speaker, what will happen in June?

(A) A competition will be held.
(B) An executive will retire.
(C) A new branch will open.
(D) A holiday will be celebrated.

화자에 따르면, 6월에 무슨 일이 일어나는가?
(A) 대회가 열릴 것이다.
(B) 임원이 은퇴할 것이다.
(C) 새 지점이 문을 열 것이다.
(D) 휴일을 기념할 것이다.

어휘 competition 대회 executive 경영진 branch 지점 celebrate 기념하다

해설　세부 사항 관련 – 화자가 말하는 6월에 일어날 일

화자가 중반부에 6월에 연례 왈츠빌 마라톤이 열리는 동안 우리는 또 바쁜 한 주를 맞이하게 된다(we have another busy week coming up in June during the annual Waltsville Marathon)고 한 것으로 보아 정답은 (A)이다.

▸▸ **Paraphrasing**　담화의 **marathon** → 정답의 **competition**

94

고난도

What does the speaker clarify?

(A) The names included on a guest list
(B) The availability of some hotel rooms
(C) The requirements for a submission
(D) The responsibilities of a position

화자는 무엇을 분명히 말하는가?
(A) 투숙객 명단에 포함된 이름들
(B) 일부 호텔 객실의 이용 가능 여부
(C) 제출 요건
(D) **직무 사항**

어휘　clarify 분명히 말하다　availability 이용 가능성　requirement 요건　submission 제출　responsibility 책무

해설　세부 사항 관련 – 화자가 명백히 말하고자 하는 것

화자가 후반부에 이는 사실 그들의(안내 데스크 직원들의) 업무가 아님을 분명히 말하고 싶다(I want to make it clear that that's not actually part of their job)며 안내 데스크 직원들의 직무에 대해서 언급하고 있는 것으로 보아 정답은 (D)이다.

95-97 전화 메시지 + 일정표

M-Au　Hi, Kioshi. I hope this message catches you before you leave work. **95As you know, today was the first day of data collection for the Gilfoy Airport employee satisfaction survey.** We administered the surveys to fifteen people, which is within our target range. **96But I just gathered the team to discuss how the project is going so far, and it seems there's a problem.** Just as we tried to warn airport management, the questionnaire is too long. Employees seem to be getting tired and not giving thoughtful answers by the end. **97I think we should shorten or at least rearrange it to address this issue.** Can we talk about this tomorrow morning? Let me know.

여보세요, 키오시. 퇴근하기 전에 이 메시지가 당도하면 좋겠네요. **알다시피, 오늘은 길포이 공항 직원 만족도 조사를 위해 데이터를 수집하는 첫날이었어요.** 우리는 설문지를 우리 목표 범위 내에 있는 열다섯 사람에게 배부했어요. **그런데 제가 방금 팀원들을 모아 프로젝트가 어떻게 진행되고 있는지 논의해봤더니 문제가 있는 것 같아 보여요.** 공항 경영진 측에 통지하려고 했던 것처럼, 설문지가 너무 길어. 직원들이 지쳐서 끝까지 사려 깊은 답변을 주지 못하는 것 같아요. 이

문제에 대처하려면 설문지를 줄이거나 아니면 최소한 재조정이라도 해야 할 것 같아요. 내일 아침에 이 사안에 대해 이야기할 수 있을까요? 알려주세요.

어휘　collection 수집　satisfaction 만족　survey 설문 조사　administer (정식으로) 주다　range 범위　gather 모으다　questionnaire 설문지　thoughtful 사려 깊은　shorten 짧게 하다　rearrange 재조정하다　address 다루다

Project Schedule

Planning	July 1–19
95Data collection	July 22–August 30
Data analysis	September 2–6
Report preparation	September 9–20
Presentation of results	September 23

프로젝트 일정표

계획	7월 1일–19일
95데이터 수집	7월 22일–8월 30일
데이터 분석	9월 2일–6일
보고 준비	9월 9일–20일
결과 보고	9월 23일

95

Look at the graphic. On which date is the speaker calling?

(A) July 1
(B) July 22
(C) September 2
(D) September 9

시각 정보에 의하면, 화자가 전화를 건 날짜는 언제인가?
(A) 7월 1일
(B) **7월 22일**
(C) 9월 2일
(D) 9월 9일

해설　시각 정보 연계 – 화자가 전화를 건 날짜

화자가 초반부에 오늘은 길포이 공항 직원 만족도 조사를 위해 데이터를 수집하는 첫날이었다(today was the first day of data collection for the Gilfoy Airport employee satisfaction survey)고 했고, 프로젝트 일정표에 따르면 데이터 수집은 7월 22일부터 시작되므로 정답은 (B)이다.

96

What has the speaker just finished doing?

(A) Calculating an expense
(B) Arranging some interviews
(C) Running some software
(D) Meeting with team members

화자는 방금 무엇을 끝냈는가?
(A) 비용 계산
(B) 면접 준비
(C) 소프트웨어 실행
(D) **팀원들과 회의**

어휘 calculate 계산하다 expense 비용 arrange 마련하다

해설 세부 사항 관련 – 화자가 방금 끝낸 일
화자가 중반부에 제가 방금 팀원들을 모아 프로젝트가 어떻게 진행되고 있는지 논의해봤더니 문제가 있는 것 같아 보인다(I just gathered the team to discuss how the project is going so far, and it seems there's a problem)고 했으므로 정답은 (D)이다.

97

What does the speaker want to discuss with the listener?

(A) The size of the research team
(B) The due date of the report
(C) The format of the questionnaire
(D) The strategy for attracting participants

화자는 청자와 무엇을 논의하기를 원하는가?
(A) 연구팀의 규모
(B) 보고서의 마감일
(C) **설문지의 구성 방식**
(D) 참가자 유치 전략

어휘 research 연구[조사] due date 만기일 format 구성 방식
strategy 전략 participant 참가자

해설 세부 관련 사항 – 화자가 청자와 논의하길 원하는 것
화자가 후반부에 이 문제에 대처하려면 설문지를 줄이거나 아니면 최소한 재조정이라도 해야 할 것 같다(I think we should shorten or at least rearrange it to address this issue)고 한 것으로 보아 정답은 (C)이다.

98-100 방송 + 평면도

W-Am **[98] In local news, the Raffden Student Arts Festival organized by the city's Office of Arts and Culture has proven popular among residents and tourists.** An average of two thousand visitors per day have come to Raffden Convention Center to see works and performances by university students. **[99] Today, the festival kicks off its second week with a special event.** Devon Keller, the young handicraft enthusiast who has become an Internet sensation, will teach thirty lucky visitors how to make one of her clay jewelry pieces. **[100] This free class will be held in the festival's "Activities Corner" at three P.M., but festival organizers recommend arriving earlier in order to reserve a seat.** Now, the weather forecast.

지역 뉴스입니다. 시의 예술 문화 사무소에서 준비한 래프덴 학생 예술 축제가 주민들과 관광객들 사이에서 인기 있는 것으로 드러났습니다. 하루 평균 2천여 명의 방문객들이 대학생들의 작품과 공연을 보기 위해 래프덴 컨벤션 센터를 방문하고 있습니다. 오늘 축제는 특별한 행사로 둘째 주를 시작합니다. 온라인에서 돌풍을 일으키고 있는 수공예품 애호가 데번 켈러가 그녀의 점토 보석 중 하나의 제작 방법을 서른 명의 행운의 방문객들에게 가르쳐줄 예정입니다. 이 무료 수업은 오후 3시에 축제의 '액티비티 코너'에서 열릴 예정이지만, 자리를 확보하려면 빨리 도착할 것을 축제 기획 측은 권합니다. 이제, 일기 예보를 듣겠습니다.

어휘 organize 준비[조직]하다 prove 드러나다, 입증하다
resident 주민 average 평균; 평균의 per ~당[마다]
performance 공연 kick off (경기 등을) 시작하다 handcraft
수공예(품) enthusiast 애호가 sensation 센세이션, 돌풍 clay
점토 jewelry 보석 organizer 조직자 reserve 예약하다

Festival Floor Plan

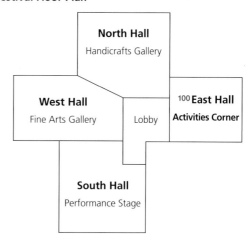

축제 평면도

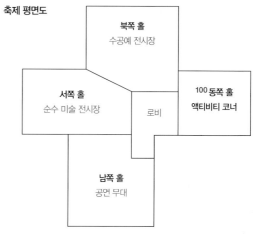

98

What kind of organization is holding the festival?

(A) An art school
(B) A museum
(C) A student-run association
(D) A city government department

어떤 조직에서 축제를 개최하고 있는가?

(A) 예술 학교
(B) 미술관
(C) 학생회
(D) 시 정부 부서

어휘 association 협회 government 정부

해설 세부 사항 관련 – 축제를 개최한 조직의 종류
화자가 초반부에 지역 뉴스에서 시의 예술 문화 사무소에서 준비한 래프덴 학생 예술 축제가 주민들과 관광객들 사이에서 인기 있는 것으로 드러났다(In local news, the Raffden Student Arts Festival organized by the city's Office of Arts and Culture has proven popular among residents and tourists)고 했으므로 정답은 (D)이다.

99

When did the festival begin?

(A) Three weeks ago
(B) Last week
(C) Yesterday
(D) This morning

축제는 언제 시작했는가?

(A) 3주 전
(B) 지난주
(C) 어제
(D) 오늘 아침

해설 세부 사항 관련 – 축제가 시작한 때
화자가 중반부에 오늘 축제는 특별한 행사로 둘째 주를 시작한다(Today, the festival kicks off its second week with a special event)고 한 것으로 보아 축제는 지난주에 시작했음을 알 수 있다. 따라서 정답은 (B)이다.

100

Look at the graphic. In which hall will a special event take place?

(A) The North Hall
(B) The West Hall
(C) The East Hall
(D) The South Hall

시각 정보에 의하면, 특별 행사는 어느 홀에서 열릴 예정인가?

(A) 북쪽 홀
(B) 서쪽 홀
(C) 동쪽 홀
(D) 남쪽 홀

해설 시각 정보 연계 – 특별 행사가 열릴 홀
화자가 후반부에 이 무료 수업은 오후 3시에 축제의 "액티비티 코너"에서 열릴 예정이지만, 자리를 확보하려면 빨리 도착할 것을 축제 기획 측이 권한다(This free class will be held in the festival's "Activities Corner" at three P.M., but festival organizers recommend arriving earlier in order to reserve a seat)고 했고, 축제 평면도에 따르면 액티비티 코너가 열리는 곳은 동쪽 홀이므로 정답은 (C)이다.

TEST 2

1 (D)	2 (C)	3 (C)	4 (A)	5 (B)
6 (A)	7 (C)	8 (B)	9 (A)	10 (C)
11 (A)	12 (B)	13 (A)	14 (B)	15 (C)
16 (A)	17 (C)	18 (A)	19 (B)	20 (B)
21 (C)	22 (B)	23 (C)	24 (A)	25 (A)
26 (B)	27 (B)	28 (B)	29 (C)	30 (A)
31 (C)	32 (D)	33 (D)	34 (B)	35 (A)
36 (D)	37 (C)	38 (A)	39 (D)	40 (B)
41 (C)	42 (B)	43 (A)	44 (B)	45 (A)
46 (C)	47 (A)	48 (C)	49 (B)	50 (D)
51 (B)	52 (A)	53 (B)	54 (A)	55 (C)
56 (D)	57 (A)	58 (D)	59 (A)	60 (C)
61 (B)	62 (A)	63 (D)	64 (C)	65 (C)
66 (D)	67 (D)	68 (B)	69 (B)	70 (C)
71 (B)	72 (D)	73 (C)	74 (D)	75 (A)
76 (B)	77 (C)	78 (D)	79 (A)	80 (C)
81 (C)	82 (D)	83 (C)	84 (A)	85 (A)
86 (B)	87 (B)	88 (C)	89 (D)	90 (B)
91 (A)	92 (A)	93 (B)	94 (D)	95 (D)
96 (A)	97 (A)	98 (C)	99 (C)	100 (B)

PART 1

1 M-Cn

(A) He's eating a cookie.
(B) He's opening a kitchen drawer.
(C) He's cooking on a stove.
(D) He's holding a baking tray.

(A) 남자는 쿠키를 먹고 있다.
(B) 남자는 주방 서랍을 열고 있다.
(C) 남자는 가스레인지에서 요리를 하고 있다.
(D) **남자는 제빵 틀을 들고 있다.**

어휘 drawer 서랍 stove (가스·전기) 레인지 baking tray 제빵 틀

해설 1인 등장 사진 – 인물의 동작 묘사

(A) 동사 오답. 남자가 쿠키를 먹고 있는(is eating a cookie) 모습이 아니므로 오답.
(B) 동사 오답. 남자가 주방 서랍을 열고 있는(is opening a kitchen drawer) 모습이 아니므로 오답.
(C) 동사 오답. 남자가 가스레인지에서 요리를 하고 있는(is cooking on a stove) 모습이 아니므로 오답.
(D) 정답. 남자가 제빵 틀을 들고 있는(is holding a baking tray) 모습이므로 정답.

2 M-Au

(A) The man is writing on a document.
(B) The man is looking in a cabinet.
(C) The woman is using a microscope.
(D) The woman is pouring some liquid.

(A) 남자는 서류에 글을 쓰고 있다.
(B) 남자는 캐비닛을 들여다보고 있다.
(C) **여자는 현미경을 사용하고 있다.**
(D) 여자는 어떤 액체를 붓고 있다.

어휘 microscope 현미경 pour 붓다, [따르다] liquid 액체

해설 2인 이상 등장 사진 – 인물의 동작 묘사

(A) 동사 오답. 남자가 서류에 글을 쓰고 있는(is writing on a document) 모습이 아니므로 오답.
(B) 동사 오답. 남자가 캐비닛을 들여다보고 있는(is looking in a cabinet) 모습이 아니므로 오답.
(C) 정답. 여자가 현미경을 사용하고 있는(is using a microscope) 모습이므로 정답.
(D) 동사 오답. 여자가 액체를 붓고 있는(is pouring some liquid) 모습이 아니므로 오답.

3 W-Br

(A) A stone barrier runs along a bridge.
(B) Some people are climbing a set of steps.
(C) A woman is working out outdoors.
(D) A path is being cleared off.

(A) 돌로 된 벽이 다리를 따라 뻗어 있다.
(B) 몇몇 사람들이 계단을 오르고 있다.
(C) **여자가 야외에서 운동하고 있다.**
(D) 길이 청소되고 있다.

어휘 barrier (장)벽 steps 계단 work out 운동하다 outdoors 야외(에서) path 길

해설 혼합 사진 – 사람 또는 사물 묘사

(A) 사진에 없는 명사를 이용한 오답. 사진에 다리(a bridge)의 모습이 보이지 않으므로 오답.
(B) 사진에 없는 명사를 이용한 오답. 사진에 사람들(people)은 보이지 않고 여자 한 명만 있으므로 오답.

(C) 정답. 여자가 야외에서 운동하고 있는(is working out outdoors) 모습이므로 정답.

(D) 동사 오답. 길(a path)이 청소되고 있는(is being cleared off) 모습이 아니므로 오답.

4 W-Am

(A) Computers have been arranged in two rows.
(B) A group of people is watching a presentation.
(C) A pair of headphones has been left on a keyboard.
(D) One of the men is distributing some papers.

(A) 컴퓨터들이 두 줄로 놓여 있다.
(B) 여러 사람들이 발표를 보고 있다.
(C) 헤드폰 하나가 키보드 위에 놓여 있다.
(D) 남자 한 명이 종이를 나눠 주고 있다.

어휘 arrange 배열하다 row 열[줄] presentation 발표 distribute 나눠주다

해설 혼합 사진 – 사람 또는 사물 묘사

(A) 정답. 컴퓨터들(computers)이 두 줄로 놓여 있는(have been arranged in two rows) 모습이므로 정답.

(B) 동사 오답. 사람들이 발표를 보고 있는(is watching a presentation) 모습이 아니므로 오답.

(C) 동사 오답. 헤드폰(a pair of headphones)이 키보드 위에 놓여 있는(has been left on a keyboard) 모습이 아니므로 오답.

(D) 동사 오답. 남자가 종이를 나눠주고 있는(is distributing some papers) 모습이 아니므로 오답.

5 W-Br [고난도]

(A) A shelving unit is being assembled.
(B) Goods are being moved around a warehouse.
(C) A technician is using tools to repair a machine.
(D) Workers are carrying a package together.

(A) 선반이 조립되고 있다.
(B) 제품이 창고 주변으로 옮겨지고 있다.
(C) 기사가 연장을 사용해 기계를 고치고 있다.
(D) 일꾼들이 함께 짐을 나르고 있다.

어휘 shelving unit 선반 assemble 조립하다 goods 제품 warehouse 창고 technician 기술자 tool 연장

해설 혼합 사진 – 사람 또는 사물 묘사

(A) 동사 오답. 선반(a shelving unit)이 조립되고 있는(is being assembled) 모습이 아니므로 오답.

(B) 정답. 제품(goods)이 창고 주변으로 옮겨지고 있는(are being moved around a warehouse) 모습이 보이므로 정답.

(C) 동사 오답. 기사(a technician)가 연장을 사용해 기계를 고치고 있는(is using tools to repair a machine) 모습이 아니므로 오답.

(D) 동사 오답. 일꾼들(workers)이 함께 짐을 나르고 있는(are carrying a package together) 모습이 아니므로 오답.

6 M-Cn

(A) There is a large rug on the floor.
(B) Curtains have been closed over windows.
(C) A wooden deck is filled with furniture.
(D) A home fireplace is being cleaned.

(A) 커다란 양탄자가 바닥에 깔려 있다.
(B) 창문 위로 커튼이 쳐져 있다.
(C) 나무 갑판이 가구로 가득 차 있다.
(D) 집 벽난로가 청소되고 있다.

어휘 rug 양탄자 deck 갑판 be filled with ~로 가득 차다 fireplace 벽난로

해설 배경 사진 – 실내 사물의 상태 묘사

(A) 정답. 커다란 양탄자(a large rug)가 바닥에(on the floor) 깔려 있으므로 정답.

(B) 동사 오답. 커튼(curtains)이 창문 위로 쳐져 있는(have been closed over windows) 모습이 아니라 열려 있는(have been pulled open) 모습이므로 오답.

(C) 동사 오답. 나무 갑판(a wooden deck)이 가구로 가득 차 있는(is filled with furniture) 모습이 아니므로 오답.

(D) 동사 오답. 집 벽난로(a home fireplace)가 청소되고 있는(is being cleaned) 모습이 아니므로 오답.

PART 2

7

M-Cn Who's coming to this afternoon's meeting?
W-Am (A) It was moved to four P.M.
      (B) I'll reserve the conference room.
      (C) Just Ms. Fisher's team.

오늘 오후 회의에 누가 참석하나요?
(A) 오후 4시로 바뀌었어요.
(B) 제가 회의실을 예약할게요.
(C) 피셔 씨 팀만요.

어휘 reserve 예약하다

해설 회의에 참석할 사람을 묻는 Who 의문문

(A) 연상 단어 오답. 질문의 afternoon에서 연상 가능한 four P.M.을 이용한 오답.

(B) 연상 단어 오답. 질문의 meeting에서 연상 가능한 conference room을 이용한 오답.

(C) 정답. 오늘 오후 회의에 참석할 사람을 묻는 질문에 피셔 씨의 팀만 참석한다고 구체적으로 응답하고 있으므로 정답.

8

M-Au Excuse me—is this your umbrella?

W-Br (A) No, I haven't.

(B) Oh, thank you!

(C) Check the weather forecast.

실례지만, 이것이 혹시 당신 우산인가요?
(A) 아니요, 안 했어요.
(B) 오, 감사합니다!
(C) 일기 예보를 확인해보세요.

해설 우산이 상대방의 것인지 묻는 Be동사 의문문

(A) 질문과 상관없는 오답. Have 의문문에 대한 응답이므로 오답.

(B) 정답. 우산 주인인지 묻는 질문에 감사하다며 본인의 것임을 우회적으로 표현하고 있으므로 정답.

(C) 연상 단어 오답. 질문의 umbrella에서 연상 가능한 weather forecast를 이용한 오답.

9

W-Am Where's the closest supermarket?

M-Cn (A) Over on Third Avenue.

(B) No, it's still open.

(C) Excellent customer service.

가장 가까운 슈퍼마켓은 어디에 있나요?
(A) 3번 가 쪽에요.
(B) 아니요, 아직 영업 중이에요.
(C) 훌륭한 고객 서비스입니다.

어휘 avenue 거리, 대로 excellent 훌륭한

해설 가장 가까운 슈퍼마켓의 위치를 묻는 Where 의문문

(A) 정답. 가장 가까운 슈퍼마켓의 위치를 묻는 질문에 3번 가 쪽에 있다며 위치를 알려주고 있으므로 정답.

(B) Yes/No 불가 오답. Where 의문문에는 Yes/No 응답이 불가능하므로 오답.

(C) 질문과 상관없는 오답.

10

W-Br When did you get back from vacation?

M-Au (A) Yes, and I got one for you too.

(B) To help with an urgent project.

(C) Today's my first day back.

휴가에서 언제 돌아오셨나요?
(A) 네, 당신 것도 하나 있어요.
(B) 긴급한 프로젝트를 돕기 위해서요.
(C) 오늘이 돌아온 첫날이에요.

어휘 vacation 휴가 urgent 긴급한

해설 휴가에서 돌아온 시점을 묻는 When 의문문

(A) Yes/No 불가 오답. When 의문문에는 Yes/No 응답이 불가능하므로 오답.

(B) 질문과 상관없는 오답. Why 의문문에 대한 응답이므로 오답.

(C) 정답. 휴가에서 돌아온 시점을 묻는 질문에 오늘이 돌아온 첫날이라며 구체적으로 응답하고 있으므로 정답.

11

W-Am What did you use to make this graphic?

M-Cn (A) The program is called "Shin Image Pro."

(B) That's right—until last year.

(C) The blue line shows our sales.

이 도표를 그리는 데 무엇을 사용하셨죠?
(A) '신 이미지 프로'라는 프로그램이요.
(B) 맞아요, 작년까지는요.
(C) 파란 선은 우리의 판매를 보여줍니다.

어휘 graphic 도표

해설 도표를 그리는 데 사용한 도구를 묻는 What 의문문

(A) 정답. 도표를 그리는 데 사용한 도구를 묻는 질문에 '신 이미지 프로'라고 불리는 프로그램이라며 구체적으로 응답하고 있으므로 정답.

(B) Yes/No 불가 오답. What 의문문에는 Yes/No 응답이 불가능한데, That's right은 일종의 Yes 응답이라고 볼 수 있으므로 오답.

(C) 연상 단어 오답. 질문의 graphic에서 연상 가능한 blue line을 이용한 오답.

12

M-Au Haven't you found a new office manager yet?

W-Am (A) I didn't know it had been lost.

(B) We're still holding interviews.

(C) At his welcome party.

새 사무실 관리자를 이미 구하지 않으셨나요?
(A) 분실된 줄 몰랐어요.
(B) 아직 면접을 진행 중이에요.
(C) 환영회에서요.

어휘 welcome party 환영회

해설 새 사무실 관리자를 구했는지 여부를 확인하는 부정의문문

(A) 연상 단어 오답. 질문의 found에서 연상 가능한 lost를 이용한 오답.

(B) 정답. 새 사무실 관리자를 구했는지 여부를 확인하는 질문에 아직 면접을 진행 중이라며 새로운 관리자를 구하지 못했음을 우회적으로 알려주고 있으므로 정답.

(C) 질문과 상관없는 오답. Where 의문문에 대한 응답이므로 오답.

13

W-Br Why was the second performance on Sunday canceled?

M-Cn (A) I hadn't heard that—how disappointing!

(B) Performance reviews will be done annually.

(C) Early Saturday evening.

일요일에 있을 두 번째 공연은 왜 취소되었나요?

(A) 저는 듣지 못했는데, 실망스럽네요!

(B) 실적 평가는 해마다 행해질 것입니다.

(C) 토요일 저녁 일찍이요.

어휘 performance 공연, 실적 review 비평[논평]; 검토하다

해설 공연이 취소된 이유를 묻는 Why 의문문

(A) 정답. 일요일에 있을 두 번째 공연이 취소된 이유를 묻는 질문에 못 들었다며 실망을 표하고 있으므로 정답.

(B) 단어 반복 오답. 질문의 performance를 반복 이용한 오답.

(C) 연상 단어 오답. 질문의 Sunday에서 연상 가능한 Saturday를 이용한 오답.

14

W-Br Is the discount just for employees, or can our families use it too?

M-Au (A) It's a great benefit, isn't it?

(B) Your close family members can.

(C) For a more reliable way of counting.

할인은 직원만 받을 수 있나요, 아니면 저희 가족들도 이용할 수 있나요?

(A) 대단한 혜택이에요, 그렇죠?

(B) 가까운 가족들은 돼요.

(C) 좀 더 믿을 수 있는 계산을 위해서요.

어휘 benefit 혜택 reliable 믿을 수 있는 counting 계산

해설 할인 적용 대상의 범위를 묻는 선택의문문

(A) 연상 단어 오답. 질문의 discount에서 연상 가능한 benefit을 이용한 오답.

(B) 정답. 할인을 받을 수 있는 대상의 범위를 묻는 선택의문문에서 가까운 가족도 가능하다며 둘 중 하나를 선택해 응답하고 있으므로 정답.

(C) 유사 발음 오답. 질문의 discount와 부분적으로 발음이 유사한 counting을 이용한 오답.

15

M-Cn How quickly could you translate this document?

W-Am (A) Some spelling mistakes.

(B) With translation software.

(C) Let me look over the contents.

이 문서를 얼마나 빨리 번역할 수 있나요?

(A) 몇몇 맞춤법 오류요.

(B) 번역 소프트웨어로요.

(C) 내용을 죽 훑어볼게요.

어휘 translate 번역하다 look over 훑어[살펴]보다

해설 문서 번역의 작업 속도를 묻는 How quickly 의문문

(A) 연상 단어 오답. 질문의 document에서 연상 가능한 spelling을 이용한 오답.

(B) 파생어 오답. 질문의 translate와 파생어 관계인 translation을 이용한 오답.

(C) 정답. 문서를 얼마나 빨리 번역할 수 있는지 묻는 질문에 내용을 훑어보겠다며 내용에 따라 번역 속도가 다를 수 있음을 우회적으로 표현하고 있으므로 정답.

16

M-Cn The cream pasta has meat in it, doesn't it?

W-Br (A) We could make it vegetarian for you.

(B) By putting it in the microwave.

(C) It's one of our lunch specials on Fridays.

이 크림 파스타에는 고기가 들어가죠, 그렇지 않나요?

(A) 당신을 위해 채식으로 만들어드릴 수 있어요.

(B) 전자레인지에 넣어서요.

(C) 금요일 점심 특선 메뉴 중 하나입니다.

어휘 vegetarian 채식주의(자)의 microwave 전자레인지

해설 크림 파스타에 고기가 들어가는지 여부를 확인하는 부가의문문

(A) 정답. 크림 파스타에 고기가 들어가는지 여부를 확인하는 질문에 채식으로 만들어줄 수 있다며 Yes를 생략하여 질문의 의도에 우회적으로 답하고 있으므로 정답.

(B) 질문과 상관없는 오답. How 의문문에 대한 응답이므로 오답.

(C) 연상 단어 오답. 질문의 pasta에서 연상 가능한 lunch specials를 이용한 오답.

17

M-Au That potted plant is in bad condition.

W-Br (A) Sarah works at a pottery plant.

(B) It's supposed to keep the air fresh.

(C) I haven't been able to water it regularly.

저 화분의 식물은 상태가 좋지 않아요.

(A) 사라는 도자기 공장에서 일해요.

(B) 공기를 맑게 해줄 거예요.

(C) 규칙적으로 물을 주지 못했어요.

어휘 potted plant 화분에 심은 식물 pottery 도자기 plant 공장 be supposed to ~라고 한다 water 물을 주다 regularly 규칙적으로

해설 정보 전달의 평서문

(A) 유사 발음 오답. 평서문의 potted와 부분적으로 발음이 유사한 pottery를 이용한 오답.

(B) 연상 단어 오답. 평서문의 condition에서 연상 가능한 fresh를 이용한 오답.

(C) 정답. 화분의 식물이 상태가 좋지 않다는 평서문에 규칙적으로 물을 주지 못했다며 그 이유를 설명하고 있으므로 정답.

18 고난도

W-Am Are you interested in attending the technology workshop?

M-Cn (A) Isn't the registration fee really expensive?
(B) The updated list of attendees.
(C) Oh, I took attendance a few minutes ago.

기술 워크숍에 참석하는 데 관심 있으신가요?
(A) 등록비가 너무 비싸지 않나요?
(B) 업데이트된 참석자 명단입니다.
(C) 오, 제가 몇 분 전에 출석을 확인했어요.

어휘 attend 참석하다 technology 기술 registration fee 등록비 attendee 참석자 take attendance 출석을 확인하다

해설 워크숍 참석에 관심이 있는지 묻는 Be동사 의문문
(A) 정답. 기술 워크숍에 참석하는 데 관심이 있는지 묻는 질문에 등록비가 너무 비싸지 않은지 되물으며 부정적인 의사를 우회적으로 표현하고 있으므로 정답.
(B) 파생어 오답. 질문의 attending과 파생어 관계인 attendees를 이용한 오답.
(C) 파생어 오답. 질문의 attending과 파생어 관계인 attendance를 이용한 오답.

19 고난도

W-Br You're picking the guest speaker up from the airport, aren't you?

W-Am (A) About his life as a photographer.
(B) I'm planning to leave at three-thirty.
(C) The director always picks the speaker.

공항에서 초청 연사를 모셔올 거죠, 그렇죠?
(A) 사진작가로서 그의 삶에 관해서요.
(B) 3시 30분에 출발할 계획이에요.
(C) 이사님께서 항상 그 연사를 고르세요.

어휘 guest speaker 초청 연사 photographer 사진작가 director 임원, 감독

해설 공항으로 사람을 마중 나갈 것인지 여부를 확인하는 부가의문문
(A) 질문과 상관없는 오답. What 의문문에 대한 응답이므로 오답.
(B) 정답. 공항에서 초청 연사를 데려올 것인지 여부를 확인하는 질문에 3시 30분에 출발할 계획이라며 직접 마중 나갈 것임을 우회적으로 응답하고 있으므로 정답.
(C) 파생어 오답. 질문의 picking과 파생어 관계인 picks를 이용한 오답.

20 고난도

M-Au Why don't we try advertising on social media?

W-Br (A) Since the site was launched.
(B) That was Lloyd's advice, too.
(C) I believe so.

소셜 미디어에 광고해보는 게 어떨까요?
(A) 웹사이트가 개설된 이후로요.
(B) 로이드도 그렇게 충고하더라고요.
(C) 그런 것 같아요.

어휘 advertise 광고하다 social media 소셜 미디어 launch 시작하다 advice 충고

해설 제안/권유의 의문문
(A) 연상 단어 오답. 질문의 social media에서 연상 가능한 site를 이용한 오답.
(B) 정답. 소셜 미디어에 광고해보자고 제안하는 질문에 같은 제안을 한 사람이 또 있다며 호응하고 있으므로 정답.
(C) 질문과 상관없는 오답. Yes/No 응답이 가능한 의문문에 대한 응답이므로 오답.

21 고난도

W-Am Where are the results of the product test?

M-Au (A) We're pleased with most of them.
(B) The quality of some sample items.
(C) Are you sure it's been completed?

제품 테스트 결과는 어디에 있죠?
(A) 우리는 그것들 대부분에 만족합니다.
(B) 일부 샘플 제품의 품질입니다.
(C) 테스트가 끝난 게 확실해요?

어휘 result 결과 quality 품질 complete 완료하다

해설 제품 테스트 결과가 있는 위치를 묻는 Where 의문문
(A) 질문과 상관없는 오답. 의견을 묻는 의문문에 대한 응답이므로 오답.
(B) 질문과 상관없는 오답. What 의문문에 대한 응답이므로 오답.
(C) 정답. 제품 테스트 결과가 있는 위치를 묻는 질문에 테스트가 끝난 게 확실하냐고 되물으며 결과지가 없다는 것을 우회적으로 알려주고 있으므로 정답.

22 고난도

W-Am What type of car do you recommend renting?

M-Cn (A) During your business trip out of state.
(B) I have some suggestions, but it's really up to you.
(C) The keys are in the top drawer of my desk.

어떤 종류의 자동차를 대여하는 것을 추천하시나요?
(A) 당신이 다른 주로 출장 가 있는 동안이요.
(B) 몇 가지 제안할 수는 있지만, 사실 당신에게 달렸어요.
(C) 열쇠는 제 책상 맨 위쪽 서랍에 있어요.

어휘 rent 빌리다; 집세 state 주 suggestion 제안 drawer 서랍

해설 대여할 만한 자동차의 종류를 묻는 What 의문문
(A) 질문과 상관없는 오답. When 의문문에 대한 응답이므로 오답.
(B) 정답. 추천할 만한 렌터카 종류를 묻는 질문에 질문자의 의견을 듣고자 함을 우회적으로 나타내고 있으므로 정답.
(C) 질문과 상관없는 오답.

23

W-Br Would you like to be contacted by text message or by e-mail?

M-Au (A) Here's our staff directory.

(B) Only if there's a problem with my order.

(C) I'd prefer to receive a phone call, actually.

문자 메시지로 연락받으시겠어요, 아니면 이메일로 연락받으시겠어요?

(A) 여기 우리 직원 명부입니다.

(B) 제 주문에 문제가 있을 경우에만요.

(C) 사실 저는 전화로 연락받고 싶은데요.

어휘 contact 연락하다 staff directory 직원 명부 order 주문 receive 받다

해설 연락받기를 원하는 수단을 묻는 선택의문문

(A) 연상 단어 오답. 질문의 contacted에서 연상 가능한 directory를 이용한 오답.

(B) 질문과 상관없는 오답.

(C) 정답. 연락받기를 원하는 수단을 묻는 선택의문문에서 전화로 연락받고 싶 다며 제3의 선택을 제시하고 있으므로 정답.

24

고난도

M-Cn Do you use the coffee machine much?

M-Au (A) I mostly drink tea.

(B) For color copies.

(C) Kenji has the invoice.

커피 머신을 자주 사용하시나요?

(A) 저는 주로 차를 마셔요.

(B) 컬러 복사용으로요.

(C) 켄지가 청구서를 갖고 있어요.

어휘 mostly 주로 invoice 송장, 청구서

해설 커피 머신을 자주 사용하는지 여부를 묻는 조동사(Do) 의문문

(A) 정답. 커피 머신을 자주 사용하는지 여부를 묻는 질문에 주로 차를 마신다 며 기기를 자주 사용하지 않음을 우회적으로 표현하고 있으므로 정답.

(B) 유사 발음 오답. 질문의 coffee과 부분적으로 발음이 유사한 copies를 이 용한 오답.

(C) 질문과 상관없는 오답.

25

M-Cn I enjoyed your article in the company newsletter.

W-Br (A) That's kind of you to say.

(B) On page two, I think.

(C) Oh, are you taking letters to the mailroom?

회사 소식지에 실린 당신의 글을 재밌게 봤어요.

(A) 그렇게 말씀해주시니 고맙습니다.

(B) 2페이지인 것 같아요.

(C) 오, 편지들을 우편실로 가져가시나요?

어휘 article 기사 newsletter 소식지 mailroom 우편실

해설 의사 전달의 평서문

(A) 정답. 회사 소식지에 실린 당신의 글을 재밌게 봤다는 칭찬의 평서문에 그 렇게 말씀해주시니 고맙다고 응답하고 있으므로 정답.

(B) 연상 단어 오답. 평서문의 newsletter에서 연상 가능한 page two를 이용 한 오답.

(C) 유사 발음 오답. 평서문의 newsletter와 부분적으로 발음이 유사한 letters를 이용한 오답.

26

W-Am How are the fitness facilities in this hotel?

M-Au (A) Whenever you're ready.

(B) I've never stayed here before.

(C) In the west wing of the ground floor.

이 호텔의 피트니스 시설은 어떤가요?

(A) 준비되시면 언제든지요.

(B) 이곳에서 숙박한 적이 없어요.

(C) 1층 서쪽 별관에서요.

어휘 facility 시설 wing 부속 건물, 별관 ground floor 1층

해설 호텔 피트니스 시설의 상태를 묻는 How 의문문

(A) 질문과 상관없는 오답. When 의문문에 대한 응답이므로 오답.

(B) 정답. 호텔 피트니스 시설의 상태를 묻는 질문에 이곳에서 숙박한 적이 없 다며 질문에 대한 답을 할 수 없음을 우회적으로 응답하고 있으므로 정답.

(C) 질문과 상관없는 오답. Where 의문문에 대한 응답이므로 오답.

27

M-Cn Why is the driver stopping the bus here?

W-Am (A) By a field on the side of the road.

(B) Go and ask the tour guide.

(C) OK, I'll tell them to stop if possible.

기사님이 왜 여기에 버스를 세우시는 거죠?

(A) 길 가에 있는 들판 옆이에요.

(B) 관광 가이드에게 가서 여쭤보세요.

(C) 좋아요, 그들에게 가능하면 멈추라고 말할게요.

해설 버스가 정차한 이유를 묻는 Why 의문문

(A) 질문과 상관없는 오답. Where 의문문에 대한 응답이므로 오답.

(B) 정답. 기사가 버스를 여기에 세운 이유를 묻는 질문에 관광 가이드에게 가 서 물어보라며 자신은 이유를 알지 못함을 우회적으로 응답하고 있으므로 정답.

(C) 파생어 오답. 질문의 stopping과 파생어 관계인 stop을 이용한 오답.

28

M-Au Would you mind taking this survey about our store?

W-Br (A) It's printed on the sign near the entrance.

(B) I'm running late to work right now.

(C) Hmm—let's revise Question Five.

우리 매장에 대한 설문 조사에 참여해주시겠습니까?

(A) 입구 근처 간판에 쓰여 있어요.

(B) 제가 지금 회사에 늦어서요.

(C) 흠, 5번 문항을 수정합시다.

어휘 survey 설문 조사 entrance 입구 revise 수정[변경]하다

해설 부탁/요청의 의문문
(A) 질문과 상관없는 오답.
(B) 정답. 설문 조사에 참여해달라고 요청하는 질문에 회사에 늦었다며 참여 거절 의사를 우회적으로 표현하고 있으므로 정답.
(C) 연상 단어 오답. 질문의 survey에서 연상 가능한 Question을 이용한 오답.

29

M-Au Does this washing machine come with the apartment?

W-Am (A) About seven kilograms of clothing.
(B) A local cleaning service does it.
(C) It belongs to the current tenant—sorry.

이 세탁기는 아파트에 딸려 있는 건가요?
(A) 약 7킬로그램의 옷이요.
(B) 지역 청소 서비스에서 그것을 해요.
(C) 그것은 지금 계신 세입자 거예요, 죄송합니다.

어휘 washing machine 세탁기 come with ~이 딸려 있다 tenant 세입자

해설 세탁기가 아파트에 딸려 있는지 여부를 확인하는 조동사(Do) 의문문
(A) 연상 단어 오답. 질문의 washing machine에서 연상 가능한 clothing을 이용한 오답.
(B) 연상 단어 오답. 질문의 washing machine에서 연상 가능한 cleaning service를 이용한 오답.
(C) 정답. 세탁기가 아파트에 딸려 있는지 여부를 묻는 질문에 지금 살고 있는 세입자 것이라며 아파트에 딸려 있는 것이 아님을 우회적으로 응답하고 있으므로 정답.

30

M-Cn Didn't our contract with that supplier end in October?

W-Am (A) This payment will settle our account.
(B) They sell manufacturing materials.
(C) Yes, it looks like I'm free then.

그 공급업체와의 계약은 10월에 끝나지 않았나요?
(A) 이 지불로 결산될 겁니다.
(B) 그들은 생산 자재를 판매합니다.
(C) 네, 그때는 제가 시간이 날 것 같네요.

어휘 contract 계약 supplier 공급자 settle 지불[정산]하다 manufacturing 제조업 material 재료

해설 계약이 10월에 끝났는지 여부를 확인하는 부정의문문
(A) 정답. 공급업체와의 계약이 10월에 끝났는지 여부를 묻는 질문에 이 지불로 결산이 완료될 것이라며 우회적으로 응답하고 있으므로 정답.
(B) 연상 단어 오답. 질문의 supplier에서 연상 가능한 manufacturing materials를 이용한 오답.
(C) 연상 단어 오답. 질문의 October에서 연상 가능한 then을 이용한 오답.

31

W-Br The shirt part of my uniform doesn't fit very well.

M-Cn (A) Does she need to be taken to a hospital?
(B) The large white logo on the back.
(C) We have a few other women's sizes available.

제 유니폼 윗도리가 잘 안 맞네요.
(A) 그녀를 병원에 데려가야 할까요?
(B) 뒷면의 큰 흰색 로고요.
(C) 다른 여성용 사이즈도 몇 개 있어요.

어휘 fit 맞다 available 이용할[구할] 수 있는

해설 정보 전달의 평서문
(A) 평서문과 상관없는 오답.
(B) 연상 단어 오답. 질문의 uniform에서 연상 가능한 logo를 이용한 오답.
(C) 정답. 유니폼 셔츠가 잘 맞지 않는다는 평서문에 다른 여성용 사이즈도 있다며 문제의 해결책을 제시하고 있으므로 정답.

PART 3

32-34

W-Br Good morning. **32 Where can I take you today?**

M-Au Holligan Square, please. And would you mind turning on the air conditioning?

W-Br No problem. So, I can guess from your suitcase that you're probably a visitor here. What brings you to Mavner City?

M-Au **33 I'm giving a presentation on my company's products to a potential client.** It's Romari Industries. Have you heard of them?

W-Br Yes—their offices are by Elmbrook Bridge, right? **34 If you get a chance, you should take a walk across there. It has some of the most famous views in the city.**

여 좋은 아침입니다. 오늘 어디로 모실까요?
남 홀리건 광장이요. 에어컨 좀 틀어주실수 있을까요?
여 그럼요. 갖고 계신 여행 가방으로 짐작건대 아마도 여기 방문객이신가 봐요. 마브너 시에는 어쩐 일이세요?
남 잠재 고객에게 저희 회사 제품에 대해 발표를 할 거예요. 로마리 인더스트리즈라고 들어보신 적 있으세요?
여 네, 사무실이 엘름브룩 다리 옆에 있어요, 맞죠? 기회가 되시면 다리를 가로질러 거닐어보세요. 이 도시에서 가장 유명한 경관을 보실 수 있을 거예요.

어휘 square 광장 suitcase 여행 가방 potential 잠재적인 client 고객 chance 기회 across 가로질러 view 전망

32

Where most likely are the speakers?

(A) At an airport
(B) At a hotel
(C) On a bus
(D) In a taxi

화자들은 어디에 있을 것 같은가?
(A) 공항
(B) 호텔
(C) 버스
(D) 택시

해설 전체 내용 관련 – 대화의 장소
여자가 첫 대사에서 오늘 어디로 모실까요(Where can I take you today?)라고 묻는 것으로 보아 택시 기사가 손님에게 목적지를 묻는 것임을 알 수 있다. 따라서 정답은 (D)이다.

33

What is the purpose of the man's trip?

(A) To evaluate a facility
(B) To attend a social event
(C) To receive some training
(D) To promote a business

남자가 여행하는 목적은 무엇인가?
(A) 시설을 평가하는 것
(B) 사교 행사에 참석하는 것
(C) 교육을 받는 것
(D) 사업을 홍보하는 것

어휘 evaluate 평가하다 facility 시설 promote 홍보하다

해설 세부 사항 관련 – 남자의 여행 목적
남자가 두 번째 대사에서 잠재 고객에게 자기 회사 제품에 대해 발표를 할 것 (I'm giving a presentation on my company's products to a potential client)이라고 한 것으로 보아 정답은 (D)이다.

34 고난도

What does the woman recommend doing?

(A) Trying a local dish
(B) Visiting a tourist attraction
(C) Storing some baggage temporarily
(D) Taking a certain route to a destination

여자는 무엇을 권하는가?
(A) 현지 음식을 먹어볼 것
(B) 관광 명소를 방문할 것
(C) 짐을 잠시 보관할 것
(D) 목적지까지 특정 경로로 갈 것

어휘 dish 요리 tourist attraction 관광 명소 store 보관하다
temporarily 일시적으로 route 경로 destination 목적지

해설 세부 사항 관련 – 여자가 권하는 것
여자가 마지막 대사에서 기회가 되면 다리를 가로질러 거닐어보라(If you get a chance, you should take a walk across there)고 권하며, 이 도시에서

가장 유명한 경관을 볼 수 있다(It has some of the most famous views in the city)고 했으므로 정답은 (B)이다.

35-37

W-Br	Alex, it's Chinami. I'm calling about my article for the industry journal. ³⁵ **Thanks again for agreeing to check it for errors.**
M-Cn	I'm happy to do it. You're sending it over today, right?
W-Br	Well, actually, I wanted to let you know that I wasn't able to finish it on time. ³⁶ **Could I send it to you on Friday instead, and get it back by Wednesday?**
M-Cn	Let me check my planner... Yeah, that should be OK.
W-Br	Great. I appreciate your flexibility. ³⁷ **Oh, but I'll send you the journal's style manual right now.** It'll give you an idea of their standards.
M-Cn	That's a good idea. I'll familiarize myself with it before Friday.

여	알렉스, 저 치나미예요. 산업 저널에 실을 제 기사 때문에 전화드렸어요. **오류를 확인해주신다고 하셔서 다시 한번 감사드려요.**
남	얼마든지요. 오늘 보내시는 거 맞죠?
여	음, 사실 제때 못 끝냈다는 걸 말씀드리려고 했어요. **대신 금요일에 보내드릴 테니 수요일까지 돌려받을 수 있을까요?**
남	제 일정표를 확인해 볼게요... 네, 괜찮겠네요.
여	다행이에요. 시간 조정해주셔서 고맙습니다. **아, 그래도 저널의 양식 설명서는 지금 바로 보내드릴게요.** 기준을 파악하실 수 있을 거예요.
남	좋은 생각이에요. 금요일 전에 숙지해야겠네요.

어휘	journal 저널, 잡지 appreciate 감사하다 flexibility 유연성 manual 설명서 standard 기준 familiarize 익숙하게 하다

35 고난도

What has the man agreed to do?

(A) Proofread some writing
(B) Participate in an interview
(C) Analyze an industry
(D) Produce some graphics

남자는 무엇을 하기로 동의했는가?
(A) 글 교정하기
(B) 면접 참여하기
(C) 산업 분석하기
(D) 삽화 제작하기

어휘 proofread (책을) 교정을 보다 analyze 분석하다

해설 세부 사항 관련 – 남자가 하기로 동의한 것
여자가 첫 대사에서 남자에게 오류를 확인해준다고 해서 다시 한번 감사하다 (Thanks again for agreeing to check it for errors)고 말한 것으로 보아 정답은 (A)이다.

▸▸ **Paraphrasing** 대화의 check ~ for errors → 정답의 **proofread**

36

Why is the woman calling?

(A) To determine a fee
(B) To check some statistics
(C) To introduce a journalist
(D) To change a schedule

여자는 왜 전화했는가?
(A) 수수료를 결정하려고
(B) 통계 자료 일부를 확인하려고
(C) 기자를 소개하려고
(D) **일정을 변경하려고**

어휘 determine 결정하다 fee 수수료 statistics 통계(자료)
         journalist 기자

해설 전체 내용 관련 – 여자가 전화한 목적

여자가 첫 대사에서 대신 금요일에 기사를 보내서 수요일까지 돌려받을 수 있을지(Could I send it to you on Friday instead, and get it back by Wednesday?)를 물으며 기사를 보내기로 한 날짜를 변경하고자 하므로 정답은 (D)이다.

37

What will the man receive today?

(A) An electronic payment
(B) A draft of an article
(C) Some guidelines
(D) Some contact information

남자는 오늘 무엇을 받을 것인가?
(A) 전자 결제
(B) 기사의 초안
(C) **지침서**
(D) 연락처

어휘 electronic 전자의 draft 초안 guideline 지침(서)

해설 세부 사항 관련 – 남자가 오늘 받을 것

여자가 두 번째 대사에서 저널의 양식 설명서를 지금 바로 보내겠다(but I'll send you the journal's style manual right now)고 했으므로 정답은 (C)이다.

▸▸ **Paraphrasing** 대화의 **manual** → 정답의 **guidelines**

38-40

M-Au	Uchenna, I just got back from lunch. What's going on? **38 Why doesn't the print shop have any electricity?**
W-Br	The wind caused a big tree to fall on a transformer on Carlton Street. The power is out across the whole neighborhood.

M-Au	Really? The restaurant I was at didn't seem to have any problems.
W-Br	**39 They must have a power generator. We should consider getting one too.** They're saying that we might not get electricity until tomorrow afternoon.
M-Au	That's going to put us behind on all of our printing jobs. **40 We'd better let our customers know.**
W-Br	Shaun is posting on social media right now. We're lucky that he could log into our company account.

남	우체나, 전 지금 막 점심을 먹고 왔어요. 무슨 일이죠? **인쇄소에 왜 전기가 안 들어오는 거예요?**
여	바람 때문에 큰 나무가 칼튼 거리에 있는 변압기로 쓰러졌어요. 인근 지역은 모두 전기가 나갔고요.
남	정말요? 제가 있던 식당은 아무 문제가 없어 보이던데요.
여	**발전기가 있어서 그럴 거예요. 우리도 하나 구비하는 걸 고려해야겠어요.** 내일 오후나 돼야 전기가 들어올 거라고 하네요.
남	인쇄 업무 일정이 전부 뒤처지겠네요. **고객들에게 알리는 게 좋겠어요.**
여	손이 지금 소셜 미디어에 게시물을 올리고 있어요. 그가 회사 계정에 로그인이 돼서 다행이에요.

어휘 electricity 전기 transformer 변압기 power 전력
         power generator 발전기 post 게시하다

38

What are the speakers mainly discussing?

(A) A power outage
(B) Some poor weather
(C) An employee absence
(D) Some roadwork

화자들은 주로 무엇을 논의하고 있는가?
(A) **정전**
(B) 악천후
(C) 직원 결근
(D) 도로 공사

어휘 absence 결근, 부재

해설 전체 내용 관련 – 대화의 주제

남자가 첫 대사에서 인쇄소에 왜 전기가 안 들어오는 것(Why doesn't the print shop have any electricity?)인지를 물으며 대화를 시작했고, 여자가 뒤이어 그에 대한 답변으로 대화를 이어가고 있는 것으로 보아 정답은 (A)이다.

▸▸ **Paraphrasing** 대화의 **doesn't ~ have any electricity** → 정답의 **power outage**

39

What does the woman suggest doing?

(A) Closing down for the day
(B) Notifying a neighboring business
(C) Teaching a skill to some workers
(D) Buying a special machine

여자는 무엇을 제안하는가?

(A) 하루 동안 문을 닫는 것
(B) 인접 업체에 알리는 것
(C) 몇몇 근로자에게 기술을 전수하는 것
(D) 특수 장치를 구입하는 것

어휘 close down 폐점하다 notify 알리다

해설 세부 사항 관련 – 여자의 제안 사항

여자가 두 번째 대사에서 식당에는 발전기가 있을 것(They must have a power generator)이라며 우리도 하나 구비하는 걸 고려해야겠다(We should consider getting one too)고 했으므로 정답은 (D)이다.

40　　　　　　　　　　　　　　　　　고난도

What does the woman mean when she says, "Shaun is posting on social media right now"?

(A) Shaun is neglecting his duties.
(B) Shaun is making an announcement.
(C) Shaun is seeking more detailed information.
(D) Shaun is more familiar with a marketing method.

여자가 "숀이 지금 소셜 미디어에 게시물을 올리고 있어요"라고 말한 의도는 무엇인가?

(A) 숀은 업무를 게을리하고 있다.
(B) 숀은 공지를 하고 있다.
(C) 숀은 좀 더 자세한 정보를 찾고 있다.
(D) 숀은 마케팅 수단에 대해 더 잘 안다.

어휘 neglect 소홀하다 duty 업무 announcement 공지 detailed 상세한 familiar 익숙한 method 방법

해설 화자의 의도 파악 – 숀이 지금 소셜 미디어에 게시물을 올리고 있다는 말의 의도

앞에서 남자가 고객들에게 상황을 알리는 게 좋겠다(We'd better let our customers know)고 하자 여자가 인용문을 언급한 것이므로 숀이 이미 고객들에게 게시물을 통해 공지를 하고 있음을 알리려는 의도임을 알 수 있다. 따라서 정답은 (B)이다

▸▸ Paraphrasing 대화의 let ~ know
　　　　　　　　 → 정답의 make an announcement

41-43

M-Au	Hi, Dora. You handle payroll, right? Well, I was looking at my electronic paycheck this week, and... I think I've been overpaid. **41 It's about a hundred dollars higher than usual.**
W-Am	Ah, you're not the first person who's come by to ask about that! **42 It's because of a change to the income tax code.** It just came into effect this month. So don't worry— that money belongs to you.
M-Au	That's great news! **43 I'm saving up for an apartment these days, so that will really help.** Thanks, Dora.

남	안녕하세요, 도라. 급여 업무를 맡고 계신 거 맞죠? 저, 이번 주에 제 전자상 급료를 확인해봤는데… 제 생각에 초과 지급된 것 같아요. **평소보다 100달러 가량 더 높았어요.**
여	아, 저한테 들러 그것에 대해 문의하는 사람이 당신이 처음이 아니에요. **소득세법이 개정되어서 그래요.** 이달부터 시행됐거든요. 그러니 걱정 마세요. 그 금액이 맞아요.
남	좋은 소식이네요! 요즘 아파트를 사려고 돈을 모으고 있는데, 정말 **도움이 되겠네요.** 고마워요, 도라.

어휘 payroll 급여 electronic 전자의 paycheck 봉급[급료](액) overpaid 초과 지급된 income 소득 tax code 세법 come into effect 시행되다 belong to ~에 속하다

41

What problem does the man mention?

(A) He has not received his paycheck.
(B) His paycheck is not itemized clearly.
(C) His pay amount is different from before.
(D) His pay was issued using an inconvenient method.

남자는 무슨 문제를 언급하는가?

(A) 봉급을 받지 못했다.
(B) 봉급이 명확하게 명목화되어 있지 않다.
(C) 급여 금액이 이전과 다르다.
(D) 급여가 불편한 방법으로 지급되었다.

어휘 itemize 항목별로 적다 clearly 분명히 issue 지급[발급]하다 inconvenient 불편한 method 방법

해설 세부 사항 관련 – 남자가 언급한 문제

남자가 첫 대사에서 급여가 평소보다 100달러 가량 더 높았다(It's about a hundred dollars higher than usual)고 말하고 있으므로 정답은 (C)이다.

42　　　　　　　　　　　　　　　　　고난도

According to the woman, what caused the problem?

(A) An address is incorrect.
(B) A tax law has been revised.
(C) A software program is not working properly.
(D) A form was misplaced.

여자에 따르면, 무엇이 문제를 유발했는가?

(A) 주소가 부정확하다.
(B) 세법이 개정되었다.
(C) 소프트웨어 프로그램이 제대로 작동하지 않고 있다.
(D) 서식을 분실했다.

어휘 revise 수정하다 properly 제대로 misplace 제자리에 두지 않다, 분실하다

해설 세부 사항 관련 – 여자가 말하는 문제의 원인

여자가 첫 대사에서 남자가 제기한 문제에 대해 소득세법이 개정되어서 그렇다(It's because of a change to the income tax code)고 응답했으므로 정답은 (B)이다.

▸▸ Paraphrasing 대화의 a change to ~
　　　　　　　　 → 정답의 ~ has been revised

43

What does the man say he is currently doing?

(A) Setting aside some money
(B) Taking overtime shifts
(C) Applying for a departmental transfer
(D) Renting an apartment

남자는 현재 무엇을 하고 있다고 말하는가?

(A) 일정 금액 비축
(B) 초과 시간 근무
(C) 부서 이동 신청
(D) 아파트 임차

어휘 set aside 챙겨 두다 shift 근무 시간 apply for 신청[지원]하다
departmental 부서의 transfer 이동 rent 임차하다

해설 세부 사항 관련 – 남자가 현재 하고 있다고 말하는 것

남자가 마지막 대사에서 요즘 아파트를 사려고 돈을 모으고 있는데, 정말 도움이 되겠다(I'm saving up for an apartment these days, so that will really help)고 말한 것으로 보아 정답은 (A)이다.

▸▸ Paraphrasing   대화의 **saving up**
→ 정답의 **setting aside some money**

44-46 3인 대화

> M-Cn OK, Edith. What did you want to speak to me about?
>
> W-Am My wrist has been sore, and I think it's from using my computer all day. **44 I'd like to find a way to make it stop hurting.**
>
> M-Cn Well, you can request ergonomic equipment, but it's a lot of paperwork. Actually, Jackie just did it. **45 You should ask her if she thinks the process was worth it.**
>
> W-Am OK. Oh, there she is now. Jackie!
>
> W-Br Hi, Edith. What's up?
>
> W-Am I heard you got some ergonomic equipment. I'm considering doing the same thing.
>
> W-Br That's a great idea. **46 I got a special computer mouse, and it has helped a lot. I'd be happy to show it to you, if you'd like.**

> 남 자, 이디스. 내게 하려던 말이 뭐였죠?
> 여1 손목이 계속 아픈데, 하루 종일 컴퓨터를 사용해서 그런 것 같아요. **통증을 멈출 방법을 찾고 싶어요.**
> 남 그럼, 인체공학 장비를 요청하면 되는데, 서류 작업이 워낙 많네요. 사실, 재키가 얼마 전 장비를 요청했어요. **그 절차를 밟을 만한 가치가 있었다고 생각하는지 재키한테 물어봐요.**
> 여1 좋아요. 아, 마침 저기 그녀가 있네요. 재키!
> 여2 안녕하세요, 이디스. 무슨 일이에요?
> 여1 인체공학 장비를 받았다고 들었어요. 똑같이 해볼까 생각 중이거든요.
> 여2 좋은 생각이에요. **특별한 컴퓨터 마우스를 받았는데 도움이 많이 되고 있어요. 원한다면 기꺼이 보여드리죠.**

어휘 wrist 손목 sore 아픈 ergonomic 인체공학의
equipment 장비 process 절차 worth ~할 가치가 있는

44 고난도

What does Edith want to do?

(A) Take on more responsibility
(B) Relieve some physical discomfort
(C) Improve a workplace relationship
(D) Increase her efficiency

이디스는 무엇을 하길 원하는가?

(A) 더 많은 책무를 맡는 것
(B) 신체적인 불편을 완화하는 것
(C) 직장에서의 대인 관계를 개선하는 것
(D) 효율성을 높이는 것

어휘 take on 떠맡다 relieve 완화하다 physical 신체의
discomfort 불편[가벼운 통증] efficiency 효율

해설 세부 사항 관련 – 이디스가 하기를 원하는 일

남자가 이디스라고 부르며 말을 건 것으로 보아 첫 번째 여자가 이디스이며, 이디스는 첫 대사에서 통증을 멈출 방법을 찾고 싶다(I'd like to make it stop hurting)고 말했으므로 정답은 (B)이다.

▸▸ Paraphrasing   대화의 **make ~ stop hurting**
→ 정답의 **relieve some physical discomfort**

45 고난도

What does the man recommend asking Jackie for?

(A) An opinion
(B) An apology
(C) Some paperwork
(D) Some equipment

남자는 재키에게 무엇을 요청하라고 권하는가?

(A) 의견
(B) 사과
(C) 서류 작업
(D) 장비

해설 세부 사항 관련 – 남자가 재키에게 요청하라고 권한 것

남자가 두 번째 대사에서 재키에 대해 언급하며, 그 절차를 밟을 만한 가치가 있었다고 생각하는지 재키한테 물어보라(You should ask her if she thinks the process was worth it)고 권하고 있으므로 정답은 (A)이다.

46

What does Jackie offer to do?

(A) Help with an installation procedure
(B) Look in the company handbook
(C) Show Edith a computer accessory
(D) Connect Edith with another coworker

재키는 무엇을 하겠다고 제안하는가?
(A) 설치 과정 돕기
(B) 회사 안내서 보기
(C) 이디스에게 컴퓨터 소품 보여주기
(D) 이디스를 다른 동료와 연결해주기

어휘   installation 설치   procedure 절차[방법]   handbook 안내서
      accessory 부속품, 장신구   coworker 동료

해설   세부 사항 관련 – 재키가 하겠다고 제안한 일
두 번째 여자가 두 번째 대사에서 특수 컴퓨터 마우스를 받았는데 도움이 많이
되고 있다(I got a special computer mouse, and it has helped a lot)
면서 원한다면 기꺼이 보여주겠다(I'd be happy to show it to you, if you'd
like)고 했으므로 정답은 (C)이다.

> ▸▸ Paraphrasing   대화의 a computer mouse
>   → 정답의 a computer accessory

47-49

W-Am	**⁴⁷Leroy, I was talking with Ms. Brissette as she checked out a book just now.** Did you know she works at an assisted living facility for elderly people?
M-Cn	No, I didn't. But—why do you bring that up?
W-Am	Well, she was saying the residents there sometimes ask her to borrow library books for them. **⁴⁸I was thinking—what if we brought some of our books directly to the facility for the residents' use?**
M-Cn	Oh, that's a great idea! And I think we already have the funds for it. **⁴⁹You should write up an official proposal for the director.**
W-Am	**⁴⁹OK, I will.** Thanks for the encouragement.

여   리로이, 브리셋 씨가 방금 전 도서를 대출할 때 얘기를 나눴는데요.
     그녀가 노인 생활 지원 시설에서 근무하는 거 알고 있었어요?
남   아니요, 몰랐어요. 그런데 그게 왜요?
여   그곳 거주자들이 가끔 그녀에게 도서관에서 책을 빌려달라고
     부탁한다고 해서요. 생각해봤는데… 거기 거주자들이 이용할 수 있게
     우리 책 일부를 직접 그 시설로 가져다드리면 어떨까요?
남   오, 그거 좋은 생각이네요! 그럴 만한 자금도 이미 있고요. 이사님께
     제출할 공식 제안서를 작성하시면 되겠어요.
여   좋아요, 할게요. 격려해줘서 고마워요.

어휘   check out (책을) 대출하다   assisted living facility
      생활 지원 시설   elderly people 노인   bring up 꺼내다
      resident 거주자   directly 바로, 직접   official 공식적인
      proposal 제안   director 임원   encouragement 격려

47

고난도

What does the woman say she just did?

(A) Spoken with a patron
(B) Read a publication
(C) Attended a lecture
(D) Posted a notice

여자는 방금 무엇을 했다고 말하는가?
(A) 이용객과의 대화
(B) 출판물 읽기
(C) 강연 참석
(D) 공지 게시

어휘   patron 고객[이용객]   publication 출판(물)   lecture 강연   post
      게시하다   notice 공지

해설   세부 사항 관련 – 여자가 방금 했다고 언급한 것
여자가 첫 대사에서 브리셋 씨가 방금 전 도서를 대출할 때 얘기를 나눴다(I
was talking with Ms. Brissette as she checked out a book just now)
고 했으므로 정답은 (A)이다.

48

고난도

What does the woman suggest offering?

(A) Private meeting facilities
(B) Classes on library resources
(C) A mobile book collection
(D) A longer borrowing period

여자는 무엇을 제공하자고 제안하는가?
(A) 개인 전용 회의 시설
(B) 도서관 자료에 대한 강좌
(C) 이동식 도서 컬렉션
(D) 더 긴 대출 기간

어휘   private (특정 개인집단) 전용의, 사적인   resource 자료[자원]
      mobile 이동식의   collection 소장품   period 기간

해설   세부 사항 관련 – 여자가 제공하자고 제안하는 것
여자가 두 번째 대사에서 거기 거주자들이 이용할 수 있게 우리 책 일부를 직
접 그 시설로 가져다드리면 어떨지(I was thinking—what if we brought
some of our books directly to the facility for the residents' use?)라
고 말한 것으로 보아 정답은 (C)이다.

49

What does the woman agree to do?

(A) Clean out a space
(B) Create a document
(C) Gather some colleagues
(D) Review a budget

여자는 무엇을 하기로 동의하는가?
(A) 공간 청소
(B) 서류 작성
(C) 동료 모집
(D) 예산 검토

어휘   space 공간   gather 모으다   colleague 동료   budget 예산

해설 세부 사항 관련 – 여자가 하기로 동의한 일

남자가 두 번째 대사에서 이사님께 제출할 공식 제안서를 작성하라(You should write up an official proposal for the director)고 권유하자 여자가 좋다고 답했으므로 정답은 (B)이다.

> ▸▸ Paraphrasing 　대화의 write up an proposal
> 　　　　　　　　 → 정답의 create a document

50-52 3인 대화

M-Cn	Hi, this is Dan Swanson. **50 You called about my car?**
W-Am	Ah, Mr. Swanson. Uh, unfortunately, **50 it seems the estimate we gave you for the repair work was incorrect...** It's going to be more like fifteen hundred dollars.
M-Cn	**51 Wow, that's a lot more than you quoted me at first...**
W-Am	Yes, sorry about that. Would you like to speak with Pete, the mechanic handling your vehicle? He's right here.
M-Cn	That would be nice.
M-Au	Hi Mr. Swanson. **52 We thought the problem was your fuel filter, but it turns out it's the catalytic converter.** That's a much more expensive part to replace, but it has to be done.
M-Cn	I see. Well, OK then.

남1	여보세요, 댄 스완슨입니다. **제 차와 관련해서 전화하셨나요?**
여	아, 스완슨 씨. 어, 안타깝게도, **수리 비용으로 뽑아드렸던 견적이 잘못된 것 같습니다…** 1,500달러 정도는 될 것 같습니다.
남1	와, 저한테 처음에 내주신 견적보다 훨씬 높은 금액이네요….
여	네, 죄송합니다. 고객님 차량을 맡고 있는 정비사인 피트와 말씀해 보시겠어요? 그가 여기 있거든요.
남1	그러면 좋겠네요.
남2	안녕하세요. 스완슨 씨. **고객님 차량의 연료 필터가 문제라고 생각했는데, 촉매 변환기가 문제였습니다.** 이 장치는 교체 부품이 훨씬 더 비싸긴 하지만 필요한 작업이에요.
남1	알겠습니다. 그럼 그렇게 하죠.

어휘 unfortunately 유감스럽게도　estimate 견적(서); 추정하다　incorrect 부정확한　quote 견적을 내다　mechanic 정비공　vehicle 차량　fuel 연료　turn out 나타나다, 드러나다　catalytic converter 촉매 변환기(자동차의 공해 방지 장치)

50

What is the main topic of the conversation?

(A) A shipping service
(B) A building process
(C) A rental contract
(D) A vehicle repair

대화의 주제는 무엇인가?

(A) 배송 서비스
(B) 건축 공정
(C) 임대 계약
(D) 차량 수리

어휘 shipping 배송　process 과정[절차]　rental 임대(료)　contract 계약　vehicle 차량

해설 전체 내용 관련 – 대화의 주제

첫 번째 남자가 첫 대사에서 본인의 차와 관련해서 전화했는지(You called about my car?) 묻자, 여자가 수리 비용으로 뽑아준 견적이 잘못된 것 같다(it seems the estimate we gave you for the repair work was incorrect)고 답한 것으로 보아 자동차 수리에 관해 대화하고 있음을 알 수 있다. 따라서 정답은 (D)이다.

51

Why is Mr. Swanson surprised?

(A) A request has been denied.
(B) A cost estimate has risen.
(C) A task has not been completed.
(D) A project manager has been replaced.

스완슨 씨는 왜 놀랐는가?

(A) 요청이 거절되어서
(B) 비용 견적액이 올라서
(C) 일이 완료되지 않아서
(D) 프로젝트 관리자가 교체되어서

어휘 deny 거절[부인]하다　task 일

해설 세부 사항 관련 – 스완슨 씨가 놀란 이유

첫 번째 남자는 첫 대사에서 자신이 댄 스완슨(this is Dan Swanson)이라고 소개했고, 두 번째 대사에서 처음에 내준 견적보다 훨씬 높은 금액(that's a lot more than you quoted me at first)이라며 놀라움을 표하고 있다. 따라서 첫 번째 남자, 즉 스완슨 씨는 높아진 견적 금액 때문에 놀란 것이므로 정답은 (B)이다.

52 고난도

What does Pete explain?

(A) The reason for a change
(B) The steps of a procedure
(C) The features of some software
(D) The options of a choice

피트는 무엇을 설명하는가?

(A) 변경에 대한 이유
(B) 절차의 단계
(C) 소프트웨어의 특징
(D) 선택 사항

어휘 step 단계　procedure 절차[방법]　feature 특징　option 선택(권)

해설 세부 사항 관련 – 피트가 설명한 것

앞에서 여자가 첫 번째 남자에게 피트를 소개했고, 두 번째 남자인 피트가 고객님 차량의 연료 필터가 문제라고 생각했는데, 촉매 변환기가 문제였다(We thought the problem was your fuel filter, but it turns out it's the catalytic converter)며 견적 금액이 오른 이유를 설명하고 있으므로 정답은 (A)이다.

53-55

> W-Am Fabian, I just saw the picture you posted of the amazing French fish dish you made. It looked delicious!
>
> M-Cn Oh thanks, Sherry. ⁵³**Now that I have more free time, I've gotten interested in making my own meals.**
>
> W-Am That's great.
>
> M-Cn Yes, I'm enjoying it. ⁵⁴**This weekend, I'm actually going to the Garrisville Farmers Market to pick up some ingredients for a special dish.**
>
> W-Am How fun! ⁵⁵**Speaking of Garrisville, did you hear that Taylor Kirby is coming there to put on a live cooking exhibition?** He's going to show how to make some of his famous recipes.
>
> M-Cn The chef who won that TV competition? Wow! I'd love to go to that.

> 여   파비안, 당신이 직접 만든 멋진 프렌치 생선 요리의 사진 게시물을 좀 전에 봤어요. 맛있어 보이던데요!
>
> 남   고마워요, 셰리. **여가 시간이 늘어나니까, 밥을 직접 해 먹는 데 흥미가 생겼어요.**
>
> 여   그거 잘됐네요.
>
> 남   네, 재미있어요. **이번 주말에는 개리스빌 파머스 마켓에 가서 특별한 요리를 위한 재료들을 구해보려고요.**
>
> 여   재미있겠네요! **개리스빌 이야기가 나왔으니 말인데, 테일러 커비가 거기 와서 라이브 요리 시범을 한다는 걸 들으셨나요?** 자신의 유명한 조리법 몇 가지를 어떻게 만드는지 보여줄 거예요.
>
> 남   TV 경연에서 우승한 요리사요? 와우! 거기에 가보고 싶네요.

어휘   post 게시하다   amazing 놀라운   delicious 맛있는   ingredient 재료   speaking of ~에 관해서 말한다면   live 생방송의; 살다   exhibition 전시회, 시범   recipe 조리법

53

What has the man become interested in?
(A) Fishing
(B) Cooking
(C) Playing an instrument
(D) Learning a new language

남자는 무엇에 흥미가 생겼는가?
(A) 낚시
(B) 요리
(C) 악기 연주
(D) 외국어 학습

해설   세부 사항 관련 – 남자가 흥미를 갖게 된 것
남자가 첫 대사에서 여가 시간이 늘어나니까 밥을 직접 해 먹는 데 흥미가 생겼다(Now that I have more free time, I've gotten interested in making my own meals)고 말했으므로 정답은 (B)이다.

▸▸ Paraphrasing   대화의 making my own meals
→ 정답의 cooking

54

What is the man planning to do this weekend?
(A) Purchase some supplies
(B) Join a hobby club
(C) Go on a group trip
(D) Stream some videos

남자는 이번 주말에 무엇을 할 계획인가?
(A) 물품 구입
(B) 동호회 가입
(C) 단체 여행
(D) 비디오 스트리밍

어휘   purchase 구입하다; 구입(품)   supplies 물품   hobby 취미   stream 스트림 처리하다(데이터 전송을 연속적으로 이어서 하다)

해설   세부 사항 관련 – 남자의 이번 주말 계획
남자가 두 번째 대사에서 이번 주말에는 개리스빌 파머스 마켓에 가서 특별한 요리를 위한 재료들을 구하려 한다(This weekend, I'm actually going to the Garrisville Farmers Market to pick up some ingredients for a special dish)고 했으므로 정답은 (A)이다.

▸▸ Paraphrasing   대화의 pick up some ingredients
→ 정답의 purchase some supplies

55

What kind of event does the woman mention?
(A) A dinner party
(B) A television show shoot
(C) A skills demonstration
(D) A competition

여자는 무슨 행사를 언급하는가?
(A) 만찬회
(B) 텔레비전 프로그램 촬영
(C) 솜씨 시연
(D) 경연

어휘   shoot 촬영; 촬영하다   demonstration 시연   competition 경쟁, 대회

해설   세부 사항 관련 – 여자가 언급한 행사
여자가 마지막 대사에서 개리스빌 이야기가 나왔으니 말인데, 테일러 커비가 거기 와서 라이브 요리 시범을 한다는 걸 들었는지(Speaking of Garrisville, did you hear that Taylor Kirby is coming there to put on a live cooking exhibition?) 묻고 있으므로 정답은 (C)이다.

W-Br 56 **Hawkins Technical Academy, Kelsie speaking.**

M-Au Hello. I'm looking to get into the computer science field, and I thought I'd start by taking classes at your school.

W-Br Sure, our academy has helped many people become qualified for jobs in computing.

M-Au Right. Uh, I just have a question about some information that's not on your Web site. 57 **How many students are there in your weekend classes, usually?**

W-Br The limit is thirty, but there are typically around twenty.

M-Au Great. 58 **Then I'd like to sign up for the information security class starting next month.**

W-Br Hmm. 58 **Given your likely knowledge level, information security would be a difficult area.** 58 **May I suggest some alternatives?**

여 호킨스 기술 학교의 켈시입니다.

남 여보세요. 컴퓨터 과학 분야에 진출하려고 하는데, 이 학교에서 수업을 듣는 것부터 시작해볼까 해서요.

여 네, 우리 학교는 많은 사람들이 컴퓨터 분야 직업에 자격을 갖추도록 돕고 있어요.

남 그렇군요. 어, 어, 학교 웹사이트에 없는 몇 가지 정보에 대해 질문이 있어요. 주말반에는 보통 학생이 몇 명이나 되나요?

여 정원은 30명이지만, 보통 20명 정도 있어요.

남 좋네요. 그러면 다음 달에 시작하는 정보 보안 수업을 신청하고 싶어요.

여 흠, 갖고 계신 지식 수준을 가늠해볼 때, 정보 보안은 어려운 분야일 수 있어요. 제가 다른 수업을 추천해드려도 될까요?

어휘 filed 분야 academy 학교 qualified 자격이 있는 computing 컴퓨터 사용 limit 한도, 허용치 typically 보통 sign up for ~을 신청하다 security 보안 given ~을 고려할 때 alternative 대안

56

What kind of business does the woman work for?

(A) An information technology consulting firm
(B) An employment agency
(C) A research laboratory
(D) An educational institute

여자는 어떤 회사에서 일하는가?
(A) 정보 기술 컨설팅 회사
(B) 직업 소개소
(C) 연구소
(D) 교육 기관

어휘 employment 직장, 고용 research 연구 laboratory 실험실 educational 교육의 institute 기관[협회]

해설 전체 내용 관련 – 여자의 근무지

여자가 첫 대사에서 호킨스 기술 학교의 켈시입니다(Hawkins Technical Academy, Kelsie speaking)라고 자신을 소개하고 있으므로 정답은 (D)이다.

▸▸ **Paraphrasing** 대화의 ~ academy
→ 정답의 educational institute

57

What does the man ask about?

(A) A number of people
(B) A source of funding
(C) A required qualification
(D) A usual start time

남자는 무엇에 관해 묻는가?
(A) 인원
(B) 자금원
(C) 필수 자격 요건
(D) 평소 시작 시간

어휘 source 원천, 출처 funding 자금 required 필수의 qualification 자격

해설 세부 사항 관련 – 남자의 문의 사항

남자가 두 번째 대사에서 주말반에는 보통 학생이 몇 명이나 되는지(How many students are there in your weekend classes, usually?)를 묻고 있으므로 정답은 (A)이다.

58　　　　　　　　　고난도

Why does the woman say, "information security would be a difficult area"?

(A) To indicate that she is impressed
(B) To recommend an additional service
(C) To justify a heavy workload
(D) To give the man a warning

여자가 "정보 보안은 어려운 분야일 수 있어요"라고 말하는 이유는 무엇인가?
(A) 감명을 받았다는 것을 보여주려고
(B) 추가 서비스를 추천하려고
(C) 과도한 업무량을 해명하려고
(D) 남자에게 주의를 주려고

어휘 indicate 나타내다 impressed 감명을 받은 additional 추가의 justify 해명[정당화]하다 workload 업무량

해설 화자의 의도 파악 – 정보 보안은 어려운 분야일 수 있다는 말의 의도

앞에서 남자가 다음 달에 시작하는 정보 보안 수업을 신청하고 싶다(Then I'd like to sign up for the information security class starting next month)고 하자, 여자가 남자의 지식 수준(your likely knowledge level)을 근거로 삼으며 인용문을 언급했다. 또한 이어서 다른 수업을 추천해도 되는지(May I suggest some alternatives?) 묻고 있으므로 입문 단계인 남자에게 정보 보안 수업은 벅찰 수 있음을 미리 알려주려는 의도로 볼 수 있다. 따라서 정답은 (D)이다.

M-Cn	Ms. Kang, welcome to our store. Have a seat.
W-Br	Thank you, Mr. Redford. **59So, you said that you became interested in distributing my company's products after you saw our advertisement in the latest issue of *Hardware Retailers Monthly.***
M-Cn	That's right. I don't know if you noticed, **60but we're renovating and expanding the southwest corner of the store.** I thought that stocking your home safe boxes could be a great use of some of that new space.
W-Br	Excellent. I think our products would sell very well here. **61What are your expectations for the distribution contract? It's helpful to make sure we have similar ideas about the major points before going forward.**
M-Cn	OK. Where would you like to start?

남	강 선생님, 저희 매장에 오신 걸 환영합니다. 앉으세요.
여	감사합니다, 레드포드 씨. 〈월간 하드웨어 소매업체〉의 최신 호에 실린 우리 광고를 보시고 나서 우리 회사 제품을 유통하는 데 관심을 가지게 되었다고요.
남	맞습니다. 아실지 모르겠지만, 저희는 매장 남서쪽 모퉁이를 보수 및 확장 공사 중입니다. 신설 공간 일부에 귀사의 가정용 금고를 비치하면 좋을 것 같습니다.
여	좋아요. 이곳에서 우리 제품이 정말 잘 팔릴 것 같습니다. 유통 계약에 대해 어떻게 예상하시나요? 일을 진행시키기 전에 주요 관점에서 비슷한 견해를 가지고 있으면 도움이 되죠.
남	그럼, 어디서부터 시작하시고 싶으신가요?

어휘	distribute (상품을) 유통시키다 advertisement 공고 latest 최신의 notice ~을 의식하다 renovate 개조[보수]하다 expand 확장하다 stock ~로 채우다[갖추다]; 재고(품) expectation 기대 go forward 전진하다

59

How did the man learn about the woman's business?

(A) From an industry magazine
(B) From an outdoor advertisement
(C) From a local newspaper
(D) From a Web site

남자는 여자의 회사에 대해 어떻게 알게 되었는가?
(A) 업계 잡지에서
(B) 옥외 광고에서
(C) 지역 신문에서
(D) 웹사이트에서

어휘 industry 산업 outdoor 야외[옥외]의

해설 세부 사항 관련 – 남자가 여자의 회사를 알게 된 경위

여자가 첫 대사에서 남자가 〈월간 하드웨어 소매업체〉의 최신 호에 실린 우리 광고를 보고 나서 우리 회사 제품을 유통하는 데 관심을 갖게 되었다고 했다 (you said that you became interested in distributing my company's products after you saw our advertisement in the latest issue of Hardware Retailers Monthly)라고 확인하는 것으로 보아 정답은 (A)이다.

60

What does the man say about his store?

(A) Some of its merchandise is out of stock.
(B) It does not have many customers.
(C) Part of it is being remodeled.
(D) A parking area is being added.

남자는 자신의 매장에 대해 무엇을 말하는가?
(A) 일부 상품이 품절되었다.
(B) 고객이 많지 않다.
(C) 매장 일부가 리모델링 중이다.
(D) 주차 구역을 추가 중이다.

어휘 merchandise 상품 out of stock 품절이 된 remodel 개조하다

해설 세부 사항 관련 – 남자가 매장에 대해 언급한 것

남자가 두 번째 대사에서 우리는 매장 남서쪽 모퉁이를 보수 및 확장 공사 중(we're renovating and expanding the southwest corner of the store)이라고 말했으므로 정답은 (C)이다.

▶▶ Paraphrasing 대화의 **renovating and expanding the southwest corner of the store**
→ 정답의 **part of it is being remodeled**

61   고난도

What does the woman propose doing first?

(A) Inspecting a manufacturing plant
(B) Discussing the terms of an agreement
(C) Distributing some product samples
(D) Reviewing some sales figures

여자는 먼저 무엇을 하라고 제안하는가?
(A) 제조 공장을 점검하는 것
(B) 계약 조건을 논의하는 것
(C) 제품 샘플을 유통하는 것
(D) 판매 수치를 검토하는 것

어휘 inspect 점검하다 manufacturing plant 제조 공장 terms 조건 figure 수치

해설 세부 사항 관련 – 여자가 먼저 하자고 제안한 것

여자가 두 번째 대사에서 유통 계약에 대해 어떻게 예상하는지(What are your expectations for the distribution contract?)를 물으며, 일을 진행시키기 전에 주요 관점에서 비슷한 견해를 가지고 있으면 도움이 된다(It's helpful to make sure we have similar ideas about the major points before going forward)고 한 것으로 보아 정답은 (B)이다.

W-Am Oh, look at those stylish watches. That reminds me—I need to get a graduation gift for one of my relatives. **62 Would you mind if we looked at the bracelets for a moment?**

M-Cn Oh, no problem. How about this gold one with green stones?

W-Am Wow, it's beautiful. **63 But look at the price! I don't want to get something so valuable that my relative never wears it because she's afraid of damaging it.**

M-Cn Good point. **64 Well, why don't you try looking for a cheaper price for it on the Internet?** I'm sure there are sites that have discounts.

W-Am You're probably right. But I'd like to walk around here a little more first.

여 오, 저 세련된 시계들을 좀 봐요. 제 친척에게 줄 졸업 선물을 사야 하는 게 떠오르네요. **잠깐 팔찌들 좀 구경해도 괜찮을까요?**

남 오, 그럼요. 녹색 장식이 박힌 이 금팔찌는 어때요?

여 와우, 예쁘네요. **그렇지만 가격을 봐요! 친척이 망가질까 신경 쓰느라 착용하지 못할 정도로 값비싼 물건은 사고 싶지 않아요.**

남 맞는 말이네요. **그럼, 인터넷으로 더 저렴한 가격의 팔찌를 찾아보는 게 어떨까요?** 할인을 하는 사이트들이 분명히 있을 거예요.

여 그 말이 맞을 것 같네요. 그래도 먼저 여기를 좀 더 돌아보고 싶어요.

어휘 graduation 졸업 relative 친척 bracelet 팔찌 valuable 귀중한 damage 손상시키다; 손상

Directory

Floor	Products
62 1	**Cosmetics & Jewelry**
2	Women's Clothing
3	Men's Clothing
4	Home Goods

층별 안내

층	제품
62 1	화장품 & 보석
2	여성 의류
3	남성 의류
4	가정용품

62

Look at the graphic. Which floor are the speakers on?

(A) The first floor
(B) The second floor
(C) The third floor
(D) The fourth floor

시각 정보에 의하면, 화자들은 몇 층에 있는가?

(A) 1층
(B) 2층
(C) 3층
(D) 4층

해설 시각 정보 연계 – 화자들이 있는 층

여자가 첫 대사에서 잠깐 팔찌들 좀 구경해도 괜찮을지(Would you mind if we looked at the bracelets for a moment?)를 묻고 있고, 층별 안내에 따르면 팔찌, 즉 보석류를 파는 곳은 1층이라고 나와 있으므로 정답은 (A)이다.

63 고난도

Why is the woman uncertain about buying an item?

(A) It may be the wrong size.
(B) It would be easy to damage.
(C) It has an unusual design.
(D) It is expensive.

여자는 왜 물건을 사는 것에 대해 확신하지 못하는가?

(A) 사이즈가 맞지 않을 수 있다.
(B) 쉽게 손상될 수 있다.
(C) 디자인이 특이하다.
(D) 비싸다.

어휘 unusual 특이한

해설 세부 사항 관련 – 여자가 물건의 구매에 대해 확신하지 못하는 이유

여자가 두 번째 대사에서 가격을 보라(look at the price!)면서, 친척이 망가질까 신경 쓰느라 착용하지 못할 정도로 값비싼 물건은 사고 싶지 않다(I don't want to get something so valuable that my relative never wears it because she's afraid of damaging it)고 했으므로 정답은 (D)이다.

64

What does the man suggest doing?

(A) Trying on an item
(B) Paying in installments
(C) Going to online stores
(D) Looking for a salesperson

남자는 무엇을 하자고 제안하는가?

(A) 제품을 써 볼 것
(B) 할부로 납부할 것
(C) 온라인 매장을 방문할 것
(D) 판매원을 찾을 것

어휘 try on ~을 시험 삼아 해[입어]보다 in installments 분납으로 salesperson 판매원

해설 세부 사항 관련 – 남자의 제안 사항

남자가 마지막 대사에서 인터넷으로 더 저렴한 가격의 팔찌를 찾아보는 게 어떨까(why don't you try looking for a cheaper price for it on the Internet?)라고 제안하고 있으므로 정답은 (C)이다.

▸▸ Paraphrasing 대화의 **try looking for ~ on the Internet** → 정답의 **going to online stores**

M-Au Hello, Ms. Bajwa. This is Craig Anderson from Rylon Group. We spoke earlier about Fiona Morris's candidacy for a job at my company.

W-Am Oh, hello again. **65 Do you need more information about Fiona's performance when she worked in my department?**

M-Au No, but it's a related issue. **66 Ms. Morris has also suggested we speak to Frank Oliver, a manager at your company. But I can't get through to the number she gave us.** Do you know why that might be?

W-Am **67 Oh, it's because Frank left the company a few weeks ago.** Fiona must not have heard. Let me see if I have his new contact information.

남 여보세요, 바자 씨. 라일론 그룹의 크레이그 앤더슨입니다. 아까 저희 회사 일자리에 피오나 모리스 지원자를 고려 중인 건으로 말씀 나누었죠.

여 오, 안녕하세요. 피오나가 저희 부서에서 일했을 때 실적에 대해 정보가 더 필요하신가요?

남 아니요, 그렇지만 관련된 문제이긴 합니다. 모리스 씨가 그쪽 회사의 관리자인 프랭크 올리버 씨와도 이야기해볼 것을 제안했어요. 그런데 그녀가 준 전화번호로는 연락이 닿질 않네요. 혹시 왜 그런지 아실까요?

여 오, 프랭크가 몇 주 전에 퇴사해서 그럴 거예요. 피오나는 소식을 못 들었을 겁니다. 그의 새로운 연락처가 제게 있는지 볼게요.

어휘 candidacy 입후보 performance 실적, 성과 related 관련된 get through to ~에 전화 연락하다

References

Timothy Ward   555-0145
(Manager at Slangal)

Maureen Jacobs   555-0182
(Supervisor at Zubina Consultants)

Anita Bajwa   555-0176
(Director at Soares Engineering)

66 Frank Oliver   555-0109
(Manager at Soares Engineering)

신원 조회처

티모시 워드 555-0145
(슬랭갈 관리자)

모린 제이콥스 555-0182
(주비나 컨설턴트 감독관)

아니타 바자 555-0176
(소아레스 엔지니어링 이사)

66 프랭크 올리버 555-0109
(소아레스 엔지니어링 관리자)

65

Who most likely is the woman?

(A) A job applicant
(B) A hiring manager
(C) A department head
(D) A corporate recruiter

여자는 누구일 것 같은가?

(A) 구직자
(B) 채용 담당자
(C) 부서 책임자
(D) 기업 모집자

어휘 applicant 지원자 head 책임자 corporate 기업(회사)의 recruiter 모집자

해설 전체 내용 관련 – 여자의 직업

여자가 첫 대사에서 피오나가 자신의 부서에서 일했을 때 실적에 대해 정보가 더 필요한 것(Do you need more information about Fiona's performance when she worked in my department?)인지를 묻고 있는 것으로 보아 여자는 부서 책임자임을 알 수 있다. 따라서 정답은 (C)이다.

66

Look at the graphic. Which phone number is the man having trouble with?

(A) 555-0145
(B) 555-0182
(C) 555-0176
(D) 555-0109

시각 정보에 의하면, 남자는 어떤 전화번호로 문제를 겪고 있는가?

(A) 555-0145
(B) 555-0182
(C) 555-0176
(D) 555-0109

해설 시각 정보 연계 – 남자가 문제를 겪고 있는 전화번호

남자가 두 번째 대사에서 모리스 씨가 그쪽 회사의 관리자인 프랭크 올리버 씨와도 이야기해볼 것을 제안했다(Ms. Morris has also suggested we speak to Frank Oliver, a manager at your company)면서 그런데 그녀가 준 전화번호로는 연락이 닿질 않는다(But I can't get through to the number she gave us)고 했고, 신원 조회처 명단에 따르면, 프랭크 올리버의 전화번호는 555-0109이므로 정답은 (D)이다.

67

What does the woman say caused a problem?

(A) A technological issue
(B) A typing error
(C) A company policy
(D) A personnel change

여자는 무엇 때문에 문제가 발생했다고 말하는가?

(A) 기술적인 문제
(B) 오타
(C) 회사 방침
(D) 인사이동

어휘 technological 기술적인 typing 타자 치기 error 오류
personnel 인원[직원들]

해설 세부 사항 관련 – 여자가 말하는 문제의 원인

여자가 마지막 대사에서 프랭크가 몇 주 전에 퇴사해서 그럴 것(it's because Frank left the company a few weeks ago)이라고 했으므로 정답은 (D)이다.

68-70 대화 + 주문서

W-Br	Hi. This is Kate at Coomer Software. **68 We ordered lunch from your deli this morning for a sales client who dropped by unexpectedly.** It just arrived, right on time, but now that we've opened up the bags, it seems there's a problem.
M-Au	OK, I've found your order form in our records. What's the problem?
W-Br	**69 We only got three of each type of sandwich.** As you can tell, that means we're missing one.
M-Au	Yes, I see. Well, I'm pretty sure that we made all seven sandwiches. **70 Let me call the employee who dropped off your order, and see what he says.**

여	안녕하세요. 쿠머 소프트웨어의 케이트입니다. **갑자기 방문하신 판매 고객을 위해 오늘 아침에 그쪽 식품 판매점에서 점심을 주문했는데요.** 방금 전 제때에 도착하긴 했는데, 가방을 열어보니 문제가 있는 것 같아요.
남	네, 제가 우리 기록에 있는 해당 주문서를 찾았습니다. 무슨 문제이시죠?
여	**샌드위치가 종류별로 3개씩만 왔어요.** 아시겠지만, 하나가 빠졌다는 얘기죠.
남	네, 그렇네요. 분명히 샌드위치를 7개 전부 다 만들었거든요. **물건을 배달한 직원에게 전화해서 확인해보겠습니다.**

어휘 deli 식품 판매점 drop by 들르다 unexpectedly 갑자기
on time 정각에 missing 빠진[누락된]

Crabtree Deli
Order Form

Item	Quantity
Ham sandwich	3
69 **Tuna sandwich**	**4**
Potato salad (container)	1
House salad	2

크랩트리 델리
주문서

제품	수량
햄 샌드위치	3
69 참치 샌드위치	4
감자 샐러드 (용기)	1
하우스 샐러드	2

68

What is taking place at the woman's company?

(A) A board meeting
(B) A client visit
(C) A sales workshop
(D) An orientation session

여자의 회사에서는 무슨 일이 일어났는가?

(A) 이사회 미팅
(B) 고객 방문
(C) 판매 워크숍
(D) 오리엔테이션

어휘 board 이사회 orientation 예비 교육 session (특정 활동을 위한)
시간

해설 세부 사항 관련 – 여자의 회사에서 일어난 일

여자가 첫 대사에서 갑자기 방문하신 판매 고객을 위해 오늘 아침에 그쪽 식품 판매점에서 점심을 주문했다(We ordered lunch from your deli this morning for a sales client who dropped by unexpectedly)고 한 것으로 보아 정답은 (B)이다.

▶▶ **Paraphrasing**   대화의 **drop by** → 정답의 **visit**

69

Look at the graphic. What is the woman missing?

(A) A ham sandwich
(B) A tuna sandwich
(C) A container of potato salad
(D) A house salad

시각 정보에 의하면, 여자는 무엇을 못 받았는가?

(A) 햄 샌드위치
(B) 참치 샌드위치
(C) 감자 샐러드 한 팩
(D) 하우스 샐러드

해설 시각 정보 연계 – 여자가 받지 못한 것

여자가 두 번째 대사에서 샌드위치가 종류별로 3개씩만 왔다(We only got three of each type of sandwich)고 했는데, 주문서에 따르면 여자는 참치 샌드위치를 4개 주문했으므로 참치 샌드위치가 한 개 빠졌음을 알 수 있다. 따라서 정답은 (B)이다.

70

What does the man say he will do next?

(A) Send a scanned copy of a form
(B) Refund the cost of the order
(C) Contact a delivery person
(D) Make some more food

남자는 다음에 무엇을 하겠다고 말하는가?

(A) 양식의 스캔본 보내기
(B) 주문 비용의 환불
(C) 배달원과의 연락
(D) 추가 음식 조리

어휘 form 양식 refund 환불하다

해설 세부 사항 관련 – 남자가 다음에 하겠다고 말한 것

남자가 마지막 대사에서 물건을 배달한 직원에게 전화해서 확인해보겠다(Let me call the employee who dropped off your order, and see what he says)고 했으므로 정답은 (C)이다.

▸▸ Paraphrasing | 대화의 **call the employee who dropped off your order**
→ 정답의 **contact a delivery person**

Part 4

71-73 회의 발췌

W-Br All right, everyone, I have some big news. **71We just signed the lease agreement for a new place of business—a whole floor of the Ashbrook Building in the Valtside neighborhood—and we'll be moving in in spring.** Now, I know that might feel like a big change, but Valtside is still within the city. **72And several bus and subway lines run through it, so it's actually easier to reach than our current area.** But best of all, we'll have more space in the Ashbrook Building than we do here. **73Let me put the layout up on the screen.** See? Our organization will finally get a real break room.

자, 여러분, 중요한 소식이 있습니다. **방금 전 새로운 사옥의 임대차 계약을 맺었습니다. 발트사이드 인근 애시브룩 빌딩의 한 층 전체이며 봄에 입주할 예정입니다.** 큰 변화라고 느껴질 수도 있지만 발트사이드는 여전히 시내에 위치해 있습니다. **몇몇 버스와 지하철 노선이 그곳을 경유해서 지금 있는 곳보다 사실 더 가기 편합니다.** 하지만 무엇보다 좋은 점은 애시브룩 빌딩에서는 여기보다 더 넓은 공간을 가지게 될 거라는 점입니다. **스크린에 배치도를 올릴게요.** 보이시죠? 우리 조직이 드디어 진짜 휴게실을 갖게 되었습니다.

어휘 lease 임대차 계약 agreement 합의 neighborhood 이웃, 인근 layout 배치 organization 조직 break room 휴게실

71

What is the purpose of the meeting?

(A) To describe a tourism campaign
(B) To announce an office relocation
(C) To report on a construction process
(D) To recommend a company outing

회의의 목적은 무엇인가?

(A) 관광 캠페인을 설명하는 것
(B) 사무실 이전을 발표하는 것
(C) 공사 과정을 보고하는 것
(D) 회사 야유회를 추천하는 것

어휘 describe 묘사하다 relocation 이전 report 알리다 process 과정[절차] recommend 추천하다 outing 야유회

해설 전체 내용 관련 – 회의의 목적

화자가 초반부에 방금 전 새로운 사옥의 임대차 계약을 맺었고 발트사이드 인근 애시브룩 빌딩의 한 층 전체를 임대해 봄에 입주할 예정(We just signed the lease agreement for a new place of business—a whole floor of the Ashbrook Building in the Valtside neighborhood—and we'll be moving in in spring)이라고 했으므로 정답은 (B)이다.

72 고난도

What does the speaker say about Valtside?

(A) It hosts an annual festival.
(B) It is beautiful in spring.
(C) It is the oldest part of the city.
(D) It is accessible by public transportation.

화자는 발트사이드에 대해 무엇을 말하는가?

(A) 매년 축제를 개최한다.
(B) 봄에 아름답다.
(C) 도시에서 가장 오래된 지역이다.
(D) 대중 교통을 이용해 갈 수 있다.

어휘 host 주최하다 annual 매년의 accessible 접근 가능한 public transportation 대중 교통

해설 세부 사항 관련 – 화자가 발트사이드에 대해 말하는 것

화자가 중반부에 몇몇 버스와 지하철 노선이 그곳을 경유해서 지금 있는 곳보다 사실 더 가기 편하다(And several bus and subway lines run through it, so it's actually easier to reach than our current area)고 했으므로 정답은 (D)이다.

▸▸ **Paraphrasing** 담화의 **several bus and subway lines run through it** → 정답의 **it is accessible by public transportation**

어휘 on one's feet 서서 comfortable 편한 researcher 연구원 manufacturing 제조 durable 오래 가는 sole 밑창 amazing 놀라운 cushioning 충격 완화 support 지지 anniversary 기념일 launch 개시[출시] select 엄선된

73

What does the speaker show the listeners?

(A) A neighborhood map
(B) A train schedule
(C) A floor plan
(D) An organization chart

화자는 청자들에게 무엇을 보여주는가?

(A) 주변 지역 안내도
(B) 기차 운행표
(C) 평면도
(D) 조직 구성도

해설 세부 사항 관련 – 화자가 청자들에게 보여주는 것

화자가 후반부에 스크린에 배치도를 올리겠다(Let me put the layout up on the screen)고 했으므로 정답은 (C)이다.

▸▸ **Paraphrasing** 담화의 **layout** → 정답의 **floor plan**

74-76 광고

> M-Cn Do you find that all you can do after a long day on your feet is sit on the sofa? 74**Then Carnahan shoes were made for you.** They're specially designed to be both stylish and comfortable. 75**Our researchers developed a new manufacturing method to create durable soles that provide amazing cushioning and support.** With Carnahan shoes, you'll be able to walk all day and still enjoy your evening. 76**And on December fourth and fifth, we'll be celebrating the one-year anniversary of the launch of Carnahan Shoes with a special sales event.** Visit one of our stores for huge discounts on select products. Carnahan Shoes—live comfortably.

긴 하루를 서서 보내고 나서 할 수 있는 일이 고작 소파에 앉는 것뿐이라고 생각하시나요? 그렇다면 카나한 슈즈는 당신을 위해 만들어졌습니다. 카나한 슈즈는 세련되면서 동시에 편하도록 특별히 디자인되었습니다. 우리 연구원들은 놀라운 충격 완화와 지지를 제공하는 오래 가는 밑창을 만들기 위해 새로운 제작 방식을 개발했습니다. 카나한 슈즈를 신으면, 하루 종일 걷고도 저녁까지 가뿐할 수 있습니다. 12월 4일과 5일에, 우리는 특별 판매 행사와 함께 카나한 슈즈의 출시 1주년을 기념할 예정입니다. 우리 매장 중 한 곳에 방문하셔서 엄선된 제품들에 대해 큰 폭의 할인을 받으세요. 카나한 슈즈로 삶이 편해집니다.

74

What type of product is being advertised?

(A) Furniture
(B) Electronics
(C) Luggage
(D) Footwear

어떤 종류의 제품이 광고되고 있는가?

(A) 가구
(B) 전자제품
(C) 짐가방
(D) 신발

해설 전체 내용 관련 – 광고되고 있는 제품

화자가 초반부에 카나한 슈즈는 당신을 위해 만들어졌다(Carnahan shoes were made for you)라고 한 것으로 보아 정답은 (D)이다.

▸▸ **Paraphrasing** 담화의 **shoes** → 정답의 **footwear**

75   고난도

According to the speaker, what has the company done?

(A) Invented a production technique
(B) Conducted market research
(C) Begun exporting to other countries
(D) Collaborated with a famous designer

화자에 따르면, 회사는 무엇을 했는가?

(A) 생산 기법 개발
(B) 시장 조사 시행
(C) 외국으로의 수출 시작
(D) 유명 디자이너와의 공동작업

어휘 invent 발명하다 technique 기법 conduct 실시[수행]하다 research 연구 export 수출하다 collaborate 협력하다

해설 세부 사항 관련 – 화자가 말하는 회사가 한 일

화자가 중반부에 우리 연구원들은 놀라운 충격 완화와 지지를 제공하는 오래 가는 밑창을 만들기 위해 새로운 제작 방식을 개발했다(Our researchers developed a new manufacturing method to create durable soles that provide amazing cushioning and support)고 했으므로 정답은 (A)이다.

▸▸ **Paraphrasing** 담화의 **developed a new manufacturing method** → 정답의 **invented a production technique**

76

What will happen on December 4 ?

(A) A new store branch will open.
(B) A sales promotion will begin.
(C) New products will be launched.
(D) The winner of a contest will be chosen.

12월 4일에 무슨 일이 일어날 것인가?
(A) 새로운 매장이 문을 열 것이다.
(B) 판촉 행사가 시작될 것이다.
(C) 신제품이 출시될 것이다.
(D) 대회의 승자가 선택될 것이다.

어휘 branch 지점 promotion 판촉[홍보]

해설 세부 사항 관련 – 12월 4일에 일어날 일
화자가 후반부에 12월 4일과 5일에, 우리는 특별 판매 행사와 함께 카나한 슈즈의 출시 1주년을 기념할 예정이다(December fourth and fifth, we'll be celebrating the one-year anniversary of the launch of Carnahan Shoes with a special sales event)고 했으므로 정답은 (B)이다.

77-79 전화 메시지

> W-Am Hi Mr. Cha. **⁷⁷This is Jody at Melting Moon Grill calling about your upcoming party for your colleague's promotion. ⁷⁸Our host said you left a message to ask if it would be all right to change your reservation from ten to fifteen people. That will be just fine.** We'll still be able to provide our special chocolate cake for everyone. ⁷⁹**Oh, and when we spoke before, you mentioned that your colleague likes live music, right?** Well, we just booked a band for that night. You can see information about them on our Web site. OK, call me back if you have any other questions or concerns.

> 여보세요 차 선생님. 곧 있을 동료 승진 축하 파티 건으로 전화드리는 멜팅 문 그릴의 조디입니다. 10명에서 15명으로 예약을 변경해도 괜찮은지 문의하려고 메시지를 남기셨다고 저희 사장님께서 말씀하시더라고요. 문제없습니다. 모든 분들을 위해 우리 특별 초콜릿 케이크도 제공해 드릴 수 있고요. 아, 전에 말씀 나눴을 때, 동료분이 라이브 뮤직을 좋아한다고 말씀하셨죠? 그날 밤을 위해 밴드를 막 예약했습니다. 그들에 대한 정보는 저희 웹사이트에서 확인하실 수 있으세요. 그럼, 다른 문의 사항이나 걱정되시는 점이 있으면 전화 주세요.

어휘 upcoming 다가오는 colleague 동료 promotion 승진 host 주인, 주최측 reservation 예약

77

What will the listener hold a party to celebrate?

(A) A marriage anniversary
(B) A retirement
(C) A promotion
(D) A birthday

청자는 무엇을 기념하려고 파티를 여는가?
(A) 결혼 기념일
(B) 은퇴
(C) 승진
(D) 생일

해설 세부 사항 관련 – 청자가 파티를 열어 기념하려는 것
화자가 초반부에 곧 있을 동료 승진 축하 파티 건으로 전화드리는 멜팅 문 그릴의 조디(This is Jody at Melting Moon Grill calling about your upcoming party for your colleague's promotion)라고 한 것으로 보아 청자는 동료의 승진 축하 파티를 계획하고 있음을 알 수 있다. 따라서 정답은 (C)이다.

78

What does the speaker confirm a change to?

(A) The menu for a celebration
(B) The theme of some decorations
(C) The time of a reservation
(D) The size of a group

화자는 무엇에 대한 변경을 확인해주는가?
(A) 기념행사를 위한 메뉴
(B) 장식의 주제
(C) 예약 시간
(D) 그룹의 규모

어휘 celebration 기념 행사 theme 주제 decoration (실내) 장식

해설 세부 사항 관련 – 화자가 변경을 확인해준 사항
화자가 초반부에 청자가 10명에서 15명으로 예약을 변경해도 괜찮은지 문의하러 메시지를 남겼다고 자신의 사장님이 말했다(Our host said you left a message to ask if it would be all right to change your reservation from ten to fifteen people)라고 하면서 문제없다(That will be just fine)고 확인해주고 있으므로 정답은 (D)이다.

---

79   고난도

What does the speaker imply when she says, "we just booked a band for that night"?

(A) A preference has been accommodated.
(B) An additional charge will be imposed.
(C) A seating arrangement must be modified.
(D) Some noise at a venue is inevitable.

화자가 "그날 밤을 위해 밴드를 막 예약했습니다"라고 말한 의미는 무엇인가?
(A) 희망 사항이 수용되었다.
(B) 추가 요금이 부과될 것이다.
(C) 좌석 배치가 수정되어야 한다.
(D) 장소에서의 소음이 불가피하다.

어휘 preference 선호(되는 것) accommodate 수용하다 impose 부과하다 modify 수정하다 venue 장소 inevitable 불가피한

해설 화자의 의도 파악 – 그날 밤을 위해 밴드를 막 예약했다는 말의 의도
앞에서 전에 말씀 나눴을 때, 동료분이 라이브 뮤직을 좋아한다고 말한 것이 맞는지(when we spoke before, you mentioned that your colleague likes live music, right?) 물으면서 인용문에서 밴드를 예약했다고 했으므로 청자가 바라던 사항을 수용하기 위한 조치를 취했음을 알리려는 의도로 볼 수 있다. 따라서 정답은 (A)이다.

80-82 방송

> M-Au UFM Radio fans, we need your help! This month, we are carrying out a survey of our regular listeners to find out who you are and what you're interested in. **80The information you provide will enable us to draw in the brand-name advertisers we need to continue broadcasting all of your favorite UFM shows.** **81To participate, either go to www.ufmradio.com/survey, or text "Survey" to 555-0182 to receive a text-message version.** That's www.ufmradio.com/survey or texting "Survey" to 555-0182. **82Everyone who fills out the entire survey will be entered into a drawing for a chance to visit our station and meet our DJs.** You might even see a famous musician while you're here! Do the survey today to secure your chance to win.

UFM 라디오 애청자 여러분, 여러분의 도움이 필요합니다! 이번 달에, 저희가 여러분이 누구이고 무엇에 관심이 있으신지를 알고자 애청자 분들께 설문 조사를 합니다. 여러분께 제공해주시는 정보로 저희가 여러분들이 아끼시는 모든 UFM 방송을 계속하는 데 필요한 유명 브랜드 광고주들을 끌어일 수 있습니다. 참여하시려면 www.ufmradio.com/survey를 방문하시거나, 문자 메시지를 받으시려면 555-0182번으로 "설문 조사"라고 문자를 보내주세요. www.ufmradio.com/survey 혹은 555-0182번으로 "설문 조사" 문자입니다. 설문지 전체를 작성해주시는 모든 분들은 저희 방송국을 방문해 DJ들을 만날 기회를 위한 추첨 행사에 응모됩니다. 여기 계시는 동안 유명 뮤지션을 보실 수도 있습니다! 오늘 설문 조사에 참여하시고 당첨될 기회를 획득하세요.

어휘 carry out 수행하다 survey 설문 조사 enable 가능하게 하다 draw 끌어들이다 advertiser 광고주 fill out 작성하다 entire 전체의 drawing 추첨 secure 획득[확보]하다

80

What will the survey results be used for?

(A) Making an expansion decision
(B) Developing new programs
(C) Attracting advertisers
(D) Planning in-person events

설문 조사 결과는 무엇에 사용될 것인가?
(A) 확장 결정
(B) 새 프로그램 개발
(C) 광고주 모집
(D) 생생한 이벤트 기획

어휘 expansion 확장 decision 결정 in-person 직접의, 생생한

해설 세부 사항 관련 – 설문 조사 결과의 용도

화자가 초반부에 여러분이 제공하는 정보로 여러분이 아끼는 모든 UFM 방송을 계속하는 데 필요한 유명 브랜드 광고주들을 끌어일 수 있다(The information you provide will enable us to draw in the brand-name advertisers we need to continue broadcasting all of your favorite UFM shows)라고 했으므로 정답은 (C)이다.

> ▸▸ **Paraphrasing** 담화의 **draw in ~ advertisers**
> → 정답의 **attract advertisers**

81   고난도

What does the speaker say about the survey?

(A) It is targeted toward listeners of a certain age.
(B) It only has multiple choice questions.
(C) There are two ways to access it.
(D) The station has conducted it before.

화자는 설문 조사에 대해 무엇을 말하는가?
(A) 특정 연령의 청취자들을 대상으로 한다.
(B) 객관식 질문만 있다.
(C) 조사에 참여하는 데는 두 가지 방법이 있다.
(D) 방송국이 전에 실시한 적이 있다.

어휘 target 목표로 삼다 certain 확실한, 어떤 multiple 많은 access 접근하다 conduct 실시[수행]하다

해설 세부 사항 관련 – 화자가 설문 조사에 대해 말하는 것

화자가 중반부에 참여하시려면 www.ufmradio.com/survey를 방문하거나, 문자 메시지를 받으려면 555-0182번으로 "설문 조사"라고 문자를 보내라(To participate, either go to www.ufmradio.com/survey, or text "Survey" to 555-0182 to receive a text-message version)라고 했으므로 정답은 (C)이다.

82

What will survey participants have the chance to win?

(A) A cash prize
(B) Concert tickets
(C) Branded merchandise
(D) A station tour

설문 조사 참여자들은 무엇에 당첨될 기회가 있는가?
(A) 상금
(B) 콘서트 입장권
(C) 유명 상표 제품
(D) 방송국 관람

어휘 cash prize 상금 branded 유명 상표의 merchandise 상품

해설 세부 사항 관련 – 설문 조사 참여자들이 당첨될 기회가 있는 것

화자가 후반부에 설문지 전체를 작성하는 모든 분들은 저희 방송국을 방문해 DJ들을 만날 기회를 위한 추첨행사에 응모된다(Everyone who fills out the entire survey will be entered into a drawing for a chance to visit our station and meet our DJs)라고 했으므로 정답은 (D)이다.

W-Br Welcome to today's workshop. **83As you know, I've been invited to your offices to discuss ethical issues that you might encounter in your role as city employees.** We'll talk about types of issues, relevant laws and regulations, and possible resolutions. **84Now, some of you might be thinking, "I'm just an entry-level employee—am I really likely to face an ethical issue?"** Well, <u>you'd be surprised</u>. So I hope that you'll all take this workshop seriously and participate wholeheartedly. **85OK, I'd like to start by sharing with you a real experience that happened to a participant in a workshop I gave last year.**

오늘 워크숍에 오신 것을 환영합니다. 아시다시피, 저는 여러분이 시 공무원으로서 역할을 하면서 맞닥뜨릴 수 있는 윤리 문제를 논의하도록 이곳에 초청받았습니다. 우리는 문제의 유형과 관련 법규 및 규정, 그리고 가능한 해결책에 대해 이야기할 겁니다. 자, 여러분 중 일부는 "나는 그저 말단 직원일 뿐인데 정말 윤리 문제에 직면할 가능성이 있을까?"라고 생각할 수도 있습니다. 글쎄요, 여러분은 놀라실 겁니다. 그러니 저는 여러분 모두가 이 워크숍을 진지하게 받아들이고 성실하게 참여하시길 바랍니다. 자, 제가 작년에 했던 워크숍 참가자에게 일어났던 실제 경험을 여러분과 공유하면서 시작하죠.

어휘 ethical 윤리적인 encounter 맞닥뜨리다 relevant 관련 있는 regulation 규정 resolution 해결 entry-level 말단인 face 직면하다 seriously 진지하게 participate 참여하다 wholeheartedly 성실하게, 진심으로 participant 참가자

83

Where most likely is the workshop taking place?
(A) At a bank
(B) At a law firm
(C) At a government office
(D) At an accounting company

워크숍은 어디에서 열리고 있을 것 같은가?
(A) 은행
(B) 법률 사무소
(C) 관공서
(D) 회계 법인

해설 세부 사항 관련 – 워크숍이 열리고 있는 장소
화자가 초반부에 여러분이 시 공무원으로서 역할을 하면서 맞닥뜨릴 수 있는 윤리 문제를 논의하도록 이곳에 초청받았다(As you know, I've been invited to your offices to discuss ethical issues that you might encounter in your role as city employees)라고 했으므로 청자들 즉, 공무원들의 근무지에서 워크숍이 열리고 있음을 알 수 있다. 따라서 정답은 (C)이다.

84
고난도

What does the speaker mean when she says, "you'd be surprised"?
(A) Some problems happen frequently.
(B) Some conflicts have already been resolved.
(C) Some mistakes have serious consequences.
(D) Some errors are easy to prevent.

화자가 "여러분은 놀라실 겁니다"라고 말한 의도는 무엇인가?
(A) 어떤 문제가 자주 발생한다.
(B) 어떤 갈등이 이미 해결되었다.
(C) 어떤 실수들은 심각한 결과를 초래한다.
(D) 어떤 오류는 예방하기 쉽다.

어휘 frequently 자주 conflict 갈등[충돌] resolve 해결하다 consequence 결과 prevent 예방하다

해설 화자의 의도 파악 – 여러분은 놀라실 겁니다라는 말의 의도
앞에서 화자가 여러분 중 일부는 "나는 그저 말단 직원일 뿐인데 정말 윤리 문제에 직면할 가능성이 있을까?"라고 생각할 수도 있다(some of you might be thinking, "I'm just an entry-level employee—am I really likely to face an ethical issue?")고 한 뒤 인용문에서 놀라게 될 것이라고 한 것으로 보아, 윤리 문제를 접할 일이 드물다고 생각하는 데 대한 반전의 의미로 한 말로 볼 수 있다. 따라서 정답은 (A)이다.

85
고난도

What does the speaker say she will do next?
(A) Tell a true story
(B) Give a short quiz
(C) Pass out an agenda
(D) Begin a slide show

화자는 그녀가 다음에 무엇을 하겠다고 말하는가?
(A) 실화를 이야기한다.
(B) 짧은 문제를 낸다.
(C) 안건을 배포하다.
(D) 슬라이드 쇼를 시작한다.

어휘 pass out 나눠주다 agenda 안건[의제]

해설 세부 사항 관련 – 화자가 다음에 하겠다고 말한 것
화자가 마지막에 자신이 작년에 했던 워크숍 참가자에게 일어났던 실제 경험을 여러분과 공유하면서 시작하겠다(I'd like to start by sharing with you a real experience that happened to a participant in a workshop I gave last year)라고 했으므로 정답은 (A)이다.

▸▸ Paraphrasing 담화의 **share with you a real experience** → 정답의 **tell a true story**

M-Cn Anna, it's Jessie. Mr. Stout just called about our bid for the landscaping project at his office. He says that Crinton Landscaping offered to do it for twelve thousand dollars. That's six hundred dollars less than what we proposed. But Mr. Stout would like to hire us if we can match that price. **86 Will you authorize me to revise our bid?** I think it's a good idea. **87 The project does require using some unusual plants and stones, but not much labor.** We could still make a profit from it. **88 Call me back as soon as you decide, because Mr. Stout wants to get started and will go with Crinton Landscaping if we take too long to respond.** Thanks.

안나, 저 제시예요. 스타우트 씨가 본인 사무실의 조경 프로젝트에 대한 우리 입찰과 관련해서 전화했는데요. 크린튼 조경이 1만 2천 달러에 일을 하겠다고 제안했다고 해요. 우리가 제안한 것보다 6백 달러나 낮은 가격이에요. 그런데 스타우트 씨는 우리가 그 가격에 맞출 수 있으면 우리를 고용하고 싶다는군요. **우리 입찰을 제가 수정하도록 허용해주시겠어요?** 저는 괜찮은 생각 같아요. **이 프로젝트는 특이한 식물과 돌들을 사용해야 하지만, 작업량은 많지 않아서요.** 여전히 수익을 낼 수 있을 거에요. **결정하시면 바로 전화 주세요. 스타우트 씨가 바로 착수하기 바라는 데다가 우리 답변이 너무 오래 걸리면 크린튼 조경과 일을 진행할 거라서요.** 감사합니다.

어휘 bid 입찰; 입찰하다 landscaping 조경 propose 제안하다 match 맞추다, 일치하다 authorize 인가하다 revise 수정하다 unusual 특이한 labor 노동 profit 이익

86

What is the purpose of the message?

(A) To offer a referral
(B) To ask for approval
(C) To apologize for a delay
(D) To answer a question

메시지의 목적은 무엇인가?

(A) 소개 제공
(B) 승인에 대한 요청
(C) 지연에 대한 사과
(D) 질문에 대한 응답

어휘 referral 보내기[소개] approval 승인 delay 지연

해설 전체 내용 관련 – 메시지의 목적

화자가 초반부에서 입찰에 대한 진행 상황을 설명한 뒤, 중반부에 우리 입찰을 본인이 수정하도록 허용해주겠는지(Will you authorize me to revise our bid?) 묻는 것으로 보아 정답은 (B)이다.

▸▸ **Paraphrasing** 담화의 **authorize me to ~** → 정답의 **approval**

87

What does the speaker say about a landscaping project?

(A) It will lead to other work opportunities.
(B) It involves special materials.
(C) It has been postponed.
(D) It requires several permits.

화자는 조경 프로젝트에 대해 무엇을 말하는가?

(A) 다른 작업 기회로 이어질 것이다.
(B) 특별한 재료가 포함된다.
(C) 연기되었다.
(D) 여러 개의 허가증이 필요하다.

어휘 lead to ~로 이어지다 opportunity 기회 involve 포함하다 material 재료 permit 허가증

해설 세부 사항 관련 – 화자가 조경 프로젝트에 대해 말하는 것

화자가 중반부에 이 프로젝트는 특이한 식물과 돌들을 사용해야 하지만 작업량은 많지 않다(The project does require using some unusual plants and stones, but not much labor)고 했으므로 정답은 (B)이다.

▸▸ **Paraphrasing** 담화의 **require using unusual plants and stones** → 정답의 **involves special materials**

88 [고난도]

What does the speaker say will happen if the listener does not act quickly?

(A) Seasonal weather will become a problem.
(B) Discounted prices will no longer be available.
(C) A potential customer will hire a competitor.
(D) A property may fail an inspection.

화자는 청자가 빨리 행동하지 않으면 무슨 일이 일어날 거라고 말하는가?

(A) 계절에 따른 날씨가 문제가 될 것이다.
(B) 할인된 가격은 더 이상 가능하지 않을 것이다.
(C) 잠재 고객이 경쟁사를 고용할 것이다.
(D) 건물이 검사에 통과하지 못 할 수 있다.

어휘 seasonal 계절적인 available 이용 가능한 potential 잠재적인 competitor 경쟁자 property 건물, 부동산 inspection 점검[검사]

해설 세부 사항 관련 – 청자가 빨리 행동하지 않으면 일어날 것이라고 화자가 말한 것

화자가 후반부에 스타우트 씨가 바로 착수하길 바라는 데다가 우리 답변이 너무 오래 걸리면 크린튼 조경과 일을 진행할 것이므로 청자가 결정하는 즉시 전화해달라(Call me back as soon as you decide, because Mr. Stout wants to get started and will go with Crinton Landscaping if we take too long to respond)고 했으므로 정답은 (C)이다.

W-Am **89Thank you all again for joining the Stoneville Farm Show as temporary event staff this week.** Starting today, you'll help us showcase the latest innovations in growing crops and raising livestock. I hope that by now, you're all clear on your duties—answering visitor questions, assisting exhibitors, reporting problems through your two-way radio. **90Please be accessible to attendees but also stay out of the way, so that they can circulate easily.** Uh, Hall C in particular gets a lot of foot traffic. So staff there will need to be aware of that. **91Finally, don't forget to see Mr. Hayashi each day to clock in and out.** He'll be in the convention center office.

이번 주 스톤빌 농장 쇼에 임시 행사 직원으로 함께주셔서 여러분 모두에게 다시 한번 감사드립니다. 오늘부터, 여러분은 작물 재배와 가축 사육 분야의 최신 혁신 기술을 전시하는 것을 돕게 됩니다. 지금쯤 여러분의 임무는 방문객 질문에 답하기, 출품자들 보조하기, 무전기로 문제 보고하기라는 것을 명확히 알고 있길 바랍니다. 참석자들이 쉽게 다가갈 수 있도록 하시되, 통행이 순조롭도록 통로에 서 있지 않도록 하세요. 어, C홀은 특히 유동 인구가 많습니다. 그러니 그곳 직원들은 이 점을 숙지하고 있어야 합니다. 끝으로, 매일 하야시 씨를 만나 출퇴근 시간을 기록하는 것을 잊지 마세요. 그는 컨벤션 센터 사무실에 있을 겁니다.

어휘 temporary 일시적인 showcase 전시하다 innovation 혁신 crop 작물 livestock 가축 duty 직무 assist 돕다 exhibitor 출품자 two-way radio 무전기 accessible 접근 가능한 circulate 순환하다 in particular 특히 foot traffic 유동 인구 be aware of ~을 알다 clock in and out 출퇴근 시간을 기록하다

89

What industry will be featured at the trade show?
(A) Pharmaceuticals
(B) Construction
(C) Energy
(D) Agriculture

무역 박람회에 어떤 산업이 소개될 것인가?
(A) 제약
(B) 건설
(C) 에너지
(D) 농업

해설 세부 사항 관련 – 교역 박람회에서 소개될 산업
화자가 도입부에 이번 주 스톤빌 농장 쇼에 임시 행사 직원으로 함께주셔서 여러분 모두에게 다시 한번 감사드린다(Thank you all again for joining the Stoneville Farm Show as temporary event staff this week)고 한 말에서 언급된 박람회의 이름으로 보아 정답은 (D)이다.

90 [고난도]

What does the speaker imply when she says, "Hall C in particular gets a lot of foot traffic"?
(A) Hall C exhibitors paid the highest registration fee.
(B) Hall C staff should take extra care not to block the aisles.
(C) Hall C would be a good place to hand out a resource.
(D) Hall C must be cleaned more often than other halls.

화자가 "C홀은 특히 유동 인구가 많습니다"라고 말한 의도는 무엇인가?
(A) C홀 출품자들은 가장 높은 등록비를 지불했다.
(B) C홀 직원들은 통로를 막지 않도록 각별히 주의해야 한다.
(C) C홀은 자료를 나눠주기 적합한 장소이다.
(D) C홀은 다른 홀보다 더 자주 청소해야 한다.

어휘 registration fee 등록비 block 막다 aisle 통로 hand out 나눠주다 resource 자료, 자원

해설 화자의 의도 파악 – C홀은 특히 유동 인구가 많다는 말의 의도
C홀에 유동 인구가 많다는 인용문을 말하기 전에 화자가 참석자들이 쉽게 다가갈 수 있도록 하되 통행이 순조롭도록 통로에 서 있지 않도록 하라(Please be accessible to attendees but also stay out of the way, so that they can circulate easily)고 주의를 준 것으로 보아 정답은 (B)이다.

▸▸ Paraphrasing 담화의 stay out of the way
→ 정답의 not to block the aisles

91 [고난도]

Why should listeners speak to Mr. Hayashi?
(A) To have their working hours recorded
(B) To obtain a communication device
(C) To report problems on the trade show floor
(D) To be reimbursed for a travel expense

왜 청자들은 하야시 씨와 이야기해야 하는가?
(A) 근무 시간을 기록하려고
(B) 통신 장비를 구하려고
(C) 무역 박람회장의 문제를 보고하려고
(D) 출장 비용을 환급 받으려고

어휘 record 기록하다 obtain 얻다 communication device 통신장비 reimburse 변제하다 expense 비용

해설 세부 사항 관련 – 청자들이 하야시 씨와 이야기해야 하는 이유
화자가 후반부에 매일 하야시 씨를 만나 출퇴근 시간을 기록하는 것을 잊지 마라(don't forget to see Mr. Hayashi each day to clock in and out)고 한 것으로 보아 정답은 (A)이다.

▸▸ Paraphrasing 담화의 clock in and out
→ 정답의 have working hours recorded

92-94 담화

W-Br　Good evening. **92As the alumni relations manager for Welksfield University, it's my honor to welcome our graduates back to campus for tonight's dinner.** This is a chance for you to share memories of your time here and make some new ones. However, that's not the only purpose of tonight's dinner. It's also for funding scholarships awarded to current and future Welksfield students. **93Please visit the booth in the back to contribute money to this worthy cause.** All right, alumni association president Gustavo Costa will give the keynote address later this evening, **94but first, you may help yourselves to the delicious spread that the caterers are setting out on the side tables now.** Thank you.

안녕하세요. 웩스필드 대학의 동문 관계 책임자로서 오늘 밤 만찬을 위해 캠퍼스로 돌아와준 우리 졸업생들을 맞이하게 되어 영광입니다. 이 행사는 이곳에서 여러분이 보냈던 시간에 대한 추억을 함께하고 새로운 추억들을 만들기 위한 기회입니다. 하지만, 이것만이 오늘 밤 만찬의 유일한 목적은 아닙니다. 현재와 미래의 웩스필드 학생들에게 수여되는 장학금 기금 조성을 위한 자리이기도 합니다. 뒤쪽에 마련된 부스를 방문하셔서 훌륭한 대의를 위해 돈을 기부해주세요. 자 그럼, 구스타보 코스타 동문회 회장님께서 오늘 저녁 잠시 후 기조 연설을 할 예정이지만, 먼저 음식업체에서 사이드 테이블에 지금 준비 중인 맛있는 진수성찬부터 즐기시기 바랍니다. 감사합니다.

어휘　alumni 졸업생　relation 관계　graduate 졸업생　purpose 목적　fund 자금을 대다; 자금　scholarship 장학금　award 수여하다　contribute 기부하다　worthy 훌륭한　cause 대의　association 협회　keynote address 기조 연설　spread 진수성찬　caterer 음식 공급자

92

What do the listeners most likely have in common?

(A) They studied at the same university.
(B) They hold the same type of job.
(C) They work for the same employer.
(D) They support the same sports team.

청자들의 공통점은 무엇일 것 같은가?
(A) 같은 대학교에서 공부했다.
(B) 직업의 종류가 같다.
(C) 같은 고용주를 위해 일한다.
(D) 같은 스포츠 팀을 응원한다.

어휘　employer 고용주　support 지지하다

해설　세부 사항 관련 - 청자들의 공통점
화자가 담화 초반부에 웩스필드 대학의 동문 관계 책임자로서 오늘 밤 만찬을 위해 캠퍼스로 돌아와준 우리 졸업생들을 맞이하게 되어 영광(As the alumni relations manager for Welksfield University, it's my honor to welcome our graduates back to campus for tonight's dinner)이라고 했으므로 청자들은 웩스필드 대학의 졸업생들임을 알 수 있다. 따라서 정답은 (A)이다.

93

What does the speaker encourage listeners to do?

(A) Stop by a photo booth
(B) Make a financial donation
(C) Join a regional association
(D) Cast a vote

화자는 청자들이 무엇을 하도록 권하는가?
(A) 사진 부스에 들르는 것
(B) 재정적인 기부를 할 것
(C) 지역 연합에 가입할 것
(D) 투표할 것

어휘　financial 금융[재정]의　donation 기부　cast a vote 투표하다

해설　세부 사항 관련 - 화자가 청자들에게 하라고 권하는 것
화자가 중반부에 뒤쪽에 마련된 부스를 방문해 훌륭한 대의를 위해 돈을 기부하라(Please visit the booth in the back to contribute money to this worthy cause)라고 권유했으므로 정답은 (B)이다.

▸▸ **Paraphrasing**　담화의 **contribute money**
　　　　　　　　　→ 정답의 **make a financial donation**

94

What will take place next?

(A) A keynote speech
(B) An award ceremony
(C) A dance performance
(D) A buffet meal

다음에 무슨 일이 있을 것인가?
(A) 기조 연설
(B) 시상식
(C) 댄스 공연
(D) 뷔페 식사

어휘　ceremony 기념식　buffet 뷔페

해설　세부 사항 관련 - 다음에 일어날 일
화자가 후반부에 구스타보 코스타 동문회 회장이 오늘 저녁 잠시 후 기조 연설을 할 예정이지만, 먼저 음식업체에서 사이드 테이블에 지금 준비 중인 맛있는 진수성찬부터 즐기기 바란다(alumni association president Gustavo Costa will give the keynote address later this evening, but first, you may help yourselves to the delicious spread that the caterers are setting out on the side tables now)고 했으므로 청자들은 뒤이어 식사를 할 것임을 알 수 있다. 따라서 정답은 (D)이다.

M-Au Hi, Carl. ⁹⁵**Thanks for putting together the list of options for replacing the meeting room table**. I'm looking over your e-mail now, and ⁹⁶**I think we should avoid the two widest ones.** I know that it was my idea to look into them, but I've changed my mind. We don't want clients to feel crowded. I think it would be better to buy a smaller table and just put chairs in the corners if needed. Uh, and the seven-foot-long table isn't very attractive, in my opinion. ⁹⁶**So I like the six-foot-long option the best.** ⁹⁷**Please go ahead and order it when you get into work tomorrow.** Then we can talk about removing the old one.

여보세요, 칼. 회의실 탁자 교체를 위한 선택안 목록을 만들어주셔서 고마워요. 보내주신 이메일을 지금 보고 있는데, 가장 넓은 것 두 개는 피해야 할 것 같아요. 제가 그것들을 살펴보자고 한 건 알지만, 생각이 바뀌었어요. 고객들이 비좁다고 느끼지 않았으면 해요. 작은 탁자를 구입하고, 필요할 경우 모퉁이에 의자들을 두는 게 더 좋을 것 같아요. 아, 그리고 제 생각엔 7피트 길이의 탁자는 그다지 매력적이지 않아 보이네요. 그래서 6피트 길이 탁자가 가장 마음에 들어요. 내일 출근하시면 그걸로 주문하세요. 그러고 나서 기존 탁자를 치우는 것에 대해 이야기하도록 해요.

어휘 put together 만들다 option 선택(권) replace 교체하다 avoid 피하다 crowded 복잡한 attractive 매력적인 opinion 의견 go ahead 진행하다 order 주문하다 remove 치우다

	Width x Length
⁹⁶Table 1	4 ft. x 6 ft.
Table 2	4 ft. x 7 ft.
Table 3	6 ft. x 6 ft.
Table 4	7 ft. x 7 ft.

	폭 x 길이
⁹⁶탁자 1	4피트 x 6피트
탁자 2	4피트 x 7피트
탁자 3	6피트 x 6피트
탁자 4	7피트 x 7피트

95
Where will a new table be placed?
(A) In a patio
(B) In a lobby
(C) In a dining room
(D) In a conference room

새 탁자는 어디에 놓일 것인가?
(A) 테라스
(B) 로비
(C) 식당
(D) 회의실

해설 세부 사항 관련 – 새 탁자가 놓일 장소
화자가 초반부에 회의실 탁자 교체를 위한 선택안 목록을 만들어줘서 고맙다(Thanks for putting together the list of options for replacing the meeting room table)고 했으므로 정답은 (D)이다.

▸▸ Paraphrasing 담화의 meeting room → 정답의 conference room

96
Look at the graphic. Which table does the speaker prefer?
(A) Table 1
(B) Table 2
(C) Table 3
(D) Table 4

시각 정보에 의하면, 화자는 어느 탁자를 선호하는가?
(A) 탁자 1
(B) 탁자 2
(C) 탁자 3
(D) 탁자 4

해설 시각 정보 연계 – 화자가 선호하는 탁자
화자는 초반부에 청자가 보낸 이메일을 지금 보고 있는데, 가장 넓은 것 두 개는 피해야 할 것 같다(I'm looking over your e-mail now, and I think we should avoid the two widest ones)고 했고, 후반부에 6피트 길이 탁자가 가장 마음에 든다(I like the six-foot-long option the best)고 했다. 시각 정보에 따르면, 가장 넓은 것 두 개(6피트, 7피트)를 제외한 나머지 중 길이가 6피트인 것은 탁자 1이므로 정답은 (A)이다.

97
What does the speaker ask the listener to do?
(A) Place a purchase order
(B) Read a reply e-mail
(C) Arrange a furniture removal
(D) Verify the space's measurements

화자는 청자에게 무엇을 하라고 요청하는가?
(A) 구매 주문을 할 것
(B) 답신 이메일을 읽을 것
(C) 가구 철거를 처리할 것
(D) 공간의 치수를 확인할 것

어휘 purchase 구매 arrange 마련[처리]하다 removal 제거 verify 확인하다 measurement 치수, 측정

해설 세부 사항 관련 – 화자가 청자에게 하라고 요청한 것
화자가 후반부에 내일 출근하면 그걸로 주문하라(Please go ahead and order it when you get into work tomorrow)고 했으므로 정답은 (A)이다.

▸▸ Paraphrasing 담화의 order → 정답의 place a purchase order

M-Cn Good morning, everyone. The reason I've asked you all to come in a little early is to see the final design of our new parking pass. **98 I'm happy to say that the graphic designer listened to your input on how she could make it easier for you to check whether vehicles in the parking area belong there.** Here's the sample pass that she made. **99 As you can see, the information on the third line is larger than it was before.** I think it's much better now. **100 The background is also a lighter shade of silver than the previous design so that all of the text is more visible.** It looks good, doesn't it?

안녕하세요, 여러분. 제가 여러분 모두를 조금 일찍 오시라고 한 이유는 새로운 주차권의 최종 디자인을 보기 위해서입니다. 차량이 해당 주차 구역에 속하는지 좀 더 쉽게 확인할 수 있는 방안에 대한 여러분의 의견을 그래픽 디자이너가 반영했다는 것을 말씀드리게 되어 기쁩니다. 여기 그녀가 만든 견본 주차권이 있습니다. 보시다시피, 세 번째 줄의 정보가 이전보다 더 커졌습니다. 지금이 훨씬 나은 것 같습니다. 글자가 더 선명해 보이도록 바탕색도 이전 디자인보다 더 밝은 계열의 은색입니다. 좋아 보이네요, 그렇죠?

어휘 reason 이유 parking pass 주차권 input 조언 vehicle 차량 background 배경 shade 색조 previous 이전의 visible 뚜렷한

98

Who most likely are the listeners?

(A) Delivery drivers
(B) Graphic designers
(C) Parking attendants
(D) Senior executives

청자들은 누구일 것 같은가?
(A) 배송 기사
(B) 그래픽 디자이너
(C) 주차 요원
(D) 고위 간부

해설 전체 내용 관련 – 청자들의 직업
화자가 초반부에 차량이 해당 주차 구역에 속하는지 좀 더 쉽게 확인할 수 있는 방안에 대한 여러분의 의견을 그래픽 디자이너가 반영했다는 것을 말씀드리게 되어 기쁘다(I'm happy to say that the graphic designer listened to your input on how she could make it easier for you to check whether vehicles in the parking area belong there)고 한 것으로 보아 청자들은 주차장에서 근무하고 있음을 알 수 있다. 따라서 정답은 (C)이다.

99

Look at the graphic. Which piece of information looked different before?

(A) The company name
(B) The pass type
(C) The pass number
(D) The expiration date

시각 정보에 의하면, 어느 부분의 정보가 예전에 달랐는가?
(A) 회사명
(B) 주차권 유형
(C) 주차권 번호
(D) 만기일

어휘 expiration 만기

해설 시각 정보 연계 – 예전과 달라진 정보

화자가 중반부에 보시다시피 세 번째 줄의 정보가 이전보다 더 커졌다(As you can see, the information on the third line is larger than it was before)고 했고, 시각 정보에서 세 번째 줄에는 #011923이라는 주차권 번호가 표기되어 있으므로 정답은 (C)이다.

100 고난도

What does the speaker mention about an earlier design?

(A) It featured an image.
(B) It was a darker color.
(C) It included additional text.
(D) It made use of a heavier material.

화자는 이전 디자인에 대해 무엇을 언급하는가?
(A) 이미지가 들어 있었다.
(B) 색이 더 어두웠다.
(C) 추가 문구가 있었다.
(D) 더 무거운 재료를 사용했다.

어휘 feature 특징으로 삼다, 특별히 포함하다 include 포함하다
       additional 추가의   material 재료

해설 세부 사항 관련 – 화자가 이전 디자인에 대해 언급한 것

화자가 후반부에 글자가 더 선명해 보이도록 바탕색도 이전 디자인보다 더 밝은 계열의 은색(The background is also a lighter shade of silver than the previous design so that all of the text is more visible)이라고 언급했으므로 정답은 (B)이다.

TEST 3

1 (C)	2 (C)	3 (A)	4 (D)	5 (B)
6 (C)	7 (A)	8 (C)	9 (A)	10 (A)
11 (C)	12 (B)	13 (B)	14 (B)	15 (A)
16 (B)	17 (C)	18 (C)	19 (C)	20 (A)
21 (C)	22 (B)	23 (A)	24 (A)	25 (C)
26 (C)	27 (B)	28 (B)	29 (A)	30 (B)
31 (A)	32 (C)	33 (A)	34 (C)	35 (A)
36 (C)	37 (C)	38 (D)	39 (C)	40 (B)
41 (B)	42 (D)	43 (A)	44 (D)	45 (D)
46 (B)	47 (D)	48 (C)	49 (A)	50 (A)
51 (D)	52 (B)	53 (A)	54 (B)	55 (C)
56 (C)	57 (B)	58 (C)	59 (B)	60 (A)
61 (C)	62 (D)	63 (B)	64 (A)	65 (B)
66 (C)	67 (D)	68 (A)	69 (B)	70 (B)
71 (D)	72 (A)	73 (D)	74 (C)	75 (B)
76 (A)	77 (B)	78 (C)	79 (D)	80 (B)
81 (A)	82 (A)	83 (B)	84 (D)	85 (B)
86 (C)	87 (B)	88 (B)	89 (D)	90 (A)
91 (D)	92 (C)	93 (D)	94 (D)	95 (A)
96 (D)	97 (A)	98 (C)	99 (A)	100 (C)

Test 3

PART 1

1 M-Cn

(A) The woman is searching in a backpack.
(B) The woman is cleaning a bottle.
(C) The woman is exploring an exhibition.
(D) The woman is standing in front of a ticket window.

(A) 여자는 배낭을 뒤지고 있다.
(B) 여자는 병을 세척하고 있다.
(C) 여자는 전시회를 답사하고 있다.
(D) 여자는 매표 창구 앞에 서 있다.

어휘 backpack 배낭 explore 답사하다 exhibition 전시회

해설 1인 등장 사진 – 인물의 동작 묘사
(A) 동사 오답. 여자가 배낭을 뒤지고 있는(is searching in a backpack) 모습이 아니므로 오답.
(B) 동사 오답. 여자가 병을 세척하고 있는(is cleaning a bottle) 모습이 아니므로 오답.
(C) 정답. 여자가 전시회를 답사하고 있는(is exploring an exhibition) 모습이므로 정답.
(D) 동사 오답. 여자가 매표 창구 앞에 서 있는(is standing in front of a ticket window) 모습이 아니므로 오답.

2 W-Am

(A) They're placing dishes in a sink.
(B) They're bending over an oven.
(C) They're looking at a piece of paper.
(D) They're stacking some clipboards.

(A) 사람들은 싱크대에 접시를 놓고 있다.
(B) 사람들은 오븐 위로 몸을 굽히고 있다.
(C) 사람들은 서류를 보고 있다.
(D) 사람들은 클립보드를 쌓고 있다.

어휘 place 놓다; 장소 sink 싱크대 bend 굽히다, 숙이다 stack 쌓다; 무더기

해설 2인 이상 등장 사진 – 인물의 동작 묘사
(A) 동사 오답. 사람들이 싱크대에 접시를 놓고 있는(are placing dishes in a sink) 모습이 아니므로 오답.
(B) 동사 오답. 사람들이 오븐 위로 몸을 굽히고 있는(are bending over an oven) 모습이 아니므로 오답.
(C) 정답. 사람들이 서류를 보고 있는(are looking at a piece of paper) 모습이므로 정답.
(D) 동사 오답. 사람들이 클립보드를 쌓고 있는(are stacking some clipboards) 모습이 아니므로 오답.

3 M-Au

(A) There is a line of customers in a store.
(B) Produce has fallen onto the floor.
(C) A cashier is handing a bag to a man.
(D) A woman is reaching out to touch a screen.

(A) 손님들이 가게에 한 줄로 서 있다.
(B) 농산물이 바닥에 떨어졌다.
(C) 계산원이 남자에게 가방을 건네주고 있다.
(D) 여자가 스크린을 만지려고 손을 뻗고 있다.

어휘 produce 농산물; 생산하다 hand 건네주다 reach out (손 등을) 뻗다

해설 혼합 사진 – 사람 또는 사물 묘사
(A) 정답. 한 줄로 늘어선 손님들이(a line of customers)이 가게에(in a store) 있는 모습이므로 정답.
(B) 동사 오답. 농산물(produce)이 바닥에 떨어져 있는(has fallen onto the floor) 모습이 보이지 않으므로 오답.
(C) 동사 오답. 계산원(a cashier)이 남자에게 가방을 건네주고 있는(is handing a bag to a man) 모습이 아니므로 오답.

(D) 동사 오답. 스크린을 만지려고 손을 뻗고 있는(is reaching out to touch a screen) 여자의 모습이 보이지 않으므로 오답.

4 W-Br 　　　　　고난도

(A) A farmer is operating some machinery.
(B) A gardener is watering some plants.
(C) Some tree branches are being trimmed.
(D) A rake is being used in a field.

(A) 농부가 기계를 작동시키고 있다.
(B) 원예사가 식물에 물을 주고 있다.
(C) 나뭇가지들이 손질되고 있다.
(D) 뜰에서 갈퀴가 사용되고 있다.

어휘　operate 작동하다　machinery 기계(류)　gardener 원예사
　　　plant 식물　branch 나뭇가지　trim 다듬다, 손질하다　rake 갈퀴

해설　혼합 사진 – 사람 또는 사물 묘사
(A) 사진에 없는 명사를 이용한 오답. 사진에 기계(machinery)의 모습이 보이지 않으므로 오답.
(B) 동사 오답. 원예사(a gardener)가 식물에 물을 주고 있는(is watering some plants) 모습이 아니므로 오답.
(C) 동사 오답. 나뭇가지들(tree branches)이 손질되고 있는(are being trimmed) 모습이 아니므로 오답.
(D) 정답. 갈퀴(a rake)가 뜰에서(in a field) 사용되고 있는(is being used) 모습이 보이므로 정답.

5 M-Cn

(A) Some people are sitting in an auditorium.
(B) Some chairs have been arranged around a table.
(C) One of the women is pointing at a bookcase.
(D) The curtains in a conference room have been closed.

(A) 사람들이 강당에 앉아 있다.
(B) 의자 몇 개가 탁자 주위에 놓여 있다.
(C) 여자들 중 한 명이 책장을 가리키고 있다.
(D) 회의실의 커튼들이 닫혀 있다.

어휘　auditorium 강당　arrange 배열하다　point at ~을 가리키다
　　　bookcase 책장　conference room 회의실

해설　혼합 사진 – 사람 또는 사물 묘사
(A) 위치 표현 오답. 사람들이 앉아 있는(are sitting) 곳이 강당(an auditorium)이 아니므로 오답.
(B) 정답. 의자들이(chairs)가 탁자 주위에 놓여 있는(have been arranged around a table) 모습이므로 정답.
(C) 동사 오답. 여자 한 명이 책장을 가리키고 있는(is pointing at a bookcase) 모습이 아니므로 오답.
(D) 사진에 없는 명사를 이용한 오답. 사진에 커튼(curtains)의 모습이 보이지 않으므로 오답.

6 W-Am

(A) There is a large sign next to a doorway.
(B) A sofa is being moved into a café.
(C) A lamp is hanging from the ceiling.
(D) A jar has been left on a display counter.

(A) 큰 간판이 출입구 옆에 있다.
(B) 소파가 카페로 옮겨지고 있다.
(C) 조명등이 천장에 매달려 있다.
(D) 병이 진열대에 놓여 있다.

어휘　sign 간판　doorway 출입구　ceiling 천장　jar 항아리, 병
　　　display counter 진열대

해설　배경 사진 – 실내 사물의 상태 묘사
(A) 사진에 없는 명사를 이용한 오답. 사진에 큰 간판(a large sign)과 출입구(a doorway)의 모습이 보이지 않으므로 오답.
(B) 동사 오답. 소파(sofa)가 카페로 옮겨지고 있는(is being moved into a café) 모습이 아니므로 오답.
(C) 정답. 조명등(lamp)이 천장에 매달려 있는(is hanging from the ceiling) 모습이므로 정답.
(D) 사진에 없는 명사를 이용한 오답. 사진에 병(a jar)과 진열대(display counter)의 모습이 보이지 않으므로 오답.

PART 2

7
M-Cn　Could you put these books back on the shelves?
W-Br　(A) Sure, I'll do that right now.
　　　(B) Here's my library card.
　　　(C) Sorry—I meant the front of the shelves.

이 책들을 책꽂이에 다시 꽂아주시겠어요?
(A) 물론이죠, 지금 당장 할게요.
(B) 여기 제 도서관 카드요.
(C) 죄송하지만 선반 앞쪽을 말한 거였어요.

어휘 shelves (shelf의 복수) 선반

해설 부탁/요청의 의문문

(A) 정답. 책들을 책꽂이에 다시 꽂아달라고 요청하는 질문에 물론(Sure)이라고 대답한 뒤, 지금 당장 하겠다며 긍정 답변과 일관된 내용을 덧붙이고 있으므로 정답.

(B) 연상 단어 오답. 질문의 books에서 연상 가능한 library를 이용한 오답.

(C) 단어 반복 오답. 질문의 shelves를 반복 이용한 오답.

8

W-Am How long will it take to prepare the appetizers?

M-Au (A) I'd love some garlic bread.

(B) About four inches each.

(C) We'll work as fast as we can.

애피타이저를 준비하는 데 얼마나 오래 걸릴까요?

(A) 저는 마늘빵이 먹고 싶어요.

(B) 각각 약 4인치입니다.

(C) 가능한 한 빨리 해볼게요.

어휘 prepare 준비하다 appetizer 애피타이저

해설 애피타이저를 준비하는 데 걸리는 시간을 묻는 How long 의문문

(A) 연상 단어 오답. 질문의 appetizers에서 연상 가능한 garlic bread를 이용한 오답.

(B) 연상 단어 오답. 질문의 how long에서 연상 가능한 four inches를 이용한 오답.

(C) 정답. 애피타이저를 준비하는 데 걸리는 시간을 묻는 질문에 가능한 한 빨리 해보겠다고 응답하고 있으므로 정답.

9

W-Br Where's the service elevator?

M-Cn (A) Around that corner and to the left.

(B) The tenth floor, please.

(C) To improve customer satisfaction.

업무용 엘리베이터는 어디 있나요?

(A) 저 모퉁이를 돌아 왼쪽이에요.

(B) 10층 좀 눌러주세요.

(C) 고객 만족도를 높이려고요.

어휘 service elevator 종업원용 엘리베이터 satisfaction 만족

해설 종업원용 엘리베이터의 위치를 묻는 Where 의문문

(A) 정답. 종업원용 엘리베이터가 있는 위치를 묻는 질문에 모퉁이를 돌아 왼쪽에 있다고 구체적으로 알려주고 있으므로 정답.

(B) 연상 단어 오답. 질문의 elevator에서 연상 가능한 tenth floor를 이용한 오답.

(C) 연상 단어 오답. 질문의 service에서 연상 가능한 customer satisfaction을 이용한 오답.

10

M-Au Did you go on the walking tour that Ivan organized?

W-Am (A) Yes—it was quite interesting.

(B) Those files are organized by type.

(C) Some tourists from out of town.

이반이 기획한 걷기 투어에 다녀오셨나요?

(A) 네, 꽤 재미있었어요.

(B) 그 파일들은 유형별로 정리되어 있어요.

(C) 외지에서 온 관광객 몇 명이요.

어휘 organize 준비하다, 정리하다 quite 꽤

해설 걷기 투어에 다녀왔는지 여부를 확인하는 조동사(Did) 의문문

(A) 정답. 이반이 기획한 걷기 투어에 다녀왔는지 여부를 묻는 질문에 네(Yes)라고 대답한 뒤, 꽤 재미있었다며 긍정 답변과 일관된 내용을 덧붙이고 있으므로 정답.

(B) 단어 반복 오답. 질문의 organized를 반복 이용한 오답.

(C) 파생어 오답. 질문의 tour와 파생어 관계인 tourists를 이용한 오답.

11

M-Au What kind of building are you designing?

W-Br (A) In the Clancy neighborhood.

(B) A freelance architect.

(C) It's a distribution center for retail goods.

어떤 종류의 건물을 설계 중이신가요?

(A) 클랜시 근방이에요.

(B) 프리랜서 건축가요.

(C) 소매 물품을 위한 유통 센터요.

어휘 neighborhood 인근, 이웃 architect 건축가 distribution 유통 retail 소매 goods 제품

해설 설계 중인 건물의 종류를 묻는 What 의문문

(A) 질문과 상관없는 오답. Where 의문문에 대한 응답이므로 오답.

(B) 질문과 상관없는 오답. 신분을 묻는 의문문에 대한 응답이므로 오답.

(C) 정답. 설계 중인 건물의 종류가 무엇인지 묻는 질문에 소매 물품을 위한 유통 센터라고 알려주고 있으므로 정답.

12

W-Am When did we last update this software program?

M-Cn (A) No—let's find another date.

(B) Near the end of January.

(C) So that it would run faster.

우리가 마지막으로 언제 이 소프트웨어 프로그램을 업데이트했죠?

(A) 아니요, 다른 날짜를 찾아봅시다.

(B) 1월 말 즈음에요.

(C) 더 빨리 실행될 수 있도록요.

해설 소프트웨어 프로그램을 최종 업데이트한 시점을 묻는 When 의문문

(A) Yes/No 불가 오답. When 의문문에는 Yes/No 응답이 불가능하므로 오답.

(B) 정답. 소프트웨어 프로그램을 마지막으로 업데이트한 시점을 묻는 질문에 1월 말 즈음이라며 구체적인 시점으로 응답하고 있으므로 정답.

(C) 질문과 상관없는 오답. Why 의문문에 대한 응답이므로 오답.

13
고난도

M-Au Didn't you complete that training course already?

W-Am (A) I've heard the instructor is great.

(B) Well, that was a long time ago.

(C) Changes to safety procedures.

그 훈련 코스를 이미 수료하지 않았나요?
(A) 강사가 좋다고 들었어요.
(B) 음, 오래 전이었어요.
(C) 안전 절차에 대한 변경이요.

어휘 complete 완수하다 instructor 강사 safety 안전 procedure 절차

해설 코스를 수료했는지 확인하는 부정의문문

(A) 연상 단어 오답. 질문의 training course에서 연상 가능한 instructor를 이용한 오답.

(B) 정답. 그 훈련 코스를 이미 수료했는지 묻는 질문에 오래 전이었다며 Yes를 생략하고 긍정의 의미로 답하고 있으므로 정답.

(C) 질문과 상관없는 오답. What 의문문에 대한 응답이므로 오답.

14

W-Br Where did you set that big box of printer paper?

M-Cn (A) From Rimson Stationery.

(B) Oh, do you need some?

(C) I used company funds.

인쇄 용지가 든 큰 상자를 어디에 두셨죠?
(A) 림슨 문구점에서요.
(B) 오, 필요하신가요?
(C) 회사 자금을 사용했어요.

어휘 stationery 문방구, 문구류 fund 자금

해설 인쇄 용지 상자의 위치를 묻는 Where 의문문

(A) 연상 단어 오답. 질문의 printer paper에서 연상 가능한 Stationery를 이용한 오답.

(B) 정답. 인쇄 용지가 든 큰 상자를 놓아둔 위치를 묻는 질문에 필요 여부를 되묻고 있으므로 정답.

(C) 질문과 상관없는 오답.

15
고난도

W-Am Do you know how to get to the warehouse from here?

M-Cn (A) I'll just use the mapping app on my smartphone.

(B) She lives in an apartment, not a house.

(C) My brother grew up here, but moved away.

여기서 창고까지 어떻게 가는지 아세요?
(A) 저는 그냥 스마트폰에 있는 지도 앱을 사용할 거예요.
(B) 그녀는 주택이 아니라 아파트에 살아요.
(C) 제 형은 여기서 자랐지만 이사를 갔어요.

어휘 warehouse 창고

해설 창고까지 가는 길을 아는지 묻는 간접의문문

(A) 정답. 창고까지 가는 길을 아는지 묻는 질문에 자신은 그냥 스마트폰에 있는 지도 앱을 사용할 거라며 우회적으로 응답하고 있으므로 정답.

(B) 유사 발음 오답. 질문의 warehouse와 부분적으로 발음이 유사한 house를 이용한 오답.

(C) 단어 반복 오답. 질문의 here를 반복 이용한 오답.

16

M-Cn Why don't you call a taxi to take you to the airport?

W-Br (A) The flight to Hong Kong.

(B) Hmm, I suppose I'd better.

(C) He's not a tax specialist.

공항에 택시를 불러 타고 가는 게 어때요?
(A) 홍콩행 항공편이요.
(B) 흠, 그러는 게 좋겠네요.
(C) 그는 세무 전문가가 아닙니다.

어휘 flight 항공편 suppose 생각하다 tax specialist 세무전문가

해설 제안/권유의 의문문

(A) 연상 단어 오답. 질문의 airport에서 연상 가능한 flight을 이용한 오답.

(B) 정답. 공항에 택시를 불러 타고 갈 것을 제안하는 질문에 그러는 게 좋겠다며 제안에 호응하므로 정답.

(C) 유사 발음 오답. 질문의 taxi와 부분적으로 발음이 유사한 tax를 이용한 오답.

17

M-Au Do you want to sweep the aisles or set up the sale display?

W-Am (A) The display will be set up between aisles.

(B) As soon as the last shopper leaves.

(C) I don't mind either job.

통로 비질을 하실래요, 아니면 매대를 진열하시겠어요?
(A) 진열품이 통로 사이에 설치될 겁니다.
(B) 마지막 쇼핑객이 나가자마자요.
(C) 어느 일이든 상관없어요.

어휘 sweep 쓸다 aisle 통로 display 진열

해설 원하는 작업을 묻는 선택의문문

(A) 단어 반복 오답. 질문의 aisles를 반복 이용한 오답.

(B) 연상 단어 오답. 질문의 sale에서 연상 가능한 shopper를 이용한 오답.

(C) 정답. 원하는 업무를 묻는 선택의문문에서 어느 일이든 상관없다고 응답하고 있으므로 정답.

---

18 고난도

W-Br Why is Mr. Hernandez treating everyone to lunch?

M-Cn (A) I think it's launching soon.

(B) Barnette Restaurant, on Fifth Street.

(C) It's just the administrators, actually.

헤르난데스 씨가 왜 모두에게 점심을 대접하는 거죠?
(A) 그것은 곧 출시될 것 같습니다.
(B) 5번 가의 바네트 식당이요.
(C) 실은 관리자들만이에요.

어휘 treat 대접하다 launch 출시[출간]하다 administrator 관리자

해설 헤르난데스 씨가 모두에게 식사 대접하는 이유를 묻는 Why 의문문

(A) 유사 발음 오답. 질문의 lunch와 부분적으로 발음이 유사한 launching을 이용한 오답.

(B) 연상 단어 오답. 질문의 lunch에서 연상 가능한 restaurant를 이용한 오답.

(C) 정답. 헤르난데스 씨가 모두에게 점심식사를 대접하는 이유를 묻는 질문에 모두가 아니라 관리자들에게만 대접한다며 반전의 답을 주고 있으므로 정답.

19

M-Au Who's writing the articles on the food festival?

W-Am (A) The cooking competition and the concert.

(B) They should be under five hundred words.

(C) Check the assignment spreadsheet.

누가 푸드 페스티벌에 관해 기사를 작성하나요?
(A) 요리 경연 대회와 콘서트요.
(B) 500자 미만이어야 합니다.
(C) 업무 배정표를 확인하세요.

어휘 competition 대회 assignment 임무, 배정 spreadsheet 데이터 문서

해설 기사의 작성자를 묻는 Who 의문문

(A) 연상 단어 오답. 질문의 food에서 연상 가능한 cooking을 이용한 오답.

(B) 연상 단어 오답. 질문의 articles에서 연상 가능한 five hundred words를 이용한 오답.

(C) 정답. 푸드 페스티벌에 관해 기사를 작성하는 사람을 묻는 질문에 업무 배정표를 확인하라며 정보의 출처를 우회적으로 알려주고 있으므로 정답.

---

20 고난도

W-Br Ga-Young is processing the results of the intern survey, isn't she?

M-Au (A) She's going to present them next week.

(B) The university's summer vacation.

(C) Thanks—I'll let her know you told me.

가영 씨가 인턴사원 설문 조사 결과를 처리 중이죠, 그렇죠?
(A) 그녀는 다음 주에 그것들을 발표할 예정입니다.
(B) 대학교의 여름 방학입니다.
(C) 고맙습니다. 당신이 말해줬다고 그녀에게 알려주겠습니다.

어휘 process 처리하다 intern 인턴사원 present 발표하다 vacation 휴가

해설 가영이 조사 결과를 처리 중인지 여부를 확인하는 부가의문문

(A) 정답. 가영이 인턴사원 설문 조사 결과를 처리 중인지 여부를 확인하는 질문에 그녀가 다음 주에 그것들을 발표할 예정이라며 현재 가영이 결과를 처리하고 있음을 우회적으로 나타내고 있으므로 정답.

(B) 질문과 상관없는 오답.

(C) 질문과 상관없는 오답.

---

21 고난도

M-Cn When will they finish renovating the café in the lobby?

W-Am (A) The menu is a lot longer now.

(B) That would be great, if you're free.

(C) Is the noise making it hard for you to focus?

로비에 있는 카페는 언제 개조가 끝나나요?
(A) 메뉴가 이제 훨씬 길어졌어요.
(B) 시간이 되신다면, 그게 좋겠네요.
(C) 소음 때문에 집중하기 힘드신가요?

어휘 renovate 개조하다 focus 집중하다

해설 카페 개조가 끝나는 시점을 묻는 When 의문문

(A) 연상 단어 오답. 질문의 café에서 연상 가능한 menu를 이용한 오답.

(B) 질문과 상관없는 오답. 도움을 베푸는 말에 대한 응답이므로 오답.

(C) 정답. 로비에 있는 카페의 개조 공사가 끝나는 시점을 묻는 질문에 소음 때문에 집중하기 힘드냐며 질문의 의도와 관련된 내용을 되묻고 있으므로 정답.

---

22 고난도

M-Cn Weren't you scheduled to work from home today?

M-Au (A) A new person in the scheduling department.

(B) Some clients asked to meet this afternoon.

(C) I'm hoping to buy a home in the suburbs.

오늘 재택근무하기로 되어 있지 않았나요?
(A) 일정 관리 부서에 새로 오신 분입니다.
(B) 고객 몇 명이 오늘 오후에 만나자고 하셨어요.
(C) 교외에 집을 사고 싶어요.

어휘 scheduling 일정 관리 suburb 교외

해설 재택근무 여부를 확인하는 부정의문문

(A) 파생어 오답. 질문의 scheduled와 파생어 관계인 scheduling을 이용한 오답.

(B) 정답. 오늘 재택근무하기로 되어 있던 것이 맞는지 확인하는 질문에 고객 몇 명이 오늘 오후에 만나자고 했다면서 출근을 하게 된 이유를 설명하고 있으므로 정답.

(C) 단어 반복 오답. 질문의 home을 반복 이용한 오답.

23 고난도

W-Am Who's on the selection committee for the research prize?

M-Au (A) Its members are appointed by the board.
(B) Oh, I've already chosen my topic.
(C) Julia Herrera won first place, I read.

연구상 선정 위원회에는 누가 있나요?
(A) 이사회가 그 위원들을 임명해요.
(B) 오, 전 이미 주제를 정했어요.
(C) 줄리아 헤레라가 1등을 차지했다는 글을 읽었어요.

어휘 selection 선발[선정] committee 위원회 research 연구
appoint 임명하다 board 이사회

해설 위원회의 구성원을 묻는 Who 의문문
(A) 정답. 연구상 선정 위원회의 구성원을 묻는 질문에 이사회가 위원들을 임명한다며 우회적으로 응답하고 있으므로 정답.
(B) 연상 단어 오답. 질문의 selection에서 연상 가능한 chosen을 이용한 오답.
(C) 연상 단어 오답. 질문의 prize에서 연상 가능한 first place를 이용한 오답.

---

24 고난도

M-Cn We need proof of your income to complete your loan application.

W-Br (A) Would a copy of my paycheck be all right?
(B) She's about to make a deposit at the bank.
(C) The money to start my own business.

당신의 대출 신청을 완료하려면 소득 증빙이 필요합니다.
(A) 제 급여 지급 사본이면 될까요?
(B) 그녀는 은행에 막 예금하려고 했어요.
(C) 제 사업을 시작하기 위한 돈입니다.

어휘 proof 증거[증명] income 수입 complete 완수하다 loan
application 대출 신청 paycheck 급여 make a deposit
예금하다

해설 부탁/요청의 평서문
(A) 정답. 대출 신청을 완료하려면 소득 증빙이 필요하다는 요청에 대해 급여 지급 사본을 내면 되냐며 관련된 정보를 구체적으로 묻고 있으므로 정답.
(B) 연상 단어 오답. 평서문의 loan application에서 연상 가능한 bank를 이용한 오답.
(C) 연상 단어 오답. 평서문의 loan application에서 연상 가능한 money를 이용한 오답.

---

25 고난도

M-Au Why aren't we having the carpets deep-cleaned this year?

W-Br (A) When everyone's at the company retreat.
(B) No, we're buying a new copy machine.
(C) Facilities maintenance is Corey's area.

올해는 왜 카펫을 대청소하지 않죠?
(A) 모두가 회사 야유회에 갔을 때요.
(B) 아니요, 우리는 새 복사기를 살 겁니다.
(C) 시설 유지는 코리 담당이에요.

어휘 retreat 피정 facility 시설 maintenance 유지, 보수

해설 카펫 청소를 하지 않는 이유를 묻는 Why 의문문
(A) 질문과 상관없는 오답. When 의문문에 대한 응답이므로 오답
(B) Yes/No 불가 오답. Why 의문문에는 Yes/No 응답이 불가능하므로 오답.
(C) 정답. 올해 카펫을 대청소하지 않는 이유를 묻는 질문에 시설 유지는 코리 담당이라며 자신은 그 이유를 알지 못함을 우회적으로 응답하고 있으므로 정답.

---

26 고난도

W-Am Am I allowed to keep travel rewards points I earn during business trips?

M-Cn (A) Samford Bank's rewards program participants.
(B) That's not necessary—just check your e-mail often.
(C) I'm not aware of any policies against it.

제가 출장 중에 쌓은 여행 보상 적립금을 보유할 수 있나요?
(A) 샘포드 은행의 보상 프로그램 참가자들입니다.
(B) 그럴 필요 없으세요. 이메일만 자주 확인하세요.
(C) 그에 반하는 어떠한 방침도 알지 못해요.

어휘 allow 허락하다 reward 보상(금) business trip 출장
participant 참가자 aware 아는 policy 정책, 방침

해설 여행 보상 적립금의 보유 가능 여부를 묻는 Be동사 의문문
(A) 단어 반복 오답. 질문의 rewards를 반복 이용한 오답.
(B) 질문과 상관없는 오답. 필요성을 묻는 질문에 대한 응답이므로 오답.
(C) 정답. 출장 중에 쌓은 여행 보상 적립금을 보유할 수 있는지 묻는 질문에 그에 반하는 어떠한 방침도 알지 못한다며 보유가 가능할 것임을 우회적으로 나타내고 있으므로 정답.

---

27 고난도

M-Au Do workers on the closing shift have any special responsibilities?

W-Am (A) Yes, the store closed down last June.
(B) Nothing that you wouldn't expect.
(C) When does it start and end?

마감 근무조 직원들은 특별 임무 사항이 있나요?
(A) 네, 가게가 지난 6월에 문을 닫았어요.
(B) 당신이 예상 못할 만한 건 없어요.
(C) 언제 시작하고 끝나나요?

어휘 shift 근무 시간, 근무조 responsibility 책무

해설 마감 근무조가 특별히 해야 할 일이 있는지 묻는 조동사(Do) 의문문
(A) 파생어 오답. 질문의 closing과 파생어 관계인 closed를 이용한 오답.
(B) 정답. 마감 근무조 직원들에게 특별 임무 사항이 있는지 묻는 질문에 당신이 예상 못할 만한 것은 없다며 이미 알고 있는 것 외에 특별히 할 일은 없음을 우회적으로 응답하고 있으므로 정답.
(C) 연상 단어 오답. 질문의 closing에서 연상 가능한 end를 이용한 오답.

28

고난도

W-Br We're issuing a press release about the expansion, aren't we?

M-Au (A) The new president is from Philadelphia.

(B) Not until all of the plans are finalized.

(C) Try pressing the "release" button on the side.

확장에 대한 보도 자료를 발표할 거죠, 그렇지 않나요?
(A) 신임 사장은 필라델피아 출신입니다.
(B) 모든 계획이 마무리되고 나서요.
(C) 측면의 "해제" 버튼을 눌러 보세요.

어휘 issue 발표하다 press release 보도 자료 expansion 확장 finalize 마무리 짓다 press 언론; 누르다 release 발표[공개], 방출; 놓아주다

해설 보도 자료 발표 여부를 묻는 부가의문문
(A) 질문과 상관없는 오답.
(B) 정답. 확장에 대한 보도 자료를 발표할 것인지 여부를 묻는 질문에 모든 계획이 마무리되고 나서라며 나중에 발표할 것임을 우회적으로 나타내고 있으므로 정답.
(C) 파생어 오답. 질문의 press와 파생어 관계인 pressing을 이용한 오답.

29

고난도

W-Am Which part of the manual did you say we should revise?

M-Cn (A) Most sections need at least some revisions.

(B) Because some of the instructions aren't clear.

(C) Each employee is given a manual at orientation.

설명서의 어느 부분을 수정해야 한다고 말씀하셨죠?
(A) 대부분이 조금씩이라도 수정이 필요합니다.
(B) 일부 설명이 명확하지 않기 때문입니다.
(C) 각 직원은 예비 교육 때 설명서를 받습니다.

어휘 manual 설명서 revise 수정하다 section 부분 at least 최소한 revision 수정 instruction 설명, 지시 orientation 예비 교육

해설 설명서에서 수정해야 할 부분을 묻는 Which 의문문
(A) 정답. 설명서의 어느 부분을 수정해야 한다고 말했는지 묻는 질문에 대부분이 조금씩이라도 수정이 필요하다고 응답하고 있으므로 정답.
(B) 연상 단어 오답. 질문의 manual에서 연상 가능한 instructions를 이용한 오답.
(C) 단어 반복 오답. 질문의 manual을 반복 이용한 오답.

30

고난도

W-Br The sales projections for this quarter are higher than I expected.

W-Am (A) There were several very good applicants.

(B) Management believes demand is going to grow.

(C) We could mount the projector on the ceiling.

이번 분기에 대한 판매 예측이 제가 기대했던 것보다 높네요.
(A) 아주 훌륭한 지원자가 몇 명 있었습니다.
(B) 경영진은 수요가 증가할 거라고 믿고 있어요.
(C) 프로젝터를 천장에 장착할 수 있어요.

어휘 projection 예측 quarter 사분기 applicant 지원자 management 경영(진) demand 수요 projector 영사기 mount 고정시키다 ceiling 천장

해설 정보 전달의 평서문
(A) 평서문과 상관없는 오답.
(B) 정답. 이번 분기에 대한 판매 예측이 기대했던 것보다 높다는 평서문에 경영진이 수요가 증가할 거라고 믿고 있다며 호응하고 있으므로 정답.
(C) 파생어 오답. 평서문의 projections와 파생어 관계인 projector를 이용한 오답.

31

고난도

M-Cn How many representatives are we sending to the negotiations?

W-Br (A) That's not as important as what our strategy is.

(B) I sent a couple out by express mail.

(C) Ellen suggested offering a five percent price cut.

협상에 대표를 몇 명이나 파견합니까?
(A) 그 점은 우리 전략이 무엇인지 만큼 중요하진 않습니다.
(B) 속달 우편으로 두어 개 보냈습니다.
(C) 엘렌이 5퍼센트 할인가를 제공하자고 제안했습니다.

어휘 representative 대표, 대리인 negotiation 협상 strategy 전략 express mail 속달 우편

해설 협상에 파견할 인원수를 묻는 How many 의문문
(A) 정답. 협상에 대표를 몇 명이나 파견하는지 묻는 질문에 그 점은 우리 전략만큼 중요하지는 않다고 우회적으로 응답하고 있으므로 정답.
(B) 파생어 오답. 질문의 sending과 파생어 관계인 sent를 이용한 오답.
(C) 연상 단어 오답. 질문의 negotiations에서 연상 가능한 price cut을 이용한 오답.

PART 3

32-34

W-Br ³²Ray, have you noticed that some customers are staying at their tables for a long time without ordering more food or drinks?

M-Au Oh yeah, it does seem like that's becoming a problem. ³³What if we posted a notice near the entrance that told people they had to leave promptly after they finish eating?

W-Br	I don't know... ³⁴ **That seems like it would make a lot of customers feel pressured and uncomfortable.** I was thinking about a more targeted approach, like just bringing the bill to slow tables before they ask.
M-Au	Ah, I see. Yes, that sounds like a better plan.

여	레이, 일부 고객들이 음식이나 음료를 더 주문하지 않으면서 오랫동안 테이블을 차지하고 있다는 것을 아세요?
남	아 네, 문제가 되고 있는 것 같아요. 식사가 끝나면 바로 나가야 한다는 안내문을 입구 옆에 게시하면 어떨까요?
여	모르겠어요… 그렇게 하면 많은 손님들이 압박감을 느끼면서 불편할 것 같아요. 저는 느린 테이블에는 손님들이 요청하기 전에 계산서를 가져다준다든지 하는 좀 더 특정 대상을 겨냥한 접근 방식에 대해 생각 중이었어요.
남	아, 알겠어요. 네, 그게 더 좋은 계획 같네요.

어휘	notice 알다: 공고[공고문] order 주문하다 post 게시[공고]하다 entrance 입구 promptly 즉시 feel pressured 압박감을 느끼다 uncomfortable 불편한 targeted (특정 대상을) 겨냥한 approach 접근 bill 계산서

32

Where do the speakers work?

(A) At a factory
(B) At an airport
(C) At a restaurant
(D) At a movie theater

화자들은 어디에서 근무하는가?

(A) 공장
(B) 공항
(C) 식당
(D) 영화관

해설 전체 내용 관련 – 화자들의 근무지

여자가 첫 대사에서 일부 고객들이 음식이나 음료를 더 주문하지 않으면서 오랫동안 테이블을 차지하고 있다는 것을 아느냐(have you noticed that some customers are staying at their tables for a long time without ordering more food or drinks?)고 묻고 있는 것으로 보아 화자들은 식당에서 근무하고 있음을 알 수 있다. 따라서 정답은 (C)이다.

33

What does the man suggest?

(A) Putting up a sign
(B) Hiring more staff
(C) Widening an entrance
(D) Automating a process

남자는 무엇을 제안하는가?

(A) 안내문 게시
(B) 추가 직원 채용
(C) 입구 확장
(D) 절차의 자동화

어휘	widen 키우다 automate 자동화하다 process 과정[절차]

해설 세부 사항 관련 – 남자의 제안 사항

남자가 첫 대사에서 식사가 끝나면 바로 나가야 한다는 안내문을 입구 옆에 게시하면 어떨지(What if we posted a notice near the entrance that told people they had to leave promptly after they finish eating?) 제안했으므로 정답은 (A)이다.

▸▸ **Paraphrasing** 대화의 **posted a notice**
→ 정답의 **putting up a sign**

34   고난도

What does the woman say the man's suggested action might cause?

(A) Service delays
(B) A shortage of space
(C) An unpleasant atmosphere
(D) A budget problem

여자는 남자가 제안한 행동이 무엇을 유발할 수도 있다고 말하는가?

(A) 서비스 지연
(B) 공간의 부족
(C) 불편한 분위기
(D) 예산 문제

어휘	delay 지연 shortage 부족 unpleasant 불편한[불쾌한] atmosphere 분위기 budget 예산

해설 세부 사항 관련 – 여자가 말하는 남자의 제안으로 유발될 수 있는 것

여자가 두 번째 대사에서 그렇게 하면 많은 손님들이 압박감을 느끼면서 불편해할 것 같다(That seems like it would make a lot of customers feel pressured and uncomfortable)고 했으므로 정답은 (C)이다.

35-37

M-Cn	Hi, Ms. Griffin. Thank you for coming.
W-Br	It's nice to meet you in person, Mr. Marsh. ³⁵ **Now, as I said on the phone, I'd like you to show me everything that you'll need my company to pack up and transport to your new apartment.**
M-Cn	Sure. Let's start with the most difficult part—the living room. ³⁶ **As you can see, I have a piano. I'm afraid that it won't survive the trip in good condition.**
W-Br	Well, we've moved pianos before with no problems. ³⁷ **And all of our work will be insured under a formal agreement drafted by lawyers. Would you like a sample copy of it?** I have one here.

남	안녕하세요, 그리핀 씨. 와주셔서 감사합니다.
여	직접 만나 뵙게 되어 반갑습니다, 마쉬 씨. **전화에서 말씀드렸듯이, 우리 회사가 포장해서 새 아파트로 운반해야 할 모든 짐을 보여주셨으면 좋겠습니다.**
남	물론이죠. 가장 어려운 부분이 거실부터 시작하죠. **보시다시피, 피아노가 있는데요. 좋은 상태로 운반을 버텨낼 수 있을지 걱정됩니다.**
여	**우리는 전에 아무 문제없이 피아노들을 옮긴 경험이 있습니다. 그리고 저희의 모든 작업은 변호사가 작성한 정식 계약서 하에 보험으로 보장될 겁니다. 계약서 견본을 보고 싶으세요?** 여기 제가 한 부를 갖고 있습니다.

어휘	pack 싸다, 포장하다 transport 수송하다 survive 견뎌 내다 condition 상태 insure 보험에 들다 formal 공식적인 agreement 합의 draft 원고를 작성하다 lawyer 변호사

35

고난도

What does the man plan to do?

(A) Move to a different residence
(B) Purchase a new appliance
(C) Put his belongings in storage
(D) Renovate an apartment

남자는 무엇을 하려고 계획하는가?

(A) 다른 거주지로 이사하는 일
(B) 새 가전제품을 구입하는 일
(C) 소지품들을 창고에 집어넣는 일
(D) 아파트를 개조하는 일

어휘   residence 주택   appliance 가전제품   belongings 소지품   storage 보관소   renovate 개조[보수]하다

해설   세부 사항 관련 – 남자가 계획하는 일

여자가 첫 대사에서 전화에서 말씀드렸듯이 우리 회사가 포장해서 새 아파트로 운반해야 할 모든 짐을 보여주셨으면 좋겠다(Now, as I said on the phone, I'd like you to show me everything that you'll need my company to pack up and transport to your new apartment)고 한 것으로 보아 남자는 곧 새 아파트로 이사할 것임을 알 수 있다. 따라서 정답은 (A)이다.

▶ Paraphrasing   대화의 your new apartment
→ 정답의 a different residence

36

Why does the man say he is concerned?

(A) A job must be completed quickly.
(B) An activity will be noisy.
(C) An item may be damaged.
(D) A room may be too small.

왜 남자는 걱정스럽다고 말하는가?

(A) 일이 빨리 마무리되어야 한다.
(B) 작업이 시끄러울 것이다.
(C) 제품이 손상될 수 있다.
(D) 방이 너무 작을 수도 있다.

어휘   complete 완수하다   activity 활동   damage 손상시키다; 손상

해설   세부 사항 관련 – 남자가 걱정하는 이유

남자의 두 번째 대사에서 보시다시피 피아노가 있다(As you can see, I have a piano)고 하면서 좋은 상태로 운반을 버텨낼 수 있을지 걱정된다(I'm afraid that it won't survive the trip in good condition)고 했으므로 정답은 (C)이다.

37

What does the woman offer to give the man?

(A) Referrals to other companies
(B) An informal cost estimate
(C) A legal document
(D) Packaging supplies

여자는 남자에게 무엇을 주겠다고 제안하는가?

(A) 다른 회사로의 의뢰서
(B) 비공식 비용 견적서
(C) 법률 문서
(D) 포장재

어휘   referral 의뢰서   informal 비공식의   estimate 견적서   legal 법률과 관련된   supplies 물품

해설   세부 사항 관련 – 여자가 남자에게 주겠다고 제안하는 것

여자가 마지막 대사에서 저희의 모든 작업은 변호사가 작성한 정식 계약서 하에 보험으로 보장될 것(And all of our work will be insured under a formal agreement drafted by lawyers)이라면서, 계약서 견본을 보고 싶냐(Would you like a sample copy of it?)고 물었으므로 정답은 (C)이다.

▶ Paraphrasing   대화의 a formal agreement drafted by
lawyers → 정답의 a legal document

38-40

W-Am	**[38] Ernest, since pay raises will be a little low this year, I think we need to find other ways to keep the staff happy.** Do you have any suggestions?
M-Au	Let me think... **[39] How about creating a company community service program?**
W-Am	Wait, why would that help?
M-Au	Well, people feel good when they help others, and spending time together outside the office would build stronger relationships between staff members.
W-Am	Those are good points, but... I don't know. Some employees might see it as a burden. **[40] Let's try to think of some other ideas before we move forward with that one.**
M-Au	Sure, Lula. I'll see what I can come up with.

여	어니스트, 올해 임금 인상이 낮을 것이기 때문에, 직원들 만족도를 유지할 만한 다른 방법들을 찾아야 할 것 같아요. 뭐 좋은 제안이 있나요?
남	글쎄요… 회사 지역 봉사 활동 프로그램을 만드는 건 어떨까요?
여	잠깐만요, 그게 어째서 도움이 되죠?
남	그게, 사람들은 다른 사람들을 도울 때 기분이 좋잖아요. 또 사무실 밖에서 함께 시간을 보내면 직원들 사이의 관계도 더 돈독해질 거고요.
여	좋은 포인트긴 하지만 잘 모르겠어요. 일부 직원들은 그것을 부담스럽게 여길 수도 있어요. **그 방안을 추진하기 전에 다른 아이디어를 생각해봅시다.**
남	그래요, 룰라. 궁리해볼게요.

어휘	raise 인상; 올리다 suggestion 제안 community service 지역(사회) 봉사 활동 relationship 관계 burden 부담

38

고난도

What is the topic of the conversation?

(A) Keeping a current client account
(B) Attracting internship applicants
(C) Meeting shareholders' expectations
(D) Maintaining employee satisfaction

대화의 주제는 무엇인가?

(A) 현재 고객 계정을 유지하는 일
(B) 인턴직 지원자를 유치하는 일
(C) 주주들의 기대를 충족하는 일
(D) 직원 만족도를 유지하는 일

어휘 account 계정, 계좌 applicant 지원자 shareholder 주주 expectation 기대 satisfaction 만족

해설 전체 내용 관련 – 대화의 주제

여자가 첫 대사에서 올해 임금 인상이 낮을 것이기 때문에 직원들 만족도를 유지할 만한 다른 방법들을 찾아야 할 것 같다(Ernest, since pay raises will be a little low this year, I think we need to find other ways to keep the staff happy)면서 직원 만족도 유지 방법에 대한 의견을 구하며 대화를 시작했으므로 정답은 (D)이다.

▶▶ Paraphrasing 대화의 keep the staff happy
→ 정답의 maintaining employee satisfaction

39

What does the man propose?

(A) Making use of a local resource
(B) Reducing time spent commuting
(C) Starting a volunteer program
(D) Expanding an orientation session

남자는 무엇을 제안하는가?

(A) 지역 자원을 활용하는 것
(B) 통근 시간을 줄이는 것
(C) 자원봉사 프로그램을 시작하는 것
(D) 예비 교육 과정을 늘리는 것

어휘 resource 자원 reduce 줄이다 commute 통근하다 expand 확대하다 orientation 예비 교육 session 시간[기간]

해설 세부 사항 관련 – 남자의 제안 사항

남자는 첫 대사에서 회사 지역 봉사 활동 프로그램을 만드는 건 어떤지(How about creating a company community service program?) 제안했으므로 정답은 (C)이다.

40

What do the speakers agree to do?

(A) Develop the man's suggestion
(B) Seek alternative options
(C) Announce a decision
(D) Ask for workers' opinions

화자들은 무엇을 하기로 동의하는가?

(A) 남자의 제안을 발전시킨다.
(B) 대체 방안을 찾는다.
(C) 결정을 발표한다.
(D) 근로자들의 의견을 묻는다.

어휘 alternative 대안이 되는 option 선택(권) announce 발표하다 opinion 의견

해설 세부 사항 관련 – 화자들이 하기로 동의한 일

여자가 세 번째 대사에서 그 방안을 추진하기 전에 다른 아이디어를 생각해 보자(Let's try to think of some other ideas before we move forward with that one)고 제안했고, 뒤이어 남자도 호응하고 있으므로 정답은 (B)이다.

41-43 3인 대화

M-Cn	Hi, everyone. **⁴¹My name is Tae-Min, and I'll be taking you around the museum today.** Are there any questions before we get started?
W-Am	I have one—is there somewhere I could leave this bag? It's quite heavy.
M-Cn	**⁴²Yes, we have lockers near the entrance.** If you head over there now, you should be able to meet us in Gilmore Hall in a few minutes.
W-Am	Thanks. I'll do that.
W-Br	Um, I'm having trouble hearing you. Would you mind speaking up?
M-Cn	Oh, sorry about that. **⁴³This is a bigger crowd than I usually handle. Yes, I'll try to speak more loudly.**

남	안녕하세요, 여러분. 제 이름은 태민입니다. 제가 오늘 여러분께 박물관을 안내해드릴 겁니다. 시작하기 전에 질문 있으십니까?
여1	한 가지 있어요. 이 가방을 맡겨둘 곳이 있을까요? 꽤 무겁거든요.
남	네, 입구 근처에 물품 보관함이 있습니다. 지금 그쪽으로 가시면, 몇 분 뒤 길모어 홀에서 저희랑 만나실 수 있을 거예요.

여1	고맙습니다. 그렇게 할게요.
여2	음, 말씀이 잘 안 들려요. 크게 말씀해주시겠어요?
남	오, 죄송합니다. 제가 보통 인솔하던 것보다 인원수가 많아서요. 좀 더 큰 소리로 말해보겠습니다.

어휘	locker (자물쇠가 달린) 물품 보관함 entrance 입구 head (특정 방향으로) 가다(향하다) handle 다루다 loudly 큰 소리로

41

Who most likely is the man?

(A) A trade show exhibitor
(B) A tour guide
(C) A workshop leader
(D) An airline representative

남자는 누구일 것 같은가?
(A) 무역 박람회 전시 참가자
(B) 관람 가이드
(C) 워크숍 리더
(D) 항공사 직원

해설 전체 내용 관련 – 남자의 직업

남자가 첫 대사에서 제 이름은 태민이고 오늘 여러분께 박물관을 안내해드릴 것(My name is Tae-Min, and I'll be taking you around the museum today)이라고 한 것으로 보아 정답은 (B)이다.

42

What does the man tell the group about?

(A) A building entrance
(B) A form of transportation
(C) An instruction manual
(D) A storage facility

남자는 단체에게 무엇에 대해 말하는가?
(A) 건물 입구
(B) 교통수단의 한 형태
(C) 사용 안내서
(D) 보관 시설

해설 세부 사항 관련 – 남자가 단체에게 말하는 것

남자가 두 번째 대사에서 입구 근처에 물품 보관함이 있다(we have lockers near the entrance)고 했으므로 정답은 (D)이다.

▸▸ Paraphrasing   대화의 lockers → 정답의 a storage facility

43

What does the man say is causing a problem?

(A) He is not used to dealing with large groups.
(B) His audio equipment is malfunctioning.
(C) Some demonstration machinery is very loud.
(D) The usual venue for a talk is unavailable.

남자는 무엇이 문제를 일으키고 있다고 말하는가?
(A) 큰 단체를 상대하는 데 익숙하지 않다.
(B) 그의 오디오 장비가 오작동하고 있다.
(C) 일부 시연 장비는 매우 시끄럽다.
(D) 평상시의 강연 장소를 이용할 수 없다.

어휘	deal with 처리하다 equipment 장비 malfunction 제대로 작동하지 않다 demonstration 시연 venue 장소 unavailable 이용할 수 없는

해설 세부 사항 관련 – 남자가 말하는 문제의 원인

남자가 마지막 대사에서 제가 보통 인솔하던 것보다 인원수가 많다(This is a bigger crowd than I usually handle)며, 좀 더 큰 소리로 말해야겠다(I'll have to speak more loudly)고 한 것으로 보아 정답은 (A)이다.

▸▸ Paraphrasing   대화의 handle → 정답의 dealing with

44-46

W-Br	**44 Hi, I have an appointment for a tune-up on my sedan.** My name is Yolanda Garcia.
M-Au	I'm sorry, Ms. Garcia, but we're pretty busy today. We might not be able to get to your car until the early evening. **45 Would you like me to check our schedule for openings tomorrow morning instead?**
W-Br	**45 Oh, I'm going out of town then.** Driving, actually. **45 That's why I scheduled my appointment for this afternoon.** Is there anything you can do to speed up the process, at least?
M-Au	Let me see... Our records say you don't really need an oil change yet. **46 Why don't we save that job for later?**
W-Br	That sounds good. Here are my keys.

여	안녕하세요, 제 자동차를 정비 받기로 약속되어 있어요. 제 이름은 율란다 가르시아입니다.
남	가르시아 씨, 죄송하지만, 오늘 저희가 일이 꽤 바빠서 초저녁이나 돼서야 고객님 차를 점검할 수 있을 것 같은데요. 대신 내일 아침 빈 시간이 있는지 스케줄을 확인해드릴까요?
여	오, 제가 그때 시외로 나갈 계획이거든요. 차를 가지고 말이죠. 그래서 제가 오늘 오후로 약속을 잡았던 거고요. 조금이라도 정비 속도를 높이기 위해 하실 수 있는 일이 있을까요?
남	어디 봅시다… 저희 기록에는 아직 오일 교체는 하실 필요가 없다고 나오네요. 그 작업은 나중으로 미루는 게 어떨까요?
여	그게 좋겠네요. 여기 제 키요.

어휘	appointment 약속 tune-up 튠업(엔진 등의 조정) sedan 세단형 자동차 opening 빈자리 instead 대신에 process 과정[절차] at least 적어도 save 남겨두다

44

Where are the speakers?

(A) At a law firm
(B) At a hair salon
(C) At a doctor's office
(D) At an auto repair shop

화자들은 어디에 있는가?
(A) 법률 사무소
(B) 미용실
(C) 의사의 진료실
(D) 자동차 정비소

해설 전체 내용 관련 – 대화의 장소

여자가 첫 대사에서 남자에게 인사를 건네며 제 자동차를 정비 받기로 약속되어 있다(I have an appointment for a tune-up on my sedan)고 한 것으로 보아 정답은 (D)이다.

45

Why did the woman schedule her appointment for today?

(A) She completed some preparations yesterday.
(B) She does not have to work this afternoon.
(C) She will attend a banquet this evening.
(D) She will leave for a trip tomorrow.

여자는 왜 오늘 약속을 잡았는가?
(A) 어제 준비 작업을 완료했다.
(B) 오늘 오후에 근무하지 않아도 된다.
(C) 오늘 저녁에 연회에 참석할 것이다.
(D) 내일 여행을 떠날 것이다.

어휘 complete 완수하다 preparation 준비 banquet 연회

해설 세부 사항 관련 – 여자가 오늘 약속을 잡은 이유

남자가 첫 대사에서 내일 아침 빈 시간이 있는지 스케줄을 확인해주기를 원하는지(Would you like me to check our schedule for openings tomorrow morning instead?) 묻자, 여자가 그때는 시외로 나갈 계획(I'm going out of town then)이라며 그래서 오늘 오후로 약속을 잡았던 것(That's why I scheduled my appointment for this afternoon)이라고 했으므로 정답은 (D)이다.

> ▸▸ **Paraphrasing** 대화의 **going out of town**
> → 정답의 **leave for a trip**

46

What does the man suggest doing?

(A) Updating some records
(B) Postponing a service
(C) Talking to a manager
(D) Saving a copy of a form

남자는 무엇을 하라고 제안하는가?
(A) 일부 기록을 업데이트하는 것
(B) 서비스를 연기하는 것
(C) 관리자와 이야기하는 것
(D) 양식의 사본을 저장하는 것

어휘 postpone 연기하다 form 양식

해설 세부 사항 관련 – 남자의 제안 사항

남자가 마지막 대사에서 그 작업은 나중으로 미루는 게 어떨지(Why don't we save that job for later?) 묻고 있으므로 정답은 (B)이다.

> ▸▸ **Paraphrasing** 대화의 **save that job for later**
> → 정답의 **postponing a service**

47-49 3인 대화

M-Cn	Hi, Jonas. What did you want to talk to us about?
M-Au	**47 Some good news—the owner of Jessup Supermarkets has given our organization a fifty-thousand-dollar gift.**
W-Am	Wow! What will it be used for?
M-Au	She only specified that we put it towards community outreach.
W-Am	**48 OK. Well, I heard about an environmental nonprofit in Florida that has been inviting famous climate scientists to give lectures... How about we plan something similar?**
M-Au	That could certainly bring us some publicity.
M-Cn	True, but educational events that are fun for schoolchildren too might engage more local citizens.
M-Au	Hmm, you both make good points. **49 I'd like to get our employees' input too. Let's set up an organization-wide meeting this week to discuss ideas.**

남1	안녕하세요, 조나스. 우리에게 뭘 얘기하려고 하셨어요?
남2	좋은 소식이에요. 제섭 슈퍼마켓츠 오너가 우리 단체에 5만 달러를 기부했어요.
여	우와! 어디에 사용될 건가요?
남2	커뮤니티 지원에 쓰라고만 하던데요.
여	그렇군요. 음, 플로리다의 한 비영리 환경 단체는 유명 기상 과학자들을 초청해서 강연을 한다고 하더군요. 우리도 비슷한 걸 계획해보면 어때요?
남2	그러면 확실히 대중의 이목을 끌 수 있을 겁니다.
남1	맞아요. 그런데 학생들도 재밌어할 만한 교육 행사라면 더 많은 시민들을 끌어들일 수 있을 거예요.
남2	흠, 두 분 다 좋은 지적을 해주셨어요. 우리 직원들 의견도 듣고 싶네요. 이번 주에 조직 전체 회의를 해서 생각을 논의해봅시다.

어휘	organization 조직, 단체 specify 명시하다 outreach 지원, 자원 nonprofit 비영리 단체; 비영리적인 climate 기후 publicity 지명도, 평판 engage 사로잡다, 끌다 input 의견

47

What has the speakers' organization received? **고난도**

(A) A grant from a government agency
(B) A prize from a national contest
(C) Additional funds from its headquarters
(D) A donation from a businessperson

화자들의 단체는 무엇을 받았는가?
(A) 정부 기관으로부터의 보조금
(B) 전국 대회 수상
(C) 본사의 추가 자금
(D) 사업가의 기부

어휘 grant 보조금 headquarters 본사 donation 기부

해설 세부 사항 관련 – 화자들이 받은 것

두 번째 남자가 첫 대사에서 기업 오너가 우리 단체에 5만 달러를 기부했다(the owner of Jessup Supermarkets has given our organization a fifty-thousand-dollar gift)고 했으므로 정답은 (D)이다.

▸▸ Paraphrasing 대화의 the owner of ~ a fifty-thousand-dollar gift → 정답의 a donation from a businessperson

48

What does the woman suggest doing with the money? **고난도**

(A) Producing some brochures
(B) Giving bonuses to employees
(C) Holding a speaker series
(D) Offering a school scholarship

여자는 돈으로 무엇을 하자고 제안하는가?
(A) 안내책자 제작
(B) 직원 보너스 제공
(C) 강연 시리즈 개최
(D) 장학금 수여

어휘 brochure 안내책자 scholarship 장학금

해설 세부 사항 관련 – 여자가 돈으로 하자고 제안하는 것

여자가 두 번째 대사에서 한 환경 단체가 유명 기상 과학자를 초청해 강연을 한다며 비슷한 것을 계획하는 게 어떨지(I heard about an environmental nonprofit ~ climate scientists to give lectures... How about we plan something similar?)라고 제안했으므로 정답은 (C)이다.

49

What does Jonas decide to do?

(A) Plan a gathering
(B) Issue a questionnaire
(C) Call a consultant
(D) Draft an article

조나스는 무엇을 하기로 결심하는가?
(A) 모임 계획
(B) 설문지 교부
(C) 자문 위원 부르기
(D) 기사 초안 작성하기

어휘 gathering 모임 issue 발급[교부]하다 draft 초안을 작성하다; 초안

해설 세부 사항 관련 – 조나스가 결심한 일

조나스가 마지막 대사에서 직원들의 의견을 듣고 싶다며, 조직 전체 회의를 해서 생각을 논의해보자(I'd like to get our employees' input ~ set up an organization-wide meeting this week to discuss ideas)고 했으므로 정답은 (A)이다.

50-52

> M-Cn Hi, Melinda? It's Chikashi. **50** I'm calling about the interior design drawings I sent you earlier this week. I'd love to hear what you think of them.
>
> W-Am Hi, Chikashi. Well, for the most part, I'm very pleased. **51** But... the chairs that you chose for the waiting room are very stylish, while our main priority is our visitors' comfort. Do you have some other options you could show me?
>
> M-Cn I do, but I want you to know that I did choose those chairs with comfort in mind. **52** Would you consider trying them out at the wholesale shop before you decide against them? It's not far from your office.
>
> W-Am **52** OK, I guess I can do that.

> 남 여보세요, 멜린다? 치카시예요. 이번 주 초에 보내드렸던 실내 디자인 도면 때문에 전화드렸어요. 어떻게 생각하시는지 듣고 싶어요.
>
> 여 안녕하세요, 치카시. 대부분에 만족했어요. 그런데… 대기실을 위해 고르신 의자들이 아주 멋스럽긴 한데, 우리의 최우선 순위는 방문객들의 편안함이에요. 제게 보여주실 다른 옵션이 있을까요?
>
> 남 있어요, 그렇지만 제가 편안함을 염두에 두고 그 의자들을 골랐다는 점을 아셨으면 해요. 반대 결정을 내리시기 전에 도매점에서 그 의자들에 앉아 보시는 걸 고려해보시겠어요? 그쪽 사무실에서 멀지 않거든요.
>
> 여 좋아요, 그럴 수 있을 것 같아요.

어휘 waiting room 대기실 priority 우선 사항 comfort 편안 option 선택(권) wholesale 도매의

50

Why is the man calling the woman?

(A) To get some feedback
(B) To notify her of a problem
(C) To confirm some instructions
(D) To volunteer for an assignment

남자는 왜 여자에게 전화하고 있는가?
(A) 피드백을 듣기 위해
(B) 여자에게 문제에 대해 알리기 위해
(C) 몇 가지 지시 사항을 확인하기 위해
(D) 임무에 자원하기 위해

어휘 notify 알리다 confirm 확인하다 instruction 지시, 설명 assignment 임무, 과제

남자가 첫 대사에서 이번 주 초에 보내드렸던 실내 디자인 도면 때문에 전화드렸다(I'm calling about the interior design drawings I sent you earlier this week)면서, 어떻게 생각하시는지 듣고 싶다(I'd love to hear what you think of them)고 했으므로 정답은 (A)이다.

▸▸ **Paraphrasing** 대화의 **hear what you think of them** → 정답의 **get some feedback**

51
고난도

What does the woman imply when she says, "our main priority is our visitors' comfort"?

(A) She is not concerned about cost.
(B) She does not mind extending a deadline.
(C) A room should have more open space.
(D) Some seating looks uncomfortable.

여자가 "우리의 최우선 순위는 방문객들의 편안함이에요"라고 말한 의미는 무엇인가?
(A) 비용에 대해 걱정하지 않는다.
(B) 마감일을 연장해도 괜찮다.
(C) 방에 좀 더 열린 공간이 있어야 한다.
(D) 좌석이 불편해 보인다.

어휘 concerned 걱정하는 extend 연장하다 seating 좌석 uncomfortable 불편한

해설 화자의 의도 파악 – 우리의 최우선 순위는 방문객들의 편안함이라는 말의 의도

여자가 인용문 앞에서 대기실을 위해 고르신 의자들이 아주 멋스럽긴 하지만(But... the chairs that you chose for the waiting room are very stylish, while)이라고 한 뒤 인용문에서 편안함을 강조한 것으로 보아, 좌석이 편해 보이지는 않는다는 의사를 전달하려는 의도로 볼 수 있다. 따라서 정답은 (D)이다.

52

What does the woman agree to do?

(A) Pay a deposit
(B) Visit a store
(C) Approve a design
(D) Wait for a shipment

여자는 무엇을 하기로 동의하는가?
(A) 보증금 지불
(B) 상점 방문
(C) 디자인 승인
(D) 배송품 기다리기

어휘 deposit 보증금 approve 승인하다 shipment 수송품

해설 세부 사항 관련 – 여자가 하기로 동의한 일

남자가 두 번째 대사에서 반대 결정을 내리기 전에 도매점에서 그 의자들에 앉아 보는 걸 고려해보겠느냐(Would you consider trying them out at the wholesale shop before you decide against them?)고 제안한 데 대해, 여자가 뒤이어 좋다(OK)며 그럴 수 있을 것 같다(I guess I can do that)고 했으므로 정답은 (B)이다.

▸▸ **Paraphrasing** 대화의 **trying them out the wholesale shop** → 정답의 **visit a store**

53-55

M-Au **53 Excuse me—I'm looking for the book *Guide to Brockler*.** You know, for the programming language "Brockler"? Your computer system says it's in stock, but **53 I can't find it on the shelf. Does that mean that another customer has bought the last copy?**

W-Br It might, but it could also mean that someone has just put it back in the wrong location. If that's the case, it's probably in the same general area. **54 Would you like me to help you look?**

M-Au That would be great, thanks. **55 I've registered to take a Brockler certification test next month, and apparently *Guide to Brockler* is the best prep book on the market.** I'm really hoping to pick it up today and start studying.

남 실례합니다. 〈브로클러 안내서〉라는 책을 찾고 있어요. 프로그래밍 언어 "브로클러" 있잖아요. 여기 컴퓨터 시스템에는 재고가 있다고 나오는데, **책장에서 찾을 수가 없어요. 다른 손님이 마지막 책을 샀다는 걸 의미하나요?**

여 가능해요, 그렇지만 누군가 책을 잘못된 위치에 꽂아 놓았을 수도 있고요. 그런 경우라면, 아마 같은 일반 구역에 있을 거예요. **찾으시는 걸 도와드릴까요?**

남 그러면 좋죠, 고맙습니다. 다음 달에 브로클러 자격 시험을 치르려고 등록했는데, 듣자 하니 〈브로클러 안내서〉가 시판되는 최고의 대비 서적이더라고요. 오늘 꼭 사서 공부를 시작할 수 있으면 좋겠어요.

어휘 shelf 책꽂이, 선반 general 일반의 register 등록하다 certification 인증 apparently 듣재[보아] 하니

53

Who most likely is the woman?

(A) A bookstore clerk
(B) A repair technician
(C) A pharmacist
(D) A librarian

여자는 누구일 것 같은가?
(A) 서점 점원
(B) 수리 기사
(C) 약사
(D) 도서관 사서

해설 전체 내용 관련 – 여자의 직업

남자가 첫 대사에서 여자에게 〈브로클러 안내서〉라는 책을 찾고 있는데(I'm looking for the book *Guide to Brockler*), 책장에서 책을 찾을 수가 없다(I can't find it on the shelf)면서 다른 손님이 마지막 책을 샀다는 걸 의미하는지(Does that mean that another customer has bought the last copy?)를 묻는 것으로 보아 여자는 서점 직원임을 알 수 있다. 따라서 정답은 (A)이다.

54

What does the woman offer to do?

(A) Provide a refund
(B) Assist with a search
(C) Restart a computer system
(D) Recommend an alternative

여자는 무엇을 하겠다고 제안하는가?
(A) 환불을 지급해준다.
(B) **찾는 것을 도와준다.**
(C) 컴퓨터 시스템을 다시 시작한다.
(D) 대안을 추천한다.

어휘 refund 환불 search 찾기 alternative 대안

해설 세부 사항 관련 – 여자가 하겠다고 제안한 일

여자가 첫 대사에서 찾는 걸 도와드릴지(Would you like me to help you look?)를 물었으므로 정답은 (B)이다.

▸▸ Paraphrasing 대화의 **help you look**
→ 정답의 **assist with a search**

55

What does the man say will happen next month?

(A) A registration period will begin.
(B) A product will be removed from the market.
(C) A certification exam will be held.
(D) A return policy will become invalid.

남자는 다음 달에 무슨 일이 일어난다고 말하는가?
(A) 등록 기간이 시작될 것이다.
(B) 제품이 시장에서 없어질 것이다.
(C) **자격 시험이 치러질 것이다.**
(D) 반품 규정이 무효화될 것이다.

어휘 period 기간 remove 치우다 exam 시험 invalid 무효한

해설 세부 사항 관련 – 남자가 말하는 다음 달에 일어날 일

남자가 마지막 대사에서 다음 달에 브로클러 자격 시험을 치르려고 등록했는데, 듣자 하니 〈브로클러 안내서〉가 시판되는 최고의 대비 서적이더라(I've registered to take a Brockler certification test next month, and apparently *Guide to Brockler* is the best prep book on the market)고 말한 것으로 보아 정답은 (C)이다.

56-58

W-Br	Oliver, I need your advice. ⁵⁶**Do you remember how I posted a quiz about the association's history on our social media account?** It's getting hundreds of comments, and not all of them are positive.
M-Cn	Hold on. Let me open up my browser... Oh, I see.
W-Br	Yeah. ⁵⁷**I didn't realize that the answer to number five is controversial.** What should I do?

M-Cn	⁵⁷**Well, the point of our social media presence is to increase member engagement,** and this got a lot of people talking.
W-Br	That's true.
M-Cn	⁵⁸**We don't want to discourage debate, so for now, just keep an eye on these comments.** You can take action later if needed.

여	올리버, 당신의 조언이 필요해요. 제가 우리 소셜 미디어 계정에 협회의 연혁에 관한 퀴즈를 어떻게 올렸는지 기억나세요? 댓글이 수백 개가 올라오고 있는데, 긍정적인 이야기만 있는 건 아니에요.
남	잠시만요. 제 브라우저를 열어볼게요. 아, 그렇네요.
여	네, 5번 답변이 논쟁이 될 줄 몰랐어요. 제가 뭘 하면 될까요?
남	글쎄요. 우리 소셜 미디어의 요점은 회원 참여를 늘리는 것인데, 이로 인해 많은 사람들이 대화를 하게 되었네요.
여	그건 사실이에요.
남	논쟁을 억제시키고 싶지는 않으니 당분간은 이 댓글들을 지켜보세요. 필요하면 나중에 조치를 취하면 돼요.

어휘 association 협회 account 계정 comment 논평, 언급 positive 긍정적인 realize 깨닫다 controversial 논란이 많은 presence 있음 engagement 참여 discourage 말리다 debate 논의

56

What did the woman post on social media?

(A) Some images
(B) Some statistics
(C) Some questions
(D) Some advice

여자는 소셜 미디어에 무엇을 게시했는가?
(A) 사진
(B) 통계 자료
(C) **질문**
(D) 조언

해설 세부 사항 관련 – 여자가 소셜 미디어에 게시한 것

여자가 첫 대사에서 제가 우리 소셜 미디어 계정에 협회의 연혁에 관한 퀴즈를 어떻게 올렸는지 기억하느냐(Do you remember how I posted a quiz about the association's history on our social media account?)고 한 것으로 보아 정답은 (C)이다.

▸▸ Paraphrasing 대화의 **a quiz** → 정답의 **some questions**

57 〔고난도〕

Why does the man say, "this got a lot of people talking"?

(A) To reject the woman's request
(B) To point out an unintended benefit of an action
(C) To express concern about some criticism
(D) To admit that he was wrong about a strategy

남자가 "이로 인해 많은 사람들이 대화를 하게 되었네요"라고 말하는 이유는 무엇인가?

(A) 여자의 요청을 거절하려고
(B) 행동으로 인한 의도하지 않은 이점을 언급하려고
(C) 비판에 대해 우려를 나타내려고
(D) 전략에 대해 오판했음을 인정하려고

어휘 reject 거절하다   unintended 의도하지 않은   benefit 이점
concern 우려[걱정]   criticism 비판   strategy 전략

해설 화자의 의도 파악 – 이로 인해 많은 사람들이 대화를 하게 되었다는 말의 의도

앞에서 여자가 5번 답변이 논쟁이 될 줄 몰랐다(I didn't realize that the answer to number five is controversial)고 걱정하자 남자가 우리 소셜 미디어의 요점은 회원 참여를 늘리는 것(the point of our social media presence is to increase member engagement)인데 이번 일로 많은 이들이 대화하게 되었다고 인용문에서 언급한 것이므로, 여자가 걱정하는 것과는 달리 의도치 않게 좋은 면도 있다는 것을 말하려는 의도로 볼 수 있다. 따라서 정답은 (B)이다.

58

What does the man ask the woman to do?

(A) Edit a sentence
(B) Write another post
(C) Monitor a discussion
(D) Respond to some comments

남자는 여자에게 무엇을 하라고 요청하는가?

(A) 문장을 편집하라고
(B) 다른 게시물을 작성하라고
(C) 토론을 지켜보라고
(D) 일부 댓글에 답을 하라고

어휘 edit 편집하다   post 온라인 게시물   monitor 모니터[감시]하다

해설 세부 사항 관련 – 남자가 여자에게 요청한 일

남자가 마지막 대사에서 논쟁을 억제시키고 싶지는 않으니 당분간은 이 댓글들을 지켜보라(We don't want to discourage debate, so for now, just keep an eye on these comments)고 했으므로 정답은 (C)이다.

▸▸ Paraphrasing   대화의 **keep an eye on these comments**
→ 정답의 **monitor a discussion**

59-61

M-Cn	OK, this is our booth space—number sixteen. ⁵⁹**Let's set up quickly so we have some time to review our recruiting strategy before the jobseekers arrive.**
W-Am	Good idea. I'll start opening the boxes. ⁶⁰**Wow, the new "About Howlert Corporation" pamphlets look great!** I think they're really going to get people interested in working for us.
M-Cn	Yes, they did turn out well, didn't they? But where's the table cover with our logo on it? We should put that down first.

W-Am	It's right here. But, Giuseppe… ⁶¹**where are the soft drinks and energy bars?** I don't see them anywhere.
M-Cn	⁶¹**Ah, I forgot to put that box in the car!** Do you think there's a supermarket nearby?

남	자, 이곳이 우리 전시 공간입니다. 16번이요. **구직자들이 도착하기 전에 우리의 채용 전략을 검토할 시간을 가질 수 있도록 서둘러 준비를 합시다.**
여	좋은 생각이에요. 상자들을 열기 시작할게요. **우와, 새 "하우러트 기업에 관하여" 팸플릿이 보기 좋네요!** 이것들 덕에 사람들이 우리 회사에 근무하는 데 정말 관심을 갖게 될 것 같아요.
남	네, 아주 잘 나왔어요, 그렇죠? 그런데 우리 로고가 들어간 탁자 덮개는 어디 있죠? 그것들부터 깔아야 해요.
여	바로 여기 있어요. 그런데 주세페… **청량음료와 에너지 바는 어디 있나요?** 도무지 보이질 않아요.
남	아, 그 상자를 차에 싣는 걸 잊었어요! 근처에 슈퍼마켓이 있을까요?

어휘 booth 부스, 전시장   review 검토하다   recruit 모집하다
strategy 전략   jobseeker 구직자   pamphlet 팸플릿
cover 덮개; 덮다

59

What type of event is about to take place?

(A) An arts festival
(B) A career fair
(C) A store opening
(D) An advertising seminar

어떤 종류의 행사가 곧 열리는가?

(A) 예술 축제
(B) 취업 박람회
(C) 점포 개점
(D) 광고 세미나

해설 세부 사항 관련 – 곧 열리는 행사의 종류

남자가 첫 대사에서 구직자들이 도착하기 전에 우리의 채용 전략을 검토할 시간을 가질 수 있도록 서둘러 준비하자(Let's set up quickly so we have some time to review our recruiting strategy before the jobseekers arrive)고 한 것으로 보아 정답은 (B)이다.

60

Why is the woman pleased?

(A) Some marketing materials are attractive.
(B) A piece of furniture is larger than expected.
(C) The man has agreed to her proposal.
(D) A space is in a busy area.

여자는 왜 기뻐하는가?

(A) 일부 마케팅 자료가 매력적이라서
(B) 가구가 예상했던 것보다 더 커서
(C) 남자가 그녀의 제안에 동의해서
(D) 공간이 붐비는 구역에 있어서

어휘 material 자료, 재료 attractive 매력적인 proposal 제안

해설 세부 사항 관련 – 여자가 기쁜 이유

여자가 첫 번째 대사에서 새 "하우러트 기업에 관하여" 팸플릿이 보기 좋다(the new "About Howlert Corporation" pamphlets look great!)며 좋아하고 있으므로 정답은 (A)이다.

61

What did the man forget to do?

(A) Clean some decorations
(B) Seal a box tightly
(C) Bring some refreshments
(D) Put fuel in a vehicle

남자는 무엇을 하기를 잊었는가?

(A) 일부 장식을 치우는 일
(B) 상자를 단단히 봉하는 일
(C) 다과를 가져오는 일
(D) 차량에 연료를 채우는 일

어휘 decoration 장식 seal 봉(인)하다 tightly 꽉, 단단히 refreshment 다과 fuel 연료 vehicle 차량

해설 세부 사항 관련 – 남자가 하기를 잊은 일

여자가 두 번째 대사에서 청량음료와 에너지 바는 어디 있냐(where are the soft drinks and energy bars?)고 묻자, 남자가 그 상자를 차에 싣는 걸 잊었다(I forgot to put that box in the car!)고 했으므로 정답은 (C)이다.

▸▸ Paraphrasing 대화의 soft drinks and energy bars
→ 정답의 refreshments

62-64 대화 + 근무 일정표

M-Au Oh no, 62 **I've been scheduled to work on Wednesday afternoon! That's when my university's Japanese class meets.** I'll have to switch shifts with somebody. You're working in the morning—could you switch with me?

W-Am 63 **Sorry, Neil, but I'm also busy on Wednesday afternoon. Try asking whoever's working the night shift that day.**

M-Au 63 **OK, I will.** But this is frustrating. I definitely told Mr. Romero that I wasn't free on Wednesday afternoons.

W-Am Well, as a manager, he has a lot of information to keep track of. 64 **You should write down your availability for him when he comes in today. Then he'll have something to refer to when he makes the next shift schedule.**

남 아 이런, 수요일 오후로 근무 일정이 잡혔어요! 그때는 제가 대학교 일본어 수업 모임이 있어요. 다른 사람과 근무 시간을 바꿔야겠어요. 아침에 근무하시죠, 저랑 바꿔주실 수 있으세요?

여 미안하지만 닐, 수요일 오후에는 나도 바빠요. 그날 밤 시간대에 근무하는 사람에게 한번 물어봐요.

남 좋아요, 그럴게요. 그렇지만 불만스럽네요. 로메로 씨한테 수요일 오후에는 시간이 되지 않는다고 확실히 말씀드렸는데요.

여 그는 관리자로서 기억해야 할 정보가 많을 거예요. 오늘 그가 오면 당신이 가능한 시간을 적어드리는 게 좋겠어요. 그럼 다음 근무 일정을 짤 때 참고할 수 있을 거예요.

어휘 switch 바꾸다 shift 근무조, 근무 시간 frustrating 불만스러운 keep track of ~을 기록하다, ~을 기억하고 있다 availability 가능성 refer to (정보를 알아내기 위해) ~을 보다

	Wednesday	Thursday
Morning shift	Christina	Christina
Afternoon shift	Neil	Ruby
63 Night shift	**Alton**	**Hakeem**

	수요일	목요일
오전 근무 시간	크리스티나	크리스티나
오후 근무 시간	닐	루비
63 밤 근무 시간	올튼	하킴

62

What is causing a scheduling conflict for the man?

(A) A family gathering
(B) Some planned travel
(C) A medical appointment
(D) A university course

무엇 때문에 남자의 일정이 겹치는가?

(A) 가족 모임
(B) 계획된 여행
(C) 진료 예약
(D) 대학 강의

어휘 conflict 충돌[갈등] gathering 모임 appointment 약속

해설 세부 사항 관련 – 남자의 일정이 겹치는 원인

남자가 첫 대사에서 수요일 오후로 근무 일정이 잡혔다(I've been scheduled to work on Wednesday afternoon!)면서 그때는 대학교 일본어 수업 모임이 있다(That's when my university's Japanese class meets)고 했으므로 근무 일정과 대학 강의가 겹치는 것을 알 수 있다. 따라서 정답은 (D)이다.

63

Look at the graphic. Who will the man next ask to take his shift?

(A) Christina
(B) Alton
(C) Ruby
(D) Hakeem

시각 정보에 의하면, 남자는 다음에 누구에게 그의 근무 시간을 맡아달라고 요청하겠는가?

(A) 크리스티나
(B) 올튼
(C) 루비
(D) 하킴

해설 시각 정보 연계 – 남자가 다음에 그의 근무 시간을 맡아달라고 요청할 사람 여자가 첫 번째 대사에서 미안하지만, 수요일 오후에는 바쁘다(Sorry, Neil, but I'm also busy on Wednesday afternoon)며 그날 밤 시간대에 근무하는 사람에게 한번 물어보라(Try asking whoever's working the night shift that day)고 제안하자 남자가 그러겠다(OK, I will)고 했고, 근무 일정표에 따르면 수요일 밤에 일하기로 되어 있는 사람은 올튼이므로 정답은 (B)이다.

64

What does the woman suggest doing when a manager arrives?

(A) Making a reminder note
(B) Getting some contact details
(C) Referring a friend for employment
(D) Reporting the status of a task

여자는 관리자가 도착하면 무엇을 하라고 제안하는가?

(A) 기억할 사항을 메모로 작성하기
(B) 연락처 정보 구하기
(C) 친구를 일자리에 추천하기
(D) 업무 상태 보고하기

어휘 reminder 상기시켜 주는 메모 details 세부 정보 refer ~을 소개[위탁]하다 status 상태 task 과업, 과제

해설 세부 사항 관련 – 여자가 관리자가 도착할 때 하라고 제안하는 일 여자가 마지막 대사에서 오늘 관리자가 오면 당신이 가능한 시간을 적어주는 게 좋겠다(You should write down your availability for him when he comes in today)며 그럼 그가 다음 근무 일정을 짤 때 참고할 수 있을 것(Then he'll have something to refer to when he makes the next shift schedule)이라고 제안하고 있으므로 정답은 (A)이다.

▸▸ **Paraphrasing** 대화의 **write down**
→ 정답의 **make a note**

65-67 대화 + 평면도

M-Au As one of the first new hires in our expanded office, you have a choice between a couple of open desks. Here's the floor plan. Where would you like to sit?

W-Br Hmm... 65 Well, I'm going to be handling sensitive information on my computer. Is there a way to ensure that people passing by me can't see it?

M-Au Oh yes, we can get you a privacy screen that fits over your monitor.

W-Br Great! 66 Then I'd like the empty desk by the copy room. That would be convenient.

M-Au All right. 67 Let's head over there now so you can see what kind of equipment and supplies you already have. Then we can order the screen and anything else you need.

남 우리 확장된 사무실의 첫 신입 사원들 중 한 사람으로서, 당신은 두 개의 빈 책상 중 하나를 택할 수 있어요. 여기 평면도가 있어요. 어디에 앉고 싶으세요?

여 흠… 저는 컴퓨터로 민감한 정보를 다룰 거예요. 제 옆을 지나가는 사람들이 그것을 확실히 못 보도록 할 수 있는 방법이 있을까요?

남 네, 당신의 모니터에 맞는 개인 정보 보호 스크린을 설치해드릴 수 있어요.

여 좋아요! 그러면 복사실 옆의 빈 책상이 마음에 들어요. 그쪽이 편할 것 같네요.

남 알겠어요. **지금 그쪽으로 가서 어떤 종류의 장비와 물품들이 이미 구비되어 있는지 보죠.** 그리고 나서 스크린과 필요한 다른 것들을 주문하면 돼요.

어휘 hire 신입 사원; 고용하다 expanded 확대된 floor plan 평면도 handle 다루다 sensitive 민감한 ensure 보장하다 privacy 사생활[프라이버시] fit 맞다 empty 빈 convenient 편리한 head 가다[향하다] equipment 장비 supplies 물품

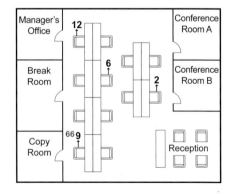

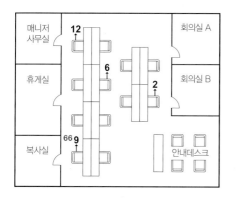

매니저 사무실	회의실 A
휴게실	회의실 B
복사실	안내데스크

65

고난도

What does the woman ask about?

(A) Computer sizes
(B) Privacy measures
(C) Meeting frequencies
(D) Temperature conditions

여자는 무엇에 대해 문의하는가?

(A) 컴퓨터 크기
(B) 개인 정보 보호 조치
(C) 회의 빈도
(D) 온도 조건

해설 세부 사항 관련 - 여자의 문의 사항

여자가 첫 대사에서 컴퓨터로 민감한 정보를 다룰 것(I'm going to be handling sensitive information on my computer)이라며, 옆을 지나가는 사람들이 그것을 확실히 못 보도록 할 수 있는 방법이 있을지(Is there a way to ensure that people passing by me can't see it?)를 묻고 있으므로 정답은 (B)이다.

▶ Paraphrasing 대화의 **a way to ensure that people passing by me can't see it** → 정답의 **privacy measures**

66

Look at the graphic. Which desk does the woman choose?

(A) 2
(B) 6
(C) 9
(D) 12

시각 정보에 의하면, 여자는 어떤 책상을 선택하는가?

(A) 2
(B) 6
(C) 9
(D) 12

해설 시각 정보 연계 - 여자가 선택하는 책상

여자가 두 번째 대사에서 복사실 옆의 빈 책상이 마음에 든다(Then I'd like the empty desk by the copy room)고 했고, 평면도에 따르면 복사실 옆의 책상은 9번이므로 정답은 (C)이다.

67

What will the speakers do next?

(A) Fill out paperwork
(B) Greet a department head
(C) Shop online for supplies
(D) Go to a workstation

화자들은 다음에 무엇을 할 것인가?

(A) 서류를 작성한다.
(B) 부서 책임자와 인사한다.
(C) 온라인으로 물품을 구매한다.
(D) 근무 자리로 간다.

어휘 fill out 작성하다   paperwork 서류 작업   greet 환영하다
workstation 일하는 자리

해설 세부 사항 관련 - 화자들이 다음에 할 일

남자가 마지막 대사에서 지금 그쪽으로 가서 어떤 종류의 장비와 물품들이 이미 구비되어 있는지 보자(Let's head over there now so you can see what kind of equipment and supplies you already have)고 제안하는 것으로 보아 화자들은 여자가 선택한 책상 쪽으로 갈 것임을 알 수 있다. 따라서 정답은 (D)이다.

68-70 대화 + 목록

W-Am	Hi. Could you help me choose a portable sound system?
M-Cn	Sure. What do you need one for?
W-Am	**68 I'm in a band, and we need equipment for performing in public places and at parties.** Do you think "The Boom" would be powerful enough for that?
M-Cn	Two thousand square feet isn't actually a very big area. **69 I'd recommend buying the model with eight thousand square feet of sound coverage instead and turning the volume down as needed.**
W-Am	Let me see the price tag... Hmm... That's not cheap.
M-Cn	**70 Well, we offer a very affordable monthly payment plan on most of our electronics, including portable sound systems.** Let me show you at the counter.

여	안녕하세요, 휴대용 사운드 시스템을 고르는 것을 도와주시겠어요?
남	물론이죠. 왜 필요하신 거죠?
여	제가 밴드에 있는데, 공공 장소와 파티에서 공연하기 위한 장비가 필요해요. "더 붐"이 충분히 강력할까요?
남	2천 평방 피트는 사실 그렇게 큰 장소는 아니에요. 대신에 음량 범위가 8천 평방 피트인 모델을 사서 필요에 따라 소리를 줄이는 것을 추천 드립니다.
여	가격표를 좀 볼게요… 흠… 싸지 않은데요.
남	휴대용 사운드 시스템을 포함한 우리 전자제품들 대부분에 매우 저렴한 월부 결제 방식을 제공해드려요. 계산대에서 보여드릴게요.

Test 3

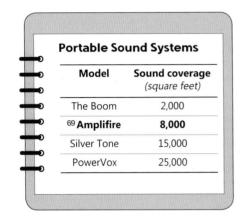

Portable Sound Systems

Model	Sound coverage (square feet)
The Boom	2,000
⁶⁹ Amplifire	8,000
Silver Tone	15,000
PowerVox	25,000

휴대용 사운드 시스템

모델	음량 범위 (평방 피트)
더 붐	2,000
⁶⁹ 앰플리파이어	8,000
실버 톤	15,000
파워박스	25,000

68

What does the woman plan to do?

(A) Perform some music
(B) Organize some lectures
(C) Host a sports event
(D) Hold a party

여자는 무엇을 하려고 계획하는가?
(A) 음악을 공연한다.
(B) 강의를 조직한다.
(C) 스포츠 행사를 주최한다.
(D) 파티를 연다.

어휘   organize 조직하다, 준비하다   lecture 강의   host 주최하다

해설   세부 사항 관련 – 여자의 계획

여자가 두 번째 대사에서 제가 밴드에 있는데 공공 장소와 파티에서 공연하기 위한 장비가 필요하다(I'm in a band, and we need equipment for performing in public places and at parties)고 했으므로 정답은 (A)이다.

69

Look at the graphic. Which model does the man recommend?

(A) The Boom
(B) Amplifire
(C) Silver Tone
(D) PowerVox

시각 정보에 의하면, 남자는 어떤 모델을 추천하는가?
(A) 더 붐
(B) 앰플리파이어
(C) 실버 톤
(D) 파워박스

해설   시각 정보 연계 – 남자가 추천하는 모델

남자가 두 번째 대사에서 음량 범위가 8천 평방 피트인 모델을 사서 필요에 따라 소리를 줄이는 것을 추천한다(I'd recommend buying the model with eight thousand square feet of sound coverage instead and turning the volume down as needed)고 했고, 시각 정보 목록에 따르면 해당 모델은 앰플리파이어이므로 정답은 (B)이다.

70   고난도

What does the man say about the store's portable sound systems?

(A) They are kept behind the counter.
(B) They can be paid for in installments.
(C) A new model will be released this month.
(D) Some of them may be rented.

남자는 상점의 휴대용 사운드 시스템에 대해 무엇을 말하는가?
(A) 계산대 뒤쪽에 보관된다.
(B) 할부로 지불할 수 있다.
(C) 신모델이 이번 달에 출시된다.
(D) 그들 중 일부는 대여가 가능하다.

어휘   in installments 할부로   release 출시[공개]하다   rent 빌리다

해설   세부 사항 관련 – 남자가 상점의 휴대용 사운드 시스템에 대해 말하는 것

남자가 마지막 대사에서 휴대용 사운드 시스템을 포함한 우리 전자제품들 대부분에 매우 저렴한 월부 결제 방식을 제공한다(we offer a very affordable monthly payment plan on most of our electronics, including portable sound systems)고 했으므로 정답은 (B)이다.

▸▸ Paraphrasing   대화의 offer a monthly payment plan → 정답의 can be paid for in installments

PART 4

71-73 공지

W-Am Good evening, shoppers. **71Did you know that EMC Furniture was voted the best value for the money by Detroit shoppers?** **72While you browse our merchandise, we invite you to compare prices by going online at any of our Internet kiosks located conveniently throughout the store**. If you can find another store offering one of our products for less, we'll beat their price. And for a limited time you can receive a fantastic deal on an extended warranty. **73Our two-hundred-dollar warranty is half price through the weekend**. Thanks for visiting EMC, where we're always looking for ways to save you money.

안녕하십니까, 쇼핑객 여러분. EMC 가구가 디트로이트 쇼핑객들에 의해 최고의 가성비 업체로 뽑혔다는 것을 알고 계셨습니까? 상품을 둘러보시는 동안 우리는 여러분이 매장 곳곳에 편리하게 위치한 인터넷 키오스크에서 온라인으로 가격을 비교해보실 것을 청합니다. 우리 제품을 더 낮은 가격에 제공하는 상점을 찾으실 수 있다면, 우리 가격을 그보다 낮춰드리겠습니다. 한시적으로 아주 좋은 가격에 더 긴 보증을 받아가실 수 있습니다. 우리의 200달러짜리 보증이 주말 내내 반값입니다. 언제나 여러분께서 비용을 절감할 수 있는 방법을 찾고 있는 EMC를 방문해주셔서 감사합니다.

어휘 vote 투표하다 value for money 가격 대비 가치 browse 둘러보다 merchandise 상품 compare 비교하다 conveniently 편리하게 beat 이기다 limited 한정된 extended 길어진 warranty 품질 보증서

71

고난도

What does the speaker say EMC Furniture received recognition for?

(A) Their excellent customer service
(B) Their innovative loyalty program
(C) Their large inventory
(D) Their reasonable prices

화자는 EMC 가구가 무엇으로 인정받았다고 말하는가?
(A) 훌륭한 고객 서비스
(B) 혁신적인 고객 보상제
(C) 다양한 재고
(D) 합리적인 가격

어휘 excellent 훌륭한 innovative 혁신적인 loyalty program 고객 보상제 inventory 물품, 재고(품) reasonable 합리적인

해설 세부 사항 관련 - 화자가 EMC 가구가 인정받았다고 말하는 것
화자가 초반부에 EMC 가구가 디트로이트 쇼핑객들에 의해 최고의 가성비 업체로 뽑혔다는 것을 알고 있느냐(Did you know that EMC Furniture was voted the best value for the money by Detroit shoppers?)고 한 것으로 보아 정답은 (D)이다.

▸▸ **Paraphrasing** 담화의 **the best value for the money** → 정답의 **their reasonable prices**

72

According to the speaker, what can shoppers do in the store?

(A) Access the Internet
(B) Watch a repair process
(C) Sit down to take a break
(D) Receive personalized advice

화자에 따르면, 쇼핑객들은 매장에서 무엇을 할 수 있는가?
(A) 인터넷에 접속할 수 있다.
(B) 수리 과정을 볼 수 있다.
(C) 앉아서 쉴 수 있다.
(D) 개인별 맞춤 조언을 받을 수 있다.

어휘 access 접근[접속]하다 process 절차[과정] personalized 개인별로 맞춤화된

해설 세부 사항 관련 - 화자가 말하는 쇼핑객들이 매장에서 할 수 있는 것
화자가 중반부에 상품을 둘러보는 동안 여러분이 매장 곳곳에 편리하게 위치한 인터넷 키오스크에서 온라인으로 가격을 비교해볼 것을 청한다(While you browse our merchandise, we invite you to compare prices by going online at any of our Internet kiosks located conveniently throughout the store)고 했으므로 정답은 (A)이다.

▸▸ **Paraphrasing** 담화의 **going online** → 정답의 **access the Internet**

73

What is currently on sale?

(A) A disposal method
(B) A club membership
(C) Furniture customization
(D) A product guarantee

현재 무엇이 할인 중인가?
(A) 처분 방법
(B) 클럽 멤버십
(C) 맞춤 가구
(D) 제품 보증

어휘 disposal 처분 method 방법 customization 주문 제작 guarantee 품질 보증서

해설 세부 사항 관련 - 현재 할인 중인 것
화자가 후반부에 우리의 200달러짜리 보증이 주말 내내 반값(Our two-hundred-dollar warranty is half price through the weekend)이라고 했으므로 정답은 (D)이다.

▸▸ **Paraphrasing** 담화의 **our warranty** → 정답의 **a product guarantee**

74-76 담화

> W-Br All right, gather around. ⁷⁴**Let me tell you what you'll be doing here today.** Dorothy and Krista, I'd like you to dust the desks and bookcases and wash the windows. Max, you vacuum the carpets. Travis and Deepak, you clean the break room. Uh, there's some mildew in there, so you'll need this bottle of Ranvex Spray. ⁷⁵**It's pretty strong, so use a small amount and keep the windows open.** ⁷⁶**Now, this isn't a big office, but I'd still like everyone to keep the two-way radio I gave you turned on, just in case.** OK, let's get started.

> 자 그럼, 집합해주세요. **오늘 이곳에서 하실 일을 알려드리겠습니다.** 도로시와 크리스타는 책상과 책장의 먼지를 털어주시고, 창문을 씻어주세요. 맥스는 카펫을 진공청소기로 청소해주세요. 트래비스와 디팩은 휴게실을 청소해주세요. 어, 거기에 곰팡이가 좀 있으니, 이 란벡스 스프레이 병이 필요할 겁니다. **이게 꽤 강하니까, 소량을 사용하시고 창문들을 열어두세요.** 자, **큰 사무실은 아니지만, 그래도 만일을 위해 모두 제가 드린 무전기를 켜놓으시기 바랍니다.** 좋습니다. 시작해봅시다.

> 어휘 gather 모이다 dust 먼지를 털다; 먼지 vacuum 진공청소기로 청소하다 mildew 곰팡이 two-way radio 무전기

74 　　　　　　　　　　　　　　　[고난도]

What is the main purpose of the talk?

(A) To promote some cleaning products
(B) To outline the schedule of a tour
(C) To give assignments to a work crew
(D) To introduce some safety videos

담화의 주요 목적은 무엇인가?
(A) 청소 제품을 홍보하는 것
(B) 관광 일정을 간략히 설명하는 것
(C) 작업반에 업무를 배정하는 것
(D) 안전 비디오를 소개하는 것

어휘 promote 홍보하다 outline 개요를 서술하다 assignment 임무, 배정 work crew 작업반

해설 전체 내용 관련 – 담화의 목적
화자가 초반부에 오늘 이곳에서 할 일을 알려주겠다(Let me tell you what you'll be doing here today)고 하면서 뒤이어 각각의 청자들이 맡게 될 작업 내용에 대해 설명하고 있는 것으로 보아 정답은 (C)이다.

75

What does the speaker say about Ranvex Spray?

(A) It smells good.
(B) It is powerful.
(C) It is a window cleaner.
(D) It comes in a small bottle.

화자는 란벡스 스프레이에 대해 무엇을 말하는가?
(A) 냄새가 좋다.
(B) 강력하다.
(C) 창문 청소 제품이다.
(D) 작은 병에 담겨 나온다.

해설 세부 사항 관련 – 화자가 란벡스 스프레이에 대해 말하는 것
화자가 중반부에 란벡스 스프레이를 언급하면서 이게 꽤 강하니까 소량을 사용하고 창문들을 열어두라(It's pretty strong, so use a small amount and keep the windows open)고 했으므로 정답은 (B)이다.

▸▸ Paraphrasing　담화의 **strong** → 정답의 **powerful**

76

According to the speaker, what has each listener received?

(A) A communication device
(B) Some protective clothing
(C) Some brochures
(D) A floor plan

화자에 따르면, 청자는 각각 무엇을 받았는가?
(A) 통신 장치
(B) 보호복
(C) 안내 책자
(D) 평면도

해설 세부 사항 관련 – 화자가 말하는 각각의 청자가 받은 물건
화자가 후반부에 큰 사무실은 아니지만, 그래도 만일을 위해 모두 제가 드린 무전기를 켜놓기 바란다(this isn't a big office, but I'd still like everyone to keep the two-way radio I gave you turned on, just in case)고 했으므로 정답은 (A)이다.

▸▸ Paraphrasing　담화의 **the two-way radio** → 정답의 **a communication device**

77-79 회의 발췌

> M-Au ⁷⁷**The last thing I'd like to discuss is, um, some news we received from the city. Apparently, they're doing some maintenance and this whole block won't have electricity for most of Tuesday.** I think it will make more sense for everyone to just work from home that day. I know it's a bit unusual, but most of us can get everything we need from our computers and make all of our calls from home. That'll be the only change. ⁷⁸**I expect everyone to be available for team calls or anything else that comes up during the workday.** ⁷⁹**We promised we'd finish making Caliban Financial's Web site by Friday, so I don't want to lose any time.**

마지막으로 제가 말씀드리고 싶은 것은 시로부터 입수한 소식입니다. 듣자 하니, 그들이 정비 작업을 하느라 화요일 대부분 시간에 이 구역 전체에 전기가 들어오지 않을 것입니다. 그날은 모두가 재택근무를 하는 것이 합리적일 것 같습니다. 평소와는 조금 다르겠지만, 우리 대부분은 컴퓨터로 필요한 모든 것을 구할 수 있고 집에서 모든 전화를 할 수 있습니다. 그 점이 유일한 변화일 것입니다. 저는 모두가 팀 통화나 근무 시간 동안 발생하는 어떤 것에도 임할 수 있기를 기대합니다. 우리는 칼리반 금융의 웹사이트를 금요일까지 끝내기로 약속했기 때문에 시간을 낭비하고 싶지 않습니다.

어휘 apparently 보아[듣자] 하니 maintenance 유지, 정비 electricity 전기 make sense 합당하다 available 시간이 있는, 이용할 수 있는 promise 약속하다 lose 잃다, 빼앗기다

77
고난도

What news from the city does the speaker mention?

(A) An inspector will visit local businesses.
(B) An area's power will be turned off.
(C) A construction project will begin.
(D) A major road will be closed.

화자는 시에서 들어온 어떤 소식을 언급하는가?
(A) 조사관이 지역 기업들을 방문할 것이다.
(B) 지역의 전력이 차단될 것이다.
(C) 건설 프로젝트가 시작될 것이다.
(D) 주요 도로가 폐쇄될 것이다.

어휘 inspector 조사관 power 전력 construction 건설 major 주요한

해설 세부 사항 관련 – 화자가 언급한 시로부터의 소식
화자가 도입부에 마지막으로 제가 말씀드리고 싶은 것은 시로부터 입수한 소식(The last thing I'd like to discuss is, um, some news we received from the city)이라며, 그들이 정비 작업을 하느라 화요일 대부분 시간에 이 구역 전체에 전기가 들어오지 않을 것(they're doing some maintenance and this whole block won't have electricity for most of Tuesday)이라고 안내하고 있으므로 정답은 (B)이다.

▸▸ Paraphrasing 담화의 this whole block won't have electricity → 정답의 an area's power will be turned off

78
고난도

What does the speaker mean when he says, "That'll be the only change"?

(A) Employees should use the same login information.
(B) Employees should not submit extra reports.
(C) Employees should work their usual hours.
(D) Employees should not prepare for an evaluation.

화자가 "그 점이 유일한 변화일 것입니다"라고 말한 의도는 무엇인가?
(A) 직원들은 동일한 로그인 정보를 사용해야 한다.
(B) 직원들은 추가 보고서를 제출하면 안 된다.
(C) 직원들은 평소 시간대로 근무해야 한다.
(D) 직원들은 평가에 대비해서는 안 된다.

어휘 submit 제출하다 evaluation 평가

해설 화자의 의도 파악 – 그 점이 유일한 변화일 것이라는 말의 의도
인용문에서 그 점이 유일한 변화일 것이라고 한 후에, 모두가 팀 통화나 근무 시간 동안 발생하는 어떤 일에도 임할 수 있기를 기대한다(I expect everyone to be available for team calls or anything else that comes up during the workday)고 한 것으로 보아 앞서 언급한 변화 이외에는 별다른 변동 사항 없이 평소 근무 시간처럼 일해야 할 것임을 전하려는 의도로 볼 수 있다. 따라서 정답은 (C)이다.

79

What type of project are the listeners working on?

(A) Doing market research
(B) Designing an automobile
(C) Remodeling an office
(D) Building a Web site

청자들은 어떤 종류의 프로젝트를 하고 있는가?
(A) 시장 조사
(B) 자동차 디자인
(C) 사무실 개조
(D) 웹사이트 구축

해설 세부 사항 관련 – 청자들이 일하고 있는 프로젝트의 종류
화자가 마지막에 우리는 칼리반 금융의 웹사이트를 금요일까지 끝내기로 약속했기 때문에 시간을 낭비하고 싶지 않다(We promised we'd finish making Calliban Financial's Web site by Friday, so I don't want to lose any time)고 했으므로 정답은 (D)이다.

80-82 전화 메시지

W-Br Hi, Anne. It's Terry. **80I got your message, and I brought the handouts for the Elsa Kwak workshop to your desk like you requested.** And they look great, by the way. **81Uh, but since you weren't at your desk, I guess that you're still trying to find the projector for the large conference room.** I have no idea why it's missing or where it would be, so I can't help you with that task. But—Ms. Kwak's flight arrives at four P.M., right? **82I could have her back here by six for the group dinner as planned. That would give you some extra time to set up.** Call me back and let me know what you think.

여보세요, 앤. 테리입니다. 당신의 메시지를 받고 요청한 대로 엘사 곽 워크숍을 위한 유인물을 당신 책상에 가져다놓았어요. 훌륭해 보이던데요. 어, 그런데 당신이 책상에 없는 걸 보니 아직도 큰 회의실용 프로젝터를 찾고 있는 것 같네요. 왜 그것이 없어졌고 어디에 있을지도 몰라서 그 일은 제가 도울 수가 없어요. 그렇지만 곽 씨의 항공편이 오후 4시에 도착하는 게 맞죠? 계획대로 단체 저녁식사를 위해 6시까지 제가 그녀를 이곳으로 모셔올 수 있어요. 그러면 당신이 준비할 시간이 좀 더 생길 거예요. 전화 주셔서 어떻게 생각하는지 알려주세요.

어휘 handout 유인물 missing 없어진

80

What is the speaker most likely talking about?

(A) Rearranging a work space
(B) Preparing for a workshop
(C) Setting up some interviews
(D) Handling some vacation requests

화자는 무엇에 대해 말하고 있는 것 같은가?

(A) 작업 공간 재배치
(B) 워크숍 준비
(C) 면접 준비
(D) 휴가 신청 처리

어휘 rearrange 재배치하다 handle 처리하다 vacation 휴가

해설 전체 내용 관련 – 전화 메시지의 주제

화자가 초반부에 당신의 메시지를 받고 요청한 대로 엘사 곽 워크숍을 위한 유인물을 당신 책상에 가져다놓았다(I got your message, and I brought the handouts for the Elsa Kwak workshop to your desk like you requested)고 했고, 뒤이어 워크숍 준비와 관련된 일에 대한 이야기를 계속하고 있으므로 정답은 (B)이다.

81   `고난도`

What problem does the speaker mention?

(A) Some equipment cannot be located.
(B) Some furniture is very heavy.
(C) A conference room is unavailable.
(D) A software program is slow.

화자는 무슨 문제를 언급하는가?

(A) 일부 장비를 찾을 수 없다.
(B) 일부 가구가 매우 무겁다.
(C) 회의실을 이용할 수 없다.
(D) 소프트웨어 프로그램이 느리다.

어휘 locate 찾다 unavailable 이용할 수 없는

해설 세부 사항 관련 – 화자가 언급한 문제

화자가 중반부에 그런데 당신이 책상에 없는 걸 보니 아직도 큰 회의실용 프로젝터를 찾고 있는 것 같다(but since you weren't at your desk, I guess that you're still trying to find the projector for the large conference room)고 언급한 것으로 보아 정답은 (A)이다.

> ▸ **Paraphrasing** 담화의 **still trying to find the projector**
> → 정답의 **some equipment cannot be located**

82   `고난도`

What does the speaker mean when she says, "Ms. Kwak's flight arrives at 4 P.M., right"?

(A) She is offering assistance to the listener.
(B) She recommends postponing a decision.
(C) She thinks a message contains incorrect information.
(D) She is grateful for the listener's support.

화자가 "곽 씨의 항공편이 오후 4시에 도착하는 게 맞죠?"라고 말한 의도는 무엇인가?

(A) 청자에게 도움을 제공하고 있다.
(B) 결정을 미룰 것을 권한다.
(C) 메시지에 부정확한 정보가 포함되어 있다고 생각한다.
(D) 청자의 지원에 감사한다.

어휘 assistance 도움 postpone 미루다 contain 포함하다 incorrect 부정확한 grateful 감사하는 support 지원

해설 화자의 의도 파악 – 곽 씨의 항공편이 오후 4시에 도착하는 게 맞냐고 물은 의도

인용문에서 곽 씨의 일정에 대해 물은 뒤, 계획대로 단체 저녁식사를 위해 6시까지 제가 그녀를 이곳으로 모셔올 수 있다(I could have her back here by six for the group dinner as planned)면서 그러면 당신이 준비할 시간이 좀 더 생길 것(That would give you some extra time to set up)이라고 했으므로 청자가 워크숍을 준비할 수 있도록 도와주려고 일정을 확인한 것임을 알 수 있다. 따라서 정답은 (A)이다.

83-85 전화 메시지

M-Cn Hello, my name is Frederick Lund, and [83] I'm calling from Patton Enterprises. I understand that you are a contractor who specializes in residential properties, and I'd like to introduce my company to you. [83] **We are the area's leading supplier of carpet remnants— that is, pieces that are left over from fitted carpet jobs.** You can pick up these pieces at incredible prices, and [84] **the items we have in stock are different every week.** [85] **Best of all, if you purchase at least three items, I can ship them to you at no cost.** Please call me back at 555-0188 to discuss this further if you're interested. Thank you.

여보세요, 제 이름은 프레데릭 룬드이고, 패튼 엔터프라이즈에서 전화드립니다. 귀하께서 주거용 부동산을 전문으로 취급하는 도급업자이라고 알고 있어서, 저희 회사를 소개해드리고자 합니다. 저희는 이 지역에서 카펫 자투리, 즉 맞춤 카펫 작업에서 남은 조각들을 공급하는 선두 업체입니다. 믿을 수 없는 가격에 이 조각들을 구입하실 수 있으며, 저희가 재고로 갖고 있는 물품들은 매주 다릅니다. 무엇보다도 귀하께서 최소 세 가지 제품을 구입하실 경우 그것들을 무료로 배송해 드립니다. 관심 있으시면 이 문제를 더 논의할 수 있도록 555-0188로 다시 전화 주십시오. 감사합니다.

어휘 contractor 도급업자 specialize in ~을 전문으로 하다 residential 주거(용)의 supplier 공급자 remnant 자투리(천), 남은 부분 incredible 믿을 수 없는 in stock 재고로

83   `고난도`

What does Patton Enterprises sell?

(A) Power tools
(B) Floor coverings
(C) Home appliances
(D) Safety gear

패튼 엔터프라이즈는 무엇을 판매하는가?

(A) 전동 공구
(B) 바닥재
(C) 가전제품
(D) 안전 장비

해설 세부 사항 관련 – 패튼 엔터프라이즈가 판매하는 것

화자가 초반부에 패튼 엔터프라이즈에서 전화드린다(I'm calling from Patton Enterprises)고 했으므로 화자는 패튼 엔터프라이즈의 직원임을 알 수 있고, 중반부에 이 지역에서 카펫 자투리, 즉 맞춤 카펫 작업에서 남은 조각들을 공급하는 선두 업체(We are the area's leading supplier of carpet remnants—that is, pieces that are left over from fitted carpet jobs)라고 소개한 것으로 보아 정답은 (B)이다.

▸▸ **Paraphrasing** 담화의 **carpet remnants**
→ 정답의 **floor coverings**

84

What does the speaker mention about the business's merchandise?

(A) It is energy-efficient.
(B) It is made from recycled materials.
(C) Its ratings are consistently positive.
(D) Its availability changes regularly.

화자는 회사의 상품에 대해 무엇을 언급하는가?

(A) 에너지 효율적이다.
(B) 재활용된 재료들로 만들어진다.
(C) 평가가 꾸준히 좋다.
(D) 구입 가능성이 정기적으로 변한다.

어휘 efficient 효율적인 recycled 재활용된 material 재료, 자료 rating 순위[평가] consistently 일관되게 availability 가능성 regularly 정기적으로

해설 세부 사항 관련 – 화자가 회사의 상품에 대해 언급한 것

화자가 중반부에 믿을 수 있는 가격에 이 조각들을 구입할 수 있으며, 저희가 재고로 갖고 있는 물품들은 매주 다르다(You can pick up these pieces at incredible prices, and the items we have in stock are different every week)고 했으므로 정답은 (D)이다.

▸▸ **Paraphrasing** 담화의 **items we have in stock are different every week**
→ 정답의 **its availability changes regularly**

85

What does the speaker offer to do for the listener?

(A) Send a catalog
(B) Deliver items for free
(C) Give a demonstration
(D) Provide a consultation

화자는 청자를 위해 무엇을 하겠다고 제안하는가?

(A) 카탈로그를 보낸다.
(B) 무료로 제품을 배송한다.
(C) 시연을 한다.
(D) 상담을 제공한다.

어휘 demonstration (사용법 등에 대한 시범) 설명 consultation 상담

해설 세부 사항 관련 – 화자가 청자를 위해 한다고 제안하는 것

화자가 후반부에 최소 세 가지 제품을 구입할 경우에는 그것들을 무료로 배송해준다(if you purchase at least three items, I can ship them to you at no cost)고 했으므로 정답은 (B)이다.

▸▸ **Paraphrasing** 담화의 **ship them to you at no cost**
→ 정답의 **deliver items for free**

86-88 방송

W-Am I'm Luisa Peters, reporting from Cavette for *Sports News Today*. As you can see, I'm here at the celebration of the Cavette Mustangs' national baseball championship. **86 There are the team's players and coaches, cruising by in open vehicles and waving at the cheering crowd.** And what a crowd it is! **87 Most of these people were here when I arrived,** and I got here at 6 A.M.! Clearly there is a lot of excitement about the Mustangs' historic win. **88 If you missed the game, you can visit sportsnewstoday.com right now to see clips of its most exciting moments.** But don't forget to tune back in to our program. At the end of the route, some of the players are going to give speeches.

카베트에서 보도하는 〈스포츠 뉴스 투데이〉의 루이사 피터스입니다. 보시다시피, 저는 이곳 카베트 머스탱의 전국 야구 선수권 대회 기념식에 와 있습니다. 팀의 선수들과 코치들이 오픈카를 타고 지나가며 환호하는 관중들에게 손을 흔들고 있습니다. 대단한 인파입니다! 이 사람들 대부분이 제가 도착했을 때 이곳에 있었는데, 저는 아침 6시에 여기 왔습니다! 머스탱의 역사적인 우승에 많이 흥분하고 있는 모습이 역력합니다. 경기를 놓치셨다면, 지금 바로 sportsnewstoday.com을 방문하시면 가장 흥분되는 순간들을 동영상으로 보실 수 있습니다. 하지만 우리 프로그램으로 다시 채널을 맞추시는 것을 잊지 마세요. 행렬 끝에 몇몇 선수들이 연설을 할 예정입니다.

어휘 celebration 기념 행사 cruise 나아가다 vehicle 차량 wave (손 등을) 흔들다 cheering 환호하는 crowd 군중 excitement 흥분 miss 놓치다 clip 동영상 route 길

86　　　　　　　　　　　고난도

What kind of event is taking place?

(A) A sports competition
(B) A groundbreaking ceremony
(C) An outdoor fund-raiser
(D) A street parade

어떤 종류의 행사가 열리고 있는가?

(A) 스포츠 대회
(B) 기공식
(C) 야외 모금 행사
(D) 거리 행진

해설 세부 사항 관련 - 행사의 종류

화자가 초반부에 팀의 선수들과 코치들이 오픈카를 타고 지나가며 환호하는 관중들에게 손을 흔들고 있다(There are the team's players and coaches, cruising by in open vehicles and waving at the cheering crowd)고 한 것으로 보아 정답은 (D)이다.

87
고난도

Why does the speaker say, "I got here at 6 A.M."?

(A) To make a recommendation about future events
(B) To emphasize how popular the event is
(C) To explain how she got an advantage
(D) To indicate frustration with a delay

화자가 "저는 아침 6시에 여기 왔습니다"라고 말한 이유는 무엇인가?

(A) 향후 행사에 대해 추천하려고
(B) 행사가 얼마나 인기 있는지 강조하려고
(C) 어떻게 이득을 보았는지 설명하려고
(D) 지연으로 인한 불만을 나타내려고

어휘 recommendation 추천 emphasize 강조하다 advantage 이점 indicate 나타내다 frustration 불만 delay 지연

해설 화자의 의도 파악 - 저는 아침 6시에 여기 왔다는 말의 의도

앞에서 이 사람들 대부분이 제가 도착했을 때 이곳에 있었다(Most of these people were here when I arrived)고 한 뒤, 인용문을 언급한 것으로 보아 자신이 아침 6시라는 이른 시간에 도착했는데도 사람들이 이미 와 있었다며 행사가 인기가 많다는 것을 알리려는 의도로 볼 수 있다. 따라서 정답은 (B)이다.

88

What is available on a Web site?

(A) A route map
(B) Game highlights
(C) Athlete biographies
(D) A public discussion

웹사이트에서 이용할 수 있는 것은 무엇인가?

(A) 노선도
(B) 경기 하이라이트
(C) 운동선수의 전기
(D) 공개 토론

어휘 route 길, 노선 biography 전기, 자서전

해설 세부 사항 관련 - 웹사이트에서 이용할 수 있는 것

화자가 후반부에 경기를 놓쳤다면 지금 바로 sportsnewstoday.com을 방문하시면 가장 흥분되는 순간들을 동영상으로 볼 수 있다(if you missed the game, you can visit sportsnewstoday.com right now to see clips of its most exciting moments)고 했으므로 정답은 (B)이다.

▸▸ Paraphrasing 담화의 clips of its most exciting moments → 정답의 game highlights

89-91 공지

M-Au Good morning, managers. **89I need to inform you of an upcoming interruption to our factory's operations.** Management approved a request from Foster Television Network to film part of an episode of the show *Bertram* here next week. **90As I understand it, the show's star is going to chase another character through the facility and have a big fight with him.** Sounds exciting, doesn't it? Anyway, both the afternoon and night shifts will be affected during the two days of filming. **91All of the important details are in the memo that I'm handing out now. Please go over it briefly with your employees so that they know what to expect.**

좋은 아침입니다, 관리자 여러분. **우리 공장 가동이 곧 중단될 것임을 알려드리겠습니다.** 경영진은 다음 주 이곳에서 〈버트람〉 쇼의 에피소드 일부를 촬영하겠다는 포스터 텔레비전 네트워크의 요청을 승인했습니다. **제가 아는 바로는 쇼의 스타가 시설물 내에서 다른 캐릭터를 쫓아가 그와 큰 싸움을 벌일 예정입니다.** 흥미진진할 것 같지 않나요? 어쨌든 낮 근무와 밤 근무조가 모두 이틀간의 촬영 기간 동안 영향을 받을 것입니다. **모든 중요한 세부 사항은 제가 지금 나눠드리고 있는 메모에 있습니다. 직원들이 무슨 일이 있을지 알 수 있도록 간단히 함께 검토해보세요.**

어휘 inform 알리다 upcoming 곧 있을 interruption 중단 approve 승인하다 film 촬영하다 chase 뒤쫓다 facility 시설 shift 근무조, 근무 시간 affect 영향을 미치다 hand out 나눠주다 go over 검토하다

89

Where most likely is the announcement being made?

(A) At a television studio
(B) At a shopping mall
(C) At a sports stadium
(D) At a manufacturing plant

어디에서 공지가 이루어지고 있는 것 같은가?

(A) 텔레비전 스튜디오
(B) 쇼핑 몰
(C) 스포츠 경기장
(D) 제조 공장

해설 전체 내용 관련 - 공지의 장소

화자가 초반부에 우리 공장 가동이 곧 중단될 것임을 알려드리겠다(I need to inform you of an upcoming interruption to our factory's operations)고 했으므로 정답은 (D)이다.

▸▸ Paraphrasing 담화의 our factory → 정답의 a manufacturing plant

90

What does the speaker say about a television show episode?

(A) It will include an action scene.
(B) It will be broadcast next week.
(C) It will feature a guest star.
(D) It will be one hour long.

화자는 텔레비전 쇼 에피소드에 대해 무엇을 말하는가?

(A) 액션 장면이 들어갈 것이다.
(B) 다음 주에 방영될 것이다.
(C) 게스트 스타가 나올 것이다.
(D) 한 시간 분량일 것이다.

어휘 include 포함하다　broadcast 방송하다　feature 특별히 포함하다

해설 세부 사항 관련 – 화자가 텔레비전 쇼 에피소드에 언급하는 것

화자가 중반부에 제가 아는 바로는 쇼의 스타가 시설물 내에서 다른 캐릭터를 쫓아가 그와 큰 싸움을 벌일 예정(As I understand it, the show's star is going to chase another character through the facility and have a big fight with him)이라고 언급했으므로 정답은 (A)이다.

91

What are the listeners asked to do?

(A) Distribute costumes to employees
(B) Conduct an inspection of a facility
(C) Avoid certain parts of a workplace
(D) Review the contents of a document

청자들은 무엇을 하라고 요청되는가?

(A) 직원들에게 의상을 나눠주기
(B) 시설 점검하기
(C) 작업장의 특정 구역 피하기
(D) 서류 내용 검토하기

어휘 distribute 나눠주다　costume 의상　conduct 실시[수행]하다 inspection 점검　avoid 피하다　content 내용

해설 세부 사항 관련 – 청자들이 요청받은 일

화자가 후반부에 모든 중요한 세부 사항은 제가 지금 나눠드리고 있는 메모에 있다(All of the important details are in the memo that I'm handing out now)면서, 직원들이 무슨 일이 있을지 알 수 있도록 간단히 함께 검토하라(Please go over it briefly with your employees so that they know what to expect)고 요청했으므로 정답은 (D)이다.

▸▸ Paraphrasing　담화의 go over → 정답의 review

92-94 회의 발췌

> **W-Br** OK, here's an idea I've been considering for improving our sales numbers. **92 A few weeks ago, I ran into a personal contact who's also in the retail industry, and she told me about a Web site called "Zatmo". 93 It sells electronic coupons for discounts on other businesses' goods.** Zatmo gets a commission if a minimum number of people buy the coupons. My contact said it really raised her store's profile. **93 I think we should try it. 94 But—does anybody see any possible downsides to working with Zatmo? If so, let's talk them over now.**

자, 여기 우리 판매 수치 개선을 위해 제가 생각해온 아이디어입니다. 몇 주 전에 마찬가지로 소매업에 종사하고 있는 지인과 우연히 마주쳤는데, 그녀가 제게 "재트모"라는 웹사이트에 대해 말해줬습니다. 그곳은 타사 제품들에 대한 온라인 할인 쿠폰을 판매합니다. 재트모는 최소한의 사람들이 쿠폰을 구입할 경우 수수료를 받습니다. 제 지인이 그 덕에 자기 매장의 인지도가 확실히 올랐다고 하더군요. 우리도 시도해봐야 한다고 생각합니다. 혹시 재트모와 함께 일하는 것에 단점이 있다고 생각하시는 분이 계신가요? 만약 그렇다면 지금 논의해보도록 하죠.

어휘 run into ~와 우연히 마주치다　contact 연줄, 인맥　retail 소매　electronic 온라인의　commission 수수료　raise 올리다 profile 인지도　downside 단점, 불리한 면

92　고난도

What does the speaker say she recently did?

(A) She went to an industry conference.
(B) She contacted a start-up company.
(C) She spoke with an acquaintance.
(D) She read a retail trade magazine.

화자는 최근에 무엇을 했다고 말하는가?

(A) 산업 회의에 참석했다.
(B) 신생 기업에 연락했다.
(C) 지인과 대화를 나눴다.
(D) 소매 업계 잡지를 읽었다.

어휘 conference 회의　start-up company 신생 기업 acquaintance 지인　trade magazine 업계지

해설 세부 사항 관련 – 화자가 최근에 했다고 말하는 것

화자가 초반부에 몇 주 전에 마찬가지로 소매업에 종사하고 있는 지인과 우연히 마주쳤는데, 그녀가 제게 "재트모"라는 웹사이트에 대해 말해줬다(A few weeks ago, I ran into a personal contact who's also in the retail industry, and she told me about a Web site called "Zatmo")고 했으므로 정답은 (C)이다.

▸▸ Paraphrasing　담화의 a personal contact → 정답의 an acquaintance

93

How does the speaker propose increasing sales?

(A) By making a deal to buy some goods in bulk
(B) By expanding into new areas of the country
(C) By selling discount vouchers through an online platform
(D) By raising the commission paid to salespeople

화자는 어떻게 판매를 높이자고 제안하는가?
(A) 제품을 대량으로 사는 거래를 함으로써
(B) 국내의 새로운 지역으로 진출함으로써
(C) 온라인 플랫폼을 통해 할인 쿠폰을 판매함으로써
(D) 영업 사원들에게 지급되는 수수료를 올림으로써

어휘 deal 거래 in bulk 대량으로 expand 확장하다 voucher 쿠폰

해설 세부 사항 관련 - 화자가 제안하는 판매 신장 방법

화자가 재트모라는 웹사이트에 대해 소개하면서 그곳은 다른 회사들의 제품에 대한 온라인 할인 쿠폰을 판매한다(It sells electronic coupons for discounts on other businesses' goods)며 우리도 시도해봐야 한다고 생각한다(I think we should try it)고 했다. 따라서 재트모를 이용해 할인 쿠폰을 판매하는 제안을 하고 있다고 볼 수 있으므로 정답은 (C)이다.

▸▸ Paraphrasing 담화의 coupons for discounts
→ 정답의 discount vouchers

94
[고난도]

What does the speaker ask the listeners to discuss?
(A) Their departments' achievements
(B) The creation of a project team
(C) A possible launch date
(D) Disadvantages of her idea

화자는 청자들에게 무엇을 논의하라고 하는가?
(A) 부서의 성과
(B) 프로젝트 팀의 조성
(C) 가능한 출시일
(D) 여자 아이디어의 단점

어휘 achievement 업적, 성취 creation 창설, 조성 launch 출시; 시작하다 disadvantage 단점

해설 세부 사항 관련 - 화자가 청자들에게 논의를 요구하는 것

화자가 후반부에 재트모와 함께 일하는 것에 단점이 있다고 생각하는 사람이 있는지(does anybody see any possible downsides to working with Zatmo?)를 묻고 있는 것으로 보아 정답은 (D)이다.

▸▸ Paraphrasing 담화의 downsides
→ 정답의 disadvantages

95-97 담화 + 조리법

M-Cn Welcome to the latest episode of Quentin's Kitchen. **95 A couple of the comments under last week's video asked for healthy snacks for summer.** So, today I'm going to show you how to make my favorite smoothies. Let's start with the blueberry kale smoothie. You'll need blueberries, baby kale, orange juice, and plain yogurt in the amounts you can see on the screen here. **96 You can add more or less yogurt depending on how creamy you want the smoothie to be.** Then, just toss it all into the

blender! It's ready once the kale is fully blended. **97 I recommend drinking it right away so that the ingredients don't separate.** It becomes a little unappetizing then.

쿠엔틴스 키친의 최신 에피소드에 오신 것을 환영합니다. 지난주 영상에 달린 몇몇 댓글들에서 여름을 위한 건강 간식을 요청하셨습니다. 그래서, 오늘은 제가 여러분에게 가장 좋아하는 스무디를 만드는 방법을 보여드리겠습니다. 블루베리 케일 스무디로 시작해볼게요. 블루베리, 베이비 케일, 오렌지 주스, 그리고 플레인 요거트가 여기 화면에 보이는 양만큼 필요합니다. 스무디가 얼마나 크리미하길 원하시는지에 따라 요거트를 더하거나 덜 넣으실 수 있습니다. 그리고 나서, 이것들을 모두 믹서기에 부어주세요! 케일이 완전히 섞이면 다 된 거예요. 재료들이 분리되지 않도록 바로 마실 것을 권해드립니다. 그러면 맛이 좀 떨어지거든요.

어휘 latest 최신의 comment 논평, 언급 kale 케일 depending on ~에 따라 toss (가볍게) 던지다 blender 믹서기 blend 섞다 ingredient 재료 separate 분리되다 unappetizing 맛없는

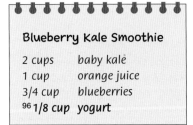

Blueberry Kale Smoothie

2 cups	baby kale
1 cup	orange juice
3/4 cup	blueberries
96 1/8 cup	yogurt

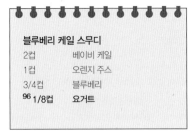

블루베리 케일 스무디

2컵	베이비 케일
1컵	오렌지 주스
3/4컵	블루베리
96 1/8컵	요거트

95
[고난도]

Who most likely are the listeners?
(A) Viewers of an online video
(B) Visitors to a supermarket
(C) Students at a cooking school
(D) The audience of a radio show

청자들은 누구일 것 같은가?
(A) 온라인 비디오의 시청자
(B) 슈퍼마켓의 방문객
(C) 요리 학교의 학생
(D) 라디오 프로그램의 청취자

해설 전체 내용 관련 - 청자들의 신분

화자가 초반부에 청자들을 향해 지난주 영상에 달린 몇몇 댓글들에서 여름을 위한 건강 간식을 요청하셨다(A couple of the comments under last week's video asked for healthy snacks for summer)고 한 것으로 보아 정답은 (A)이다.

96

Look at the graphic. Which amount does the speaker say can be adjusted?

(A) 2 cups
(B) 1 cup
(C) 3/4 cup
(D) 1/8 cup

시각 정보에 의하면, 화자는 어떤 양을 조절할 수 있다고 말하는가?

(A) 2컵
(B) 1컵
(C) 3/4컵
(D) 1/8컵

┤ 해설 시각 정보 연계 – 화자가 조절할 수 있다고 말하는 양

화자가 중반부에 스무디가 얼마나 크리미하길 원하는지에 따라 요거트를 더하거나 덜 넣을 수 있다(You can add more or less yogurt depending on how creamy you want the smoothie to be)고 했고, 시각 정보에 나온 조리법에 따르면 요거트는 1/8컵으로 나와 있으므로 정답은 (D)이다.

97

What does the speaker recommend doing?

(A) Consuming the smoothie immediately
(B) Refrigerating the ingredients beforehand
(C) Serving small amounts as appetizers
(D) Using a special setting on the blender

화자는 무엇을 하기를 권하는가?

(A) 스무디를 즉시 마실 것
(B) 재료들을 사전에 냉장 보관할 것
(C) 전채로서 조금만 섭취할 것
(D) 믹서기의 특정 설정을 이용할 것

┤ 어휘 consume 소비하다 immediately 즉시 refrigerate 냉장보관하다 beforehand 사전에 serve 제공하다 appetizer 전채

┤ 해설 세부 사항 관련 – 화자의 권고사항

화자가 후반부에 스무디 재료들이 분리되지 않도록 바로 마실 것을 권한다(I recommend drinking it right away so that the ingredients don't separate)고 했으므로 정답은 (A)이다.

▸▸ **Paraphrasing** 담화의 **drinking it right away**
→ 정답의 **consuming the smoothie immediately**

98-100 전화 메시지 + 웹페이지 레이아웃

M-Au Hi Wakana, it's Leo. I'm just looking over the layout options for our Web site that you sent over. 98 **If I have to choose, I prefer the one that has both our logo and the drop-down menus on the left side of the screen.** 99 **But will it allow us to feature high-quality photographs of our property listings?** That's the most important feature, anyway. 100 **Uh, also, I know you wanted**

to interview me for the site's "About Us" **section, but I'm just too busy to meet in person this week.** I do have a long car drive to meet a prospective buyer tomorrow morning, though. 100 **Could we talk on the phone as I drive?** Let me know.

여보세요 와카나, 레오입니다. 당신이 보낸 우리 웹사이트를 위한 레이아웃 옵션을 지금 막 보고 있어요. 제가 골라야 한다면, 저는 화면 왼쪽에 우리 로고와 드롭다운 메뉴가 둘 다 있는 것이 마음에 들어요. 그런데 우리 부동산 목록의 고화질 사진을 포함시킬 수 있을까요? 어쨌든 이게 가장 중요한 특징이거든요. 어, 또, 사이트의 "회사 소개" 부분을 위해 저를 인터뷰하길 원하는 건 알지만, 이번 주에는 너무 바빠서 직접 만날 수가 없어요. 내일 아침에 구매 예정자를 만나러 장시간 운전을 해야 해요. 제가 운전하면서 통화할 수 있을까요? 알려주세요.

┤ 어휘 layout 레이아웃[배치] option 선택(권) feature 특별히포함하다; 특징 property 부동산 listing 목록 section 부분 in person 직접 prospective 예상되는, 장래의

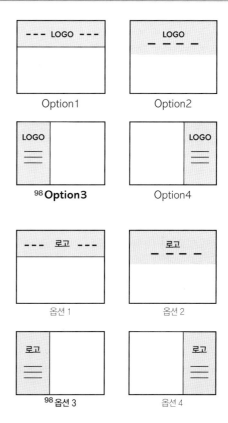

Option1   Option2

98 **Option3**   Option4

옵션 1   옵션 2

98 **옵션 3**   옵션 4

98

Look at the graphic. Which option does the speaker prefer?

(A) Option 1
(B) Option 2
(C) Option 3
(D) Option 4

시각 정보에 의하면, 화자는 어느 옵션을 선호하는가?
(A) 옵션 1
(B) 옵션 2
(C) **옵션 3**
(D) 옵션 4

해설 시각 정보 연계 – 화자가 선호하는 옵션

화자가 초반부에 제가 골라야 한다면, 저는 화면 왼쪽에 우리 로고와 드롭다운 메뉴가 둘 다 있는 것이 마음에 든다(If I have to choose, I prefer the one that has both our logo and the drop-down menus on the left side of the screen)고 했고, 웹페이지 레이아웃에 따르면 해당 옵션은 옵션 3이므로 정답은 (C)이다.

99

Where most likely does the speaker work?

(A) At a real estate firm
(B) At a photography studio
(C) At a hotel chain
(D) A tour agency

화자는 어디에서 일할 것 같은가?

(A) 부동산 회사
(B) 사진 스튜디오
(C) 호텔 체인
(D) 여행사

해설 전체 내용 관련 – 화자의 근무지

화자가 중반부에 우리 부동산 목록의 고화질 사진을 포함시킬 수 있을지(will it allow us to feature high-quality photographs of our property listings?)를 묻고 있는 것으로 보아 정답은 (A)이다.

100

What does the speaker suggest doing over the phone?

(A) Discussing layout styles
(B) Apologizing to a client
(C) Carrying out an interview
(D) Giving some driving directions

화자는 전화로 무엇을 하자고 제안하는가?

(A) 레이아웃 스타일 논의하기
(B) 고객에게 사과하기
(C) 인터뷰 수행하기
(D) 운전 길 안내하기

어휘 apologize 사과하다 carry out 수행하다 directions 길 안내

해설 세부 사항 관련 – 화자가 전화로 하자고 제안하는 일

화자가 후반부에 사이트의 "회사 소개" 부분을 위해 저를 인터뷰하길 원하는 건 알지만 이번 주에는 너무 바빠서 직접 만날 수가 없다(I know you wanted to interview me for the site's "About Us" section, but I'm just too busy to meet in person this week)고 한 뒤, 운전하면서 통화할 수 있을지(Could we talk on the phone as I drive?)를 묻고 있으므로 정답은 (C)이다.

TEST 4

1 (D)	**2** (A)	**3** (D)	**4** (B)	**5** (C)
6 (A)	**7** (B)	**8** (C)	**9** (C)	**10** (A)
11 (B)	**12** (A)	**13** (A)	**14** (C)	**15** (B)
16 (C)	**17** (A)	**18** (B)	**19** (A)	**20** (C)
21 (B)	**22** (B)	**23** (C)	**24** (A)	**25** (C)
26 (A)	**27** (A)	**28** (A)	**29** (B)	**30** (C)
31 (B)	**32** (C)	**33** (B)	**34** (A)	**35** (A)
36 (D)	**37** (C)	**38** (D)	**39** (A)	**40** (C)
41 (A)	**42** (C)	**43** (D)	**44** (C)	**45** (D)
46 (B)	**47** (B)	**48** (A)	**49** (D)	**50** (D)
51 (B)	**52** (A)	**53** (A)	**54** (C)	**55** (B)
56 (D)	**57** (B)	**58** (B)	**59** (B)	**60** (C)
61 (D)	**62** (C)	**63** (A)	**64** (C)	**65** (A)
66 (A)	**67** (B)	**68** (B)	**69** (D)	**70** (C)
71 (C)	**72** (D)	**73** (A)	**74** (A)	**75** (B)
76 (D)	**77** (D)	**78** (A)	**79** (C)	**80** (B)
81 (A)	**82** (B)	**83** (A)	**84** (C)	**85** (A)
86 (B)	**87** (D)	**88** (A)	**89** (C)	**90** (D)
91 (D)	**92** (D)	**93** (C)	**94** (B)	**95** (D)
96 (A)	**97** (C)	**98** (B)	**99** (C)	**100** (D)

PART 1

1   W-Br

(A) They're lifting a box in an office.
(B) They're shaking hands with each other.
(C) One of the men is checking his watch.
(D) One of the men is touching a keyboard.

(A) 사람들은 사무실에서 상자를 들어올리고 있다.
(B) 사람들은 서로 악수를 하고 있다.
(C) 남자들 중 한 명이 시계를 확인하고 있다.
(D) 남자들 중 한 명이 키보드를 만지고 있다.

어휘   lift 들어 올리다   shake hands 악수하다

해설   2인 이상 등장 사진 – 인물의 동작 묘사

(A) 동사 오답. 사람들이 사무실에서 상자를 들어 올리고 있는(are lifting a box in an office) 모습이 아니므로 오답.
(B) 동사 오답. 사람들이 서로 악수를 하고 있는(are shaking hands with each other) 모습이 아니므로 오답.
(C) 동사 오답. 남자들 중 한 명이 시계를 확인하고 있는(is checking his watch) 모습이 아니므로 오답.
(D) 정답. 남자들 중 한 명이 키보드를 만지고 있는(is touching a keyboard) 모습이므로 정답.

2   M-Au

(A) A man is using a pole for a task.
(B) A man is watering some plants.
(C) A man is swimming in a pool.
(D) A man is painting a deck.

(A) 남자는 작업을 위해 막대기를 사용하고 있다.
(B) 남자는 식물에 물을 주고 있다.
(C) 남자는 수영장에서 수영하고 있다.
(D) 남자는 테라스를 페인트칠하고 있다.

어휘   pole 막대기   task 일   deck 테라스, 갑판

해설   1인 등장 사진 – 인물의 동작 묘사

(A) 정답. 남자가 작업을 위해 막대기를 사용하고 있는(is using a pole for a task) 모습이므로 정답.
(B) 동사 오답. 남자가 식물에 물을 주고 있는(is watering some plants) 모습이 아니므로 오답.
(C) 동사 오답. 남자가 수영장에서 수영하고 있는(is swimming in a pool) 모습이 아니므로 오답.
(D) 동사 오답. 남자가 테라스를 페인트칠하고 있는(is painting a deck) 모습이 아니므로 오답.

3   M-Cn

(A) Some people are standing around a conference table.
(B) Images are being projected on a whiteboard.
(C) A woman is handing out bottles of water.
(D) A woman is addressing meeting participants.

(A) 사람들이 회의 테이블 주변에 서 있다.
(B) 이미지들이 화이트보드에 비춰지고 있다.
(C) 여자는 물병을 나눠주고 있다.
(D) 여자는 회의 참가자들에게 발표를 하고 있다.

어휘   conference 회의   hand out 나눠주다   address 연설하다   participant 참가자

해설   혼합 사진 – 사람 또는 사물 묘사

(A) 동사 오답. 사람들이 회의 테이블 주변에 서 있는(are standing around a conference table) 모습이 아니므로 오답.
(B) 동사 오답. 이미지들이 화이트보드에 비춰지고 있는(are being projected on a whiteboard) 모습이 아니므로 오답.

(C) 동사 오답. 여자가 물병을 나눠주고 있는(is handing out bottles of water) 모습이 아니므로 오답.

(D) 정답. 여자가 회의 참가자들에게 발표를 하고 있는(is addressing meeting participants) 모습이므로 정답.

4 W-Am

고난도

(A) One of the glass jars is empty.
(B) There are several pieces of silverware in a cup.
(C) A kitchen knife has been left on a plate.
(D) Bowls have been stacked on a counter.

(A) 유리병 중 하나는 비어 있다.
(B) 컵에 은식기가 몇 개 있다.
(C) 부엌칼이 접시에 놓여 있다.
(D) 우묵한 그릇들이 카운터에 쌓여 있다.

어휘 jar 병 empty 빈 silverware 은식기 plate 접시 bowl (우묵한) 그릇 stack 쌓다

해설 배경 사진 – 실내 사물의 상태 묘사

(A) 상태 표현 오답. 유리병 중 하나(one of the glass jars)가 비어 있는(is empty) 상태가 아니므로 오답.

(B) 정답. 은식기 여러 개(several pieces of silverware)가 컵에 들어 있는 (in a cup) 모습이므로 정답.

(C) 사진에 없는 명사를 이용한 오답. 사진에 부엌칼(a kitchen knife)의 모습이 보이지 않으므로 오답.

(D) 사진에 없는 명사를 이용한 오답. 사진에 우묵한 그릇(bowls)의 모습이 보이지 않으므로 오답.

5 W-Br

(A) A gallery tour is taking place.
(B) A man is putting a picture in a frame.
(C) A group of people is being photographed.
(D) Lights have been turned toward some artwork.

(A) 미술관 관람이 진행 중이다.
(B) 남자는 액자에 사진을 끼우고 있다.
(C) 한 무리의 사람들이 사진 촬영되고 있다.
(D) 조명들이 예술 작품을 향해 있다.

어휘 take place 열리다 frame 액자 photograph ~의 사진을 찍다; 사진 artwork 예술 작품

해설 혼합 사진 – 사람 또는 사물 묘사

(A) 동사 오답. 미술관 관람(a gallery tour)이 진행 중인(is taking place) 모습이 아니므로 오답.

(B) 사진에 없는 명사를 이용한 오답. 사진에 사진(a picture)과 액자(a frame)의 모습이 보이지 않으므로 오답.

(C) 정답. 한 무리의 사람들이 사진 촬영되고 있는(is being photographed) 모습이므로 정답.

(D) 사진에 없는 명사를 이용한 오답. 사진에 예술 작품(artwork)의 모습이 보이지 않으므로 오답.

6 M-Au

고난도

(A) Some shirts have been hung on racks.
(B) Some hats have been placed in a shopping cart.
(C) A woman is laying a product on a shelf.
(D) A window display is being rearranged.

(A) 셔츠 몇 장이 옷걸이에 걸려 있다.
(B) 모자 몇 개가 쇼핑 카트에 담겨 있다.
(C) 여자는 선반에 제품을 놓고 있다.
(D) 쇼윈도 상품 진열이 재배치되고 있다.

어휘 rack 걸이[거치대], 선반 lay 놓다[두다] shelf 선반 rearrange 재배치하다

해설 혼합 사진 – 사람 또는 사물 묘사

(A) 정답. 셔츠 몇 장(some shirts)이 옷걸이에 걸려 있는(have been hung on racks) 모습이므로 정답.

(B) 사진에 없는 명사를 이용한 오답. 사진에 쇼핑 카트(a shopping cart)의 모습이 보이지 않으므로 오답.

(C) 동사 오답. 여자가 선반에 제품을 놓고 있는(is laying a product on a shelf) 모습이 아니므로 오답.

(D) 동사 오답. 쇼윈도 상품 진열(a window display)이 재배치되고 있는(is being rearranged) 모습이 아니므로 오답.

PART 2

7

M-Au Why did you nominate Melanie for an employee award?

W-Br (A) I wish I could, but I'm busy.
(B) Because she works really hard.
(C) The "Team Player" award.

왜 멜라니를 직원 상에 지명하셨나요?
(A) 저도 그러고 싶지만, 바빠서요.
(B) 그녀는 열심히 일하니까요.
(C) "팀 플레이어" 상입니다.

어휘 nominate (상 등에) 지명하다 employee 직원 award 상

해설 멜라니를 직원 상에 지명한 이유를 묻는 Why 의문문

(A) 질문과 상관없는 오답. 요청·부탁의 의문문에 대한 응답이므로 오답.

(B) 정답. 멜라니를 직원 상에 지명한 이유를 묻는 질문에 그녀가 열심히 일하기 때문이라고 이유를 제시하고 있으므로 정답.

(C) 단어 반복 오답. 질문의 award를 반복 이용한 오답.

8

W-Am Would you mind picking up some napkins next time you go to the store?

M-Cn (A) Sometime this morning.

(B) I already picked up my trash.

(C) We might have some in storage, though.

다음에 상점에 가시면 냅킨 좀 사다 주시겠어요?

(A) 오늘 아침 중에요.

(B) 저는 이미 제 쓰레기를 치웠어요.

(C) 근데 창고에 좀 있을 텐데요.

어휘 pick up (어디에서) ~을 찾아오다, 치우다 trash 쓰레기 storage 창고, 저장소

해설 부탁/요청의 의문문

(A) 연상 단어 오답. 질문의 next time에서 연상 가능한 sometime을 이용한 오답.

(B) 파생어 오답. 질문의 picking과 파생어 관계인 picked를 이용한 오답.

(C) 정답. 냅킨을 사달라고 요청하는 질문에 창고에 있을 거라며 구매가 불필요함을 우회적으로 나타내고 있으므로 정답.

9

고난도

M-Au Will I need to reserve a table for dinner?

W-Br (A) A pasta dish with vegetables on the side.

(B) Let me see—Mr. Carter, party of four?

(C) The restaurant isn't full in the evenings.

저녁 식사 테이블을 예약해야 할까요?

(A) 채소를 곁들인 파스타 요리요.

(B) 확인해보겠습니다, 카터 씨, 일행 네 분이요?

(C) 그 식당은 저녁에는 붐비지 않아요.

어휘 reserve 예약하다 party 일행, 단체

해설 식사 예약을 해야 하는지 여부를 묻는 조동사(Will) 의문문

(A) 연상 단어 오답. 질문의 dinner에서 연상 가능한 pasta를 이용한 오답.

(B) 연상 단어 오답. 질문의 reserve에서 연상 가능한 party of four를 이용한 오답.

(C) 정답. 저녁 식사 예약을 해야 하는지 묻는 질문에 그 식당은 저녁에는 붐비지 않는다며 예약할 필요가 없음을 우회적으로 응답하고 있으므로 정답.

10

W-Am The interview with Ellen Bradley went well, didn't it?

M-Cn (A) I think we should hire her.

(B) Her career history and skills.

(C) I prefer the view from Paul's work station.

엘렌 브래들리와의 면접은 잘 진행됐죠, 그렇죠?

(A) 그녀를 고용해야 할 것 같아요.

(B) 그녀의 경력과 능력이요.

(C) 저는 폴의 근무 자리에서의 전망이 더 좋아요.

어휘 career 직업, 경력 view 전망

해설 면접이 잘 진행됐는지 여부를 확인하는 부가의문문

(A) 정답. 엘렌 브래들리와의 면접이 잘 진행되었는지 여부를 확인하는 질문에 그녀를 고용해야 할 것 같다며 우회적으로 Yes의 뜻을 밝히고 있으므로 정답.

(B) 연상 단어 오답. 질문의 interview에서 연상 가능한 career를 이용한 오답.

(C) 유사 발음 오답. 질문의 interview와 부분적으로 발음이 유사한 view를 이용한 오답.

11

M-Au Who should I talk to if I have questions about payroll?

W-Am (A) I think the receptionist did.

(B) That would be Jin-Woo.

(C) Yes—how often will I be paid?

급여에 대해 질문이 있으면 누구와 이야기해야 하죠?

(A) 접수원이 한 것 같아요.

(B) 진우 씨일 거예요.

(C) 네, 얼마나 자주 돈을 받게 되나요?

어휘 payroll 급여 receptionist 접수원

해설 질문이 있을 때 이야기해야 할 사람을 묻는 Who 의문문

(A) 연상 단어 오답. 질문의 who에서 연상 가능한 receptionist를 이용했지만 did는 과거에 했음을 의미하여 질문에 어울리는 응답이 아니므로 오답.

(B) 정답. 급여에 대한 질문이 있을 경우 이야기할 수 있는 사람을 묻는 질문에 진우 씨일 것이라고 알려주고 있으므로 정답.

(C) Yes/No 불가 오답. Who 의문문에는 Yes/No 응답이 불가능하므로 오답.

12

M-Cn Where do you usually get your news?

W-Br (A) From the local newspaper.

(B) I haven't heard anything about it.

(C) Every few hours.

소식을 주로 어디에서 접하시나요?

(A) 지역 신문에서요.

(B) 그것에 대해 들은 바가 없습니다.

(C) 몇 시간마다요.

해설 소식 매체를 묻는 Where 의문문

(A) 정답. 소식을 주로 어디에서 접하는지 묻는 질문에 지역 신문이라고 구체적으로 알려주고 있으므로 정답.

(B) 연상 단어 오답. 질문의 news에서 연상 가능한 heard를 이용한 오답.

(C) 질문과 상관없는 오답. How often 의문문에 대한 응답이므로 오답.

Test 4

13

W-Am How do I use the hotel's dry-cleaning service?

M-Au (A) Did you ask the front desk staff?

(B) For my suit and shirts.

(C) Our rooms are cleaned twice daily.

호텔의 드라이클리닝 서비스는 어떻게 이용하나요?
(A) 안내 데스크 직원에게 문의해보셨나요?
(B) 제 정장과 셔츠를 위해서요.
(C) 우리 방은 매일 두 번 청소됩니다.

어휘 front desk 안내 데스크 suit 정장

해설 서비스의 이용 방법을 묻는 How 의문문
(A) 정답. 호텔의 드라이클리닝 서비스를 이용하는 방법을 묻는 질문에 안내 데스크 직원에게 문의해봤는지 되물으며 자신은 답변을 알지 못함을 우회적으로 표현하고 있으므로 정답.
(B) 연상 단어 오답. 질문의 dry-cleaning에서 연상 가능한 suit and shirts를 이용한 오답.
(C) 파생어 오답. 질문의 cleaning과 파생어 관계인 cleaned를 이용한 오답.

14

W-Br Did you pack up all of the equipment in the seminar room?

M-Au (A) An overseas manufacturer.

(B) It was quite easy to operate.

(C) There weren't enough boxes for everything.

세미나실에 있는 장비를 전부 챙기셨나요?
(A) 해외 제조업체입니다.
(B) 작동하기 꽤 쉬웠습니다.
(C) 전부 담기에는 상자가 부족했어요.

어휘 pack up (짐을) 싸다 equipment 장비 overseas 해외의 manufacturer 제조업체 operate 작동하다

해설 장비를 챙겼는지 묻는 조동사(Did) 의문문
(A) 연상 단어 오답. 질문의 equipment에서 연상 가능한 manufacturer를 이용한 오답.
(B) 연상 단어 오답. 질문의 equipment에서 연상 가능한 operate를 이용한 오답.
(C) 정답. 세미나실에 있는 장비를 전부 챙겼는지 묻는 질문에 전부 담기에는 상자가 부족했다며, 장비를 모두 챙기지는 못했음을 우회적으로 응답하고 있으므로 정답.

15
고난도

M-Cn When does the lease on our current space end?

W-Am (A) We pay rent plus property taxes.

(B) Oh, we just got a notice about that.

(C) How much space are you looking for?

지금 있는 공간에 대한 임대 계약은 언제 끝납니까?
(A) 우리는 임대료와 재산세를 지불합니다.
(B) 오, 그에 관한 공지를 지금 막 받았어요.
(C) 얼마나 큰 공간을 찾고 계십니까?

어휘 lease 임대차 계약 current 현재의 space 공간 rent 임차료 property tax 재산세 notice 공고문

해설 임대 계약의 종료 시점을 묻는 When 의문문
(A) 연상 단어 오답. 질문의 lease에서 연상 가능한 rent를 이용한 오답.
(B) 정답. 지금 있는 공간에 대한 임대 계약이 끝나는 시점을 묻는 질문에 관련 공지를 지금 막 받았다며 확인 의사를 우회적으로 밝히고 있으므로 정답.
(C) 단어 반복 오답. 질문의 space를 반복 이용한 오답.

16
고난도

M-Au Aren't you the sales clerk I spoke to on the phone?

W-Am (A) Yes, a buy-one-get-one-free sale.

(B) I believe it's 555-0130.

(C) My shift only started five minutes ago.

저와 통화하셨던 판매원 아니세요?
(A) 네, 1+1 할인이에요.
(B) 555-0130번일 겁니다.
(C) 제 근무 시간은 기껏해야 5분 전에 시작됐는데요.

어휘 sales clerk 판매원 shift 근무 시간, 근무조

해설 통화를 했던 판매원인지 확인하는 부정의문문
(A) 파생어 오답. 질문의 sales와 파생어 관계인 sale을 이용한 오답.
(B) 연상 단어 오답. 질문의 phone에서 연상 가능한 전화번호를 이용한 오답.
(C) 정답. 통화를 했던 판매원인지 묻는 질문에 근무 시간이 5분 전에 시작됐다며 자신은 통화를 했던 판매원이 아님을 우회적으로 밝히고 있으므로 정답.

17

W-Br Do staff here usually bring lunch from home or go out to eat?

M-Au (A) Most people bring their own food.

(B) In the cafeteria on the ground floor.

(C) Sure, that sounds good.

직원들이 보통 집에서 점심 도시락을 싸 오나요, 아니면 나가서 사 먹나요?
(A) 대부분의 사람들이 본인 음식을 가져옵니다.
(B) 1층에 있는 구내식당에서요.
(C) 물론이죠, 그게 좋겠어요.

어휘 cafeteria 구내식당

해설 직원들의 점심식사 해결 방식을 묻는 선택의문문
(A) 정답. 직원들이 보통 점심식사를 해결하는 방식을 묻는 선택의문문에서 대부분의 사람들이 본인 음식을 가져온다며 둘 중 하나를 선택해 응답하고 있으므로 정답.
(B) 연상 단어 오답. 질문의 lunch에서 연상 가능한 cafeteria를 이용한 오답.
(C) 질문과 상관없는 오답. 제안·권유의 의문문에 대한 응답이므로 오답.

18

고난도

M-Cn How are you preparing for your conference speech?

W-Am (A) It's going to be in the auditorium.

(B) Well, it's still a month away.

(C) Some stories about my research.

회의 연설을 어떻게 준비하고 계신가요?
(A) 강당에서 열릴 예정입니다.
(B) 글쎄요, 아직 한 달이나 남았는걸요.
(C) 제 연구에 대한 이야기들이요.

어휘 auditorium 강당   research 연구

해설 연설 준비 방법을 묻는 How 의문문

(A) 질문과 상관없는 오답. Where 의문문에 대한 응답이므로 오답.

(B) 정답. 회의 연설을 준비하는 방법을 묻는 질문에 아직 한 달이나 남았다며 준비를 서두르지 않고 있음을 우회적으로 밝히고 있으므로 정답.

(C) 질문과 상관없는 오답. What 의문문에 대한 응답이므로 오답.

19

고난도

W-Br Ms. Hardin's goodbye party has been scheduled for May second.

M-Cn (A) I didn't know she was leaving.

(B) No, it will be the first time.

(C) There was a cake and some gifts.

하딘 씨의 송별회는 5월 2일로 예정되었습니다.
(A) 그녀가 떠나는 줄 몰랐어요.
(B) 아니요, 처음일 겁니다.
(C) 케이크와 선물 몇 개가 있었어요.

해설 정보 전달의 평서문

(A) 정답. 하딘 씨의 송별회가 5월 2일로 예정되었다는 평서문에 그녀가 떠나는 줄 몰랐다며 반전의 응답을 하고 있으므로 정답.

(B) 연상 단어 오답. 평서문의 second에서 연상 가능한 first를 이용한 오답.

(C) 연상 단어 오답. 평서문의 party에서 연상 가능한 cake를 이용한 오답.

20

W-Am What does this error message mean?

M-Au (A) Mr. Walsh stopped by while you were out.

(B) I didn't find any errors when I looked.

(C) Isn't it listed in the product manual?

이 오류 메시지는 무슨 의미입니까?
(A) 나가 계시는 동안 월쉬 씨가 들르셨어요.
(B) 제가 봤을 때는 오류를 발견하지 못했어요.
(C) 제품 설명서에 나와 있지 않아요?

어휘 stop by 들르다   list 작성하다, 열거하다   manual 설명서

해설 오류 메시지의 의미를 묻는 What 의문문

(A) 질문과 상관없는 오답.

(B) 단어 반복 오답. 질문의 error를 반복 이용한 오답.

(C) 정답. 오류 메시지의 의미를 묻는 질문에 제품 설명서에 나와 있지 않은지 되물으며 관련 사항에 대해 언급하고 있으므로 정답.

21

M-Cn Isn't that the actor from that television show you watch?

W-Br (A) Tuesday nights at eight.

(B) I think that man just looks like him.

(C) Thanks—my brother asked for a watch for his birthday.

저 사람은 당신이 시청하는 그 텔레비전 쇼의 배우가 아닌가요?
(A) 화요일 저녁 8시요.
(B) 저 남자는 그냥 그와 닮은 것 같아요.
(C) 고맙습니다. 제 남동생이 생일에 손목시계를 사달래요.

어휘 look like ~처럼 보이다

해설 지칭하는 사람이 배우가 맞는지 확인하는 부정의문문

(A) 질문과 상관없는 오답. When 의문문에 대한 응답이므로 오답.

(B) 정답. 지칭하는 사람이 상대가 시청하는 텔레비전 쇼의 배우가 맞는지 묻는 질문에 그냥 닮은 사람인 것 같다며 우회적으로 No를 의미하고 있으므로 정답.

(C) 단어 반복 오답. 질문의 watch를 반복 이용한 오답.

22

W-Am Where can I learn about financial investing?

M-Au (A) Yes, very interesting.

(B) How about taking a course online?

(C) Into a savings account.

어디에서 금융 투자에 대해 배울 수 있을까요?
(A) 네, 아주 흥미로워요.
(B) 온라인 강좌를 듣는 게 어때요?
(C) 저축 예금으로요.

어휘 financial 금융의   investing 투자   savings account 저축 예금

해설 금융 투자를 배울 수 있는 곳을 묻는 Where 의문문

(A) Yes/No 불가 오답. Where 의문문에는 Yes/No 응답이 불가능하므로 오답.

(B) 정답. 금융 투자를 배울 수 있는 곳을 묻는 질문에 온라인 강좌를 듣는 게 어떻겠냐고 제안하고 있으므로 정답.

(C) 연상 단어 오답. 질문의 financial에서 연상 가능한 savings account를 이용한 오답.

23

고난도

W-Br Did Mr. Chae approve the designs for the lobby renovation?

M-Cn (A) Unfortunately, it isn't.

(B) We have enough proof already.

(C) After a few revisions.

채 씨는 로비 개조 디자인을 승인했나요?
(A) 안타깝게도, 그게 아닙니다.
(B) 우리에게는 이미 증거가 충분히 있습니다.
(C) 몇 번 수정한 후에요.

어휘 approve 승인하다 renovation 개조[수리] proof 증거
revision 수정

해설 채 씨가 디자인을 승인했는지 여부를 묻는 조동사(Did) 의문문

(A) 질문과 상관없는 오답. 채 씨에 대해 묻는 질문에 사물 주어인 it으로 응답하고 있으므로 오답.

(B) 유사 발음 오답. 질문의 approve와 부분적으로 발음이 유사한 proof를 이용한 오답.

(C) 정답. 채 씨가 로비 개조 디자인을 승인했는지 여부를 묻는 질문에 몇 번 수정한 후에라며 승인이 이루어졌음을 우회적으로 밝히고 있으므로 정답.

24

M-Au Who collected the most donations for the fund-raiser?

W-Am (A) We're announcing it at tomorrow's meeting.

(B) Over six hundred dollars.

(C) I really care about this cause.

누가 모금 행사를 위해 가장 많은 기부금을 모았나요?
(A) 내일 회의 때 발표할 겁니다.
(B) 600달러 이상이요.
(C) 저는 이 대의에 대해 정말 신경 쓰고 있습니다.

어휘 donation 기부 fund-raiser 모금 행사 announce 발표하다
cause 대의

해설 가장 많은 기부금을 모은 사람을 묻는 Who 의문문

(A) 정답. 모금 행사를 위해 가장 많은 기부금을 모은 사람을 묻는 질문에 내일 회의 때 발표할 것이라며 아직 답변을 알려줄 수 없음을 우회적으로 밝히고 있으므로 정답.

(B) 연상 단어 오답. 질문의 donations에서 연상 가능한 six hundred dollars를 이용한 오답.

(C) 연상 단어 오답. 질문의 fund-raiser에서 연상 가능한 cause를 이용한 오답.

25

W-Br Would you prefer Thursday afternoon or Friday morning for your next appointment?

M-Cn (A) Three days' worth of medicine.

(B) I want to hear my test results in person.

(C) Let me open up my calendar app.

다음 예약은 목요일 오후가 좋으세요, 아니면 금요일 오전이 좋으세요?
(A) 3일치 약입니다.
(B) 제 테스트 결과를 직접 듣고 싶습니다.
(C) 제 일정 앱을 확인해볼게요.

어휘 appointment 약속, 예약 medicine 약 calendar 달력

해설 예약 희망 일정을 묻는 선택의문문

(A) 연상 단어 오답. 병원 관련 질문에 연상 가능한 medicine을 이용한 오답.

(B) 연상 단어 오답. 병원 관련 질문에 연상 가능한 test result를 이용한 오답.

(C) 정답. 다음 예약 희망 일정을 묻는 선택의문문에서 일정 앱을 확인해보겠다며, 정보를 확인한 후 답변을 줄 수 있음을 우회적으로 표현하고 있으므로 정답.

26 고난도

W-Br The parking area's going to be remodeled soon, isn't it?

M-Au (A) Oh, I take the commuter train here.

(B) It's past the stoplight, on your left.

(C) One of our older models, actually.

주차장이 곧 리모델링 되는 거죠, 그렇죠?
(A) 오, 저는 통근 열차를 타고 다녀요.
(B) 정지 신호를 지나서 왼쪽에 있어요.
(C) 사실 우리의 구모델 중 하나예요.

어휘 remodel 개조하다 commuter train 통근 열차 stoplight 정지 신호 actually 사실은

해설 주차장이 곧 리모델링 되는지 여부를 확인하는 부가의문문

(A) 정답. 주차장이 곧 리모델링 되는지 여부를 확인하는 질문에 통근 열차를 타고 다닌다며 관련 정보를 알지 못함을 우회적으로 표현하고 있으므로 정답.

(B) 질문과 상관없는 오답. Where 의문문에 대한 응답이므로 오답.

(C) 유사 발음 오답. 질문의 remodeled와 부분적으로 발음이 유사한 models를 이용한 오답.

27

W-Am Are we still accepting submissions for the new logo?

M-Au (A) The deadline is today at five.

(B) A white "M" on a blue circle.

(C) I submitted mine by e-mail.

새 로고를 위한 제출물을 아직 받고 있나요?
(A) 마감 시한이 오늘 5시예요.
(B) 파란 동그라미 위에 하얀 M자요.
(C) 제 것은 이메일로 제출했어요.

어휘 accept 받아주다 submission (제안서 등의) 제출 deadline 기한

해설 아직 제출물을 받고 있는지 여부를 묻는 Be동사 의문문

(A) 정답. 새 로고를 위한 제출물을 아직 받고 있는지 묻는 질문에 마감 시한이 오늘 5시라며 아직 받고 있음을 우회적으로 밝히고 있으므로 정답.

(B) 연상 단어 오답. 질문의 logo에서 연상 가능한 로고 디자인 묘사를 이용한 오답.

(C) 파생어 오답. 질문의 submissions와 파생어 관계인 submitted를 이용한 오답.

28 고난도

M-Cn When did Vaskin Apparel start selling household goods?

W-Am (A) I guess you missed the big promotional campaign.

(B) That's kind of you, but I don't need anything.

(C) No, they don't let you put items on hold.

배스킨 어패럴은 가정용품을 언제 판매하기 시작했나요?
(A) 대규모 판촉 캠페인을 놓치신 것 같군요.
(B) 감사하지만, 저는 아무것도 필요하지 않습니다.
(C) 아니요, 물건에 예약을 걸어두실 수 없어요.

어휘 household goods 가정용품 miss 놓치다 promotional 판촉의
on hold 보류 중인, 기다리게 하는

해설 업체의 가정용품 판매 시작 시점을 묻는 When 의문문
(A) 정답. 배스킨 어패럴이 가정용품을 판매하기 시작한 시점을 묻는 질문에 질
문자가 판촉 캠페인을 놓친 것 같다며 상황을 이해하는 입장을 우회적으로
나타내고 있으므로 정답.
(B) 질문과 상관없는 오답. 제안·권유의 의문문에 대한 응답이므로 오답.
(C) Yes/No 불가 오답. When 의문문에는 Yes/No 응답이 불가능하므로 오답.

29

M-Au The scanner in this self-service kiosk won't
recognize my passport.

W-Br (A) A major international airline.
(B) You'll have to check in at the counter, then.
(C) He's probably a new employee.

이 셀프서비스 키오스크의 스캐너가 제 여권을 인식하지 못해요.
(A) 주요 국제 항공사입니다.
(B) 그럼, 카운터에서 수속을 밟으셔야 합니다.
(C) 그는 아마 신입 직원일 겁니다.

어휘 recognize 인식하다 passport 여권 international 국제적인
airline 항공사

해설 정보 전달의 평서문
(A) 연상 단어 오답. 평서문의 passport에서 연상 가능한 airline을 이용한
오답.
(B) 정답. 셀프서비스 키오스크의 스캐너가 여권을 인식하지 못한다는 평서문
에 카운터에서 수속을 밟아야 한다며 문제에 대한 해결책을 제시하고 있으
므로 정답.
(C) 평서문과 상관없는 오답.

30

고난도

W-Am Which section of Harrison Street is closed?

W-Br (A) OK, I'll take Stokes Avenue instead.
(B) The city is repairing a water pipe.
(C) They finished up the roadwork yesterday.

해리슨 가의 어느 구역이 폐쇄되었죠?
(A) 알겠습니다, 대신 스톡스 가로 가겠습니다.
(B) 시에서 수도관을 수리 중입니다.
(C) 도로 공사는 어제 끝났어요.

어휘 section 부분 instead 대신에 repair 수리하다 roadwork 도로
공사

해설 거리의 폐쇄된 구역을 묻는 Which 의문문
(A) Yes/No 불가 오답. Which 의문문에는 Yes/No 응답이 불가능한데, OK
도 일종의 Yes 응답이라고 볼 수 있으므로 오답.
(B) 질문과 상관없는 오답. Why 의문문에 대한 응답이므로 오답.
(C) 정답. 해리슨 가에서 어느 구역이 폐쇄되었는지 묻는 질문에 도로 공사가
어제 끝났다며 폐쇄 구간이 개통되었음을 우회적으로 알려주고 있으므로
정답.

31

고난도

M-Cn Please examine our utility bills for any extra
charges.

W-Am (A) To save money on electricity.
(B) There's never been a mistake in them before.
(C) You can pay by check or automatic withdrawal.

추가 징수된 게 있는지 공과금을 확인해주십시오.
(A) 전기료를 절감하기 위해서요.
(B) 이전에는 한 번도 오류가 없었는데요.
(C) 수표나 자동 이체로 결제하실 수 있어요.

어휘 utility bill 공과금 charge 요금 electricity 전기 by check
수표로 withdrawal 인출

해설 부탁/요청의 평서문
(A) 질문과 상관없는 오답. Why 의문문에 대한 응답이므로 오답.
(B) 정답. 추가 징수된 것이 있는지 공과금을 확인해달라는 요청에 이전에는 오
류가 한 번도 없었다며 요청 사항에 대한 의구심을 나타내고 있으므로 정답.
(C) 연상 단어 오답. 평서문의 charges에서 연상 가능한 pay를 이용한 오답.

PART 3

32-34

M-Cn Ah, there you are, Alice. **32 Do you know
why the party guests are finishing the
appetizers so quickly? Our servers are
coming back with empty trays in just
minutes.**

W-Br I was just coming to talk to you about
that. **33 The greeter we stationed at the
entrance says that she's already counted
more than fifty guests.**

M-Cn Really? **33 There were only supposed
to be thirty!** OK, I'll call Gene and ask
him to bring some extra food from our
kitchen. **34 Could you drive to the nearest
supermarket and pick up some more? The
truck is parked by the back door.**

W-Br Sure. Let's see, I'll get dinner rolls and
lettuce… Anything else?

남 아, 여기 계시군요, 앨리스. 파티 손님들이 애피타이저를 왜 이렇게 빨리
먹어 치우고 있는지 아세요? 우리 종업원들이 단 몇 분 만에 쟁반이 빈
채로 돌아오고 있어요.
여 그 점에 관해서 말씀드리려고 오던 중이에요. 입구에 배치한 손님 맞이
직원이 이미 50명 이상의 손님을 셌다고 하네요.
남 정말요? 30명만 있어야 하는데요! 알겠어요, 진에게 전화해서
주방에서 추가로 음식을 가져오라고 요청할게요. 제일 가까운
슈퍼마켓에 차를 몰고 가서 음식을 좀 더 사다 주시겠어요? 뒷문 옆에
트럭이 주차되어 있어요.
여 물론이죠. 어디 봅시다, 디너 롤과 양상추를 사 올게요… 또 필요한
건요?

32

What are the speakers most likely doing?

(A) Delivering some groceries
(B) Giving a cooking demonstration
(C) Catering a celebration
(D) Holding a bake sale

화자들은 무엇을 하는 중일 것 같은가?
(A) 식료품 배달
(B) 요리 시연
(C) **기념 행사에 음식 공급**
(D) 빵 바자회 개최

어휘 grocery 식료품 demonstration 시연 cater 음식을 공급하다
      celebration 기념 행사 bake sale 빵 바자(기금을 모으기 위해 빵,
      케이크 등을 구워 파는 행사)

해설 세부 사항 관련 – 화자들이 하고 있는 일
남자가 첫 대사에서 파티 손님들이 애피타이저를 왜 이렇게 빨리 먹어 치우고
있는지 아느냐(Do you know why the party guests are finishing the
appetizers so quickly?)고 물으며, 우리 웨이터들이 단 몇 분 만에 쟁반이
빈 채로 돌아오고 있다(Our servers are coming back with empty trays
in just minutes)고 한 것으로 보아 정답은 (C)이다.

33

According to the woman, what is causing a problem?

(A) An inefficient process
(B) A large number of people
(C) Damage to an appliance
(D) Bad weather

여자에 따르면, 무엇이 문제를 일으키고 있는가?
(A) 비효율적인 절차
(B) **많은 수의 사람들**
(C) 가전제품의 손상
(D) 악천후

어휘 inefficient 비효율적인 process 절차[과정] damage 손상
      appliance 가전제품

해설 세부 사항 관련 – 여자가 말하는 문제의 원인
여자가 첫 대사에서 입구에 배치한 손님 맞이 직원이 그녀가 이미 50명 이상
의 손님을 셌다고 한다(The greeter we stationed at the entrance says
that she's already counted more than fifty guests)고 하자, 남자가 30
명만 있어야 한다(There were only supposed to be thirty!)고 한 것으로
보아 예상 손님 수가 초과된 것임을 알 수 있다. 따라서 정답은 (B)이다.

34

Where will the woman most likely go next?

(A) To an automobile
(B) To a front entrance
(C) To a storage area
(D) To a kitchen

여자는 다음에 어디로 갈 것 같은가?
(A) **자동차**
(B) 정문
(C) 창고
(D) 주방

해설 세부 사항 관련 – 여자가 다음에 갈 곳
남자가 두 번째 대사에서 제일 가까운 슈퍼마켓에 차를 몰고 가서 음식을 좀 더
사다 주겠냐(Could you drive to the nearest supermarket and pick up
some more?)고 부탁하며 뒷문 옆에 트럭이 주차되어 있다(The truck is
parked by the back door)고 자동차가 있는 곳을 알려주자 여자가 수긍했으
므로 정답은 (A)이다.

▸▸ Paraphrasing   대화의 **the truck**
                  → 정답의 **an automobile**

35-37 3인 대화

M-Au	**35 Finally, here are the conference rooms that you and your employees could use.** As you can see, each one has state-of-the-art presentation equipment. You can reserve them through a convenient online system.
W-Am	OK. I think this would fit our start-up's needs pretty well. **36 What do you think, Theresa?**
W-Br	I agree, but I'm still uncertain about sharing a space with other companies. **36 I mean, what happens if there's a disagreement between us and another tenant?**
M-Au	Those are very rare. **37 And remember, we offer month-to-month usage contracts.** If you choose that, you'd be free to leave relatively quickly even if a problem did arise.

남	마지막으로, 이곳이 여러분과 직원들이 사용하게 되는 회의실입니다. 보시다시피, 각 회의실에는 최첨단 프레젠테이션 장비가 있습니다. 편리한 온라인 시스템을 통해 장비들을 예약하실 수 있습니다.
여1	좋네요. 우리 신생 기업이 필요로 하는 것과 잘 맞을 것 같아요. **어떻게 생각하세요, 테레사?**
여2	동의해요, 하지만 다른 기업들과 공간을 공유한다는 것에 대해 아직도 확신이 없어요. **제 말은, 우리와 다른 세입자 사이에 의견 차이가 생기면 어떻게 되죠?**
남	그런 일은 매우 드뭅니다. **그리고 기억하세요, 저희는 월 단위 이용 계약을 제공합니다.** 이 계약을 선택하시면, 문제가 발생하더라도 비교적 빨리 철수하실 수 있을 겁니다.

어휘 state-of-the-art 최첨단의 equipment 장비 reserve 예약하다 fit 맞다 start-up 신생 기업 uncertain 확신이 없는 share 공유하다 disagreement 의견 차이 tenant 세입자 rare 드문 usage 이용 contract 계약 relatively 비교적 arise 발생하다

35

What are the women doing?

(A) Touring an office space
(B) Shopping for electronics
(C) Checking in at a conference
(D) Learning to use a software program

여자들은 무엇을 하고 있는가?

(A) 사무실 공간 둘러보기
(B) 전자제품 쇼핑
(C) 회의 입장 수속
(D) 소프트웨어 프로그램 이용법 학습

어휘 electronics 전자제품 check in 체크인하다, 수속을 밟다 conference 회의

해설 세부 사항 관련 – 여자들이 하고 있는 일

남자가 첫 대사에서 여자들에게 마지막으로 여러분과 직원들이 사용할 수 있는 회의실이다(Finally, here are the conference rooms that you and your employees could use)라고 한 것으로 보아 화자들은 지금 근무 공간을 둘러보고 있음을 알 수 있다. 따라서 정답은 (A)이다.

36

Why is Theresa concerned?

(A) A retail price is high.
(B) A piece of equipment is large.
(C) An opportunity might be missed.
(D) A conflict might occur.

테레사는 왜 걱정하는가?

(A) 소매가격이 높아서
(B) 장비가 커서
(C) 기회를 놓칠까 봐서
(D) 의견 충돌이 일어날까 봐서

해설 세부 사항 관련 – 테레사가 걱정하는 이유

첫 번째 여자가 첫 대사에서 테레사의 이름을 부르며 어떻게 생각하는지(What do you think, Theresa?)를 묻자, 두 번째 여자가 대답하며 우리와 다른 세입자 사이에 의견 차이가 생기면 어떻게 되느냐(I mean, what happens if there's a disagreement between us and another tenant?)고 한 것으로 보아 두 번째 여자가 테레사이며 세입자간 의견 충돌 가능성에 대해 걱정하는 것임을 알 수 있다. 따라서 정답은 (D)이다.

▸▸ Paraphrasing 대화의 a disagreement
→ 정답의 a conflict

37

What does the man emphasize the availability of?

(A) A special transportation service
(B) A form of commercial insurance
(C) A short-term commitment option
(D) A free training resource

남자는 무엇을 이용할 수 있다고 강조하는가?

(A) 특별 운송 서비스
(B) 상업 보험의 한 형태
(C) 단기 계약 선택권
(D) 무료 교육 자원

어휘 transportation 운송 commercial 상업적인 insurance 보험 commitment 약속, 책무 option 선택(권) resource 자원

해설 세부 사항 관련 – 남자가 이용할 수 있다고 강조하는 것

남자가 마지막 대사에서 저희는 월 단위 이용 계약을 제공한다는 것을 기억하라(remember, we offer month-to-month usage contracts)라고 했으므로 정답은 (C)이다.

▸▸ Paraphrasing 대화의 month-to-month usage contracts
→ 정답의 a short-term commitment

38-40

M-Cn Good evening, and [38]**welcome to Flatner Art Gallery. Are you here for Ms. Greenbaum's lecture?**

W-Am [38]**Yes—I loved her book on famous exhibitions. I couldn't miss the chance to hear her speak in person.**

M-Cn We're glad that she agreed to come. [39]**Uh, may I see your "Friends of the Gallery" membership card?**

W-Am Here it is. Oh, and since I'm a little early, could I take a quick walk through Garrett Hall? I heard that it was just renovated.

M-Cn [40]**I'm sorry, but since it's past six P.M., all parts of the gallery are closed except for the lecture area.**

남 안녕하세요. 플래트너 미술관에 오신 것을 환영합니다. 그린바움 씨의 강연 때문에 여기 오셨나요?

여 네, 유명한 전시회에 관한 그녀의 책이 좋았거든요. 그녀가 말하는 걸 직접 들을 기회를 놓칠 수 없었어요.

남 그녀가 와준다고 동의해주셔서 저희도 기뻤습니다. 어, "프렌즈 오브 더 갤러리" 회원 카드를 좀 볼 수 있을까요?

여 여기 있어요. 아, 그리고 제가 좀 일찍 와서 그러는데, 가렛 홀을 빠르게 둘러봐도 될까요? 최근에 개조했다고 들었어요.

남 죄송하지만, 오후 6시가 지나서 강연 장소를 제외하고는 미술관 전 구역이 문을 닫았습니다.

어휘 lecture 강의 exhibition 전시회 miss 놓치다 renovate 보수[개조]하다 except for ~을 제외하고는

38

Why has the woman come to the gallery?

(A) To see a new piece of artwork
(B) To inquire about exhibiting
(C) To finalize a purchase
(D) To listen to a talk

여자는 미술관에 왜 왔는가?

(A) 새로운 미술품을 보려고
(B) 전시에 관해 문의하려고
(C) 구매를 확정 지으려고
(D) 강연을 들으려고

어휘 artwork 미술품 inquire 묻다 finalize 마무리 짓다

해설 세부 사항 관련 - 여자가 미술관에 온 이유

남자가 플래트너 미술관에 오신 것을 환영한다(welcome to Flatner Art Gallery)며 그린바움 씨의 강연 때문에 여기 오는지(Are you here for Ms. Greenbaum's lecture?)를 묻자 여자가 그렇다(Yes)고 대답했으므로 정답은 (D)이다.

▸▸ **Paraphrasing** 대화의 lecture → 정답의 talk

39

What does the man ask the woman to provide?

(A) Proof of a membership
(B) The name of her friend
(C) The title of a painting
(D) A credit card

남자는 여자에게 무엇을 제공하라고 요청하는가?

(A) 회원증
(B) 친구의 이름
(C) 그림의 제목
(D) 신용카드

해설 세부 사항 관련 - 남자가 여자에게 제공하라고 한 것

남자가 두 번째 대사에서 여자에게 "프렌즈 오브 더 갤러리" 회원 카드를 좀 볼 수 있느냐(may I see your "Friends of the Gallery" membership card?)고 물었으므로 정답은 (A)이다.

▸▸ **Paraphrasing** 대화의 your membership card
→ 정답의 proof of a membership

40

Why will the woman be unable to enter Garrett Hall?

(A) Its contents have been loaned out.
(B) It is being renovated.
(C) Business hours are over.
(D) A pass has some restrictions.

여자는 왜 가렛 홀에 들어갈 수 없는가?

(A) 전시물이 대여되고 없어서
(B) 보수 공사 중이라서
(C) 개관 시간이 끝나서
(D) 입장권에 일부 제약이 있어서

어휘 content 내용물 loan 빌려주다 pass 입장권 restriction 제한

해설 세부 사항 관련 - 여자가 가렛 홀에 들어갈 수 없는 이유

남자가 마지막 대사에서 죄송하지만 오후 6시가 지나서 강연 장소를 제외하고는 미술관 전 구역이 문을 닫았다(I'm sorry, but since it's past six P.M., all parts of the gallery are closed except for the lecture area)라고 했으므로 정답은 (C)이다.

▸▸ **Paraphrasing** 대화의 all parts of the gallery are closed
→ 정답의 business hours are over

41-43

W-Br	Hi. **41 My name is Glinda Stokes, and I made an appointment to have my dog washed and groomed on Saturday.**
M-Cn	Hello, Ms. Stokes. Yes, the miniature poodle at two o'clock. How can I help you today?
W-Br	**42 Well, when I made that appointment, I forgot that a friend from out of town will be visiting that afternoon. Do you happen to have any openings in the morning, instead?** I'm sorry about the mistake.
M-Cn	Oh, no problem. **43 We're always happy to try to satisfy customer requests as long as we have some advance notice.** Let's see… Would nine A.M. be too early?
W-Br	No, that would be perfect. Thank you so much.

여	여보세요. 제 이름은 글린다 스톡스이고, 토요일에 제 개를 목욕시키고 손질받기로 예약을 했어요.
남	안녕하세요, 스톡스 씨. 네, 2시에 미니어처 푸들이요. 오늘은 무엇을 도와드릴까요?
여	저, 제가 예약을 했을 때 외지에서 제 친구가 그날 오후에 방문하기로 한 것을 깜박 했어요. 대신에 혹시 그날 아침에 자리가 남아 있을까요? 실수해서 죄송해요.
남	오, 아닙니다. 미리 알려만 주신다면 저희는 항상 고객의 요구를 만족시킬 수 있도록 기꺼이 노력합니다. 확인해 볼게요… 오전 9시는 너무 이른가요?
여	아니요, 아주 좋은 것 같아요. 정말 감사합니다.

어휘	appointment 약속 groom 손질하다 opening 빈자리, 공석 instead 대신에 satisfy 만족시키다 advance notice 사전 통고

41

What service does the woman plan to receive?

(A) Pet care
(B) Vehicle washing
(C) Interior decorating
(D) Plumbing repair

여자는 무슨 서비스를 받을 계획인가?

(A) 애완동물 관리
(B) 세차
(C) 실내 장식
(D) 배관 수리

해설 세부 사항 관련 - 여자가 받으려는 서비스의 종류

여자가 첫 대사에서 자신의 이름은 글린다 스톡스이고, 토요일에 개를 목욕시키고 손질받기로 예약을 했다(My name is Glinda Stokes, and I made an appointment to have my dog washed and groomed on Saturday)고 했으므로 정답은 (A)이다.

▸▸ Paraphrasing 대화의 **have my dog washed and groomed** → 정답의 **pet care**

42

What mistake did the woman make?

(A) She gave the wrong address.
(B) She failed to provide an important detail.
(C) She chose an inconvenient appointment time.
(D) She did not realize that a deal had ended.

여자는 어떤 실수를 했는가?
(A) 주소를 잘못 알려줬다.
(B) 중요한 세부 사항을 알려주지 않았다.
(C) 곤란한 예약 시간을 선택했다.
(D) 거래가 끝났음을 깨닫지 못했다.

어휘 detail 세부 사항 inconvenient 불편한, 곤란한 realize 깨닫다 deal 거래

해설 세부 사항 관련 - 여자가 한 실수

여자가 두 번째 대사에서 예약을 했을 때 외지에서 친구가 그날 오후에 방문하기로 한 것을 깜빡 했다(when I made that appointment, I forgot that a friend from out of town will be visiting that afternoon)며 대신에 혹시 그날 아침에 자리가 남아 있을지(Do you happen to have any openings in the morning, instead?)를 묻고 있는 것으로 보아 정답은 (C)이다.

43 [고난도]

What does the man say about his business?

(A) It uses advanced technology.
(B) It charges a fee to fulfill certain requests.
(C) It encourages staff to receive certifications.
(D) It tries to accommodate customers.

남자는 자신의 업체에 대해 무엇을 말하는가?
(A) 선진 기술을 사용한다.
(B) 특정 요청을 수행하는 데는 수수료를 부과한다.
(C) 직원들이 자격증을 따도록 권장한다.
(D) 고객을 수용하고자 노력한다.

어휘 advanced 선진의 charge 부과하다 fee 수수료 fulfill 이행하다 certification 증명(서) accommodate 수용하다

해설 세부 사항 관련 - 남자가 자신의 사업에 대해 말하는 것

남자가 마지막 대사에서 미리 알려만 주면 항상 고객의 요구를 만족시킬 수 있도록 기꺼이 노력한다(We're always happy to try to satisfy customer requests as long as we have some advance notice)고 했으므로 정답은 (D)이다.

▸▸ Paraphrasing 대화의 **satisfy customer requests** → 정답의 **accommodate customers**

44-46

M-Au Hi, Myra? This is Juan from Haslop Global calling. **44I'm happy to say that, based on your qualifications and yesterday's interview, we'd like to invite you to join the company as an in-house financial consultant.**

W-Br Oh, that's great! I was really impressed by everything I heard yesterday. **45I'm particularly excited about the chance to decide for myself when to start and finish work.**

M-Au Yes, our current staff really enjoy that perk. Now, the terms of our contract can be complex. **46Could you come in to the office tomorrow to look over them together?**

W-Br **46Sure.** But I hope you don't expect me to make a decision right then.

남 여보세요, 마이라? 해슬롭 글로벌에서 전화드리는 후안입니다. 당신의 자격과 어제 치른 면접을 토대로, 당신을 저희 회사에 사내 금융 자문 위원으로 모시고자 합니다.

여 오, 잘됐네요! 어제 제가 들은 모든 것이 정말 인상 깊었거든요. 언제 일을 시작하고 마칠지 제 스스로 정할 수 있다는 점이 특히 기대됩니다.

남 네, 지금 우리 직원이 그 특전을 아주 좋아합니다. 자, 우리 계약 조건이 복잡할 수 있습니다. 내일 사무실로 오셔서 함께 검토해 보시겠어요?

여 좋아요. 그런데 제가 그때 바로 결정을 내릴 거라고 생각하지 않으셨으면 좋겠습니다.

어휘 based on ~을 근거하여 qualification 자격 in-house (회사·조직) 내부의 impressed 감명을 받은 particularly 특히 perk 특전 term 조건 complex 복잡한

44

Why is the man calling the woman?

(A) To arrange an interview with her
(B) To ask for a document
(C) To offer her a job
(D) To assess her professional qualifications

남자는 왜 여자에게 전화하고 있는가?
(A) 여자와 면접 약속을 잡으려고
(B) 서류를 요청하려고
(C) 여자에게 일자리를 제안하려고
(D) 여자의 직업적 자질을 평가하려고

어휘 arrange 주선[마련]하다 assess 평가하다

해설 전체 내용 관련 – 남자가 전화를 건 목적

남자가 첫 대사에서 당신의 자격과 어제 치른 면접을 토대로, 당신을 사내 금융 자문위원으로 모시고 싶다(I'm happy to say that, based on your qualifications and yesterday's interview, we'd like to invite you to join the company as an in-house financial consultant)고 했으므로 정답은 (C)이다.

▸▸ Paraphrasing 대화의 **invite you to join the company as ~** → 정답의 **offer her a job**

45

What does the woman say is attractive about a position?

(A) The salary for it is high.
(B) The work involved seems enjoyable.
(C) It is with a famous company.
(D) Its hours are flexible.

여자는 일자리에 대해 무엇이 매력적이라고 말하는가?

(A) 급여가 높다.
(B) 관련된 업무가 즐거워 보인다.
(C) 회사가 유명하다.
(D) **근무 시간이 유동적이다.**

어휘 salary 급여 involved 관련된 enjoyable 즐거운 flexible 유연한

해설 세부 사항 관련 – 여자가 일자리에 대해 매력적이라고 말하는 점

여자가 첫 대사에서 언제 일을 시작하고 마칠지 스스로 정할 수 있다는 점이 특히 기대된다(I'm particularly excited about the chance to decide for myself when to start and finish work)고 한 것으로 보아 정답은 (D)이다.

▸▸ Paraphrasing 대화의 **decide for myself when to start and finish work**
→ 정답의 **its hours are flexible**

46

What does the woman agree to do?

(A) Send some paperwork
(B) Visit a workplace
(C) Make a phone call
(D) Prepare a presentation

여자는 무엇을 하기로 동의하는가?

(A) 서류를 보내는 것
(B) **근무 현장을 방문하는 것**
(C) 전화를 거는 것
(D) 발표를 준비하는 것

어휘 paperwork 서류 workplace 직장 prepare 준비하다

해설 세부 사항 관련 – 여자가 하기로 동의한 것

남자가 두 번째 대사에서 내일 사무실로 오셔서 함께 검토해보겠느냐(Could you come in to the office tomorrow to look over them together?)고 묻자, 여자가 네(Sure)라고 대답했으므로 정답은 (B)이다.

▸▸ Paraphrasing 대화의 **come in to the office**
→ 정답의 **visit a workplace**

47-49 3인 대화

W-Am Oh, hi, Keith and Randy. **47 I noticed you haven't been coming to my cycling class lately.** Is everything all right?

M-Au Hi, Fuyuko. My work schedule changed, so now we exercise in the evenings instead of the mornings.

M-Cn But we do miss your class! **48 You don't offer personal training, do you?**

M-Au **48 Yes, we'd love to have you lead just the two of us through a tailored cycling routine once a week or so.**

W-Am I'd be happy to do that.

M-Cn Great! How about on Thursdays?

W-Am That could work. **49 Could you wait a moment while I go to my desk to review my calendar?**

M-Cn Sure. We'll be lifting weights over here for a while.

M-Au Yes, take your time.

여 오, 안녕하세요, 키스 그리고 랜디. **최근 들어 제 사이클링 수업에 오시지 않는 것 같던데요.** 괜찮으신 거죠?

남1 안녕하세요, 푸유코. 제 업무 일정이 바뀌어서, 요즘 우리는 오전 대신에 저녁에 운동을 해요.

남2 그래도 당신의 수업이 정말 그리워요! 개인 훈련은 제공하지 않으시나요?

남1 맞아요, 일주일에 한 번 정도 당신이 맞춤 사이클링 루틴에 따라 우리 둘만 이끌어주시면 좋겠어요.

여 저도 그러면 좋겠네요.

남2 좋아요. 목요일마다 어때요?

여 괜찮을 것 같아요. **제 책상으로 가서 달력을 확인하는 동안 잠깐 기다려주시겠어요?**

남2 물론이죠. 여기서 잠시 역기를 들어올리고 있을게요.

남1 그래요, 천천히 하세요.

어휘 notice ~을 알다 lately 최근에 lead 이끌다 tailored 맞춤형의 lift 들어올리다 weight 역기

47

Who most likely is the woman?

(A) An auto mechanic
(B) A fitness instructor
(C) A medical clinic receptionist
(D) A real estate agent

여자는 누구일 것 같은가?

(A) 자동차 정비사
(B) **피트니스 강사**
(C) 병원 접수 안내원
(D) 부동산 중개인

해설 전체 내용 관련 - 여자의 직업

여자가 첫 대사에서 최근 들어 제 사이클링 수업에 오시지 않는 것 같던데요(I noticed you haven't been coming to my cycling class lately)라고 한 것으로 보아 정답은 (B)이다.

48
고난도

What do the men want to know about?

(A) A customized service
(B) A routine inspection
(C) Some test results
(D) Some safety rules

남자들은 무엇에 대해 알고 싶어 하는가?

(A) 맞춤형 서비스
(B) 정기 점검
(C) 테스트 결과
(D) 안전 수칙

어휘 customized 맞춤의 routine 정례적인 inspection 점검
safety 안전

해설 세부 사항 관련 - 남자들이 알고 싶어 하는 것

두 번째 남자가 첫 대사에서 개인 훈련은 제공하지 않는지(You don't offer personal training, do you?)를 물었고, 뒤이어 첫 번째 남자가 맞아요(Yes)라고 맞장구를 치며 일주일에 한 번 정도 당신이 맞춤 사이클링 루틴에 따라 우리 둘만 이끌어주면 좋겠다(we'd love to have you lead just the two of us through a tailored cycling routine once a week or so)고 한 것으로 보아 두 남자 모두 개별 맞춤 훈련에 관해 궁금해하고 있음을 알 수 있다. 따라서 정답은 (A)이다.

▶▶ Paraphrasing 대화의 tailored → 정답의 customized

49

Why does the woman ask the men to wait?

(A) A supervisor must approve a request.
(B) A budget has not been finalized yet.
(C) She must rearrange some furniture.
(D) She needs to check a schedule.

여자는 왜 남자들에게 기다리라고 하는가?

(A) 관리자가 요청을 승인해야 해서
(B) 예산안이 아직 마무리되지 않아서
(C) 가구를 재배치해야 해서
(D) 일정을 확인해야 해서

어휘 supervisor 관리자 approve 승인하다 budget 예산(안)
finalize 마무리짓다 rearrange 재배치하다

해설 세부 사항 관련 - 여자가 남자들에게 기다리라고 한 이유

여자가 마지막 대사에서 책상으로 가서 달력을 확인하는 동안 잠깐 기다려 줄 수 있는지(Could you wait a moment while I go to my desk to review my calendar?)를 물었으므로 정답은 (D)이다.

▶▶ Paraphrasing 대화의 review my calendar
→ 정답의 check a schedule

50-52

M-Cn Oh, hi, Rosemary. Do you need the conference room? [50] **I just brought my laptop in here because I was having trouble concentrating. The noise from the construction site next door is so loud out in the office.**

W-Am I came in here for the same reason. It's frustrating, isn't it? [51] **Actually, yesterday I told my boss that I was having a hard time with it.** I was hoping she'd have some ideas for solutions.

M-Cn What did she say?

W-Am [52] **She promised to ask the company to pay for noise-cancelling headphones staff can use at their seats.** I hope that they agree.

M-Cn If they do, I might have to look into getting a pair as well.

남 오, 안녕하세요, 로즈마리. 회의실을 쓰실 건가요? 전 집중이 잘 안 돼서 지금 막 제 노트북 컴퓨터를 들고 여기 들어왔어요. 사무실은 옆 공사 현상에서 오는 소음으로 너무 시끄럽거든요.

여 사실, 저도 같은 이유로 여기 왔어요. 불만스럽지 않아요? 사실은 어제 제가 제 상관에게 그것 때문에 힘들다고 말했어요. 그녀가 해결책을 내주시길 바라고 있었어요.

남 그녀가 뭐라고 하던가요?

여 직원들이 자리에서 사용할 수 있는 소음 차단 헤드폰에 대한 비용을 지불해달라고 회사에 요청할 거라고 약속했어요. 회사에서 동의해주면 좋겠어요.

남 그렇게 되면, 저도 하나 구입하는 걸 고려해봐야 할 것 같아요.

어휘 concentrate 집중하다 loud 시끄러운 frustrating
불만스러운

50

Why is the man in the conference room?

(A) To have a quick snack
(B) To prepare for a seminar
(C) To lead a videoconference
(D) To work in a quiet place

남자는 왜 회의실에 있는가?

(A) 간단한 간식을 먹으려고
(B) 세미나를 준비하려고
(C) 화상 회의를 주도하려고
(D) 조용한 장소에서 일하려고

어휘 prepare 준비하다 videoconference 화상 회의

해설 세부 사항 관련 - 남자가 회의실에 있는 이유

남자가 첫 대사에서 집중이 잘 안 돼서 지금 막 노트북 컴퓨터를 들고 여기 들어왔다(I just brought my laptop in here because I was having trouble concentrating)며, 사무실은 옆 공사 현장에서 오는 소음으로 너무 시끄럽다(The noise from the construction site next door is so loud out in the office)고 했으므로 정답은 (D)이다.

51

What does the woman say she recently did?

(A) She calculated some costs.
(B) She complained to a manager.
(C) She made plans to travel abroad.
(D) She went to another floor of the building.

여자는 최근에 무엇을 했다고 말하는가?

(A) 비용을 계산했다.
(B) 관리자에게 불만을 토로했다.
(C) 해외로 여행할 계획을 세웠다.
(D) 건물의 다른 층으로 갔다.

어휘 calculate 계산하다 complain 항의하다 abroad 해외로

해설 세부 사항 관련 – 여자가 최근에 했다고 말하는 것

여자가 첫 대사에서 사실은 어제 상관에게 그것 때문에 힘들다고 말했다 (Actually, yesterday I told my boss that I was having a hard time with it)고 했으므로 정답은 (B)이다.

> ▶ **Paraphrasing** 대화의 told my boss that I was having a hard time with it → 정답의 complained to a manager

52

What might the speakers' company buy for employees?

(A) Some audio equipment
(B) Some special seating
(C) A cooling appliance
(D) A beverage machine

화자들의 회사는 직원들을 위해 무엇을 살 것 같은가?

(A) 오디오 장비
(B) 특별 좌석
(C) 냉각 장치
(D) 음료 기계

어휘 equipment 장비 appliance 기기 beverage 음료

해설 세부 사항 관련 – 화자들의 회사가 직원을 위해 구입할 것

여자가 마지막 대사에서 상관이 직원들이 자리에서 사용할 수 있는 소음 차단 헤드폰에 대한 비용을 지불해달라고 회사에 요청할 거라고 약속했다 (She promised to ask the company to pay for noise-cancelling headphones staff can use at their seats)고 했으므로 정답은 (A)이다.

> ▶ **Paraphrasing** 대화의 noise-cancelling headphones → 정답의 some audio equipment

53-55

W-Br ⁵³Omar, Matt has been telling me that your employee book club is really fun. How can I join?

M-Au I'm glad to hear that you're interested, Ursula! I'll just put you on the e-mail list. That's all there is to it.

W-Br Great! When's the next meeting?

M-Au It's this Thursday. Here's the book we're reading now. ⁵⁴It's a bestseller that has some great tips on management techniques. You'll need to get your own copy.

W-Br Oh! That sounds great but… that's a really big book. ⁵⁵And the meeting is on Thursday?

M-Au ⁵⁵Ah, you don't have to finish the whole thing by then. Just chapters three and four.

여 오마르, 매트가 제게 당신네 직원 독서 클럽이 정말 재미있다고 얘기하더라고요. 어떻게 들어갈 수 있죠?

남 관심 있으시다는 이야기를 들으니 좋은데요. 어슐라! 이메일 리스트에 당신을 올려드릴게요. 그게 다예요.

여 좋아요! 다음 모임은 언제죠?

남 이번 주 목요일이요. 여기 지금 우리가 읽고 있는 책이에요. **경영 기법에 관한 몇 가지 훌륭한 조언이 있는 베스트셀러예요.** 당신이 볼 책을 사야 할 거예요.

여 오! 좋긴 한데… 정말 큰 책이네요. 모임은 목요일이고요?

남 아, 그때까지 책을 전부 끝낼 필요는 없어요. 3, 4장만 읽으면 돼요.

어휘 interested 관심 있는 management 경영 technique 기법, 기술

53

What are the speakers mainly discussing?

(A) An activity group
(B) A business trip
(C) A promotional event
(D) An employee newsletter

화자들은 주로 무엇을 논의하고 있는가?

(A) 활동 그룹
(B) 출장
(C) 판촉 행사
(D) 사원 소식지

해설 전체 내용 관련 – 대화의 주제

여자가 첫 대사에서 매트가 당신네 직원 독서 클럽이 정말 재미있다고 얘기하더라(Omar, Matt has been telling me that your employee book club is really fun)고 하며 독서 클럽에 대한 이야기를 이어가고 있으므로 정답은 (A)이다.

54

What does the man say about a book?

(A) He has not started reading it.
(B) He owns several copies.
(C) It is very popular.
(D) It gives investment tips.

남자는 책에 대해 무엇을 말하는가?

(A) 아직 읽기 시작하지 않았다.
(B) 여러 권을 가지고 있다.
(C) 매우 인기 있다.
(D) 투자 조언을 제공한다.

어휘 own 소유하다 investment 투자

해설 세부 사항 관련 – 남자가 책에 대해 말하는 것

남자가 두 번째 대사에서 경영 기법에 관한 몇 가지 훌륭한 조언이 있는 베스트셀러(It's a bestseller that has some great tips on management techniques)라고 책을 소개하고 있는 것으로 보아 정답은 (C)이다.

▸▸ Paraphrasing 대화의 a bestseller → 정답의 very popular

55
고난도

What does the woman imply when she says, "that's a really big book"?

(A) The book will not fit in a display.
(B) It will take a long time to read the book.
(C) The book probably contains certain information.
(D) It will be uncomfortable to carry the book.

여자가 "정말 큰 책이네요"라고 말한 의미는 무엇인가?
(A) 책이 진열대에 들어가지 않을 것이다.
(B) 책을 읽는 데 오래 걸릴 것이다.
(C) 아마 특정 정보가 들어 있을 것이다.
(D) 들고 다니기 불편할 것이다.

어휘 fit 맞다 contain 들어 있다 uncomfortable 불편한 carry 나르다

해설 화자의 의도 파악 – 정말 큰 책이라는 말의 의도

여자가 인용문을 언급한 직후에 모임이 목요일인 것(And the meeting is on Thursday?)을 재차 확인하자, 남자가 그때까지 책을 전부 끝낼 필요는 없다(you don't have to finish the whole thing by then)고 한 것으로 보아 다음 모임까지 시간이 얼마 남지 않았는데 책이 너무 두꺼워 다 읽기 힘들겠다는 의도로 한 말임을 알 수 있다. 따라서 정답은 (B)이다.

56-58

M-Cn Hello. This is Wallace Dunn calling from Lensard Incorporated. ⁵⁶I ordered some office supplies from you last week, and the invoice said they'd arrive by March third. But that was yesterday, and we haven't gotten anything. What's going on?

W-Br Let me just find your account... OK. It appears that your shipment was delayed by a road closure. It should arrive tomorrow.

M-Cn Well, I hope so. ⁵⁷My colleagues are running out of the supplies required to keep our business running smoothly.

W-Br I'm sorry about that. ⁵⁸We don't usually allow this, but—would you like the shipment's ID code? If you enter it into a box on our Web site, you can follow your order's progress along its route.

남   여보세요. 렌사드 주식회사에서 전화드리는 월리스 던입니다. 지난주에 귀사에서 사무 용품을 주문했고, 송장에는 5월 3일까지 물건이 도착한다고 나와 있습니다. 하지만 어제가 그날이었고 우리는 아무것도 받지 못했습니다. 어떻게 된 거죠?

여   고객님 계정을 확인해보겠습니다… 아, 네. 도로 폐쇄로 배송이 지연된 것으로 나오네요. 내일 도착할 겁니다.

남   그러길 바랍니다. 제 동료들이 우리 사업을 순조롭게 운영하는 데 필요한 물품들이 바닥나고 있어요.

여   죄송합니다. 보통은 이를 허용하지 않습니다만, 배송 ID 코드를 원하시나요? 저희 웹사이트의 검색란에 입력하시면, 경로에 따라 주문품의 배송 상태를 확인하실 수 있으세요.

어휘 incorporated 주식회사 order 주문하다 supply 용품 invoice 송장, 청구서 shipment 수송(품) delay 연기하다 closure 폐쇄 colleague 동료 smoothly 순조롭게 allow 허용하다 progress 진척[진행] route 경로

56

What is the purpose of the call?

(A) To order some office supplies
(B) To complain about the quality of some goods
(C) To ask about a charge on an invoice
(D) To check the status of a shipment

전화의 목적은 무엇인가?
(A) 사무 용품을 주문하는 것
(B) 일부 제품의 품질에 대해 항의하는 것
(C) 청구서에 나온 요금에 대해 문의하는 것
(D) 배송 상황을 확인하는 것

어휘 complain 항의하다 goods 제품 charge 요금; 청구하다 status 상황

해설 전체 내용 관련 – 전화의 목적

남자가 첫 대사에서 지난주에 귀사에서 사무 용품을 주문했고, 송장에는 5월 3일까지 물건이 도착한다고 나와 있다(I ordered some office supplies from you last week, and the invoice said they'd arrive by March third)고 했고, 하지만 어제가 그날이었고 우리는 아무것도 받지 못했다(But that was yesterday, and we haven't gotten anything. What's going on?)인지를 묻고 있는 것으로 보아 정답은 (D)이다.

57
고난도

Why does the man mention his coworkers?

(A) To describe how a mistake was noticed
(B) To explain the need for some items
(C) To clarify whom the woman should contact
(D) To highlight an advantage of a proposal

남자는 왜 자신의 동료들을 언급하는가?
(A) 어떻게 실수를 발견했는지 설명하려고
(B) 일부 제품의 필요성을 설명하려고
(C) 여자가 연락해야 할 사람을 명확히 말하려고
(D) 제안의 이점을 강조하려고

어휘 describe 말하다 notice ~을 알다 explain 설명하다 clarify 분명히 말하다 highlight 강조하다 advantage 이점 proposal 제안

남자가 두 번째 대사에서 제 동료들이 우리 사업을 순조롭게 운영하는 데 필요한 물품들이 바닥나고 있다(My colleagues are running out of the supplies required to keep our business running smoothly)고 했으므로 물품이 필요한 이유를 설명하려는 의도로 한 말임을 알 수 있다. 따라서 정답은 (B)이다.

58

What does the woman offer the man?

(A) A discount coupon
(B) A tracking number
(C) A branded gift
(D) A return authorization

여자는 남자에게 무엇을 제공하는가?
(A) 할인 쿠폰
(B) 추적 번호
(C) 유명 상표 선물
(D) 반품 승인

어휘　track 추적하다　branded 유명 상표의　return 반품
authorization 인가

해설　세부 사항 관련 – 여자가 남자에게 제안하는 것
여자가 마지막 대사에서 보통은 이를 허용하지 않지만, 배송 ID 코드를 원하는지(We don't usually allow this, but—would you like the shipment's ID code?)를 물으며 자사 웹사이트의 검색란에 입력하면, 경로에 따라 주문품의 진척 상황을 확인할 수 있다(If you enter it into a box on our Web site, you can follow your order's progress along its route)고 했으므로 정답은 (B)이다.

▸▸ Paraphrasing　대화의 **the shipment's ID code**
→ 정답의 **a tracking number**

59-61

W-Am ⁵⁹**Aaron, those displays of blue jeans that you set up look very nice.** I think you're really starting to master this job.

M-Au Thanks, Ms. Soto. I'm enjoying the work. It's fun to help customers find what they need.

W-Am That's great. Well, I'm going to head home. Is there anything I should know before I go?

M-Au ⁶⁰**Oh, did you see that we're completely out of the Rothland-brand padded jackets?**

W-Am Aren't there some in the stockroom?

M-Au No, we sold those too. ⁶¹**Though I didn't realize they were back there, actually, when the first customer asked me about them.** It's lucky that Chae-Young was here.

W-Am Yes, I see. Well, I'll order some more, then.

여 아론, 당신이 해놓은 청바지 디스플레이가 정말 멋져 보이네요. 이 일에 숙달되기 시작한 것 같아요.

남 고맙습니다. 소토 씨. 일이 즐거워요. 고객들이 필요한 것을 찾도록 돕는 것이 재미있습니다.

여 잘됐네요. 자, 저는 집에 가 보려고요. 제가 가기 전에 알아야 할 게 있을까요?

남 아, 로트랜드 브랜드 패딩 재킷이 완전히 소진된 걸 아셨나요?

여 창고에 좀 있지 않나요?

남 아니요, 그것들도 팔았습니다. 실은 첫 번째 손님이 그것들에 대해 물으셨을 때 저는 거기에 있는지 몰랐지만요. 채영 씨가 여기 있어서 다행이었어요.

여 네, 알겠어요. 그럼 좀 더 주문할게요.

어휘　padded jacket 패딩 재킷　stockroom 창고, 보관실

59

Where is the conversation taking place?

(A) At a flower shop
(B) At a clothing retailer
(C) At an art supply store
(D) At a supermarket

대화가 이루어지고 있는 장소는 어디인가?
(A) 꽃 가게
(B) 의류 소매점
(C) 미술품 가게
(D) 슈퍼마켓

해설　전체 내용 관련 – 대화의 장소
여자가 첫 대사에서 남자에게 당신이 해놓은 청바지 디스플레이가 정말 멋져 보인다(those displays of blue jeans that you set up look very nice)고 한 것으로 보아 정답은 (B)이다.

60

What does the man say about some merchandise?

(A) It should be added to a display.
(B) It is in the stockroom.
(C) It has sold out.
(D) It needs to be organized.

남자는 일부 상품에 대해 무엇을 말하는가?
(A) 진열대에 추가해야 한다.
(B) 창고에 있다.
(C) 매진되었다.
(D) 정리할 필요가 있다.

어휘　add 추가하다　stockroom 저장실, 창고　sell out 다 팔리다, 매진되다

해설　세부 사항 관련 – 남자가 상품에 대해 말하는 것
남자가 두 번째 대사에서 로트랜드 브랜드 패딩 재킷이 완전히 소진된 걸 알았는지(did you see that we're completely out of the Rothland-brand padded jackets?)를 묻고 있으므로 정답은 (C)이다.

61

고난도

What does the man imply when he says, "It's lucky that Chae-Young was here"?

(A) A task required two people.
(B) He was very busy today.
(C) Chae-Young has a special skill.
(D) Chae-Young provided useful information.

남자가 "채영 씨가 여기 있어서 다행이었어요"라고 말한 의미는 무엇인가?

(A) 업무에 두 사람이 필요했다.
(B) 오늘 매우 바빴다.
(C) 채영이 특별한 기술을 가지고 있다.
(D) 채영이 유용한 정보를 제공했다.

해설 화자의 의도 파악 – 채영 씨가 여기 있어서 다행이었다는 말의 의도
앞에서 실은 첫 번째 손님이 그것들에 대해 물으셨을 때 저는 그것들이 거기에 있는지 몰랐다(Though I didn't realize they were back there, actually, when the first customer asked me about them)고 하면서 인용문을 언급한 것으로 보아, 채영 씨가 물건이 있는 곳을 알려주어 다행이었다는 의도로 한 말임을 알 수 있다. 따라서 정답은 (D)이다.

62-64 대화 + 업무 배정표

M-Cn	Kara, hi. I got your latest status update on the construction and wanted to stop by. What's going on?
W-Am	Well, the rain has put the framing work behind by several days, and I just heard that the flooring materials won't arrive until May.
M-Cn	Uh-oh. **62 So will we be ready for guests in time for tourist season?**
W-Am	It's going to be close. **63 To be safe, I think we should bring in a specialist company to handle the flooring.**
M-Cn	OK, I'll think about it. For now, can you show me how the framing is going? **64 Let's start with the walls.**
W-Am	**64 Sure, I'll take you to the crew leader.** Follow me.

남	카라, 안녕하세요. 최근 건설 현황 업데이트를 받아 보고 들르고 싶었어요. 어떻게 되어가고 있죠?
여	비 때문에 골조 작업이 며칠 뒤처졌어요. 그리고 바닥재는 5월이나 되어서야 도착할 거고요.
남	이런. **그러면 휴가철에 맞춰 손님을 맞을 준비가 될까요?**
여	아슬아슬해요. **안전하려면, 전문 회사를 불러들여 바닥재를 처리하도록 해야 할 것 같아요.**
남	좋아요, 생각해보죠. 일단은, 골조 작업이 어떻게 되어가고 있는지 보여주시겠어요? **벽부터 시작합시다.**
여	**네, 작업 반장에게 모셔다드릴게요.** 따라오세요.

어휘 latest 최신의 status 상황 construction 건설 framing 틀, 뼈대 flooring 바닥재 material 자재 in time for ~에 시간 맞춰 specialist 전문가 handle 다루다 crew (특정한 기술을 가지고 함께 일하는) 팀, 조

Framing Assignments

Area	Crew Leader
Stairs	Whitney
Roof	Grant
64 **Walls**	**Santos**
Windows	Jim

골조 업무배정

구역	작업 반장
계단	휘트니
지붕	그랜트
64 **벽**	**산토스**
창문	짐

62

What most likely is being built?

(A) An apartment complex
(B) A store
(C) A hotel
(D) A school building

무엇을 건설 중일 것 같은가?

(A) 아파트 단지
(B) 상점
(C) 호텔
(D) 학교 건물

해설 세부 사항 관련 – 건설 중인 것
남자가 두 번째 대사에서 휴가철에 맞춰 손님을 맞을 준비가 될지(will we be ready for guests in time for tourist season?)를 물으며 휴가철과 손님을 언급한 것으로 보아 호텔을 짓고 있음을 알 수 있다. 따라서 정답은 (C)이다.

63

고난도

What does the woman suggest doing?

(A) Hiring some subcontractors
(B) Postponing an opening day
(C) Installing a protective covering
(D) Contacting other suppliers

여자는 무엇을 하자고 제안하는가?

(A) 하도급 업체 고용
(B) 개관일 연기
(C) 보호 덮개 설치
(D) 다른 공급업자에 연락

어휘 subcontractor 하도급 업체 postpone 미루다 install 설치 protective 보호하는 supplier 공급업자

해설 세부 사항 관련 – 여자의 제안 사항

여자가 두 번째 대사에서 안전하려면 전문 회사를 불러들여 바닥재를 처리하도록 해야 할 것 같다(To be safe, I think we should bring in a specialist company to handle the flooring)고 했으므로 정답은 (A)이다.

> ▸▸ Paraphrasing 대화의 bring in a specialist company
> → 정답의 hiring some subcontractors

64

Look at the graphic. Whom are the speakers going to see?

(A) Whitney
(B) Grant
(C) Santos
(D) Jim

시각 정보에 의하면, 화자들은 누구를 만나러 가는가?

(A) 휘트니
(B) 그랜트
(C) 산토스
(D) 짐

해설 시각 정보 연계 – 화자들이 만나러 가는 사람

남자가 세 번째 대사에서 벽부터 둘러보기 시작하자(Let's start with the walls)고 하자 여자가 작업반장에게 모셔다 드리겠다(Sure, I'll take you to the crew leader)고 했고, 업무 배정표에 따르면 벽 담당자는 산토스이므로 정답은 (C)이다.

65-67 대화 + 진열대

W-Br	Howard, could you come over here for a second?
M-Au	Sure, Ms. Quinn. What's up?
W-Br	65These carrots are looking a little dry. When was the last time you sprayed water on them?
M-Au	Oh, do they need to be sprayed with water? I thought it was only the broccoli in this section.
W-Br	No, it isn't. You know, this isn't the first time there's been confusion about this. 66I'm going to make a list of the fruits and vegetables that need regular spraying. I'll post it in the staff room.
M-Au	That would be really helpful. 67And I'll go get a spray bottle to take care of these carrots.

여	하워드, 잠깐 이쪽으로 와 주시겠어요?
남	물론이죠, 퀸 씨. 무슨 일입니까?
여	이 당근들이 약간 시들어 보여요. 마지막으로 물을 주신 게 언제였나요?
남	오, 그것들에도 물을 줘야 하나요? 이 칸에서는 브로콜리만 해당된다고 생각했습니다.

여	아니요, 그렇지 않아요. 아시다시피, 이 일에 대해 혼선이 있었던 게 이번이 처음이 아니네요. 규칙적으로 물을 줘야 하는 과일과 채소 목록을 작성해야겠어요. 직원실에 붙여놓을게요.
남	그러면 정말 도움이 될 것 같습니다. 그럼 저는 이 당근들을 돌보기 위해 스프레이 병을 가져오겠습니다.

어휘	spray 뿌리다 section 부분 confusion 혼동 vegetable 채소 regular 규칙적인 take care of ~을 돌보다

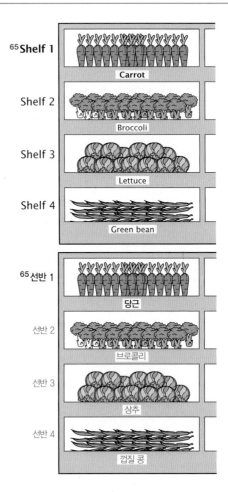

65

Look at the graphic. Which shelf's vegetables is the woman concerned about?

(A) Shelf 1
(B) Shelf 2
(C) Shelf 3
(D) Shelf 4

시각 정보에 의하면, 여자는 어느 선반의 채소들을 걱정하는가?

(A) 선반 1
(B) 선반 2
(C) 선반 3
(D) 선반 4

해설 **시각 정보 연계 – 여자가 걱정하는 채소의 선반**

여자가 두 번째 대사에서 당근들이 약간 시들어 보인다(These carrots are looking a little dry)며 우려를 표했고, 진열대에 따르면 당근들은 선반 1에 있으므로 정답은 (A)이다.

66

What does the woman say she will make a list of?

(A) Types of produce
(B) Staff members
(C) Cleaning tasks
(D) Purchase dates

여자는 무슨 목록을 만들겠다고 말하는가?

(A) 농산물 종류
(B) 직원들
(C) 청소 업무
(D) 구매일자

해설 **세부 사항 관련 – 여자가 만들 목록의 종류**

여자가 세 번째 대사에서 규칙적으로 물을 줘야 하는 과일과 채소 목록을 작성해야겠다(I'm going to make a list of the fruits and vegetables that need regular spraying)고 했으므로 정답은 (A)이다.

▸▸ **Paraphrasing** 대화의 **fruits and vegetables**
→ 정답의 **produce**

67

What will the man most likely do next to some vegetables?

(A) Carry them to another area
(B) Spray water on them
(C) Examine them for defects
(D) Rearrange them into piles

남자는 다음에 일부 채소들에 무엇을 할 것 같은가?

(A) 다른 구역으로 옮긴다.
(B) 스프레이로 물을 준다.
(C) 하자가 있는지 살펴본다.
(D) 다시 정리하여 쌓는다.

해설 **세부 사항 관련 – 남자가 다음에 일부 채소에 할 일**

남자가 마지막 대사에서 그럼 저는 이 당근들을 돌보기 위해 스프레이 병을 가져오겠다(I'll go get a spray bottle to take care of these carrots)고 했으므로 정답은 (B)이다.

68-70 대화 + 강좌 정보

M-Au Colland Studios. How can I help you?

W-Am **68 I'm interested in taking a social dance class, but I was wondering—is it OK to go without a partner?**

M-Au Absolutely. Your instructor will partner you up with one of your classmates at each session.

W-Am That's good. But I guess I'd better choose a class with a lot of participants. **69 Could you sign me up for whichever beginner class has the most people registered so far?**

M-Au **70 Sorry, but we don't allow sign-ups over the phone. You can either stop by our studio or follow the directions on our Web site.**

W-Am Oh, I see. **70 I'll go to your Web site.** Thanks.

남 콜랜드 스튜디오입니다. 무엇을 도와드릴까요?
여 소셜 댄스 강좌를 듣고 싶은데 파트너 없이 가도 괜찮은지 궁금해요.
남 물론이죠. 강사가 매 시간마다 수강생 중 한 분과 짝을 지어 주실 겁니다.
여 좋네요. 그런데 수강생이 많은 반을 선택하는 게 좋을 것 같아요. 입문반에서 지금까지 가장 많은 사람이 등록한 수업에 저를 등록해 주시겠어요?
남 죄송하지만, 전화로는 등록해드릴 수가 없습니다. 저희 스튜디오에 방문하시거나 웹사이트에서 지시를 따라 하시면 됩니다.
여 아, 알겠어요. 웹사이트에 들어가볼게요. 고맙습니다.

어휘 interested 관심 있는 instructor 강사 partner up with ～와 파트너가 되다 session 시간 sign up for ～에 신청하다 register 등록하다 stop by 들르다 direction 지시, 방향

Beginners' Classes	
Class	**Current Registrants/Capacity**
Rumba	7 / 22
Salsa	16 / 16 (FULL)
Swing	11 / 18
69 Waltz	**19 / 20**

입문반	
강좌	**현재 등록생/수용 인원**
룸바	7 / 22
살사	16 / 16 (마감됨)
스윙	11 / 18
69 왈츠	**19 / 20**

68 고난도

What does the woman ask about?

(A) How long each session lasts
(B) Whether she can attend alone
(C) How much experience an instructor has
(D) What kind of dance the man recommends

여자는 무엇에 관해 문의하는가?

(A) 각 수업 시간이 지속되는 시간
(B) 혼자 참여할 수 있는지 여부
(C) 강사의 경력 수준
(D) 남자가 추천하는 댄스의 종류

여자가 첫 대사에서 소셜 댄스 강좌를 듣고 싶은데 파트너 없이 가도 괜찮은지 궁금하다(I'm interested in taking a social dance class, but I was wondering—is it OK to go without a partner?)고 했으므로 정답은 (B)이다.

▸▸ **Paraphrasing** 대화의 **go without a partner**
→ 정답의 **attend alone**

69

Look at the graphic. Which class does the woman want to sign up for?

(A) Rumba
(B) Salsa
(C) Swing
(D) Waltz

시각 정보에 의하면, 여자는 어느 강좌에 등록하길 원하는가?

(A) 룸바
(B) 살사
(C) 스윙
(D) 왈츠

해설 시각 정보 연계 – 여자가 등록하길 원하는 강좌

여자가 두 번째 대사에서 입문반에서 지금까지 가장 많은 사람이 등록한 수업에 저를 등록해줄 수 있는지(Could you sign me up for whichever beginner class has the most people registered so far?)라고 물었고, 입문반 강좌 정보에 따르면 등록 인원이 가장 많은 수업은 왈츠이므로 정답은 (D)이다.

70

What does the woman agree to do online?

(A) Order some merchandise
(B) Get driving directions
(C) Register for a class
(D) Read some advice

여자는 온라인으로 무엇을 하기로 동의하는가?

(A) 상품 주문
(B) 운전 경로 파악
(C) 강좌 등록
(D) 몇 가지 조언 읽기

해설 세부 사항 관련 – 여자가 온라인으로 하기를 동의한 일

남자가 세 번째 대사에서 죄송하지만, 전화로는 등록해드릴 수가 없다(Sorry, but we don't allow sign-ups over the phone)며 저희 스튜디오에 방문하시거나 웹사이트에서 지시를 따라 하면 된다(You can either stop by our studio or follow the directions on our Web site)고 안내하자, 여자가 웹사이트에 들어가보겠다(I'll go to your Web site)고 했으므로 정답은 (C)이다.

PART 4

71-73 설명

W-Br All right, everyone. **71Now that you've been given an overview of our operations here at the warehouse, it's time to talk about some specific tasks.** I'll start by showing you how to use the forklift to move items around. **72Now, safety is important, so the first thing you need to do is look carefully at each component of the forklift.** You should make sure there is no damage, especially to the tires. **73For a full list of what you need to check, please refer to the printout I'm giving you now.**

자, 여러분. 여기 창고에서 우리가 할 작업 개요를 받아보셨으니, 이제 몇 가지 구체적인 업무에 대해 이야기하겠습니다. 제품들을 옮기는 데 지게차를 어떻게 사용하는지부터 보여드리겠습니다. 자, 안전이 중요하므로, 가장 먼저 하실 일은 지게차의 각 부품을 유심히 살펴보는 겁니다. 아무 손상도 없는지, 특히 타이어에 손상이 없는지 확인하셔야 합니다. 확인하셔야 할 것에 대한 전체 목록은 지금 제가 드리는 인쇄물을 참고하십시오.

어휘 overview 개요 operation 작업 warehouse 창고 specific 구체적인 task 업무 forklift 지게차 safety 안전 component 부품, 요소 damage 손상 printout 인쇄물

71

Where do the listeners work?

(A) At a moving company
(B) At a manufacturing plant
(C) At a storage facility
(D) At a construction firm

청자들은 어디에서 일하는가?

(A) 이삿짐 센터
(B) 제조 공장
(C) 보관 시설
(D) 건설 회사

해설 전체 내용 관련 – 청자들의 근무지

화자가 초반부에 여기 창고에서 우리가 할 작업 개요를 받아보셨으니, 이제 몇 가지 구체적인 업무에 대해 이야기하겠다(Now that you've been given an overview of our operations here at the warehouse, it's time to talk about some specific tasks)고 한 것으로 보아 청자들은 창고 시설에서 근무하고 있음을 알 수 있다. 따라서 정답은 (C)이다.

▸▸ **Paraphrasing** 담화의 **the warehouse**
→ 정답의 **a storage facility**

72

고난도

What does the speaker remind the listeners to do first?

(A) Put on some safety gear
(B) Refer to a floor plan
(C) Study a warning label
(D) Inspect the parts of a machine

화자는 청자들에게 먼저 무엇부터 하라고 상기시키는가?

(A) 보호 장비 착용
(B) 평면도 참고
(C) 경고 라벨 검토
(D) 기계의 부품 점검

어휘 gear 장비 refer to ~을 참고하다 floor plan 평면도 warning 경고 inspect 점검하다 part 부품

해설 세부 사항 관련 - 화자가 청자들에게 먼저 하라고 한 것

화자가 중반부에 안전이 중요하므로 가장 먼저 할 일은 지게차의 각 부품을 유심히 살펴보는 것(Now, safety is important, so the first thing you need to do is look carefully at each component of the forklift)이라고 했으므로 정답은 (D)이다.

▸ Paraphrasing 담화의 **look carefully at each component of the forklift**
→ 정답의 **inspect the parts of a machine**

73

According to the speaker, where can listeners find additional information?

(A) On a handout
(B) In a user manual
(C) On a Web site
(D) In a break room

화자에 따르면, 청자들은 어디에서 추가 정보를 찾을 수 있는가?

(A) 유인물
(B) 사용 설명서
(C) 웹사이트
(D) 휴게실

해설 세부 사항 관련 - 청자들이 추가 정보를 찾을 수 있는 곳

화자가 마지막에 확인하셔야 할 것에 대한 전체 목록은 지금 제가 드리는 인쇄물을 참고하라(For a full list of what you need to check, please refer to the printout I'm giving you now)고 했으므로 정답은 (A)이다.

▸ Paraphrasing 담화의 **the printout I'm giving you**
→ 정답의 **a handout**

74-76 전화 메시지

W-Am Hi Don, it's me. I'm about to fly home. Sorry I didn't call you until now—it's been a busy day. 74But I'm happy to say that the meetings went extremely well—both Ervitt Partners and Wyant Capital said they would

be interested in funding our business! We can expect their offers within the week. Oh, my flight just started boarding. 75But, uh, I'd love to tell you more when I land. 76Can we meet up for dinner? I should be back in the city by seven. Let me know.

여보세요, 돈, 저예요. 곧 돌아가는 비행기를 탈 거예요. 지금에서야 전화해서 미안해요. 바쁜 하루였어요. 그래도 회의가 아주 잘 풀렸다고 말하게 돼서 기뻐요. 얼빗 파트너스와 와이언트 캐피널 모두 우리 사업에 자금을 대는 데 관심이 있다고 말했어요! 우리는 이번 주 내로 그들의 제안을 기대할 수 있어요. 아, 제 비행기가 막 탑승을 시작했어요. 그런데 착륙해서 더 말씀드리고 싶은 게 있어요. 만나서 저녁 식사를 같이 할 수 있을까요? 7시까지 그곳에 돌아갈 수 있을 거예요. 알려주세요.

어휘 be about to 막 ~하려고 하다 extremely 극히 interested 관심 있는 fund 자금을 대다 offer 제안; 제안하다 board 탑승하다 land 착륙하다

74

고난도

Whom did the speaker meet with today?

(A) Potential investors
(B) Current clients
(C) Business consultants
(D) Government regulators

화자는 오늘 누구와 만났는가?

(A) 잠재적 투자자
(B) 현 고객
(C) 사업 자문 위원
(D) 정부 규제 기관 담당자

어휘 potential 잠재적인 investor 투자자 regulator 규제[단속] 기관[담당자]

해설 세부 사항 관련 - 화자가 오늘 만난 사람

화자가 초반부에 회의가 아주 잘 풀렸다고 말하게 돼서 기쁘다(I'm happy to say that the meetings went extremely well)면서, 얼빗 파트너스와 와이언트 캐피널 모두 우리 사업에 자금을 대는 데 관심이 있다고 말했다(both Ervitt Partners and Wyant Capital said they would be interested in funding our business!)고 한 것으로 보아 정답은 (A)이다.

75

What does the speaker mean when she says, "my flight just started boarding"?

(A) Her trip is behind schedule.
(B) She has to end the call.
(C) It is too late to make a change.
(D) She will be unable to get a message.

화자가 "제 비행기가 막 탑승을 시작했어요"라고 말한 의도는 무엇인가?

(A) 여행이 일정보다 늦어진다.
(B) 통화를 끝내야 한다.
(C) 변경하기에는 너무 늦었다.
(D) 메시지를 받을 수 없을 것이다.

어휘 back lot 야외 촬영지 preserved 보존된 production (영화 등의) 제작 last 지속되다 electric 전기의

77

Where is the tour taking place?

(A) A city street
(B) A nature reserve
(C) An aircraft factory
(D) A movie studio

투어가 열리고 있는 장소는 어디인가?

(A) 도심 거리
(B) 자연 보호 구역
(C) 항공기 공장
(D) **영화 스튜디오**

어휘 reserve 보호 구역 aircraft 항공기

해설 전체 내용 관련 – 담화의 장소

화자가 초반부에 이번 프레이저 픽처스 야외 촬영지 투어에 오신 것을 환영한다(Hello, and welcome to this tour of Frazier Pictures' back lot)며, 우리의 가장 유명한 영화들이 만들어졌던 잘 보존된 세트들을 보여드리게 되어 매우 기쁘다(I'm so excited to show you the well-preserved sets on which our most famous movies were made)고 한 것으로 보아 정답은 (D)이다.

▸▸ Paraphrasing 담화의 the ~ sets on which our ~ movies were made → 정답의 a movie studio

78

What are the listeners asked to do?

(A) Remain seated in a vehicle
(B) Save questions until the end
(C) Watch an introductory video
(D) Turn off personal electronics

청자들은 무엇을 하라고 요청되는가?

(A) **차량에 계속 앉아 있기**
(B) 마지막까지 질문 보류하기
(C) 소개 비디오 보기
(D) 개인용 전자 장치 끄기

어휘 seated 앉아 있는 introductory 소개용의 electronics 전자 장치

해설 세부 사항 관련 – 청자들이 요청받은 것

화자가 중반부에 투어는 45분 정도 지속될 것이며, 그 시간 내내 이 전동 카트에 앉아 계실 것을 요청드린다(the tour will last about forty-five minutes, and we ask that you stay seated in these electric carts the whole time)고 했으므로 정답은 (A)이다.

▸▸ Paraphrasing 담화의 stay seated in these electric carts → 정답의 remain seated in a vehicle

76

What does the speaker ask the listener to do?

(A) Reply to an e-mail
(B) Pick her up from the airport
(C) Set up a morning meeting
(D) Eat a meal with her

화자는 청자에게 무엇을 하라고 요청하는가?

(A) 이메일에 회신할 것
(B) 공항에 마중 나올 것
(C) 오전 회의를 준비할 것
(D) **함께 식사할 것**

해설 세부 사항 관련 – 화자가 청자에게 하라고 요청하는 것

화자가 후반부에 만나서 저녁 식사를 같이 할 수 있을지(Can we meet up for dinner?)를 묻고 있으므로 정답은 (D)이다.

▸▸ Paraphrasing 담화의 meet up for dinner → 정답의 eat a meal with

77-79 여행 정보

M-Au ⁷⁷Hello, and welcome to this tour of Frazier Pictures' back lot. I'm so excited to show you the well-preserved sets on which our most famous movies were made. If we're lucky, you may even see one or two productions being filmed today! ⁷⁸Now, the tour will last about forty-five minutes, and we ask that you stay seated in these electric carts the whole time. If you have any problems or questions, you may speak to me or an assistant guide at any time. OK, we're coming up on our first stop— Soundstage 1. ⁷⁹Let me tell you the colorful past of this building, which was one of the first constructed on our lot.

안녕하세요. 이번 프레이저 픽처스 야외 촬영지 투어에 오신 것을 환영합니다. 우리의 가장 유명한 영화들이 만들어졌던 잘 보존된 세트들을 보여드리게 되어 매우 기쁩니다. 운이 좋으시면, 오늘 촬영 중인 한두 편의 작품들을 보실 수 있을 겁니다! 자, 투어는 45분 정도 지속될 것이며, 그 시간 내내 이 전동 카트에 앉아 계실 것을 요청드립니다. 문제나 궁금하신 점이 있으시면, 저나 보조 가이드에게 언제든지 말씀하시면 됩니다. 자, 우리는 첫 번째 목적지인 사운드스테이지 1로 들어가고 있습니다. 우리 촬영지에 처음으로 세워진 것 중 하나인 이 건물의 화려한 과거를 말씀드리겠습니다.

79

What will the speaker talk about next?

(A) A company's expansion plans
(B) The course of the tour
(C) The history of a site
(D) An upcoming celebration

화자는 다음에 무엇에 대해 말할 것인가?
(A) 회사의 확장 계획
(B) 투어의 코스
(C) 촬영지의 역사
(D) 곧 있을 기념 행사

어휘 expansion 확장 site 부지 upcoming 곧 있을 celebration 기념 행사

해설 세부 사항 관련 – 화자가 다음에 말할 것
화자가 마지막에 우리 촬영지에 처음으로 세워진 것 중 하나인 이 건물의 화려한 과거를 말씀드리겠다(Let me tell you the colorful past of this building, which was one of the first constructed on our lot)고 한 것으로 보아 정답은 (C)이다.

▶▶ **Paraphrasing** 담화의 **the ~ past of this building**
→ 정답의 **the history of a site**

80-82 방송

M-Cn This is your hourly local news update on CWT, Winnipeg's most trusted news source. **⁸⁰The Canadian Board of Better Business Practices is hosting a job fair in the Arabesque Convention Center downtown this Saturday, starting at ten A.M.** Anyone looking for a job should stop by to meet hiring directors from some of the largest Winnipeg employers. There will also be career counselors offering free consultations and career aptitude tests for anyone interested. **⁸¹The event is free to attend, but it is expected to fill up quickly, so consider arriving early to make sure you get in.** **⁸²Now, let's hear about the incoming storm from Kyung-Ho Jang.** Hi, Kyung-Ho.

위니펙에서 가장 신뢰받는 뉴스 소식통 CWT의 시간별 지역 뉴스 업데이트입니다. 캐나다 경영 실무 개선 위원회가 이번 주 토요일 오전 10시부터 시내의 아라베스크 컨벤션 센터에서 취업 박람회를 주최합니다. 구직자 누구든 들러서 위니펙에서 가장 큰 몇몇 업체들의 채용 책임자들을 만나보길 권합니다. 관심 있는 사람 누구에게나 무료 상담과 진로 적성 검사를 해주는 직업 상담사들도 있을 것입니다. 행사 참석은 무료이지만 인원이 빨리 찰 것으로 예상되므로, 확실히 입장하기 위해서는 일찍 도착하는 것을 고려하십시오. 자, 이제 장경호 씨로부터 다가오는 폭풍 소식을 들어보도록 하죠. 안녕하세요, 경호 씨.

어휘 hourly 매시간의 trusted 신뢰받는 source 소식통[정보원] director 책임자 counselor 상담사 consultation 상담 aptitude 적성 fill up (~으로) 차다 incoming 들어오는

80

According to the broadcast, what type of event will occur on Saturday?

(A) An athletic competition
(B) A career fair
(C) An exhibition opening
(D) A trade show

방송에 따르면, 토요일에 어떤 종류의 행사가 열릴 것인가?
(A) 체육 대회
(B) 취업 박람회
(C) 전시 개관
(D) 무역 박람회

해설 세부 사항 관련 – 토요일에 열릴 행사의 종류
화자가 초반부에 캐나다 경영 실무 개선 위원회가 이번 주 토요일 오전 10시부터 시내의 아라베스크 컨벤션 센터에서 취업 박람회를 주최한다(The Canadian Board of Better Business Practices is hosting a job fair in the Arabesque Convention Center downtown this Saturday, starting at ten A.M.)고 했으므로 정답은 (B)이다.

▶▶ **Paraphrasing** 담화의 **a job fair** → 정답의 **a career fair**

81

Why does the speaker say attendees should arrive to the event early?

(A) To ensure entrance
(B) To meet a local celebrity
(C) To gain discounted admission
(D) To find parking nearby

화자는 왜 참가자들이 행사에 일찍 도착해야 한다고 말하는가?
(A) 입장을 확실히 하기 위해
(B) 지역의 유명 인사를 만나기 위해
(C) 할인된 입장권을 획득하기 위해
(D) 근처 주차 공간을 찾기 위해

어휘 ensure 반드시 ~하게 하다 entrance 입장 celebrity 유명 인사 admission 입장(료) nearby 근처에

해설 세부 사항 관련 – 참가자들이 행사에 일찍 도착해야 한다고 말한 이유
화자가 후반부에 행사 참석은 무료이지만 인원이 빨리 찰 것으로 예상되므로 확실히 입장하기 위해서는 일찍 도착하는 것을 고려하라(The event is free to attend, but it is expected to fill up quickly, so consider arriving early to make sure you get in)고 했으므로 정답은 (A)이다.

▶▶ **Paraphrasing** 담화의 **to make sure you get in**
→ 정답의 **to ensure entrance**

82

What will listeners most likely hear next?

(A) An interview
(B) A weather report
(C) A sports update
(D) An advertisement

청자들은 다음에 무엇을 들을 것 같은가?
(A) 인터뷰
(B) 일기 예보
(C) 스포츠 업데이트
(D) 광고

해설 **세부 사항 관련 – 청자들이 다음에 들을 것**

화자가 마지막에 이제 장경호 씨로부터 다가오는 폭풍 소식을 들어보도록 하자 (Now, let's hear about the incoming storm from Kyung-Ho Jang)라고 했으므로 정답은 (B)이다.

83-85 연설

> W-Am **83Congratulations, everyone, on completing the first annual Employee Enrichment Week at Jenson and Grieves Marketing. This week, we challenged ourselves with rigorous team-building activities,** and we learned a lot about each other. I saw bonds formed between colleagues, and new talents discovered in each of you. **84It makes me very happy as your operations manager to see such remarkable growth in everyone.** I'm sure the work we did this week will contribute to a more productive work environment for all of us. **85Since this is the first time we conducted the Employee Enrichment Week, I wasn't sure if it would be worth repeating next year. Now, I know we need to do this again.** Thank you.

> 여러분, 젠슨 앤 그리브스 마케팅에서 제1회 연례 직원 능력 계발 주간 행사를 마친 것을 축하합니다. 이번 주, 우리는 엄격한 팀 구축 활동으로 스스로에게 도전했으며, 서로에 대해 많은 것을 배웠습니다. 저는 동료들 사이에 맺어진 유대감과 여러분 각자에게서 발견된 새로운 재능들을 보았습니다. 여러분의 업무 관리자로서 모두에게서 주목할 만한 성장을 보게 되어 매우 기쁩니다. 이번 주에 우리가 했던 일이 우리 모두에게 보다 생산적인 업무 환경을 만들어줄 것이라고 저는 확신합니다. 직원 능력 계발 주간 행사를 진행한 것은 이번이 처음이라서, 내년에 또 진행할 가치가 있을지 확신하지 못했습니다. 이제, 저는 이것을 다시 해야 한다는 것을 압니다. 감사합니다.

> 어휘 annual 연례의 enrichment 강화 challenge 도전하다 rigorous 엄격한 bond 유대 form 형성하다 colleague 동료 talent 재능 remarkable 주목할 만한 contribute to ~에 기여하다 productive 생산적인 environment 환경 conduct 실시[수행]하다 worth ~할 가치가 있는

83

What does the speaker congratulate the listeners on?

(A) Finishing a team-building program
(B) Launching a new product
(C) Breaking a sales record
(D) Receiving promotions

화자는 청자들에게 무엇에 관해 축하하는가?

(A) 팀 구축 프로그램 수료
(B) 신제품 출시
(C) 판매 기록 경신
(D) 승진

어휘 launch 출시하다 break 깨다 record 기록 promotion 승진

해설 **세부 사항 관련 – 화자가 청자들에게 축하하는 것**

화자가 도입부에 젠슨 앤 그리브스 마케팅에서 제1회 연례 직원 능력 계발 주간 행사를 마친 것을 축하한다(Congratulations, everyone, on completing the first annual Employee Enrichment Week at Jenson and Grieves Marketing)고 했고, 이번 주에 우리는 엄격한 팀 구축 활동으로 스스로에게 도전했다(This week, we challenged ourselves with rigorous team-building activities)고 했으므로 정답은 (A)이다.

84

Who is the speaker?

(A) A previous customer
(B) A business researcher
(C) A current supervisor
(D) A city official

화자는 누구인가?

(A) 이전 고객
(B) 사업 연구원
(C) 현직 관리자
(D) 시 공무원

어휘 previous 이전의 researcher 연구원 supervisor 관리자 official 공무원

해설 **전체 내용 관련 – 화자의 직업**

화자가 중반부에 여러분의 업무 관리자로서 모두에게서 주목할 만한 성장을 보게 되어 매우 기쁘다(It makes me very happy as your operations manager to see such remarkable growth in everyone)고 한 것으로 보아 정답은 (C)이다.

> ▸▸ Paraphrasing 담화의 **your operations manager**
> → 정답의 **a ~ supervisor**

85 [고난도]

Why does the speaker say, "Now, I know we need to do this again"?

(A) An activity was effective.
(B) Some results were unexpected.
(C) Participants performed poorly.
(D) Other people should observe an activity.

화자가 "이제, 저는 이것을 다시 해야 한다는 것을 압니다"라고 말한 이유는 무엇인가?

(A) 행사가 효과적이었다.
(B) 일부 결과들은 예상 밖이었다.
(C) 참가자들이 형편없이 일을 수행했다.
(D) 다른 사람들이 활동을 관찰해야 한다.

어휘 effective 효과적인 unexpected 예상 밖의 participant 참가자 perform 수행하다 observe 관찰하다

해설 화자의 의도 파악 – 이제 이것을 다시 해야 한다는 것을 안다고 말한 의도
앞에서 직원 능력 계발 주간 행사를 진행한 것은 이번이 처음이라서, 내년
에도 반복할 가치가 있을지 확신하지 못했다(Since this is the first time
we conducted the Employee Enrichment Week, I wasn't sure if it
would be worth repeating next year)고 말한 뒤, 인용문을 언급한 것으로
보아 직원 능력 계발 프로그램을 내년에도 다시 시행하는 것에 대해 확신이 생
길 만큼 효과적이었다는 의도로 한 말임을 알 수 있다. 따라서 정답은 (A)이다.

86-88 담화

> W-Br Hi, I'm Stella Hogan. Thanks for watching
> the latest in my line of home improvement
> how-to videos. ⁸⁶**In this one, I'm going to show
> you how to paint the inside walls of your home
> without damaging your windows or anything
> else.** All right, here are my supplies. There are
> details about them in the notes for this video.
> Uh, you may be wondering why I chose Dewitt-
> brand paint. ⁸⁷**It's because it's inexpensive and
> sold in most stores, so I thought that many
> people would be likely to use it.** ⁸⁸**Now, as you
> can see, I've already removed all of the furniture
> and other objects from this room.** Next, I'll lay
> down this plastic sheet to protect the carpet.

안녕하세요, 저는 스텔라 호건입니다. 집 개선 방법 영상의 최신 게시물을 시청
해주셔서 고맙습니다. **이번 영상에서는, 창문이나 다른 것을 훼손시키지 않고 집
내벽을 페인트칠하는 방법을 보여드리겠습니다.** 자, 여기 제 용품들이 있습니다.
이것들에 대한 세부 정보는 이 영상의 메모란에 있는데요. 어, 제가 왜 드위트
브랜드 페인트를 선택했는지 궁금하실 수 있는데요. **비싸지 않으면서 대부분의
매장에서 판매되고 있기 때문에, 많은 사람들이 사용할 것 같다고 생각했습니다.**
자, 보시다시피, 이 방에서 가구와 다른 물건들을 이미 모두 치웠습니다. 다음
으로, 카펫을 보호하기 위해 이 플라스틱 시트를 깔겠습니다.

어휘 latest 최신의 것: 최신의 improvement 개선 inside 안의
damage 손상시키다 supplies 용품 details 세부 사항 wonder
궁금해하다 inexpensive 비싸지 않은 remove 치우다 object
물건 protect 보호하다

86
What is the topic of the talk?
(A) Carpet cleaning
(B) House painting
(C) Light fixture repair
(D) Window installation

담화의 주제는 무엇인가?
(A) 카펫 청소
(B) 집 페인트칠
(C) 조명 기구 수리
(D) 창문 설치

해설 전체 내용 관련 – 담화의 주제
화자가 초반부에 이번 영상에서는, 창문이나 다른 것을 훼손시키지 않고 집 내
벽을 페인트칠하는 방법을 보여드리겠다(In this one, I'm going to show
you how to paint the inside walls of your home without damaging
your windows or anything else)고 했으므로 정답은 (B)이다.

87
What does the speaker say about a product?
(A) It is durable.
(B) It comes with instructions.
(C) It is sold in a variety of colors.
(D) It is affordable.

화자는 제품에 대해 무엇을 말하는가?
(A) 내구성이 있다.
(B) 설명서가 함께 나온다.
(C) 다양한 색상으로 판매된다.
(D) 가격이 적당하다.

어휘 durable 내구성이 있는 instructions 설명서 a variety of 여러
가지의 affordable (가격이) 알맞은

해설 세부 사항 관련 – 화자가 제품에 대해 말하는 것
화자가 중반부에 비싸지 않으면서 대부분의 매장에서 판매되고 있기 때문에 많
은 사람들이 사용할 것 같다고 생각했다(It's because it's inexpensive and
sold in most stores, so I thought that many people would be likely
to use it)고 했으므로 정답은 (D)이다.

▸▸ **Paraphrasing** 담화의 inexpensive → 정답의 affordable

88
What does the speaker say she did before the talk?
(A) Cleared out a room
(B) Mixed some chemicals
(C) Covered some surfaces
(D) Measured an object

화자는 담화 전에 무엇을 했다고 말하는가?
(A) 방을 치웠다.
(B) 일부 화학약품을 혼합했다.
(C) 표면들을 덮었다.
(D) 물건의 치수를 쟀다.

어휘 mix 섞다 chemical 화학물질 surface 표면 measure
측정하다

해설 세부 사항 관련 – 화자가 담화 전에 했다고 말하는 것
화자가 후반부에 보시다시피 이 방에서 가구와 다른 물건들을 이미 모두 치웠
다(Now, as you can see, I've already removed all of the furniture
and other objects from this room)고 했으므로 정답은 (A)이다.

▸▸ **Paraphrasing** 담화의 **removed all of the furniture and
other objects from this room**
→ 정답의 **cleared out a room**

M-Cn **89 OK, let's talk about the new office space we're moving into. 90First—I've heard some people say they'll miss our current location, but I really think you're all going to love the new building.** Have you seen the amenities they offer? **90It's a big step up.** Now, we can move into our new space on October fifth, and the lease on this building ends three days later. We have to move everything in between those days. **91We've hired a mover to handle the bigger items, like desks and computers, but I'd like you all to move your own belongings. You should start boxing those up this week.** Does that seem doable?

좋아요, 우리가 입주할 새 사무실 공간에 대해 이야기해봅시다. 먼저 몇몇 사람들이 지금 장소가 그리울 거라고 말하는 것을 들었지만, 여러분 모두가 새 건물을 좋아하게 될 거라고 생각합니다. 그들이 제공하는 편의시설을 보셨나요? 훨씬 업그레이드됐습니다. 자, 우리는 10월 5일에 새로운 공간으로 입주할 수 있고, 이 건물의 임대차 계약은 3일 후에 종료됩니다. 그 사이에 모든 것을 옮겨야 합니다. 책상과 컴퓨터 같은 큰 물건들을 처리할 이삿짐 센터를 고용했지만, 소지품들은 여러분 모두가 각자 옮기면 좋겠습니다. 이번 주에 짐을 싸기 시작해야 할 겁니다. 할 수 있을 것 같습니까?

어휘 miss 그리워하다 location 장소, 위치 amenity 편의시설
lease 임대차 계약 handle 처리하다 belongings 소지품 box
상자에 넣다 doable 할 수 있는

89

What is the announcement mainly about?

(A) A project for a client
(B) A corporate merger
(C) An office relocation
(D) An annual budget

공지는 주로 무엇에 관한 것인가?
(A) 고객을 위한 프로젝트
(B) 기업 합병
(C) 사무실 이전
(D) 연간 예산

어휘 merger 합병 relocation 이전 budget 예산

해설 전체 내용 관련 – 공지의 주제
화자가 도입부에 우리가 입주할 새 사무실 공간에 대해 이야기해보자(let's talk about the new office space we're moving into)고 했으므로 정답은 (C)이다.

▸▸ Paraphrasing 담화의 **moving into** → 정답의 **relocation**

90

Why does the speaker say, "Have you seen the amenities they offer"?

(A) To inquire about some facilities
(B) To suggest a policy change
(C) To criticize a venue's management
(D) To emphasize some benefits

화자가 "그들이 제공하는 편의시설을 보셨나요"라고 말한 이유는 무엇인가?
(A) 일부 시설에 대해 문의하려고
(B) 정책 변경을 제안하려고
(C) 행사장 관리를 비판하려고
(D) 일부 혜택을 강조하려고

어휘 inquire 문의하다 facility 시설 policy 정책 criticize 비판하다
venue 행사장 emphasize 강조하다

해설 화자의 의도 파악 – 그들이 제공하는 편의시설을 봤냐고 말한 의도
앞에서 몇몇 사람들이 지금 장소가 그리울 거라고 말하는 것을 들었지만, 여러분 모두가 새 건물을 좋아하게 될 거라고 생각한다(I've heard some people say they'll miss our current location, but I really think you're all going to love the new building)고 했고, 인용문을 언급한 뒤, 훨씬 업그레이드됐다(It's a big step up)고 한 것으로 보아 새 건물에 대한 장점을 부각시키려는 뜻으로 한 말임을 알 수 있다. 따라서 정답은 (D)이다.

91

What does the speaker ask listeners to do?

(A) Download some computer software
(B) Pack up their personal items
(C) Register for a meeting time
(D) Look at an employee handbook

화자는 청자들에게 무엇을 하라고 요청하는가?
(A) 컴퓨터 소프트웨어 다운로드
(B) 개인 물품 챙기기
(C) 회의 시간 등록
(D) 직원 안내서 보기

해설 세부 사항 관련 – 화자가 청자들에게 하라고 요청한 일
화자가 후반부에 책상과 컴퓨터 같은 큰 물건들을 처리할 이삿짐 센터를 고용했지만, 소지품들은 여러분 모두가 각자 옮기면 좋겠다(We've hired a mover to handle the bigger items, like desks and computers, but I'd like you all to move your own belongings)면서, 이번 주에 짐을 싸기 시작해야 할 것(You should start boxing those up this week)이라고 했으므로 정답은 (B)이다.

▸▸ Paraphrasing 담화의 **your own belongings**
→ 정답의 **personal items**

92-94 담화

M-Au Hello, ladies and gentleman. My name is Wayne Beck, and I'm the president of the Western Cosmetics Association. **92The WCA is proud to have organized this incredible** gathering of cosmetics professionals, and glad that you have all come. ⁹³Over the next two days, you'll listen to expert lecturers and meet many other members of this exciting field. We hope that you enjoy your time. Oh, but before you head to the first workshops, I need to make an announcement. ⁹⁴Due to some unavoidable circumstances, tonight's after-dinner networking party cannot be held in the Grand Ballroom, as it says in your program. Instead, it will be held in the Rose Ballroom. Thank you.

안녕하십니까, 신사 숙녀 여러분. 제 이름은 웨인 벡이고, 서부 화장품 협회의 회장입니다. WCA는 이런 굉장한 화장품 전문가 모임을 주선한 것을 자랑스럽게 여기며, 여러분이 모두 와 주셔서 기쁩니다. 향후 이틀간 여러분은 전문 강사들의 강연을 듣고 이 흥미진진한 분야에 종사하는 다른 많은 회원들을 만나게 될 것입니다. 우리는 여러분이 즐거운 시간을 보내길 바랍니다. 아, 그런데 첫 번째 워크숍으로 향하기 전에 발표할 것이 있습니다. 불가피한 사정으로 인해 오늘 밤 식후 인맥 형성 파티는 프로그램에 나와 있는 것처럼 그랜드 대연회장에서 열릴 수 없게 되었습니다. 대신 로즈 대연회장에서 열릴 예정입니다. 감사합니다.

어휘 association 협회 organize 조직하다 incredible 믿을 수 없는 gathering 모임 professional 전문가; 전문적인 expert 전문적인; 전문가 lecturer 강사 field 분야 head 향하다 announcement 발표 unavoidable 불가피한 circumstance 상황 networking 인맥 형성 instead 대신에

92
고난도

What is taking place?

(A) A charity dinner
(B) A music festival
(C) A groundbreaking ceremony
(D) An industry conference

무엇이 열리고 있는가?
(A) 자선 만찬
(B) 음악 축제
(C) 기공식
(D) 업계 회의

해설 세부 사항 관련 – 열리고 있는 행사
화자가 초반부에 WCA는 이런 굉장한 화장품 전문가 모임을 주선한 것을 자랑스럽게 여기며, 여러분이 모두 와주셔서 기쁘다(The WCA is proud to have organized this incredible gathering of cosmetics professionals, and glad that you have all come)고 했으므로 화장품 업계의 모임이 열리고 있음을 알 수 있다. 따라서 정답은 (D)이다.

▸▸ Paraphrasing 담화의 gathering of ~ professionals → 정답의 industry conference

93
고난도

What does the speaker say the listeners can do?

(A) Purchase event merchandise
(B) Meet a company executive
(C) Network with others
(D) Sample some refreshments

화자는 청자들이 무엇을 할 수 있다고 말하는가?
(A) 행사 상품 구매하기
(B) 회사 임원 만나기
(C) 다른 사람들과 친분 쌓기
(D) 다과 맛보기

어휘 merchandise 상품 executive 임원 network 인맥을 형성하다 sample 맛보다, 시식하다

해설 세부 사항 관련 – 청자들이 할 수 있는 것
화자가 중반부에 향후 이틀간 청자들이 전문 강사들의 강연을 듣고 다른 많은 회원들을 만나게 될 것(Over the next two days, you'll listen to expert lecturers and meet many other members of this exciting field)이라고 했으므로 정답은 (C)이다.

▸▸ Paraphrasing 담화의 meet many other members → 정답의 network with others

94

What does the speaker say has changed?

(A) The focus of an organization
(B) The location of an event
(C) The date of a launch
(D) The cost of a ticket

화자는 무엇이 바뀌었다고 말하는가?
(A) 조직의 주안점
(B) 행사 장소
(C) 출시일
(D) 입장권 비용

어휘 organization 조직 location 장소 launch 출시[개시]

해설 세부 사항 관련 – 화자가 바뀌었다고 말하는 것
화자가 후반부에 불가피한 사정으로 인해 오늘 밤 식후 인맥 형성 파티는 프로그램에 나와 있는 것처럼 그랜드 볼룸에서 열릴 수 없게 되었다(Due to some unavoidable circumstances, tonight's after-dinner networking party cannot be held in the Grand Ballroom, as it says in your program)면서, 대신 로즈 볼룸에서 열릴 예정이다(Instead, it will be held in the Rose Ballroom)고 장소 변경에 대해 안내하고 있으므로 정답은 (B)이다.

95-97 회의 발췌 + 도표

W-Am Let's get started. ⁹⁵As you know, our firm's promotional campaign for Dorints Foods' new line of potato chips has been a huge success. Take a look at this graph of the company's sales revenues over the last few months. [96]**The month that their new line actually came out, there was only this small, temporary increase. Then we took over the marketing for it, and the numbers skyrocketed.** Just amazing. Now other clients are asking for similar campaigns. [97]**That's why Takuya, the leader of the team responsible for the campaign, is going to speak next. He's going to present some of the innovative marketing methods they developed for it so that you can start making use of them yourselves.**

시작합니다. 아시다시피, 도린츠 식품의 신제품 감자칩에 대한 우리 회사의 홍보 캠페인이 큰 성공을 거뒀습니다. 지난 몇 간간의 회사의 매출액 그래프를 한번 보시죠. 신제품이 실제로 나온 달에는 미미한 일시적 증가만 있었을 뿐입니다. 그리고 나서 우리가 그 제품에 대한 마케팅에 착수했고 수치가 급등했습니다. 그저 놀랍습니다. 다른 고객들이 유사한 캠페인을 요청해오고 있습니다. 그래서 이 캠페인을 책임지고 있는 타쿠야 팀장이 다음으로 발언을 하겠습니다. 그는 그들이 개발한 획기적인 마케팅 방법 중 일부를 제시해 여러분이 직접 활용할 수 있도록 할 것입니다.

어휘 promotional 홍보의 revenue 수익 temporary 일시적인 increase 증가 skyrocket 급등하다 amazing 놀라운 similar 비슷한 responsible 책임지고 있는 present 제시하다 innovative 획기적인 method 방법

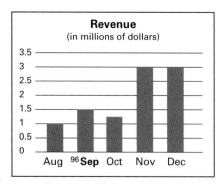
Revenue
(in millions of dollars)

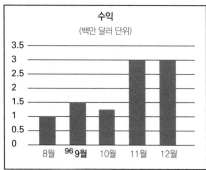
수익
(백만 달러 단위)

95

Who most likely are the listeners?

(A) Snack food developers
(B) Financial analysts
(C) Grocery store managers
(D) Advertising professionals

청자들은 누구일 것 같은가?
(A) 스낵 푸드 개발자
(B) 재무 분석가
(C) 식료품점 관리자
(D) 광고 전문가

해설 전체 내용 관련 – 청자들의 직업

화자가 초반부에 아시다시피 도린츠 식품의 신제품 감자칩에 대한 우리 회사의 홍보 캠페인이 큰 성공을 거뒀다(As you know, our firm's promotional campaign for Dorints Foods' new line of potato chips has been a huge success)고 한 것으로 보아 청자들은 광고 회사에 근무하는 사람들임을 알 수 있다. 따라서 정답은 (D)이다.

▸▸ Paraphrasing 담화의 promotional campaign
→ 정답의 advertising

96

Look at the graphic. In which month was a product line released?

(A) September
(B) October
(C) November
(D) December

시각 정보에 의하면, 어느 달에 제품이 출시되었는가?
(A) 9월
(B) 10월
(C) 11월
(D) 12월

해설 시각 정보 연계 – 제품이 출시된 달

화자가 중반부에 신제품이 실제로 나온 달에는 미미한 일시적 증가만 있었을 뿐이다(The month that their new line actually came out, there was only this small, temporary increase)고 했고, 그리고 나서 우리가 그 제품에 대한 마케팅에 착수했고 수치가 급등했다(Then we took over the marketing for it, and the numbers skyrocketed)고 했는데, 도표에 따르면 수익이 급등하기 전에 미미한 일시적 증가가 있었던 달은 9월이므로 정답은 (A)이다.

97

What will Takuya most likely do?

(A) Assign some responsibilities to the listeners
(B) Address the listeners' concerns about a policy
(C) Teach the listeners some promotional techniques
(D) Present an award to one of the listeners

타쿠야는 무엇을 할 것 같은가?

(A) 청자들에게 일부 업무를 배정한다.
(B) 정책에 대한 청자들의 우려를 처리한다.
(C) 청자들에게 몇 가지 홍보 기법을 가르쳐준다.
(D) 청자들 중 한 명에게 상을 수여한다.

어휘 assign 배정하다 address (문제 등을) 다루다 concern 우려
technique 기법 present 주다 award 상

해설 세부 사항 관련 – 타쿠야가 할 것 같은 일
화자가 후반부에 이 캠페인을 책임지고 있는 타쿠야 팀장이 다음으로 발언을
하겠다(That's why Takuya, the leader of the team responsible for
the campaign, is going to speak next)고 했고, 그는 그들이 개발한 획
기적인 마케팅 방법 중 일부를 제시해 여러분이 직접 활용할 수 있도록 할 것
(He's going to present some of the innovative marketing methods
they developed for it so that you can start making use of them
yourselves)이라고 했으므로 정답은 (C)이다.

▶ Paraphrasing   담화의 present some of the innovative
marketing methods
→ 정답의 teach some promotional
techniques

98-100 공지 + 표

M-Cn Before we start today's meeting, let's
take a minute to recognize the employees
who represented our company in the recent
community center fund-raiser. Could you all
stand up? 98 I know that singing in a talent show
was a big challenge for some of you, but you
did it anyway. Your dedication to the community
is inspiring. 99 And I'm proud to announce that
all of you collected enough donations to earn a
tote bag and even a T-shirt—wow! Feel free to
wear the T-shirt on casual Fridays. 100 Thanks to
citizens like you, the center will be able to offer
courses for elderly people hoping to improve
their computer skills. Great job.

오늘 회의를 시작하기 전에, 최근 주민 센터 모금 행사에서 우리 회사를 대표했
던 직원들께 감사하는 시간을 갖도록 합시다. 모두 일어서 주시겠습니까? 장기
자랑에서 노래하는 것이 여러분 중 몇몇에게는 큰 도전이었다는 것을 알지만 어
쨌든 여러분은 해내셨습니다. 지역 사회에 대한 여러분의 헌신은 고무적입니다.
그리고 여러분 모두가 토트백과 심지어 티셔츠를 얻기에 충분한 기부금을 모았다
고 발표하게 되어 자랑스럽습니다. 왜! 평상복을 입는 금요일에 그 티셔츠를 마
음껏 입으세요. 여러분과 같은 시민들 덕분에 센터는 컴퓨터 기술을 향상시키고
싶어하는 노인들을 위한 강좌를 제공할 수 있게 될 것입니다. 훌륭합니다.

어휘 recognize 알아보다, 인정[표창]하다 represent 대표하다
community 주민, 지역 사회 fund-raiser 모금 행사 talent
재능 challenge 도전 dedication 헌신 inspiring 고무[격려]하는
donations 기부금 citizen 시민 elderly 연세가 드신 improve
향상시키다

Rewards for Fund-raiser Participants		
Level	Minimum amount raised	Prize(s)
1	$10	Certificate
2	$50	Certificate + bag
99 3	$100	Certificate + bag + T-shirt
4	$200	Certificate + bag + T-shirt + movie tickets

모금 행사 참여자를 위한 답례		
등급	최소 모금액	상
1	10달러	인증서
2	50달러	인증서 + 가방
99 3	100달러	인증서 + 가방 + 티셔츠
4	200달러	인증서 + 가방 + 티셔츠 + 영화표

98

What did some fund-raiser participants do?

(A) They completed a sports challenge.
(B) They gave a musical performance.
(C) They donated some homemade food.
(D) They decorated an outdoor space.

일부 모금 행사 참여자들은 무엇을 했는가?

(A) 스포츠 챌린지를 완수했다.
(B) 음악 공연을 했다.
(C) 집에서 만든 음식을 기부했다.
(D) 야외 공간을 꾸몄다.

어휘 complete 끝마치다 performance 공연 donate 기부하다
decorate 꾸미다 outdoor 야외의

해설 세부 사항 관련 – 일부 모금 행사 참여자들이 한 일
화자가 초반부에 장기자랑에서 노래하는 것이 여러분 중 몇몇에게는 큰 도
전이었다는 것을 알지만 어쨌든 여러분은 해냈다(I know that singing in
a talent show was a big challenge for some of you, but you did it
anyway)고 했으므로 정답은 (B)이다.

▶ Paraphrasing   담화의 singing in a talent show
→ 정답의 gave a musical performance

99

Look at the graphic. Which level did the participating
listeners most likely reach?

(A) Level 1
(B) Level 2
(C) Level 3
(D) Level 4

시각 정보에 의하면, 참여한 청자들은 어떤 등급에 도달했을 것 같은가?

(A) 1등급
(B) 2등급
(C) 3등급
(D) 4등급

화자가 중반부에 여러분 모두가 토트백과 심지어 티셔츠를 얻기에 충분한 기부금을 모았다고 발표하게 되어 자랑스럽다(I'm proud to announce that all of you collected enough donations to earn a tote bag and even a T-shirt)고 했고, 표에 따르면 토트백과 티셔츠가 수여되는 등급은 3등급이므로 정답은 (C)이다.

100

What will the funds be used for?

(A) Medical research

(B) Improvements to a park

(C) The renovation of a community center

(D) An educational program

기금은 무엇에 사용될 것인가?

(A) 의료 연구

(B) 공원 개선

(C) 주민 센터 보수

(D) 교육 프로그램

어휘 improvement 개선 renovation 보수[수선] educational 교육의

해설 세부 사항 관련 – 기금이 사용될 곳

화자는 후반부에 여러분과 같은 시민들 덕분에 센터는 컴퓨터 기술을 향상시키고 싶어 하는 노인들을 위한 강좌를 제공할 수 있게 될 것(Thanks to citizens like you, the center will be able to offer courses for elderly people hoping to improve their computer skills)이라고 한 것으로 보아 기금이 노인을 위한 컴퓨터 교육에 사용될 것임을 알 수 있다. 따라서 정답은 (D)이다.

▸▸ Paraphrasing   담화의 courses ~ to improve their computer skills
→ 정답의 an educational program

TEST 5

1 (D)	**2** (A)	**3** (B)	**4** (C)	**5** (A)
6 (C)	**7** (A)	**8** (B)	**9** (C)	**10** (B)
11 (A)	**12** (C)	**13** (C)	**14** (A)	**15** (C)
16 (A)	**17** (B)	**18** (A)	**19** (B)	**20** (C)
21 (B)	**22** (A)	**23** (A)	**24** (B)	**25** (B)
26 (B)	**27** (C)	**28** (C)	**29** (A)	**30** (C)
31 (B)	**32** (B)	**33** (D)	**34** (C)	**35** (A)
36 (C)	**37** (B)	**38** (A)	**39** (D)	**40** (D)
41 (B)	**42** (A)	**43** (C)	**44** (D)	**45** (C)
46 (A)	**47** (C)	**48** (C)	**49** (B)	**50** (D)
51 (A)	**52** (C)	**53** (D)	**54** (D)	**55** (D)
56 (D)	**57** (B)	**58** (A)	**59** (A)	**60** (D)
61 (D)	**62** (C)	**63** (B)	**64** (B)	**65** (B)
66 (B)	**67** (A)	**68** (B)	**69** (D)	**70** (C)
71 (B)	**72** (D)	**73** (A)	**74** (A)	**75** (C)
76 (B)	**77** (C)	**78** (A)	**79** (D)	**80** (D)
81 (D)	**82** (A)	**83** (C)	**84** (B)	**85** (A)
86 (A)	**87** (B)	**88** (C)	**89** (C)	**90** (A)
91 (D)	**92** (A)	**93** (D)	**94** (C)	**95** (A)
96 (C)	**97** (B)	**98** (B)	**99** (C)	**100** (B)

PART 1

1　M-Au

(A) He's rolling down a window.
(B) He's replacing a tire.
(C) He's putting fuel in a vehicle.
(D) He's examining an engine.

(A) 남자는 창문을 내리고 있다.
(B) 남자는 타이어를 교체하고 있다.
(C) 남자는 차에 연료를 채우고 있다.
(D) **남자는 엔진을 점검 중이다.**

어휘　roll down ~을 내리다[열다]　replace 교체하다　fuel 연료
　　　vehicle 차량　examine 조사하다

해설　1인 등장 사진 – 인물의 동작 묘사

(A) 동사 오답. 남자가 창문을 내리고 있는(is rolling down a window) 모습
　　이 아니므로 오답.
(B) 동사 오답. 남자가 타이어를 교체하고 있는(is replacing a tire) 모습이
　　아니므로 오답.
(C) 동사 오답. 남자가 차에 연료를 채우고 있는(is putting fuel in a
　　vehicle) 모습이 아니므로 오답.
(D) 정답. 남자가 엔진을 점검하고 있는(is examining an engine) 모습이므
　　로 정답.

2　W-Am

(A) The woman is pointing upward.
(B) They're looking at a clipboard.
(C) They're wearing safety glasses.
(D) The man is wrapping a box in plastic.

(A) **여자는 위쪽을 가리키고 있다.**
(B) 사람들은 클립보드를 보고 있다.
(C) 사람들은 보안경을 쓰고 있다.
(D) 남자가 상자를 비닐로 싸고 있다.

어휘　point 가리키다　upward 위쪽으로　safety glasses 보안경
　　　wrap 싸다　plastic 비닐

해설　2인 이상 등장 사진 – 인물의 동작 묘사

(A) 정답. 여자가 위를 가리키고 있는(is pointing upward) 모습이므로 정답.
(B) 동사 오답. 사람들이 클립보드를 보고 있는(are looking at a clipboard)
　　모습이 아니므로 오답.
(C) 동사 오답. 사람들이 보안경을 쓰고 있는(are wearing safety glasses)
　　모습이 아니므로 오답.
(D) 동사 오답. 남자가 상자를 비닐로 싸고 있는(is wrapping a box in
　　plastic) 모습이 아니므로 오답.

3　W-Br

(A) She's cooking on a stove.
(B) She's standing at a buffet.
(C) She's carrying a tray of food.
(D) She's pouring soup into a bowl.

(A) 여자는 가스레인지에서 요리를 하고 있다.
(B) **여자는 뷔페에 서 있다.**
(C) 여자는 음식이 든 쟁반을 들고 있다.
(D) 여자는 그릇에 수프를 따르고 있다.

어휘　stove 레인지, 스토브　buffet 뷔페　tray 쟁반　pour 붓다[따르다]
　　　bowl 그릇

해설　1인 등장 사진 – 인물의 동작 묘사

(A) 동사 오답. 여자가 가스레인지에서 요리를 하고 있는(is cooking on a
　　stove) 모습이 아니므로 오답.
(B) 정답. 여자가 뷔페에 서 있는(is standing at a buffet) 모습이므로 정답.
(C) 동사 오답. 여자가 음식이 든 쟁반을 들고 있는(is carrying a tray of
　　food) 모습이 아니므로 오답.

(D) 동사 오답. 여자가 그릇에 수프를 따르고 있는(is pouring soup into a bowl) 모습이 아니므로 오답.

4 M-Cn

(A) Some people are applauding a performance.
(B) A floor is being polished.
(C) A mirror covers most of one wall.
(D) A man is dancing on a stage.

(A) 몇몇 사람들은 공연에 박수를 치고 있다.
(B) 바닥이 닦이고 있다.
(C) 거울이 한쪽 벽의 대부분을 뒤덮고 있다.
(D) 남자는 무대에서 춤을 추고 있다.

어휘 applaud 박수를 치다 performance 공연 polish (윤이 나도록) 닦다 cover 덮다

해설 혼합 사진 – 사람 또는 사물 묘사
(A) 동사 오답. 공연에 박수를 치고 있는(are applauding a performance) 사람들의 모습이 보이지 않으므로 오답.
(B) 동사 오답. 바닥이 닦이고 있는(is being polished) 모습이 보이지 않으므로 오답.
(C) 정답. 거울(a mirror)이 한쪽 벽의 대부분을 뒤덮고 있는(covers most of one wall) 모습이므로 정답.
(D) 사진에 없는 명사를 이용한 오답. 사진에 무대(a stage)의 모습이 보이지 않으므로 오답.

5 W-Am [고난도]

(A) Cars are parked along a waterway.
(B) Boats are being rowed toward the shore.
(C) A bridge connects two parts of a forest.
(D) A row of tents faces the ocean.

(A) 수로를 따라 차들이 주차되어 있다.
(B) 배가 해안을 향해 노 저어지고 있다.
(C) 다리는 숲의 두 부분을 연결한다.
(D) 한 줄로 늘어선 텐트들이 바다를 향한다.

어휘 waterway 수로 row (노를 써서) 배를 젓다; 줄[열] shore 해안 forest 숲 face ~을 향하다 ocean 바다

해설 배경 사진 – 실외 사물의 상태 묘사
(A) 정답. 차들이 수로를 따라 주차되어 있는(are parked along a waterway) 모습이므로 정답.
(B) 동사 오답. 배(boats)가 해안을 향해 노 저어지고 있는(are being rowed toward the shore) 모습이 보이지 않으므로 오답.
(C) 사진에 없는 명사를 이용한 오답. 사진에 숲(a forest)의 모습이 보이지 않으므로 오답.
(D) 사진에 없는 명사를 이용한 오답. 사진에 텐트들(tents)의 모습이 보이지 않으므로 오답.

6 M-Au

(A) The woman is drinking from a glass.
(B) One of the men is gesturing at a projector screen.
(C) A laptop computer has been opened.
(D) There are file folders on the table.

(A) 여자는 잔을 들고 음료를 마시고 있다.
(B) 남자들 중 한 명은 영사기 화면을 향해 손짓하고 있다.
(C) 노트북 컴퓨터가 열려 있다.
(D) 탁자에 파일 폴더들이 있다.

어휘 gesture 손짓을 하다

해설 혼합 사진 – 사람 또는 사물 묘사
(A) 동사 오답. 여자가 잔을 들고 음료를 마시고 있는(is drinking from a glass) 모습이 아니므로 오답.
(B) 사진에 없는 명사를 이용한 오답. 사진에 영사기 스크린(a projector screen)의 모습이 보이지 않으므로 오답.
(C) 정답. 노트북 컴퓨터(a laptop computer)가 열려 있는(has been opened) 모습이므로 정답.
(D) 사진에 없는 명사를 이용한 오답. 사진에 파일 폴더들(file folders)의 모습이 보이지 않으므로 오답.

PART 2

7

W-Am When does the last train to Montreal leave from this station?
M-Cn (A) At eleven-fifteen at night.
(B) Just a few more stations.
(C) No, I'm going to Toronto today.

이 역에서 몬트리올행 마지막 기차는 언제 떠나나요?
(A) 밤 11시 15분예요.
(B) 몇 정거장만 더요.
(C) 아니요, 저는 오늘 토론토로 갑니다.

해설 몬트리올행 마지막 기차의 출발 시점을 묻는 When 의문문
(A) 정답. 몬트리올행 마지막 기차가 출발하는 시점을 묻는 질문에 밤 11시 15분이라고 구체적인 시간으로 응답하고 있으므로 정답.
(B) 연상 단어 오답. 질문의 train에서 연상 가능한 stations를 이용한 오답.
(C) Yes/No 불가 오답. When 의문문에는 Yes/No 응답이 불가능하므로 오답.

8

W-Br Have you ever heard of Williamson Appliances?

M-Au (A) I need a new refrigerator.

(B) That name does seem familiar.

(C) Go ahead and turn up the volume.

윌리엄슨 가전에 대해 들어보셨나요?
(A) 새 냉장고가 필요해요.
(B) **익숙한 이름 같네요.**
(C) 볼륨을 높이세요.

어휘 appliances 가전 제품 refrigerator 냉장고 familiar 익숙한

해설 윌리엄슨 가전에 대해 들어본 적이 있는지 여부를 묻는 조동사(Have) 의문문
(A) 연상 단어 오답. 질문의 Appliances에서 연상 가능한 refrigerator를 이용한 오답.
(B) 정답. 윌리엄슨 가전에 대해 들어본 적이 있는지 묻는 질문에 익숙한 이름이라며 들어본 적이 있음을 우회적으로 나타내고 있으므로 정답.
(C) 연상 단어 오답. 질문의 heard에서 연상 가능한 volume을 이용한 오답.

9

M-Cn I could reserve a conference room for the performance reviews.

W-Br (A) It's down the hall to your left.

(B) The top performers in each department.

(C) That would be great.

제가 실적 평가를 위해 회의실을 예약할 수 있어요.
(A) 복도 아래 왼쪽에 있어요.
(B) 각 부서의 최고 성과자들이요.
(C) **그게 좋겠네요.**

어휘 reserve 예약하다 conference 회의 performance 실적, 성과

해설 제안/권유의 평서문
(A) 평서문과 상관없는 오답. Where 의문문에 대한 응답이므로 오답
(B) 파생어 오답. 평서문의 performance와 파생어 관계인 performers를 이용한 오답.
(C) 정답. 실적 평가를 위해 회의실을 예약할 수 있다고 제안하는 평서문에 그렇게 하면 좋겠다고 호응하고 있으므로 정답.

10   고난도

W-Am Isn't this Angela's desk?

M-Cn (A) Oh, where did you find it?

(B) She said I could sit here when she's away.

(C) Yes, the latest lab test.

이것은 안젤라의 책상이 아닌가요?
(A) 아, 어디에서 그것을 찾으셨어요?
(B) **그녀가 자리를 비울 때 제가 여기 앉아도 된다고 했어요.**
(C) 네, 최신 실험실 테스트예요.

어휘 latest 최신의 lab 실험실

해설 안젤라의 책상 여부를 확인하는 부정의문문
(A) 질문과 상관없는 오답.
(B) 정답. 가리키는 책상이 안젤라의 책상이 아닌지 묻는 질문에 그녀가 자리를 비울 때 여기 앉아도 된다고 했다며, 안젤라의 책상이 맞다는 것을 우회적으로 알려주고 있으므로 정답.
(C) 질문과 상관없는 오답.

11

W-Am Which button do I click on to create a graph?

M-Au (A) The one with three colored lines.

(B) It's a good way to display figures.

(C) I didn't know you took photographs.

그래프를 만들려면 어느 버튼을 클릭해야 하나요?
(A) **삼색선이 있는 거요.**
(B) 수치를 표시하기 좋은 방법이에요.
(C) 당신이 사진을 찍은 줄 몰랐어요.

어휘 display 내보이다 figure 수치 photograph 사진

해설 그래프를 만들려면 클릭해야 하는 버튼을 묻는 Which 의문문
(A) 정답. 그래프를 만들려면 어느 버튼을 클릭해야 하는지 묻는 질문에 삼색선이 있는 것이라고 구체적으로 알려주고 있으므로 정답.
(B) 연상 단어 오답. 질문의 graph에서 연상 가능한 figures를 이용한 오답.
(C) 유사 발음 오답. 질문의 graph와 부분적으로 발음이 유사한 photographs를 이용한 오답.

12   고난도

W-Br Do you think Chris Cole or Jane Barr is a better candidate for the job?

M-Cn (A) That's the hiring manager's opinion.

(B) Yes, the earliest date possible.

(C) Based on the interviews, I'd choose Chris.

크리스 콜과 제인 바 중에 누가 그 일에 더 적합한 후보라고 생각하세요?
(A) 그것은 채용 담당자의 의견입니다.
(B) 네, 가능한 가장 빠른 날짜예요.
(C) **면접을 바탕으로, 전 크리스를 선택하겠어요.**

어휘 candidate 후보자 based on ~을 근거하여

해설 일자리에 더 적합한 후보를 묻는 선택의문문
(A) 연상 단어 오답. 질문의 candidate for the job에서 연상 가능한 hiring을 이용한 오답.
(B) Yes/No 불가 오답. 문장과 문장을 연결하는 경우를 제외하고는 선택의문문에는 Yes/No 응답이 불가능하므로 오답.
(C) 정답. 일자리에 더 적합하다고 생각하는 후보를 묻는 선택의문문에서 면접을 바탕으로 크리스를 택하겠다며 둘 중 하나를 선택해 응답하고 있으므로 정답.

13

M-Au This is the first day of the city arts festival, isn't it?

W-Am (A) An exhibition of works by local artists.

(B) This painting won second prize, actually.

(C) Check the official event Web site.

오늘이 시 예술 축제의 첫날이죠, 그렇죠?
(A) 지역 예술가들의 작품 전시회입니다.
(B) 사실, 이 그림은 2등 상을 수상했어요.
(C) 공식 행사 웹사이트를 확인해보세요.

어휘 exhibition 전시회 work 작품 prize 상 official 공식의

해설 오늘이 축제의 첫날인지 여부를 확인하는 부가의문문
(A) 파생어 오답. 질문의 arts와 파생어 관계인 artists를 이용한 오답.
(B) 연상 단어 오답. 질문의 arts에서 연상 가능한 painting을 이용한 오답.
(C) 정답. 오늘이 시 예술 축제의 첫날인지 여부를 확인하는 질문에 공식 행사 웹사이트를 확인해보라며 원하는 답변을 알려줄 수 없음을 우회적으로 표현하고 있으므로 정답.

14

W-Br Where can I exchange these dollars for British pounds?

M-Cn (A) There's a bank across the street.

(B) Sure, we have plenty of change.

(C) A little lower than yesterday.

어디서 이 달러들을 영국 파운드로 환전할 수 있을까요?
(A) 길 건너에 은행이 있어요.
(B) 물론이죠, 잔돈은 얼마든지 있습니다.
(C) 어제보다 조금 낮네요.

어휘 exchange 교환하다 plenty of 충분한 change 잔돈

해설 환전이 가능한 곳을 묻는 Where 의문문
(A) 정답. 달러를 영국 파운드로 환전할 수 있는 곳을 묻는 질문에 길 건너에 은행이 있다고 알려주고 있으므로 정답.
(B) Yes/No 불가 오답. Where 의문문에는 Yes/No 응답이 불가능한데, Sure도 일종의 Yes 응답이라고 볼 수 있으므로 오답.
(C) 연상 단어 오답. 질문의 exchange에서 환율을 연상하게 하는 lower를 이용한 오답.

15 고난도

M-Au Excuse me—why does this form ask for an e-mail address?

M-Cn (A) Try looking in the staff directory first.

(B) I e-mailed it to jsmith@rppo.com.

(C) You can leave that part blank if you want.

실례지만, 이 양식에서 이메일 주소를 요구하는 이유가 뭐죠?
(A) 직원 명부부터 살펴보세요.
(B) jsmith@rppo.com으로 이메일을 보냈어요.
(C) 원하시면 그 부분은 빈칸으로 두셔도 돼요.

어휘 form 양식 directory (이름 등을 알파벳 순으로 나열한) 안내 책자 blank 빈

해설 양식에서 이메일 주소를 요구하는 이유를 묻는 Why 의문문
(A) 질문과 상관없는 오답. Where 의문문에 대한 응답이므로 오답.
(B) 파생어 오답. 질문의 e-mail과 파생어 관계인 e-mailed를 이용한 오답.
(C) 정답. 양식에서 이메일 주소를 요구하는 이유를 묻는 질문에 원하면 비워두라는 말로 직접적인 답변을 대신하고 있으므로 정답.

16

M-Au Don't you have any winter clothing in stock yet?

W-Br (A) What exactly are you looking for?

(B) A group skiing trip in January.

(C) We're having a heating unit installed soon.

아직 겨울 옷은 재고가 없나요?
(A) 정확히 무엇을 찾고 계시나요?
(B) 1월에 단체 스키 여행이요.
(C) 조만간 난방 장치를 설치할 겁니다.

어휘 in stock 재고의 heating 난방 unit (상품의) 한 개[단위] install 설치하다

해설 겨울 옷의 재고 유무를 확인하는 부정의문문
(A) 정답. 겨울 옷의 재고를 갖고 있는지 묻는 질문에 구체적으로 찾는 것이 무엇인지 되묻고 있으므로 정답.
(B) 연상 단어 오답. 질문의 winter에서 연상 가능한 January를 이용한 오답.
(C) 연상 단어 오답. 질문의 winter에서 연상 가능한 heating을 이용한 오답.

17 고난도

M-Cn Who's the director of digital marketing?

W-Am (A) At Creldon Associates.

(B) I've only met the assistant director.

(C) It's a series of Web advertisements.

디지털 마케팅 이사는 누구입니까?
(A) 크렐던 협회에서요.
(B) 저는 부장님만 만나 봤어요.
(C) 웹 광고 시리즈입니다.

어휘 director 이사 associate 협회 advertisement 광고

해설 디지털 마케팅 이사를 묻는 Who 의문문
(A) 질문과 상관없는 오답. Where 의문문에 대한 응답이므로 오답.
(B) 정답. 디지털 마케팅의 이사가 누구인지 묻는 질문에 자신은 부장님만 만나 봤다며 관련 정보를 알지 못함을 우회적으로 응답하고 있으므로 정답.
(C) 연상 단어 오답. 질문의 marketing에서 연상 가능한 advertisements를 이용한 오답.

18 고난도

M-Cn How do you keep your uniform so clean?

W-Br (A) You have to use the right laundry detergent.

(B) Just to wipe down the counters.

(C) I thought we had to keep it there.

유니폼을 어떻게 그렇게 깨끗하게 유지하시나요?
(A) 올바른 세탁 세제를 사용해야 해요.
(B) 카운터를 닦으려고요.
(C) 거기에 보관해야 한다고 생각했어요.

어휘　laundry 세탁　detergent 세제　wipe 닦다

해설　유니폼의 유지 방법을 묻는 How 의문문
(A) 정답. 유니폼을 깨끗하게 유지하는 방법을 묻는 질문에 올바른 세탁 세제를 사용해야 한다고 구체적으로 응답하고 있으므로 정답.
(B) 연상 단어 오답. 질문의 clean에서 연상 가능한 wipe를 이용한 오답.
(C) 단어 반복 오답. 질문의 keep을 반복 이용한 오답.

19　고난도
W-Am　Please place any metal items in this basket.
W-Br　(A) A couple pounds of apples.
　　　(B) Let me get my keys out of my pocket.
　　　(C) So-Hee is training to replace Mark.

이 바구니에 금속 물체를 넣어주십시오.
(A) 사과 2파운드요.
(B) 주머니에서 열쇠를 꺼내겠습니다.
(C) 소희가 마크의 후임으로 교육 중입니다.

어휘　metal 금속　basket 바구니　pound 파운드(약 453그램)　replace 대신하다

해설　부탁/요청의 평서문
(A) 평서문과 상관없는 오답. What 의문문에 대한 응답이므로 오답.
(B) 정답. 바구니에 금속 물체를 넣어달라는 요청에 대해 주머니에서 열쇠를 꺼내겠다며 요청에 응하고 있으므로 정답.
(C) 유사 발음 오답. 평서문의 place와 부분적으로 발음이 유사한 replace를 이용한 오답.

20
W-Am　You're going to the post office this afternoon, aren't you?
M-Cn　(A) No, it wasn't on the poster.
　　　(B) Here's a roll of first-class stamps.
　　　(C) After I repackage this shipment.

오늘 오후에 우체국에 가실 거죠, 그렇죠?
(A) 아니요, 포스터에 없었어요.
(B) 여기 1급 우표 한 묶음입니다.
(C) 이 배송물을 재포장하고 나서요.

어휘　post office 우체국　roll 통, 두루마리　stamp 우표　repackage 재포장하다　shipment 배송품

해설　우체국에 가는지 여부를 확인하는 부가의문문
(A) 파생어 오답. 질문의 post와 파생어 관계인 poster를 이용한 오답.
(B) 연상 단어 오답. 질문의 post office에서 연상 가능한 stamps를 이용한 오답.
(C) 정답. 오늘 오후에 우체국에 가는지 여부를 확인하는 질문에 이 배송물을 재포장하고 나서라며 간다는 것을 우회적으로 표현하고 있으므로 정답.

21
M-Au　Where's this law firm's reference library?
W-Am　(A) Our large collection of law books and documents.
　　　(B) I'll show you the building's floor plan.
　　　(C) Ms. Garcia certainly writes good reference letters.

이 법률 회사의 열람 전용 도서관은 어디인가요?
(A) 저희가 소장하고 있는 방대한 법률 서적과 문서들입니다.
(B) 건물 평면도를 보여드릴게요.
(C) 가르시아 씨는 확실히 좋은 추천서를 씁니다.

어휘　law firm 법률 회사　reference library 열람 전용 도서관　collection 소장품　floor plan 평면도　certainly 틀림없이　reference letter 추천서

해설　열람 전용 도서관의 위치를 묻는 Where 의문문
(A) 연상 단어 오답. 질문의 library에서 연상 가능한 books를 이용한 오답.
(B) 정답. 열람 전용 도서관의 위치를 묻는 질문에 평면도를 보여주겠다며 우회적으로 응답하고 있으므로 정답.
(C) 단어 반복 오답. 질문의 reference를 반복 이용한 오답.

22
W-Br　Could I borrow your mobile phone charger?
M-Au　(A) Did you lose yours again?
　　　(B) The charges are explained on your invoice.
　　　(C) Almost one hundred percent.

휴대폰 충전기를 빌릴 수 있을까요?
(A) 본인 것을 또 잃어버리셨어요?
(B) 청구서에 요금이 설명되어 있습니다.
(C) 거의 백 퍼센트입니다.

어휘　charger 충전기　lose 잃어버리다　charge 요금　invoice 청구서, 송장

해설　부탁/요청의 의문문
(A) 정답. 휴대폰 충전기를 빌릴 수 있는지 요청하는 질문에 본인의 것을 또 분실했는지 되묻고 있으므로 정답.
(B) 파생어 오답. 질문의 charger와 파생어 관계인 charges를 이용한 오답.
(C) 연상 단어 오답. 질문의 charger에서 연상 가능한 one hundred percent를 이용한 오답.

23　고난도
W-Am　Who can I ask about the status of my maintenance request?
M-Cn　(A) I'd wait another day before following up.
　　　(B) Yes, during the question-and-answer session.
　　　(C) Because this electrical outlet still isn't working.

제 유지 관리 요청에 대한 진행 상황은 누구에게 물어보면 될까요?
(A) 저라면 더 알아보기 전에 하루 더 기다려보겠어요.
(B) 네, 질의응답 시간에요.
(C) 이 콘센트가 여전히 작동하지 않아서요.

어휘 status (진행 과정의) 상황 maintenance 유지 follow up
더 알아보다, 후속 조치하다 session (특정 활동을 위한) 시간[기간]
electrical outlet 콘센트

해설 요청 관련 진행 상황에 대해 물어볼 사람을 묻는 Who 의문문
(A) 정답. 유지 관리 요청에 대한 진행 상황을 물어볼 수 있는 사람을 묻는 질문
에 본인이라면 더 알아보기 전에 하루 더 기다려볼 것이라며 조언하고 있으
므로 정답.
(B) Yes/No 불가 오답. Who 의문문에는 Yes/No 응답이 불가능하므로 오답.
(C) 연상 단어 오답. 질문의 maintenance request에서 연상 가능한 isn't
working을 이용한 오답.

24

W-Am How long do you expect the research study to
take?

M-Au (A) It was carefully inspected in June.
(B) There is a lot of data to gather.
(C) Through an Internet search portal.

연구 조사가 얼마나 걸릴 것으로 예상하십니까?
(A) 6월에 꼼꼼하게 검사 받았습니다.
(B) 수집해야 할 자료가 많습니다.
(C) 인터넷 검색 포털을 통해서요.

어휘 research 연구, 조사 study 연구 inspect 검사하다

해설 연구 조사의 예상 소요 시간을 묻는 How long 의문문
(A) 유사 발음 오답. 질문의 expect와 부분적으로 발음이 유사한 inspected를
이용한 오답.
(B) 정답. 연구 조사에 걸릴 것으로 예상하는 시간을 묻는 질문에 수집해야 할
자료가 많아 오래 걸릴 수 있음을 우회적으로 표현하고 있으므로 정답.
(C) 유사 발음 오답. 질문의 research와 부분적으로 발음이 유사한 search를
이용한 오답.

25

M-Cn Are the handouts ready to be distributed?

W-Br (A) It's a summary of my main points.
(B) We just need to staple them.
(C) Each person in the seminar.

유인물을 나눠줄 준비가 되었나요?
(A) 제 요점에 대한 요약본입니다.
(B) 스테이플러로 고정만 하면 돼요.
(C) 세미나에 참석한 각 인원이요.

어휘 handout 유인물 distribute 나눠주다 summary 요약 staple
스테이플러로 고정하다

해설 유인물의 배포 준비 여부를 묻는 Be동사 의문문
(A) 질문과 상관없는 오답. What 의문문에 대한 응답이므로 오답.
(B) 정답. 유인물을 나눠줄 준비가 되었는지 묻는 질문에 스테이플러로 고정만 하
면 된다면서 준비가 거의 다 되었음을 우회적으로 응답하고 있으므로 정답.
(C) 질문과 상관없는 오답.

26

M-Au What are these small ceramic bowls for?

W-Br (A) Five thousand won for a set of three.
(B) The waiter will let us know when he comes
back.
(C) Do you remember where you last saw it?

이 작은 도자기 그릇들은 무슨 용도인가요?
(A) 세 개짜리 한 세트에 5,000원입니다.
(B) 웨이터가 돌아오면 알려줄 거예요.
(C) 언제 그것을 마지막으로 봤는지 기억하세요?

어휘 ceramic 도자기

해설 그릇의 용도를 묻는 What 의문문
(A) 질문과 상관없는 오답. How much 의문문에 대한 응답이므로 오답.
(B) 정답. 작은 그릇들의 용도를 묻는 질문에 웨이터가 알려줄 거라며 우회적으
로 응답하고 있으므로 정답.
(C) 질문과 상관없는 오답. 질문에 it이 가리키는 명사가 없으므로 오답.

27

M-Cn Would you like me to order a new copy machine?

W-Am (A) Yokoyama Office Electronics, I believe.
(B) The user's manual is in the box.
(C) The technician is still trying to fix the old one.

새 복사기를 주문해드릴까요?
(A) 요코야마 사무용 전자제품인 것 같아요.
(B) 상자 안에 사용 설명서가 있습니다.
(C) 기사가 아직 기존 것을 고치려고 노력 중이에요.

어휘 order 주문하다 copy machine 복사기 manual 설명서 fix
고치다

해설 제안/권유의 의문문
(A) 연상 단어 오답. 질문의 copy machine에서 연상 가능한 Office
Electronics를 이용한 오답.
(B) 연상 단어 오답. 질문의 copy machine에서 연상 가능한 user's manual
을 이용한 오답.
(C) 정답. 새 복사기를 주문할지 제안하는 질문에 기사가 아직 기존 것을 고치
려고 노력 중이라며 거절의 의사를 우회적으로 표현하고 있으므로 정답.

28

W-Br Are we going to have an employee picnic again this
year?

M-Au (A) I'd love to go with you.
(B) That's OK—the park is within walking distance.
(C) If the weather allows it.

올해에도 직원 야유회를 가나요?
(A) 당신과 함께 가고 싶어요.
(B) 괜찮아요. 공원은 걸어갈 수 있는 거리에 있어요.
(C) 날씨가 허락한다면요.

어휘 employee 직원 distance 거리 allow 허락하다

해설   직원 야유회 개최 여부를 묻는 Be동사 의문문

(A) 파생어 오답. 질문의 going과 파생어 관계인 go를 이용한 오답.

(B) 연상 단어 오답. 질문의 picnic에서 연상 가능한 park를 이용한 오답.

(C) 정답. 올해에도 직원 야유회를 가는지 묻는 질문에 날씨를 언급하며 여건이 될 경우 야유회를 갈 것임을 우회적으로 응답하고 있으므로 정답.

29 고난도

W-Br   Do I have to return this contract in person, or can I mail it back?

M-Au   (A) That's your copy to keep.

(B) Once you've signed and dated it.

(C) I'm sorry, but we don't accept returns.

이 계약서를 직접 반납해야 하나요, 아니면 우편으로 보내도 되나요?

(A) 당신이 가지면 되는 사본입니다.

(B) 당신이 서명하고 날짜를 적고 나서요.

(C) 죄송하지만, 반품은 받지 않습니다.

어휘   return 반송하다; 반품   contract 계약서   in person 직접   once ~하자마자   date 날짜를 적다; 날짜   accept 수락하다

해설   계약서의 반환 방법을 묻는 선택의문문

(A) 정답. 계약서의 반환 방법을 묻는 선택의문문에서 가지면 되는 사본이라며 제3의 답변을 주고 있으므로 정답.

(B) 연상 단어 오답. 질문의 contract에서 연상 가능한 signed를 이용한 오답.

(C) 단어 반복 오답. 질문의 return을 반복 이용한 오답.

30 고난도

M-Cn   Why is there a moving truck parked out front?

W-Am   (A) It's all right as long as it's not moving quickly.

(B) We'll need permission from the building supervisor.

(C) They must have found a tenant for the office next door.

왜 앞쪽에 이삿짐 트럭이 주차되어 있죠?

(A) 빨리 움직이지만 않으면 괜찮습니다.

(B) 건물 관리자로부터 허가가 필요할 겁니다.

(C) 옆 사무실에 세입자를 찾은 모양이에요.

어휘   permission 허가   supervisor 관리자, 감독관   tenant 세입자

해설   이삿짐 트럭이 주차되어 있는 이유를 묻는 Why 의문문

(A) 단어 반복 오답. 질문의 moving을 반복 이용한 오답.

(B) 연상 단어 오답. 질문의 parked에서 연상 가능한 permission을 이용한 오답.

(C) 정답. 이삿짐 트럭이 앞쪽에 주차되어 있는 이유를 묻는 질문에 옆 사무실에 세입자를 찾은 모양이라며 이유를 추측하는 응답을 하고 있으므로 정답.

31 고난도

M-Au   Fonson Bridge is closed, and I don't know another route.

W-Am   (A) No, we're still pretty far from the river.

(B) Oh, I forgot that you're not from around here.

(C) Whichever is the fastest.

폰슨 다리가 폐쇄되었는데, 전 다른 길은 몰라요.

(A) 아니요, 아직 강에서 꽤 멀리 떨어져 있습니다.

(B) 아, 이 근처 출신이 아니라는 걸 잊었네요.

(C) 어느 쪽이든 가장 빠른 쪽으로요.

어휘   route 길   pretty 꽤   whichever 어느 쪽이든 ~한 것

해설   정보 전달의 평서문

(A) 연상 단어 오답. 평서문의 Bridge에서 연상 가능한 river를 이용한 오답.

(B) 정답. 폰슨 다리가 폐쇄되었는데 다른 길은 모른다는 평서문에 당신이 이 근처 출신이 아니라는 걸 잊었다며 길을 모르는 이유를 이해함을 표현하고 있으므로 정답.

(C) 평서문과 상관없는 오답. 선택의문문에 대한 응답이므로 오답.

PART 3

32-34

M-Cn   OK, Georgia, **32 I can install the rest of the flooring myself. I'd like you to climb up onto the roof and help Rick attach the tiles. 33 Say, is that a new toolbox?**

W-Br   **33 Oh—yes, it is. You know, my old blue toolkit was falling apart and never could carry that much anyway. So I thought I'd invest in a new one.**

M-Cn   It's really nice. Wait, is it a Wenton X Series? With the adjustable handle feature? I thought those cost like a hundred dollars.

W-Br   **34 Well, now that it's been on the market for a few years, its price has dropped.** If you like it, you should look into getting one, too.

남   좋아요, 조지아, 나머지 바닥은 제가 직접 설치할 수 있어요. 지붕 위로 올라가서 릭이 타일을 붙이는 것을 도와주면 좋겠어요. 저, 그거 새 공구 상자예요?

여   아, 네. 아시다시피, 제 오래된 파란색 연장 세트가 너덜너덜해졌고, 어쨌든 그렇게 많이 담을 수가 없었어요. 그래서 새로운 것에 **투자해야겠다고 생각했죠.**

남   정말 좋네요. 잠깐, 이거 웬튼 X 시리즈예요? 조정 가능한 손잡이가 달린 거요? 그거 100달러 정도 하는 줄 아는데요.

여   **글쎄, 시장에 나온 지도 몇 년 되어서 가격이 떨어졌어요.** 만약 마음에 드시면, 사는 쪽으로 알아보세요.

32

What kind of business do the speakers most likely work for?

(A) A hardware store
(B) A construction firm
(C) A building equipment manufacturer
(D) A landscaping company

화자들은 어떤 종류의 업체에서 일하는 것 같은가?
(A) 철물점
(B) 건설 회사
(C) 건설 장비 제조업체
(D) 조경 회사

해설 전체 내용 관련 – 화자들의 근무지
남자가 첫 대사에서 나머지 바닥은 직접 설치할 수 있다(I can install the rest of the flooring myself)며 여자에게 지붕 위로 올라가서 릭이 타일을 붙이는 것을 도와주면 좋겠다(I'd like you to climb up onto the roof and help Rick attach the tile)고 한 것으로 보아 정답은 (B)이다.

33   고난도

What has the woman recently done?

(A) Rearranged a storage area
(B) Met with potential investors
(C) Attended a live demonstration
(D) Replaced one of her belongings

여자가 최근에 한 일은 무엇인가?
(A) 보관 구역을 재배치했다.
(B) 잠재 투자자를 만났다.
(C) 실시간 시연회에 참석했다.
(D) 소지품 중 하나를 교체했다.

어휘 rearrange 재배치하다 storage 보관 potential 잠재적인
      investor 투자자 demonstration 시연 belongings 소유물

해설 세부 사항 관련 – 여자가 최근에 한 일
남자가 첫 대사에서 공구 상자가 새것(is that a new toolbox?)인지를 물었고, 여자가 네(yes)라며 오래된 파란색 연장 세트가 너덜너덜해졌고, 어쨌든 그렇게 많이 담을 수가 없었다(You know, my old blue toolkit was falling apart and never could carry that much anyway)고 한 뒤, 그래서 새로운 것에 투자해야겠다고 생각했다(So I thought I'd invest in a new one)고 했으므로 정답은 (D)이다.

34

What does the woman say has changed about the Wenton X Series?

(A) It now has additional features.
(B) It is now made of a different metal.
(C) It has become less expensive.
(D) It has become safer to use.

여자는 웬튼 X 시리즈에 대해 무엇이 바뀌었다고 말하는가?
(A) 지금은 추가적인 특징들이 더해졌다.
(B) 지금은 다른 금속으로 만들어진다.
(C) 가격이 낮아졌다.
(D) 사용하기 더 안전해졌다.

어휘 additional 추가적인 metal 금속 expensive 비싼

해설 세부 사항 관련 – 여자가 웬튼 X 시리즈에 대해 바뀌었다고 말한 것
여자가 마지막 대사에서 시장에 나온 지도 몇 년 되어서 가격이 떨어졌다(now that it's been on the market for a few years, its price has dropped)고 했으므로 정답은 (C)이다.

▸▸ Paraphrasing   대화의 its price has dropped
                   → 정답의 it has become less expensive

35-37

W-Am	**35 Devon, did you hear about the television ad the marketing department is creating? It will feature some real employees working in our office.**
M-Au	Really? That's interesting.
W-Am	Yeah. So, tomorrow they're going to send a film crew here to record us working.
M-Au	**36 Wow! I never thought I'd be on TV for working in the accounting department.**
W-Am	I don't think anyone thought that!
M-Au	**37 I guess I'll wear my best-looking suit tomorrow, then.** I want to make sure I look good on camera!

여	데본, 마케팅 부서에서 만들고 있는 텔레비전 광고에 대해 들었어요? 우리 사무실에서 근무하는 실제 직원들도 몇 명 나올 거예요.
남	정말요? 그거 재미있는데요.
여	네. 그래서 내일 여기로 촬영팀을 보내 우리가 일하고 있는 걸 녹화할 거예요.
남	와! 회계부서에서 근무하는 걸로 TV에 나올 거라고는 생각도 못했어요.
여	아무도 그렇게 생각 못했을 것 같아요!
남	그럼 내일 제일 근사한 양복을 입어야겠어요. 카메라에 잘 나오고 싶거든요!

어휘	feature 특별히 포함하다 crew (특정 기술을 가지고 함께 일하는) 팀, 반 record 녹화[녹음]하다 accounting 회계

35

What are the speakers mainly discussing?

(A) A video shoot
(B) A department supervisor
(C) A training program
(D) An upcoming presentation

화자들이 주로 논의하고 있는 것은 무엇인가?
(A) 비디오 촬영
(B) 부서 책임자
(C) 교육 프로그램
(D) 곧 있을 발표

어휘 shoot 촬영; 촬영하다 supervisor 관리자 upcoming 곧 있을

해설 전체 내용 관련 – 대화의 주제
여자가 첫 대사에서 마케팅 부서에서 만들고 있는 텔레비전 광고에 대해 들었는지(did you hear about the television ad the marketing department is creating?)를 물으며 우리 사무실에서 근무하는 실제 직원들도 몇 명 나올 것(It will feature some real employees working in our office)이라고 광고 촬영에 대한 이야기를 꺼냈고 뒤이어 그에 대한 대화가 이어지고 있으므로 정답은 (A)이다.

36

고난도

Why does the woman say, "I don't think anyone thought that"?

(A) To decline an offer
(B) To justify a decision
(C) To agree with the man
(D) To correct a misunderstanding

여자가 "아무도 그렇게 생각 못했을 것 같아요!"라고 말하는 이유는 무엇인가?
(A) 제안을 거절하려고
(B) 결정을 정당화하려고
(C) 남자의 말에 동의하려고
(D) 오해를 바로잡으려고

어휘 decline 거절하다 offer 제안 justify 정당화하다 correct 정정하다 misunderstanding 오해

해설 화자의 의도 파악 – 아무도 그렇게 생각 못했을 것 같다는 말의 의도
남자가 앞에서 회계부서에서 근무하는 걸로 TV에 나올 거라고는 생각도 못 했다(I never thought I'd be on TV for working in the accounting department)고 하자 여자가 인용문을 언급했으므로 남자의 말에 공감을 표하려는 의도로 한 말임을 알 수 있다. 따라서 정답은 (C)이다.

37

What does the man say he will do tomorrow?

(A) Arrive to work late
(B) Wear attractive clothes
(C) Watch a television broadcast
(D) Bring in his camera

남자는 내일 무엇을 하겠다고 말하는가?
(A) 직장에 늦게 도착한다.
(B) 멋진 옷을 입는다.
(C) 텔레비전 방송을 본다.
(D) 카메라를 가져온다.

해설 세부 사항 관련 – 남자가 내일 할 일
남자가 마지막 대사에서 그럼 내일 제일 근사한 양복을 입어야겠다(I guess I'll wear my best-looking suit tomorrow, then)고 했으므로 정답은 (B)이다.

▶▶ Paraphrasing 대화의 **wear my best-looking suit**
→ 정답의 **wear attractive clothes**

38-40 3인 대화

M-Au	Eastlake Printing. How can I help you?
W-Am	Hi, I'd like to have some posters printed and covered in protective plastic. 38 **How large of a document can you do that for?** Would three feet by two feet be too big?
M-Au	Hmm, let me check with my coworker. 39 **Demetri, can we laminate a three-foot-by-two-foot poster?**
M-Cn	39 **No, but we could print it on special, thicker paper instead.** That gives a similar effect.
M-Au	OK. Thanks, Demetri. Ma'am, did you hear that?
W-Am	I did. 40 **But I don't think that's a good idea. Paper wouldn't be durable enough for my needs.** I'll try some other print shops.

남1	이스트레이크 인쇄입니다. 무엇을 도와드릴까요?
여	안녕하세요, 포스터 몇 장을 인쇄해서 보호용 필름을 붙이고 싶어요. **얼마나 큰 서류를 해 주실 수 있나요?** 가로 3피트×세로 2피트는 너무 클까요?
남1	흠, 제 동료에게 확인해보겠습니다. **드미트리, 가로 3피트×세로 2피트짜리 포스터에 비닐 코팅을 할 수 있을까요?**
남2	**아니요, 대신 두꺼운 특수 용지에 인쇄할 수 있어요.** 그러면 비슷한 효과가 날 거예요.
남1	알겠어요. 고마워요, 드미트리. 선생님, 들으셨습니까?
여	네. 하지만 그건 좋은 생각이 아닌 것 같네요. 종이 재질은 제가 필요한 만큼 충분히 오래가지 못할 거예요. 다른 인쇄소에 가봐야겠어요.

어휘 coworker 동료 laminate 비닐로 코팅하다 durable 내구성이 있는

38

What does the woman ask about?

(A) A size limit
(B) A bulk price
(C) A minimum quantity
(D) A likely completion date

여자는 무엇에 대해서 묻는가?
(A) 크기 제한
(B) 대량 구매가
(C) 최소 수량
(D) 가능한 완료 날짜

해설 세부 사항 관련 – 여자의 문의 사항
여자가 첫 대사에서 얼마나 큰 서류를 해 줄 수 있는지(How large of a document can you do that for?)를 묻고 있으므로 정답은 (A)이다.

Test 5

39

What does Demetri recommend that the woman do?

(A) Inquire at other print shops
(B) Wait until new stock is delivered
(C) Look at some samples online
(D) Choose a different material

드미트리는 여자에게 무엇을 하라고 권하는가?

(A) 다른 인쇄소에 문의할 것
(B) 새 재고가 배송될 때까지 기다릴 것
(C) 온라인으로 몇몇 견본들을 살펴볼 것
(D) 다른 재료를 선택할 것

어휘 inquire 문의하다 stock 재고(품) material 재료

해설 세부 사항 관련 – 드미트리가 여자에게 하라고 권하는 것

첫 번째 남자가 두 번째 대사에서 드미트리를 부르며 가로 3피트×세로 2피트짜리 포스터에 비닐 코팅을 할 수 있을지(Demetri, can we laminate a three-foot-by-two-foot poster?)를 묻자 두 번째 남자 즉, 드미트리가 아니(No)라고 하고 나서, 대신 두꺼운 특수 용지에 인쇄할 수 있다(but we could print it on special, thicker paper instead)라고 답했으므로 정답은 (D)이다.

40

What does the woman say about Demetri's recommendation?

(A) She will consider it.
(B) She will implement it.
(C) She wants to hear more about it.
(D) She does not believe it is suitable.

여자는 드미트리의 권고에 대해 무엇을 말하는가?

(A) 고려해보겠다.
(B) 실행에 옮길 것이다.
(C) 정보를 더 듣고 싶다.
(D) 적절하다고 생각하지 않는다.

어휘 implement 실행하다 suitable 적절한

해설 세부 사항 관련 – 여자가 드미트리의 권고에 대해 말하는 것

여자가 마지막 대사에서 그건 좋은 생각이 아닌 것 같다(But I don't think that's a good idea)며, 종이 재질은 제가 필요한 만큼 충분히 오래가지 못할 것(Paper wouldn't be durable enough for my needs)이라고 한 것으로 보아 정답은 (D)이다.

41-43

W-Br	Hi, my name is Natalie Reeves. **41 I have a two o'clock appointment with Dr. Dhawan.**
M-Cn	Let me see… yes, there you are. **41 Did you bring the patient update paperwork we sent to your address on Evans Drive?**
W-Br	**42 Oh, I actually moved last month, so no, I never even got those documents. Is that going to be a problem?**

M-Cn **43 No, it just means you'll need to complete them now, before your appointment. Would you like the paper version, or the electronic version on this tablet computer?**

여 안녕하세요, 제 이름은 나탈리 리브스이고요. 2시에 다완 선생님과의 진료 예약이 있어요.

남 확인해 볼게요… 네, 오셨군요. 에반스 드라이브의 주소로 보내드린 환자 업데이트 서류는 가지고 오셨어요?

여 아, 사실 제가 지난달에 이사를 해서, 아니요, 그런 서류를 받은 적이 없어요. 문제가 되나요?

남 아니요, 그냥 진료 전에 지금 그것들을 작성하시면 됩니다. 종이 버전을 원하세요, 아니면 이 태블릿 컴퓨터에 있는 전자 버전을 원하세요?

어휘 appointment 예약 patient 환자 paperwork 서류, 문서 업무 address 주소 actually 사실은 document 서류 complete 완료하다 electronic 전자의

41

Where most likely does the conversation take place?

(A) At a real estate agency
(B) At a medical clinic
(C) At a post office
(D) At a law firm

대화가 이루어지고 있는 장소는 어디일 것 같은가?

(A) 부동산 중개소
(B) 병원
(C) 우체국
(D) 법률 사무소

해설 전체 내용 관련 – 대화의 장소

여자가 첫 대사에서 2시에 다완 선생님과 진료 약속이 있다(I have a two o'clock appointment with Dr. Dhawan)고 했고, 뒤이어 남자가 에반스 드라이브의 주소로 보내드린 환자 업데이트 서류를 가지고 왔는지(Did you bring the patient update paperwork we sent to your address on Evans Drive?)를 묻고 있는 것으로 보아 정답은 (B)이다.

42

What problem does the woman describe?

(A) She did not receive a piece of mail.
(B) She did not understand some instructions.
(C) She misplaced a document.
(D) She is uncertain about a proposal.

여자는 무슨 문제를 설명하는가?

(A) 우편물을 받지 못했다.
(B) 일부 지침을 이해하지 못했다.
(C) 서류를 잃어버렸다.
(D) 제안에 대해 확신하지 못한다.

어휘 receive 받다 mail 우편(물) instruction 지시 misplace 제자리에 두지 않다, 분실하다 uncertain 확신이 없는 proposal 제안

여자가 두 번째 대사에서 사실 지난달에 이사를 해서 그런 서류를 받은 적이 없다(I actually moved last month, so no, I never even got those documents)고 했으므로 정답은 (A)이다.

43

What does the man ask the woman to choose?

(A) When an appointment will be rescheduled for
(B) Whether she will authorize a transaction
(C) How she will fill out some forms
(D) Where a shipment will be sent

남자는 여자에게 무엇을 선택하라고 하는가?

(A) 예약을 언제로 다시 잡을지
(B) 거래를 승인할지 아닐지
(C) 양식을 어떻게 작성할지
(D) 배송물을 어디로 보낼지

어휘 reschedule 일정을 변경하다 authorize 인가하다 transaction 거래 form 양식 shipment 수송품

해설 세부 사항 관련 – 남자가 여자에게 선택하라고 한 것

남자가 마지막 대사에서 그냥 진료 전에 지금 그것들을 작성하면 된다(it just means you'll need to complete them now, before your appointment)면서, 종이 버전을 원하는지 아니면 태블릿 컴퓨터에 있는 전자 버전을 원하는지(Would you like the paper version, or the electronic version on this tablet computer?)를 묻고 있으므로 정답은 (C)이다.

44-46

M-Au	Hi, Ms. Griffith. ⁴⁴**I just wanted to remind you that elevator technicians will be coming in next week to perform routine maintenance.**
W-Br	Thanks, Lester. ⁴⁵**Actually—I've been thinking about improving or maybe even replacing our elevators to speed them up. When the technicians are here, I'd like to ask them what the possibilities are.**
M-Au	Well, they're maintenance technicians, so I'm not sure they'd know much about important factors like pricing.
W-Br	Good point. Hmm… ⁴⁶**Then please call the company and arrange for a consultant to come in and talk to me.** Sometime in the next few weeks would be great.

남 안녕하세요, 그리피스 씨. 엘리베이터 기사들이 다음 주에 정기 정비를 하기 위해 방문할 예정이라는 것을 상기시켜드리려고요.

여 고마워요, 레스터. 실은… 엘리베이터의 속도를 높이기 위해 엘리베이터를 개선하거나 아예 교체하는 것에 대해 생각하고 있었어요. 기사들이 이곳에 오면 어떤 가능성이 있는지 물어보려고요.

남 글쎄요, 정비 기사들이라 가격과 같은 중요한 요소에 대해 많이 알고 있을지 모르겠네요.

여 좋은 지적이네요. 흠… 그럼 그 회사에 전화해서 컨설턴트가 방문해서 저와 얘기할 수 있게 주선해주세요. 다음 몇 주 내로 아무 때나 괜찮아요.

어휘 remind 상기시키다 technician 기사, 기술자 perform 행하다 possibility 가능성 maintenance 유지 factor 요인 arrange 주선하다

44 고난도

What is the main topic of the conversation?

(A) An employee's performance evaluation
(B) A technical difficulty with some software
(C) A system for issuing scheduling reminders
(D) A convenience facility in a building

대화의 주제는 무엇인가?

(A) 직원의 성과 평가
(B) 일부 소프트웨어의 기술적 어려움
(C) 일정 알림 발송 시스템
(D) 건물의 편의시설

어휘 performance 성과 evaluation 평가 issue 발행하다 scheduling 일정 관리 reminder 상기시키는 것 convenience 편의 facility 시설

해설 전체 내용 관련 – 대화의 주제

남자가 첫 대사에서 엘리베이터 기사들이 다음 주에 정기 정비를 하기 위해 방문할 예정이라는 것을 상기시키고 싶었다(I just wanted to remind you that elevator technicians will be coming in next week to perform routine maintenance)며 대화를 시작했고, 뒤이어 여자도 엘리베이터에 관한 이야기를 이어가고 있으므로 정답은 (D)이다.

▸▸ Paraphrasing 대화의 elevator
→ 정답의 a convenience facility

45

What does the woman want to do?

(A) Administer a companywide survey
(B) Lower some maintenance spending
(C) Learn about upgrade options
(D) Clarify some guidelines

여자는 무엇을 하길 원하는가?

(A) 전사적 조사 실시하기
(B) 일부 유지 관리 비용 절감하기
(C) 업그레이드 선택 사항에 대해 알아보기
(D) 일부 지침을 명확히 하기

어휘 administer 실시하다 companywide 회사 전반의 lower 낮추다 maintenance 유지 spending 지출 option 선택(권) clarify 명확히 하다 guideline 지침

Test 5

해설 세부 사항 관련 – 여자가 하기를 원하는 일

여자가 첫 대사에서 엘리베이터의 속도를 높이기 위해 엘리베이터를 개선하거나 아예 교체하는 것에 대해 생각하고 있었다(I've been thinking about improving or maybe even replacing our elevators to speed them up)면서, 기사들이 이곳에 오면 어떤 가능성이 있는지 물어보려 한다(When the technicians are here, I'd like to ask them what the possibilities are)고 했으므로 정답은 (C)이다.

46

What does the woman ask the man to do?

(A) Set up a meeting
(B) Draft a notice
(C) Clean out a room
(D) Search a database

여자는 남자에게 무엇을 하라고 요청하는가?

(A) 회의 잡기
(B) 공고문 작성
(C) 방 청소
(D) 데이터베이스 검색

어휘 draft 초안[원고]을 작성하다 notice 공고문

해설 세부 사항 관련 – 여자가 남자에게 하라고 요청한 것

여자가 마지막 대사에서 그 회사에 전화해서 컨설턴트가 방문해서 자신과 얘기할 수 있게 주선해줄 것(please call the company and arrange for a consultant to come in and talk to me)을 요청하고 있으므로 정답은 (A)이다.

▸▸ Paraphrasing 대화의 arrange for a consultant to come in and talk to me
→ 정답의 set up a meeting

47-49

W-Am	Welcome to Nashlin Shoes.
M-Cn	Hi. I was given this pair of sneakers as a gift, but they're not really my style. **47 I'd like to exchange them for a refund.**
W-Am	I can help you with that. **48 I'll need to see the receipt, though—do you happen to have it?**
M-Cn	Yes, the person who gave me the sneakers included it in the box, just in case. Here it is.
W-Am	Great. **49 Oh, I'm sorry, but since it's been more than thirty days since these were purchased, we can't give you a cash refund.** You'll only be able to get store credit.

여	내슐린 슈즈에 오신 걸 환영합니다.
남	안녕하세요. 이 운동화 한 켤레를 선물로 받았는데, 내 스타일이 정말 아니에요. 환불하고 싶습니다.
여	제가 도와드리겠습니다. **그래도 영수증을 좀 확인해야 합니다. 혹시 가지고 계세요?**

남 네, 혹시 몰라서 운동화를 주신 분이 상자에 넣어두셨어요. 여기 있네요.

여 잘됐네요. 아, **죄송합니다만, 이게 구매된 지 30일이 지나서 현금 환불은 해드릴 수가 없습니다.** 상점 교환권으로만 받으실 수 있으세요.

어휘 pair 쌍 exchange 교환하다 refund 환불 receipt 영수증 purchase 구입하다 store credit 상점 교환권

47

Why is the man at the store?

(A) To have some footwear repaired
(B) To buy a gift for a family member
(C) To return some unwanted goods
(D) To place an advance order

남자는 왜 가게에 있는가?

(A) 신발을 수선 받으려고
(B) 가족을 위해 선물을 사려고
(C) 원하지 않는 제품을 반품하려고
(D) 예약 주문을 하려고

어휘 repair 수선[수리]하다 unwanted 원치 않는 advance order 예약 주문, 선주문

해설 세부 사항 관련 – 남자가 가게에 있는 이유

남자가 첫 대사에서 물건들을 환불하고 싶다(I'd like to exchange them for a refund)고 했으므로 정답은 (C)이다.

▸▸ Paraphrasing 대화의 exchange them for a refund
→ 정답의 return some unwanted goods

48

What does the woman request that the man do?

(A) Estimate a person's shoe size
(B) Complete some paperwork
(C) Provide proof of a purchase
(D) Show her the problem with an item

여자는 남자에게 무엇을 할 것을 요청하는가?

(A) 신발 사이즈를 가늠해 줄 것
(B) 서류 작업을 완료할 것
(C) 구매 증명서를 제공할 것
(D) 여자에게 제품의 문제점을 보여줄 것

어휘 estimate 추정하다 complete 완료하다 paperwork 서류 작업 proof 증명(서)

해설 세부 사항 관련 – 여자가 남자에게 해달라고 요청한 일

여자가 두 번째 대사에서 그래도 영수증을 좀 확인해야 한다(I'll need to see the receipt, though)면서, 혹시 가지고 있는지(do you happen to have it?) 묻고 있으므로 정답은 (C)이다.

▸▸ Paraphrasing 대화의 the receipt
→ 정답의 proof of a purchase

49

고난도

What does the woman apologize for?

(A) A long shipping duration
(B) An unfavorable store policy
(C) The small selection of merchandise
(D) A malfunctioning payment system

여자는 무엇에 대해 사과하는가?

(A) 긴 배송 기간
(B) 불리한 상점 정책
(C) 좁은 상품 선택의 폭
(D) 고장난 지불 시스템

어휘 shipping 배송 duration 기간 unfavorable 불리한 policy
정책 selection 선택, 선택된 것들 merchandise 상품
malfunctioning 고장난 payment 지불

해설 세부 사항 관련 – 여자가 사과하는 이유

여자가 마지막 대사에서 죄송하지만 이게 구매된 지 30일이 지나서 현금 환불은 해드릴 수가 없다(I'm sorry, but since it's been more than thirty days since these were purchased, we can't give you a cash refund)며 사과하고 있으므로 정답은 (B)이다.

50-52 3인 대화

W-Am	Hi. **50My colleague and I just used the kiosk to print out our reserved tickets, and we see that we've been seated in different rows.**
W-Br	We were planning to get some work done on the train. **50Could we possibly sit together?** Here are our tickets.
M-Au	Oh, you're going down to Hingdon? **51I'm sorry, but all of the trains going there are completely full.** The Hingdon Music Festival is this weekend.
W-Am	I see. Well, that's disappointing. But thanks anyway.
M-Au	No problem.
W-Br	Well, what should we do, Tara? We need to get ready for our presentation.
W-Am	We'll have to do the preparations separately. **52Let's sit down and figure out who will handle what.**

여1 안녕하세요. 제 동료와 제가 방금 키오스크를 이용해서 예약한 표를 출력했는데, 서로 다른 줄에 앉게 됐네요.
여2 기차 안에서 일을 좀 할 계획이었거든요. 혹시 같이 앉을 수 있을까요? 여기 우리의 티켓이에요.
남 아, 힝돈으로 가시는 거예요? 죄송하지만, 그쪽으로 가는 모든 열차가 **완전히 만원이에요.** 힝돈 음악 축제가 이번 주말이거든요.
여1 그렇군요. 아쉽네요. 어쨌든 고맙습니다.
남 전혀요.

여2 그럼, 어떻게 할까요, 타라? 발표를 준비해야 하는데요.
여1 준비는 따로 해야 할 것 같아요. **앉아서 누가 뭘 할지 생각해보도록 해요.**

어휘 reserve 예약하다 row 줄[열] possibly 아마
completely 완전히 full 가득한 disappointing
실망스러운 separately 따로따로 handle 처리하다

50

What do the women hope to do?

(A) Reserve an earlier train
(B) Use a self-service machine
(C) Take advantage of a promotion
(D) Change their seating assignments

여자들은 무엇을 하기를 바라는가?

(A) 더 이른 기차 예약
(B) 셀프서비스 기계 사용
(C) 판촉 행사 이용
(D) 좌석 배치 변경

어휘 take advantage of ~을 이용하다 promotion 판촉 (활동)
assignment 배정[배치]

해설 세부 사항 관련 – 여자들이 하기를 원하는 일

첫 번째 여자가 첫 대사에서 제 동료와 제가 방금 키오스크를 이용해서 예약한 표를 출력했는데 서로 다른 줄에 앉게 됐다(My colleague and I just used the kiosk to print out our reserved tickets, and we see that we've been seated in different rows)고 했고, 두 번째 여자가 뒤이어 혹시 같이 앉을 수 있는지(Could we possibly sit together?)를 묻고 있는 것으로 보아 정답은 (D)이다.

51

What problem does the man describe?

(A) Some tickets have sold out.
(B) Some departures will be delayed.
(C) A computer server is down.
(D) A voucher has expired.

남자는 무슨 문제를 설명하는가?

(A) 일부 표가 매진되었다.
(B) 일부 출발이 지연될 것이다.
(C) 컴퓨터 서버가 다운되었다.
(D) 상품권이 만료되었다.

어휘 departure 출발 delay 미루다 voucher 상품권 expire
만료되다

해설 세부 사항 관련 – 남자가 설명하는 문제

남자가 첫 대사에서 죄송하지만, 그쪽으로 가는 모든 열차가 완전히 만원이다(I'm sorry, but all of the trains going there are completely full)라고 했으므로 정답은 (A)이다.

▸▸ **Paraphrasing** 대화의 **all of the trains going there are completely full**
→ 정답의 **some tickets have sold out**

52

고난도

What will the women most likely do next?

(A) Notify a coworker
(B) Reevaluate a budget
(C) Divide up some work tasks
(D) Consider other travel methods

여자들은 다음에 무엇을 할 것 같은가?

(A) 동료에게 알린다.
(B) 예산을 재평가한다.
(C) 일부 업무를 분담한다.
(D) 다른 이동 수단을 고려한다.

어휘 notify 알리다 coworker 동료 reevaluate 재평가하다 budget 예산 divide up 나누다 consider 고려하다 method 방법, 수단

해설 세부 사항 관련 – 여자들이 다음에 할 일

여자가 마지막 대사에서 앉아서 누가 뭘 할지 생각해보도록 하자(Let's sit down and figure out who will handle what)고 했으므로 정답은 (C)이다.

▶▶ **Paraphrasing** 대화의 **figure out who will handle what**
→ 정답의 **divide up some work tasks**

53-55

M-Cn	**53 Pinterville Times front desk, this is Matt.** How can I help you?
W-Br	Hi, I was hoping to speak to one of your reporters—uh, Denise Webber.
M-Cn	May I ask what this is about?
W-Br	I'd like to express my dissatisfaction about her article on Pinterville Park. **54 There's some incorrect information in it that needs to be cleared up.**
M-Cn	**55 Ah, in that case, please fill out the reporting form on our Web site.** You can access it from the "Contact Us" menu.
W-Br	Oh, OK. Once I do that, how long will it take for a correction to be printed?
M-Cn	Well, we have to verify the information, so it usually takes a few days.

남	〈핀터빌 타임스〉 안내 데스크의 매트입니다. 무엇을 도와드릴까요?
여	안녕하세요, 기자들 중 한 분과 통화하고 싶었는데… 음, 데니스 웨버 씨요.
남	무엇에 관한 건지 여쭤봐도 될까요?
여	핀터빌 파크에 대한 그녀의 기사에 불만을 표하고 싶어요. **정정되어야 하는 잘못된 정보가 들어 있어요.**
남	아, 그렇다면 저희 웹사이트에서 신고서를 작성해주세요. "연락처" 메뉴에서 찾으시면 됩니다.
여	아, 알겠습니다. 일단 그렇게 하고 나면, 정정 기사가 실리는 데 얼마나 걸릴까요?
남	그게, 정보를 검증해야 하기 때문에 보통 며칠이 걸립니다.

어휘 front desk 안내 데스크 express 표현하다 dissatisfaction 불만 article 기사 incorrect 부정확한 clear up 정리하다, 설명하다 fill out 작성하다 form 양식 access 접근하다 correction 정정 verify 입증하다

53

What most likely is the man's job?

(A) A journalist
(B) A graphic designer
(C) A newspaper editor
(D) A receptionist

남자의 직업은 무엇일 것 같은가?

(A) 기자
(B) 그래픽 디자이너
(C) 신문 편집자
(D) 안내 접수원

해설 전체 내용 관련 – 남자의 직업

남자가 첫 번째 대사에서 〈핀터빌 타임스〉 안내 데스크의 매트입니다(Pinterville Times front desk, this is Matt)라고 자신을 소개하고 있으므로 정답은 (D)이다.

54

According to the woman, what is the problem with an article?

(A) Some details are missing.
(B) There are some errors.
(C) The meaning of its title is unclear.
(D) It was placed in the wrong section.

여자에 따르면, 기사의 문제점은 무엇인가?

(A) 일부 정보가 누락되었다.
(B) 몇 가지 오류가 있다.
(C) 제목의 의미가 명확하지 않다.
(D) 잘못된 구획에 배치되었다.

어휘 details 세부 사항 missing 빠진 error 오류 section 부분

해설 세부 사항 관련 – 여자가 말하는 기사의 문제점

여자가 두 번째 대사에서 정정되어야 하는 잘못된 정보가 들어 있다(There's some incorrect information in it that needs to be cleared up)고 했으므로 정답은 (B)이다.

▶▶ **Paraphrasing** 대화의 **some incorrect information**
→ 정답의 **some errors**

55

What does the man ask the woman to do?

(A) Verify her professional qualifications
(B) Check the online version of the article
(C) Wait for him to locate a colleague
(D) File her complaint electronically

남자는 여자에게 무엇을 하라고 요청하는가?

(A) 직업적인 자격을 입증할 것
(B) 기사의 온라인 버전을 확인할 것
(C) 남자가 동료를 찾기를 기다릴 것
(D) 불만을 온라인으로 접수할 것

어휘 professional 직업의 qualification 자격 locate ~의 위치를 찾아내다 complaint 불만 electronically 온라인으로

해설 세부 사항 관련 – 남자가 여자에게 하라고 요청한 것
남자가 세 번째 대사에서 저희 웹사이트에서 신고서를 작성하라(in that case, please fill out the reporting form on our Web site)고 요청하고 있으므로 정답은 (D)이다.

▸▸ Paraphrasing   대화의 on our Web site
→ 정답의 electronically

56-58

M-Cn	Ms. Bowers? This is Orlando from Ankins Electronics. **56 I'm calling about the order for spare camera parts that you placed through our Web site.**
W-Am	Yes, this is Emily Bowers. Is there a problem?
M-Cn	No, we just need a little more information to make sure we send you the right products. **57 Could you look at the underside of your camera and tell me its full model number?**
W-Am	Oh, I'm at work right now. **57 And I don't have the number memorized or anything.**
M-Cn	All right. **58 Can I give you the direct phone number for customer service so you can call us from home later?**
W-Am	Sure. **58 Let me just get a pen. OK, I'm ready.**

남	바우어스 씨? 앙킨스 일렉트로닉스의 올란도입니다. 저희 웹사이트를 통해 주문하신 여분의 카메라 부품 주문 건 때문에 전화했습니다.
여	네, 에밀리 바우어스입니다. 무슨 문제라도 있나요?
남	아니요, 제품을 제대로 보낼 수 있도록 정보가 조금 더 필요할 뿐입니다. 카메라 아래쪽을 보시고 전체 모델 번호를 알려주시겠습니까?
여	아, 제가 지금 직장에 있어요. 번호를 외우고 있거나 뭐 그런 것도 아니고요.
남	알겠습니다. 나중에 집에서 전화하실 수 있도록 고객 서비스 직통 전화 번호를 알려드릴까요?
여	네, 펜 좀 가져올게요. 좋아요, 준비됐어요.

어휘 order 주문 spare 여분의 part 부품 underside 아랫면 memorize 외우다 direct 직통[직행]의

56

What is the man calling about?

(A) A sales event
(B) A repair service
(C) A new business
(D) A product order

남자는 무엇에 관해 전화하고 있는가?

(A) 할인 행사
(B) 수리 서비스
(C) 새로운 사업
(D) 제품 주문

해설 전체 내용 관련 – 전화의 목적
남자가 첫 대사에서 저희 웹사이트를 통해 주문한 여분의 카메라 부품 주문 건 때문에 전화했다(I'm calling about the order for spare camera parts that you placed through our Web site)고 전화한 목적을 밝혔으므로 정답은 (D)이다.

57   고난도

What does the woman mean when she says, "I'm at work right now"?

(A) She does not have access to an item.
(B) She forgot about an appointment.
(C) She does not have time to talk.
(D) She is unaware of an issue that has arisen.

여자가 "제가 지금 직장에 있어요"라고 말한 의도는 무엇인가?

(A) 제품에 접근할 수 없다.
(B) 약속에 대해 잊었다.
(C) 말할 시간이 없다.
(D) 발생한 문제에 대해 몰랐다.

어휘 access 접근 forget 잊다 appointment 약속 unaware ~을 알지 못하는 issue 문제 arise 발생하다

해설 화자의 의도 파악 – 제가 지금 직장에 있다는 말의 의도
남자가 인용문 앞에서 카메라 아래쪽을 보고 전체 모델 번호를 알려달라 (Could you look at the underside of your camera and tell me its full model number?)고 요청하자, 여자가 인용문을 언급하며 번호를 외우고 있거나 뭐 그런 것도 아니다(I don't have the number memorized or anything)라며 남자의 요청에 응할 수 없다고 한 것으로 보아 직장에 있어서 제품을 확인할 수 없다는 의도로 한 말임을 알 수 있다. 따라서 정답은 (A)이다.

58

What will the woman most likely do next?

(A) Write down some contact information
(B) Stand near the entrance to a building
(C) Make a drawing of a space
(D) Take a bus to her house

여자가 다음에 할 것 같은 일은 무엇인가?

(A) 연락처 정보를 기록한다.
(B) 건물 입구 가까이에 선다.
(C) 공간 도면을 그린다.
(D) 집으로 가는 버스를 탄다.

해설 세부 사항 관련 – 여자가 다음에 할 일

남자가 세 번째 대사에서 나중에 집에서 전화할 수 있도록 고객 서비스 직통 전화번호를 알려드릴지(Can I give you the direct phone number for customer service so you can call us from home later?)를 묻자, 여자가 펜을 가져오겠다(Let me just get a pen)고 했고, 준비됐다(I'm ready)고 한 것으로 보아 정답은 (A)이다.

> **Paraphrasing** 대화의 **the ~ phone number**
> → 정답의 **some contact information**

59-61

M-Au	Hi, Michelle. It's Leland. **59I wanted to call and thank you for letting me borrow that book by Theresa Riley.** I ended up referring to it a lot while writing my article.
W-Am	Oh, it was no problem. I'm glad I could help.
M-Au	You really did. **60If I'd had to wait for the university library to order the book, I'd never have been able to get the article to the journal last week before the cutoff date.**
W-Am	Yeah, the library's system is pretty slow sometimes.
M-Au	I've certainly learned that lesson. **61 Anyway, do you have a free hour sometime this week?** I'd like to meet up to return the book and buy you a coffee.

남	여보세요, 미셸. 릴랜드예요. **전화해서 테레사 라일리가 쓴 그 책을 빌려줘서 고맙다고 말하고 싶었어요.** 기사를 쓰면서 결국 그 책을 많이 참고하게 됐네요.
여	아, 천만에요. 도움이 되었다니 기쁘네요.
남	정말 그랬어요. 대학 도서관에서 책을 주문할 때까지 기다렸더라면, 전 그 기사를 지난주 마감일 전에 결코 저널에 올릴 수 없었을 거예요.
여	맞아요, 도서관 시스템은 때때로 꽤나 느려요.
남	그 교훈은 확실히 배웠어요. 어쨌든 **이번 주 중에 시간 있어요?** 만나서 책도 돌려주고 커피도 사고 싶어요.

어휘	borrow 빌리다 end up 결국 (어떤 처지에) 처하게 되다 refer to ~을 참고하다 article 기사 cutoff date 마감일 pretty 꽤 lesson 교훈

59

What does the man thank the woman for?

(A) Lending him a resource
(B) Introducing him to an acquaintance
(C) Allowing him to use a workstation
(D) Looking over his writing

남자는 여자에게 무엇을 감사하는가?

(A) 자료를 빌려준 것
(B) 지인을 소개해준 것
(C) 작업 공간을 쓰도록 해준 것
(D) 글을 검토해 준 것

어휘 lend 빌려주다 resource 자원[재료] introduce 소개하다 acquaintance 지인 workstation 작업장

해설 세부 사항 관련 – 남자가 여자에게 감사하는 것

남자가 첫 대사에서 전화해서 테레사 라일리가 쓴 그 책을 빌려줘서 고맙다고 말하고 싶었다(I wanted to call and thank you for letting me borrow that book by Theresa Riley)고 했으므로 정답은 (A)이다.

> **Paraphrasing** 대화의 **letting ~ borrow that book**
> → 정답의 **lending ~ a resource**

60 [고난도]

What does the man say happened last week?

(A) A publishing decision was announced.
(B) A research interview took place.
(C) A university institution was closed.
(D) A submission was made.

남자는 지난주에 무슨 일이 일어났다고 말하는가?

(A) 출판 결정이 발표되었다.
(B) 연구 인터뷰가 이루어졌다.
(C) 한 대학 기관이 문을 닫았다.
(D) 제출이 이루어졌다.

어휘 publishing 출판 decision 결정 announce 발표하다 research 연구 take place 일어나다 institution 기관 submission 제출

해설 세부 사항 관련 – 남자가 지난주에 일어났다고 말한 일

남자가 두 번째 대사에서 대학 도서관에서 책을 주문할 때까지 기다렸더라면, 그 기사를 지난주 마감일 전에 결코 저널에 올릴 수 없었을 것(If I'd had to wait for the university library to order the book, I'd never have been able to get the article to the journal last week before the cutoff date)이라고 했으므로 남자는 지난주에 기사를 제출했음을 알 수 있다. 따라서 정답은 (D)이다.

61

What does the man ask the woman about?

(A) Her experience with a process
(B) Her favorite coffee drink
(C) Her opinions on a book
(D) Her availability in the near future

남자는 여자에게 무엇에 관해 묻는가?

(A) 절차에 대한 경험
(B) 좋아하는 커피 음료
(C) 책에 대한 의견
(D) 가까운 미래에 시간이 되는지 여부

어휘 process 절차[과정] favorite 좋아하는 opinion 의견 availability 시간이 되는지 여부

해설 세부 사항 관련 – 남자가 여자에게 묻는 것

남자가 마지막 대사에서 이번 주 중에 시간 있는지(do you have a free hour sometime this week?)를 묻고 있으므로 정답은 (D)이다.

> **Paraphrasing** 대화의 **a free hour sometime this week**
> → 정답의 **availability in the near future**

W-Br	Hi, Dave. ⁶²**I wanted to check how your preparations for Byung-Hoon Han's first day are going. I'd like to get him ready to start contributing to the team right away.**
M-Cn	Sure, Claudette. ⁶³**I'm arranging his orientation sessions right now.** It looks like we should be able to get them all done on the first day.
W-Br	That's great. And how about the office supplies he'll need? Have you ordered them yet?
M-Cn	Oh, I'd like your opinion on that, actually. Here's the order form I filled out. Does it look all right? Or did I forget anything?
W-Br	Hmm… ⁶⁴**That seems like too many paper clips. Two boxes would probably be enough.** Otherwise, it looks good.

여	안녕하세요, 데이브. 한병훈 씨의 첫날을 위한 준비는 어떻게 되어가고 있는지 확인하고 싶어서요. 그가 곧바로 팀에 기여할 수 있도록 준비가 되었으면 해요.
남	물론이죠, 클로데트. 지금 그의 오리엔테이션 시간을 짜고 있어요. 첫날에 다 끝낼 수 있을 것 같아 보여요.
여	잘됐네요. 그리고 그가 필요로 할 사무용품은 어떤가요? 이미 주문하셨나요?
남	아, 사실 그 부분에 대해 당신의 의견을 듣고 싶어요. 여기 제가 작성한 주문서예요. 괜찮아 보이나요? 아니면 제가 놓친 게 있나요?
여	흠… 종이 클립이 너무 많은 것 같네요. 아마 두 박스면 충분할 거예요. 그것 말고는 좋아 보여요.

어휘	preparation 준비 contribute 기여하다 arrange 마련하다 orientation 예비 교육 session (특정 활동을 위한) 시간 office supplies 사무 용품 order 주문하다 opinion 의견 fill out 작성하다 otherwise 그 외에는

Order Form

Item	No.
File organizers	3
⁶⁴Paper clips boxes	5
Pen sets	2
Staplers	1
Sticky notes pads	4

주문서

제품	수량
파일 정리 케이스	3
⁶⁴ 종이 클립함	5
펜 세트	2
스테이플러	1
포스트잇	4

62

Who most likely is Mr. Han?

(A) A government inspector
(B) A board member
(C) A new hire
(D) A vendor

한 씨는 누구일 것 같은가?
(A) 정부 감찰관
(B) 이사진
(C) 신입 사원
(D) 판매자

해설 세부 사항 관련 – 한 씨의 직업

여자가 첫 대사에서 한병훈 씨의 첫날을 위한 준비는 어떻게 되어가고 있는지 확인하고 싶다(I wanted to check how your preparations for Byung-Hoon Han's first day are going)며, 그가 곧바로 팀에 기여할 수 있도록 준비가 되었으면 한다(I'd like to get him ready to start contributing to the team right away)고 한 것으로 보아 정답은 (C)이다.

63 고난도

What does the man say he is currently doing?

(A) Organizing some files
(B) Making a schedule
(C) Reviewing an agreement
(D) Collecting some supplies

남자는 현재 무엇을 하고 있다고 말하는가?
(A) 일부 파일의 정리
(B) 일정 짜기
(C) 계약서 검토
(D) 일부 물품 수거

어휘 organize 정리하다 review 검토하다 collect 모으다 supplies 물품

해설 세부 사항 관련 – 남자가 현재 하고 있다고 말한 것

남자가 첫 대사에서 지금 그의 오리엔테이션 시간을 짜고 있다(I'm arranging his orientation sessions right now)고 했으므로 정답은 (B)이다.

Test 5

64

Look at the graphic. Which number does the woman recommend changing?

(A) 3
(B) 5
(C) 2
(D) 4

시각 정보에 의하면, 여자는 어느 수량을 바꾸라고 권하는가?

(A) 3
(B) 5
(C) 2
(D) 4

해설   시각 정보 연계 – 여자가 바꾸라고 권하는 수량

여자가 마지막 대사에서 종이 클립이 너무 많은 것 같다(That seems like too many paper clips)며 아마 두 박스면 충분할 것(Two boxes would probably be enough)이라고 했고, 주문서에 따르면 종이 클립함의 수량은 5이므로 정답은 (B)이다.

65-67 대화 + 평면도

W-Br	[65] **Hi, I'm calling to make an evening reservation for my office's annual holiday party.** Can you serve twenty-five people? Preferably in one of your private rooms.
M-Au	Certainly. [66] **We just renovated our largest dining room besides the main one, and I must say it's lovely. We'll put your party in there.** What day and time will you be coming?
W-Br	Well, the party's this Friday and we'll be coming at six o'clock.
M-Au	Let's see... Yes, we do have an opening at six. [67] **Now, we require a one-hundred-dollar deposit to hold a dining room for an event.**
W-Am	That shouldn't be a problem.

여	여보세요. 사무실 연례 휴일 파티를 위해 저녁 예약을 하려고 전화드렸어요. 스물다섯 명인데 가능할까요? 가급적이면 분리된 방으로요.
남	당연하죠. 얼마 전 메인 다이닝 룸 다음으로 가장 큰 다이닝 룸을 개조했는데, 정말 예뻐요. 손님 일행을 거기 배정해드릴게요. 며칠 몇 시에 오실 예정인가요?
여	음, 파티는 이번 주 금요일이고, 6시에 갈 거예요.
남	확인하겠습니다… 네, 6시에 자리가 있네요. 그럼, 행사를 위해 다이닝 룸을 잡으려면 100달러의 보증금이 필요합니다.
여	그건 문제없어요.

어휘   reservation 예약   annual 연례의   preferably 가급적
private 사적인   renovate 개조[보수]하다   besides ~외에
I must say 정말, 진짜로   party 일행, 단체   deposit 보증금

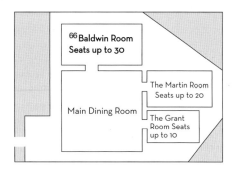

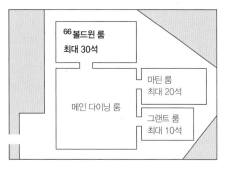

65

What is the woman organizing?

(A) A fund-raiser
(B) An office dinner
(C) An awards ceremony
(D) A retirement party

여자는 무엇을 주선하고 있는가?

(A) 모금 행사
(B) 사무실 저녁 회식
(C) 시상식
(D) 은퇴 파티

해설   세부 사항 관련 – 여자가 주선하고 있는 것

여자가 첫 대사에서 사무실 연례 휴일 파티를 위해 저녁 예약을 하려고 전화했다(I'm calling to make an evening reservation for my office's annual holiday party)고 했으므로 정답은 (B)이다.

66

Look at the graphic. What room will the woman's group use?

(A) The Main Dining Room
(B) The Baldwin Room
(C) The Martin Room
(D) The Grant Room

시각 정보에 의하면, 여자의 일행은 어느 룸을 사용할 것인가?

(A) 메인 다이닝 룸
(B) 볼드윈 룸
(C) 마틴 룸
(D) 그랜트 룸

해설 시각 정보 연계 – 여자의 일행이 사용할 룸

남자가 첫 대사에서 얼마 전 메인 다이닝 룸 다음으로 가장 큰 다이닝 룸을 개조했는데 정말 예쁘다(We just renovated our largest dining room besides the main one, and I must say it's lovely)며 손님 일행을 그쪽으로 배정하겠다(We'll put your party in there)고 했고, 평면도에 따르면 메인 다이닝 룸 외에 가장 큰 다이닝 룸은 볼드윈 룸이므로 정답은 (B)이다.

67

What does the man say the woman will have to do?

(A) Make a partial payment beforehand
(B) Approve a fixed menu of dishes
(C) Vacate the room by a certain time
(D) Read some guidelines for patrons

남자는 여자가 무엇을 해야 한다고 말하는가?

(A) 미리 부분 결제를 해야 한다.
(B) 고정 메뉴를 승인해야 한다.
(C) 일정 시간까지 방을 비워야 한다.
(D) 고객을 위한 몇 가지 지침을 읽어야 한다.

어휘 partial 부분적인 payment 지불 beforehand 미리 approve 승인하다 fixed 고정된 vacate 비우다 guideline 지침 patron 고객

해설 세부 사항 관련 – 남자가 말하는 여자가 해야 할 일

남자가 마지막 대사에서 행사를 위해 다이닝 룸을 잡으시려면 100달러의 보증금이 필요하다(we require a one-hundred-dollar deposit to hold a dining room for an event)고 했으므로 정답은 (A)이다.

> ▶ Paraphrasing   대화의 require a ~ deposit
> → 정답의 make a partial payment
> beforehand

68-70 대화 + 웹페이지

M-Au **68 Ms. Tucker, I think I've discovered why we haven't been getting enough applicants for job openings lately.** Take a look at the Web page on my tablet. It shows our average ratings on Gold-Star-Employers.com, a Web site for reviewing employers.

W-Am Ah... yes, these numbers could be better. **69 Well, there isn't much that we can do about our compensation package at present, but this other low rating seems like something we could address.** Can you find out more about it?

M-Au Sure. The site also has some longer reviews of our company. **70 I'll read through them and prepare an outline of the important points for you by the end of the day.**

남 터커 씨, 최근에 낸 채용 공고에 지원자를 충분히 구하지 못하고 있는 이유를 발견한 것 같네요. 제 태블릿에서 이 웹페이지를 한번 보세요. 사업주들을 평가하기 위한 웹사이트인 Gold-Star-Employers.com에 나온 우리의 평균 등급을 보여주고 있어요.

여 아, 네, 이 수치들은 아쉬움이 있네요. 글쎄, 현재 우리의 보수에 대해 우리가 할 수 있는 것은 별로 없지만, 이 다른 낮은 등급은 우리가 다룰 수 있을 것으로 보이네요. 좀 더 자세히 알아봐주시겠어요?

남 물론이죠. 이 사이트에는 우리 회사에 대한 좀 더 긴 평가들도 있어요. 오늘 중으로 제가 다 읽고 중요한 요점들에 대해 간략한 설명을 준비할게요.

어휘 discover 발견하다 applicant 지원자 job opening (직장의) 빈 자리 rating 등급 review 검토하다, 논평하다; 검토, 논평 employer 사업주 compensation package (급여와 복리 후생을 포함한) 보수 at present 현재 address (문제 등에 대해) 다루다 outline 개요를 서술하다

http://gold-star-employers.com

Average ratings for Custas Associates

Career Opportunities ★ ★ ★ ☆ ☆

Management ★ ★ ★ ★ ☆

Pay and Benefits ★ ★ ☆ ☆ ☆

69 Work-Life Balance ★ ★ ☆ ☆ ☆

http://gold-star-employers.com

커스터스 어소시에이츠 평균 등급

취업 전망 ★ ★ ★ ☆ ☆

관리 ★ ★ ★ ★ ☆

급여 및 복리 후생 ★ ★ ☆ ☆ ☆

69 일과 삶의 균형 ★ ★ ☆ ☆ ☆

68

What problem does the man mention?

(A) A news report criticized the company.
(B) It is difficult to attract new staff.
(C) A client did not renew a contract.
(D) Several employees have quit their jobs.

남자는 무슨 문제를 언급하는가?

(A) 뉴스 보도가 회사를 비판했다.
(B) 신입 직원을 유치하기가 어렵다.
(C) 한 고객이 계약을 갱신하지 않았다.
(D) 몇몇 직원이 일을 그만뒀다.

어휘 criticize 비판하다 attract 끌어모으다 renew 갱신하다 contract 계약 quit 그만두다

해설 세부 사항 관련 - 남자가 언급한 문제

남자가 첫 대사에서 최근에 낸 채용 공고에 지원자를 충분히 구하지 못하고 있는 이유를 발견한 것 같다(I think I've discovered why we haven't been getting enough applicants for job openings lately)고 한 것으로 보아 정답은 (B)이다.

69
고난도

Look at the graphic. Which category does the woman want to know more about?

(A) Career Opportunities
(B) Management
(C) Pay and Benefits
(D) Work-Life Balance

시각 정보에 의하면, 여자는 어느 카테고리에 대해 더 알고 싶어 하는가?

(A) 취업 전망
(B) 관리
(C) 급여 및 복리 후생
(D) 일과 삶의 균형

해설 시각 정보 연계 - 여자가 더 알고 싶어 하는 카테고리

여자가 첫 대사에서 현재 우리의 보수에 대해 우리가 할 수 있는 것은 별로 없지만 이 다른 낮은 등급은 우리가 다룰 수 있을 것으로 보인다(there isn't much that we can do about our compensation package at present, but this other low rating seems like something we could address)고 했고, 웹페이지 시각 정보에 따르면 급여 및 복리 후생 외에 등급이 낮은 항목은 일과 삶의 균형이므로 정답은 (D)이다.

70

What will the man do today?

(A) Share a Web link with the woman
(B) Alert other supervisors about a discovery
(C) Create a summary of some content
(D) Post a review on the Web site

남자는 오늘 무엇을 할 것인가?

(A) 여자와 웹 링크를 공유한다.
(B) 발견에 대해 다른 관리자에게 알린다.
(C) 일부 내용의 요약본을 작성한다.
(D) 웹사이트에 대한 평가를 게시한다.

어휘 share 공유하다 alert (위험 등을) 알리다 supervisor 관리자
discovery 발견 summary 요약 content 내용 post 게시하다

해설 세부 사항 관련 - 남자가 오늘 할 일

남자가 마지막 대사에서 오늘 중으로 다 읽고 중요한 요점들에 대해 간략한 설명을 준비하겠다(I'll read through them and prepare an outline of the important points for you by the end of the day)고 했으므로 정답은 (C)이다.

> ▸▸ Paraphrasing 대화의 prepare an outline
> → 정답의 create a summary

PART 4

71-73 음성 메시지

M-Cn You have reached the Menning Community College's Gardening Hotline. **71Our crew of Master Gardeners is happy to give you guidance on all types of problems related to gardening and plant care.** **72Please keep in mind, however, that this is a free service staffed by volunteers, so we may not always be right.** We take calls from nine A.M. to noon, Monday through Friday. **73Because our hours are short, we ask that callers take care to ask their question quickly and simply.** Thank you.

메닝 커뮤니티 칼리지의 원예 상담 전화입니다. 우리 마스터 정원사 팀은 당신에게 원예 및 식물 돌보기와 관련된 모든 종류의 문제에 대해 기꺼이 안내를 제공해 드립니다. 그러나 이것은 자원봉사자들로 구성된 무료 서비스이므로 우리가 항상 옳은 것은 아닐 수 있다는 점을 염두에 두십시오. 우리는 월요일부터 금요일, 오전 9시부터 정오까지 전화를 받습니다. 시간이 짧기 때문에 전화하시는 분들은 빠르고 간단하게 문의하도록 신경 써주시기를 부탁드립니다. 감사합니다.

어휘 reach (특히 전화로) 연락하다 gardening 원예 crew (같은 일에 종사하는) 조, 팀 gardener 정원사 guidance 지도 related to ~와 관련 있는 staff 직원을 제공하다; 직원

71

What is the purpose of the hotline?

(A) To give updates
(B) To provide advice
(C) To accept donations
(D) To take reports on community problems

상담 전화의 목적은 무엇인가?

(A) 업데이트 제공
(B) 조언 제공
(C) 기부금 수령
(D) 지역 사회 문제에 대한 신고 접수

어휘 advice 조언 accept 받아들이다 donation 기부(금)
community 지역 사회

해설 세부 사항 관련 - 상담 전화의 목적

화자가 초반부에 우리 마스터 정원사 팀은 당신에게 원예 및 식물 돌보기와 관련된 모든 종류의 문제에 대해 기꺼이 안내를 제공한다(Our crew of Master Gardeners is happy to give you guidance on all types of problems related to gardening and plant care)고 했으므로 정답은 (B)이다.

> ▸▸ Paraphrasing 담화의 give you guidance
> → 정답의 provide advice

72

 고난도

What does the speaker mention about potential call recipients?

(A) They follow strict rules.
(B) They are currently busy.
(C) They are given regular training.
(D) They are not paid workers.

잠재적인 전화 수신인에 대해 화자는 무엇을 언급하는가?

(A) 엄격한 규칙을 따른다.
(B) 현재 바쁜 상태이다.
(C) 정기 교육을 받는다.
(D) 유급 직원이 아니다.

어휘 potential 잠재적인 recipient 받는 사람 strict 엄격한 currently 현재 regular 정기적인 paid 유급의

해설 세부 사항 관련 – 잠재적인 전화 수신인에 대해 화자가 언급한 사항
화자가 중반부에 이것은 자원봉사자들로 구성된 무료 서비스이므로 우리가 항상 옳은 것은 아닐 수 있다는 점을 염두에 두라(Please keep in mind, however, that this is a free service staffed by volunteers, so we may not always be right)고 했으므로 정답은 (D)이다.

73

What does the speaker ask listeners to do during their call?

(A) Be brief
(B) Take notes
(C) Speak clearly
(D) Remain polite

화자는 청자들에게 통화 중에 무엇을 하라고 요청하는가?

(A) 간략할 것
(B) 필기할 것
(C) 명확히 말할 것
(D) 정중할 것

어휘 brief 간단한 take notes 기록하다 clearly 명확히 polite 예의 바른

해설 세부 사항 관련 – 화자가 청자들에게 통화 중에 하라고 요청한 것
화자가 후반부에 시간이 짧기 때문에 전화하는 분들은 빠르고 간단하게 문의하도록 신경 써달라(Because our hours are short, we ask that callers take care to ask their question quickly and simply)고 했으므로 정답은 (A)이다.

▸▸ Paraphrasing 담화의 quickly and simply
→ 정답의 brief

74-76 회의 발췌

M-Au Thanks for joining me, everyone. I'm excited to talk about my experiences at the Office Wellness Conference. There were lots of memorable presentations, but the one that impressed me the most was given by Edge Thinking. 74 **They're a consulting firm that specializes in helping companies make their offices healthier and happier places to work.** 75 **I contracted them to come in later this month to look around our office and determine how to improve it.** 76 **But there's one idea from their presentation that I want to try right away—standing desks. You can see some pictures of them up here on the screen.** They're supposed to have a variety of health benefits. What do you think?

와주셔서 감사합니다, 여러분. 오피스 웰니스 컨퍼런스에서의 제 경험에 대해 이야기하게 되어 흥분되네요. 기억에 남는 발표들이 많았지만, 가장 인상 깊었던 것은 엣지 씽킹의 발표였습니다. 그 회사는 기업들이 더 건강하고 행복한 근무지를 만들 수 있도록 전문적으로 도와주는 컨설팅 회사입니다. 그 회사가 이달 말에 방문해서 우리 사무실을 둘러보고 개선 방안을 결정하기로 계약을 했습니다. 하지만 그들의 프레젠테이션에서 나온 아이디어 한 가지는 바로 시도해보고 싶은데, 바로 스탠딩 책상입니다. 여기 스크린에서 그 책상들의 사진을 몇 장 보실 수 있습니다. 이 책상으로 다양한 건강상의 혜택을 볼 수 있다고 합니다. 어떻게 생각하시나요?

어휘 memorable 기억할 만한 impress 깊은 인상을 주다 specialize in ~을 전문으로 하다 contract 계약하다 determine 결정하다, 알아내다 improve 개선하다 be supposed to ~하다고 여겨지다 a variety of 여러 가지의 benefit 혜택

74

고난도

What is Edge Thinking?

(A) A company that promotes healthy workplaces
(B) A government campaign targeting an industry
(C) An annual human resources conference
(D) A Web site operated by a research organization

엣지 씽킹은 무엇인가?

(A) 건강한 직장을 도모하는 회사
(B) 업계를 대상으로 하는 정부 캠페인
(C) 연례 인사 회의
(D) 연구 기관이 운영하는 웹사이트

어휘 promote 촉진[고취]하다 target 목표로 삼다 industry 산업 human resources 인사(부) operate 운영하다 organization 기구

해설 세부 사항 관련 – 엣지 씽킹의 업종
화자가 중반부에 엣지 씽킹은 기업들이 더 건강하고 행복한 근무지를 만들 수 있도록 전문적으로 도와주는 컨설팅 회사이다(They're a consulting firm that specializes in helping companies make their offices healthier and happier places to work)라고 했으므로 정답은 (A)이다.

75

고난도

What did the speaker arrange?

(A) A tour of a factory
(B) A team-building outing
(C) An assessment of an office
(D) A seminar on well-being

화자는 무엇을 주선했는가?
(A) 공장 견학
(B) 팀워크 야유회
(C) 사무실 평가
(D) 웰빙 세미나

어휘 outing 야유회 assessment 평가

해설 세부 사항 관련 – 화자가 주선한 것

화자가 중반부에 그 회사가 이달 말에 방문해서 우리 사무실을 둘러보고 개선 방안을 결정하기로 계약을 했다(I contracted them to come in later this month to look around our office and determine how to improve it)고 했으므로 정답은 (C)이다.

▸▸ Paraphrasing 담화의 look around our office and determine how to improve it → 정답의 an assessment of an office

76

What does the speaker show the listeners?

(A) Some revisions to a floor plan
(B) Images of furniture
(C) A list of job benefits
(D) A potential itinerary

화자는 청자들에게 무엇을 보여주는가?
(A) 평면도 수정안
(B) 가구 이미지
(C) 직장 혜택 목록
(D) 잠정적 여행 일정

어휘 revision 수정 floor plan 평면도 potential 잠재적인 itinerary 여행 일정

해설 세부 사항 관련 – 화자가 청자들에게 보여주는 것

화자가 후반부에 그들의 프레젠테이션에서 나온 아이디어 한 가지는 바로 시도해보고 싶은데, 바로 스탠딩 책상(there's one idea from their presentation that I want to try right away—standing desks)이라며, 여기 스크린에서 책상들의 사진을 몇 장 볼 수 있다(You can see some pictures of them up here on the screen)고 했으므로 화자는 청자들에게 스탠딩 책상의 사진을 보여주고 있음을 알 수 있다. 따라서 정답은 (B)이다.

▸▸ Paraphrasing 담화의 some pictures → 정답의 images

77-79 전화 메시지

> **W-Am** Hi, Dominick. It's Melody, calling from the event in Newark. It's going really well, I guess. **77A lot of potential distributors have stopped by our booth to pick up samples of our fruit juice. 78Uh, the problem is that we've been much more popular than we expected. There are two more days in the show** and I have about twenty sample bottles left. I think if you shipped another few cases overnight, they would arrive by lunch tomorrow. **79I'll e-mail you all the details you'll need, so please check your inbox as soon as you get this.**

여보세요, 도미닉. 멜로디예요. 뉴어크의 행사에서 전화하고 있어요. 정말 잘 되어가는 것 같아요. 많은 잠재적 유통업자들이 우리 부스에 들러서 과일 주스 샘플을 받아 갔어요. 어, 문제는 우리가 예상했던 것보다 훨씬 더 인기가 있다는 점이에요. 행사가 이틀 더 남았는데 샘플 병이 20개 정도 남았어요. 밤사이에 추가 몇 상자를 보내주면 내일 점심때쯤 도착할 것 같아요. 필요한 세부 사항을 전부 이메일로 보낼 테니, 이것을 확인하는 즉시 받은 편지함을 확인해주세요.

어휘 distributor 유통업자 stop by 들르다 ship 수송하다 overnight 밤사이에 details 세부 사항 inbox 받은 편지함

77

What kind of event is the speaker most likely attending?

(A) A cosmetics convention
(B) An arts and crafts festival
(C) A food and beverage exposition
(D) A pharmaceutical trade show

화자는 어떤 종류의 행사에 참석하고 있는 것 같은가?
(A) 화장품 컨벤션
(B) 예술 공예 축제
(C) 식음료 박람회
(D) 제약 무역 박람회

어휘 craft 공예 beverage 음료 exposition 박람회, 전시회 pharmaceutical 제약의

해설 세부 사항 관련 – 화자가 참석하고 있는 행사의 종류

화자가 초반부에 많은 잠재적 유통업자들이 우리 부스에 들러서 과일 주스 샘플을 받아 갔다(A lot of potential distributors have stopped by our booth to pick up samples of our fruit juice)고 한 것으로 보아 정답은 (C)이다.

78

What does the speaker imply when she says, "I have about twenty sample bottles left"?

(A) More giveaway stock is urgently needed.
(B) Her return journey will not be difficult.
(C) A prediction about a product was correct.
(D) A display should be removed from a booth.

화자가 "샘플 병이 20개 정도 남았어요"라고 말한 의미는 무엇인가?

(A) 더 많은 증정품 물량이 긴급히 필요하다.
(B) 돌아오는 여정이 어렵지 않을 것이다.
(C) 제품에 대한 예측이 옳았다.
(D) 진열품을 부스에서 치워야 한다.

어휘 giveaway 증정품 stock 재고(품) urgently 급히 journey 여행
prediction 예측 correct 옳은 display 진열

해설 화자의 의도 파악 – 샘플 병이 20개 정도 남았다는 말의 의도
화자가 앞에서 문제는 우리가 예상했던 것보다 훨씬 더 인기가 있다는 점(the problem is that we've been much more popular than we expected)이고 행사는 이틀 더 남았다(There are two more days in the show)고 하면서 인용문을 언급했으므로, 음료의 인기가 많은데 행사가 이틀이나 남아 20병으로는 부족하므로 빨리 물량을 추가로 구비해야 한다는 것을 설명하려는 의도로 한 말이라고 볼 수 있다. 따라서 정답은 (A)이다.

79

What does the speaker say she will do?

(A) Have lunch with a possible distributor
(B) Check the details of a contract
(C) Take an overnight flight
(D) Send the listener an e-mail

화자는 무엇을 하겠다고 말하는가?
(A) 잠재 유통업자와 점심을 먹는다.
(B) 계약의 세부 내용을 확인한다.
(C) 야간 비행기를 탄다.
(D) 청자에게 이메일을 보낸다.

해설 세부 사항 관련 – 화자가 하겠다고 말하는 것
화자가 마지막에 필요한 세부 사항을 전부 이메일로 보낼 테니, 이것을 확인하는 즉시 받은 편지함을 확인해달라(I'll e-mail you all the details you'll need, so please check your inbox soon as you get this)고 했으므로 정답은 (D)이다.

80-82 광고

M-Cn Cooking is a fun and rewarding hobby, and whether you're an experienced cook or a beginner in the kitchen, the Cessna Institute can help you to improve your skills. [80]**Thanks to a government grant, we are able to offer admission fees that are affordable to everyone, as they are income-based. You may be eligible to pay nothing at all!** Among the institute's instructors are several highly experienced local chefs, including Nelson Duncan. [81]**His restaurant just won the Armenta Prize!** [82]**Slots in all of our courses are going fast, so call us today at 555-0182 to sign up.** Don't miss your chance to become a more confident cook.

요리는 재미있고 보람 있는 취미로, 경험이 많은 요리사이든, 주방 초보자이든 세스나 학원은 당신이 실력을 향상하도록 도울 수 있습니다. 정부 보조금 덕분에 입학금은 소득을 기준으로 하므로, 누구에게나 부담이 없는 입학금을 제공할 수 있습니다. 당신은 아무것도 지불하지 않아도 될 수 있습니다! 이 학원의 강사 중에는 넬슨 던컨을 포함해 경험이 풍부한 여러 명의 현지 요리사들이 있습니다. 그의 식당은 얼마 전 아멘타상을 받았습니다! 모든 강좌의 자리가 빠르게 차고 있으니, 오늘 555-0182번으로 전화하셔서 등록하십시오. 더욱 자신감 있는 요리사가 될 기회를 놓치지 마세요.

어휘 rewarding 보람 있는 experienced 경험이 많은 institute 기관(협회) government 정부 grant 보조금 admission 입장 affordable 감당할 수 있는 income 소득 based 기반을 둔 eligible 자격이 되는 instructor 강사 prize 상 slot 자리, 시간 sign up ~에 등록하다 confident 자신감 있는

80

What does the speaker emphasize about the Cessna Institute?

(A) Its long history
(B) Its convenient location
(C) Its high admission requirements
(D) Its variable entrance costs

화자는 세스나 학원에 대해 무엇을 강조하는가?
(A) 긴 역사
(B) 편리한 위치
(C) 높은 입학 자격 요건
(D) 가변적인 입학 비용

어휘 convenient 편리한 location 위치, 장소 requirement 요건 variable 가변적인 entrance 입학, 입장

해설 세부 사항 관련 – 화자가 세스나 학원에 관해 강조하는 것
화자가 초반부에 정부 보조금 덕분에 입학금은 소득을 기준으로 하므로 누구에게나 부담이 없는 입학금을 제공할 수 있다(Thanks to a government grant, we are able to offer admission fees that are affordable to everyone as they are income-based)고 했고, 당신은 아무것도 지불하지 않아도 될 수 있다(You may be eligible to pay nothing at all!)고 했으므로 입학 비용이 사람마다 다를 수 있다는 것에 대해 설명하고 있음을 알 수 있다. 따라서 정답은 (D)이다.

81

What does the speaker say about Mr. Duncan?

(A) He opened a new restaurant.
(B) His classroom is well-equipped.
(C) He studied at the Cessna Institute.
(D) His business received an award.

화자는 던컨 씨에 대해 무엇을 말하는가?
(A) 새 식당을 열었다.
(B) 그의 교실은 장비가 잘 갖춰져 있다.
(C) 세스나 학원에서 공부했다.
(D) 그의 사업체는 상을 받았다.

어휘 equipped 장비를 갖춘 institute (특히 교육 관련) 기관 award 상

해설 세부 사항 관련 – 화자가 던컨 씨에 대해 말하는 것

화자가 중반부에 던컨 씨에 대해 언급한 뒤 그의 식당은 얼마 전 아멘타상을 받았다(His restaurant just won the Armenta Prize!)고 했으므로 정답은 (D)이다.

> ▸▸ **Paraphrasing** 담화의 **won the ~ prize**
> → 정답의 **received an award**

82

Why are the listeners encouraged to register soon?

(A) Classes are filling up quickly.
(B) A special offer is about to end.
(C) The deadline is approaching.
(D) A new policy will be adopted shortly.

청자들은 왜 서둘러 등록하도록 권장되는가?

(A) 강좌들이 빨리 차고 있어서
(B) 특별 할인이 곧 끝나서
(C) 마감일이 다가오고 있어서
(D) 곧 새로운 규정이 채택될 것이라서

어휘 fill up 가득 차다 be about to 막 ~하려고 하다 approach 다가오다 adopt 채택하다 shortly 곧

해설 세부 사항 관련 – 청자들이 등록을 서두르라고 권장 받는 이유

화자가 후반부에 모든 강좌의 자리가 빠르게 차고 있으니, 오늘 555-0182번으로 전화해 등록하라(Slots in all of our courses are going fast, so call us today at 555-0182 to sign up)고 했으므로 정답은 (A)이다.

> ▸▸ **Paraphrasing** 담화의 **slots in all of our courses are going fast** → 정답의 **classes are filling up quickly**

83-85 공지

W-Br ⁸³**Attention, Dugan Fitness Center customers.** Please take a short break to listen to the following announcement. ⁸⁴**There is currently no hot water in the shower rooms.** We have called a repair service and they will arrive within the hour, but we don't know how long it will take to fix the problem. Also, while the repair work is taking place, the shower rooms may be entirely unavailable. We are deeply sorry for this inconvenience. ⁸⁵**To make it up to you, we would like to extend your membership by one week for free. The front desk staff will set that up when you leave today.**

두간 피트니스 센터 고객 여러분께 알립니다. 잠시 쉬면서 다음 안내 방송을 들어 주시기 바랍니다. 현재 샤워실에 온수가 나오지 않습니다. 수리 업체에 전화를 했고 그들은 한 시간 안에 도착할 예정이지만, 문제를 해결하는 데 얼마나 오래 걸릴지 모르겠습니다. 또한, 보수 작업이 진행되는 동안 샤워실은 완전히 이용이 불가능할 수 있습니다. 불편을 끼쳐드려 대단히 죄송합니다. 보상을 위해 여러분의 회원권을 무료로 1주일만큼 연장해드리고자 합니다. 오늘 나가실 때 안내 데스크 직원이 그렇게 설정해드릴 것입니다.

어휘 attention (안내 방송에서) 알립니다 break 휴식 announcement 발표 currently 현재 repair 수리 fix 바로잡다 take place 일어나다 entirely 전적으로 unavailable 이용할 수 없는 inconvenience 불편 extend 연장하다

83

Who is the announcement most likely for?

(A) Theater patrons
(B) Shoppers
(C) Gym users
(D) Travelers

안내 방송은 누구를 위한 것이겠는가?

(A) 극장 이용객들
(B) 쇼핑객들
(C) 헬스클럽 이용자들
(D) 여행자들

해설 전체 내용 관련 – 청자의 신분

화자가 도입부에 두간 피트니스 센터 고객 여러분께 알린다(Attention, Dugan Fitness Center customers)고 한 것으로 보아 정답은 (C)이다.

> ▸▸ **Paraphrasing** 담화의 **fitness center customers**
> → 정답의 **gym users**

84

What does the speaker announce?

(A) A correction to an advertisement
(B) An issue with some plumbing
(C) A shortage of inventory
(D) A change in venue

화자는 무엇을 발표하는가?

(A) 광고 정정
(B) 배수 문제
(C) 재고 부족
(D) 장소 변경

어휘 correction 정정[수정] plumbing 배관, 배수 shortage 부족 inventory 재고 venue 장소

해설 세부 사항 관련 – 화자의 발표 내용

화자가 초반부에 현재 샤워실에 온수가 나오지 않는다(There is currently no hot water in the shower rooms)고 했으므로 정답은 (B)이다.

85

What does the speaker say some staff members will do?

(A) Arrange a form of compensation
(B) Oversee the sharing of a resource
(C) Make further announcements
(D) Help listeners leave the area

화자는 일부 직원들이 무엇을 할 것이라고 말하는가?

(A) 어떤 형태의 보상을 마련해준다.
(B) 자원의 공유를 감독한다.
(C) 추가 공지를 한다.
(D) 청자들이 나가는 것을 돕는다.

어휘 arrange 마련하다 form 방식 compensation 보상 oversee 감독하다 share 공유하다 resource 자원

해설 세부 사항 관련 – 화자가 일부 직원들이 할 것이라고 말하는 것
화자가 마지막에 보상을 위해 여러분의 회원권을 무료로 1주일만큼 연장해 드리겠다(To make it up to you, we would like to extend your membership by one week for free)면서, 오늘 나갈 때 안내 데스크 직원이 그렇게 설정해줄 것(The front desk staff will set that up when you leave today)이라고 했으므로 정답은 (A)이다.

▸▸ Paraphrasing 담화의 **make it up to you**
→ 정답의 **compensation**

86-88 담화

M-Au **86 As I said in my e-mail, I called you all here to talk about a serious problem at the laboratory.** When I returned from lunch yesterday, **87 I found the doors of Chemical Storage Cabinet Two left wide open. It appears that nothing is missing, but this is still a major safety breach. You've all seen the sign saying "Cabinets Must Be Locked At All Times."** Please, please remember that there's a reason we put that sign up. All right. **88 Uh, I know that this was one person's mistake, so I'm sorry to have to speak to all of you like this.** I hope you'll understand.

이메일에서 말씀드린 대로 실험실에서의 심각한 문제에 대해 이야기하기 위해 여러분을 모두 여기로 불렀습니다. 어제 점심을 먹고 돌아왔을 때, 저는 화학품 보관 캐비닛 2의 문이 활짝 열려 있는 것을 발견했습니다. 분실된 것은 없는 것으로 보이지만 이는 여전히 중대한 안전 위반입니다. '캐비닛은 항상 잠겨 있어야 한다'는 표지판을 모두 보셨을 겁니다. 우리가 그 표지판을 붙인 이유가 있다는 것을 꼭 기억하시기 바랍니다. 자, 음, 이것이 한 사람의 실수라는 것을 알고 있는데 이렇게 여러분 모두에게 말을 해야 해서 미안합니다. 이해해주시길 바랍니다.

어휘 call (오라고) 부르다 serious 심각한 laboratory 실험실 chemical 화학 물질 storage 보관 appear ~인 것 같다 missing 분실된 major 중대한 breach 위반 lock 잠그다

86

Where does the speaker work?

(A) At a research facility
(B) At a manufacturing plant
(C) At a city government agency
(D) At a shipping center

화자는 어디에서 일하는가?

(A) 연구 시설
(B) 제조 공장
(C) 시 정부 기관
(D) 물류 센터

해설 전체 내용 관련 – 화자의 근무지
화자가 도입부에 이메일에서 말씀드린대로 실험실에서의 심각한 문제에 대해 이야기하기 위해 여러분을 모두 여기로 불렀다(As I said in my e-mail, I called you all here to talk about a serious problem at the laboratory)고 했으므로 정답은 (A)이다.

▸▸ Paraphrasing 담화의 **the laboratory**
→ 정답의 **a research facility**

87   고난도

What does the speaker mean when he says, "there's a reason we put that sign up"?

(A) An activity can be dangerous.
(B) Storage spaces must be kept secure.
(C) Visitors need special assistance.
(D) Some old equipment is fragile.

화자가 "우리가 그 표지판을 붙인 이유가 있다"라고 말한 의도는 무엇인가?

(A) 활동이 위험할 수 있다.
(B) 보관 공간은 안전하게 유지되어야 한다.
(C) 방문객들은 특별한 도움이 필요하다.
(D) 일부 오래된 장비는 손상되기 쉽다.

어휘 dangerous 위험한 space 공간 secure 안전한 assistance 도움 equipment 장비 fragile 손상되기 쉬운

해설 화자의 의도 파악 – 우리가 그 표지판을 붙인 이유가 있다는 말의 의도
앞에서 화학품 보관 캐비닛 2의 문이 열려 있는 것을 발견했다(I found the doors of Chemical Storage Cabinet Two left wide open)고 했고, 분실된 것은 없어 보이지만 이는 여전히 중대한 안전 위반(It appears that nothing is missing, but this is still a major safety breach)이라고 안전 수칙이 제대로 지켜지지 않고 있음을 상기시키면서, "캐비닛은 항상 잠겨 있어야 한다"는 표지판을 모두 보셨을 것(You've all seen the sign saying "Cabinets Must Be Locked At All Times.")이라고 한 뒤 인용문을 언급했다. 따라서 인용문은 안전을 위해 캐비닛이 항상 잠겨 있어야 한다는 것을 강조하기 위한 의도로 한 말이므로 정답은 (B)이다.

88

What does the speaker apologize for?

(A) Not noticing a mistake earlier
(B) Not explaining a procedure
(C) Addressing all of the listeners
(D) Limiting access to an amenity

화자는 무엇에 대해 사과하는가?

(A) 실수를 일찍 알아차리지 못한 것
(B) 절차를 설명하지 않은 것
(C) 청자들 모두에게 말을 한 것
(D) 편의시설에 접근을 제한한 것

───────────────────────

어휘 notice 알아차리다 procedure 절차 address (누구에게) 말을
하다 limit 제한하다 access 접근 amenity 편의시설

해설 세부 사항 관련 – 화자가 사과하는 것

화자가 후반부에 이것이 한 사람의 실수였다는 것을 알고 있는데 이렇게 여러
분 모두에게 말을 해야 해서 미안하다(I know that this was one person's
mistake, so I'm sorry to have to speak to all of you like this)고 했으
므로 정답은 (C)이다.

▸▸ Paraphrasing 담화의 **speak to all of you**
　　　　　　　　　→ 정답의 **addressing all of the listeners**

89-91 소개

> **W-Br** Everyone, could I have your attention for a
> moment? [89] **Welcome to the launch of Ammett
> Gallery's show of Carlos Valdez's work**. We're
> so glad you could join us. We've collected more
> than forty of Mr. Valdez's paintings from various
> periods of his career. [90] **And as the highlight of
> tonight's event, I'd like to introduce Professor
> Mona Carlson of Flonning University. She's
> a leading expert on Mr. Valdez's work,** and
> she's agreed to say a few words about the
> contents and meaning of our show. [91] **We hope
> her speech will help you appreciate what you
> see as you continue circulating throughout
> the gallery this evening.** All right, please give a
> warm welcome to Professor Mona Carlson!

> 여러분, 잠깐 주목해 주시겠습니까? 아메트 미술관의 카를로스 발데즈 작품 전
> 시회의 개최 행사에 오신 것을 환영합니다. 여러분이 우리와 함께할 수 있어서
> 정말 기쁩니다. 우리는 발데즈 씨의 경력 중 다양한 시기에 그려진 그림 40여
> 점을 수집해왔습니다. 그리고 오늘 밤 행사의 하이라이트로 플로닝 대학의 모나
> 칼슨 교수님을 소개해드리고자 합니다. 그녀는 발데즈 씨의 작품에 관한 일류
> 전문가로, 우리 전시회의 내용과 의미에 대해 몇 말씀해주시는 데 동의하셨습
> 니다. 그녀의 연설이 오늘 저녁 미술관 곳곳을 돌면서 보시게 될 것들을 제대로
> 감상하는 데 도움이 되기를 바랍니다. 자, 모나 칼슨 교수님께 따뜻한 환대 부탁
> 드립니다!

> 어휘 attention 주목 launch 개시 (행사) collect 모으다
> period 시기 introduce 소개하다 professor 교수 leading
> 일류의 expert 전문가 content 내용물 meaning 의미
> appreciate 감상하다, 진가를 알아보다 continue 계속하다
> circulate 돌아다니다

89

What event are the listeners attending?

(A) A guest lecture
(B) A welcome reception
(C) An exhibition opening
(D) A tour of an artist's workshop

청자들은 무슨 행사에 참석 중인가?
(A) 초청 강연
(B) 환영회
(C) 전시회 개막식
(D) 예술가 워크숍 투어

───────────────────────

해설 세부 사항 관련 – 청자들이 참석 중인 행사

화자가 초반부에 아메트 미술관의 카를로스 발데즈 작품 전시회의 개최 행사에
오신 것을 환영한다(Welcome to the launch of Ammett Gallery's show
of Carlos Valdez's work)고 했으므로 정답은 (C)이다.

▸▸ Paraphrasing 담화의 **the launch of ~ Gallery's show**
　　　　　　　　　→ 정답의 **an exhibition opening**

90　　　　　　　　　　　　　　　　　[고난도]

Who most likely is Ms. Carlson?

(A) An art scholar
(B) A painter
(C) A gallery owner
(D) A museum donor

칼슨 씨는 누구일 것 같은가?
(A) 미술 학자
(B) 화가
(C) 미술관 소유주
(D) 박물관 기부자

───────────────────────

해설 세부 사항 관련 – 칼슨 씨의 직업

화자가 중반부에 오늘 밤 행사의 하이라이트로 플로닝 대학의 모나 칼슨 교
수님을 소개하려고 한다(as the highlight of tonight's event, I'd like to
introduce Professor Mona Carlson of Flonning University)고 했고, 그
녀는 발데즈 씨의 작품에 관한 일류 전문가(She's a leading expert on Mr.
Valdez's work)라고 했으므로 정답은 (A)이다.

▸▸ Paraphrasing 담화의 **professor** → 정답의 **scholar**

91

According to the speaker, what will happen after
Ms. Carlson speaks?

(A) Some refreshments will be served.
(B) Some photographs will be taken.
(C) The listeners will ask questions.
(D) The listeners will walk around.

화자에 따르면, 칼슨 씨의 강연 후 무슨 일이 일어날 것인가?
(A) 다과가 제공될 것이다.
(B) 사진을 촬영할 것이다.
(C) 청자들이 질문을 할 것이다.
(D) 청자들이 돌아다닐 것이다.

어휘 refreshment 다과 serve 제공하다

해설 세부 사항 관련 – 칼슨 씨의 강연 후 일어날 일

화자가 후반부에 그녀의 연설이 오늘 저녁 미술관 곳곳을 돌면서 보게 될 것들을 제대로 감상하는 데 도움이 되기를 바란다(We hope her speech will help you appreciate what you see as you continue circulating throughout the gallery this evening)고 했으므로 정답은 (D)이다.

▶▶ **Paraphrasing** 담화의 **circulate** → 정답의 **walk around**

92-94 방송

> W-Am You're listening to *Bondella Today*, the show about current affairs in our city. Up next today, ⁹² **there's the possible designation of the old Kirkland house on Third Street as a historic home.** Its newest owner, Albert Reynolds, submitted his application to the Bondella Cultural Heritage Board this week. ⁹³ **Mr. Reynolds probably hopes to receive some of the city funding available for the restoration of historic homes**—the building is in bad condition. Personally, I hope he succeeds, because with a few improvements, the property could be quite striking. ⁹⁴ **If you feel the same, why not speak up in support of Mr. Reynold's application at the board's next open meeting?** It will be held on Tuesday evening at City Hall.

> 여러분은 지금 우리 시의 시사에 관한 쇼인 〈본델라 투데이〉를 듣고 계십니다. 오늘 다음 순서입니다. 3번 가에 있는 커클랜드 고택이 역사적인 주택으로 지정될 수도 있다고 합니다. 고택의 새 주인인 알버트 레이놀즈는 이번 주에 본델라 문화 위원회에 그의 신청서를 제출했습니다. 레이놀즈 씨는 아마도 고택 복구 작업을 위해 마련된 시의 재정 지원을 받고 싶어 할 것입니다. 그 건물은 상태가 좋지 않습니다. 몇 가지 개선만으로도 그 건물은 굉장히 매력적일 수 있기 때문에 개인적으로 저는 그가 성공하기를 바랍니다. 같은 생각이시라면 다음 공개 위원회에서 레이놀즈 씨의 신청을 지지하는 목소리를 내주시면 어떨까요? 위원회는 시청에서 화요일 저녁에 열릴 예정입니다.

> 어휘 current affairs 시사 up next 다음 순서로는 designation 지정 historic 역사적인 newest 최신의 submit 제출하다 application 신청(서) cultural heritage 문화재 board 이사회, 위원회 funding 재정 지원, 자금 restoration 복구[복원] condition 상태 improvement 개선 striking 굉장히 매력적인 in support of ~을 지지하여

92
고난도

What is the main topic of the broadcast?

(A) A special status for a residence
(B) The activities of a citizens' organization
(C) The possible purchase of a structure
(D) A publication on a city's history

방송의 주제는 무엇인가?

(A) 주택에 대한 특별 자격
(B) 시민 단체의 활동
(C) 건축물의 매입 가능성
(D) 도시 역사에 관한 출판물

어휘 status (법적) 자격[지위] residence 주택 citizen 시민 organization 단체 structure 건축물 publication 출판(물)

해설 전체 내용 관련 – 방송의 주제

화자가 초반부에 3번 가에 있는 커클랜드 고택이 역사적인 주택으로 지정될 수도 있다(there's the possible designation of the old Fitzgerald house on Third Street as a historic home)면서 관련 소식을 전하고 있는 것으로 보아 정답은 (A)이다.

▶▶ **Paraphrasing** 담화의 **the ~ house** → 정답의 **a residence**

93
고난도

Why does the speaker say, "the building is in bad condition"?

(A) To express disapproval of a proposal
(B) To report the result of an official inspection
(C) To suggest that a project will be harder than expected
(D) To explain an assumption she has made

화자가 "그 건물은 상태가 좋지 않습니다"라고 말하는 이유는 무엇인가?

(A) 제안에 대해 찬성하지 않음을 나타내려고
(B) 공식 점검 결과를 보고하려고
(C) 프로젝트가 예상보다 어려울 것임을 암시하려고
(D) 그녀가 한 가정에 대해 설명하려고

어휘 express 나타내다 disapproval 불찬성 result 결과 official 공식적인 inspection 점검 assumption 가정

해설 화자의 의도 파악 – 그 건물은 상태가 좋지 않다고 말한 의도

앞에서 레이놀즈씨는 아마도 고택 복구 작업을 위해 마련된 시의 재정 지원을 받고 싶어 할 것(Mr. Reynolds probably hopes to receive some of the city funding available for the restoration of historic homes)이라면서 인용문을 언급했으므로, 레이놀즈 씨가 지원금을 신청한 이유에 대한 본인의 가정을 뒷받침하려는 의도로 한 말임을 알 수 있다. 따라서 정답은 (D)이다.

94
고난도

What does the speaker encourage some listeners to do?

(A) Apply for membership in a group
(B) Provide financial support for a cause
(C) Make a public comment on a matter
(D) See a property in person

화자는 일부 청자들에게 무엇을 하라고 권하는가?

(A) 단체의 구성원 자격 신청
(B) 대의를 위한 재정적 지원 제공
(C) 문제에 대한 공개 발언
(D) 건물 직접 보기

어휘 apply for 신청하다 financial 재정의 cause 대의명분 comment 언급, 논평 property 건물, 부동산

해설 세부 사항 관련 - 화자가 청자들에게 하라고 격려하는 것

화자가 후반부에 같은 생각이라면 다음 공개 위원회에서 레이놀즈 씨의 신청을 지지하는 목소리를 내주시면 어떨까요(If you feel the same, why not speak up in support of Mr. Reynold's application at the board's next open meeting?)라고 했으므로 정답은 (C)이다.

▸▸ **Paraphrasing** 담화의 **speak up** → 정답의 **make a public comment**

95-97 공지 + 도표

> M-Cn All right, everyone, I have an announcement to make. As you know, our survey to choose our new salad dressing flavor ended yesterday. **⁹⁵First, thank you again for asking our customers to vote when you took their order at the counter.** We collected over two hundred votes in a week, which I think is quite good. So, here are the results. **⁹⁶Look at how many votes the first-place dressing got!** It's the clear choice. Now, we want to make the launch of the new dressing a fun event. **⁹⁷So I've decided that, for the first week, we're going to give diners two dollars off if they order the new dressing with their salad.** I think this will attract new customers.

자, 여러분, 발표할 게 있습니다. 여러분도 아시다시피, 새로운 샐러드 드레싱 맛을 선택하기 위한 설문 조사는 어제 끝이 났습니다. 먼저 카운터에서 주문을 받을 때 고객분들께 투표해 달라고 요청해주셔서 다시 한번 감사드립니다. 우리는 일주일에 200표 이상을 모았고 꽤 잘했다고 생각합니다. 자, 여기 결과입니다. **1등 드레싱이 얼마나 많은 표를 받았는지 보세요!** 선택은 확실합니다. 이제 우리는 새로운 드레싱의 출시를 재미있는 행사로 만들기를 원합니다. 그래서 저는 첫 주 동안 손님들이 샐러드와 함께 새로운 드레싱을 주문하면 2달러를 할인해주기로 결정했습니다. 이렇게 하면 새 고객들을 끌 것이라고 생각합니다.

어휘 announcement 발표 survey 설문 조사 flavor 맛 vote 투표하다; 표 collect 모으다 quite 꽤 first-place 1등 launch 출시; 출시하다 diner 식사하는 사람[손님] attract 끌어들이다

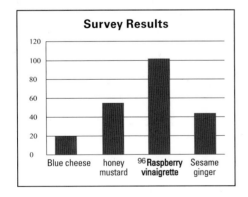

Survey Results

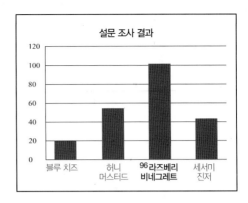

설문 조사 결과

어휘 raspberry 산딸기 vinaigrette 비네그레트(식초·기름·양념으로 만든 소스) sesame 참깨 ginger 생강

95

Who most likely are the listeners?

(A) Restaurant staff
(B) Lunch customers
(C) Product developers
(D) Marketing specialists

청자들은 누구일 것 같은가?

(A) 식당 직원
(B) 점심 손님
(C) 제품 개발자
(D) 마케팅 전문가

해설 전체 내용 관련 - 청자들의 직업

화자가 초반부에 카운터에서 주문을 받을 때 고객분들께 투표해달라고 요청해줘서 다시 한번 감사드린다(thank you again for asking our customers to vote when you took their order at the counter)고 한 것으로 보아 정답은 (A)이다.

96
고난도

Look at the graphic. Which type of salad dressing does the speaker point out?

(A) Blue cheese
(B) Honey mustard
(C) Raspberry vinaigrette
(D) Sesame ginger

시각 정보에 의하면, 화자는 어떤 종류의 샐러드 드레싱을 언급하는가?

(A) 블루 치즈
(B) 허니 머스터드
(C) 라즈베리 비네그레트
(D) 세서미 진저

해설 시각 정보 연계 - 화자가 언급하는 샐러드 드레싱의 종류

화자가 중반부에 1등 드레싱이 얼마나 많은 표를 받았는지 보라(Look at how many votes the first-place dressing got!)고 했고, 도표에 따르면 가장 많은 표를 받은 1등 드레싱은 라즈베리 비네그레트이므로 정답은 (C)이다.

97

What has the speaker decided to do?

(A) Contact an outside consultant
(B) Offer a promotional discount
(C) Discontinue two types of dressing
(D) Increase a regular supply order

화자는 무엇을 하기로 결정했는가?

(A) 외부 컨설턴트에 연락할 것
(B) 판촉 할인을 제공할 것
(C) 드레싱 두 종류를 중단할 것
(D) 정기 공급 주문을 늘릴 것

어휘 promotional 홍보[판촉]의 discontinue 중단하다 increase
늘리다 regular 정기적인 supply 공급

해설 세부 사항 관련 – 화자의 결정 사항

화자가 후반부에 첫 주 동안 손님들이 샐러드와 함께 새로운 드레싱을 주문하면 2달러를 할인해주기로 결정했다(I've decided that, for the first week, we're going to give diners two dollars off if they order the new dressing with their salad)고 한 것으로 보아 정답은 (B)이다.

▸ Paraphrasing 담화의 give ~ two dollars off
→ 정답의 offer a ~ discount

98-100 전화 메시지 + 가격표

W-Br Hi. My name is Ichika Hironaka, and I'm calling with a question about tickets for the Boheim Horse Show. **98 I'm planning to take my family to the show to celebrate my son's birthday.** **99 There are four of us, so I'd like to take advantage of the group discount we're eligible for.** But I'm not yet sure that my daughter will be able to go. **100 If I have to cancel her ticket, will I be able to get my money back? I'm worried that the rules on that kind of thing might be stricter for group tickets.** Please give me a call back at 555-0185.

여보세요. 제 이름은 이치카 히로나카입니다. 보하임 호스 쇼의 표에 관해 질문이 있어서 전화드립니다. 아들의 생일을 축하하려고 가족들을 쇼에 데려갈 계획입니다. 우리가 4명이니까, 자격이 되는 단체 할인을 이용하고 싶습니다. 하지만 제 딸이 갈 수 있을지 아직 확실하지가 않습니다. 만약 제가 그녀의 표를 취소해야 할 경우, 제 돈을 돌려받을 수 있을까요? 단체 티켓은 이런 일에 관한 규정이 더 엄격할까 봐 걱정이 됩니다. 555-0185번으로 제게 전화 주십시오.

어휘 celebrate 기념하다 take advantage of 이용하다
eligible 자격이 있는 strict 엄격한

BOHEIM HORSE SHOW

Ticket pricing (per person)

1–3 people	£30
99 4–10 people	**£27**
11+ people	£24

보하임 호스 쇼

표 가격 (1인당)

1–3명	30파운드
99 4–10명	**27파운드**
11명 이상	24파운드

98

Who will the speaker attend the show with?

(A) Work colleagues
(B) Relatives
(C) Potential clients
(D) Fellow members of a club

화자는 누구와 함께 쇼에 참석할 예정인가?

(A) 직장 동료
(B) 가족
(C) 잠재 고객
(D) 클럽의 동료 회원

해설 세부 사항 관련 – 화자가 함께 쇼에 참석할 사람

화자가 초반부에 아들의 생일을 축하하려고 가족들을 쇼에 데려갈 계획(I'm planning to take my family to the show to celebrate my son's birthday)이라고 했으므로 정답은 (B)이다.

▸ Paraphrasing 담화의 my family → 정답의 relatives

99

Look at the graphic. How much would the speaker like to pay per person?

(A) £33
(B) £30
(C) £27
(D) £24

시각 정보에 의하면, 화자는 1인당 얼마를 지불하길 원하는가?

(A) 33파운드
(B) 30파운드
(C) 27파운드
(D) 24파운드

해설 시각 정보 연계 – 화자가 원하는 1인당 지불 금액

화자가 중반부에 우리가 4명이니까, 자격이 되는 단체 할인을 이용하고 싶다 (There are four of us, so I'd like to take advantage of the group discount we're eligible for)고 했고, 가격표에 따르면 4인은 4~10명 구간에 해당하므로 정답은 (C)이다.

100 `고난도`

What is the speaker concerned about?

(A) Rules may prohibit bringing certain items.
(B) The tickets may not be refundable.
(C) Part of the show may be canceled.
(D) A sale period may have ended.

화자는 무엇에 관해 걱정하는가?

(A) 규정상 특정 품목의 반입이 금지될 수도 있다.
(B) 표가 환불되지 않을 수 있다.
(C) 쇼의 일부가 취소될 수 있다.
(D) 판매 기간이 끝났을 수 있다.

어휘 rule 규정 prohibit 금지하다 bring 가져오다 refundable 환불 가능한 cancel 취소하다 period 기간

해설 세부 사항 관련 – 화자의 걱정 사항

화자가 후반부에 만약 딸의 표를 취소해야 할 경우, 돈을 돌려받을 수 있을지 (If I have to cancel her ticket, will I be able to get my money back?)를 물으며, 단체 티켓은 이런 일에 관한 규정이 더 엄격할까 봐 걱정이 된다(I'm worried that the rules on that kind of thing might be stricter for group tickets)고 했으므로 정답은 (B)이다.

> ▸▸ Paraphrasing   담화의 **be able to get my money back**
> → 정답의 **be refundable**

TEST 6

1 (C)	**2** (A)	**3** (C)	**4** (A)	**5** (D)
6 (B)	**7** (B)	**8** (C)	**9** (A)	**10** (A)
11 (B)	**12** (B)	**13** (A)	**14** (C)	**15** (B)
16 (B)	**17** (A)	**18** (C)	**19** (B)	**20** (A)
21 (C)	**22** (B)	**23** (C)	**24** (A)	**25** (B)
26 (C)	**27** (A)	**28** (A)	**29** (C)	**30** (C)
31 (B)	**32** (D)	**33** (D)	**34** (A)	**35** (B)
36 (C)	**37** (C)	**38** (C)	**39** (D)	**40** (C)
41 (A)	**42** (D)	**43** (B)	**44** (C)	**45** (A)
46 (D)	**47** (A)	**48** (C)	**49** (B)	**50** (C)
51 (C)	**52** (A)	**53** (B)	**54** (B)	**55** (D)
56 (D)	**57** (D)	**58** (C)	**59** (D)	**60** (D)
61 (B)	**62** (B)	**63** (B)	**64** (D)	**65** (D)
66 (B)	**67** (D)	**68** (A)	**69** (A)	**70** (B)
71 (A)	**72** (A)	**73** (B)	**74** (C)	**75** (B)
76 (A)	**77** (C)	**78** (B)	**79** (D)	**80** (B)
81 (C)	**82** (C)	**83** (B)	**84** (C)	**85** (D)
86 (C)	**87** (A)	**88** (C)	**89** (C)	**90** (A)
91 (C)	**92** (D)	**93** (C)	**94** (A)	**95** (A)
96 (C)	**97** (D)	**98** (B)	**99** (A)	**100** (D)

PART 1

1   W-Am

(A) They're carrying a ladder.
(B) They're assembling some furniture.
(C) They're walking on a ramp.
(D) They're stacking boxes in a truck.

(A) 사람들은 사다리를 옮기고 있다.
(B) 사람들은 가구를 조립하고 있다.
(C) **사람들은 경사로 위를 걷고 있다.**
(D) 사람들은 트럭에 상자를 쌓고 있다.

어휘   assemble 조립하다   ramp 경사로   stack 쌓다

해설   2인 이상 등장 사진 – 인물의 동작 묘사

(A) 동사 오답. 사람들이 사다리를 옮기고 있는(are carrying a ladder) 모습이 아니므로 오답.
(B) 동사 오답. 사람들이 가구를 조립하고 있는(are assembling some furniture) 모습이 아니므로 오답.
(C) 정답. 사람들이 경사로 위를 걷고 있는(are walking on a ramp) 모습이므로 정답.
(D) 동사 오답. 사람들이 트럭에 상자를 쌓고 있는(are stacking boxes in a truck) 모습이 아니므로 오답.

2   M-Cn

(A) She's examining some merchandise.
(B) She's adjusting the handle of a shopping cart.
(C) She's trying a food sample in a store.
(D) She's reaching into her handbag.

(A) **여자는 상품을 살펴보고 있다.**
(B) 여자는 쇼핑 카트의 손잡이를 조정하고 있다.
(C) 여자는 가게에서 시식을 하고 있다.
(D) 여자는 핸드백에 손을 넣고 있다.

어휘   examine 조사[검토]하다   merchandise 상품   adjust 조정하다
reach into ~안에 손을 넣다

해설   1인 등장 사진 – 인물의 동작 묘사

(A) 정답. 여자가 상품을 살펴보고 있는(is examining some merchandise) 모습이므로 정답.
(B) 사진에 없는 명사를 이용한 오답. 사진에 쇼핑 카트(a shopping cart)의 모습이 보이지 않으므로 오답.
(C) 동사 오답. 여자가 가게에서 시식을 하고 있는(is trying a food sample in a store) 모습이 아니므로 오답.
(D) 동사 오답. 여자가 핸드백에 손을 넣고 있는(is reaching into her handbag) 모습이 아니므로 오답.

3   M-Au

(A) He's putting on a safety helmet.
(B) He's photographing a construction site.
(C) He's writing on a clipboard.
(D) He's leaning against a railing.

(A) 남자는 안전모를 쓰고 있다.
(B) 남자는 공사장의 사진을 찍고 있다.
(C) **남자는 클립보드에 글을 쓰고 있다.**
(D) 남자는 난간에 기대고 있다.

어휘   photograph ~의 사진을 찍다; 사진   construction site 공사장
lean against ~에 기대다   railing 난간

해설　1인 등장 사진 – 인물의 동작 묘사

(A) 동사 오답. 남자가 안전모를 쓰고 있는(is putting on a safety helmet) 모습이 아니라 이미 착용하고 있는(is wearing) 모습이므로 오답. 참고로 이미 착용 중인 상태를 나타내는 wearing과 무언가를 착용하는 동작을 묘사하는 putting on을 혼동하지 않도록 주의한다.

(B) 동사 오답. 남자가 공사장의 사진을 찍고 있는(is photographing a construction site) 모습이 아니므로 오답.

(C) 정답. 남자가 클립보드에 글을 쓰고 있는(is writing on a clipboard) 모습이므로 정답.

(D) 동사 오답. 남자가 난간에 기대고 있는(is leaning against a railing) 모습이 아니므로 오답.

4　W-Br

(A) Some buildings overlook the water.
(B) Boats are sailing on a lake.
(C) A walkway stretches over a road.
(D) A field is surrounded by trees.

(A) 몇몇 건물들이 물을 내려다보고 있다.
(B) 배들이 호수 위를 나아가고 있다.
(C) 길 위에 보도가 뻗어 있다.
(D) 들판이 나무로 둘러싸여 있다.

어휘　overlook 내려다보다　sail 항해하다　lake 호수　walkway 보도
stretch 펼쳐지다　field 들판　surround 둘러싸다

해설　배경 사진 – 실외 사물의 상태 묘사

(A) 정답. 몇몇 건물(some buildings)들이 물을 내려다보고 있는(overlook the water) 모습이므로 정답.

(B) 사진에 없는 명사를 이용한 오답. 사진에 배(boats)의 모습이 보이지 않으므로 오답.

(C) 동사 오답. 보도(a walkway)가 길 위에 뻗어 있는(stretches over a road) 모습이 아니므로 오답.

(D) 사진에 없는 명사를 이용한 오답. 사진에 들판(a field)의 모습이 보이지 않으므로 오답.

5　M-Cn

(A) The door of a car has been opened.
(B) Some repair work is taking place.
(C) A man is winding up a hose.
(D) Fuel is being put into a vehicle.

(A) 자동차의 문이 열려 있다.
(B) 보수 공사가 진행 중이다.
(C) 남자는 호스를 감고 있다.
(D) **연료가 차에 주입되고 있다.**

어휘　repair 보수　take place (일 등이) 일어나다　wind up (실·끈 등을) 감다　hose 호스　fuel 연료　vehicle 차량

해설　혼합 사진 – 사람 또는 사물 묘사

(A) 동사 오답. 자동차의 문(the door of a car)이 열려 있는(has been opened) 모습이 아니므로 오답.

(B) 동사 오답. 보수 공사(repair work)가 진행 중인(is taking place) 모습이 보이지 않으므로 오답.

(C) 동사 오답. 남자가 호스를 감고 있는(is winding up a hose) 모습이 아니므로 오답.

(D) 정답. 연료(fuel)가 차에 주입되고 있는(is being put into a vehicle) 모습이므로 정답.

6　W-Br　 고난도

(A) Leaves are being raked into piles in a park.
(B) Some passers-by are walking in the same direction.
(C) Seats have been set up in front of a stage.
(D) Musical instruments are being laid out on a mat.

(A) 공원에서 낙엽이 갈퀴질 되어 쌓이고 있다.
(B) **행인들이 같은 방향으로 걷고 있다.**
(C) 무대 앞에 좌석이 설치되어 있다.
(D) 악기들이 매트 위에 놓이고 있다.

어휘　rake 갈퀴질하다　pile 더미　passer-by 행인　direction 방향
musical instrument 악기　lay 놓다

해설　혼합 사진 – 사람 또는 사물 묘사

(A) 동사 오답. 낙엽이 갈퀴질 되어 쌓이고 있는(are being raked into piles) 모습이 아니므로 오답.

(B) 정답. 행인들(passers-by)이 같은 방향으로 걷고 있는(are walking in the same direction) 모습이므로 정답.

(C) 사진에 없는 명사를 이용한 오답. 사진에 좌석(seats)과 무대(a stage)의 모습이 보이지 않으므로 오답.

(D) 동사 오답. 악기들(musical instruments)이 매트 위에 놓이고 있는(are being laid out) 모습이 아니므로 오답.

PART 2

7

W-Br When do you think we'll hear from the caterer?

M-Au (A) Yes, I think so.

(B) Sometime this afternoon.

(C) A lower price quote.

음식 공급업체한테 언제 연락이 올 것 같습니까?
(A) 네, 그렇게 생각합니다.
(B) 오늘 오후 중으로요.
(C) 더 낮은 견적가입니다.

어휘 caterer 음식 공급자[사] quote 견적

해설 업체에서 연락이 올 시점을 묻는 When 의문문
(A) Yes/No 불가 오답. When 의문문에는 Yes/No 응답이 불가능하므로 오답.
(B) 정답. 음식 공급업체한테 연락이 올 것 같은 시점을 묻는 질문에 오늘 오후 중이라고 응답하고 있으므로 정답.
(C) 질문과 상관없는 오답. What 의문문에 대한 응답이므로 오답.

8

M-Cn Have you found a good graduate program yet?

W-Br (A) So that I can get a master's degree.

(B) She graduated with honors.

(C) Yes, and I've been accepted!

좋은 대학원 과정은 찾으셨나요?
(A) 석사 학위를 받으려고요.
(B) 그녀는 우등으로 졸업했어요.
(C) 네, 합격도 했답니다!

어휘 graduate 졸업생; 졸업하다 master 석사 degree 학위
honors (학업의) 우등 accept 받아주다

해설 좋은 대학원 과정을 찾았는지 여부를 묻는 조동사(Have) 의문문
(A) 연상 단어 오답. 질문의 graduate program에서 연상 가능한 master's degree를 이용한 오답.
(B) 파생어 오답. 질문의 graduate와 파생어 관계인 graduated를 이용한 오답.
(C) 정답. 좋은 대학원 과정을 찾았는지 묻는 질문에 네(Yes)라고 대답한 뒤, 합격도 했다며 긍정 답변과 일관된 내용을 덧붙이고 있으므로 정답.

9

고난도

W-Am Where should I put up the posters?

M-Cn (A) Start with the notice boards.

(B) I put them on your desk.

(C) By the end of the day.

포스터를 어디에 붙여야 할까요?
(A) 게시판부터 시작하세요.
(B) 책상 위에 뒀습니다.
(C) 오늘 중으로요.

어휘 notice board 게시판

해설 포스터를 붙일 위치를 묻는 Where 의문문
(A) 정답. 포스터를 붙일 위치를 묻는 질문에 게시판부터 시작하라고 구체적으로 알려주고 있으므로 정답.
(B) 연상 단어 오답. 질문의 Where에서 연상 가능한 desk를 이용한 오답.
(C) 질문과 상관없는 오답. When 의문문에 대한 응답이므로 오답.

10

M-Au I want to attend the training workshop this Thursday.

W-Am (A) How long would you be gone?

(B) Around one hundred employees.

(C) In the meeting room.

이번 주 목요일에 교육 워크숍에 참석하고 싶습니다.
(A) 얼마나 오래 가 계실 겁니까?
(B) 직원 100여 명 정도입니다.
(D) 회의실에서요.

어휘 attend 참석하다 training 교육, 훈련 employee 직원

해설 의사 전달의 평서문
(A) 정답. 이번 주 목요일에 교육 워크숍에 참석하고 싶다는 의사를 전달하는 평서문에 얼마나 오래 가 있을 것인지 물으며 관련 정보를 묻고 있으므로 정답.
(B) 평서문과 상관없는 오답. How many 의문문에 대한 응답이므로 오답.
(C) 연상 단어 오답. 평서문의 workshop에서 연상 가능한 meeting room을 이용한 오답.

11

M-Au Would you like me to order you some lunch?

W-Br (A) The bakery downstairs.

(B) I brought a sandwich with me.

(C) I really liked it, too.

점심 식사를 주문해드릴까요?
(A) 아래층 빵집이요.
(B) 샌드위치를 가져왔어요.
(C) 저도 정말 마음에 들었어요.

어휘 order 주문하다 bakery 빵집 downstairs 아래층

해설 제안/권유의 의문문
(A) 연상 단어 오답. 질문의 lunch에서 연상 가능한 bakery를 이용한 오답.
(B) 정답. 점심 식사를 주문해줄지 묻는 질문에 샌드위치를 가져왔다며 거절의 의사를 우회적으로 나타내고 있으므로 정답.
(C) 파생어 오답. 평서문의 like와 파생어 관계인 liked를 이용한 오답.

12

W-Am How can we attract more customers to our bookshop?

W-Br (A) Yes, it's a busy place.

(B) I'm not really a marketing expert.

(C) Many people have already read it.

어떻게 하면 우리 서점에 더 많은 손님을 유치할 수 있을까요?
(A) 네, 붐비는 곳이에요.
(B) 저는 마케팅 전문가가 아니에요.
(C) 많은 사람들이 그것을 이미 읽었어요.

어휘 attract 끌어 모으다 expert 전문가

해설 손님 유치 방법을 묻는 How 의문문
(A) Yes/No 불가 오답. How 의문문에는 Yes/No 응답이 불가능하므로 오답.
(B) 정답. 서점에 더 많은 손님을 유치할 수 있는 방법을 묻는 질문에 마케팅 전문가가 아니라며 답변할 수 없음을 우회적으로 밝히고 있으므로 정답.
(C) 연상 단어 오답. 질문의 bookshop에서 연상 가능한 read를 이용한 오답.

13

M-Cn Is the cafeteria renovation this week or next week?

W-Am (A) It began this morning.

(B) That's a long time to wait.

(C) Replacing the ovens.

구내식당 보수 공사가 이번 주인가요 아니면 다음 주인가요?
(A) 오늘 아침에 시작했어요.
(B) 기다리기에는 긴 시간이네요.
(C) 오븐을 교체하는 거요.

어휘 cafeteria 구내식당 renovation 개보수 replace 교체하다

해설 보수공사 시기를 묻는 선택의문문
(A) 정답. 구내식당의 보수공사 시기를 묻는 선택의문문에서 오늘 아침에 시작했다며 이번 주가 공사 기간임을 우회적으로 응답하고 있으므로 정답.
(B) 질문과 상관없는 오답.
(C) 연상 단어 오답. 질문의 cafeteria에서 연상 가능한 ovens를 이용한 오답.

14

W-Br What part of the sales presentation do you want to practice first?

M-Cn (A) For the clients from Lorman Associates.

(B) It's a good way to increase your sales.

(C) Let's run through the introduction.

영업 발표의 어느 부분을 먼저 연습하고 싶으신가요?
(A) 로만사에서 오신 고객들을 위해서요.
(B) 판매를 높이기 위한 좋은 방법입니다.
(C) 도입부를 연습해봅시다.

어휘 presentation 발표 practice 연습하다 increase 늘리다 run through 연습하다

해설 먼저 연습하고 싶은 발표 부분을 묻는 What 의문문
(A) 질문과 상관없는 오답.
(B) 단어 반복 오답. 질문의 sales를 반복 이용한 오답.
(C) 정답. 영업 발표의 어느 부분을 먼저 연습하고 싶은지 묻는 질문에 도입부를 연습해보자고 구체적으로 응답하고 있으므로 정답.

15

W-Br You bought a music festival ticket already, correct?

M-Au (A) A three-day pass, please.

(B) I'm still deciding whether to go.

(C) No, it's an annual event.

음악 축제 티켓은 이미 사셨죠, 그렇죠?
(A) 3일권으로 주세요.
(B) 아직 갈지 말지 고민 중이에요.
(C) 아니요, 연례 행사입니다.

어휘 festival 축제 pass 통행권 annual 연례의

해설 티켓의 구입 여부를 확인하는 부가의문문
(A) 연상 단어 오답. 질문의 ticket에서 연상 가능한 pass를 이용한 오답.
(B) 정답. 음악 축제 티켓을 구입했는지 여부를 확인하는 질문에 아직 갈지 말지 고민 중이라고 응답하고 있으므로 정답.
(C) 연상 단어 오답. 질문의 festival에서 연상 가능한 event를 이용한 오답.

16

M-Cn Where did you park your bicycle?

W-Am (A) Jackie has the same model in red.

(B) Oh, I took the bus today.

(C) From a shop on Barnhart Street.

자전거를 어디에 주차하셨나요?
(A) 재키는 빨간색으로 같은 모델이 있어요.
(B) 아, 오늘은 버스를 탔어요.
(C) 바나트 가에 있는 가게에서요.

해설 자전거를 주차한 위치를 묻는 Where 의문문
(A) 연상 단어 오답. 질문의 bicycle에서 연상 가능한 model을 이용한 오답.
(B) 정답. 자전거를 주차한 위치를 묻는 질문에 오늘은 버스를 탔다며 자전거를 타고 오지 않았음을 우회적으로 나타내고 있으므로 정답.
(C) 질문과 상관없는 오답. Where 의문문에 대한 응답이므로 오답.

17

W-Br Is the IT crew going to install the new software today?

M-Cn (A) As soon as we go out for lunch.

(B) Sure, I'll show you how to do it.

(C) They wear their uniforms every day.

IT 팀이 오늘 새 소프트웨어를 설치할 겁니까?
(A) 우리가 점심을 먹으러 나가자마자요.
(B) 물론이죠, 어떻게 하는지 보여드릴게요.
(C) 그들은 매일 유니폼을 입습니다.

어휘 install 설치하다 as soon as ~하자마자

해설 IT 팀이 오늘 소프트웨어를 설치하는지 여부를 묻는 Be동사 의문문

(A) 정답. IT 팀이 오늘 새 소프트웨어를 설치하는지 여부를 묻는 질문에 우리가 점심을 먹으러 나가자마자라며 구체적으로 응답하고 있으므로 정답.

(B) 연상 단어 오답. 질문의 new software에서 연상 가능한 show you how to를 이용한 오답

(C) 질문과 상관없는 오답.

18

M-Au I could also show you some smaller apartments downtown.

W-Am (A) Collect any small parts in this bag.
(B) Wasn't it difficult to relocate?
(C) I prefer to have more space.

시내에 있는 더 작은 아파트들도 보여드릴 수 있어요.
(A) 이 가방에 작은 부품들을 모으세요.
(B) 이사하는 데 힘들지 않았나요?
(C) 공간이 좀 더 넓은 것이 좋습니다

어휘 downtown 시내에 part 부품 relocate 이전하다 space 공간

해설 제안/권유의 평서문

(A) 파생어 오답. 평서문의 smaller와 파생어 관계인 small을 이용한 오답.

(B) 연상 단어 오답. 질문의 apartments에서 연상 가능한 relocate를 이용한 오답.

(C) 정답. 시내에 있는 소형 아파트들도 보여줄 수 있다고 제안하는 평서문에 공간이 좀 더 넓은 것이 좋다며 우회적으로 거절하고 있으므로 정답.

19

고난도

M-Cn Which elevator goes to the top floor?

M-Au (A) Yes, the fifty-second floor.
(B) You'll need a special access code.
(C) The CEO's office.

어느 엘리베이터가 꼭대기층으로 갑니까?
(A) 네, 52층입니다.
(B) 특수 접근 코드가 필요할 거예요.
(C) 대표이사님 사무실입니다.

어휘 access code 접근 코드

해설 꼭대기층으로 가는 엘리베이터를 묻는 Which 의문문

(A) Yes/No 불가 오답. Which 의문문에는 Yes/No 응답이 불가능하므로 오답.

(B) 정답. 어느 엘리베이터가 꼭대기층으로 가는지 묻는 질문에 특수 접근 코드가 있어야 한다며 이용이 제한되어 있음을 우회적으로 알리고 있으므로 정답.

(C) 질문과 상관없는 오답.

20

W-Br Can you tell us about potential safety issues with the project?

M-Cn (A) That information's on the next slide.
(B) I have some safety shoes right here, actually.
(C) Not that I am aware of.

프로젝트와 관련된 잠재적인 안전 문제에 대해 말씀해주시겠습니까?
(A) 그 정보는 다음 슬라이드에 있습니다.
(B) 사실 여기 안전화가 몇 켤레 있습니다.
(C) 제가 알기로는 아닙니다.

어휘 potential 잠재적인 safety 안전 issue 문제 aware 알고 있는

해설 부탁/요청의 의문문

(A) 정답. 프로젝트와 관련된 잠재적인 안전 문제에 대해 말해줄 것을 요청하는 질문에 해당 정보가 곧 소개됨을 알리고 있으므로 정답.

(B) 단어 반복 오답. 질문의 safety를 반복 이용한 오답.

(C) 질문과 상관없는 오답.

21

M-Au Who's delivering the office supplies to our customer in the Trident Building?

W-Br (A) A few boxes of pens.
(B) Thanks, I appreciate that.
(C) Becky said she could do it.

누가 트라이던트 빌딩에 있는 우리 고객에게 사무용품을 배송하나요?
(A) 펜 몇 상자요.
(B) 고맙습니다, 감사드려요.
(C) 베키가 할 수 있다고 했어요.

어휘 deliver 배송하다 office supplies 사무용품 appreciate 고마워하다

해설 사무용품을 배송하는 사람을 묻는 Who 의문문

(A) 질문과 상관없는 오답. What 의문문에 대한 응답이므로 오답.

(B) 질문과 상관없는 오답.

(C) 정답. 트라이던트 빌딩에 있는 고객에게 사무용품을 배송하는 사람을 묻는 질문에 베키가 할 수 있다고 했다고 알려주고 있으므로 정답.

22

W-Am When are we leaving for the movie?

M-Au (A) That's fine with me.
(B) It depends—what's the traffic like?
(C) I moved it already.

우리 언제 영화 보러 나가나요?
(A) 전 그거 괜찮습니다.
(B) 상황 봐서요. 교통 상황이 어떤가요?
(C) 제가 벌써 옮겼어요.

어휘 depend ~에 달려 있다 traffic 교통

해설 영화를 보러 가는 시점을 묻는 When 의문문
(A) 질문과 상관없는 오답. 제안문에 대한 응답이므로 오답.
(B) 정답. 영화를 보러 나가는 시점을 묻는 질문에 상황 봐서라고 응답한 뒤, 교통 상황이 어떤지 되묻고 있으므로 정답.
(C) 유사 발음 오답. 질문의 movie와 부분적으로 발음이 유사한 moved를 이용한 오답.

23

M-Cn Didn't Martin direct the advertisement for our spring clothing range?
W-Am (A) It's on several cable TV channels.
      (B) His clothing designs are excellent.
      (C) No, he only offered suggestions.

마틴이 우리 봄 의류 세트 광고를 총괄하지 않았나요?
(A) 몇몇 케이블 TV 채널에 나와요.
(B) 그의 옷 디자인은 훌륭해요.
(C) 아니요, 그는 제안만 했어요.

어휘 direct 총괄하다 advertisement 광고 range 범위, 세트 excellent 훌륭한 offer 제공하다 suggestion 제안

해설 마틴의 광고 총괄 여부를 확인하는 부정의문문
(A) 연상 단어 오답. 질문의 advertisement에서 연상 가능한 TV를 이용한 오답.
(B) 단어 반복 오답. 질문의 clothing을 반복 이용한 오답.
(C) 정답. 마틴이 봄 의류 세트 광고를 총괄했는지 묻는 질문에 아니요(No)라고 대답한 뒤, 그는 제안만 했다며 부정 답변과 일관된 내용을 덧붙이고 있으므로 정답.

24 고난도

W-Br Do we have to use a company mobile phone, or is it optional?
M-Cn (A) Well, there are major advantages to it.
      (B) To handle business while traveling.
      (C) Of course—just let your supervisor know.

회사 휴대폰을 사용해야 하나요, 아니면 선택 사항인가요?
(A) 음, 그것에는 큰 이점이 몇 가지 있어요.
(B) 출장 중에 업무를 처리하려고요.
(C) 물론이죠, 그냥 상관에게 알려주세요.

어휘 optional 선택적인 major 주요한 advantage 이점, 장점 handle 처리하다 supervisor 관리자

해설 회사 휴대폰의 사용 의무 여부를 묻는 선택의문문
(A) 정답. 회사 휴대폰을 사용해야 하는지 묻는 선택의문문에서 그것에 큰 이점이 몇 가지 있다며 회사 휴대폰 사용을 우회적으로 권장하고 있으므로 정답.
(B) 질문과 상관없는 오답. Why 의문문에 대한 응답이므로 오답.
(C) 질문과 상관없는 오답. Of course(물론이죠)가 어떤 선택인지 알 수 없으므로 오답.

25 고난도

M-Au Who received the award for Most Improved Employee?
W-Br (A) Right, she's doing much better now.
      (B) I missed that part of the banquet.
      (C) Great—you deserve it!

최고 향상 직원상은 누가 수상했나요?
(A) 맞아요, 그녀는 지금 훨씬 잘 하고 있어요.
(B) 연회에서 그 부분을 놓쳤어요.
(C) 잘됐네요, 당신은 자격이 있어요!

어휘 receive 받다 award 상 improved 향상된 banquet 연회 deserve ~을 받을 만하다

해설 수상자를 묻는 Who 의문문
(A) Yes/No 불가 오답. Who 의문문에는 Yes/No 응답이 불가능한데, Right도 일종의 Yes 응답이라고 볼 수 있으므로 오답.
(B) 정답. 최고 향상 직원상을 수상한 사람을 묻는 질문에 그 대목을 놓쳤다며 모른다는 답을 우회적으로 표현하고 있으므로 정답.
(C) 연상 단어 오답. 질문의 award에서 연상 가능한 deserve를 이용한 오답.

26 고난도

W-Am We should assign the new interns to General Affairs.
M-Au (A) Please check the building directory.
      (B) About ten vacant positions.
      (C) I believe Human Resources needs some help, too.

신입 인턴들을 총무과에 배치해야 합니다.
(A) 건물 안내도를 확인하십시오.
(B) 공석 10여 개요.
(C) 인사과도 일손이 필요한 것 같아요.

어휘 assign (사람을) 배치하다 General Affairs 총무과 directory 안내 책자 vacant 비어 있는 position 직책 Human Resources 인사과

해설 의사 전달의 평서문
(A) 평서문과 상관없는 오답.
(B) 평서문과 상관없는 오답. How many 의문문에 대한 응답이므로 오답.
(C) 정답. 신입 인턴들을 총무과에 배치해야 한다는 의사를 전달하는 평서문에 인사과도 일손이 필요한 것 같다며 인력 배치와 관련해 추가적인 의사를 제시하고 있으므로 정답.

27

M-Cn Why didn't Jeremy apply for the branch manager role?
W-Am (A) He didn't meet the requirements.
      (B) Only if there are no other applicants.
      (C) I'd be happy to give you a reference.

제레미는 왜 지점장 직에 지원하지 않았나요?
(A) 그는 요건을 갖추지 못했어요.
(B) 다른 지원자가 없는 경우에만요.
(C) 기꺼이 추천서를 드릴게요.

어휘 apply for ~에 지원하다 branch 지점 role 역할 meet
충족시키다 requirement 요건 applicant 지원자 reference
추천서

해설 제레미가 지점장 직에 지원하지 않은 이유를 묻는 Why 의문문
(A) 정답. 제레미가 지점장 직에 지원하지 않은 이유를 묻는 질문에 그는 요건
을 갖추지 못했다고 이유를 제시하고 있으므로 정답.
(B) 파생어 오답. 질문의 apply와 파생어 관계인 applicants를 이용한 오답.
(C) 연상 단어 오답. 질문의 apply에서 연상 가능한 reference를 이용한 오답.

28
M-Au Ms. Blaine is picking up the investors from the
airport, isn't she?
W-Br (A) I thought she had a schedule conflict.
(B) To the Regency Hotel.
(C) Their flight departs at two.

블레인 씨가 공항에서 투자자들을 픽업하는 거죠, 그렇죠?
(A) 일정이 겹치는 것 같던데요.
(B) 리젠시 호텔로요.
(C) 그들의 비행기는 2시에 출발해요.

어휘 pick up ~을 데리러 가다 investor 투자자 schedule conflict
일정 충돌 flight 항공편 depart 출발하다

해설 블레인 씨가 공항에 투자자들을 마중 나가는지 여부를 확인하는 부가의문문
(A) 정답. 블레인 씨가 공항에서 투자자들을 픽업하는지 여부를 확인하는 질문
에 일정이 겹치는 것 같다며 픽업이 어렵다는 것을 우회적으로 나타내고 있
으므로 정답.
(A) 질문과 상관없는 오답. Where 의문문에 대한 응답이므로 오답.
(C) 연상 단어 오답. 질문의 airport에서 연상 가능한 flight를 이용한 오답.

29
M-Cn Would you like these scented candles gift-
wrapped?
W-Br (A) I sent them to my sister.
(B) They smell wonderful.
(C) Does that cost extra?

이 향초들을 선물 포장해드릴까요?
(A) 언니에게 그것들을 보냈어요.
(B) 좋은 향기가 나요.
(C) 추가 비용이 드나요?

어휘 scented 향기로운 gift-wrapped 선물 포장하다 cost 비용이 들다
extra 추가로

해설 제안/권유의 의문문
(A) 유사 발음 오답. 질문의 scented와 부분적으로 발음이 유사한 sent를 이
용한 오답.
(B) 연상 단어 오답. 질문의 scented candles에서 연상 가능한 smell을 이
용한 오답.
(C) 정답. 향초 선물 포장을 제안하는 질문에 추가 비용이 드냐며 추가적인 관
련 정보를 묻고 있으므로 정답.

30
[고난도]
W-Am How can I help out with the organization's
fundraising event?
M-Cn (A) I'm just glad I could participate.
(B) We raised more than expected.
(C) Wendy can give you some tasks.

단체의 모금 행사를 어떻게 도우면 될까요?
(A) 제가 참여할 수 있어서 다행이에요.
(B) 우리가 예상했던 것보다 많이 모았어요.
(C) 웬디가 몇 가지 할 일을 줄 거예요.

어휘 organization 단체 fundraising 모금 participate 참여하다
raise (자금 등을) 모으다 expect 예상하다 task 일

해설 행사를 도울 방법을 묻는 How 의문문
(A) 연상 단어 오답. 질문의 event에서 연상 가능한 participate를 이용한 오답.
(B) 연상 단어 오답. 질문의 fundraising에서 연상 가능한 raised를 이용한
오답.
(C) 정답. 단체의 모금 행사를 도울 방법을 묻는 질문에 웬디가 몇 가지 할 일을
줄 것이라며 다른 이에게 문의하라는 것을 우회적으로 나타내고 있으므로
정답.

31
W-Am Did you remember to ask Hiroto to clean the air
conditioner?
M-Au (A) Don't forget the ceiling fans.
(B) I haven't seen him since yesterday.
(C) It is a bit cold in here.

잊지 않고 히로토에게 에어컨을 청소해달라고 하셨어요?
(A) 천장 선풍기를 잊지 마세요.
(B) 어제 이후로 그를 못 봤어요.
(C) 여기는 좀 추워요.

어휘 air conditioner 에어컨 ceiling 천장 fan 선풍기

해설 에어컨 청소 요청 여부를 묻는 조동사(Did) 의문문
(A) 연상 단어 오답. 질문의 remember에서 연상 가능한 forget을 이용한 오답.
(B) 정답. 히로토에게 에어컨을 청소해달라고 했는지 묻는 질문에 어제 이후로
그를 보지 못했다며 말할 기회가 없었음을 우회적으로 나타내고 있으므로
정답.
(C) 연상 단어 오답. 질문의 air conditioner에서 연상 가능한 cold를 이용한
오답.

PART 3

32-34

> W-Br　Hello. ³²**I made a reservation to hire a Montoya sedan from your company.** Here's the confirmation e-mail you sent me.
>
> M-Au　Thank you. OK, I see that you'll have the vehicle for two days. Here are the keys. Do you have any questions?
>
> W-Br　Yes. ³³**Is the satellite navigation system complicated? I've never used one before, so I'm a bit worried about whether I'll be able to figure it out.**
>
> M-Au　³⁴**It's fairly simple, but also—there's a user manual in the glove compartment.**
>
> W-Br　Oh, great. ³⁴**I'll take a look at that before I set off.**

> 여　안녕하세요. 귀사에서 몬토야 세단을 대여하기로 예약을 했어요. 여기 당신이 보내준 확인 이메일이 있어요.
>
> 남　고맙습니다. 네, 이틀 동안 차를 쓰실 거네요. 여기 열쇠입니다. 질문 있으세요?
>
> 여　네, 위성 내비게이션 시스템이 복잡한가요? 한 번도 써본 적이 없어서 과연 그것을 파악할 수 있을지 조금 걱정이 돼요.
>
> 남　상당히 간단하기도 하지만 앞좌석 보관함에 사용자 설명서도 있어요.
>
> 여　아, 다행이네요. 출발하기 전에 그것을 좀 살펴볼게요.

> 어휘　reservation 예약　hire 빌리다　confirmation 확인 satellite 위성　complicated 복잡한　figure out 알아내다 user manual 사용자 설명서　glove compartment (자동차 앞좌석의) 보관함　set off 출발하다

32

Where are the speakers?

(A) At a restaurant
(B) At a vacation resort
(C) At a conference center
(D) At a car rental agency

화자들은 어디에 있는가?

(A) 식당
(B) 휴양지 리조트
(C) 컨퍼런스 센터
(D) 자동차 대여점

해설　전체 내용 관련 – 대화의 장소

여자가 첫 대사에서 귀사에서 몬토야 세단을 대여하기로 예약을 했다(I made a reservation to hire a Montoya sedan from your company)고 한 것으로 보아 정답은 (D)이다.

▸▸ **Paraphrasing**　대화의 **hire a ~ sedan**
→ 정답의 **car rental**

33

What problem does the woman mention?

(A) She has misplaced a set of keys.
(B) She does not know how long a trip will take.
(C) She did not receive an e-mail.
(D) She is unsure about operating a device.

여자는 무슨 문제를 언급하는가?

(A) 열쇠 묶음을 잃어버렸다.
(B) 여행이 얼마나 오래 걸릴지 모른다.
(C) 이메일을 받지 못했다.
(D) 기기 작동에 대해 자신이 없다.

어휘　misplace 제자리에 두지 않다, 분실하다　receive 받다　unsure 자신 없는, 확신하지 못하는　operate 작동하다　device 장치[기구]

해설　세부 사항 관련 – 여자가 언급한 문제

여자가 두 번째 대사에서 위성 내비게이션 시스템이 복잡한지(Is the satellite navigation system complicated?)를 물으며, 한 번도 써본 적이 없어서 과연 그것을 파악할 수 있을지 조금 걱정이 된다(I've never used one before, so I'm a bit worried about whether I'll be able to figure it out)고 했으므로 정답은 (D)이다.

34

What does the woman say she will do?

(A) Check some instructions
(B) Use a storage compartment
(C) Make an initial payment
(D) Watch a video

여자는 무엇을 하겠다고 말하는가?

(A) 일부 지침을 확인한다.
(B) 보관함을 사용한다.
(C) 초기 지불을 한다.
(D) 동영상을 본다.

어휘　instruction 지시, 설명　storage compartment 보관함, 짐칸 initial 초기의　payment 지불

해설　세부 사항 관련 – 여자가 하겠다고 말하는 것

남자가 두 번째 대사에서 (기기 작동이) 상당히 간단하기도 하지만 앞좌석 사물함에 사용자 설명서도 있다(It's fairly simple, but also—there's a user manual in the glove compartment)고 설명하자, 여자가 출발하기 전에 그것을 좀 살펴보겠다(I'll take a look at that before I set off)고 했으므로 정답은 (A)이다.

▸▸ **Paraphrasing**　대화의 **a user manual**
→ 정답의 **instructions**

35-37

W-Br Excuse me, Norman. ³⁵**I'd like to speak with you about something after you receive the delivery today.**

M-Cn Oh, the delivery was this morning.

W-Br Ah, great! ³⁶**Well, the CEO wants to add a few more healthy dishes to our catering options.** What do you think about developing some soups?

M-Cn Hmm... I don't know. We'd have to invest in special containers to transport them. That might be costly.

W-Br Good point. But I don't want to give up on this idea yet. ³⁷**I'm going to get on the Internet and see what kinds of containers are available.**

여 실례합니다, 노먼 씨. 오늘 배송을 받으신 후에 말씀드리고 싶은 게 있어요.

남 아, 배송은 오늘 아침이었어요.

여 아, 잘됐네요! 대표이사님이 저희 음식 납품 목록에 건강에 좋은 음식을 몇 개 더 추가하기를 원하세요. 수프를 개발하는 것에 대해 어떻게 생각하세요?

남 음... 잘 모르겠어요. 그것들을 운반하려면 특별한 용기에 투자를 해야 할 거예요. 그건 비용이 많이 들 수도 있어요.

여 좋은 지적입니다. 하지만 아직 이 아이디어를 포기하고 싶지는 않네요. 인터넷에 접속해서 어떤 종류의 용기가 가능한지 알아봐야겠어요.

어휘 receive 받다 delivery 배송 add 추가하다 dish 요리 catering 음식 공급 option 선택(할 수 있는 것) develop 개발하다 invest 투자하다 container 용기 transport 수송하다 costly 비용이 드는 give up 포기하다 available 이용 가능한

35

고난도

What does the man mean when he says, "the delivery was this morning"?

(A) He needs to put away some stock.
(B) He is available to have a discussion.
(C) He does not require the woman's help.
(D) He is confused about a work schedule.

남자가 "배송은 오늘 아침이었어요"라고 말하는 의도는 무엇인가?
(A) 재고품을 치워야 한다.
(B) 이야기를 나누는 것이 가능하다.
(C) 여자의 도움이 필요하지 않다.
(D) 업무 일정에 대해 혼란스럽다.

어휘 stock 재고(품) confused 혼란스러운

해설 화자의 의도 파악 – 배송은 오늘 아침이었다는 말의 의도
여자가 첫 대사에서 오늘 배송을 받으신 후에 말씀드리고 싶은 게 있다(I'd like to speak with you about something after you receive the delivery today)고 하자 남자가 인용문을 언급했으므로, 배송은 이미 아침에 받았으니 지금 대화할 시간이 있다는 뜻으로 한 말임을 알 수 있다. 따라서 정답은 (B)이다.

36

According to the woman, what does the CEO want to do?

(A) Open a new branch
(B) Hire more servers
(C) Expand a menu
(D) Offer a discount

여자에 따르면, 대표이사는 무엇을 하기를 원하는가?
(A) 신규 지점 개점
(B) 웨이터 추가 고용
(C) 메뉴 확장
(D) 할인 제공

어휘 branch 지점 server 서빙하는 사람 expand 확장하다

해설 세부 사항 관련 – 대표이사가 하기를 원한다고 여자가 말하는 일
여자가 두 번째 대사에서 대표이사님이 저희 음식 납품 목록에 건강에 좋은 음식을 몇 개 더 추가하기를 원하신다(the CEO wants to add a few more healthy dishes to our catering options)고 했으므로 정답은 (C)이다.

▸▸ Paraphrasing 대화의 add a few more ~ dishes → 정답의 expand a menu

37

What does the woman decide to do?

(A) Share an idea with an executive
(B) Visit a competitor
(C) Conduct online research
(D) Make an official announcement

여자는 무엇을 하기로 결정하는가?
(A) 경영진과 아이디어 공유
(B) 경쟁사 방문
(C) 온라인 조사 실시
(D) 공식 발표

어휘 share 공유하다 executive 경영[운영]진 competitor 경쟁 상대 conduct 실시[수행]하다 official 공식의 announcement 발표

해설 세부 사항 관련 – 여자가 하기로 결정한 것
여자가 마지막 대사에서 인터넷에 접속해서 어떤 종류의 용기가 가능한지 알아봐야겠다(I'm going to get on the Internet and see what kinds of containers are available)고 했으므로 정답은 (C)이다.

▸▸ Paraphrasing 대화의 get on the Internet and see ~ → 정답의 conduct online research

38-40

W-Am ³⁸**Hi, this is Kathy in the IT department. How can I help you?**

M-Cn Hi, Kathy. I just started working here in the marketing department, and I'm having trouble logging into my work computer.

W- Am I see. Are you using the user name and password you were assigned at the orientation?

M- Cn Yes, and I double-checked those with HR, but ³⁹**whenever I enter them, the computer just freezes and then shuts down.**

W- Am That's strange. ⁴⁰**I'll send an employee up to take a look at it.** He'll be there in a few minutes.

여 여보세요. IT 부서의 캐시입니다. 무엇을 도와드릴까요?

남 안녕하세요, 캐시. 제가 이제 막 마케팅 부서에서 일하기 시작했는데 업무용 컴퓨터에 로그인하는 데 문제가 있어요.

여 그렇군요. 예비 교육에서 배정받은 사용자 이름과 암호를 사용하고 계신가요?

남 네, 인사부와도 이중으로 확인을 했는데, **그것들을 입력할 때마다 컴퓨터가 멈추고 꺼져버리네요.**

여 이상하네요. **직원을 보내서 살펴보게 할게요.** 그가 곧 그리로 갈 거예요.

어휘 department 부서 trouble 문제 password 비밀번호 assign 배정하다 orientation 예비 교육 HR 인사부 freeze (시스템 고장으로 컴퓨터 화면이) 멈추다 shut down (기계가) 멈추다 strange 이상한 employee 직원

38

Who most likely is the woman?

(A) An office receptionist
(B) A human resources manager
(C) An information technology technician
(D) A maintenance supervisor

여자는 누구일 것 같은가?

(A) 사무 접수원
(B) 인사 담당자
(C) IT 기사
(D) 유지 보수 관리자

해설 전체 내용 관련 – 여자의 직업
여자가 첫 대사에서 여보세요, IT 부서의 캐시입니다(Hi, this is Kathy in the IT department)라고 했고 무엇을 도와드릴지(How can I help you?)를 묻고 있는 것으로 보아 정답은 (C)이다.

39

What problem does the man have?

(A) He forgot a password.
(B) He missed an orientation.
(C) He cannot get into his office.
(D) His computer is malfunctioning.

남자에게 무슨 문제가 있는가?

(A) 비밀번호를 잊어버렸다.
(B) 예비 교육에 빠졌다.
(C) 사무실에 들어갈 수 없다.
(D) **컴퓨터가 제대로 작동하고 있지 않다.**

어휘 miss 놓치다 malfunctioning 오작동하는

해설 세부 사항 관련 – 남자가 겪고 있는 문제
남자가 두 번째 대사에서 그것들을 입력할 때마다 컴퓨터가 멈추고 꺼져버린다(whenever I enter them, the computer just freezes and then shuts down)고 했으므로 정답은 (D)이다.

▶▶ Paraphrasing 대화의 the computer freezes and shuts down → 정답의 his computer is malfunctioning

40

What will the woman probably do next?

(A) Go to pick up a machine
(B) Search for a publication
(C) Assign a task to a worker
(D) Approve a spending request

여자는 다음에 무엇을 하겠는가?

(A) 기계를 가지러 간다.
(B) 출판물을 검색한다.
(C) **작업자에게 업무를 할당한다.**
(D) 지출 요청을 승인한다.

어휘 publication 출판물 task 일 approve 승인하다 spending 지출

해설 세부 사항 관련 – 여자가 다음에 할 일
여자가 마지막 대사에서 직원을 보내서 살펴보게 하겠다(I'll send an employee up to take a look at it)고 했으므로 정답은 (C)이다.

▶▶ Paraphrasing 대화의 send an employee up to take a look → 정답의 assign a task to a worker

41-43

W- Am Hi, Terry. ⁴¹**I haven't seen you since you started fixing cars at Sheldon Auto.** Are you enjoying the job so far?

M- Au It could be better. I get along well with my coworkers, but ⁴²**I'm getting tired of the fifty-five-minute bus ride to work every day.**

W- Am That does sound frustrating. ⁴³**Well, I'm planning to go to a career fair at the community center this Saturday at two. Why don't you come with me?** You might find a job that suits you better.

M- Au That's not a bad idea at all. Would you like to get lunch first? I could pick you up at noon.

여	안녕하세요, 테리. **셸던 오토에서 자동차 수리를 시작한 이후로 만나지 못했네요.** 지금까지 일은 재미있나요?
남	약간 아쉬움이 있어요. 직장 동료들과는 잘 지내지만 **매일 출근하려고 55분씩 버스를 타는 데 지쳐가고 있어요.**
여	그것 참 힘들겠네요. 음, 제가 이번 주 토요일 2시에 주민 센터에서 열리는 취업 박람회에 갈 예정인데요. 저랑 같이 가시지 않을래요? 더 잘 맞는 일자리를 찾을지도 몰라요.
남	그거 괜찮은 생각인데요. 먼저 점심부터 드시겠어요? 제가 정오에 모시러 갈 수 있어요.

어휘	fix 수리하다 so far 지금까지 get along with ~와 잘 지내다 coworker 동료 ride (차량 등을) 타고 가기 frustrating 불만스러운 career fair 취업 박람회 community center 주민 센터 suit (~에게) 맞다

41

What most likely is the man's job?

(A) Vehicle mechanic
(B) Parking attendant
(C) Car salesperson
(D) Delivery driver

남자의 직업은 무엇일 것 같은가?

(A) 자동차 정비사
(B) 주차 안내원
(C) 자동차 판매사원
(D) 택배 기사

해설 전체 내용 관련 – 남자의 직업

여자가 첫 대사에서 남자에게 셸던 오토에서 자동차 수리를 시작한 이후로 만나지 못했다(I haven't seen you since you started fixing cars at Sheldon Auto)고 인사를 건네는 것으로 보아 정답은 (A)이다.

42

고난도

What does the man say he dislikes about his job?

(A) The lack of promotion opportunities
(B) The competitive colleagues
(C) The irregular finish time
(D) The long commute

남자는 자신의 직업에 대해 무엇이 마음에 들지 않는다고 말하는가?

(A) 승진 기회의 부족
(B) 경쟁심이 강한 동료들
(C) 불규칙적인 마감 시간
(D) 장거리 통근

어휘	lack 부족 promotion 승진 opportunity 기회 competitive 경쟁심이 강한 commute 통근

해설 세부 사항 관련 – 남자가 자신의 직업에 대해 싫어하는 점

남자가 첫 대사에서 매일 출근하려고 55분씩 버스를 타는 데 지쳐가고 있다(I'm getting tired of the fifty-five-minute bus ride to work every day)고 했으므로 정답은 (D)이다.

▸▸ Paraphrasing 대화의 **the fifty-five-minute bus ride to work** → 정답의 **the long commute**

43

What does the woman suggest that the man do?

(A) Submit an application form
(B) Accompany her to an event
(C) Speak to their mutual friend
(D) Read a job advertisement

여자는 남자에게 무엇을 하라고 제안하는가?

(A) 신청서를 제출할 것
(B) 행사에 자신과 동행할 것
(C) 서로 아는 친구와 이야기할 것
(D) 구인 광고를 읽을 것

어휘	submit 제출하다 application form 신청서 accompany 동행하다 mutual 상호 간의, 서로의

해설 세부 사항 관련 – 여자가 남자에게 하라고 제안하는 것

여자가 두 번째 대사에서 이번 주 토요일 2시에 주민 센터에서 열리는 취업 박람회에 갈 예정(I'm planning to go to a career fair at the community center this Saturday at two)이라면서, 같이 가지 않겠냐(Why don't you come with me?)고 권하고 있으므로 정답은 (B)이다.

▸▸ Paraphrasing 대화의 **come with me** → 정답의 **accompany her**

44-46 3인 대화

M-Cn	Hi, Olivia. Thanks for inviting us to your new home for this consultation. **44I'm James, and I'll be handling the decoration and arrangement of your living room and bedrooms.** This is my colleague, Joe.
M-Au	**44Hi, I'll be taking care of your bathrooms and kitchen.**
W-Br	It's a pleasure to meet the two of you. **45Uh, as you can see, I don't even have any furniture, so you'll really have a lot to do.**
M-Au	Well, we love a challenge! **46Now, why don't you show us around?** That way, we can get some ideas for how to begin.
W-Br	**46Sure.** Let's start with the upstairs rooms and work our way down.
M-Cn	Sounds good.

남1	안녕하세요, 올리비아. 이번 상담을 위해 새 집으로 초대해주셔서 고맙습니다. 저는 제임스이고, 거실과 침실의 장식과 정리를 담당할 겁니다. 이쪽은 제 동료 조입니다.
남2	안녕하세요, 저는 욕실과 부엌을 맡을 겁니다.
여	두 분을 만나뵙게 되어 기뻐요. 어, 보시다시피 가구조차 없어서 하실 일이 정말 많을 거예요.
남2	저희는 도전을 좋아합니다! 그럼, 저희를 안내해주시겠어요? 그렇게 하면, 어떻게 시작해야 할지 아이디어를 좀 얻을 수 있을 거예요.
여	물론이죠. 위층 방부터 시작해서 아래로 내려가도록 하죠.
남1	좋습니다.

어휘	consultation 상담 handle 다루다 decoration 장식
	arrangement 정리 colleague 동료 take care of
	~을 책임지고 떠맡다 bathroom 욕실 pleasure 기쁨
	challenge 도전 upstairs 위층

44

Who most likely are the men?

(A) City officials
(B) Real estate agents
(C) Interior decorators
(D) Event planners

남자들은 누구일 것 같은가?

(A) 시 공무원
(B) 부동산 중개인
(C) 실내 장식가
(D) 행사 기획자

해설 전체 내용 관련 – 남자들의 직업

첫 번째 남자는 첫 대사에서 본인이 제임스이고 거실과 침실의 장식과 정리를 담당할 것(I'm James, and I'll be handling the decoration and arrangement of your living room and bedrooms)이라고 했고, 두 번째 남자는 인사하면서 자신은 욕실과 부엌을 맡을 것(Hi, I'll be taking care of your bathrooms and kitchen)이라고 한 것으로 보아 정답은 (C)이다.

45

What does the woman mention about the property?

(A) It is currently unfurnished.
(B) It will also be used for business.
(C) It is located downtown.
(D) It is in need of repairs.

여자는 집에 대해 무엇을 언급하는가?

(A) 현재 가구가 비치되어 있지 않다.
(B) 사업용으로도 사용될 것이다.
(C) 시내에 위치해 있다.
(D) 수리가 필요하다.

어휘	property 부동산, 건물 currently 현재 unfurnished 가구가
	비치되어 있지 않은 located ~에 위치한 downtown 시내에

해설 세부 사항 관련 – 여자가 집에 대해 언급하는 것

여자가 첫 대사에서 보시다시피 가구조차 없어서 하실 일이 정말 많을 것(as you can see, I don't even have any furniture, so you'll really have a lot to do)이라고 한 것으로 보아 정답은 (A)이다.

> ▸▸ **Paraphrasing** 대화의 **I don't even have any furniture**
> → 정답의 **It is currently unfurnished**

46

What will the men probably do next?

(A) Show the woman some paperwork
(B) Unload some equipment
(C) Interview the woman
(D) Tour the residence

남자들은 다음에 무엇을 하겠는가?
(A) 여자에게 서류를 보여준다.
(B) 몇몇 장비를 내린다.
(C) 여자를 인터뷰한다.
(D) 거주지를 둘러본다.

어휘	paperwork 서류 unload (짐을) 내리다 equipment 장비
	residence 거주지

해설 세부 사항 관련 – 남자들이 다음에 할 일

두 번째 남자가 두 번째 대사에서 그럼 저희를 안내해주시겠냐(Now, why don't you show us around?)고 묻자 여자가 물론(Sure)이라고 했으므로 남자들은 여자의 안내로 집을 둘러볼 것임을 알 수 있다. 따라서 정답은 (D)이다.

47-49

W-Am	Peter, I just saw your e-mail. ⁴⁷**I'm sorry, but I won't be able to write that report by Friday. I have too many other tasks to take care of.**
M-Cn	Well, I really need that report this week. ⁴⁸**Could any of your other work be redistributed to your coworkers?**
W-Am	Hmm... ⁴⁸**Angelina could add the new client details to the database.** She's done that before, when I've gone on vacation.
M-Cn	OK. ⁴⁹**Let me check her schedule for the week.** If she's not too busy, I'll ask her to handle that. Will that give you enough time to write the report?
W-Am	Yes, I think it would.

여	피터, 방금 당신의 이메일을 봤어요. 미안하지만 금요일까지는 그 보고서를 쓸 수 없겠어요. 처리해야 할 다른 일이 너무 많아요.
남	어, 이번 주에 그 보고서가 꼭 필요해요. 당신의 다른 업무 중에서 동료에게 재배정할 수 있는 일이 있을까요?
여	흠… 안젤리나가 신규 고객 정보를 데이터베이스에 추가할 수 있어요. 제가 휴가 중일 때 그녀가 그 일을 했거든요.
남	네. 이번 주 그녀의 일정을 확인해볼게요. 그녀가 너무 바쁘지 않다면 내가 그녀에게 그것을 처리해달라고 요청할게요. 그러면 보고서를 작성할 시간이 충분할까요?
여	네, 그럴 것 같네요.

어휘	redistribute 재분배하다 coworker 동료 detail 세부
	사항 handle 다루다

47

Why does the woman say she is unable to accept an assignment?

(A) Her workload is too heavy.
(B) She does not have a necessary skill.
(C) It would violate a company policy.
(D) She is going out of town soon.

여자는 왜 임무를 수락할 수 없다고 말하는가?

(A) 업무량이 너무 많다.
(B) 필요한 기술이 없다.
(C) 회사 규정에 위배될 수 있다.
(D) 곧 외지로 나간다.

어휘 accept 수락하다 assignment 임무, 과제 workload 업무량
violate 위반하다 policy 규정

해설 세부 사항 관련 – 여자가 임무를 수락할 수 없다고 말하는 이유

여자가 첫 대사에서 미안하지만 금요일까지는 그 보고서를 쓸 수 없겠다(I'm sorry, but I won't be able to write that report by Friday)면서, 처리해야 할 다른 일이 너무 많다(I have too many other tasks to take care of)고 했으므로 정답은 (A)이다.

▶▶ Paraphrasing 대화의 I have too many other tasks
→ 정답의 Her workload is too heavy

48

What does the woman suggest asking Angelina to do?

(A) Provide some training
(B) Contact new clients
(C) Update a database
(D) Postpone a vacation

여자는 안젤리나에게 무엇을 부탁하라고 제안하는가?

(A) 교육을 시켜줄 것
(B) 신규 고객에게 연락할 것
(C) 데이터베이스를 업데이트할 것
(D) 휴가를 미룰 것

어휘 training 교육 postpone 미루다

해설 세부 사항 관련 – 여자가 안젤리나에게 부탁해달라고 제안한 일

남자가 첫 대사에서 당신의 다른 업무 중에서 동료에게 재배정할 수 있는 일이 있는지(Could any of your other work be redistributed to your coworkers?)를 묻자 여자가 안젤리나가 신규 고객 정보를 데이터베이스에 추가할 수 있다(Angelina could add the new client details to the database)고 했으므로 여자는 안젤리나에게 데이터베이스에 정보를 입력하는 일을 부탁할 것을 제안하고 있음을 알 수 있다. 따라서 정답은 (C)이다.

▶▶ Paraphrasing 대화의 add the new ~ details to the database → 정답의 update a database

49

What does the man say he will check?

(A) A building directory
(B) A work calendar
(C) A staff handbook
(D) A survey report

남자는 무엇을 확인하겠다고 말하는가?

(A) 건물 안내도
(B) 업무 일정표
(C) 직원 안내서
(D) 설문 조사 보고서

해설 세부 사항 관련 – 남자가 확인하겠다고 말하는 것

남자가 두 번째 대사에서 이번 주 그녀의 일정을 확인해보겠다(Let me check her schedule for the week)고 했으므로 정답은 (B)이다.

▶▶ Paraphrasing 대화의 her schedule
→ 정답의 a work calendar

50-52

M-Au	Hi, this is Scott Rubin. I ordered some posters from your store earlier this week. **50 Uh, I'm looking at the sample you sent me, and I don't think my company's logo is visible enough. Maybe dark blue wasn't a good choice for it.**
W-Am	OK, we can make it a lighter shade of blue. **51 I'll have my assistant do that this morning, and she'll e-mail you the revised sample this afternoon.** And since it's a minor change, there won't be any additional cost.
M-Au	Great. Oh, and one other thing—regarding the scheduled pick-up time tomorrow, can we make it one P.M. instead of eleven A.M.? **52 I have an early business lunch.**

남	여보세요, 스콧 루빈입니다. 이번 주 초에 당신의 가게에서 포스터를 주문했습니다. 음, 보내주신 샘플을 보고 있는데 우리 회사 로고가 충분히 또렷하게 보이지 않는 것 같네요. 아무래도 짙은 파란색이 좋은 선택이 아니었나 봅니다.
여	알겠습니다. 그 부분을 좀 더 밝은 파란색으로 해보겠습니다. 제 조수에게 오늘 아침에 그것을 해서 오후에 수정된 샘플을 이메일로 보내도록 하겠습니다. 그리고 사소한 변경이라서 추가 비용은 없을 겁니다.
남	잘됐네요. 아, 그리고 한 가지 더 있어요. 내일 픽업 예정 시간 말인데, 오전 11시 대신에 오후 1시로 할 수 있을까요? 제가 업무상 이른 점심 약속이 있어서요.

어휘	visible (눈에) 보이는, 뚜렷한 shade 색조 revised 수정된
	minor 작은[가벼운] regarding ~에 관하여

50 고난도

What is the man concerned about?

(A) The price of a service
(B) The quality of an image
(C) The color of a logo
(D) The size of an order

남자는 무엇에 대해 걱정하는가?

(A) 서비스의 가격
(B) 이미지의 품질
(C) 로고의 색상
(D) 주문품의 크기

해설 세부 사항 관련 – 남자의 우려 사항

남자가 첫 대사에서 보내주신 샘플을 보고 있는데 우리 회사 로고가 충분히 또렷하게 보이지 않는 것 같다(I'm looking at the sample you sent me, and I don't think my company's logo is visible enough)면서 아무래도 짙은 파란색이 좋은 선택이 아니었나 보다(Maybe dark blue wasn't a good choice for it)라고 했으므로 정답은 (C)이다.

51

What does the woman say her assistant will do this afternoon?

(A) Prepare a revised invoice
(B) Print additional copies
(C) Send a design electronically
(D) Pack up some posters

여자는 오늘 오후에 자신의 조수가 무엇을 할 것이라고 말하는가?
(A) 수정된 청구서 준비
(B) 추가 사본 인쇄
(C) 온라인으로 디자인 발송
(D) 포스터 포장

어휘 invoice 청구서 electronically 온라인으로 pack up 포장하다

해설 세부 사항 관련 – 여자가 오늘 오후 자신의 조수가 할 것이라고 말하는 일

여자가 첫 대사에서 자신의 조수에게 오늘 아침에 그렇게 해서 오후에 수정된 샘플을 이메일로 보내도록 하겠다(I'll have my assistant do that this morning, and she'll e-mail you the revised sample this afternoon)고 했으므로 정답은 (C)이다.

▸▸ Paraphrasing 대화의 e-mail you ~
→ 정답의 send ~ electronically

52

Why does the man want to change an appointment time?

(A) He has to attend a business gathering.
(B) His coworker is using a company car.
(C) He needs to pick up some clients.
(D) His office is scheduled to close early.

남자는 왜 약속 시간을 바꾸길 원하는가?
(A) 비즈니스 모임에 참석해야 한다.
(B) 동료가 회사 차량을 이용하고 있다.
(C) 고객을 몇 명 데려와야 한다.
(D) 사무실이 일찍 문을 닫을 예정이다.

어휘 gathering 모임

해설 세부 사항 관련 – 남자가 약속 시간을 바꾸길 원하는 이유

남자가 마지막 대사에서 업무상 이른 점심 약속이 있다(I have an early business lunch)고 했으므로 정답은 (A)이다.

▸▸ Paraphrasing 대화의 have an ~ business lunch
→ 정답의 attend a business gathering

53-55

M-Au 53Rachel, you know how our guests sometimes ask if we offer neighborhood tours? I'd like to try doing that. I think it would make their stay with us more memorable.

W-Br That's a great idea. 54So many fascinating events have happened around here— there would be a lot to talk about.

M-Au Exactly! 55So, do you think any of our workers could lead a tour, or should we try to find a professional tour guide?

W-Br Hmm... Well, Michael knows the area pretty well. And he's very outgoing. Why don't you mention the idea to him when he comes in for his shift?

남 레이첼, 손님들이 가끔 우리가 동네 관광을 해주는지 물어보는 거 아시죠? 그걸 시도해봤으면 해요. 우리 숙소에 머무는 것이 더 기억에 남게 할 수 있을 것 같아요.

여 멋진 생각이에요. 이 주변에서 매혹적인 일들이 아주 많이 일어났잖아요. 이야깃거리가 많을 거예요.

남 바로 그거예요! 그럼 우리 직원 중에 관광을 이끌 수 있는 사람이 있을까요, 아니면 전문 관광 가이드를 찾아봐야 할까요?

여 음, 마이클이 이 지역을 꽤 잘 알아요. 그리고 그는 매우 사교적이고요. 그가 교대 근무를 하러 올 때 그에게 그 생각을 말해보는 게 어때요?

어휘 neighborhood 근처 memorable 기억할 만한 fascinating 매력적인 professional 전문적인 pretty 꽤 outgoing 사교적인 shift 교대 근무 (시간)

53

What type of business do the speakers most likely work for?

(A) A movie theater
(B) A hotel
(C) A museum
(D) A travel agency

화자들은 무슨 종류의 사업에 종사할 것 같은가?
(A) 영화 극장
(B) 호텔
(C) 박물관
(D) 여행사

해설 전체 내용 관련 – 화자들의 직업

남자가 첫 대사에서 여자에게 손님들이 가끔 우리가 동네 관광을 해주는지 물어보는 것을 아는지(you know how our guests sometimes ask if we offer neighborhood tours?)를 물으며, 그걸 시도해봤으면 한다(I'd like to try doing that)고 했고, 우리 숙소에 머무는 것이 더 기억에 남게 할 수 있을 것 같다(I think it would make their stay with us more memorable)고 한 것으로 보아 화자들은 숙박 업체에서 근무하고 있음을 알 수 있다. 따라서 정답은 (B)이다.

54

What does the woman mention about the surrounding neighborhood?

(A) It has a new leisure facility.
(B) It has an interesting history.
(C) It has a confusing layout.
(D) It lacks parking.

여자는 주변 동네에 대해 무엇을 언급하는가?
(A) 새로운 레저 시설을 갖추고 있다.
(B) 흥미로운 역사가 있다.
(C) 구조가 복잡하다.
(D) 주차 공간이 부족하다.

어휘 facility 시설 confusing 혼란스러운 layout (건물 등의)
레이아웃[배치] lack ~이 부족하다

해설 세부 사항 관련 – 여자가 주변 동네에 대해 언급하는 것

여자가 첫 대사에서 이 주변에서 매혹적인 일들이 아주 많이 일어났다(So many fascinating events have happened around here)고 했고, 이야깃거리가 많을 것(there would be a lot to talk about)이라고 한 것으로 보아 정답은 (B)이다.

55

What does the woman imply when she says, "Michael knows the area pretty well"?

(A) It is surprising that Michael made a mistake.
(B) Michael might be able to answer a question.
(C) The man should not be concerned about a delay.
(D) She thinks Michael is suitable for a role.

여자가 "마이클이 이 지역을 꽤 잘 알아요"라고 말하는 의미는 무엇인가?
(A) 마이클이 실수했다는 것이 놀랍다.
(B) 마이클이 질문에 답할 수 있을지도 모른다.
(C) 남자가 지연에 대해 걱정하지 말아야 한다.
(D) 마이클이 역할에 적합하다고 생각한다.

해설 화자의 의도 파악 – 마이클이 이 지역을 꽤 잘 안다는 말의 의도

앞에서 남자가 우리 직원 중에 관광을 이끌 수 있는 사람이 있을지, 아니면 전문 관광 가이드를 찾아봐야 할지(do you think any of our workers could lead a tour, or should we try to find a professional tour guide?)를 여자에게 묻자 인용문을 언급한 것으로 보아, 관광을 이끌 사람으로 마이클을 추천하려는 의도로 한 말임을 알 수 있다. 따라서 정답은 (D)이다.

56-58 3인 대화

W-Br **56 Mr. Tarrant, many people are wondering what the best wireless earphones are these days. I'd like to review some of the most popular ones on our Web site.**

M-Cn **56 Great idea, Harumi!** That should increase our traffic. **57 But, can you work out an agreement with manufacturers to get some free items to review?** Our budget wouldn't allow us to buy them ourselves.

W-Br Oh, I'm not sure. I don't have many contacts in the electronics industry, actually.

M-Cn Well, Janelle used to cover that field. Janelle?

W-Am Yes, Mr. Tarrant?

M-Cn **58 Harumi needs some help with a new project. Could you sit down with her to talk it over?**

W-Am Absolutely. Is now a good time, Harumi?

여1 타랜트 씨, 요즘 가장 좋은 무선 이어폰이 무엇인지 궁금해하는 사람들이 많아요. 우리 웹사이트에서 가장 인기 있는 것들 중 몇 개를 평가하면 좋겠어요.

남 좋은 생각이에요, 하루미! 그러면 우리의 방문량이 늘어날 거예요. 하지만 평가할 무료 제품을 몇 가지 구할 수 있도록 제조업체와 협약을 맺을 수 있을까요? 우리 예산으로는 그것들을 직접 살 수 없을 거예요.

여1 아, 잘 모르겠어요. 사실 전 전자업계 쪽에 인맥이 많지 않거든요.

남 자넬이 그 분야를 관장했었죠. 자넬?

여2 네, 타랜트 씨?

남 하루미가 새로운 프로젝트에 도움을 필요로 해요. 그녀와 앉아서 얘기 좀 할 수 있나요?

여2 당연하죠. 지금 시간이 괜찮은가요, 하루미?

어휘 wonder 궁금해하다 wireless 무선의 traffic 방문량
work out ~을 해결하다 agreement 협의
manufacturer 제조사 budget 예산 contact 연줄(이
닿는 사람) electronics industry 전자 산업 cover 다루다
field 분야

56

What types of products does Harumi want to review?

(A) Security systems
(B) Digital cameras
(C) Game consoles
(D) Audio equipment

하루미는 어떤 종류의 제품을 평가하기를 원하는가?
(A) 보안 시스템
(B) 디지털 카메라
(C) 게임기
(D) 오디오 장비

해설 세부 사항 관련 – 하루미가 평가하기를 원하는 제품의 종류

첫 번째 여자가 남자에게 요즘 가장 좋은 무선 이어폰이 무엇인지 궁금해하는 사람들이 많다(Mr. Tarrant, many people are wondering what the best wireless earphones are these days)면서, 우리 웹사이트에서 가장 인기 있는 것들 중 몇 개를 평가하면 좋겠다(I'd like to review some of the most popular ones on our Web site)고 하자, 남자가 좋은 생각이에요, 하루미!(Great idea, Harumi!)이라고 답했으므로 첫 번째 여자가 하루미이고, 하루미는 무선 이어폰을 평가하길 원하고 있음을 알 수 있다. 따라서 정답은 (D)이다.

▶ Paraphrasing 대화의 earphones
→ 정답의 audio equipment

57

고난도

What does the man ask Harumi about?

(A) Determining some standards
(B) Encouraging readers to leave comments
(C) Clearing out a space for shipments
(D) Negotiating a deal with manufacturers

남자는 하루미에게 무엇에 대해 묻는가?
(A) 어떤 기준을 결정하는 일
(B) 독자들에게 댓글을 남기라고 장려하는 일
(C) 배송품을 위해 공간을 치우는 일
(D) 제조업체들과 협상하는 일

어휘 determine 결정하다 standard 기준, 표준 encourage
장려하다 comment 논평, 언급 space 공간 shipment 수송물
negotiate 협상하다 deal 거래

해설 세부 사항 관련 – 남자가 하루미에게 묻는 것
남자가 첫 대사에서 하루미의 이름을 부르면서 평가할 무료 제품을 몇 가지
구할 수 있도록 제조업체와 협약을 맺을 수 있는지(can you work out an
agreement with manufacturers to get some free items to review?)
를 묻고 있으므로 정답은 (D)이다.

▸▸ Paraphrasing 대화의 work out an agreement with
manufacturers
→ 정답의 negotiating a deal with
manufacturers

58

What does the man request that Janelle do?

(A) Monitor an online discussion
(B) Locate a project file
(C) Meet with a coworker
(D) Edit some articles

남자는 자넬에게 무엇을 하라고 요청하는가?
(A) 온라인 토론 모니터링
(B) 프로젝트 파일 찾기
(C) 동료와 만나기
(D) 일부 기사 편집

어휘 monitor 모니터[감시]하다 locate 찾다 coworker 동료 edit
편집하다 article 기사

해설 세부 사항 관련 – 남자가 자넬에게 하라고 요청한 것
남자가 두 번째 대사에서 자넬을 불렀고 자넬이 대답하자, 하루미가 새로운
프로젝트에 도움을 필요로 한다(Harumi needs some help with a new
project)면서 그녀와 앉아서 얘기를 할 수 있는지(Could you sit down with
her to talk it over?)를 묻고 있으므로 정답은 (C)이다.

▸▸ Paraphrasing 대화의 sit down with her to talk it over
→ 정답의 meet with a coworker

59-61

M-Cn	Veronica, I'd like your advice. Our gym's membership has been dropping over the last few months. **⁵⁹How could we bring in some new members?**
W-Am	**⁶⁰Let me think… well, we could try to advertise more.** Instead of just putting ads in the newspaper, we could also hand out flyers, put up posters, and so on.
M-Cn	I like it, but ⁶¹**I'm concerned about whether our funds can stretch that far**. The cost of regularly printing flyers and posters would add up pretty quickly.
W-Am	Good point. Oh, then how about social media? I don't know if that would be as effective, but it would certainly be cheaper.

남	베로니카, 조언 좀 해주세요. 우리 헬스클럽의 회원수가 지난 몇 달 동안 계속 떨어지고 있어요. **어떻게 하면 신규 회원들을 모집할 수 있을까요?**
여	**생각 좀 해볼게요… 글쎄요. 광고를 더 많이 할 수도 있어요.** 신문에만 광고하는 게 아니라 전단지를 나눠주고 포스터를 붙이는 등의 일도 할 수 있어요.
남	마음에 드는데, **우리 자금을 그렇게까지 늘릴 수 있을지 걱정돼요.** 정기적으로 전단지와 포스터를 인쇄하는 비용이 꽤 빨리 늘어날 거예요.
여	좋은 지적이예요. 아, 그럼 소셜 미디어는 어때요? 그게 효과적일지는 모르겠지만, 확실히 더 저렴할 거예요.

어휘 drop 떨어지다 bring in (장소·사업에) 유치하다 ad 광고
hand out 배포하다 flyer 전단지 concerned 걱정하는
fund 자금 stretch 늘리다 regularly 정기적으로
effective 효과적인 certainly 확실히

59

What does the man ask for the woman's advice on?

(A) Evaluating suppliers
(B) Recruiting volunteers
(C) Participating in conferences
(D) Attracting customers

남자는 무엇에 대해 여자의 조언을 구하는가?
(A) 공급업체 평가
(B) 자원봉사자 모집
(C) 컨퍼런스 참가
(D) 고객 유치

어휘 evaluate 평가하다 supplier 공급업체 recruit 모집하다
volunteer 자원봉사자 attract 끌어 모으다

해설 세부 사항 관련 – 남자가 여자의 조언을 구하는 것
남자가 첫 대사에서 어떻게 하면 신규 회원들을 모집할 수 있을지(How could
we bring in some new members?)를 묻고 있으므로 정답은 (D)이다.

60

What does the woman recommend?

(A) Relaxing some communication rules
(B) Analyzing posts on a Web platform
(C) Subscribing to a news source
(D) Increasing marketing activities

여자는 무엇을 추천하는가?
(A) 일부 의사소통 규칙의 완화
(B) 웹 플랫폼의 게시물 분석
(C) 뉴스 자료 구독
(D) 마케팅 활동 증가

어휘   relax 완화하다   communication 의사소통   rule 규칙   analyze
       분석하다   post 우편물, 게시물   subscribe to ~을 구독하다
       source 자료[(자료의) 출처]   increase 늘리다   activity 활동

해설   세부 사항 관련 - 여자의 추천 사항

여자가 첫 대사에서 광고를 더 많이 할 수도 있다(we could try to advertise
more)고 했으므로 정답은 (D)이다.

▸▸ Paraphrasing   대화의 **advertise more**
                   → 정답의 **increasing marketing activities**

61   고난도

Why is the man uncertain about the woman's
suggestion?

(A) A venue may not be available.
(B) A budget may not be large enough.
(C) A timeline cannot be extended.
(D) A law may not allow a change.

남자는 왜 여자의 제안에 대해 확신하지 못하는가?
(A) 장소를 이용하지 못할 수 있다.
(B) 예산이 충분하지 않을 수 있다.
(C) 일정을 연장할 수 없다.
(D) 법적으로 변경이 허용되지 않을 수 있다.

어휘   venue 장소   available 이용 가능한   budget 예산   timeline
       시각표, 일정   extend 연장하다   law 법   allow 허락하다

해설   세부 사항 관련 - 남자가 여자의 제안에 대해 확신하지 못하는 이유

남자가 두 번째 대사에서 우리 자금을 그렇게까지 늘릴 수 있을지 걱정된다
(I'm concerned about whether our funds can stretch that far)고 했으
므로 정답은 (B)이다.

▸▸ Paraphrasing   대화의 **funds** → 정답의 **a budget**
                   대화의 **stretch** → 정답의 **extended**

62-64 대화 + 지도

M-Au   Hello, Ms. Bailey? This is Tyler from
       Yenville Services. **⁶²I'm supposed to mow
       the lawn and pull up some weeds at your
       house this morning,** but I can't seem to
       find it.

W-Br   **⁶³OK—well, it's the white house on the
       corner of Flint and Poole, across from the
       bank.**

M-Au   Oh, really? That's the six hundred block.
       **⁶⁴Aren't you located at five-sixty-one Flint
       Street?**

W-Br   **⁶⁴Ah, no, I'm at six-fifty-one Flint Street.**

M-Au   Got it. Sorry for the confusion. I'll see you
       in a few minutes.

남   여보세요, 베일리 씨? 옌빌 서비스의 타일러입니다. 오늘 아침에
    당신의 집에서 잔디를 깎고 잡초를 뽑기로 되어 있는데 집을 찾을 수가
    없어요.

여   그래요. 음, 플린트 가와 풀 로 모퉁이에 있는 하얀 집이요. 은행
    건너편에 있어요.

남   아, 정말요? 거기는 600번 단지인데요. 플린트 가 561번지에 계신 거
    아니세요?

여   아, 아니요, 플린트 가 651번지에 있어요.

남   알겠습니다. 혼동해서 죄송해요. 몇 분 뒤 뵙겠습니다.

어휘   be supposed to ~하기로 되어 있다   mow (잔디를) 깎다
       lawn 잔디   weed 잡초   corner 모퉁이   across from
       ~의 맞은편에   located ~에 위치한   confusion 혼동

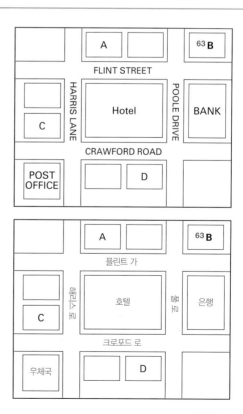

62

Who most likely is the man?

(A) A painter
(B) A gardener
(C) A caterer
(D) A repair person

남자는 누구일 것 같은가?

(A) 페인트공
(B) 정원사
(C) 음식 납품업자
(D) 수리공

해설　전체 내용 관련 – 남자의 직업

남자가 첫 대사에서 오늘 아침에 당신의 집에서 잔디를 깎고 잡초를 뽑기로 되어 있다(I'm supposed to mow the lawn and pull up some weeds at your house this morning)고 한 것으로 보아 정답은 (B)이다.

63

Look at the graphic. Where does the woman live?

(A) At Location A
(B) At Location B
(C) At Location C
(D) At Location D

시각 정보에 의하면, 여자는 어디에 살고 있는가?

(A) 위치 A
(B) 위치 B
(C) 위치 C
(D) 위치 D

해설　시각 정보 연계 – 여자의 거주 위치

여자가 첫 대사에서 은행 건너편 플린트 가와 풀 로 모퉁이에 있는 하얀 집으로 은행 건너편에 있다(it's the white house on the corner of Flint and Poole, across from the bank)라고 설명했고, 지도에 따르면 해당 위치는 B이므로 정답은 (B)이다.

64

What is the problem?

(A) A service has been canceled.
(B) The man had the wrong address.
(C) A road has been closed to traffic.
(D) The woman's house has been renovated.

무엇이 문제인가?

(A) 서비스가 취소되었다.
(B) 남자는 잘못된 주소를 갖고 있었다.
(C) 도로는 교통이 통제되었다.
(D) 여자의 집은 개조되었다.

어휘　cancel 취소하다　traffic 교통　renovate 개조[보수]하다

해설　세부 사항 관련 – 문제점

남자가 두 번째 대사에서 플린트 가 561번지에 계신 거 아니냐(Aren't you located at five-sixty-one Flint Street?)고 묻자 여자가 아니요, 플린트 가 651번지에 있어요(no, I'm at six-fifty-one Flint Street)라고 대답한 것으로 보아 남자는 주소를 잘못 알고 있었음을 알 수 있다. 따라서 정답은 (B)이다.

65-67 대화 + 광고

W-Br	Are you finding everything you need today, sir?
M-Cn	I have a question about these beautiful Shanter dinnerware sets, actually. **65 Can I use them to warm food up in the microwave?**
W-Br	Yes, all of the pieces are made of microwave-safe ceramic. And, as you can see, they're on sale right now. How large of a set are you thinking of getting?
M-Cn	Well, that sale makes me want to buy a big one. **66 But I really only need a four-person set.**
W-Br	Sure. You can always come back and buy more later.
M-Cn	Oh, really? Won't they be gone in a few months?
W-Br	**67 No—Shanter tends to offer the same designs for years.** You'll have time.

여	오늘 필요하신 건 다 찾고 계신가요, 손님?
남	사실 이 아름다운 샨터 식기 세트에 대해 질문이 있어요. **전자레인지에 음식을 데우는 데 써도 되나요?**
여	그럼요, 모든 식기들은 전자레인지에 안전한 세라믹으로 만들어졌어요. 그리고 보시다시피 지금 할인 중이랍니다. 얼마나 큰 세트를 사실 생각이세요?
남	음, 할인 때문에 큰 걸로 사고 싶어지네요. **하지만 실은 4인용 세트만 있으면 돼요.**
여	그러시죠. 나중에 언제든지 다시 오셔서 더 구입하실 수 있으세요.
남	아, 정말요? 몇 달 후면 없어지지 않을까요?
여	**아니요, 샨터는 몇 년 동안 같은 디자인을 제공하는 경향이 있어요.** 시간은 충분하실 거예요.

어휘	dinnerware 식기　warm up (음식을) 데우다　microwave 전자레인지　on sale 할인 중인　tend to ~하는 경향이 있다

Northside Home Goods

Sale on Shanter brand
❧ **floral dinnerware sets!** ❧

sets for 2 people: $5 off	66 sets for 4 people: $10 off	sets for 8+ people: $15 off

---

노스사이드 가정용품
샨터 브랜드 할인
❀ 꽃무늬 식기 세트! ❀

2인용
세트: 5달러
할인

⁶⁶ 4인용
세트: 10달러
할인

8인 이상
세트: 15달러
할인

65

What does the man want to know about the dinnerware sets?

(A) Why they are on sale
(B) How they should be washed
(C) How many pieces they include
(D) Whether they can be heated

남자는 식기 세트에 대해 무엇을 알고 싶어 하는가?
(A) 할인 중인 이유
(B) 세척 방법
(C) 포함되어 있는 제품의 개수
(D) 가열 가능 여부

해설 세부 사항 관련 – 남자가 식기 세트에 대해 알고 싶은 사항

남자가 첫 대사에서 전자레인지에 음식을 데우는 데 써도 되는지(Can I use them to warm food up in the microwave?)를 묻고 있으므로 정답은 (D)이다.

▸▸ **Paraphrasing** 대화의 **warm food up in the microwave** → 정답의 **they can be heated**

66

Look at the graphic. How much money will the man save?

(A) $5
(B) $10
(C) $15
(D) $20

시각 정보에 의하면, 남자는 얼마를 절약할 수 있는가?
(A) 5달러
(B) 10달러
(C) 15달러
(D) 20달러

해설 시각 정보 연계 – 남자가 절약할 수 있는 금액

남자가 두 번째 대사에서 실은 4인용 세트만 있으면 된다(I really only need a four-person set)고 했고, 광고에 따르면 4인용 세트는 10달러를 할인 받을 수 있으므로 정답은 (B)이다.

67 〔고난도〕

What does the woman say about Shanter's products?

(A) They are easy to return.
(B) They are designed to be long-lasting.
(C) They are not offered by many retailers.
(D) They are not discontinued often.

여자는 샨터의 제품에 대해 무엇을 말하는가?
(A) 반품하기 쉽다.
(B) 오래가도록 디자인되었다.
(C) 많은 소매업자들에 의해 제공되지 않는다.
(D) 자주 단종되지 않는다.

어휘 return 돌려주다 long-lasting 오래가는 offer 제공하다
retailer 소매업자 discontinue 중단하다

해설 세부 사항 관련 – 여자가 샨터의 제품에 대해 말하는 것

여자가 마지막 대사에서 샨터는 몇 년 동안 같은 디자인을 제공하는 경향이 있다(Shanter tends to offer the same designs for years)고 했으므로 정답은 (D)이다.

▸▸ **Paraphrasing** 대화의 **offer the same designs for years** → 정답의 **not discontinued often**

68-70 대화 + 출발 안내 전광판

M-Au Good morning, Nobuko. I got to the station a little early, so I bought you a coffee.

W-Am Oh, thank you, Jay!

M-Au No problem. Are you all ready to present to our clients?

W-Am Absolutely. ⁶⁸ **I have the presentation file on a portable storage drive, and I also e-mailed it to myself, just in case.** So, what platform are we leaving from?

M-Au Let's check the departure board... ⁶⁹ **Oh no, our train is delayed by a half an hour!**

W-Am How annoying! Well, the presentation isn't until after lunch, so we should still be on time. ⁷⁰ **Why don't we go over our presentation strategy again while we wait?**

남 좋은 아침입니다, 노부코. 역에 조금 일찍 도착해서 커피를 한 잔 사왔어요.

여 오, 고마워요, 제이!

남 무슨 말씀을요. 우리 고객들에게 발표할 준비는 다 되었나요?

여 당연하죠. 휴대용 저장 드라이브에 발표 파일이 있고, 혹시나 해서 제 계정으로 이메일도 보내뒀어요. 그럼, 어느 플랫폼에서 출발하는 거죠?

남 출발 안내 전광판을 확인해보죠… 이런, 우리 열차가 30분 연착됐어요!

여 짜증나네요! 음, 발표가 점심시간 이후이니까 아직 시간은 맞출 수 있을 거예요. 기다리는 동안 발표 전략을 다시 한번 검토해볼까요?

어휘 present 발표하다 absolutely 물론 portable 휴대용의 storage 저장 departure 출발 board 게시판 delay 지연시키다 annoying 짜증스러운 strategy 전략

Destination	Scheduled Departure	Status
[69]Detroit	07:35	Delayed (30 minutes)
Indianapolis	07:55	On Time
Toledo	08:15	Delayed (45 minutes)
Milwaukee	08:25	Delayed (2 hours)

목적지	예정 출발 시간	상황
[69]디트로이트	07:35	연착 (30분)
인디애나폴리스	07:55	정시
톨레도	08:15	연착 (45분)
밀워키	08:25	연착 (2시간)

68

What does the woman say she has brought?

(A) A computer accessory
(B) Some refreshments
(C) Some gifts
(D) A printout

여자는 무엇을 가져왔다고 말하는가?

(A) 컴퓨터 소품
(B) 다과
(C) 선물
(D) 인쇄물

해설 세부 사항 관련 – 여자가 가져왔다고 말하는 것

여자가 두 번째 대사에서 휴대용 저장 드라이브에 발표 파일이 있고, 혹시나 해서 제 계정으로 이메일도 보내뒀다(I have the presentation file on a portable storage drive, and I also e-mailed it to myself, just in case)고 했으므로 정답은 (A)이다.

▸▸ Paraphrasing 대화의 a portable storage drive → 정답의 a computer accessory

69

Look at the graphic. What is the speakers' destination?

(A) Detroit
(B) Indianapolis
(C) Toledo
(D) Milwaukee

시각 정보에 의하면, 화자들의 목적지는 어디인가?

(A) 디트로이트
(B) 인디애나폴리스
(C) 톨레도
(D) 밀워키

해설 시각 정보 연계 – 화자들의 목적지

남자가 세 번째 대사에서 우리 열차가 30분 연착됐다(our train is delayed by a half an hour!)고 했고, 출발 안내 전광판에 따르면 30분 연착된 기차는 디트로이트행 기차이므로 정답은 (A)이다.

70

What does the woman suggest doing?

(A) Making a phone call
(B) Reviewing some plans
(C) Going to a departure platform
(D) Reserving some accommodations

여자는 무엇을 하자고 제안하는가?

(A) 전화 걸기
(B) 몇몇 계획의 검토
(C) 출발 플랫폼으로 가기
(D) 숙소 예약

어휘 review 검토하다 reserve 예약하다 accommodation 숙소

해설 세부 사항 관련 – 여자의 제안 사항

여자가 마지막 대사에서 기다리는 동안 발표 전략을 다시 한번 검토해보자(Why don't we go over our presentation strategy again while we wait?)고 제안하고 있으므로 정답은 (B)이다.

▸▸ Paraphrasing 대화의 go over → 정답의 reviewing

PART 4

71-73 전화 메시지

M-Au Hello, Ms. Singh. This is Matt Miller calling from Wells Beaumont UK. [71]**Thank you for your interest in our senior laboratory researcher position. I'm happy to say that you are one of just a few candidates that we have chosen to move forward with.** [72]**We like that you've already been successfully managing teams of researchers and technicians for several years, as proven leadership ability is required for the role.** So, we would like you to come in for an interview next Tuesday at 9 A.M. [73]**Please call me back at your earliest convenience so that we can confirm this arrangement.** Thank you.

안녕하십니까, 싱 씨. 웰스 보몽 영국 지사의 매트 밀러입니다. 우리 수석 실험실 연구원 자리에 관심을 가져주셔서 감사합니다. 당신이 우리가 다음 단계를 위해 선택한 몇 안 되는 후보 중 한 명이라는 것을 알려드리게 되어 기쁘게 생각합니다. 이 역할에는 입증된 리더십 능력이 요구되기 때문에, 우리는 당신이 이미 몇 년간 연구자와 기술자들로 구성된 팀을 성공적으로 관리해왔다는 점이 마음에 듭니다. 그래서 다음 주 화요일 오전 9시에 면접을 보러 와주셨으면 합니다. 우리가 이 계획을 확정할 수 있도록 가능한 한 빨리 전화 회신을 주시기 바랍니다. 고맙습니다.

71

Who most likely is the listener?

(A) A job applicant
(B) A reference provider
(C) An external recruiter
(D) A career coach

청자는 누구일 것 같은가?

(A) **구직자**
(B) 추천서 제공자
(C) 외부 채용 담당자
(D) 진로 지도자

어휘 applicant 지원자 reference 추천서 provider 제공자
external 외부의 recruiter 모집자 career 진로, 경력 coach
지도자, 코치

해설 전체 내용 관련 – 청자의 신분
화자가 초반부에 우리 수석 실험실 연구원 자리에 관심을 가져주셔서 감사하다(Thank you for your interest in our senior laboratory researcher position)면서, 당신이 우리가 다음 단계를 위해 선택한 몇 안 되는 후보 중 한 명이라는 것을 알려드리게 되어 기쁘게 생각한다(I'm happy to say that you are one of just a few candidates that we have chosen to move forward with)고 했으므로 정답은 (A)이다.

72

`고난도`

What does the speaker say the listener has?

(A) Relevant experience
(B) A large number of contacts
(C) A sample legal agreement
(D) Generous funding

화자는 청자에게 무엇이 있다고 말하는가?

(A) **관련 경력**
(B) 다수의 인맥
(C) 법률 계약서 견본
(D) 넉넉한 자금

어휘 relevant 관련이 있는 legal 법률과 관련된 agreement 계약서,
합의 generous 넉넉한 funding 자금

해설 세부 사항 관련 – 화자가 청자에게 있다고 말하는 것
화자가 중반부에 이 역할에는 입증된 리더십 능력이 요구되기 때문에, 우리는 당신이 이미 몇 년간 연구자와 기술자들로 구성된 팀을 성공적으로 관리해왔다는 점이 마음에 든다(We like that you've already been successfully managing teams of researchers and technicians for several years, as proven leadership ability is required for the role)고 했으므로 정답은 (A)이다.

73

What does the speaker ask the listener to do?

(A) Submit a document
(B) Return his call
(C) Visit a Web site
(D) Confirm some data

화자는 청자에게 무엇을 하라고 요청하는가?

(A) 서류 제출
(B) **전화 회신**
(C) 웹사이트 방문
(D) 데이터 확인

어휘 submit 제출하다 document 서류 confirm 확인하다

해설 세부 사항 관련 – 화자의 요청 사항
화자가 마지막에 우리가 이 계획을 확정할 수 있도록 가능한 한 빨리 전화 회신을 주시기 바란다(Please call me back at your earliest convenience so that we can confirm this arrangement)고 했으므로 정답은 (B)이다.

▸▸ Paraphrasing 담화의 call me back
→ 정답의 return his call

74-76 회의 발췌

W-Am Good morning, team. ⁷⁴**Today we begin development of our new range of office chairs.** ⁷⁵**Now, according to our market research data, office workers are looking for more comfortable chairs.** Because they sit at their desks for several hours a day, they prefer ergonomic seats that will reduce muscle and joint pain. So that will be the focus of this line. I know that some of you are familiar with this kind of design, but I want everyone to have an in-depth understanding as we begin this project. ⁷⁶**So, I've hired an expert in ergonomics to come in and speak to us today.** She'll be here in about an hour.

좋은 아침입니다, 팀 여러분. 오늘 우리는 새로운 사무용 의자들을 개발하기 시작합니다. 현재 우리의 시장 조사 자료에 따르면, 회사원들은 더 편한 의자를 찾고 있습니다. 하루에 몇 시간씩 책상에 앉아 있기 때문에, 근육과 관절 통증을 줄여줄 인체공학적 좌석을 선호합니다. 그래서 이것이 이 제품군의 주안점이 될 겁니다. 이런 디자인에 익숙한 사람도 일부 있다는 것은 알지만 이 프로젝트를 시작하면서 저는 모두가 깊이 있는 이해를 갖추기를 바랍니다. 그래서 오늘 인체공학 전문가를 영입해 이곳을 방문해서 우리와 이야기를 나눌 수 있도록 했습니다. 그녀는 한 시간쯤 있으면 올 겁니다.

어휘 development 개발 comfortable 편한 prefer 선호하다
ergonomic 인체공학의 reduce 줄이다 muscle 근육 joint 관절
pain 통증 familiar 익숙한 in-depth 깊이 있는 understanding
이해 expert 전문가

74

What product does the speaker's company sell?

(A) Automobiles
(B) Electronics
(C) Furniture
(D) Luggage

화자의 회사는 어떤 제품을 판매하는가?

(A) 자동차
(B) 전자제품
(C) 가구
(D) 짐 가방

해설　세부 사항 관련 – 화자의 회사에서 판매하는 제품
화자가 도입부에 오늘 우리는 새로운 사무용 의자들을 개발하기 시작한다 (Today we begin development of our new range of office chairs)고 했으므로 정답은 (C)이다.

➤➤ **Paraphrasing**　담화의 **office chairs** → 정답의 **furniture**

75

What does the company's target market want?

(A) Better durability
(B) Increased comfort
(C) Improved safety
(D) Reduced cost

회사의 목표 시장은 무엇을 원하는가?

(A) 내구성 향상
(B) 편안함 향상
(C) 안전성 향상
(D) 비용 절감

어휘　durability 내구성　increased 증가된　comfort 편안함
improved 개선된　safety 안전

해설　세부 사항 관련 – 회사의 목표 시장이 원하는 사항
화자가 초반부에 현재 우리의 시장 조사 자료에 따르면, 회사원들은 더 편한 의자를 찾고 있다(according to our market research data, office workers are looking for more comfortable chairs)고 했으므로 정답은 (B)이다.

➤➤ **Paraphrasing**　담화의 **more comfortable** → 정답의 **increased comfort**

76

What does the speaker say she has done?

(A) Employed a consultant
(B) Ordered some materials
(C) Talked to a facility manager
(D) Made a list of features

화자는 무엇을 했다고 말하는가?

(A) 자문 위원 고용
(B) 일부 자재 주문
(C) 시설 관리자와 대화
(D) 특징 목록 작성

어휘　employ 고용하다　consultant 자문 위원　order 주문하다
material 자재　facility 시설　feature 특징

해설　세부 사항 관련 – 화자가 했다고 말하는 것
화자가 후반부에 오늘 인체공학 전문가를 영입해 이곳을 방문해서 우리와 이야기를 나눌 수 있도록 했다(I've hired an expert in ergonomics to come in and speak to us today)고 했으므로 정답은 (A)이다.

➤➤ **Paraphrasing**　담화의 **hired an expert**
→ 정답의 **Employed a consultant**

77-79 전화 메시지

M-Cn Hi, Catherine, this is David. [77]**I'm calling about your trip to San Francisco this Thursday for the skills development workshop.** [78]**As you know, you were given special permission to turn in the travel request form on very short notice, several days after the usual deadline.** Luckily, we've still been able to accommodate most of your preferences—except one. [79]**You asked to take Coastal Airlines because of your rewards membership, but I've booked you on West Coast Air instead.** West Coast Air flies direct to San Francisco, and [79]**it's our policy to book direct flights when possible.** I hope you understand.

여보세요, 캐서린, 데이비드예요. 능력 계발 워크숍 때문에 이번 주 목요일 샌프란시스코로 가는 출장 건으로 전화했어요. 아시다시피, 평소 마감일이 며칠 지난 후 출장 신청서를 촉박하게 제출할 수 있도록 특별 허가를 받으셨어요. 다행히도 우리는 한 가지를 제외하고는 당신의 선호 사항 대부분을 수용할 수 있었어요. 멤버십 포인트 때문에 코스탈 항공을 이용하겠다고 요청하셨지만 웨스트 코스트 항공으로 대신 예약했어요. 웨스트 코스트 항공은 샌프란시스코 직항편이 있어요. 직항이 있을 시 직항편을 예약하는 것이 저희 방침이고요. 이해해주시기를 바랍니다.

어휘　permission 허가　turn in 제출하다　on short notice 급히, 촉박하게　accommodate 수용하다　preference 선호
reward 보상　direct flight 직항편

77

What event will the listener attend on Thursday?

(A) A trade exposition
(B) A recruitment fair
(C) A training workshop
(D) A grand opening

목요일에 청자는 무슨 행사에 참석할 것인가?

(A) 무역 박람회
(B) 채용 박람회
(C) 교육 워크숍
(D) 개업식

해설 세부 사항 관련 – 청자가 목요일에 참석할 행사

화자가 초반부에 능력 계발 워크숍 때문에 이번 주 목요일 샌프란시스코로 가는 출장 건으로 전화했다(I'm calling about your trip to San Francisco this Thursday for the skills development workshop)고 한 것으로 보아 정답은 (C)이다.

▸▸ Paraphrasing 담화의 the skills development workshop
→ 정답의 a training workshop

78 고난도

What does the speaker say about a form?
(A) It is incomplete.
(B) It was submitted relatively late.
(C) It includes an unusual request.
(D) It has been misplaced.

화자는 양식에 대해 무엇을 말하는가?
(A) 불완전하다.
(B) 비교적 늦게 제출되었다.
(C) 특이한 요청이 포함되어 있다.
(D) 분실되었다.

어휘 incomplete 불완전한 misplace 제자리에 두지 않다, 분실하다

해설 세부 사항 관련 – 화자가 양식에 대해 말하는 것

화자가 중반부에 아시다시피 평소 마감일이 며칠 지난 후 출장 신청서를 촉박하게 제출할 수 있도록 특별 허가를 받으셨다(As you know, you were given special permission to turn in the travel request form on very short notice, several days after the usual deadline)고 한 것으로 보아 정답은 (B)이다.

▸▸ Paraphrasing 담화의 turn in → 정답의 submitted

79 고난도

Why does the speaker say, "West Coast Air flies direct to San Francisco"?
(A) To point out a mistake that he discovered
(B) To answer a question about an itinerary
(C) To suggest an alternative travel option
(D) To explain why he made a decision

화자가 "웨스트 코스트 항공은 샌프란시스코 직항편이 있어요"라고 말하는 이유는 무엇인가?
(A) 그가 발견한 실수를 지적하려고
(B) 여행 일정에 대한 질문에 답하려고
(C) 대체 여행 선택 사항을 제안하려고
(D) 결정을 내린 이유를 설명하려고

어휘 itinerary 여행 일정 alternative 대안의; 대안

해설 화자의 의도 파악 – 웨스트 코스트 항공은 샌프란시스코 직항편이 있다고 말한 의도

청자는 코스탈 항공을 이용하겠다고 요청했지만 화자가 웨스트 코스트 항공으로 대신 예약했다(You asked to take Coastal Airlines ~ but I've booked you on West Coast Air instead)며, 직항이 있을 시 직항을 예약하는 것이 방침(it's our policy to book direct flights when possible)이라고 했으므로 인용문은 요청과 다르게 항공편을 예약한 이유를 설명하려는 의도임을 알 수 있다. 따라서 정답은 (D)이다.

80-82 광고

W-Br It's the middle of May, and that means it's time for Castleford's weeklong "Screenings Under the Stars" festival. ⁸⁰**Every evening from May eighteenth through twenty-fourth, the city will be showing a classic film on a large outdoor screen at Spruce Park.** No tickets are necessary. ⁸¹**Simply come to the west side of the park with something comfortable to sit on.** Food trucks will be available each night from seven P.M., and the film will be introduced by an expert at eight. Don't miss this chance to enjoy classic cinema in a unique setting! ⁸²**To learn which films will be shown, visit our Web site, www.castleford-sus. com.** We hope to see you under the stars!

지금은 5월 중순이고, 그 말은 일주일간 열리는 캐슬포드의 "별 아래 영화 상영" 축제 기간이라는 뜻입니다. 5월 18일부터 24일까지 매일 저녁, 도시는 스프루스 공원의 대형 야외 스크린에 명작 영화를 상영할 예정입니다. 표는 필요하지 않습니다. 그냥 편하게 앉을 수 있는 것을 들고 공원의 서쪽으로 오세요. 푸드 트럭은 매일 밤 7시부터 이용할 수 있으며, 8시에 전문가가 영화를 소개할 것입니다. 독특한 장소에서 명작 영화를 감상할 수 있는 이 기회를 놓치지 마세요! 어떤 영화가 상영될 것인지 알아보려면, 저희 웹사이트 www.castleford-sus.com을 방문하세요. 별 아래에서 여러분을 만나뵙기 바랍니다!

어휘 weeklong 1주일에 걸친 screening (영화) 상영 classic 명작, 고전 outdoor 야외의 necessary 필요한 comfortable 편한 available 이용 가능한 introduce 소개하다 expert 전문가 chance 기회 unique 독특한 setting 장소[환경]

80

What type of event is the speaker advertising?
(A) An outdoor concert
(B) A movie festival
(C) A street parade
(D) A sports tournament

화자는 어떤 종류의 행사를 광고하고 있는가?
(A) 야외 음악회
(B) 영화 축제
(C) 거리 행진
(D) 스포츠 경기

해설 세부 사항 관련 – 화자가 광고 중인 행사

화자가 초반부에 5월 18일부터 24일까지 매일 저녁 도시는 스프루스 공원의 대형 야외 스크린에 명작 영화를 상영할 예정(Every evening from May eighteenth through twenty-fourth, the city will be showing a classic film on a large outdoor screen at Spruce Park)이라고 했으므로 정답은 (B)이다.

81

What are listeners encouraged to do?

(A) Try a special kind of food
(B) Wear warm clothing
(C) Bring their own seating
(D) Use public transportation

청자들은 무엇을 하라고 권장되는가?
(A) 특별한 종류의 음식을 먹어볼 것
(B) 따뜻한 옷을 입을 것
(C) 자신의 좌석을 가져올 것
(D) 대중교통을 이용할 것

어휘 seating 좌석 public transportation 대중교통

해설 세부 사항 관련 – 청자들이 하라고 권장되는 일

화자가 중반부에 그냥 편하게 앉을 수 있는 것을 들고 공원의 서쪽으로 오라(Simply come to the west side of the park with something comfortable to sit on)고 권하고 있으므로 정답은 (C)이다.

▸▸ **Paraphrasing** 담화의 **something ~ to sit on**
→ 정답의 **bring their own seating**

82

Why should listeners visit a Web site?

(A) To become a volunteer worker
(B) To download a map of a venue
(C) To see an entertainment lineup
(D) To purchase tickets in advance

청자들은 왜 웹사이트를 방문해야 하는가?
(A) 자원봉사자가 되기 위해
(B) 장소의 지도를 다운로드하기 위해
(C) 상영물 일정표를 보기 위해
(D) 표를 미리 구입하기 위해

어휘 venue 장소 entertainment 오락(물) lineup (행사 등의) 예정표 purchase 구매하다 in advance 미리

해설 세부 사항 관련 – 청자들이 웹사이트를 방문해야 하는 이유

화자가 후반부에 어떤 영화가 상영될 것인지 알아보려면 저희 웹사이트 www.castleford-sus.com을 방문하라(To learn which films will be shown, visit our Web site, www.castleford-sus.com)고 했으므로 정답은 (C)이다.

▸▸ **Paraphrasing** 담화의 **films** → 정답의 **entertainment**

83-85 회의 발췌

> W-Am **83I'd like to give you all an update on the project to add a new wing to the community center.** As you know, we're currently collecting funding donations from local businesses. **84Well, I'm happy to say that we've already received more than sixty thousand dollars, and** we're still waiting for Joslyn Associates! **84It looks like we will easily meet our fund-raising goal.** This

> is great, because it means that construction can start on time and probably finish in early summer. **85I had been concerned about the August storms causing delays.**

> 주민 센터에 새로운 별관을 추가하기 위한 프로젝트에 대한 최신 정보를 모두에게 알려드리고자 합니다. 아시다시피, 우리는 현재 지역 사업체로부터 자금 기부를 받고 있습니다. 벌써 6만 달러 이상을 받았다고 말씀드리게 되어 기쁘며, 아직 조슬린 어소시에이츠를 기다리고 있습니다! 모금 목표를 쉽게 달성할 것 같습니다. 이는 공사가 제때 시작되어 아마 초여름에 끝날 수 있다는 것을 의미하기 때문에 대단한 일입니다. 저는 지연의 원인이 되는 8월의 태풍에 대해 걱정했거든요.

어휘 add 추가하다 wing 부속 건물 community center 주민 센터 currently 현재 collect 모으다 funding 자금 donation 기부 local 지역의 receive 받다 fund-raising 모금 goal 목표 construction 공사 probably 아마 concerned 걱정하는 cause ~을 야기하다 delay 지연

83 [고난도]

What is being discussed?

(A) A park restoration
(B) A building expansion
(C) An educational program
(D) An election campaign

무엇이 논의되고 있는가?
(A) 공원 복구
(B) 건물 확장
(C) 교육 프로그램
(D) 선거 운동

해설 전체 내용 관련 – 담화의 주제

화자가 도입부에 주민 센터에 새로운 별관을 추가하기 위한 프로젝트에 대한 최신 정보를 모두에게 알려주고자 한다(I'd like to give you all an update on the project to add a new wing to the community center)고 했으므로 정답은 (B)이다.

▸▸ **Paraphrasing** 담화의 **add a new wing to the community center** → 정답의 **a building expansion**

84 [고난도]

What does the speaker imply when she says, "we're still waiting for Joslyn Associates"?

(A) She is worried that a deadline will not be met.
(B) She is unable to grant a request at this time.
(C) Joslyn Associates will contribute to an initiative.
(D) Joslyn Associates has a lot of influence in the city.

화자가 "아직 조슬린 어소시에이츠를 기다리고 있습니다"라고 말하는 의미는 무엇인가?
(A) 마감일이 지켜지지 않을까 걱정한다.
(B) 현재 요청을 승인할 수 없다.
(C) 조슬린 어소시에이츠가 계획에 기여할 것이다.
(D) 조슬린 어소시에이츠는 도시에 많은 영향력을 갖고 있다.

어휘 deadline 마감 시한 grant 승인하다 request 요청 contribute to ~에 기여하다 initiative 계획 influence 영향(력)

해설 화자의 의도 파악 – 아직 조슬린 어소시에이츠를 기다리고 있다는 말의 의도

화자가 앞에서 벌써 6만 달러 이상을 기부 받았다고 말씀드리게 되어 기쁘다(I'm happy to say that we've already received more than sixty thousand dollars)고 하면서 인용문을 언급했고, 인용문 뒤에서 모금 목표를 쉽게 달성할 것 같다(It looks like we will easily meet our fund-raising goal)고 한 것으로 보아 조슬린 어소시에이츠라는 업체에서도 프로젝트에 기부를 할 예정임을 알리려는 의도로 한 말임을 알 수 있다. 따라서 정답은 (C)이다.

85

What was the speaker concerned about before?

(A) Expensive permit fees
(B) A shortage of personnel
(C) Negative public opinion
(D) Poor seasonal weather

화자는 전에 무엇을 걱정했는가?

(A) 비싼 허가 수수료
(B) 인력 부족
(C) 부정적 여론
(D) 안 좋은 계절성 날씨

어휘 permit 허가증 fee 수수료 shortage 부족 personnel 직원들 negative 부정적인 public 대중의 seasonal 계절적인

해설 세부 사항 관련 – 화자가 전에 걱정한 것

화자가 마지막에 지연의 원인이 되는 8월의 태풍에 대해 걱정했다(I had been concerned about the August storms causing delays)고 했으므로 정답은 (D)이다.

▸▸ Paraphrasing 담화의 August storms
→ 정답의 poor seasonal weather

86-88 방송

W-Br **86 Hi everyone, and welcome to another week of** *Unwritten*, **the podcast about the lives of great novelists**. Today, we're going to talk about Dorothy Pearson, the genius who wrote *Rose Branches* when she was just twenty years old. But first, I need to say something about last week's episode on Joong-Soo Ahn. **87 Yes, you heard that right—it's "Joong-Soo", not "Juhng-Soo", which is what I called him throughout the episode. I'm sorry about that.** Some very kind listeners alerted me to the mistake through the show's social media accounts. **88 I hope that all of you will let me know when I've gotten something wrong like that.** I always appreciate it.

안녕하세요 여러분, 이번 주에도 위대한 소설가들의 삶을 다루는 팟캐스트 〈언리튼〉을 찾아주신 것을 환영합니다. 오늘은 갓 스무 살 때 〈장미나무 가지〉를 쓴 천재 도로시 피어슨에 대해 이야기해볼 겁니다. 하지만 먼저, 지난주에 다뤘던 안 중수에 대한 에피소드에 대해 말씀드릴 것이 있습니다. 네, 제대로 들으셨습니다. 제가 에피소드 내내 불렀던 '정수가 아니라 '중수'가 맞습니다. 죄송합니다. 매우 친절하신 청취자 몇 분께서 쇼의 소셜 미디어 계정을 통해 제게 실수를 지적해주셨습니다. 제가 그런 실수를 했을 때 여러분 모두가 저에게 알려주시기 바랍니다. 항상 감사하게 생각하고 있습니다.

어휘 novelist 소설가 genius 천재 alert 알리다 account 계정 appreciate 고마워하다

86

What is the topic of the podcast?

(A) Writing advice
(B) Book reviews
(C) Famous authors
(D) Publishing trends

팟캐스트의 주제는 무엇인가?

(A) 작문 조언
(B) 서평
(C) 유명 작가
(D) 출판 동향

해설 전체 내용 관련 – 담화의 주제

화자가 도입부에 이번 주에도 위대한 소설가들의 삶을 다루는 팟캐스트 〈언리튼〉을 찾아주신 것을 환영한다(welcome to another week of *Unwritten*, the podcast about the lives of great novelists)고 했으므로 정답은 (C)이다.

▸▸ Paraphrasing 담화의 great novelists
→ 정답의 famous authors

87

What does the speaker apologize for?

(A) Pronouncing a name incorrectly
(B) Misunderstanding a listener question
(C) Including a segment with bad sound quality
(D) Interrupting the show for an advertisement

화자는 무엇에 대해 사과하는가?

(A) 이름을 잘못 발음한 일
(B) 청자의 질문을 오해한 일
(C) 음질이 안 좋은 부분이 포함된 일
(D) 광고를 위해 쇼를 중단한 일

어휘 pronounce 발음하다 incorrectly 부정확하게 misunderstand 오해하다 segment 부분 interrupt 중단시키다

해설 세부 사항 관련 – 화자가 사과한 것

화자가 중반부에 제대로 들으셨다(you heard that right)면서, 제가 에피소드 내내 불렀던 '정수가 아니라 '중수'가 맞다(it's "Joong-Soo", not "Juhng-Soo", which is what I called him throughout the episode)며 죄송하다(I'm sorry about that)고 사과하고 있으므로 정답은 (A)이다.

Test 6

88

What does the speaker encourage listeners to do?

(A) Report any errors she makes
(B) Recommend ideas for future episodes
(C) Support the podcast's sponsor
(D) Follow her social media account

화자는 청자들에게 무엇을 하라고 권하는가?

(A) 그녀가 한 어떤 실수든 알려줄 것
(B) 향후 에피소드를 위한 아이디어를 추천할 것
(C) 팟캐스트의 광고주를 지원할 것
(D) 그녀의 소셜 미디어 계정을 팔로우할 것

어휘 report 알리다 error 실수[오류] recommend 추천하다
support 지원하다 sponsor 후원자, 광고주

해설 세부 사항 관련 – 화자가 청자들에게 하라고 권한 것

화자가 후반부에 제가 그런 실수를 했을 때 여러분 모두가 저에게 알려주시기 바란다(I hope that all of you will let me know when I've gotten something wrong like that)고 했으므로 정답은 (A)이다.

▶▶ Paraphrasing 담화의 let me know when I've gotten something wrong
→ 정답의 report any errors she makes

89-91 회의 발췌

> M-Au Hi, everyone. I called you in for this meeting because I'd like your help. **89As you probably know, I'll be introducing the Axion mobile phone at the Sydney Technology Expo this weekend.** Though it won't be released until August, this will be the first time that the world hears about it. So the marketing team and I have been working hard on my presentation. **90Today, I'd like to practice it for you and hear your opinions and suggestions for revision.** All right? Good. **91Now, these printouts contain the latest version of the speech. Barbara, would you mind passing those out?** Everyone can make notes on them while I speak.

안녕하십니까, 여러분. 여러분의 도움이 필요해서 이 회의에 여러분을 소집했습니다. 아마 아시겠지만, 이번 주말 시드니 테크놀로지 엑스포에서 액시온 휴대전화를 소개할 겁니다. 비록 8월에나 출시되겠지만, 전 세계가 이것을 접하는 것은 이번이 처음이 될 것입니다. 그래서 마케팅팀과 저는 프레젠테이션을 열심히 준비해왔습니다. 오늘은 여러분에게 이것을 연습해보고 여러분의 의견과 수정에 대한 제안을 듣고 싶습니다. 괜찮으시죠? 좋습니다. 자, 이 인쇄물에는 최신 버전의 연설이 포함되어 있습니다. 바바라, 이것 좀 나눠주시겠어요? 제가 말하는 동안 누구나 메모를 하실 수 있습니다.

어휘 call in 부르다 introduce 소개하다 release 공개하다
practice 연습하다 opinion 의견 suggestion 제안 revision
수정 printout 인쇄(물) contain 포함하다 latest 최신의
pass out 나눠주다 make notes on 주를 달다

89

According to the speaker, what will happen soon?

(A) A project team will be formed.
(B) A leadership position will be filled.
(C) A product will be announced.
(D) A mobile app will be released.

화자에 따르면, 곧 무슨 일이 일어날 것인가?

(A) 프로젝트 팀이 구성될 것이다.
(B) 관리자급 직위가 충원될 것이다.
(C) 제품이 발표될 것이다.
(D) 모바일 앱이 출시될 것이다.

어휘 form 형성시키다 position 자리 fill 채우다 announce 발표하다

해설 세부 사항 관련 – 화자가 곧 일어난다고 말하는 일

화자가 초반부에 이번 주말 시드니 테크놀로지 엑스포에서 액시온 휴대전화를 소개할 것(I'll be introducing the Axion mobile phone at the Sydney Technology Expo this weekend)이라고 했으므로 정답은 (C)이다.

▶▶ Paraphrasing 담화의 introducing the ~ mobile phone
→ 정답의 A product will be announced

90

What does the speaker want the listeners to do?

(A) Provide some feedback
(B) Create a recording
(C) Gather some supplies
(D) Revise some sales figures

화자는 청자들이 무엇을 하기를 원하는가?

(A) 피드백 제공
(B) 기록 작성
(C) 물품 수집
(D) 매출 수치 정정

어휘 provide 제공하다 recording 기록 gather 모으다 supplies
물품 revise 수정하다 figure 수치

해설 세부 사항 관련 – 화자가 청자들이 하기를 원하는 것

화자가 중반부에 오늘은 여러분에게 이것을 연습해보고 여러분의 의견과 수정에 대한 제안을 듣고 싶다(Today, I'd like to practice it for you and hear your opinions and suggestions for revision)고 했으므로 정답은 (A)이다.

▶▶ Paraphrasing 담화의 your opinions and suggestions
→ 정답의 some feedback

91

What does the speaker ask Barbara to hand out?

(A) Entrance passes
(B) A set of prototypes
(C) A draft of a script
(D) Notepads

화자는 바바라에게 무엇을 나눠주라고 부탁하는가?

(A) 입장권
(B) 시제품 세트
(C) 대본의 초안
(D) 메모장

해설 세부 사항 관련 – 화자가 바바라에게 나눠주라고 부탁한 것

화자가 후반부에 이 인쇄물에는 최신 버전의 연설이 포함되어 있다(these printouts contain the latest version of the speech)면서, 바바라에게 인쇄물을 나눠주겠는지(Barbara, would you mind passing those out?) 부탁하고 있으므로 정답은 (C)이다.

92-94 담화

M-Cn Welcome, everyone, to your first day of work at Royston Industrial. **⁹²My name is Manuel Gomez, and I'm going to give you a tour of this manufacturing plant.** By the end, you will be familiar with the facility and should have a good understanding of the process by which our products are made. Now, before we start, **⁹³I need each of you to grab a helmet and goggles from the boxes here and put them on. ⁹⁴I know they're uncomfortable, but you can't be in the plant without them.** Just look around at the other workers. OK, are we ready to begin?

여러분 모두 로이스턴 산업에 첫 출근하신 것을 환영합니다. 제 이름은 마누엘 고메즈이고 이 제조 공장을 견학시켜드리겠습니다. 견학이 마무리될 무렵 시설물에 익숙해지고 제품이 만들어지는 과정에 대해 잘 이해하실 수 있게 될 겁니다. 자, 시작하기 전에 여러분 각자 여기 박스에서 헬멧과 고글을 집어 가셔서 착용해주셔야 합니다. 불편하다는 거 알고 알고 있습니다만 장비 없이는 공장에 들어가실 수 없습니다. 다른 근무자들을 한번 둘러보십시오. 좋습니다. 시작할 준비가 되었나요?

어휘 tour 견학 manufacturing plant 제조 공장 familiar 익숙한, ~을 잘 아는 facility 시설 process 과정 grab 움켜잡다 uncomfortable 불편한

92

Where most likely is the talk taking place?

(A) At a fitness center
(B) At a construction site
(C) In a hospital
(D) In a factory

담화가 열리는 장소는 어디일 것 같은가?
(A) 피트니스 센터
(B) 건설 현장
(C) 병원
(D) 공장

해설 전체 내용 관련 – 담화의 장소

화자가 초반부에 제 이름은 마누엘 고메즈이고 이 제조 공장을 견학시켜드리겠다(My name is Manuel Gomez, and I'm going to give you a tour of this manufacturing plant)고 했으므로 정답은 (D)이다.

▸▸ Paraphrasing 담화의 **manufacturing plant**
→ 정답의 **factory**

93

What does the speaker ask the listeners to do?

(A) Wear safety gear
(B) Watch a demonstration
(C) Clean some machines
(D) Pack some boxes

화자는 청자들에게 무엇을 하라고 요청하는가?
(A) 안전 장비 착용하기
(B) 시연 보기
(C) 기계 청소하기
(D) 박스 포장하기

어휘 safety gear 안전 장비 demonstration 시연 pack 포장하다

해설 세부 사항 관련 – 화자가 청자들에게 요청한 일

화자가 중반부에 각자 박스에서 헬멧과 고글을 집어 가서 착용해야 한다(I need each of you to grab a helmet and goggles from the boxes here and put them on)고 했으므로 정답은 (A)이다.

▸▸ Paraphrasing 담화의 **a helmet and goggles**
→ 정답의 **safety gear**

94   고난도

What does the speaker mean when he says "Just look around at the other workers"?

(A) A requirement applies to everyone at a workplace.
(B) The listeners can learn a task by observing others.
(C) The listeners' negative feelings are common.
(D) There is serious competition for an opportunity.

화자가 '다른 근무자들을 한번 둘러보십시오'라고 말하는 의도는 무엇인가?
(A) 요구 사항이 작업장의 모두에게 적용된다.
(B) 청자들은 다른 사람들을 관찰함으로써 업무를 배울 수 있다.
(C) 청자들의 부정적인 감정은 일반적인 것이다.
(D) 기회를 놓고 치열한 경쟁이 있다.

어휘 requirement 요구 사항 apply to ~에 적용되다 workplace 작업장 task 업무 observe 관찰하다 common 일반적인, 흔한 serious 심각한 competition 경쟁 opportunity 기회

해설 세부 사항 관련 – 청자들이 다음에 할 일

안전 장비 착용을 요청하며 장비 없이는 공장에 들어갈 수 없다고 한 뒤 인용문을 언급한 것은 다른 근무자들 모두 안전 장비를 착용하고 있는 모습을 확인시키려는 의도로 볼 수 있다. 따라서 정답은 (A)이다.

95-97 전화 메시지 + 양식

W-Br Hi Brian, it's Sophia Hines. ⁹⁵**I'm calling about the company's plan to supply wireless keyboards to all of our software helpline staff.** ⁹⁶**I just learned that some of the workers at our branch already have them. So instead of the forty that I originally requested, we're only going to need twenty-eight.** I sent you an e-mail about this too, but I wanted to call you directly so that you got the message as soon as possible. Am I too late? ⁹⁷**Has the order been processed already?** Let me know.

안녕하세요, 브라이언, 저 소피아 하인즈입니다. 우리 소프트웨어 전화 상담 서비스 전 직원에게 무선 키보드를 공급하려는 회사의 계획과 관련해 전화드렸습니다. 방금 우리 지사의 직원 일부가 이미 그것을 가지고 있다는 것을 알게 되었습니다. 그래서 제가 원래 요청했던 40개 대신 28개만 있으면 됩니다. 이에 대해 이메일도 보내긴 했는데 가능한 한 빨리 메시지를 받으실 수 있도록 직접 전화드리고 싶었습니다. 제가 너무 늦었으려나요? 주문이 이미 처리되었을까요? 알려주시기 바랍니다.

어휘 supply 공급하다 helpline 전화 상담 서비스 branch 지점 instead of ~ 대신에 originally 원래 directly 직접 order 주문 process 처리하다; 절차

Requested Quantities of Wireless Keyboards

Branch	Quantity
Bristol	25
Manchester	35
⁹⁶Norwich	40
Liverpool	45

무선 키보드 요청 수량

지사	수량
브리스톨	25
맨체스터	35
⁹⁶노리치	40
리버풀	45

95

Who most likely will use the keyboards?

(A) Customer service representatives
(B) Data entry specialists
(C) Software designers
(D) Newspaper staff

누가 키보드를 사용할 것 같은가?

(A) 고객 서비스 직원
(B) 데이터 입력 전문가
(C) 소프트웨어 설계자
(D) 신문사 직원

해설 세부 사항 관련 – 키보드를 사용할 것 같은 사람
화자가 초반부에 우리 소프트웨어 전화 상담 서비스 전 직원에게 무선 키보드를 공급하려는 회사의 계획과 관련해 전화드렸다(I'm calling about the company's plan to supply wireless keyboards to all of our software helpline staff)고 했으므로 정답은 (A)이다.

▸▸ Paraphrasing 담화의 helpline staff → 정답의 customer service representatives

96

Look at the graphic. Which branch does the speaker work for?

(A) Bristol
(B) Manchester
(C) Norwich
(D) Liverpool

시각 정보에 의하면, 화자는 어느 지사에 근무하는가?

(A) 브리스톨
(B) 맨체스터
(C) 노리치
(D) 리버풀

해설 시각 정보 연계 – 화자가 근무하는 지사
화자가 중반부에 방금 우리 지사의 직원 일부가 이미 그것을 가지고 있다는 것을 알게 되었다(I just learned that some of the workers at our branch already have them)면서, 그래서 제가 원래 요청했던 40개 대신 28개만 있으면 된다(So instead of the forty that I originally requested, we're only going to need twenty-eight)고 했는데, 양식에 따르면 원래 40개가 요청되었던 지사는 노리치 지사이므로 정답은 (C)이다.

97 고난도

What does the speaker ask about?

(A) When a shipment will arrive
(B) How to start a return process
(C) Whom to notify about an issue
(D) Whether an order has been finalized

화자는 무엇에 대해 묻는가?

(A) 배송물이 도착할 시기
(B) 반품 절차를 시작하는 방법
(C) 문제에 대해 통지할 사람
(D) 주문이 완료되었는지 여부

어휘 shipment 배송(물) return 반환 notify 알리다 issue 문제 finalize 완결하다

해설 세부 사항 관련 – 화자의 문의 사항

화자가 후반부에 주문이 이미 처리되었는지(Has the order been processed already?)를 묻고 있으므로 정답은 (D)이다.

▸▸ Paraphrasing 담화의 the order been processed
→ 정답의 an order has been finalized

98-100 담화 + 일정표

M-Au All right, there's a change to today's demonstration schedule that I need to let you know about. Unfortunately, the materials we need to construct windmill sails didn't arrive in time, so the Miniature Windmill demonstration is cancelled. 98**We've decided to run the eleven A.M. demonstration again in its place, as that one's sure to be popular.** 99**I'll put up a notice at the museum entrance to alert visitors to the change.** And in addition to Family Fun Day, today is exciting because we're welcoming a new employee—John Dixon. Hi, John! 100**He's going to observe some of your tours today so that he can learn how to give them.**

자, 오늘 시연 일정에 변경 사항이 있어서 알려드리겠습니다. 안타깝게도, 풍차 날개를 제작하는 데 필요한 자재들이 제때 도착하지 않아서, 미니어처 풍차 시연이 취소되었습니다. 대신 오전 11시 시연은 인기가 있을 것이 확실하므로 11시 시연을 한 번 더 진행하기로 했습니다. 박물관 입구에 안내문을 내걸어 방문객들에게 변경 사항을 공지하겠습니다. 그리고 패밀리 펀 데이 외에도, 오늘은 신입 사원 존 딕슨을 맞이하기 때문에 신나는 날입니다. 안녕하세요, 존! 그는 오늘 투어를 안내하는 방법을 배울 수 있도록 여러분의 투어를 일부 관찰할 것입니다.

어휘 demonstration 시연 unfortunately 불행하게도 material 자재 construct 건설하다, 구성하다 windmill sail 풍차 날개 notice 안내문 entrance 입구 alert 알리다 exciting 신나는 observe 관찰하다

Exeter Science Museum

Family fun Day Demonstrations

9:00 A.M.	Invisible Ink
98 11:00 A.M.	**Homemade Slime**
1:00 P.M.	Glitter Volcano
3:00 P.M.	Miniature Windmill
5:00 P.M.	Rocket Balloon Car

엑스터 과학 박물관

패밀리 펀 데이 시연

오전 9시 – 투명 잉크
98 오전 11시 – 홈메이드 슬라임
오후 1시 – 번쩍이는 화산
오후 3시 – 미니어처 풍차
오후 5시 – 로켓 풍선 자동차

98

Look at the graphic. Which demonstration does the speaker say will take place twice?

(A) Invisible Ink
(B) Homemade Slime
(C) Glitter Volcano
(D) Rocket Balloon Car

시각 정보에 의하면, 화자는 어떤 시연이 두 번 열릴 것이라고 말하는가?

(A) 투명 잉크
(B) 홈메이드 슬라임
(C) 번쩍이는 화산
(D) 로켓 풍선 자동차

어휘 homemade 집에서 만든, 손으로 만든

해설 시각 정보 연계 – 화자가 두 번 열릴 것이라고 말하는 시연

화자가 중반부에 대신 오전 11시 시연은 인기가 있을 것이 확실하므로 11시 시연을 한 번 더 진행하기로 했다(We've decided to run the eleven A.M. demonstration again in its place, as that one's sure to be popular)고 했고, 일정표에 따르면, 오전 11시 시연에 있을 행사는 홈메이드 슬라임이므로 정답은 (B)이다.

99

What does the speaker say he will do?

(A) Post an announcement
(B) Lead visitors on a tour
(C) Set up a temporary exhibit
(D) Hand out some badges

화자는 무엇을 하겠다고 말하는가?

(A) 공고문 게시
(B) 방문객 관람 안내
(C) 임시 전시품 설치
(D) 배지 배포

어휘 post 게시하다 announcement 발표 (내용) temporary 임시의 exhibit 전시품 hand out 나눠주다

해설 세부 사항 관련 – 화자가 하겠다고 말하는 것

화자가 중반부에 박물관 입구에 안내문을 내걸어 방문객들에게 변경 사항을 공지하겠다(I'll put up a notice at the museum entrance to alert visitors to the change)고 했으므로 정답은 (A)이다.

▸▸ Paraphrasing 담화의 put up a notice
→ 정답의 post an announcement

100

Why will Mr. Dixon observe some of the listeners? 고난도

(A) To prepare to write an article
(B) To give performance evaluations
(C) To carry out scientific research
(D) To receive training for his job

딕슨 씨는 왜 일부 청자들을 관찰할 것인가?

(A) 기사 작성을 준비하기 위해
(B) 업무 평가를 하기 위해
(C) 과학 연구를 수행하기 위해
(D) 직무 교육을 받기 위해

어휘   prepare 준비하다   article 기사   performance 성과
      evaluation 평가   carry out 수행하다   scientific 과학의
      research 연구   receive 받다

해설   세부 사항 관련 – 딕슨 씨가 일부 청자들을 관찰할 예정인 이유

화자가 후반부에 딕슨 씨를 소개하며, 그는 오늘 투어를 안내하는 방법을 배울
수 있도록 여러분의 투어를 일부 관찰할 것(He's going to observe some of
your tours today so that he can learn how to give them)이라고 설명
했으므로 정답은 (D)이다.

> ▸▸ Paraphrasing   담화의 **learn how to**
>   → 정답의 **receive training**

TEST 7

1 (C)	**2** (D)	**3** (D)	**4** (A)	**5** (C)
6 (B)	**7** (C)	**8** (B)	**9** (B)	**10** (A)
11 (C)	**12** (A)	**13** (B)	**14** (C)	**15** (A)
16 (B)	**17** (B)	**18** (A)	**19** (B)	**20** (C)
21 (A)	**22** (C)	**23** (A)	**24** (B)	**25** (C)
26 (B)	**27** (C)	**28** (C)	**29** (B)	**30** (A)
31 (C)	**32** (A)	**33** (D)	**34** (C)	**35** (D)
36 (D)	**37** (A)	**38** (C)	**39** (A)	**40** (D)
41 (A)	**42** (D)	**43** (B)	**44** (D)	**45** (B)
46 (A)	**47** (C)	**48** (C)	**49** (B)	**50** (D)
51 (B)	**52** (C)	**53** (B)	**54** (C)	**55** (A)
56 (B)	**57** (A)	**58** (B)	**59** (A)	**60** (B)
61 (B)	**62** (C)	**63** (B)	**64** (C)	**65** (D)
66 (D)	**67** (B)	**68** (C)	**69** (D)	**70** (D)
71 (B)	**72** (C)	**73** (A)	**74** (D)	**75** (C)
76 (D)	**77** (A)	**78** (B)	**79** (C)	**80** (C)
81 (A)	**82** (B)	**83** (B)	**84** (D)	**85** (D)
86 (A)	**87** (C)	**88** (C)	**89** (B)	**90** (A)
91 (C)	**92** (C)	**93** (B)	**94** (A)	**95** (B)
96 (A)	**97** (D)	**98** (A)	**99** (B)	**100** (B)

PART 1

1 M-Au

고난도

(A) A woman is framing a piece of art.
(B) A woman is removing a lid from a jar.
(C) A woman is kneeling by some decorative objects.
(D) A woman is positioning a vase on a stand.

(A) 여자는 예술품을 액자에 넣고 있다.
(B) 여자는 병 뚜껑을 열고 있다.
(C) 여자는 장식물 옆에 무릎을 꿇고 있다.
(D) 여자는 스탠드에 꽃병을 놓고 있다.

어휘 frame 액자에 넣다; 액자 remove 치우다 lid 뚜껑 jar 병, 단지
kneel 무릎을 꿇다 decorative 장식용의 object 물건 position
(특정한 위치에) 두다 vase 꽃병 stand 스탠드

해설 1인 등장 사진 – 인물의 동작 묘사

(A) 동사 오답. 여자가 예술품을 액자에 넣고 있는(is framing a piece of art) 모습이 아니므로 오답.
(B) 동사 오답. 여자가 병 뚜껑을 열고 있는(is removing a lid from a jar) 모습이 아니므로 오답.
(C) 정답. 여자가 장식물 옆에 무릎을 꿇고 있는(is kneeling by some decorative objects) 모습이므로 정답.
(D) 동사 오답. 여자가 스탠드에 꽃병을 놓고 있는(is positioning a vase on a stand) 모습이 아니므로 오답.

2 W-Am

(A) They are putting on safety gloves.
(B) They are walking up some steps.
(C) They are using handheld measuring devices.
(D) They are standing close together.

(A) 사람들이 안전 장갑을 끼고 있다.
(B) 사람들이 계단을 걸어 올라가고 있다.
(C) 사람들이 휴대용 측정기를 사용하고 있다.
(D) 사람들이 서로 가까이 서 있다.

어휘 put on ~을 입다 safety 안전 glove 장갑 step 계단
handheld 손에 들고 쓰는 measuring device 측정 기구

해설 2인 이상 등장 사진 – 인물의 동작 묘사

(A) 동사 오답. 사람들이 안전 장갑을 끼고 있는(are putting on safety gloves) 모습이 아니라 남자 한 명이 이미 착용하고 있는(are wearing) 모습이므로 오답. 참고로 이미 착용 중인 상태를 나타내는 wearing과 무언가를 착용하는 동작을 가리키는 putting on을 혼동하지 않도록 주의한다.
(B) 동사 오답. 사람들이 계단을 걸어 올라가고 있는(are walking up some steps) 모습이 아니므로 오답.
(C) 사진에 없는 명사를 이용한 오답. 사진에 휴대용 측정기(handheld measuring devices)의 모습이 보이지 않으므로 오답.
(D) 정답. 사람들이 서로 가까이 서 있는(standing close together) 모습이므로 정답.

3 M-Cn

(A) One of the men is using a pen to take notes.
(B) The woman is reaching for a calculator.
(C) The men are seated across from each other.
(D) One of the men is placing a cup to his mouth.

(A) 남자들 중 한 명이 메모를 하기 위해 펜을 사용하고 있다.
(B) 여자는 계산기 쪽으로 손을 뻗고 있다.
(C) 남자들은 서로 마주 앉아 있다.
(D) 남자들 중 한 명이 컵을 입에 대고 있다.

어휘 take notes 기록하다 reach for ~쪽으로 손을 뻗다 calculator
계산기 across from ~의 맞은편에 place 놓다[두다]

해설 2인 이상 등장 사진 – 인물의 동작 묘사

(A) 동사 오답. 메모를 하기 위해 펜을 사용하고 있는(is using a pen to take notes) 남자의 모습이 보이지 않으므로 오답.

(B) 동사 오답. 여자가 계산기 쪽으로 손을 뻗고 있는(is reaching for a calculator) 모습이 아니므로 오답.

(C) 동사 오답. 남자들이 서로 마주 앉아 있는(are seated across from each other) 모습이 아니므로 오답.

(D) 정답. 남자들 중 한 명이 컵을 입에 대고 있는(is placing a cup to his mouth) 모습이므로 정답.

---

4 W-Br   고난도

(A) Outdoor chairs are arranged in a row.
(B) Patio umbrellas have been closed.
(C) Seat cushions are leaning against a tree.
(D) Tables have been stacked upside down.

(A) 실외용 의자가 일렬로 배열되어 있다.
(B) 테라스 파라솔이 접혀 있다.
(C) 좌석 쿠션이 나무에 기대어 있다.
(D) 탁자는 거꾸로 쌓여 있다.

어휘 outdoor 실외의 arrange 배열하다 row 줄 patio 테라스 lean against ~에 기대다 stack 쌓다 upside down 거꾸로

해설 배경 사진 – 실외 사물의 상태 묘사

(A) 정답. 실외용 의자(outdoor chairs)가 일렬로 배열되어 있는(are arranged in a row) 모습이므로 정답.

(B) 동사 오답. 테라스 파라솔(patio umbrellas)이 접혀 있는(have been closed) 모습이 아니므로 오답.

(C) 사진에 없는 명사를 이용한 오답. 사진에 좌석 쿠션(seat cushions)의 모습이 보이지 않으므로 오답.

(D) 사진에 없는 명사를 이용한 오답. 사진에 탁자(tables)의 모습이 보이지 않으므로 오답.

---

5 M-Au   고난도

(A) Some flowers are being packed into a basket.
(B) Some bushes are being lifted out of the ground.
(C) Some potted plants are lined up on shelves.
(D) Some workers are planting a garden.

(A) 몇몇 꽃들이 바구니에 담기고 있다.
(B) 몇몇 덤불이 땅에서 들어올려지고 있다.
(C) 화분 몇 개가 선반 위에 줄지어 있다.
(D) 몇몇 작업자들이 뜰에 식물을 심고 있다.

어휘 pack (짐을) 싸다 bush 덤불 lift 들어올리다 ground 땅 potted plant 화분에 담긴 식물 line up 한 줄로 세우다 shelves (shelf의 복수) 선반 plant (나무 등을) 심다

해설 혼합 사진 – 사람 또는 사물 묘사

(A) 동사 오답. 몇몇 꽃들이 바구니에 담기고 있는(are being packed into a basket) 모습이 아니므로 오답.

(B) 동사 오답. 몇몇 덤불(some bushes)이 땅에서 들어올려지고 있는(are being lifted out of the ground) 모습이 아니므로 오답.

(C) 정답. 화분들(potted plants)이 선반 위에 줄지어 있는(are lined up on shelves) 모습이므로 정답.

(D) 사진에 없는 명사를 이용한 오답. 작업자들(workers)의 모습은 보이지 않고 남자 한 명만 있으므로 오답.

---

6 W-Am   고난도

(A) A display is being stocked with sandwiches.
(B) Prepared food is being weighed on a scale.
(C) Some people are clearing trays from a work area.
(D) Baking tools have been stored in cabinets.

(A) 진열장이 샌드위치로 채워지고 있다.
(B) 조리 식품이 저울에 무게가 달리고 있다.
(C) 몇몇 사람들이 작업장에서 쟁반을 치우고 있다.
(D) 제빵 도구가 캐비닛에 보관되어 있다.

어휘 stock 채우다 weigh 무게를 달다 scale 저울 tray 쟁반 baking tool 제빵 도구 store 보관하다

해설 혼합 사진 – 사람 또는 사물 묘사

(A) 동사 오답. 진열장(a display)이 샌드위치로 채워지고 있는(is being stocked with sandwiches) 모습이 아니므로 오답.

(B) 정답. 조리 식품(prepared food)이 저울에 달리고 있는(is being weighed on a scale) 모습이므로 정답.

(C) 동사 오답. 사람들이 작업장에서 쟁반을 치우고 있는(are clearing trays from a work area) 모습이 아니므로 오답.

(D) 동사 오답. 제빵 도구(baking tools)가 캐비닛에 보관되어 있는(have been stored in cabinets) 모습이 아니므로 오답.

PART 2

7

M-Cn Who's going to organize our shop window this week?

W-Am (A) For her organizational skills.
　　　 (B) They opened last week.
　　　 (C) Karen said she would.

누가 이번 주 우리 가게 진열창을 준비하나요?
(A) 그녀의 조직력을 위해서요.
(B) 그들은 지난주에 개업했어요.
(C) 카렌이 하겠다고 했어요.

어휘 organize 준비하다, 정리하다 organizational 조직의

해설 가게 진열창을 준비할 사람을 묻는 Who 의문문
(A) 파생어 오답. 질문의 organize와 파생어 관계인 organizational을 이용한 오답.
(B) 단어 반복 오답. 질문의 week를 반복 이용한 오답.
(C) 정답. 이번 주에 가게 진열창을 준비할 사람을 묻는 질문에 카렌이 하겠다고 했다고 응답하고 있으므로 정답.

8
W-Br Shouldn't there be music playing during this video?
M-Au (A) Once the pop song ends.
(B) Check if the speakers are turned on.
(C) There're a few in that drawer.

이 영상에 배경 음악이 있어야 하지 않나요?
(A) 팝송이 끝나자마자요.
(B) 스피커가 켜져 있는지 확인하세요.
(C) 저 서랍 안에 몇 개 있어요.

어휘 once ~하자마자 a few 약간의 drawer 서랍

해설 영상에 배경 음악이 있는지 여부를 확인하는 부정의문문
(A) 질문과 상관없는 오답. When 의문문에 대한 응답이므로 오답.
(B) 정답. 영상에 배경 음악이 있어야 하지 않는지 묻는 질문에 스피커가 켜져 있는지 확인하라며 소리가 날 수 있음을 우회적으로 알려주고 있으므로 정답.
(C) 단어 반복 오답. 질문의 'there + be'를 반복 이용한 오답

9
M-Cn How were our revenues for the first quarter?
W-Am (A) By giving a brief summary.
(B) Here's the report.
(C) On Third Avenue.

1분기 동안 우리 수익이 어땠나요?
(A) 간단한 요약본을 주는 것으로요.
(B) 여기 보고서가 있어요.
(C) 3번 가에서요.

어휘 revenue 수익 quarter 분기 brief 간단한

해설 1분기 수익의 상태를 묻는 How 의문문
(A) 질문과 상관없는 오답. 방법을 묻는 How 의문문에 대한 응답이므로 오답.
(B) 정답. 1분기 동안 수익이 어땠는지 묻는 질문에 여기 보고서가 있다고 수익을 직접 확인해볼 것을 우회적으로 나타내고 있으므로 정답.
(C) 유사 발음 오답. 질문의 revenues와 부분적으로 발음이 유사한 Avenue를 이용한 오답.

10
W-Br Why don't we have our luncheon at a sushi restaurant?
M-Cn (A) Do you know of one nearby?
(B) The sales director plans to launch it online.
(C) The rest of them arrived late.

초밥집에서 오찬을 하는 게 어떨까요?
(A) 근처에 아는 곳이 있나요?
(B) 영업 이사가 온라인으로 출시할 계획입니다.
(C) 나머지는 늦게 도착했어요.

어휘 luncheon 오찬 launch 시작[착수]하다 rest 나머지

해설 제안/권유의 의문문
(A) 정답. 초밥집에서 오찬을 하는 게 어떨지 묻는 질문에 근처에 아는 곳이 있는지 권유에 호응하는 추가 정보를 묻고 있으므로 정답.
(B) 유사 발음 오답. 질문의 luncheon과 부분적으로 발음이 유사한 launch를 이용한 오답.
(C) 유사 발음 오답. 질문의 restaurant과 부분적으로 발음이 유사한 rest of를 이용한 오답.

11
M-Au The copy machine on the second floor is out of order.
W-Br (A) You can cancel the order via their Web site.
(B) Denby's Café has good coffee.
(C) I've already called a technician.

2층 복사기가 고장났습니다.
(A) 웹사이트를 통해 주문을 취소하실 수 있습니다.
(B) 덴비스 카페는 커피가 좋아요.
(C) 기술자를 이미 불렀어요.

어휘 copy machine 복사기 out of order 고장난 cancel 취소하다 order 주문 via ~을 통해 technician 기술자

해설 정보 전달의 평서문
(A) 단어 반복 오답. 평서문의 order를 반복 이용한 오답.
(B) 유사 발음 오답. 평서문의 copy와 부분적으로 발음이 유사한 coffee를 이용한 오답.
(C) 정답. 2층 복사기가 고장났다는 평서문에 기술자를 이미 불렀다며 문제 상황에 대한 해결책을 제시하고 있으므로 정답.

12
고난도
W-Am Why is there so little merchandise on this shelf?
M-Au (A) Haruki is about to restock it.
(B) I think I sold one last year.
(C) A larger size may be available.

왜 이 선반에는 상품이 거의 없나요?
(A) 하루키가 막 재고를 다시 채우려 하고 있어요.
(B) 작년에 하나를 팔았던 것 같아요.
(C) 더 큰 사이즈를 구할 수 있어요.

Test 7

어휘 merchandise 상품 shelf 선반 be about to 막 ~하려는 참이다
restock 다시 채우다 available 구입[이용할] 수 있는

해설 선반에 상품이 거의 없는 이유를 묻는 Why 의문문
(A) 정답. 선반에 상품이 거의 없는 이유를 묻는 질문에 하루키가 막 재고를 다시 채우려 하고 있다며, 선반이 비어 있는 문제 상황이 곧 해결될 것임을 알리고 있으므로 정답.
(B) 연상 단어 오답. 질문의 merchandise에서 연상 가능한 sold를 이용한 오답.
(C) 연상 단어 오답. 질문의 little에서 연상 가능한 larger size를 이용한 오답.

13

M-Cn Could you help me hang these party banners?
W-Br (A) I didn't know you went to that party.
(B) Sure, I can give you a hand.
(C) No, the band didn't play that song.

이 파티 현수막 거는 것 좀 도와주시겠어요?
(A) 그 파티에 가신 줄 몰랐어요.
(B) 물론이죠, 제가 도와드릴게요.
(C) 아니요, 그 밴드는 그 곡을 연주하지 않았습니다.

어휘 hang 걸다 banner 현수막 hand 도움

해설 부탁/요청의 의문문
(A) 단어 반복 오답. 질문의 party를 반복 이용한 오답.
(B) 정답. 파티 현수막을 거는 것을 좀 도와줄 수 있는지 부탁하는 질문에 물론이라며 도와드리겠다고 수락하고 있으므로 정답.
(C) 연상 단어 오답. 질문의 party에서 연상 가능한 band를 이용한 오답.

14

M-Au Does this office have bins for recyclables?
W-Am (A) I've never been on a long cycling trip.
(B) Their products have improved over the years.
(C) Everything goes in the blue container over there.

이 사무실에 재활용품 수거함이 있나요?
(A) 긴 자전거 여행은 해본 적이 없어요.
(B) 그들의 제품은 몇 년간 개선되었어요.
(C) 저쪽에 있는 파란 용기에 다 담아요.

어휘 bin 통 recyclables 재활용품 improve 개선하다 container 용기

해설 사무실에 재활용품 수거함이 있는지 묻는 조동사(Does) 의문문
(A) 유사 발음 오답. 질문의 recyclables와 부분적으로 발음이 유사한 cycling을 이용한 오답.
(B) 질문과 상관없는 오답.
(C) 정답. 사무실에 재활용품 수거함이 있는지 묻는 질문에 저쪽에 있는 파란 용기에 다 담는다며 재활용품 수거함이 따로 없음을 우회적으로 나타내고 있으므로 정답.

15

고난도

W-Br When does the symphony orchestra hold its free concerts?
W-Am (A) Aren't those often crowded, though?
(B) Yes, I'm a season ticket holder.
(C) At various venues throughout the city.

교향악단은 언제 무료 콘서트를 개최하나요?
(A) 그런데 그건 보통 너무 붐비지 않나요?
(B) 네, 저는 시즌 티켓 소지자예요.
(C) 도시 전역의 다양한 장소에서요.

어휘 symphony orchestra 교향악단 crowded 붐비는 though 하지만 holder 소지자 various 다양한 venue 장소

해설 무료 연주회의 개최 시점을 묻는 When 의문문
(A) 정답. 교향악단의 무료 콘서트 개최 시점을 묻는 질문에 무료 콘서트는 보통 너무 붐비지 않냐며 행사 참여에 대해 부정적인 의견을 우회적으로 나타내고 있으므로 정답.
(B) Yes/No 불가 오답. When 의문문에는 Yes/No 응답이 불가능하므로 오답.
(C) 질문과 상관없는 오답. Where 의문문에 대한 응답이므로 오답.

16

고난도

W-Br Where do you keep the keys to the supply room?
M-Cn (A) On the first day of work.
(B) The door should be open.
(C) He asked for late check-in.

비품실 열쇠를 어디에 보관하시나요?
(A) 근무 첫날에요.
(B) 문이 열려 있을 거예요.
(C) 그가 늦은 체크인을 요청했어요.

어휘 supply room 비품실

해설 비품실 열쇠의 보관 위치를 묻는 Where 의문문
(A) 질문과 상관없는 오답. When 의문문에 대한 응답이므로 오답.
(B) 정답. 비품실 열쇠를 어디에 보관하는지 묻는 질문에 문이 열려 있을 것이라고 열쇠가 필요 없음을 우회적으로 알려주고 있으므로 정답.
(C) 연상 단어 오답. 질문의 room에서 연상 가능한 check-in을 이용한 오답.

17

고난도

W-Am Is the traffic always this heavy here?
M-Au (A) Yes, he can't lift them.
(B) It's rush hour.
(C) The earlier shipment.

여기는 항상 이렇게 교통량이 많나요?
(A) 네, 그는 그것들을 들어올릴 수 없어요.
(B) 러시아워거든요.
(C) 이전 배송물입니다.

어휘 traffic 교통 lift 들어올리다 rush hour (출퇴근) 혼잡 시간대 shipment 수송품

해설 교통량이 항상 많은지 여부를 묻는 Be동사 의문문
(A) 연상 단어 오답. 질문의 heavy에서 연상 가능한 lift를 이용한 오답.
(B) 정답. 교통량이 항상 많은지 여부를 묻는 질문에 러시아워라며 특정 시간대에 교통량이 몰리고 있음을 우회적으로 나타내고 있으므로 정답.
(C) 연상 단어 오답. 질문의 heavy에서 연상 가능한 shipment를 이용한 오답.

18
M-Cn Who's leading the next staff workshop?
W-Am (A) The board will decide.
(B) Thanks, I'll read over them.
(C) When did you hire him?

누가 다음 직원 워크숍을 주도할 건가요?
(A) 이사회에서 결정할 겁니다.
(B) 고맙습니다, 다시 읽어볼게요.
(C) 언제 그를 고용하셨나요?

어휘 lead 이끌다 board 이사회 read over 다시 읽다
해설 다음 워크숍을 주도할 사람을 묻는 Who 의문문
(A) 정답. 다음 직원 워크숍을 주도할 사람을 묻는 질문에 이사회에서 결정할 것이라며 자신도 답을 알지 못함을 우회적으로 응답하고 있으므로 정답.
(B) 유사 발음 오답. 질문의 leading과 부분적으로 발음이 유사한 read를 이용한 오답.
(C) 질문과 상관없는 오답.

19
W-Br Where is the best place to buy a tablet?
M-Au (A) They don't use gaming apps that often.
(B) The best deals are from online stores.
(C) You can plug it into this power outlet.

태블릿 컴퓨터를 사기에 가장 좋은 곳은 어디입니까?
(A) 그들은 게임 앱을 그렇게 자주 사용하지 않습니다.
(B) 가장 좋은 거래는 온라인 상점에서 사는 거죠.
(C) 이 전기 콘센트에 꽂으시면 돼요.

어휘 tablet 태블릿 컴퓨터 that often 그렇게 자주 deal 거래 power outlet 전기 콘센트
해설 태블릿을 사기에 좋은 장소를 묻는 Where 의문문
(A) 연상 단어 오답. 질문의 tablet에서 연상 가능한 apps를 이용한 오답.
(B) 정답. 태블릿 컴퓨터를 사기에 가장 좋은 곳을 묻는 질문에 가장 좋은 거래는 온라인 상점에서 사는 것이라고 구체적으로 응답하고 있으므로 정답.
(C) 유사 발음 오답. 질문의 tablet과 부분적으로 발음이 유사한 outlet을 이용한 오답.

20 고난도
W-Am These photos of the new product line look great.
M-Cn (A) At the main production facility.
(B) Most of the phone lines were busy.
(C) We had a professional take them.

이 신제품 라인 사진들이 좋아 보이네요.
(A) 주 생산 시설에서요.
(B) 전화선은 대부분 통화 중이었어요.
(C) 전문가가 촬영하도록 했어요.

어휘 main 주요한 facility 시설 professional 전문가; 전문적인
해설 의사 전달의 평서문
(A) 파생어 오답. 평서문의 product와 파생어 관계인 production을 이용한 오답.
(B) 파생어 오답. 평서문의 line과 파생어 관계인 lines를 이용한 오답.
(C) 정답. 신제품 라인 사진들이 좋아 보인다는 의사를 전달하는 평서문에 전문가가 촬영하도록 했다며 그 이유에 대해 설명하고 있으므로 정답.

21 고난도
M-Au Isn't there an alternative date for the art festival in case of rain?
W-Br (A) It would just be moved indoors.
(B) That isn't one of the exhibition themes.
(C) I turned in my submission yesterday.

우천 시 예술제의 대체 날짜가 있지 않나요?
(A) 그냥 실내로 옮길 겁니다.
(B) 그것은 전시 주제 중 하나가 아닙니다.
(C) 어제 제 제출물을 제출했어요.

어휘 alternative 대안; 대안의 in case of ~한 경우에 indoors 실내로 exhibition 전시 theme 주제 turn in ~을 제출하다 submission 제출
해설 우천 시에 대비해 예술제의 대체일이 있는지 여부를 확인하는 부정의문문
(A) 정답. 우천 시 예술제 대체 날짜가 있지 않는지 묻는 질문에 그냥 실내로 옮길 것이라며 대체일이 따로 없음을 우회적으로 나타내고 있으므로 정답.
(B) 연상 단어 오답. 질문의 art festival에서 연상 가능한 exhibition을 이용한 오답.
(C) 연상 단어 오답. 질문의 date에서 연상 가능한 yesterday를 이용한 오답.

22 고난도
W-Am What time is the factory inspection scheduled for?
M-Au (A) On a first-come, first-served basis.
(B) Usually two to three hours.
(C) It may be postponed.

공장 점검은 몇 시로 예정되어 있나요?
(A) 선착순으로요.
(B) 보통 두세 시간이요.
(C) 연기될 수도 있어요.

어휘 inspection 점검 basis 기준 postpone 미루다
해설 공장 점검 예정 시각을 묻는 What 의문문
(A) 질문과 상관없는 오답. How 의문문에 대한 응답이므로 오답.
(B) 질문과 상관없는 오답. How long 의문문에 대한 응답이므로 오답.
(C) 정답. 공장 점검이 몇 시로 예정되어 있는지 묻는 질문에 연기될 수도 있다며 시간이 확정되지 않은 상태임을 우회적으로 나타내고 있으므로 정답.

Test 7

23

M-Cn It looks like Conference Room B is double-booked for this afternoon.

W-Br (A) It's OK—it's two meetings for the same team.

(B) They don't sell many cooking supplies.

(C) You can try requesting a single bedroom instead.

고난도

회의실 B가 오늘 오후에 이중으로 예약된 것 같아요.
(A) 괜찮아요. 동일 팀의 회의가 두 개예요.
(B) 그들은 요리 용품을 많이 팔지 않습니다.
(C) 대신 1인실을 요청하실 수 있으세요.

어휘 conference room 회의실 double 이중의 supplies 물품 request 요청하다 instead 대신에

해설 정보 전달의 평서문
(A) 정답. 회의실 B가 오늘 오후에 이중으로 예약된 것 같다는 평서문에 괜찮다 며 동일 팀의 회의가 두 개라고 상황을 설명하고 있으므로 있으므로 정답.
(B) 질문과 상관없는 오답.
(C) 단어 반복 오답. 평서문의 room을 반복 이용한 오답.

24

M-Au Have you sent me the Gilliam account file yet?

W-Br (A) That was a mistake—sorry.

(B) Isn't it on our internal Web site?

(C) One hundred and twenty, by my count.

고난도

제게 길리엄 거래 파일을 이미 보내셨나요?
(A) 그건 실수였어요, 죄송합니다.
(B) 우리 내부 웹사이트에 있지 않나요?
(C) 제 계산으로는 120입니다.

어휘 account 거래, 계정 internal 내부의 count 계산

해설 파일을 보냈는지 여부를 묻는 조동사(Have) 의문문
(A) 질문과 상관없는 오답.
(B) 정답. 자신에게 길리엄 거래 파일을 이미 보냈는지 묻는 질문에 우리 내부 웹사이트에 있지 않은지 되물으며 파일을 보내지 않아도 확인할 수 있음을 우회적으로 알려주고 있으므로 정답.
(C) 유사 발음 오답. 질문의 account와 부분적으로 발음이 유사한 count를 이 용한 오답.

25

W-Am I can put this jacket in the washing machine, right?

M-Cn (A) Would you like help putting it on?

(B) Our collection of winter apparel.

(C) Just make sure it's set to cold water.

이 재킷을 세탁기에 세탁해도 되죠, 그렇죠?
(A) 입는 것을 도와드릴까요?
(B) 우리의 겨울 의류 제품군입니다.
(C) 반드시 냉수에 맞춰지도록 하세요.

어휘 apparel 의류 make sure 확실히 하다 be set to ~에 맞추다

해설 세탁 방법을 확인하는 부가의문문
(A) 연상 단어 오답. 질문의 jacket에서 연상 가능한 put on을 이용한 오답.
(B) 연상 단어 오답. 질문의 jacket에서 연상 가능한 apparel을 이용한 오답.
(C) 정답. 재킷을 세탁기에 세탁해도 되는지 여부를 확인하는 질문에 냉수에 맞 추라는 주의 사항을 언급하며 우회적으로 Yes를 뜻하고 있으므로 정답.

26

M-Au Do the interns arrive Thursday or next Monday?

M-Cn (A) The new application deadline.

(B) I haven't gotten any updates about that.

(C) All right, we'll be finished shortly.

인턴들은 목요일에 도착하나요, 아니면 다음 주 월요일인가요?
(A) 새로운 지원 마감일이에요.
(B) 그에 대한 어떤 새로운 소식도 받지 못했어요.
(C) 좋아요, 곧 끝나겠네요.

어휘 application 지원 deadline 기한 shortly 곧

해설 인턴들이 도착하는 요일을 묻는 선택의문문
(A) 연상 단어 오답. 질문의 interns에서 연상 가능한 application을 이용한 오답.
(B) 정답. 인턴들이 도착하는 요일을 묻는 선택의문문에서 그에 대한 어떤 새로 운 소식도 받지 못했다며 답변을 줄 수 없음을 우회적으로 나타내고 있으므 로 정답.
(C) 질문과 상관없는 오답.

27

M-Au Whose headset is this?

W-Br (A) I'm heading the Planning Committee.

(B) Mostly for its comfort.

(C) Just set it on the side table.

이것은 누구의 헤드셋이죠?
(A) 저는 기획 위원회를 책임지고 있습니다.
(B) 주로 편의를 위해서요.
(C) 그냥 사이드 테이블에 두세요.

어휘 head ~을 이끌다[책임지다] mostly 주로

해설 헤드셋의 주인을 묻는 Whose 의문문
(A) 유사 발음 오답. 질문의 headset과 부분적으로 발음이 유사한 heading을 이용한 오답.
(B) 질문과 상관없는 오답. Why 의문문에 대한 응답이므로 오답.
(C) 정답. 헤드셋의 주인을 묻는 질문에 그냥 사이드 테이블에 두라며 우회적으 로 응답하고 있으므로 정답.

28

W-Am Why was construction stopped on that shopping center project?

M-Cn (A) We can stop somewhere else.

(B) Is there a sale going on now?

(C) The developer ran out of money.

그 쇼핑센터의 공사가 왜 중단되었나요?
(A) 다른 곳에서 멈춰도 돼요.
(B) 지금 세일 중인가요?
(C) 개발업체가 자금이 떨어졌어요.

어휘 construction 공사 somewhere 어딘가에서 developer 개발업자 run out of ~이 바닥나다

해설 공사가 중단된 이유를 묻는 Why 의문문
(A) 파생어 오답. 질문의 stopped와 파생어 관계인 stop을 이용한 오답.
(B) 연상 단어 오답. 질문의 shopping center에서 연상 가능한 sale을 이용한 오답.
(C) 정답. 쇼핑센터의 공사가 중단된 이유를 묻는 질문에 개발업체가 돈이 떨어졌다며 이유를 제시하고 있으므로 정답.

29

고난도

M-Au These old documents are finally going to be shredded.
W-Am (A) No, it doesn't need a title page.
(B) That should free up some space.
(C) For increasing the font size.

이 오래된 서류들은 최종적으로 분쇄될 겁니다.
(A) 아니요, 제목 페이지는 필요 없어요.
(B) 그러면 공간이 생기겠네요.
(C) 글자 크기를 키우려고요.

어휘 shred 찢다, 절단하다 free up 공간이 생기게 하다 increase 늘리다

해설 정보 전달의 평서문
(A) 연상 단어 오답. 평서문의 documents에서 연상 가능한 page를 이용한 오답.
(B) 정답. 서류들이 분쇄될 거라는 평서문에 공간이 생기겠다며 반기고 있으므로 정답.
(C) 연상 단어 오답. 평서문의 documents에서 연상 가능한 font size를 이용한 오답.

30

W-Br This brochure design is attractive, isn't it?
M-Au (A) I'd prefer a simpler layout, to be honest.
(B) Because the rooftop patio is closed.
(C) No, it's already been assigned to Derek.

이 책자 디자인이 매력적이네요, 그렇지 않나요?
(A) 솔직히 저는 더 간단한 레이아웃이면 좋겠어요.
(B) 옥상 테라스가 닫혀 있기 때문입니다.
(C) 아니요, 그건 이미 데릭에게 배정되었습니다.

어휘 brochure 책자 attractive 매력적인 prefer 선호하다 layout 배치 honest 정직한 rooftop 옥상 patio 파티오 assign 배정하다

해설 책자 디자인이 매력적인지 여부를 확인하는 부가의문문
(A) 정답. 책자의 디자인이 매력적인지 여부를 확인하는 질문에 솔직히 더 간단한 레이아웃이면 좋겠다며 동의하지 않음을 간접적으로 나타내고 있으므로 정답.
(B) 질문과 상관없는 오답. Why 의문문에 대한 응답이므로 오답.
(C) 유사 발음 오답. 질문의 design과 부분적으로 발음이 유사한 assigned를 이용한 오답.

31

고난도

M-Cn Do you think two hours is enough time to fit in all the presentations?
W-Am (A) Well, smaller images will fit better on your slides.
(B) That projector is mounted closer to the screen.
(C) As long as none of the speakers run over time.

2시간이 모든 발표를 하기에 충분한 시간이라고 생각하세요?
(A) 음, 더 작은 이미지가 슬라이드에 더 적합하겠어요.
(B) 그 프로젝터는 스크린에 더 가깝게 설치되어 있어요.
(C) 시간을 넘기는 발표자가 없다면요.

어휘 enough 충분한 fit in ~에 들어맞다 presentation 발표 mount 고정시키다

해설 2시간이 발표하기에 충분한 시간인지 묻는 조동사(Do) 의문문
(A) 단어 반복 오답. 질문의 fit을 반복 이용한 오답.
(B) 연상 단어 오답. 질문의 presentations에서 연상 가능한 projector를 이용한 오답.
(C) 정답. 2시간이 모든 발표를 하기에 충분한 시간이라고 생각하는지 묻는 질문에 시간을 넘기는 발표자가 없다면 충분할 것임을 우회적으로 나타내고 있으므로 정답.

PART 3

32-34

W-Am Excuse me—do you know if bus number 7 goes to Bryson Rotary?

M-Au Yes, it does. **32 Are you trying to get to Valmont Shopping Plaza?**

W-Am **32 Actually, yes.** It's near the rotary, right?

M-Au That's right. This outbound bus will stop in front of the mall. **33 But there's some paving work underway on the south side of Bryson Rotary.** Bus number 7 coming back this direction is being re-routed away from the rotary. It's confusing, so...

W-Am Oh, I see.

M-Au **34 For your return trip, I'd recommend taking bus number 22 instead.** It stops about two blocks from here.

여	실례지만, 7번 버스가 브라이슨 로터리까지 가는지 아세요?
남	네, 그렇습니다. **발몬트 쇼핑 플라자에 가시려는 겁니까?**
여	네, 그래요. 로터리 근처에 있는 거 맞죠?
남	맞습니다. 시외로 가는 이 버스는 쇼핑몰 앞에 정차할 겁니다. **하지만 브라이슨 로터리 남쪽에는 도로 포장 작업이 진행 중이에요.** 이 방향으로 돌아오는 7번 버스는 로터리에서 떨어진 곳으로 경로가 변경되어 운행 중입니다. 헷갈리시니까….
여	아, 그렇군요.
남	**돌아오실 때는 대신 22번 버스를 타실 것을 추천드립니다.** 여기서 두 블록 정도 떨어져서 정차합니다.

어휘	**rotary** 로터리; 회전하는 **outbound** (어떤 장소에서) 나가는 **paving** (도로 등의) 포장 **underway** 진행 중인 **direction** 방향 **re-route** 경로를 변경하다 **confusing** 혼란스러운

32

Where most likely is the woman going?

(A) To a shopping mall
(B) To a city park
(C) To a conference center
(D) To a railway terminal

여자는 어디로 가고 있는 것 같은가?

(A) 쇼핑몰
(B) 도시 공원
(C) 컨퍼런스 센터
(D) 철도 터미널

해설 세부 사항 관련 – 여자가 가고 있는 장소

남자가 첫 대사에서 발몬트 쇼핑 플라자에 가시려는 것(Are you trying to get to Valmont Shopping Plaza?)인지 묻자, 여자가 그렇다(Actually, yes)고 대답했으므로 정답은 (A)이다.

▸▸ Paraphrasing 대화의 **Valmont Shopping Plaza**
→ 정답의 **a shopping mall**

33

`고난도`

What is mentioned about Bryson Rotary?

(A) It usually has heavy traffic.
(B) It is the site of a city festival.
(C) It has a subway stop.
(D) It is partially under construction.

브라이슨 로터리에 대해 언급된 것은 무엇인가?

(A) 평소 교통량이 많다.
(B) 도시 축제의 장소이다.
(C) 지하철역이 있다.
(D) **부분적으로 공사가 진행 중이다.**

어휘 **site** 장소 **partially** 부분적으로 **construction** 공사

해설 세부 사항 관련 – 브라이슨 로터리에 대해 언급된 것

남자가 두 번째 대사에서 브라이슨 로터리 남쪽에는 도로 포장 작업이 진행 중(But there's some paving work underway on the south side of Bryson Rotary)이라고 했으므로 정답은 (D)이다.

▸▸ Paraphrasing 대화의 **some paving work underway**
→ 정답의 **partially under construction**

34

What does the man recommend doing?

(A) Parking in a garage
(B) Walking along a pedestrian street
(C) Returning via a different bus route
(D) Postponing a trip for a few hours

남자는 무엇을 하라고 추천하는가?

(A) 차고에 주차할 것
(B) 보도를 따라 걸을 것
(C) **다른 버스 노선으로 돌아올 것**
(D) 몇 시간 동안 이동을 미룰 것

어휘 **garage** 차고 **pedestrian** 보행자 **via** ~을 통해 **postpone** 미루다

해설 세부 사항 관련 – 남자의 추천 사항

남자가 마지막 대사에서 돌아올 때는 대신 22번 버스를 타실 것을 추천드린다(For your return trip, I'd recommend taking bus number 22 instead)고 했으므로 정답은 (C)이다.

▸▸ Paraphrasing 대화의 **taking bus number 22 instead**
→ 정답의 **via a different bus route**

35-37

M-Au	Hi, Samantha. **35I just finished setting up all the displays for all the eco-friendly apparel we stock here in the store.**
W-Br	I see. They look great. **36We'll put the collection boxes for Saturday's recycling initiative right in front of those windows.** That way, people will notice those brands when they're dropping off their old clothing.
M-Au	Excellent. Oh, that reminds me… **37I have to print out the 10%-off coupons we're giving each customer who brings in used items.** I'll do that right now.

남	안녕하세요, 사만다. 여기 매장에 우리가 입고하는 모든 친환경 의류를 위한 진열대 설치를 방금 완료했어요.
여	알겠어요, 멋지네요. 토요일 재활용 계획을 위한 수거함을 저 창문 바로 앞에 놓을 거예요. 그렇게 하면 사람들이 낡은 옷을 가져다 놓을 때 저 브랜드들을 알아보게 될 거예요.
남	훌륭하군요. 아, 그러고 보니… 중고 물품을 가지고 오는 각각의 고객에게 우리가 드리는 10퍼센트 할인 쿠폰을 출력해야 해요. 지금 당장 할게요.

어휘	**set up** 설치하다 **eco-friendly** 친환경적인 **apparel** 의류 **stock** (판매용 상품을 갖춰 두고) 있다 **collection** 수거 **recycling** 재활용 **initiative** (목적 달성 등을 위한 새로운) 계획 **notice** 알아보다 **drop off** 갖다주다 **used** 중고의

35

Where most likely do the speakers work?

(A) At a fitness center
(B) At a home furnishings store
(C) At a coffee shop
(D) At a clothing store

화자들은 어디에서 일할 것 같은가?
(A) 피트니스 센터
(B) 가정용 가구점
(C) 커피숍
(D) 옷 가게

해설 전체 내용 관련 – 화자들의 근무지

남자가 첫 대사에서 여기 매장에 우리가 입고하는 모든 친환경 의류를 위한 진열대 설치를 방금 완료했다(I just finished setting up all the displays for all the eco-friendly apparel we stock here in the store)고 한 것으로 보아 화자들은 의류 매장에서 일하고 있음을 알 수 있다. 따라서 정답은 (D)이다.

▸▸ **Paraphrasing** 대화의 **apparel** ➔ 정답의 **clothing**

36

What is scheduled to take place Saturday?

(A) A grand opening celebration
(B) A safety inspection
(C) A closure for inventory
(D) A recycling collection event

토요일에 무슨 일이 있을 예정인가?
(A) 개업식
(B) 안전 점검
(C) 재고 마감
(D) 재활용 수거 행사

어휘 inspection 점검 closure 종료 inventory 재고(품)

해설 세부 사항 관련 – 토요일에 일어날 일

여자가 첫 대사에서 토요일 재활용 활동을 위한 수거함을 저 창문 바로 앞에 놓을 것(We'll put the collection boxes for Saturday's recycling initiative right in front of those windows)이라고 말한 것으로 보아 정답은 (D)이다.

37

What does the man say he will do next?

(A) Prepare some discount vouchers
(B) Place some boxes in storage
(C) Update a planning spreadsheet
(D) Process a customer refund

남자는 다음에 무엇을 하겠다고 말하는가?
(A) 할인 쿠폰 준비하기
(B) 창고에 상자 몇 개 두기
(C) 기획 정산표 업데이트하기
(D) 고객 환불 처리하기

어휘 voucher 상품권 storage 보관소 spreadsheet 스프레드시트, 정산표 process 처리하다 refund 환불

해설 세부 사항 관련 – 남자가 다음에 하겠다고 하는 일

남자가 마지막 대사에서 중고 물품을 가지고 오는 각각의 고객에게 우리가 드리는 10퍼센트 할인 쿠폰을 출력해야 한다(I have to print out the 10%-off coupons we're giving each customer who brings in used items)면서, 지금 당장 하겠다(I'll do that right now)고 했으므로 정답은 (A)이다.

▸▸ **Paraphrasing** 대화의 **print out the 10%-off coupons** ➔ 정답의 **prepare some discount vouchers**

38-40

W-Am	Hi, welcome to the Electric Bike Superstore. How can I help you?
M-Cn	38 **Well, I'm a do-it-yourself enthusiast and would like to buy an electric cargo bike to bring lumber and bricks home from the hardware store.** I'd want the model with the biggest carrying capacity.
W-Am	Your best choice would be the Y10. It's durable and has a long-lasting battery. 39 **Its one drawback is that it's quite large and requires a lot of storage space.**
M-Cn	Can I see one?
W-Am	Sure, follow me. 40 **Also... this week only, our store will attach any accessories, including cargo baskets, to your bike at no charge.**

여	안녕하세요, 일렉트릭 바이크 슈퍼스토어에 오신 걸 환영합니다. 어떻게 도와드릴까요?
남	음, 저는 직접 만드는 것을 좋아하는 사람인데, 철물점에서 목재와 벽돌을 집으로 가져올 수 있는 전기 화물 자전거를 구입하고 싶어요. 운반 용량이 가장 큰 모델을 원해요.
여	최선의 선택은 Y10일 거예요. 내구성이 좋고 배터리가 오래 가거든요. 한 가지 단점은 상당히 크고 보관 공간을 많이 차지한다는 점이에요.
남	하나 볼 수 있을까요?
여	물론이죠, 절 따라오세요. 또한… 이번 주에만 우리 가게는 당신의 자전거에 화물 바구니를 포함한 모든 부속품을 무료로 부착해드려요.

어휘 electric 전기의 do-it-yourself 손수 만드는 취미(D.I.Y.) enthusiast 열광적인 팬 cargo 화물 lumber 목재 brick 벽돌 hardware store 철물점 capacity 용량 choice 선택 durable 내구성이 있는 long-lasting 오래가는 drawback 결점 storage 보관 space 공간 attach 붙이다 accessories 부속품

38

고난도

Why does the man want to purchase an electric bike?

(A) To add to a city's bike-share program
(B) To replace an older sport bike
(C) To transport building materials
(D) To shorten his daily commute

남자는 왜 전기 자전거를 사고 싶어 하는가?

(A) 시의 자전거 공유 프로그램에 추가하려고
(B) 구형 스포츠 자전거를 교체하려고
(C) 건축 자재를 운반하려고
(D) 일일 통근 시간을 단축하려고

어휘 purchase 구입하다 share 공유하다 replace 교체하다
transport 수송[운송]하다 material 재료 shorten 단축하다
commute 통근 (거리)

해설 세부 사항 관련 – 남자가 전기 자전거를 사고 싶은 이유
남자가 첫 대사에서 본인은 직접 만드는 것을 좋아하는 사람인데, 철물점에서 목재와 벽돌을 집으로 가져올 수 있는 전기 화물 자전거를 구입하고 싶다(Well, I'm a do-it-yourself enthusiast and would like to buy an electric cargo bike to bring lumber and bricks home from the hardware store)고 했으므로 정답은 (C)이다.

▶▶ Paraphrasing 대화의 bring lumber and bricks
→ 정답의 transport building materials

39

According to the woman, what is a disadvantage of the Y10 bike?

(A) Its size
(B) Its appearance
(C) Its battery life
(D) Its cost

여자에 따르면, Y10 자전거의 단점은 무엇인가?

(A) 크기
(B) 외관
(C) 배터리 수명
(D) 가격

해설 세부 사항 관련 – 여자가 말하는 Y10 자전거의 단점
여자가 두 번째 대사에서 한 가지 단점은 상당히 크고 보관 공간을 많이 차지한다는 점(Its one drawback is that it's quite large and requires a lot of storage space)이라고 했으므로 정답은 (A)이다.

40

What does the woman say the store is offering that week?

(A) Trial use of a charging station
(B) Extended warranties on bikes
(C) Reduced prices for repair services
(D) Free installation of accessories

여자는 가게가 그 주에 무엇을 제공한다고 말하는가?

(A) 충전소 체험 사용
(B) 자전거에 대한 보증 기간 연장
(C) 수리 서비스의 가격 인하
(D) 부속품의 무료 설치

어휘 trial 체험, 시험 charging 충전 extend 연장하다 warranty
보증서 reduce 줄이다 repair 수리 installation 설치

해설 세부 사항 관련 – 여자가 말하는 가게가 그 주에 제공하는 것
여자가 마지막 대사에서 이번 주에만 우리 가게는 당신의 자전거에 화물 바

구니를 포함한 모든 부속품을 무료로 부착해드린다(Also... this week only, our store will attach any accessories, including cargo baskets, to your bike at no charge)고 했으므로 정답은 (D)이다.

▶▶ Paraphrasing 대화의 attach any accessories ~ at no
charge → 정답의 free installation of
accessories

41-43

M-Au Hi, Myra. **⁴¹Some of the customer service representatives I oversee have pointed out an issue with our order entry software.** Uh...

W-Am What exactly is the problem?

M-Au Some promotional discounts aren't being applied properly. I tried to update the pricing feature of the program, but...

W-Am Oh, I've done that before. **⁴²What happens with the program is that it has trouble processing promotional discounts without additional information.**

M-Au I see.

W-Am On the screen, go to the window that says, "assign discount" and select the products that it applies to. **⁴³You'll want to look at the instruction manual as you do it to ensure everything is accurate.**

남 안녕하세요, 마이라. 제가 감독하는 고객 서비스 담당자 몇 명이 우리의 주문 입력 소프트웨어에 문제를 지적했어요. 어….

여 문제가 정확히 뭐죠?

남 일부 판촉 할인이 제대로 적용되지 않고 있어요. 프로그램의 가격 책정 기능을 업데이트하려고 했지만….

여 아, 그거 해본 적 있어요. 추가 정보가 없으면 판촉 할인을 처리하는 데 문제가 생기는 일이 프로그램에서 발생해요.

남 그렇군요.

여 화면에서 "할인 지정"이라고 적힌 창으로 가서 적용되는 제품을 선택하세요. 모든 것이 정확한지 확실히 하려면 하시면서 사용 설명서를 보시는 게 좋을 거예요.

어휘 representative 대표 oversee 감독하다 entry 입력
exactly 정확히 promotional 홍보[판촉]의 apply 적용하다
properly 제대로 pricing 가격 책정 feature 기능, 특징
process 처리하다 additional 추가의 assign 지정하다
instruction manual 사용 설명서 ensure 반드시 ~하게
하다 accurate 정확한

41

Who most likely is the man?

(A) A customer service manager
(B) A software designer
(C) A shipping clerk
(D) An event planner

남자는 누구일 것 같은가?

(A) 고객 서비스 관리자
(B) 소프트웨어 설계자
(C) 선적 사무원
(D) 행사 기획자

해설 전체 내용 관련 – 남자의 직업

남자가 첫 대사에서 제가 감독하는 고객 서비스 담당자 몇 명이 우리의 주문 입력 소프트웨어에 문제를 지적했다(Some of the customer service representatives I oversee have pointed out an issue with our order entry software)고 한 것으로 보아 정답은 (A)이다.

42

고난도

Why most likely does the woman say, "I've done that before"?

(A) To argue that a task must be possible
(B) To acknowledge a mistake she made
(C) To explain why she is working alone
(D) To show understanding of a problem

여자가 "그거 해본 적 있어요"라고 말하는 이유는 무엇일 것 같은가?

(A) 작업이 가능해야 한다고 주장하려고
(B) 실수를 했다는 점을 인정하려고
(C) 혼자 일하고 있는 이유를 설명하려고
(D) 문제에 대한 이해를 보여주려고

어휘 argue 주장하다 task 일 acknowledge 인정하다

해설 화자의 의도 파악 – 그거 해본 적 있다는 말의 의도

인용문 뒤에 여자가 추가 정보가 없으면 판촉 할인을 처리하는 데 문제가 생기는 일이 프로그램에서 발생한다(What happens with the program is that it has trouble processing promotional discounts without additional information)며 남자가 언급한 문제에 대해서 설명하고 있는 것으로 보아 경험상 문제 상황에 대해 알고 있다는 점을 보여주려고 한 말임을 알 수 있다. 따라서 정답은 (D)이다.

43

What does the woman suggest doing?

(A) Asking a team leader for additional help
(B) Referring to an instruction book during a process
(C) Sending a product back to its manufacturer
(D) Keeping a record of some actions

여자는 무엇을 하라고 제안하는가?

(A) 팀장에게 추가적인 도움 요청하기
(B) 절차 중에 설명서 참고하기
(C) 제조업체에 제품 반송하기
(D) 특정 행위에 대해 기록해두기

어휘 refer to ~을 참고하다 process 과정[절차] manufacturer 제조업체

해설 세부 사항 관련 – 여자의 제안 사항

여자가 마지막 대사에서 모든 것이 정확한지 확실히 하려면 하면서 사용 설명서를 보는 게 좋을 것(You'll want to look at the instruction manual as you do it to ensure everything is accurate)이라고 했으므로 정답은 (B)이다.

▸▸ **Paraphrasing** 대화의 look at the instruction manual during a process → 정답의 referring to an instruction book as you do it

44-46 3인 대화

W-Br **⁴⁴Thank you again, Mr. Taylor, for coming over today. Will you need to make another visit to finish the job?**

M-Au **⁴⁴No, it's all done now. Your sink simply needed a new washer for the faucet. It was an easy fix.**

W-Br Wow, that was fast. Your service is outstanding. **⁴⁵I'll definitely tell my friends to call you when they have a plumbing problem.**

M-Au Oh, thank you.

W-Br Sure. And Tom, you had a question, right?

M-Cn Yes. **⁴⁶Mr. Taylor, I'm wondering roughly what you would charge to put in a new showerhead—you know, the kind that saves water.**

M-Au Yes, that would be about sixty dollars for materials and installation.

여 테일러 씨, 오늘 와주셔서 다시 한번 감사드려요. 그 일을 끝내려면 한 번 더 방문해야 하시나요?

남1 아니요, 이제 다 끝났습니다. 당신의 싱크대에는 단지 수도꼭지에 새 나사받이가 필요했을 뿐이에요. 간단한 수리였어요.

여 와, 빠르네요. 서비스가 훌륭하세요. 제 친구들에게 배관 문제가 생기면 꼭 당신에게 전화하라고 말할게요.

남1 아, 고맙습니다.

여 당연한 걸요. 그리고 톰, 질문이 있었죠?

남2 맞아요. 테일러 씨, 새 샤워기를 다는 데 대략 얼마를 청구하시는지 궁금해요. 물을 절약하는 그런 종류로 말이에요.

남1 네, 재료와 설치 비용으로 60달러 정도 될 겁니다.

어휘 washer 나사받이 faucet 수도꼭지 outstanding 뛰어난 definitely 분명히 plumbing 배관 wonder 궁금하다 roughly 대략 charge 청구하다 showerhead 샤워기 installation 설치

44

What did Mr. Taylor just finish doing?

(A) Cleaning a power tool
(B) Unloading a truck
(C) Landscaping a yard
(D) Repairing a sink

테일러 씨는 방금 무엇을 끝냈는가?

(A) 전동 공구 청소
(B) 트럭 하역
(C) 마당 조경
(D) 싱크대 수리

해설 세부 사항 관련 – 테일러 씨가 방금 끝낸 일

여자가 첫 대사에서 테일러 씨, 오늘 와주셔서 다시 한번 감사드려요(Thank you again, Mr. Taylor, for coming over today)라며 그 일을 끝내려면 한 번 더 방문해야 하는지(Will you need to make another visit to finish the job?)를 묻자, 첫 번째 남자가 이제 다 끝났다(No, it's all done now)며, 싱크대에는 단지 수도꼭지에 새 나사받이가 필요했고 간단한 수리였다(Your sink simply needed a new washer for the ~ was an easy fix)고 했으므로 남자는 테일러이고 싱크대를 수리했음을 알 수 있다. 따라서 정답은 (D)이다.

▸▸ Paraphrasing 대화의 **fix** → 정답의 **repairing**

45

What does the woman say she will do?

(A) Organize a neighborhood event
(B) Refer others to Mr. Taylor's business
(C) Pay for services with a credit card
(D) Move a parked vehicle

여자는 무엇을 하겠다고 말하는가?

(A) 동네 행사 기획
(B) 다른 사람들에게 테일러 씨의 업체 추천
(C) 신용카드로 결제
(D) 주차된 차량의 이동

─ 어휘 organize 기획하다 refer (사람을) ~에게 보내다

해설 세부 사항 관련 – 여자가 하겠다고 말하는 것

여자가 두 번째 대사에서 친구들에게 배관 문제가 생기면 꼭 당신에게 전화하라고 말하겠다(I'll definitely tell my friends to call you when they have a plumbing problem)고 했으므로 정답은 (B)이다.

▸▸ Paraphrasing 대화의 **tell my friends to call ~**
→ 정답의 **refer others to ~**

46

What does Tom ask Mr. Taylor for?

(A) A cost estimate
(B) A regular client discount
(C) A printed receipt
(D) A copy of a contract

톰은 테일러 씨에게 무엇에 대해 묻는가?

(A) 비용 견적
(B) 단골 고객 할인
(C) 인쇄된 영수증
(D) 계약서 사본

─ 어휘 estimate 추정(치), 견적 regular client 단골 고객 receipt 영수증 contract 계약(서)

해설 세부 사항 관련 – 톰이 테일러 씨에게 묻는 것

여자가 세 번째 대사에서 톰의 이름을 부르자, 두 번째 남자인 톰이 등장하며 테일러에게 새 샤워기를 다는 데 대략 얼마를 청구하는지 궁금하다(Mr. Taylor, I'm wondering roughly what you would charge to put in a new showerhead)며 물을 절약하는 샤워기(you know, the kind that saves water)의 비용에 대해 물었으므로 정답은 (A)이다.

▸▸ Paraphrasing 대화의 roughly what you would charge
→ 정답의 a cost estimate

47-49

W-Am	Hi, is there anything I can help you find here in the gift shop?
M-Cn	Yes, ⁴⁷do you have any books with photos of your museum's permanent exhibits?
W-Am	Sure, there's this one here titled *Highlights of the City History Museum*. ⁴⁸It has a whole chapter devoted to our collection of vintage memorabilia that trace the history of athletics in the region—no other area museum has exhibits like this.
M-Cn	Interesting. I'd like to purchase it.
W-Am	Great. ⁴⁹I'll get a new, sealed copy for you from this cabinet. I have to ask the store manager for a key to open it—just one moment.

여	안녕하세요, 여기 선물가게에서 찾고 계신 걸 도와드릴 게 있을까요?
남	네, 박물관의 영구 전시품 사진이 담긴 책이 있으십니까?
여	물론이죠, 여기 (도시 역사 박물관의 하이라이트)라는 제목이 붙은 게 있네요. 이 책의 한 챕터 전체가 저희가 소장하고 있는 빈티지 기념품에 관한 것으로 이 지역의 운동 경기 역사를 보여주고 있어요. 타 지역 박물관에는 이런 전시물이 없답니다.
남	흥미롭네요. 이것을 구입하고 싶어요.
여	좋아요. 이 캐비닛에서 포장된 새 책으로 꺼내드릴게요. 매장 관리자에게 열쇠를 달라고 해야 해요. 잠시만요.

어휘	permanent 영구적인 exhibit 전시품; 전시하다 title 제목을 붙이다 devote 할애하다 collection 소장품 vintage 빈티지 memorabilia 수집품[기념품] trace 추적하다 athletics 운동 경기 region 지역 purchase 구입하다 sealed 봉인된

47

What does the man say he is looking for?

(A) A souvenir T-shirt
(B) A camera carrying bag
(C) An illustrated guidebook
(D) A set of drawing tools

남자는 무엇을 찾고 있다고 말하는가?

(A) 기념품 티셔츠
(B) 카메라 운반용 가방
(C) 삽화가 담긴 안내서
(D) 화구 세트

─ 어휘 souvenir 기념품 illustrated 삽화를 넣은 guidebook 안내서 drawing 그림 tool 도구

해설 세부 사항 관련 – 남자가 찾고 있다고 말하는 것

남자가 첫 대사에서 박물관의 영구 전시품 사진이 담긴 책이 있는지(do you have any books with photos of your museum's permanent exhibits?)를 묻고 있으므로 정답은 (C)이다.

> ▸▸ Paraphrasing 대화의 books with photos
> → 정답의 an illustrated guidebook

48

고난도

According to the woman, why is the museum special?

(A) It has free admission.
(B) It is the city's oldest museum.
(C) It has exhibits on sporting history.
(D) It allows visitors to take photographs.

여자에 따르면, 박물관이 특별한 이유는 무엇인가?

(A) 무료 입장이 있다.
(B) 시에서 가장 오래된 박물관이다.
(C) 스포츠 역사에 관한 전시물이 있다.
(D) 방문객들의 사진 촬영을 허용한다.

어휘 admission 입장 allow 허락하다

해설 세부 사항 관련 – 여자가 말하는 박물관이 특별한 이유

여자가 두 번째 대사에서 이 책의 한 챕터 전체가 박물관에서 소장하고 있는 빈티지 기념품에 관한 것으로 이 지역의 운동 경기 역사를 보여주고 있다(It has a whole chapter devoted to our collection of vintage memorabilia that trace the history of athletics in the region)면서, 타 지역 박물관에는 이런 전시물이 없다(no other area museum has exhibits like this)고 했으므로 정답은 (C)이다.

> ▸▸ Paraphrasing 대화의 athletics → 정답의 sporting

49

What will the woman ask a manager for?

(A) A product code
(B) A key to a cabinet
(C) Some gift wrapping
(D) Some business cards

여자는 관리자에게 무엇을 요구할 것인가?

(A) 제품 코드
(B) 캐비닛 열쇠
(C) 선물 포장
(D) 명함 몇 장

해설 세부 사항 관련 – 여자가 관리자에게 요구할 것

여자가 마지막 대사에서 이 캐비닛에서 포장된 새 책으로 꺼내드리겠다(I'll get a new, sealed copy for you from this cabinet)며, 매장 관리자에게 열쇠를 달라고 해야 한다(I have to ask the store manager for a key to open it)고 했으므로 정답은 (B)이다.

50-52

M-Au Hi, Mona. **50 We have a production problem with our line of spices that are packaged in the smallest sized jars**—our company label is being applied crookedly. It's strange because there are no issues with the labeling for our cans of pasta sauce.

W-Br Oh, that happens with Labeling Machine Number 2. **51 You need to slow down its conveyor belt by changing the settings manually. I can help you with that.**

M-Au That would be great. It'll take time to resolve the issue, right? So we won't have much of that product to package this morning. **52 I'll go to the packaging area and tell that team to take a break.**

남 안녕하세요, 모나. **가장 작은 크기의 병에 포장되는 우리 향신료 라인 생산에 문제가 있어요.** 우리 회사 라벨이 비뚤게 적용되고 있어요. 우리 파스타 소스 캔의 라벨 작업에는 문제가 없어서 이상해요.

여 아, 라벨 작업 기계 2번에서 그런 일이 발생해요. **수동으로 설정을 변경해서 컨베이어 벨트를 늦춰야 해요. 제가 도와드릴 수 있어요.**

남 그러면 좋겠네요. 문제를 해결하는 데 시간이 걸리겠죠? 그러면 오늘 아침에는 그 제품을 포장할 게 많지 않겠어요. **포장 구역으로 가서 그 팀에게 휴식을 취하라고 말할게요.**

어휘 production 생산 spice 향신료 package 포장하다 jar 병, 항아리 label 라벨[상표]; 라벨을 붙이다 apply 적용하다 crookedly 비뚤게 strange 이상한 manually 손으로 resolve 해결하다 break 휴식 (시간)

50

고난도

What does the speakers' company most likely manufacture?

(A) Soft drinks
(B) Skin care products
(C) Eating utensils
(D) Food seasonings

화자의 회사는 무엇을 생산할 것 같은가?

(A) 청량 음료
(B) 스킨케어 제품
(C) 식기류
(D) 음식 양념

해설 세부 사항 관련 – 화자의 회사의 생산 제품

남자가 첫 대사에서 가장 작은 크기의 병에 포장되는 우리 향신료 라인 생산에 문제가 있다(We have a production problem with our line of spices that are packaged in the smallest sized jars)고 말하고 있는 것으로 보아 정답은 (D)이다.

> ▸▸ Paraphrasing 대화의 spices → 정답의 food seasonings

Test 7

51

What will the woman help the man do?

(A) Place products into shipping boxes
(B) Adjust a machine's operating speed
(C) Change the design of a logo
(D) Order additional equipment

여자는 남자가 무엇을 하도록 도울 것인가?

(A) 제품을 배송 상자에 넣는 일
(B) 기계의 작동 속도를 조절하는 일
(C) 로고 디자인을 바꾸는 일
(D) 추가 장비를 주문하는 일

어휘 place 두다 adjust 조절하다 operating (기계의) 조작상의
order 주문하다 additional 추가의 equipment 장비

해설 세부 사항 관련 – 여자가 남자가 하도록 도울 일

여자가 첫 대사에서 수동으로 설정을 변경해서 컨베이어 벨트를 늦춰야 한다
(You need to slow down its conveyor belt by changing the settings
manually)면서, 도와드릴 수 있다(I can help you with that)라고 했으므로
정답은 (B)이다.

▶▶ Paraphrasing 대화의 **slow down its conveyor belt**
→ 정답의 **adjust a machine's operating**
speed

52

What will the man most likely do next?

(A) Phone a company technician
(B) Search for an instruction manual
(C) Inform a team of a work interruption
(D) Choose an alternative type of packaging

남자는 다음에 무엇을 할 것 같은가?

(A) 회사 기술자에게 전화한다.
(B) 사용 설명서를 찾는다.
(C) 팀에게 작업 중단을 알린다.
(D) 대체 포장 유형을 선택한다.

어휘 phone 전화하다 technician 기술자 search for 찾다
instruction manual 사용 설명서 inform 알리다
interruption 중단 alternative 대안이 되는

해설 세부 사항 관련 – 남자가 다음에 할 일

남자가 마지막 대사에서 포장 구역으로 가서 그 팀에게 휴식을 취하라고 말
하겠다(I'll go to the packaging area and tell that team to take a
break)고 했으므로 정답은 (C)이다.

▶▶ Paraphrasing 대화의 **tell that team to take a break**
→ 정답의 **inform a team of a work**
interruption

53-55 3인 대화

M-Cn	Thank you, both, for stopping by my office. **53 I recently did a walk-through of our largest property, Eastern Shopping Mall, and, well… the store directory and interior directional signs could be a lot better.**
W-Am	I noticed that recently too. Some are quite confusing. **54 I'm actually running a focus group meeting next week with some of the owners of the shops in the mall.** Hopefully, they'll provide useful input. And Susan, you have an idea, right?
W-Br	Well, **55 I used to work with Drew Hiller. He runs a firm that advises clients about design considerations for signs. I could get in touch with him.**
M-Cn	Yes, that's an excellent idea.

남	두 분 다 제 사무실에 들러주셔서 감사합니다. **최근에 우리의 가장 큰 부동산인 이스턴 쇼핑몰을 둘러보았는데, 음… 가게 안내도와 내부 안내 표지판이 많이 아쉬웠어요.**
여1	저도 최근에 그것을 알게 되었어요. 몇몇은 꽤 혼란스럽더라고요. 실은 다음 주에 쇼핑몰의 점주 몇 분과 포커스 그룹 회의를 할 예정이에요. 그들이 유용한 조언을 제공해주면 좋겠네요. 수잔, 아이디어가 있다고 했죠?
여2	음, 저는 드류 힐러와 함께 일했었어요. 그는 고객들에게 표지판 디자인에서 고려할 사항에 대해 조언하는 회사를 운영하고 있어요. 제가 그에게 연락을 해볼 수 있어요.
남	네, 그거 훌륭한 생각이네요.

어휘 walk-through 둘러보기 property 부동산 directory
안내도 interior 내부의 directional 지시[안내]의, 방향의
notice 알아채다 confusing 혼란스러운 focus group
포커스 그룹(조사나 실험을 위해 각 계층을 대표하도록 뽑은 소수의
사람들로 구성된 그룹) hopefully 바라건대 input 조언, 의견
firm 회사 advise 조언하다 consideration 고려 사항
get in touch with ~와 연락하다

53

According to the man, what needs improvement?

(A) A promotional flyer
(B) Some guidance signs
(C) Some outdoor gardens
(D) A restaurant in a food court

남자에 따르면, 개선이 필요한 것은 무엇인가?

(A) 홍보 전단
(B) 일부 안내 표지판
(C) 일부 야외 정원
(D) 푸드코트의 식당

어휘 promotional 홍보의 flyer 전단 guidance 안내 outdoor
야외의

194

해설 세부 사항 관련 - 남자가 말하는 개선이 필요한 점

남자가 첫 대사에서 최근에 우리의 가장 큰 부동산인 이스턴 쇼핑몰을 둘러보았는데 가게 안내도와 내부 안내 표지판이 많이 아쉬웠다(I recently did a walk-through of our largest property, Eastern Shopping Mall, and, well... the store directory and interior directional signs could be a lot better)고 한 것으로 보아 가게 안내도 및 표지판에 개선이 필요하다는 것임을 알 수 있다. 따라서 정답은 (B)이다.

54

Who most likely will participate in next week's focus group?

(A) Maintenance workers
(B) Mall shoppers
(C) Store owners
(D) Real estate developers

누가 다음 주의 포커스 그룹에 참여할 것 같은가?

(A) 유지 보수 작업자
(B) 쇼핑몰 쇼핑객
(C) 매장 주인
(D) 부동산 개발업자

해설 세부 사항 관련 - 다음 주의 포커스 그룹에 참여할 사람

여자가 첫 대사에서 실은 다음 주에 쇼핑몰의 점주 몇 명과 포커스 그룹 회의를 할 예정(I'm actually running a focus group meeting next week with some of the owners of the shops in the mall)이라고 했으므로 정답은 (C)이다.

55

What does Susan offer to do?

(A) Contact a consultant
(B) Post notices in a building
(C) Lead a training session
(D) Redesign a questionnaire

수잔은 무엇을 하겠다고 제안하는가?

(A) 컨설턴트에게 연락
(B) 건물 내 공고문 게시
(C) 교육 진행
(D) 설문지 재작성

어휘 post 게시하다 notice 공고문 session (특정 활동을 위한) 시간
questionnaire 설문지

해설 세부 사항 관련 - 수잔이 하겠다고 제안한 일

첫 번째 여자가 대사 후반부에 수잔을 부르자 두 번째 여자가 등장하는 것으로 보아 이 여자가 수잔이고, 드류 힐러와 함께 일했었다(I used to work with Drew Hiller)며 그는 고객들에게 표지판 디자인에서 고려할 사항에 대해 조언하는 회사를 운영하고 있다(He runs a firm that advises clients about design considerations for signs)면서, 제가 그에게 연락을 해볼 수 있다(I could get in touch with him)고 했으므로 정답은 (A)이다.

▸▸ Paraphrasing 대화의 get in touch with
→ 정답의 contact

56-58

W-Am 56 **Dan, we've gotten some employee feedback about the floor plan of our office.** And fortunately, it seems that most of the staff likes our setup.

M-Cn That's encouraging. 57 **Any issues that stand out?**

W-Am 57 **Yes, our data analysts complained that it's difficult to locate previous research reports, because they're stored in the large filing cabinets in the research room. That's rather far from our work area.**

M-Cn Oh, that is a problem.

W-Am 58 **Mr. Kim, the office manager, could buy a small bookshelf for this office. We could put the more recent reports there. I'll ask him to do that.**

여 댄, 우리 사무실의 도면에 대한 직원들의 피드백을 받았어요. 다행히도 직원들 대부분이 우리의 배치를 마음에 들어 하는 것 같아요.

남 고무적이네요. 눈에 띄는 문제가 있나요?

여 네, 우리의 데이터 분석가들이 이전의 연구 보고서가 연구실의 큰 파일 캐비닛에 보관되어 있어서 찾기 힘들다고 불평했어요. 그곳은 우리 근무 장소에서 상당히 멀거든요.

남 아, 그거 문제네요.

여 사무장인 김씨가 이 사무실에 작은 책장을 살 수 있을 거예요. 거기에 더 최근의 보고서를 둘 수 있고요. 그에게 그렇게 해달라고 요청할게요.

어휘 floor plan 평면도 fortunately 다행히도 seem ~인 것 같다 setup 배치, 설정 encouraging 고무적인 stand out 눈에 띄다 analyst 분석가 complain 불평하다 locate 찾아내다 previous 이전의 research 연구 store 보관하다 rather 다소 bookshelf 책장

56

What are the speakers mainly discussing?

(A) A new work-from-home policy
(B) The layout of a workplace
(C) An upcoming video shoot
(D) New procedures for collecting data

화자들은 주로 무엇을 논의하고 있는가?

(A) 새로운 재택근무 정책
(B) 업무 현장의 배치
(C) 곧 있을 영상 촬영
(D) 데이터 수집을 위한 새로운 절차

어휘 policy 정책 layout 배치 workplace 업무 현장 upcoming 곧 있을 shoot 촬영 procedure 절차

해설 전체 내용 관련 - 대화의 주제

여자가 첫 대사에서 우리 사무실의 도면에 대한 직원들의 피드백을 받았다(we've gotten some employee feedback about the floor plan of our office)며 그에 관한 이야기를 이어가고 있으므로 정답은 (B)이다.

▸▸ **Paraphrasing**   대화의 **the floor plan of our office**
→ 정답의 **the layout of a workplace**

57

What problem does the woman report?

(A) Some documents are hard to access.
(B) Some employees have long commutes to work.
(C) Some storage areas have no more space.
(D) Some hallways are often noisy.

여자는 어떤 문제를 보고하는가?

(A) 일부 문서에 접근하기 어렵다.
(B) 일부 직원은 통근 시간이 길다.
(C) 일부 보관 구역에 더 이상 공간이 없다.
(D) 일부 복도는 자주 소란스럽다.

어휘   access 접근하다   commute 통근   storage 보관   space 공간
hallway 복도

해설   세부 사항 관련 – 여자가 보고하는 문제

남자가 첫 대사에서 눈에 띄는 문제가 있는지(Any issues that stand out?)
를 묻자, 여자가 데이터 분석가들이 이전의 연구 보고서가 연구실의 큰 파
일 캐비닛에 보관되어 있어서 찾기 힘들다고 불평했다(our data analysts
complained that it's difficult to locate previous research reports,
because they're stored in the large filing cabinets in the research
room)면서, 그곳은 우리 근무 장소에서 상당히 멀다(That's rather far from
our work area)라고 한 것으로 보아 정답은 (A)이다.

▸▸ **Paraphrasing**   대화의 **it's difficult to locate previous
research reports** → 정답의 **Some
documents are hard to access**

58

What will the woman ask Mr. Kim to do?

(A) Move to a smaller office
(B) Purchase a piece of furniture
(C) Revise a research report
(D) Extend a submission deadline

여자는 김 씨에게 무엇을 하라고 요청할 것인가?

(A) 더 작은 사무실로의 이동
(B) 가구 구입
(C) 연구 보고서 수정
(D) 제출 기한 연장

어휘   purchase 구입하다   revise 수정하다   extend 연장하다
submission 제출

해설   세부 사항 관련 – 여자가 김씨에게 부탁할 사항

여자가 마지막 대사에서 사무장인 김씨가 이 사무실에 작은 책장을 살 수 있
을 것(Mr. Kim, the office manager, could buy a small bookshelf for
this office)이라고 했고, 거기에 더 최근의 보고서를 둘 수 있다(We could
put the more recent reports there)면서 그에게 그렇게 해달라고 요청하
겠다(I'll ask him to do that)고 했으므로 정답은 (B)이다.

▸▸ **Paraphrasing**   대화의 **buy a small bookshelf**
→ 정답의 **purchase a piece of furniture**

59-61

M-Au	Hi, Sarah. [59]**We've gotten a lot of compliments from customers in the three weeks since we added organic baked goods to our other health food selections.**
W-Br	Good to hear. [60]**I'm wondering what else we can do to build interest in our business.**
M-Au	I've been thinking about that too, and... other organic grocery stores have hands-on cooking classes.
W-Br	Hmm. [60]**That's something worth exploring.** We had Isaiah, our herbal gardening expert, come in and answer customers' questions, but that's about it. OK, well...
M-Au	Let's definitely consider it. [61]**Right now, I'll head over to the Kelley orchard down the road to pick up some blueberries for the store.**

남	안녕하세요, 사라. 기타 건강식품 상품군에 유기농 제과 제품을 추가하고 나서 3주 동안 고객들로부터 많은 칭찬을 받았어요.
여	잘됐네요. 우리 업체에 대한 관심을 쌓기 위해 또 무엇을 할 수 있을지 생각 중이에요.
남	저도 생각해봤는데, 다른 유기농 식료품점들은 요리 실습 수업이 있어요.
여	흠. 연구해볼 만한 일이네요. 우리 약초 원에 전문가인 이사야를 불러서 고객의 질문에 답하도록 하긴 했지만, 그게 다였어요. 좋아요, 그럼….
남	그것을 확실히 고려해봅시다. 전 지금 가게에 쓸 블루베리를 가지러 길 아래쪽에 있는 켈리 과수원으로 갈 겁니다.

어휘   compliment 칭찬   organic 유기농의   baked goods
제과 제품   wonder ~이 어떨까 생각하다   interest 관심
hands-on 직접 해 보는   worth ~할 가치가 있는   explore
탐구[분석]하다   herbal 약초의   gardening 원예   expert
전문가   that's (about) it 그게 다예요   definitely 확실히
head 향하다   orchard 과수원

59

What did the speakers' business do recently?

(A) Expanded its range of products
(B) Held an anniversary celebration
(C) Joined an industry association
(D) Renovated a shopping area

화자의 업체는 최근에 무엇을 했는가?

(A) 제품군 확대
(B) 기념식 개최
(C) 산업 협회 가입
(D) 쇼핑 구역 개조

어휘   expand 확대하다   range 범위   anniversary 기념일
celebration 축하 행사   industry 산업   association 협회
renovate [개조]보수하다

해설 세부 사항 관련 – 화자의 업체가 최근에 한 일

남자가 첫 대사에서 기타 건강식품 상품군에 유기농 제과 제품을 추가하고 나서 3주 동안 고객들로부터 많은 칭찬을 받았다(We've gotten a lot of compliments from customers in the three weeks since we added organic baked goods to our other health food selections)고 한 것으로 보아 정답은 (A)이다.

▸▸ Paraphrasing   대화의 added ~ goods to our ~ selections → 정답의 expanded its range of products

60   고난도

Why most likely does the man say, "other organic grocery stores have hands-on cooking classes"?

(A) To show surprise at a local trend
(B) To suggest offering in-store activities
(C) To highlight the health benefits of organic foods
(D) To express doubt about the effectiveness of a promotion

남자가 "다른 유기농 식료품점들은 요리 실습 수업이 있어요"라고 말하는 이유는 무엇일 것 같은가?

(A) 현지 트렌드에 놀라움을 보여주기 위해
(B) 매장 내 활동을 제공하자고 제안하기 위해
(C) 유기농 식품의 건강상 이점을 강조하기 위해
(D) 홍보 효과에 대해 의구심을 표하기 위해

어휘 in-store 매장 내의 highlight 강조하다 benefit 이점 express 표현하다 effectiveness 효과 promotion 홍보[판촉]

해설 화자의 의도 파악 – 다른 유기농 식료품점들은 요리 실습 수업이 있다는 말의 의도

여자가 첫 대사에서 우리 업체에 대한 관심을 쌓기 위해 또 무엇을 할 수 있을지 생각 중(I'm wondering what else we can do to build interest in our business)이라고 하자 남자가 인용문을 언급했고, 뒤이어 여자가 연구해 볼 만한 가치가 있는 일(That's something worth exploring)이라고 한 것으로 보아 고객의 관심을 끌기 위해 업체에서 시도해볼 수 있는 활동에 대한 아이디어를 내고자 한 말임을 알 수 있다. 따라서 정답은 (B)이다.

61   고난도

What will the man probably do next?

(A) Water some plants
(B) Visit a nearby farm
(C) Clear off a display shelf
(D) Request a catalog

남자는 다음에 무엇을 하겠는가?

(A) 일부 식물에 물을 준다.
(B) 근처 농장을 방문한다.
(C) 진열대를 치운다.
(D) 카탈로그를 요청한다.

어휘 water 물을 주다 nearby 근처의 clear off 치우다

해설 세부 사항 관련 – 남자가 다음에 할 일

남자가 마지막 대사에서 전 지금 가게에 쓸 블루베리를 가지러 길 아래쪽에 있는 켈리 과수원으로 갈 것(Right now, I'll head over to the Kelley orchard down the road to pick up some blueberries for the store)이라고 했으므로 정답은 (B)이다.

▸▸ Paraphrasing   대화의 head over to the ~ orchard down the road → 정답의 visit a nearby farm

62-64 대화 + 지도

M-Cn Megan, I've updated our Web site. ⁶²**On the homepage, I added a quote from the article in _City-Life Review_ that named us the best property management company in the area.**

W-Br Good. ⁶³**Next Tuesday I'll interview Anna Lopez, the owner of the flower shop nearby, for our neighborhood guide section of our site.**

M-Cn Ah, I almost forgot... Here is a map I made—it shows four of the district's favorite restaurants. See?

W-Br Oh, there's one problem. ⁶⁴**The Italian restaurant on Main Street just moved—it's next door to the Korean place on Fir Street now.**

M-Cn OK. I'll change that part then.

남 메건, 우리 웹사이트를 업데이트했어요. 홈페이지에 우리를 지역 최고의 부동산 관리 회사라고 명명한 〈시티-라이프 리뷰〉 기사의 인용문을 추가했어요.
여 좋아요. 다음 주 화요일에 저는 우리 사이트의 우리 동네 안내 코너를 위해 근처 꽃가게 주인인 안나 로페즈를 인터뷰할 거예요.
남 아, 잊어버릴 뻔했는데… 여기 제가 만든 지도인데, 이 구역에서 가장 인기 있는 네 곳의 식당을 보여줘요. 보이죠?
여 아, 한 가지 문제가 있네요. 메인 가에 있던 이탈리안 레스토랑이 얼마 전 이전했어요. 지금은 퍼 가에 있는 한식당 옆에 있어요.
남 알겠어요. 그럼 그 부분을 수정할게요.

어휘 quote 인용문 article 기사 name 명명하다 property 부동산 nearby 근처에 neighborhood 지역 guide 안내 section (신문 등의) 난, 코너 district 지구[지역]

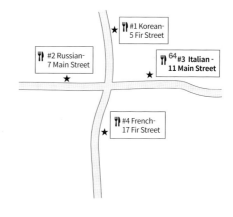

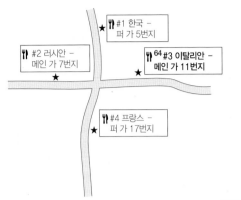

#1 한국 –
퍼 가 5번지

#2 러시안 –
메인 가 7번지

#3 이탈리안 –
메인 가 11번지

#4 프랑스 –
퍼 가 17번지

62

고난도

What does the man say he put on the business's Web site?

(A) A link
(B) An apology
(C) Some praise
(D) Some prices

남자는 업체의 웹사이트에 무엇을 게시했다고 말하는가?

(A) 링크
(B) 사과
(C) 칭찬
(D) 가격

해설 세부 사항 관련 – 남자가 업체의 웹사이트에 올린 것

남자가 첫 대사에서 홈페이지에 우리를 지역 최고의 부동산 관리 회사라고 명명한 시티-라이프 리뷰 기사의 인용문을 추가했다(On the homepage, I added a quote from the article in *City-Life Review* that named us the best property management company in the area)고 했으므로 정답은 (C)이다.

63

What does the woman say she will do next week?

(A) Arrange a staff appreciation party
(B) Speak with a local business owner
(C) Purchase a navigation device
(D) View some vacant apartments

여자는 다음 주에 무엇을 하겠다고 말하는가?

(A) 직원 감사 파티 주선
(B) 지역 업체 주인과 대화
(C) 내비게이션 기기 구입
(D) 몇몇 비어 있는 아파트 보기

어휘 arrange 주선하다 appreciation 감사 purchase 구입하다
device 기기 vacant 비어 있는

해설 세부 사항 관련 – 여자가 다음 주에 하겠다고 말한 일

여자가 첫 대사에서 다음 주 화요일에 우리 사이트의 우리 동네 안내 코너를 위해 근처 꽃가게 주인인 안나 로페즈를 인터뷰할 것(Next Tuesday I'll interview Anna Lopez, the owner of the flower shop nearby, for our neighborhood guide section of our site)이라고 했으므로 정답은 (B)이다.

▸▸ Paraphrasing 대화의 interview the owner of the ~ shop nearby → 정답의 speak with a local business owner

64

Look at the graphic. Which location number is no longer accurate?

(A) #1
(B) #2
(C) #3
(D) #4

시각 정보에 의하면, 어떤 위치 번호가 더 이상 정확하지 않은가?

(A) #1
(B) #2
(C) #3
(D) #4

해설 시각 정보 연계 – 더 이상 정확하지 않은 위치 번호

여자가 두 번째 대사에서 메인 가에 있던 이탈리안 레스토랑이 얼마 전 이전했다(The Italian restaurant on Main Street just moved)면서 지금은 퍼 가에 있는 한식당 옆에 있다(it's next door to the Korean place on Fir Street now)고 했으므로 이탈리안 레스토랑은 더 이상 기존 위치에 있지 않음을 알 수 있다. 지도에 따르면 이탈리안 레스토랑은 3번이므로 정답은 (C)이다.

65-67 대화 + 일정표

W-Am I'm all ready for tomorrow's interviews. **65We have to hire someone soon to help with the bimonthly special issues that we're going to start publishing next month.**

M-Au Yes, that's going to be a lot of extra work. We really need the interviews to go smoothly. **66I'll text each candidate a link to a map of our building so that they don't have trouble finding us.**

W-Am Good idea.

M-Au **67Oh, and by the way, the first candidate, David Meyer, will also take his proofreading test tomorrow in the conference room. So we can only do one interview in there before lunch.**

W-Am No problem. **67We can interview the other candidate coming in tomorrow morning in a small meeting room.**

여 내일 면접을 위한 준비는 다 됐어요. **다음 달부터 출판을 시작할 격월 특별 간행물을 도와줄 사람을 곧 채용해야 해요.**

남 네, 추가 작업이 많을 겁니다. 면접이 정말 순조롭게 진행되어야 해요. **각 후보자에게 우리 건물 지도의 링크를 문자로 보내서 그들이 우리를 찾는 데 문제가 없도록 할게요.**

여 좋은 생각이에요.

남	아, 그나저나 첫 번째 후보자인 데이비드 마이어가 내일 회의실에서 교정 시험도 치를 예정이에요. 그래서 점심 전에는 거기서 인터뷰 하나만 진행할 수 있어요.
여	문제없어요. 내일 아침에 오는 다른 후보를 작은 회의실에서 인터뷰할 수 있어요.

어휘	hire 채용하다 bimonthly 격월의 issue (정기 간행물의) 호 publish 출판하다 smoothly 순조롭게 text 문자를 보내다 candidate 후보자 proofreading 교정

Interview Schedule
Conference Room

David Meyer	10:00 A.M.
67 Erica Yang	11:00 A.M.
LUNCH BREAK	12:00 P.M.-1:00 P.M.
Lance Dedham	1:30 P.M.
Joy Nelson	3:00 P.M.

면접 일정
회의실

데이비드 마이어	오전 10:00
67 에리카 양	오전 11:00
점심 시간	오후 12:00 −1:00
랜스 데덤	오후 1:30
조이 넬슨	오후 3:00

65

What does the woman say the magazine will start doing next month?

(A) Reducing rates for advertisements
(B) Publishing letters from subscribers
(C) Giving tours of its headquarters complex
(D) Releasing special issues regularly

여자는 다음 달에 잡지가 무엇을 시작할 것이라고 말하는가?

(A) 광고료 인하
(B) 구독자 편지 출판
(C) 본사 건물 견학 제공
(D) 정기 특별 간행물 출간

어휘 rate 요금 subscriber 구독자 headquarters 본사 complex
복합 건물, 단지 release 출시하다 regularly 정기적으로

해설 세부 사항 관련 – 여자가 다음 달에 잡지에서 시작할 것이라고 말한 것
여자가 첫 대사에서 다음 달부터 출판을 시작할 격월 특별 간행물을 도와줄 사람을 곧 채용해야 한다(We have to hire someone soon to help with the bimonthly special issues that we're going to start publishing next month)고 한 것으로 보아 정답은 (D)이다.

▸▸ Paraphrasing   대화의 bimonthly → 정답의 regularly
대화의 start publishing → 정답의 releasing

66

What does the man plan to do?

(A) Take photos for a Web site
(B) Proofread some writing
(C) Set up audiovisual equipment
(D) Send out text messages

남자는 무엇을 할 계획인가?

(A) 웹사이트를 위한 사진 촬영
(B) 일부 글의 교정
(C) 시청각 장비 설치
(D) 문자 메시지 발송

어휘 audiovisual 시청각의 equipment 장비

해설 세부 사항 관련 – 남자의 계획
남자가 첫 대사에서 각 후보자에게 우리 건물 지도의 링크를 문자로 보내서 그들이 우리를 찾는 데 문제가 없도록 하겠다(I'll text each candidate a link to a map of our building so that they don't have trouble finding us)고 했으므로 정답은 (D)이다.

67   고난도

Look at the graphic. Which candidate will be interviewed in a different room?

(A) David Meyer
(B) Erica Yang
(C) Lance Dedham
(D) Joy Nelson

시각 정보에 의하면, 어느 후보자가 다른 방에서 면접을 볼 것인가?

(A) 데이비드 마이어
(B) 에리카 양
(C) 랜스 데덤
(D) 조이 넬슨

해설 시각 정보 연계 – 다른 방에서 면접을 볼 후보자
남자가 두 번째 대사에서 첫 번째 후보자인 데이비드 마이어가 내일 회의실에서 교정 시험도 치를 예정(the first candidate, David Meyer, will also take his proofreading test tomorrow in the conference room)이라며, 그래서 점심 전에는 거기서 인터뷰 하나만 진행할 수 있다(So we can only do one interview in there before lunch)고 하자, 여자가 내일 아침에 오는 다른 후보를 작은 회의실에서 인터뷰할 수 있다(We can interview the other candidate coming in tomorrow morning in a small meeting room)고 했다. 일정표에 의하면, 데이비드 마이어를 제외한 나머지 아침 면접 후보자는 에리카 양이므로 정답은 (B)이다.

W-Br	Hi, Darnell. **68I heard we're having challenges with our store's level of staffing.**
M-Cn	**68Yes, it's been low, especially considering how busy it is.**
W-Br	Well, it's lucky some of our cashiers can work overtime today, then.
M-Cn	True. All right, let's work on getting inventory onto the store floor. **69This afternoon, I'd like us to focus on one aisle only and restock all its shelves with printer paper, notebooks, and report covers.**
W-Br	Sure. **70That part of the store does look a little empty, because of last week's fall clearance event.**
M-Cn	Exactly. And the clerks on the night shift can handle the other aisles, since they're less urgent.

여	안녕하세요, 다넬. 우리 가게의 직원 수에 문제가 있다고 들었어요.
남	네, 특히 얼마나 바쁜지를 고려하면 적었어요.
여	그럼 오늘 우리 출납원들 중 몇 명이 초과 근무를 할 수 있어서 다행이네요.
남	맞아요. 자, 재고를 매장 층으로 올려놓는 작업을 합시다. 오늘 오후는 한 통로에만 집중하고 모든 선반을 프린터 용지, 공책, 보고서 표지로 다시 채워주면 좋겠어요.
여	물론이죠. 지난주 가을 재고 정리 행사 때문에 매장의 그 부분이 좀 비어 보여요.
남	정확해요. 그리고 다른 통로들은 덜 급하니까 야간 근무 점원들이 그쪽을 처리하면 돼요.

어휘	challenge 문제 staffing 직원 채용[배치] especially 특히 considering ~을 고려하면 cashier 출납원 overtime 초과 근무 inventory 재고(품) aisle 통로 restock 다시 채우다[보충하다] clearance 없애기[정리] clerk 점원 shift 근무조, 근무 시간 handle 처리하다 urgent 긴급한

General Goods Section

Aisle 1	Garden supplies
Aisle 2	Carpet and flooring
Aisle 3	Sports equipment
69Aisle 4	Office stationery

일반 상품 구역

1번 통로	정원 용품
2번 통로	카펫 및 바닥재
3번 통로	스포츠 장비
69 4번 통로	사무실 문구류

68

What problem do the speakers mention?

(A) A missing form
(B) A delayed delivery
(C) A shortage of employees
(D) An out-of-date training manual

화자들은 무슨 문제를 언급하는가?
(A) 분실된 양식
(B) 지연된 배송
(C) **직원 부족**
(D) 구식 교육 설명서

어휘 missing 분실된 form 양식 delayed 지연된 shortage 부족 out-of-date 구식의 manual 설명서

해설 세부 사항 관련 – 화자들이 언급하는 문제
여자가 첫 대사에서 우리 가게의 직원 수에 문제가 있다고 들었다(I heard we're having challenges with our store's level of staffing)고 하자 남자가 뒤이어 특히 얼마나 바쁜지를 고려하면 적었다(Yes, it's been low, especially considering how busy it is)고 한 것으로 보아 정답은 (C)이다.

69

Look at the graphic. Which aisle will the speakers work in that afternoon?

(A) Aisle 1
(B) Aisle 2
(C) Aisle 3
(D) Aisle 4

시각 정보에 의하면, 화자들은 그날 오후에 어느 통로에서 일할 것인가?
(A) 1번 통로
(B) 2번 통로
(C) 3번 통로
(D) **4번 통로**

해설 시각 정보 연계 – 화자들이 그날 오후에 일할 통로
남자가 두 번째 대사에서 오늘 오후는 한 통로에만 집중하고 모든 선반을 프린터 용지, 공책, 보고서 표지로 다시 채워주면 좋겠다(This afternoon, I'd like us to focus on one aisle only and restock all its shelves with printer paper, notebooks, and report covers)고 했고, 매장 안내표에 따르면 사무실 문구류를 취급하는 통로는 4번 통로이므로 정답은 (D)이다.

70

고난도

According to the woman, what happened last week?

(A) A staff recruiting event
(B) A district managers' meeting
(C) A building renovation
(D) A seasonal sale

여자에 따르면, 지난주에 무슨 일이 일어났는가?

(A) 직원 채용 행사
(B) 지점장 회의
(C) 건물 개조
(D) 정기 세일

어휘 recruiting 채용 district 지구[지역] renovation 개조[보수]
seasonal 계절에 따른, 정기적인

해설 세부 사항 관련 – 여자가 말하는 지난주에 발생한 일

여자가 마지막 대사에서 지난주 가을 재고 정리 행사 때문에 매장의 그 부분이 좀 비어 보인다(That part of the store does look a little empty, because of last week's fall clearance event)고 했으므로 정답은 (D)이다.

▸▸ **Paraphrasing** 대화의 **fall clearance event**
→ 정답의 **a seasonal sale**

PART 4

71-73 안내 방송

M-Cn Attention riders. ⁷¹**Once all the passengers from this arriving flight have boarded our shuttle, we will depart for Gate 2 of Delray Airport's main terminal.** From there you can proceed directly to the immigration inspection lanes. ⁷²**As a major gateway to overseas, Delray Airport handles a wide variety of aircraft.** ⁷³**During our ride, you are invited to look out the window and watch these planes being serviced in the runway parking area.** Please hold onto the safety rails while the vehicle is in motion, as it may make sudden stops. Thank you.

승객 여러분께 알립니다. 도착하는 이 비행기의 모든 승객들이 우리 셔틀에 탑승하면 델레이 공항의 주 터미널 2번 게이트로 출발하겠습니다. 거기서부터 출입국 심사 통로로 직행하실 수 있습니다. 해외로의 주요 관문으로서 델레이 공항은 다양한 항공기를 취급합니다. 탑승해 계신 동안 여러분은 창밖을 내다보고 활주로 주차 구역에서 정비를 받고 있는 비행기들을 보실 수 있습니다. 차량이 갑자기 멈출 수 있으므로 차량이 이동하는 동안 안전 손잡이를 잡으십시오. 고맙습니다.

어휘 depart 출발하다 proceed 나아가다 directly 곧장
immigration inspection 출입국 심사 lane 통로 overseas
해외로 service 정비하다 runway 활주로 safety rail 안전 손잡이
in motion 이동 중인

71

Where is the announcement being given?

(A) On a high-speed train
(B) On an airport shuttle bus
(C) In a baggage claim area
(D) At an airport departure lounge

안내 방송은 어디에서 나오고 있는가?

(A) 고속 열차
(B) 공항 셔틀버스
(C) 수하물 찾는 곳
(D) 공항 출국장

해설 전체 내용 관련 – 안내 방송의 장소

화자가 초반부에 도착하는 이 비행기의 모든 승객들이 우리 셔틀에 탑승하면 델레이 공항의 주 터미널 2번 게이트로 출발하겠다(Once all the passengers from this arriving flight have boarded our shuttle, we will depart for Gate 2 of Delray Airport's main terminal)고 한 것으로 보아 정답은 (B)이다.

72

고난도

What does the speaker mention about Delray Airport?

(A) It is one of two airports in the city.
(B) It mainly handles cargo planes.
(C) It offers international flights.
(D) It was recently expanded.

화자는 델레이 공항에 대해 무엇을 언급하는가?

(A) 시내에 있는 두 공항 중 한 곳이다.
(B) 화물 항공기를 주로 취급한다.
(C) 국제선 항공편을 제공한다.
(D) 최근에 확장되었다.

어휘 mainly 주로 cargo 화물 offer 제공하다 international
국제적인 expand 확장하다

해설 세부 사항 관련 – 화자가 델레이 공항에 대해 언급한 것

화자가 중반부에 해외로의 주요 관문으로서 델레이 공항은 다양한 항공기를 취급한다(As a major gateway to overseas, Delray Airport handles a wide variety of aircraft)고 했으므로 정답은 (C)이다.

▸▸ **Paraphrasing** 담화의 **overseas**
→ 정답의 **international**

73

고난도

What does the speaker encourage listeners to do?

(A) Observe airport operations
(B) Make use of luggage racks
(C) Request additional station stops
(D) Register for a notification service

Test 7

화자는 청자들에게 무엇을 하라고 권하는가?

(A) 공항 작업 관찰
(B) 수하물 선반 사용
(C) 추가 역 정차 요청
(D) 알림 서비스 등록

어휘 observe ~을 보다, 관찰하다 operation 작업, 운용 luggage
수하물 rack 선반 additional 추가의 register for ~에 등록하다
notification 알림

해설 세부 사항 관련 – 화자가 청자들에게 권하는 사항

화자가 후반부에 탑승해 있는 동안 여러분은 창밖을 내다보고 활주로 주차
구역에서 정비를 받고 있는 비행기들을 볼 수 있다(During our ride, you
are invited to look out the window and watch these planes being
serviced in the runway parking area)고 했으므로 정답은 (A)이다.

▸▸ Paraphrasing 담화의 look out the window and watch
these planes being serviced
→ 정답의 observe airport operations

74-76 회의 발췌

> W-Br Welcome to today's meeting. **74Recently
> our technology advisor, Ms. Sharma, oversaw
> user testing for our new Language Learning
> Max mobile phone app. Her report on our app
> arrived yesterday, so I'd like to use this time to
> go over some of its key points.** Overall, users
> were positive about the app's design features.
> **75However, a number of people indicated
> that the digital images used to represent
> the vocabulary items were somewhat fuzzy
> and hard to see.** That's an important concern
> we need to address. **76So I made a short
> presentation on this issue. Let's turn our
> attention now to the first slide, which shows a
> sample image.**

오늘 회의에 오신 것을 환영합니다. 최근에 저희 기술 고문인 샤르마 씨가 새로
운 랭귀지 러닝 맥스 휴대전화 앱의 사용자 테스트를 두루 살펴보셨습니다. 우리
앱에 관한 그녀의 보고서가 어제 도착해서 이 시간을 이용해 앱의 몇몇 주요 사항
들을 검토하고 싶습니다. 전반적으로 사용자들은 앱의 디자인적인 특징에 대해
긍정적이었습니다. 하지만 많은 사람들이 어휘 항목을 나타내려고 사용된 디지털
이미지가 다소 흐릿하고 보기 힘들다고 지적했습니다. 그것은 우리가 해결해야
할 중요한 우려 사항입니다. 그래서 제가 이 문제에 대해 짧은 프레젠테이션을
만들었습니다. 이제 샘플 이미지를 보여주는 첫 번째 슬라이드에 주목해봅시다.

어휘 advisor 고문 oversee 두루 살피다, 감독하다 overall
전반적으로 positive 긍정적인 feature 특징 indicate 시사하다
represent 나타내다 somewhat 다소 fuzzy 흐릿한 address
(문제 등을) 다루다

---

74 〔고난도〕

What is the main purpose of the meeting?

(A) To address listeners' feedback on a plan
(B) To brainstorm names for a product
(C) To familiarize attendees with a software program
(D) To review a consultant's report

회의의 주요 목적은 무엇인가?
(A) 계획에 대한 청자들의 피드백을 다루는 것
(B) 제품의 이름을 브레인스토밍하는 것
(C) 참석자들에게 소프트웨어 프로그램을 숙지시키는 것
(D) **컨설턴트의 보고서를 검토하는 것**

어휘 brainstorm 브레인스토밍하다, 아이디어를 모으다 familiarize
익숙하게 하다 attendee 참석자

해설 전체 내용 관련 – 회의의 목적

화자가 초반부에 최근에 기술 고문인 샤르마 씨가 새로운 랭귀지 러닝 맥스
휴대전화 앱의 사용자 테스트를 두루 살펴봤다(Recently our technology
advisor, Ms. Sharma, oversaw user testing for our new Language
Learning Max mobile phone app)면서, 우리 앱에 관한 그녀의 보고서가
어제 도착해서 이 시간을 이용해 앱의 몇몇 주요 사항들을 검토하고 싶다(Her
report on our app arrived yesterday, so I'd like to use this time to
go over some of its key points)고 했으므로 정답은 (D)이다.

▸▸ Paraphrasing 담화의 go over → 정답의 review

75 〔고난도〕

According to the speaker, what is the problem with a
mobile phone app?

(A) High user fees
(B) Slow loading speed
(C) Unclear illustrations
(D) Complex navigation

화자에 따르면, 휴대전화 앱의 문제는 무엇인가?
(A) 높은 이용료
(B) 느린 로딩 속도
(C) **불분명한 그림**
(D) 복잡한 조작

어휘 fee 수수료 loading 로딩 unclear 불분명한 illustration
삽화[도해] navigation 조종[운항]

해설 세부 사항 관련 – 화자가 말하는 휴대전화 앱의 문제

화자가 중반부에 많은 사람들이 어휘 항목을 나타내려고 사용된 디지털 이미지
가 다소 흐릿하고 보기 힘들다고 지적했다(a number of people indicated
that the digital images used to represent the vocabulary items
were somewhat fuzzy and hard to see)고 했으므로 정답은 (C)이다.

▸▸ Paraphrasing 담화의 fuzzy and hard to see
→ 정답의 unclear

76

What will the speaker probably do next?

(A) Evaluate design proposals
(B) Welcome a guest speaker
(C) Pass out sample items
(D) Discuss a presentation slide

화자는 다음에 무엇을 하겠는가?

(A) 설계 제안서 평가
(B) 초청 연사 환영
(C) 샘플 항목 배포
(D) 프레젠테이션 슬라이드 논의

어휘 evaluate 평가하다 proposal 제안서 pass out 나눠주다
discuss 논의하다

해설 세부 사항 관련 – 화자가 다음에 할 일

화자가 마지막에 자신이 이 문제에 대해 짧은 프레젠테이션을 만들었다(I made a short presentation on this issue)면서, 이제 샘플 이미지를 보여주는 첫 번째 슬라이드에 주목해보자(Let's turn our attention now to the first slide, which shows a sample image)고 했으므로 정답은 (D)이다.

77-79 안내 방송

M-Au Thank you for shopping at Lorna's Market, the region's number-one full-service grocery store. **77We hope you are pleased with the recent upgrades we made to our layout and lighting.** To match the new interior, we are now looking for new members to join our team. **78Lorna's Market is currently hiring in the meat, grocery, and deli departments. 79We are also seeking drivers for our new door-to-door delivery service, which we'll launch on June first.** Both full- and part-time hours are available. Apply online by visiting www.lornas-market. com.

지역의 1순위 풀서비스 식료품점인 로나스 마켓에서 쇼핑해주셔서 감사합니다. 최근 우리의 배치와 조명을 업그레이드한 것이 마음에 드셨기를 바랍니다. 새로운 인테리어에 걸맞게 이제 우리 팀에 합류할 새 멤버를 찾고 있습니다. 로나스 마켓은 현재 육류, 식료품, 델리 부서에서 인력을 채용하고 있습니다. 6월 1일에 출시할 집 앞 배송 신규 서비스를 위해서도 운전자를 모집 중입니다. 풀타임과 파트타임 모두 가능합니다. www.lornas-market.com을 방문하여 온라인으로 지원하세요.

어휘 region 지역 grocery 식료품 pleased 기쁜 layout 배치 lighting 조명 match 맞추다[부응하다] currently 현재 deli 델리(수입 식품 등을 파는 가게) seek 구하다 launch 출시하다

77

What does the speaker mention about Lorna's Market?

(A) It was recently remodeled.
(B) It has a seafood department.
(C) It has a loyalty card program.
(D) Its management has changed.

화자는 로나스 마켓에 대해 무엇을 언급하는가?

(A) **최근에 리모델링 되었다.**
(B) 해산물 부서가 있다.
(C) 카드 포인트 적립제가 있다.
(D) 경영진이 바뀌었다.

어휘 recently 최근에 remodel 개조하다 loyalty card 포인트 적립 카드 management 경영진

해설 세부 사항 관련 – 화자가 로나스 마켓에 대해 언급한 것

화자가 초반부에 최근 우리의 배치와 조명을 업그레이드한 것이 마음에 드셨기를 바란다(We hope you are pleased with the recent upgrades we made to our layout and lighting)고 한 것으로 보아 정답은 (A)이다.

▸▸ Paraphrasing 담화의 the recent upgrades we made to our layout and lighting
→ 정답의 recently remodeled

78

What is the main purpose of the announcement?

(A) To remind shoppers about extended hours
(B) To publicize current job openings
(C) To encourage use of self-checkout machines
(D) To share the results of a survey

이 안내 방송의 주요 목적은 무엇인가?

(A) 쇼핑객들에게 연장된 시간에 대해 상기시키는 것
(B) **현재 채용 공고를 알리는 것**
(C) 셀프 계산 기계의 사용을 권장하는 것
(D) 설문 조사 결과를 공유하는 것

어휘 remind 상기시키다 extended 연장된 publicize 알리다 job opening 채용 공고 encourage 권장하다 share 공유하다 result 결과 survey 설문 조사

해설 전체 내용 관련 – 안내 방송의 목적

화자가 중반부에 로나스 마켓은 현재 육류, 식료품, 델리 부서에서 인력을 채용하고 있다(Lorna's Market is currently hiring in the meat, grocery, and deli departments)고 했으므로 정답은 (B)이다.

▸▸ Paraphrasing 담화의 currently hiring
→ 정답의 current job openings

79

According to the announcement, what will start on June 1?

(A) A series of cooking demonstrations
(B) The construction of a new location
(C) A home delivery service
(D) A prize giveaway contest

안내 방송에 따르면, 6월 1일에 무엇이 시작되는가?

(A) 일련의 요리 시연
(B) 새로운 장소의 건설
(C) **가정 배달 서비스**
(D) 경품 제공 행사

어휘 a series of 일련의 demonstration 시연 construction 건설
location 장소 prize 경품 giveaway 증정품

해설 세부 사항 관련 – 6월 1일에 시작되는 일

화자가 후반부에 6월 1일에 출시할 집 앞 배송 신규 서비스를 위해서도 운전자를 모집 중(We are also seeking drivers for our new door-to-door delivery service, which we'll launch on June first)이라고 했으므로 정답은 (C)이다.

80-82 관광 정보

W-Br Greetings, all. I'm Ellen Hoon. I'll be your volunteer guide for this tour of the city's historic district. **80I've studied this community for over twenty years in my role as professor of regional studies at South Central University,** and it's my favorite part of the city. Now...remember that people do live here. **81Please try not to look into windows or lean against gates as we explore the area.** Before we tour a replica of one of the historical homes, we'll now walk over to the Culture Center. **82It has detailed sketches created by the district's original architects that show some of the structures' floor plans.** Follow me this way.

인사드립니다, 여러분. 저는 엘렌 훈입니다. 이번 시 역사 지구 관광을 위한 여러분의 자원봉사 가이드입니다. 저는 사우스 센트럴 대학교 지역학과 교수로서 20년 넘게 이 지역 사회를 연구해왔으며, 이곳은 제가 시에서 가장 좋아하는 구역입니다. 자… 여기에 사람들이 살고 있다는 것을 기억하십시오. 우리가 그 지역을 답사할 때 창문을 들여다보거나 문에 기대지 않도록 하십시오. 역사적 가옥의 복원 모형을 둘러보기 전에, 우리는 지금 문화 센터로 걸어갈 것입니다. 그곳에는 상세한 스케치가 있는데, 이 구역의 최초 건축가들이 그린 것으로 건축물의 평면도를 보여줍니다. 이쪽으로 저를 따라오십시오.

어휘 greeting 인사 volunteer 자원봉사자 district 지구[구역]
regional 지역의 lean against ~에 기대다 explore 답사하다
replica 복제품, 모형 original 원래의 architect 설계자, 건축가
floor plan 평면도

80

Where most likely does the speaker work?

(A) At a transportation service
(B) At an architecture firm
(C) At an educational institution
(D) At a dining establishment

화자는 어디에서 일할 것 같은가?

(A) 운송 서비스
(B) 건축 회사
(C) **교육 기관**
(D) 식당

해설 전체 내용 관련 – 화자의 근무지

화자가 초반부에 저는 사우스 센트럴 대학교 지역학과 교수로서 20년 넘게 이 지역 사회를 연구해왔다(I've studied this community for over twenty years in my role as professor of regional studies at South Central University)고 한 것으로 보아 정답은 (C)이다.

▶ Paraphrasing 담화의 University
  → 정답의 an educational institution

81

What does the speaker mean when she says, "remember that people do live here"?

(A) Listeners should be respectful toward residents.
(B) Older homes are more attractive to buyers.
(C) Residents depend on tourism revenue.
(D) It is unusual for a historic district to be occupied.

화자가 "여기에 사람들이 살고 있다는 것을 기억하십시오"라고 말하는 의도는 무엇인가?

(A) **청자들은 주민에게 예의를 갖춰야 한다.**
(B) 노후 주택이 매입자에게 더 매력적이다.
(C) 주민은 관광 수입에 의존한다.
(D) 역사 지구에 사람이 거주하는 것은 흔치 않은 일이다.

어휘 respectful 공손한 resident 주민 attractive 매력적인
depend on ~에 의존하다 tourism 관광 revenue 수익
unusual 흔하지 않은 occupy (주택 등을) 사용하다[거주하다]

해설 화자의 의도 파악 – 여기에 사람들이 살고 있다는 것을 기억하라는 말의 의도

화자가 인용문을 언급한 뒤, 우리가 그 지역을 답사할 때 창문을 들여다보거나 문에 기대지 않도록 하라(Please try not to look into windows or lean against gates as we explore the area)고 한 것으로 보아 실제 거주지역이므로 주민들에 대한 배려를 당부하려는 의도로 한 말임을 알 수 있다. 따라서 정답은 (A)이다.

82

What does the speaker say the listeners will see next?

(A) A live performance
(B) Some architectural drawings
(C) Some classic vehicles
(D) A body of water

화자는 청자들이 다음에 무엇을 볼 것이라고 말하는가?

(A) 라이브 공연
(B) **건축 도면**
(C) 클래식 차량
(D) 수역

해설　세부 사항 관련 – 화자가 청자들이 다음에 볼 것이라고 말하는 것

화자가 후반부에 그곳(문화 센터)에는 상세한 스케치가 있는데, 이 구역의 최초 건축가들이 그린 것으로 건축물의 평면도를 보여준다(It has detailed sketches, created by the district's original architects, that show some of the structures' floor plans)고 안내하고 있는 것으로 보아 정답은 (B)이다.

▸▸ **Paraphrasing**　담화의 **the structures' floor plans**
　　　　　　　　　　→ 정답의 **architectural drawings**

83-85 뉴스 보도

M-Au　This is a WRB News Radio update. ⁸³**This Sunday at one P.M., the city library kicks off its summer series of family movies with a screening of *Trek Across Peru*, an exciting adventure story.** All film showings are free and open to the public. For a complete schedule, visit www.wenville-library.org. ⁸⁴**The library also invites all residents to look through its entire collection of books and magazines by clicking on the "Browse" button on its homepage.** ⁸⁵**And to specially encourage our listeners to do that, WRB News Radio will be holding a call-in trivia contest about the library's offerings later today. This is how it will work.**

WRB 뉴스 라디오 업데이트입니다. 이번 주 일요일 오후 1시에 시립 도서관은 흥미로운 모험 이야기인 〈페루 일주 트레킹〉의 상영과 함께 가족 영화 여름 시리즈를 시작합니다. 모든 영화 상영은 무료이며 대중에게 개방됩니다. 전체 일정을 보시려면 www.wenville-library.org를 방문하세요. 도서관은 또한 모든 주민들이 홈페이지의 "검색" 버튼을 클릭하여 도서와 잡지의 전 소장 목록을 살펴보실 것을 권합니다. 그리고 특별히 우리 청취자들의 참여를 장려하고자, WRB 뉴스 라디오는 오늘 나중에 도서관의 제공 서비스에 대한 청취자 전화 참여 상식 콘테스트를 열 예정입니다. 방법을 알려드리겠습니다.

어휘　kick off 시작하다　screening 상영　free 무료의　public 대중　complete 완전한　invite 권하다, 요청하다　resident 주민　entire 전체의　browse 둘러보다　encourage 장려하다　call-in (라디오 등의) 시청자 전화 참가 프로　trivia 일반 상식　contest 대회

83

What is the main topic of the news report?

(A) A profile of a local politician
(B) An upcoming community activity
(C) Driving conditions on area roadways
(D) Problems with an environmental project

뉴스 보도의 주요 주제는 무엇인가?
(A) 지역 정치인의 프로필
(B) 곧 있을 지역 사회 활동
(C) 지역 도로의 주행 여건
(D) 환경 프로젝트의 문제점

어휘　profile 프로필　politician 정치인　upcoming 곧 있을　community 지역 사회　activity 활동　condition 조건, 상태　roadway 도로　environmental 환경의

해설　전체 내용 관련 – 뉴스 보도의 주제

화자가 초반부에 이번 주 일요일 오후 1시에 시립 도서관은 흥미로운 모험 이야기인 〈페루 일주 트레킹〉의 상영과 함께 가족 영화 여름 시리즈를 시작한다(This Sunday at one P.M., the city library kicks off its summer series of family movies with a screening of *Trek Across Peru*, an exciting adventure story)며 곧 있을 지역 행사에 대한 소식을 알리고 있으므로 정답은 (B)이다.

84

What are listeners invited to do?

(A) Participate in an opinion poll
(B) Attend an outdoor event
(C) Join a volunteer organization
(D) View an online catalog

청자들은 무엇을 하라고 요청되는가?
(A) 여론 조사 참여
(B) 야외 행사 참석
(C) 자원봉사 단체 가입
(D) 온라인 카탈로그 보기

어휘　participate 참여하다　opinion 의견　poll 여론 조사　attend 참석하다　outdoor 야외의　volunteer 자원봉사자　organization 단체　view 보다

해설　세부 사항 관련 – 청자들이 요청받은 일

화자가 중반부에 도서관은 모든 주민들이 홈페이지의 "검색" 버튼을 클릭하여 도서와 잡지의 전 소장 목록을 살펴볼 것을 권한다(The library also invites all residents to look through its entire collection of books and magazines by clicking on the "Browse" button on its homepage)고 했으므로 정답은 (D)이다.

▸▸ **Paraphrasing**　담화의 **look through its entire collection of books and magazines ~ on its homepage** → 정답의 **view an online catalog**

85　고난도

What most likely will be heard next?

(A) A list of business closures
(B) A paid advertisement
(C) A call from a radio listener
(D) An explanation of a competition

다음에 들을 내용은 무엇인가?
(A) 폐업 목록
(B) 유료 광고
(C) 라디오 청취자의 전화
(D) 콘테스트에 대한 설명

어휘　list 목록　closure 폐쇄, 종료　paid 유료의　advertisement 광고　explanation 설명　competition 콘테스트

Test 7

해설 세부 사항 관련 – 다음에 들을 내용
화자가 마지막에 특별히 우리 청취자들의 참여를 장려하고자, WRB 뉴스 라디오는 오늘 나중에 도서관의 제공 서비스에 대한 청취자 전화 참여 상식 콘테스트를 열 예정(to specially encourage our listeners to do that, WRB News Radio will be holding a call-in trivia contest about the library's offerings later today)이라며, 방법을 알려드리겠다(This is how it will work)고 했으므로 청취자들은 뒤이어 콘테스트에 대한 설명을 들을 것임을 알 수 있다. 따라서 정답은 (D)이다.

86-88 전화 메시지

W-Am Hi, Mr. Bowers. It's Nina Estrada, calling to follow up on our consultation yesterday. **86As senior designer at my firm, I'm confident I can guide you through every step of your hotel's renovation project.** Now, during my visit, you showed me some guest rooms, and... the wallpaper and lamps are quite old. **87So we'll want to focus on that element during the improvement process.** As we discussed, your hotel will be able to remain operational while the contractors do their work, so that will minimize revenue losses. **88Later today, I'll send you an e-mail with my recommendations, estimated costs, and so on in detail.** Take a look at it and let me know what you think.

안녕하십니까, 바우어스 씨. 니나 에스트라다입니다. 어제 우리 상담에 관해 더 말씀드리려고 전화드립니다. 저희 회사의 수석 디자이너로서, 저는 귀하의 호텔 개조 프로젝트를 모든 단계에 걸쳐 안내할 수 있다고 확신합니다. 일단, 제가 방문드렸을 때 객실을 몇 곳 보여주셨는데 벽지와 램프가 꽤 낡았습니다. 그래서 저희는 개조 과정에서 그 부분에 집중하고자 합니다. 논의했던 대로 귀하의 호텔은 도급업자가 일을 하는 동안 계속 운영될 수 있으므로 수익 손실을 최소화할 수 있을 것입니다. 오늘 이따가 제 권고안, 견적 비용 등을 상세하게 이메일로 보내드리겠습니다. 한번 보시고 어떻게 생각하시는지 알려주십시오.

어휘 follow up 후속 조치하다 confident 확신하는 guide 안내하다 wallpaper 벽지 element 요소 contractor 도급업자 minimize 최소화하다 revenue 수익 loss 손실 estimated 견적의 in detail 상세하게

86

Who most likely is the speaker?

(A) An interior designer
(B) A convention organizer
(C) A hotel manager
(D) A real estate agent

화자는 누구일 것 같은가?

(A) 인테리어 디자이너
(B) 컨벤션 조직자
(C) 호텔 관리자
(D) 부동산 중개인

해설 전체 내용 관련 – 화자의 직업
화자가 초반부에 회사의 수석 디자이너로서 귀하의 호텔 개조 프로젝트를 모든 단계에 걸쳐 안내할 수 있다고 확신한다(As senior designer at my firm, I'm confident I can guide you through every step of your hotel's renovation project)고 했으므로 정답은 (A)이다.

87 [고난도]

Why most likely does the speaker say, "the wallpaper and lamps are quite old"?

(A) To indicate that she is impressed by some materials' durability
(B) To justify the decision to change a venue
(C) To emphasize the need to make updates
(D) To compliment a structure's vintage decorations

화자가 "벽지와 램프가 꽤 낡았습니다"라고 말하는 이유는 무엇일 것 같은가?

(A) 일부 재료의 내구성에 놀랐다는 것을 나타내기 위해
(B) 장소 변경 결정을 정당화하기 위해
(C) 업데이트 필요성을 강조하기 위해
(D) 건축물의 빈티지 장식을 칭찬하기 위해

어휘 indicate 나타내다 impressed 감명받은 material 재료 durability 내구성 justify 정당화하다 decision 결정 venue 장소 emphasize 강조하다 compliment 칭찬하다 structure 건축물 vintage 빈티지 decoration 장식

해설 화자의 의도 파악 – 벽지와 램프가 꽤 낡았다는 말의 의도
화자가 인용문 뒤에 그래서 저희는 개조 과정에서 그 부분에 집중하고자 한다(So we'll want to focus on that element during the improvement process)고 했으므로, 낡은 벽지와 램프에 대해 집중적인 개선이 필요함을 강조하고자 한 말임을 알 수 있다. 따라서 정답은 (C)이다.

88

What does the speaker say she will do later that day?

(A) Recruit additional workers
(B) Introduce the listener to a colleague
(C) Provide a written proposal
(D) Issue a partial refund

화자는 그날 나중에 무엇을 하겠다고 말하는가?

(A) 추가 인력 모집
(B) 동료에게 청자 소개
(C) 서면 제안서 제공
(D) 부분 환불 지급

어휘 recruit 모집하다 additional 추가의 introduce 소개하다 colleague 동료 provide 제공하다 proposal 제안서 issue 지급하다 partial 부분적인 refund 환불

해설 세부 사항 관련 – 화자가 그날 늦게 하겠다고 말하는 것
화자가 후반부에 오늘 이따가 제 권고안, 견적 비용 등을 상세하게 이메일로 보내드리겠다(Later today, I'll send you an e-mail with my recommendations, estimated costs, and so on in detail)고 했으므로 정답은 (C)이다.

M-Cn **89Welcome, all, to the home of the city's most extensive collection of paintings and photographs from all different time periods.** All tours of our facility are self-guided—you don't need a tour guide or a special mobile phone app. **90Instead, you can hear explanations of all the exhibits through this pushbutton audio guide that I'll give you in a minute.** You simply push the button corresponding to the exhibit you are viewing, and then you'll hear a description of the work in the headphones. **91Finally, uh, I recommend beginning your tour in Gallery B, since our main gallery is already quite full at the moment.**

다양한 시대의 회화 및 사진 작품을 시에서 최대로 보유하고 있는 이곳에 오신 모두를 환영합니다. 우리 시설의 모든 관람은 셀프 가이드로 되어 있습니다. 관람 가이드나 특별한 휴대전화 앱이 필요 없습니다. 대신, 제가 잠시 후 여러분께 드릴 이 버튼식 오디오 가이드를 통해 모든 전시품에 대한 설명을 들으실 수 있습니다. 지금 보고 계시는 전시품에 해당하는 버튼을 누르시면, 헤드폰으로 작품에 대한 설명을 들으실 수 있을 겁니다. 마지막으로, 현재 우리 메인 갤러리는 이미 꽤 꽉 찼기 때문에 갤러리 B에서 관람을 시작하시기를 권해드립니다.

어휘 extensive 광범위한 collection 수집 period 시대 facility 시설 explanation 설명 exhibit 전시품 corresponding to ~에 해당하는 description 설명[서술]

89

고난도

Where most likely is the introduction taking place?

(A) At a university student center
(B) At an art museum
(C) At a formal garden
(D) At a photo studio

어디에서 소개가 이루어지고 있는 것 같은가?

(A) 대학 학생회관
(B) 미술관
(C) 잘 갖춰진 정원
(D) 사진관

해설 전체 내용 관련 – 소개가 이루어지는 장소

화자가 도입부에 다양한 시대의 회화 및 사진 작품을 시에서 최대로 보유하고 있는 이곳에 오신 모두를 환영한다(Welcome, all, to the home of the city's most extensive collection of paintings and photographs from all different time periods)고 한 것으로 보아 정답은 (B)이다.

▸▸ Paraphrasing 담화의 the home of the city's most extensive collection of paintings and photographs → 정답의 an art museum

90

What will the speaker give the listeners?

(A) An audio device
(B) A gift shop coupon
(C) A guide map to a facility
(D) A link to a mobile phone app

화자는 청자들에게 무엇을 줄 것인가?

(A) 오디오 장치
(B) 선물 가게 쿠폰
(C) 시설 안내도
(D) 휴대전화 앱 링크

해설 세부 사항 관련 – 화자가 청자들에게 줄 것

화자가 중반부에 제가 잠시 후 여러분께 드릴 이 버튼식 오디오 가이드를 통해 모든 전시품에 대한 설명을 들으실 수 있다(you can hear explanations of all the exhibits through this pushbutton audio guide that I'll give you in a minute)고 했으므로 정답은 (A)이다.

▸▸ Paraphrasing 담화의 this pushbutton audio guide → 정답의 an audio device

91

What does the speaker suggest doing?

(A) Watching an introductory film
(B) Ordering a meal in advance
(C) Starting a tour in a less crowded area
(D) Filling out a feedback survey

화자는 무엇을 하라고 제안하는가?

(A) 소개 영상 보기
(B) 미리 식사 주문하기
(C) 덜 붐비는 곳에서 관람 시작하기
(D) 피드백 설문지 작성하기

어휘 introductory 소개용의 meal 식사 in advance 미리 crowded 붐비는 fill out 작성하다 survey 설문 조사

해설 세부 사항 관련 – 화자가 하라고 제안하는 것

화자가 마지막에 현재 우리 메인 갤러리는 이미 꽤 꽉 찼기 때문에 갤러리 B에서 관람을 시작하시기를 권한다(I recommend beginning your tour in Gallery B, since our main gallery is already quite full at the moment)고 했으므로 정답은 (C)이다.

▸▸ Paraphrasing 담화의 full → 정답의 crowded

92-94 전화 메시지

W-Am Hi, Tony. **92I heard you got approval for your transfer to the company's overseas office in Hong Kong. Congratulations!** Related to that, you had asked me last week about having your belongings moved out of your apartment and

Test 7

put into storage. And, well...**there are a lot of moving companies in this area.** [93]**I wouldn't worry at all.** [94]**If you have time, go online and visit www.hongkong-sources.com. It has useful information about living in that area, and it'll help you out a lot I think.** Hope to talk again soon. Bye.

안녕하세요, 토니. 홍콩에 있는 회사의 해외 지사로 전근 허가를 받았다고 들었어요. 축하드려요! 그와 관련해서 지난주에 제게 당신의 물건을 아파트에서 옮겨서 창고에 넣는 것에 대해 물어보셨잖아요. 음… 이 지역에는 이삿짐 센터가 많아요. 저라면 전혀 걱정하지 않을 거예요. 시간이 되시면 온라인에 접속해 www. hongkong-sources.com을 방문해보세요. 그 지역에 사는 것에 대한 유용한 정보도 있고 제 생각엔 당신에게 많은 도움이 될 것 같아요. 조만간 다시 이야기하기를 바랍니다. 안녕히 계세요.

어휘 approval 승인 transfer 전근 overseas 해외의 related to ~와 관련있는 belongings 소유물 storage 보관소

92

Why most likely does the speaker congratulate the listener?

(A) He gave a successful presentation.
(B) He recently purchased a new house.
(C) His transfer request was granted.
(D) His sales team won an award.

화자는 왜 청자를 축하하는 것 같은가?
(A) 그가 성공적인 발표를 했다.
(B) 최근에 새 집을 샀다.
(C) 전근 요청이 승인되었다.
(D) 그의 영업팀이 상을 받았다.

어휘 successful 성공적인 presentation 발표 recently 최근에 purchase 구입하다 grant 승인하다 award 상

해설 세부 사항 관련 – 화자가 청자를 축하하는 이유
화자가 초반부에 홍콩에 있는 회사의 해외 지사로 전근 허가를 받았다고 들었다(I heard you got approval for your transfer to the company's overseas office in Hong Kong)면서, 축하드린다(Congratulations!)고 한 것으로 보아 정답은 (C)이다.

▸▸ Paraphrasing 담화의 got approval for your transfer → 정답의 His transfer request was granted

93

What does the speaker imply when she says, "there are a lot of moving companies in this area"?

(A) She needs more details about a project.
(B) The region has many new residents.
(C) It will not be difficult to hire a mover.
(D) A new company might struggle at first.

화자가 "이 지역에는 이삿짐 센터가 많아요"라고 말하는 의미는 무엇인가?
(A) 프로젝트에 대한 더 많은 정보가 필요하다.
(B) 그 지역에는 신규 거주자가 많다.
(C) 이삿짐 센터를 고용하기 어렵지 않을 것이다.
(D) 신생 회사는 처음에 고전할 수도 있다.

어휘 details 세부 사항 region 지역 resident 거주자 hire 고용하다 mover 이삿짐 센터 struggle 고군분투하다

해설 화자의 의도 파악 – 이 지역에는 이삿짐 센터가 많다는 말의 의도
화자가 인용문 뒤에 저라면 전혀 걱정하지 않을 것(I wouldn't worry at all)이라고 한 것으로 보아 주변에 이삿짐 센터가 많이 있어서 구하기 힘들지 않을 거라 걱정할 필요 없다는 의도로 한 말임을 알 수 있다. 따라서 정답은 (C)이다.

94

What does the speaker say will be helpful for the listener?

(A) Browsing a Web site
(B) Modifying a travel itinerary
(C) Completing an electronic form
(D) Holding a special staff meeting

화자는 무엇이 청자에게 도움이 될 것이라고 말하는가?
(A) 웹사이트 검색
(B) 여행 일정 수정
(C) 전자 양식 작성
(D) 특별 직원 회의 개최

어휘 browse 검색하다 modify 수정하다 itinerary 여행 일정 complete 작성하다 electronic 전자의 form 양식 hold (회의 등) 개최하다

해설 세부 사항 관련 – 화자가 청자에게 도움이 될 것이라고 말하는 것
화자가 후반부에 시간이 되면, 온라인에 접속해 www.hongkong-sources.com을 방문해보라(If you have time, go online and visit www.hong-kong-sources.com)면서, 그 지역에 사는 것에 대한 유용한 정보도 있고, 제 생각엔 당신에게 많은 도움이 될 것 같다(It has useful information about living in that area, and it'll help you out a lot I think)고 했으므로 정답은 (A)이다.

▸▸ Paraphrasing 담화의 go online and visit www.hongkong-sources.com → 정답의 browsing a Web site

95-97 회의 발췌 + 차트

M-Cn As you know, the interns will start next week. [95]**They'll first receive classroom instruction to become familiar with all the inventory management software products we've created for various industries.** Then we'll give them hands-on training in our newest program, Merchandise-Wiz, aimed at the shoe industry. [96]**This will help them to perform their**

duties related to monitoring our online customer service forum. Now, we have one last-minute change for the practical module. ⁹⁷**The air conditioning is malfunctioning in the room Yuko was assigned, so we won't use that one.** Her trainee group is small, so we'll combine it with Jim's group and they'll meet in his assigned room.

아시다시피, 인턴들이 다음 주에 일을 시작할 겁니다. 그들은 먼저 다양한 산업을 위해 우리가 제작한 재고 관리 소프트웨어 전 제품에 익숙해지도록 강의실 교육을 받을 것입니다. 그런 다음 신발 산업을 겨냥한 우리의 최신 프로그램인 머천다이즈 위즈로 실습 교육을 그들에게 제공할 것입니다. 이는 인턴들이 우리 온라인 고객 서비스 포럼을 모니터링하는 것과 관련된 임무를 수행하는 데 도움이 될 것입니다. 자, 실습 모듈에 막판 변경 사항이 하나 있습니다. 유코가 배정받은 강의실의 에어컨이 오작동하고 있어서 그 강의실은 사용하지 않을 것입니다. 그녀의 연수생 그룹은 작으니 짐의 그룹과 합쳐서 그가 배정받은 강의실에서 만날 것입니다.

어휘 instruction 교육, 지시 familiar ~을 잘 아는 inventory 재고(품) hands-on 직접 해 보는 aim 겨냥하다 perform 수행하다 duty 임무 related to ~와 관련 있는 monitor 감시하다 last-minute 마지막 순간의 practical 실습의 module 모듈, 교과목 단위 malfunctioning 오작동하는 assign 배정하다 trainee 연수생 combine 결합하다

Name of Trainer	Room number
Gregor	305
Jim	307
Becky	309
⁹⁷Yuko	311

강사명	강의실 번호
그레고르	305
짐	307
베키	309
⁹⁷유코	311

95

What kind of business does the speaker most likely work for?

(A) At a merchandise display distributor
(B) At a software development firm
(C) At a footwear manufacturer
(D) At a package shipping company

화자는 어떤 종류의 회사에서 일할 것 같은가?

(A) 상품 진열 유통업체
(B) 소프트웨어 개발 회사
(C) 신발 제조업체
(D) 택배 운송 회사

어휘 merchandise 상품 display 진열 distributor 유통업체 development 개발 firm 회사 footwear 신발 manufacturer 제조업체 package 소포 shipping 운송

해설 전체 내용 관련 – 화자의 근무지
화자가 초반부에 그들(인턴들)은 먼저 다양한 산업을 위해 우리가 제작한 재고 관리 소프트웨어 전 제품에 익숙해지도록 강의실 교육을 받을 것(They'll first receive classroom instruction to become familiar with all the inventory management software products we've created for various industries)이라고 한 것으로 보아 정답은 (B)이다.

96

고난도

According to the speaker, what will interns be required to do?

(A) Oversee an online messaging board
(B) Create posts for a social media account
(C) Test a feature of a computer program
(D) Compile statistics about clients

화자에 따르면, 인턴들은 무엇을 해야 하는가?

(A) 온라인 메시지 게시판 감독
(B) 소셜 미디어 계정을 위한 게시물 작성
(C) 컴퓨터 프로그램의 기능 테스트
(D) 고객에 대한 통계 작성

어휘 oversee 감독하다 board 게시판 create 만들다 post 게시물 account 계정 feature 특징 compile 작성하다 statistics 통계

해설 세부 사항 관련 – 화자가 말하는 인턴들이 해야 할 일
화자가 중반부에 이는 인턴들이 우리 온라인 고객 서비스 포럼을 모니터링하는 것과 관련된 임무를 수행하는 데 도움이 될 것(This will help them to perform their duties related to monitoring our online customer service forum)이라고 했으므로 정답은 (A)이다.

▸▸ Paraphrasing 담화의 monitoring our online customer service forum → 정답의 oversee an online messaging board

97

Look at the graphic. Which room will most likely NOT be used for training?

(A) 305
(B) 307
(C) 309
(D) 311

시각 정보에 의하면, 어느 강의실이 교육에 사용되지 않을 것 같은가?

(A) 305
(B) 307
(C) 309
(D) 311

화자가 후반부에 유코가 배정받은 강의실의 에어컨이 오작동하고 있어서 그 강의실은 사용하지 않을 것(The air conditioning is malfunctioning in the room Yuko was assigned, so we won't use that one)이라고 했고, 차트에 의하면 유코가 배정받은 강의실은 311호이므로 정답은 (D)이다.

98-100 공지 + 표지판

W-Am OK, big announcement... **98 In June, we're going to move all warehouse staff to a "four-ten workweek". You'll have four days of ten-hour shifts and then three days off.** **99 This will make it easier for our temporary staff to help out as we approach the summer season, when we experience peak demand for our services.** There will be a full meeting on this change next Monday. **100 Also, yesterday I put up a new sign in the loading dock area. It informs visitors that they need to wear identification badges.** There's now a lot of information on that wall. But we do need to ensure procedures are being followed correctly.

자, 중대 발표가 있습니다… 6월에 모든 창고 직원을 '주 4–10 근무제'로 바꿀 겁니다. 4일간 10시간 근무를 한 뒤 3일을 쉬게 됩니다. 이렇게 하면 우리 서비스에 대한 수요가 최고조인 여름철이 다가올 때 임시직원들이 도움을 주는 것이 쉬워질 것입니다. 다음 주 월요일에 이 변경에 대한 전체 회의가 있을 겁니다. 또, 어제는 제가 하역장에 새 표지판을 달았습니다. 방문객들에게 신분증 배지를 착용하고 있어야 한다는 점을 알리는 것입니다. 그 벽에는 지금 많은 정보가 있습니다. 그러나 절차가 바르게 준수되고 있는지 확실히 해야 할 필요가 있습니다.

어휘 announcement 발표 warehouse 창고 workweek 주당 근무 시간 shift 근무 시간, 근무조 temporary 임시의 approach 다가가다[오다] experience 경험하다 peak 절정, 최고조 demand 수요 loading dock 하역장 inform 알리다 identification 신분증 badge 배지 ensure 반드시 ~하게 하다 procedure 절차 correctly 바르게

Sign

1	Delivery Drivers Must Sign in at Office
2	100 Visitors Must Wear ID Badges
3	Area Monitored by Security Camera
4	Parking for Delivery Vehicles Only

표지판

1	배달 기사 사무실 출입 시 필히 서명
2	100 방문객 신분증 배지 필히 착용
3	보안 카메라 감시 구역
4	배송 차량 전용 주차 공간

98

What does the speaker first announce a change to?

(A) A work schedule
(B) The staff dress code
(C) A stocking system
(D) A floor plan

화자는 무엇에 대한 변경을 첫 번째로 발표하는가?

(A) 근무 일정
(B) 직원 복장 규정
(C) 재고 시스템
(D) 평면도

해설 세부 사항 관련 – 화자가 첫 번째로 발표하는 변경 사항

화자가 초반부에 6월에 모든 창고 직원을 '주 4-10 근무제'로 바꿀 것(In June, we're going to move all warehouse staff to a "four-ten workweek")이라며, 4일간 10시간 근무를 한 뒤 3일을 쉬게 된다(You'll have four days of ten-hour shifts and then three days off)고 근무 시간이 변경될 것임을 가장 먼저 발표했으므로 정답은 (A)이다.

99 고난도

According to the speaker, what will happen in the summer?

(A) A new product will be launched.
(B) A busy period will begin.
(C) A facility will close temporarily.
(D) A sales contest will take place.

화자에 따르면, 여름에 무슨 일이 일어날 것인가?

(A) 신상품이 출시될 것이다.
(B) 바쁜 기간이 시작될 것이다.
(C) 시설이 일시적으로 폐쇄될 것이다.
(D) 판매 경쟁이 있을 것이다.

어휘 launch 출시하다 period 기간 facility 시설 temporarily 일시적으로 contest 경연, 경쟁

해설 세부 사항 관련 – 화자가 여름에 일어난다고 말하는 일

화자가 중반부에 이렇게 하면 우리 서비스에 대한 수요가 최고조인 여름철이 다가올 때 임시직원들이 도움을 주는 것이 쉬워질 것(This will make it easier for our temporary staff to help out as we approach the summer season, when we experience peak demand for our services)이라고 했으므로 정답은 (B)이다.

▶▶ Paraphrasing 담화의 when we experience peak demand for our services → 정답의 a busy period

100

Look at the graphic. Which sign did the speaker install yesterday?

(A) Sign #1
(B) Sign #2
(C) Sign #3
(D) Sign #4

시각 정보에 의하면, 화자는 어제 무슨 표지판을 설치했는가?

(A) 표지판 1
(B) 표지판 2
(C) 표지판 3
(D) 표지판 4

해설 시각 정보 연계 – 화자가 어제 설치한 표지판

화자가 후반부에 어제 하역장에 새 표지판을 달았다(yesterday I put up a new sign in the loading dock area)며, 이는 방문객들에게 신분증 배지를 착용하고 있어야 한다는 점을 알리는 것(It informs visitors that they need to wear identification badges)이라고 했고, 시각 정보에 의하면 방문객의 신분증 착용에 관한 표지판은 2번 표지판이므로 정답은 (B)이다.

TEST 8

1 (C)	2 (D)	3 (A)	4 (C)	5 (C)
6 (D)	7 (A)	8 (C)	9 (B)	10 (A)
11 (C)	12 (B)	13 (A)	14 (A)	15 (C)
16 (B)	17 (B)	18 (C)	19 (A)	20 (B)
21 (C)	22 (C)	23 (A)	24 (B)	25 (C)
26 (C)	27 (A)	28 (B)	29 (A)	30 (B)
31 (C)	32 (A)	33 (D)	34 (A)	35 (B)
36 (A)	37 (C)	38 (C)	39 (B)	40 (B)
41 (D)	42 (C)	43 (A)	44 (C)	45 (A)
46 (B)	47 (A)	48 (D)	49 (D)	50 (B)
51 (C)	52 (B)	53 (D)	54 (B)	55 (C)
56 (C)	57 (D)	58 (C)	59 (A)	60 (A)
61 (D)	62 (B)	63 (B)	64 (A)	65 (C)
66 (D)	67 (C)	68 (B)	69 (B)	70 (A)
71 (B)	72 (A)	73 (A)	74 (D)	75 (C)
76 (D)	77 (C)	78 (C)	79 (B)	80 (B)
81 (D)	82 (B)	83 (A)	84 (D)	85 (A)
86 (C)	87 (C)	88 (B)	89 (D)	90 (B)
91 (D)	92 (A)	93 (B)	94 (D)	95 (D)
96 (A)	97 (D)	98 (A)	99 (C)	100 (C)

PART 1

1 W-Am

(A) He is carrying a bucket.
(B) He is adjusting his hat.
(C) He is leaning against a ladder.
(D) He is painting the side of a house.

(A) 남자는 양동이를 나르고 있다.
(B) 남자는 모자를 고쳐 쓰고 있다.
(C) 남자는 사다리에 기대고 있다.
(D) 남자는 집의 측면을 페인트칠하고 있다.

어휘 bucket 양동이 adjust 조절하다 lean against 기대다 ladder
사다리

해설 1인 등장 사진 – 인물의 동작 묘사
(A) 동사 오답. 남자가 양동이를 나르고 있는(is carrying a bucket) 모습이
아니므로 오답.
(B) 동사 오답. 남자가 모자를 고쳐 쓰고 있는(is adjusting his hat) 모습이
아니라 쓰고 있는(is wearing) 모습이므로 오답.
(C) 정답. 남자가 사다리에 기대고 있는(is leaning against a ladder) 모습
이므로 정답.
(D) 동사 오답. 남자가 집의 측면을 페인트칠하고 있는(is painting the side
of a house) 모습이 아니므로 오답.

2 M-Au

(A) They are clapping their hands.
(B) They are running side by side.
(C) They are drinking from bottles.
(D) They are facing one another.

(A) 사람들은 박수를 치고 있다.
(B) 사람들은 나란히 달리고 있다.
(C) 사람들은 병에 든 음료를 마시고 있다.
(D) 사람들은 서로 마주보고 있다.

어휘 clap 박수를 치다 side by side 나란히 bottle 병 face ~을
마주보다 one another 서로

해설 2인 이상 등장 사진 – 인물의 동작 묘사
(A) 동사 오답. 사람들이 박수를 치고 있는(are clapping their hands) 모습
이 아니므로 오답.
(B) 동사 오답. 사람들이 나란히 달리고 있는(are running side by side) 모
습이 아니므로 오답.
(C) 동사 오답. 사람들이 병에 든 음료를 마시고 있는(are drinking from
bottles) 모습이 아니므로 오답.
(D) 정답. 사람들이 서로 마주보고 있는(are facing one another) 모습이므
로 정답.

3 M-Cn

(A) A man is working with a hand tool.
(B) Bricks are being stacked in piles.
(C) An outdoor garden is being planted.
(D) A man is sweeping a walking path.

(A) 남자는 수공구를 가지고 일하고 있다.
(B) 벽돌이 수북하게 쌓이고 있다.
(C) 야외 정원에 식물이 심어지고 있다.
(D) 남자는 보도를 쓸고 있다.

어휘 hand tool 수공구 brick 벽돌 stack 쌓다 in piles 수북하게
outdoor 야외의 plant 심다 sweep (빗자루로) 쓸다 path 길

해설 혼합 사진 – 사람 또는 사물 묘사
(A) 정답. 남자가 수공구를 가지고 일하고 있는(is working with a hand
tool) 모습이므로 정답.
(B) 동사 오답. 벽돌(bricks)이 수북하게 쌓이고 있는(are being stacked in
piles) 모습이 아니므로 오답.

(C) 동사 오답. 야외 정원(an outdoor garden)에 식물이 심어지고 있는(is being planted) 모습이 아니므로 오답.

(D) 동사 오답. 남자가 보도를 쓸고 있는(is sweeping a walking path) 모습이 아니므로 오답.

---

4 W-Br 고난도

(A) The door of a laundry machine is being opened.
(B) There is a seating area in the center of the room.
(C) A bin has been set up near some appliances.
(D) Some laundry is being folded beside a basket.

(A) 세탁기의 문이 열리고 있다.
(B) 방의 중앙에 좌석 공간이 있다.
(C) 통이 가전제품 가까이에 놓여 있다.
(D) 세탁물이 바구니 옆에서 개켜지고 있다.

어휘 laundry 세탁, 세탁물 seating 좌석 bin (저장용) 통, 쓰레기통 appliances 가전제품 fold 개키다[접다]

해설 배경 사진 – 실내 사물의 상태 묘사

(A) 동사 오답. 세탁기의 문(the door of a laundry machine)이 열리고 있는(is being opened) 모습이 아니므로 오답.

(B) 사진에 없는 명사를 이용한 오답. 사진에 좌석 공간(a seating area)의 모습이 보이지 않으므로 오답.

(C) 정답. 통(a bin)이 가전제품 가까이에 놓여 있는(has been set up near some appliances) 모습이므로 정답.

(D) 동사 오답. 세탁물(some laundry)이 바구니 옆(beside a basket)에서 개켜지고 있는(is being folded) 모습이 아니므로 오답.

---

5 M-Au 고난도

(A) People are stepping onto an escalator.
(B) Baggage is being pulled off a cart.
(C) A walkway is lined with columns.
(D) The woman is inspecting the man's luggage.

(A) 사람들은 에스컬레이터에 오르고 있다.
(B) 짐이 카트에서 꺼내지고 있다.
(C) 보도에 기둥이 늘어서 있다.
(D) 여자는 남자의 짐을 검사하고 있다.

어휘 step 움직이다 baggage 짐[수하물] walkway 보도 line ~을 따라 늘어서다 column 기둥 inspect 검사하다 luggage 짐[수하물]

해설 혼합 사진 – 사람 또는 사물 묘사

(A) 사진에 없는 명사를 이용한 오답. 사진에 에스컬레이터(an escalator)의 모습이 보이지 않으므로 오답.

(B) 동사 오답. 짐(baggage)이 카트에서 꺼내지고 있는(is being pulled off a cart) 모습이 아니므로 오답.

(C) 정답. 보도(a walkway)에 기둥이 늘어서 있는(is lined with columns) 모습이므로 정답.

(D) 동사 오답. 여자가 남자의 짐을 검사하고 있는(is inspecting the man's luggage) 모습이 아니므로 오답.

---

6 W-Am

(A) Cars are parked along a parade route.
(B) Performers are climbing onto a raised stage.
(C) There are spectators watching from windows.
(D) Musical instruments are being played on a street.

(A) 자동차들이 퍼레이드 경로를 따라 주차되어 있다.
(B) 연주자들이 솟은 무대 위로 올라가고 있다.
(C) 창문에서 구경하는 관중들이 있다.
(D) 악기들이 거리에서 연주되고 있다.

어휘 parade 퍼레이드 route 경로 performer 연주자 climb 오르다 spectator 관중 musical instrument 악기

해설 혼합 사진 – 사람 또는 사물 묘사

(A) 사진에 없는 명사를 이용한 오답. 사진에 차(cars)들의 모습이 보이지 않으므로 오답.

(B) 사진에 없는 명사를 이용한 오답. 사진에 솟은 무대(a raised stage)의 모습이 보이지 않으므로 오답.

(C) 위치 오답. 창문에서 구경하고 있는(watching from windows) 관중들(spectators)의 모습이 보이지 않으므로 오답.

(D) 정답. 악기들(musical instruments)이 거리에서 연주되고 있는(are being played on a street) 모습이므로 정답.

PART 2

7

W-Am What time do you close this evening?

M-Cn (A) We're open until ten o'clock.

(B) This tie matches with those clothes.

(C) On Friday the twelfth.

오늘 저녁 몇 시에 문을 닫나요?
(A) 저희는 10시까지 영업합니다.
(B) 이 넥타이는 저 옷들과 잘 어울려요.
(C) 12일 금요일입니다.

어휘 tie 넥타이; 묶다 match 어울리다

해설 문 닫는 시각을 묻는 What 의문문
(A) 정답. 오늘 저녁 몇 시에 문을 닫는지 묻는 질문에 10시까지 영업한다며 간접적으로 응답하고 있으므로 정답.
(B) 유사 발음 오답. 질문의 close와 부분적으로 발음이 유사한 clothes를 이용한 오답.
(C) 질문과 상관없는 오답. 날짜를 묻는 When 의문문에 대한 응답이므로 오답.

8

M-Au Who made this brochure for the trade show?

W-Br (A) Yes, with a special printer.

(B) Sorry—this copy is for Valerie.

(C) Someone on the design team.

누가 이 무역 박람회용 책자를 만들었죠?
(A) 네, 특수 프린터로요.
(B) 죄송하지만 이 복사본은 발레리를 위한 겁니다.
(C) 디자인팀의 누군가요.

어휘 brochure 책자 trade 무역 copy 복사본

해설 책자의 작성자를 묻는 Who 의문문
(A) Yes/No 불가 오답. Who 의문문에는 Yes/No 응답이 불가능하므로 오답.
(B) 연상 단어 오답. 질문의 brochure에서 연상 가능한 copy를 이용한 오답.
(C) 정답. 무역 박람회용 책자를 만든 사람을 묻는 질문에 디자인팀의 누군가라고 응답하고 있으므로 정답.

9

M-Cn Do you have any extra paper?

W-Am (A) A one-year subscription.

(B) I'll look in the storage closet.

(C) That dish is already pretty spicy.

여분의 종이가 있으십니까?
(A) 1년 구독입니다.
(B) 수납장을 볼게요.
(C) 그 요리는 이미 꽤 매워요.

어휘 extra 추가의 subscription 구독 storage closet 수납장 pretty 꽤 spicy 매운

해설 여분의 종이가 있는지 묻는 조동사(Do) 의문문
(A) 질문과 상관없는 오답.
(B) 정답. 여분의 종이가 있는지 묻는 질문에 수납장을 보겠다며 도움을 주고 있으므로 정답.
(C) 연상 단어 오답. 질문의 paper와 발음이 비슷한 pepper(후추)에서 연상 가능한 spicy를 이용한 오답.

10

W-Br When will the renovation project be finished?

M-Au (A) Probably by early spring.

(B) For the new staff lounge.

(C) Due to some budget concerns.

보수 공사는 언제 끝날까요?
(A) 아마 이른 봄쯤에요.
(B) 새로운 직원 휴게실을 위해서요.
(C) 일부 예산 걱정 때문에요.

어휘 renovation 보수 probably 아마 early 이른 lounge 휴게실 budget 예산 concern 우려[걱정]

해설 카페 개조가 끝나는 시점을 묻는 When 의문문
(A) 정답. 보수 공사가 끝나는 시점을 묻는 질문에 아마 이른 봄쯤이라며 구체적인 시기를 알려주고 있으므로 정답.
(B) 질문과 상관없는 오답. Why 의문문에 대한 응답이므로 오답.
(C) 질문과 상관없는 오답. Why 의문문에 대한 응답이므로 오답.

11

W-Am Where should we go to have the posters made?

M-Cn (A) No, it isn't that difficult.

(B) Because I need to frame them.

(C) Elm Street Printing does good work.

포스터를 만들려면 어디로 가야 할까요?
(A) 아니요, 그렇게 어렵지 않아요.
(B) 그것들을 액자에 넣어야 해서요.
(C) 엘름 스트리트 프린팅이 일을 잘 해요.

어휘 frame 액자에 넣다

해설 포스터 제작할 수 있는 장소를 묻는 Where 의문문
(A) Yes/No 불가 오답. Where 의문문에는 Yes/No 응답이 불가능하므로 오답.
(B) 질문과 상관없는 오답. Why 의문문에 대한 응답이므로 오답.
(C) 정답. 포스터를 만들기 위해 가야 하는 장소를 묻는 질문에 엘름 스트리트 프린팅이 일을 잘 한다고 알려주고 있으므로 정답.

12

W-Br How can I join a video conference with this software?

M-Cn (A) Yes, I enjoyed listening to her presentation.

(B) Click the camera button on the screen.

(C) The cashier will check their membership cards.

이 소프트웨어로 어떻게 화상 회의에 참가할 수 있나요?

(A) 네, 그녀의 발표를 즐겁게 들었습니다.
(B) **화면에 있는 카메라 버튼을 클릭하세요.**
(C) 계산대 점원이 회원증을 확인할 겁니다.

어휘 video conference 화상 회의 presentation 발표 cashier 출납원

해설 소프트웨어를 이용한 화상 회의 참가 방법을 묻는 How 의문문
(A) Yes/No 불가 오답. How 의문문에는 Yes/No 응답이 불가능하므로 오답.
(B) 정답. 소프트웨어를 이용해 화상 회의에 참가하는 방법을 묻는 질문에 화면에 있는 카메라 버튼을 클릭하라며 구체적인 방법을 알려주고 있으므로 정답.
(C) 연상 단어 오답. 질문의 join에서 연상 가능한 membership을 이용한 오답.

13

M-Au Are you looking for a part-time or a full-time position?

W-Br (A) I'm hoping to work twenty hours per week.
(B) Not anymore—Kazuki let me borrow his.
(C) The dental clinic might be hiring.

시간제 근무를 찾고 계시나요, 아니면 정규직을 찾고 계시나요?
(A) **주당 20시간을 근무하고 싶어요.**
(B) 이제 아니에요. 가즈키가 제게 자기 것을 빌려줬어요.
(C) 치과에서 채용 중일 수도 있어요.

어휘 per ~당 borrow 빌리다 dental clinic 치과 hire 채용하다

해설 구직 중인 직종을 묻는 선택의문문
(A) 정답. 시간제 근무와 정규직 중 찾고 있는 직종을 묻는 선택의문문에서 주당 20시간을 근무하고 싶다며 시간제 근무를 찾고 있다는 것을 우회적으로 나타내고 있으므로 정답.
(B) 연상 단어 오답. 질문의 looking for에서 연상 가능한 borrow를 이용한 오답.
(C) 연상 단어 오답. 질문의 position에서 연상 가능한 hiring을 이용한 오답.

14

M-Cn Who is in charge of ordering cleaning supplies?

W-Am (A) Are we running low already?
(B) A charger for mobile devices.
(C) That surprised me too.

누가 청소 용품 주문을 담당하나요?
(A) **벌써 바닥났나요?**
(B) 휴대 장치용 충전기입니다.
(C) 저도 놀랐어요.

어휘 in charge of ~을 담당하다 supplies 용품 run low 바닥나다 charger 충전기 mobile 이동하는 device 장치

해설 청소 용품 주문 담당자를 묻는 Who 의문문
(A) 정답. 청소 용품 주문을 담당하는 사람을 묻는 질문에 벌써 바닥났는지 주문과 관련하여 되묻고 있으므로 정답.
(B) 유사 발음 오답. 질문의 charge와 부분적으로 발음이 유사한 charger를 이용한 오답.
(C) 유사 발음 오답. 질문의 supplies와 부분적으로 발음이 유사한 surprised를 이용한 오답.

---

15 고난도

M-Au Wasn't Frank supposed to lead tomorrow's workshop?

W-Am (A) I've read only the first one.
(B) I doubt he did it.
(C) Haven't you seen the updated schedule?

프랭크가 내일 워크숍을 이끌기로 되어 있었지 않나요?
(A) 첫 번째 것만 읽었어요.
(B) 저는 그가 그랬다고 생각하지 않아요.
(C) **변경된 스케줄을 못 보셨나요?**

어휘 be supposed to ~하기로 되어 있다 lead 이끌다 doubt 의심을 갖다, 의심하다

해설 프랭크가 워크숍을 주도하는지 여부를 확인하는 부정의문문
(A) 유사 발음 오답. 질문의 lead와 부분적으로 발음이 유사한 read를 이용한 오답.
(B) 질문과 상관없는 오답. 내일 일정을 묻는 질문에 과거형으로 답하고 있으므로 오답.
(C) 정답. 프랭크가 내일 워크숍을 이끌기로 되어 있는지 여부를 묻는 질문에 변경된 스케줄을 보지 못했는지 되물으며 프랭크가 맡지 않을 수도 있음을 우회적으로 암시하고 있으므로 정답.

---

16 고난도

W-Br Why don't we take the subway to get to the airport?

M-Cn (A) He has to change planes in Madrid.
(B) We have too many heavy bags.
(C) To register for flight update texts.

지하철을 타고 공항에 가는 게 어떨까요?
(A) 그는 마드리드에서 비행기를 갈아타야 해요.
(B) **무거운 가방이 너무 많아요.**
(C) 항공편 업데이트 문자를 신청하려고요.

어휘 subway 지하철 plane 비행기 register for 신청[등록]하다 flight 항공편 text 문자

해설 제안/권유의 의문문
(A) 연상 단어 오답. 질문의 airport에서 연상 가능한 planes를 이용한 오답.
(B) 정답. 지하철을 타고 공항에 가자고 제안하는 질문에 무거운 가방이 너무 많다며 거절의 의사를 우회적으로 나타내고 있으므로 정답.
(C) 연상 단어 오답. 질문의 airport에서 연상 가능한 flight을 이용한 오답.

17

M-Au Have we ever advertised in local magazines?

W-Br (A) She used to work as a television reporter.
(B) No, but we could consider it.
(C) When did you send it?

우리가 지역 잡지에 광고를 낸 적이 있나요?
(A) 그녀는 텔레비전 리포터로 일했어요.
(B) **아니요, 그렇지만 고려해볼 수 있어요.**
(C) 언제 그것을 보내셨어요?

Test 8

advertise 광고하다 local 지역의 consider 고려하다

해설 지역 잡지에 광고를 낸 적이 있는지 여부를 묻는 조동사(Have) 의문문

(A) 연상 단어 오답. 질문의 magazines에서 연상 가능한 reporter를 이용한 오답.

(B) 정답. 지역 잡지에 광고를 낸 적이 있는지를 묻는 질문에 아니요(No)라고 대답한 뒤, 그렇지만 고려해볼 수 있다며 관련 의견을 덧붙였으므로 정답.

(C) 질문과 상관없는 오답.

18

M-Cn It's chilly in here, isn't it?

W-Am (A) We couldn't hear the sound.

(B) He's on another line now.

(C) I just turned the heat up.

여기는 춥네요, 그렇지 않나요?

(A) 소리를 듣지 못했어요.

(B) 그는 지금 다른 전화를 받고 있어요.

(C) 방금 난방을 올렸어요.

어휘 chilly 추운 turn up (소리·난방을) 올리다 heat 난방, 온도

해설 장소가 추운지 여부를 확인하는 부가의문문

(A) 유사 발음 오답. 질문의 here와 부분적으로 발음이 유사한 hear를 이용한 오답.

(B) 질문과 상관없는 오답.

(C) 정답. 장소가 춥다는 것에 동의를 구하는 질문에 방금 난방을 올렸다며 의견에 동의함을 우회적으로 나타내고 있으므로 정답.

19

W-Br When does this gift card expire?

M-Au (A) It's good for five years.

(B) They retired from their positions last month.

(C) Thank you for thinking of me.

이 상품권은 언제 만료되나요?

(A) 5년간 유효합니다.

(B) 그들은 지난달에 퇴직했어요.

(C) 생각해주셔서 고맙습니다.

어휘 expire 만료되다 good 유효한 retire 은퇴하다

해설 상품권의 만료 시점을 묻는 When 의문문

(A) 정답. 상품권이 만료되는 시점을 묻는 질문에 5년간 유효하다며 5년 뒤에 만료된다는 점을 우회적으로 나타내고 있으므로 정답.

(B) 연상 단어 오답. 질문의 When에서 연상 가능한 last month를 이용한 오답.

(C) 연상 단어 오답. 질문의 gift에서 연상 가능한 thank you를 이용한 오답.

20   고난도

W-Am I heard a Mexican restaurant opened up nearby.

M-Cn (A) Oh, where did you find the key?

(B) We had Mexican for lunch on Monday.

(C) The maximum weight for packages.

근처에 멕시칸 식당이 문을 열었다고 들었어요.

(A) 아, 어디서 열쇠를 찾으셨나요?

(B) 우리는 월요일에 점심으로 멕시칸 음식을 먹었어요.

(C) 소포의 최대 중량입니다.

어휘 nearby 근처에 maximum 최대의 weight 무게 package 소포, 포장물

해설 정보 전달의 평서문

(A) 평서문과 상관없는 오답.

(B) 정답. 근처에 멕시칸 식당이 문을 열었다고 들었다는 평서문에 월요일에 점심으로 멕시칸 음식을 이미 먹었다며 멕시칸 식당에 갈 의사가 없다는 것을 우회적으로 알리고 있으므로 정답.

(C) 유사 발음 오답. 질문의 Mexican과 부분적으로 발음이 유사한 maximum을 이용한 오답.

21

M-Au Isn't the shipment of office furniture going to arrive here today?

W-Am (A) Check the assembly instructions.

(B) By using a mobile phone app.

(C) Yes, it's out for delivery now.

사무용 가구 배송이 오늘 이곳에 도착하지 않나요?

(A) 조립 설명서를 확인하세요.

(B) 휴대전화 앱을 이용해서요.

(C) 네, 현재 배송을 위해 출고되었습니다.

어휘 shipment 배송 assembly 조립 instruction 설명(서)

해설 배송물이 오늘 도착하는지 여부를 확인하는 부정의문문

(A) 연상 단어 오답. 질문의 furniture에서 연상 가능한 assembly를 이용한 오답.

(B) 질문과 상관없는 오답. How 의문문에 대한 응답이므로 오답.

(C) 정답. 사무용 가구 배송물이 오늘 이곳에 도착하는지를 묻는 질문에 네(Yes)라고 대답한 뒤, 현재 배송을 위해 출고되었다며 긍정 답변과 일관된 내용을 덧붙였으므로 정답.

22

W-Br Should we add a video to our next presentation?

M-Au (A) I haven't watched that one yet.

(B) The previous marketing director.

(C) Only if it's really necessary.

다음 프레젠테이션에 영상을 추가할까요?

(A) 아직 그것을 못 봤어요.

(B) 이전 마케팅 이사입니다.

(C) 정말 필요한 경우에만요.

어휘 add 추가하다 previous 이전의 director 이사 necessary 필수적인

해설 제안/권유의 의문문

(A) 연상 단어 오답. 질문의 video에서 연상 가능한 watched를 이용한 오답.

(B) 질문과 상관없는 오답. Who 의문문에 대한 응답이므로 오답.

(C) 정답. 다음 프레젠테이션에 영상을 추가할지 묻는 질문에 정말 필요한 경우에만이라며 조건부 동의의 의사를 전달하고 있으므로 정답.

23

M-Cn How have sales been for our newest energy drink?

W-Br (A) The figures are being compiled now.
(B) Solar is a good option for clean energy.
(C) I went to a discount supermarket.

우리의 최신 에너지 음료의 판매는 어땠나요?
(A) 지금 수치를 집계하는 중입니다.
(B) 태양열은 청정 에너지를 위한 좋은 선택입니다.
(C) 저는 할인 마트에 갔습니다.

어휘 newest 최신의 figure 수치 compile (자료 등을) 모으다, 집계하다
option 선택(권) discount 할인

해설 음료의 판매 상태를 묻는 How 의문문
(A) 정답. 최신 에너지 음료의 판매 상태를 묻는 질문에 지금 수치를 집계하는 중이라며 아직 판매 결과를 정확히 알지 못함을 우회적으로 응답하고 있으므로 정답.
(B) 단어 반복 오답. 질문의 energy를 반복 이용한 오답.
(C) 연상 단어 오답. 질문의 sales에서 연상 가능한 discount supermarket을 이용한 오답.

24

M-Cn The vending machine in the break room is out of order.

M-Au (A) All the guest rooms were booked.
(B) I already called the technician.
(C) Bending exercises to stay healthy.

휴게실의 자판기가 고장났어요.
(A) 모든 객실이 예약되었어요.
(B) 이미 기술자에게 전화했어요.
(C) 건강을 유지하기 위한 굽히기 운동이에요.

어휘 vending machine 자판기 break room 휴게실 out of order
고장난 book 예약하다 technician 기술자 bending 굽힘

해설 정보 전달의 평서문
(A) 단어 반복 오답. 평서문의 room을 반복 이용한 오답.
(B) 정답. 휴게실의 자판기가 고장났다는 평서문에 이미 기술자에게 전화했다며 문제 해결을 위한 후속 조치를 했다는 것을 알려주고 있으므로 정답.
(C) 유사 발음 오답. 평서문의 vending과 부분적으로 발음이 유사한 bending을 이용한 오답.

25　　　　　　　　　　　　　　고난도

W-Br Where is the ticket office located?

M-Au (A) Sure, I'll ask a parking attendant.
(B) Before the performance begins.
(C) Mark picked up our tickets yesterday.

매표소는 어디에 있나요?
(A) 물론이죠, 주차 요원에게 물어볼게요.
(B) 공연이 시작하기 전에요.
(C) 마크가 어제 우리 표를 찾아왔어요.

어휘 attendant 안내원, 종업원 performance 공연

해설 매표소의 위치를 묻는 Where 의문문
(A) Yes/No 불가 오답. Where 의문문에는 Yes/No 응답이 불가능한데, Sure도 일종의 Yes 응답이라고 볼 수 있으므로 오답.
(B) 연상 단어 오답. 질문의 ticket에서 연상 가능한 performance를 이용한 오답.
(C) 정답. 매표소가 있는 위치를 묻는 질문에 마크가 어제 우리 표를 찾아왔다며 매표소에 갈 필요가 없음을 우회적으로 알려주고 있으므로 정답.

26　　　　　　　　　　　　　　고난도

W-Am This notebook shouldn't be sitting out, should it?

M-Cn (A) At the employee performance review.
(B) He prefers electronic books.
(C) An intern may have left it there.

이 노트는 밖에 놓여 있으면 안 되죠, 그렇죠?
(A) 직원 업무 평가에서요.
(B) 그는 전자책을 선호해요.
(C) 인턴이 거기에 두었나 보네요.

어휘 sit 놓여 있다 performance review 업무 평가 prefer 선호하다
electronic 전자의

해설 공책이 밖에 있어도 되는지 여부를 확인하는 부가의문문
(A) 질문과 상관없는 오답. When 의문문에 대한 응답이므로 오답.
(B) 파생어 오답. 질문의 notebook과 파생어 관계인 books를 이용한 오답.
(C) 정답. 노트가 밖에 놓여 있는 것을 지적하는 질문에 인턴이 거기에 둔 것 같다며 관련 내용을 추측하고 있으므로 정답.

27

M-Au Why was this week's meeting so short?

W-Br (A) There wasn't much new agenda.
(B) Usually twice a week.
(C) No, our team is actually overstaffed.

이번 주 회의는 왜 그렇게 짧았나요?
(A) 새로운 안건이 별로 없었어요.
(B) 보통 일주일에 두 번이요.
(C) 아니요, 우리 팀은 사실 인원이 너무 많아요.

어휘 agenda 안건 actually 사실 overstaffed 인원 과잉인

해설 회의가 짧은 이유를 묻는 Why 의문문
(A) 정답. 이번 주 회의가 짧았던 이유를 묻는 질문에 새로운 안건이 별로 없었다며 이유를 제시하고 있으므로 정답.
(B) 질문과 상관없는 오답. How often 의문문에 대한 응답이므로 오답
(C) Yes/No 불가 오답. Why 의문문에는 Yes/No 응답이 불가능하므로 오답.

28

M-Cn Is the landscaping crew coming today or tomorrow?

W-Br (A) Probably some fences and gardens.

(B) They should be here this afternoon.

(C) The candidate's recent résumé.

조경 작업팀이 오늘 오나요, 아니면 내일 오나요?
(A) 아마 일부 울타리와 정원일 겁니다.
(B) 오늘 오후에 올 겁니다.
(C) 후보자의 최근 이력서입니다.

어휘 landscaping 조경 crew 인부, 팀원 probably 아마 fence 울타리 candidate 후보자 recent 최근의 résumé 이력서

해설 조경 인부들이 오는 날을 묻는 선택의문문
(A) 연상 단어 오답. 질문의 landscaping에서 연상 가능한 fences와 gardens를 이용한 오답.
(B) 정답. 조경 인부들이 오는 날을 묻는 선택의문문에서 오늘 오후에 올 것이라며 두 선택안 중 하나를 택해 응답하고 있으므로 정답.
(C) 질문과 상관없는 오답. What 의문문에 대한 응답이므로 오답.

29

M-Au Someone will have to let me into the warehouse.

W-Br (A) I have an access card.

(B) Most of our workers live in apartments, not houses.

(C) They're trying to save money on shipping.

누군가가 저를 창고 안으로 들여보내줘야겠어요.
(A) 제가 출입 카드를 갖고 있어요.
(B) 우리 근로자 대부분이 주택이 아니라 아파트에 살고 있어요.
(C) 그들은 운송비를 절약하려고 노력 중이에요.

어휘 warehouse 창고 access 접근[입장]

해설 부탁/요청의 평서문
(A) 정답. 누군가가 자신을 창고 안으로 들여보내줘야겠다고 요청하는 평서문에 출입 카드를 갖고 있다며 해결책을 우회적으로 제시하고 있으므로 정답.
(B) 파생어 오답. 평서문의 warehouse와 파생어 관계인 houses를 이용한 오답.
(C) 질문과 상관없는 오답.

30

W-Am The new carpeting looks great, doesn't it?

M-Cn (A) A few of them arrived late.

(B) The color is quite attractive.

(C) From an online clothing store.

새 카페트가 좋아 보이네요, 그렇죠?
(A) 그들 중 몇 명은 늦게 도착했어요.
(B) 색상이 꽤 매력적이에요.
(C) 온라인 의류 매장에서요.

어휘 quite 꽤 attractive 매력적인

해설 새 카페트가 좋아 보이는지 여부를 확인하는 부가의문문
(A) 질문과 상관없는 오답.
(B) 정답. 새 카페트가 좋아 보이는지 여부를 묻는 질문에 색상이 꽤 매력적이라며 좋아 보인다는 의사를 우회적으로 표현하고 있으므로 정답.
(C) 질문과 상관없는 오답. Where 의문문에 대한 응답이므로 오답.

31

W-Am Could you help me set up this display case?

W-Br (A) She was able to log on successfully.

(B) Why did they raise prices?

(C) Let's do that after our break.

이 진열장을 설치하는 걸 좀 도와주시겠어요?
(A) 그녀는 성공적으로 로그인할 수 있었어요.
(B) 그들은 왜 가격을 올렸을까요?
(C) 그 일은 쉬고 난 뒤에 합시다.

어휘 set up 설치하다 display case 진열장 successfully 성공적으로 raise 올리다 break 휴식

해설 부탁/요청의 의문문
(A) 연상 단어 오답. 질문의 Could에서 연상 가능한 was able to를 이용한 오답.
(B) 질문과 상관없는 오답.
(C) 정답. 진열장을 설치하는 것을 도와달라고 부탁하는 질문에 휴식 후 도와줄 의사가 있음을 나타내고 있으므로 정답.

PART 3

32-34

M-Cn Hi, Karen. While you were away, the maintenance crew took away all the old file cabinets. **³²So now we have more space to set up desks for the part-time staff. See?**

W-Br **³²Oh, I'm really happy to see that.** Everything looks terrific. **³³But... the carpets still have some stains. Shouldn't we get them cleaned professionally?**

M-Cn I was thinking the same thing. **³³I heard B & R Services does good work.** Plus, they use eco-friendly cleaning equipment. **³⁴Their Web site is B-and-R.com.**

W-Br **³⁴Great. Let's take a look now—we can go over all their service options.**

남 안녕하세요, 카렌. 당신이 없는 동안, 유지 보수 팀이 낡은 파일 캐비닛을 전부 치웠어요. 그래서 이제 우리는 시간제 직원들을 위해 책상을 설치할 더 많은 공간을 확보했어요. 보이죠?

여 아, 이걸 보니 정말 기분이 좋네요. 모든 것이 멋져 보여요. 하지만… 카펫에 아직 얼룩이 좀 있어요. 전문적으로 청소를 해야 하지 않을까요?

218

남 　나도 같은 생각을 하고 있었어요. B&R 서비스가 일을 잘한다고 들었어요. 게다가, 그들은 환경 친화적인 청소 장비를 사용해요. 그들의 웹사이트는 B-and-R.com이에요.

여 　좋아요. 지금 살펴봅시다. 그들의 서비스 옵션을 전부 검토해봐요.

어휘　maintenance 유지 보수　crew 팀, 반　terrific 멋진
　　　stain 얼룩　professionally 전문적으로　eco-friendly
　　　친환경적인　equipment 장비　go over 검토하다

32

What does the woman say she is pleased with?

(A) A larger work area
(B) An extended vacation
(C) Some budget decisions
(D) Some recent sales results

여자는 무엇에 만족한다고 말하는가?

(A) 더 넓은 작업 구역
(B) 늘어난 휴가
(C) 예산 결정
(D) 최근 판매 결과

어휘　extended 늘어난　vacation 휴가　budget 예산　decision 결정
　　　recent 최근의　result 결과

해설　세부 사항 관련 – 여자가 만족한다고 말한 것
남자가 첫 대사에서 이제 우리는 시간제 직원들을 위해 책상을 설치할 더 많은 공간을 확보했다(now we have more space to set up desks for the part-time staff)고 하자 여자가 뒤이어 이걸 보니 정말 기분이 좋다(I'm really happy to see that)고 했으므로 정답은 (A)이다.

▶▶ **Paraphrasing**　대화의 more space to set up desks for
　　　　　　　　　the part-time staff
　　　　　　　→ 정답의 a larger work area

33

What kind of business most likely is B & R Services?

(A) An event planning firm
(B) A temporary staffing agency
(C) An interior decorating provider
(D) A carpet cleaning company

B&R 서비스는 어떤 종류의 업체일 것 같은가?

(A) 행사 기획사
(B) 임시 직원 파견 업체
(C) 실내 장식 업체
(D) 카펫 청소 회사

어휘　planning 계획　temporary 임시의　staffing 직원 채용
　　　agency 대리점　decorating 장식　provider 제공자

해설　세부 사항 관련 – B&R 서비스의 업종
여자가 첫 대사에서 카펫에 아직 얼룩이 좀 있다(the carpets still have some stains)면서 전문적으로 청소를 해야 하지 않을지(Shouldn't we get them cleaned professionally?)를 묻자 남자가 B&R서비스가 일을 잘한다고 들었다(I heard B & R Services does good work)고 추천했으므로 B&R은 카펫을 청소하는 업체임을 알 수 있다. 따라서 정답은 (D)이다.

34

What will the speakers probably do next?

(A) Review information on a Web site
(B) Prepare a presentation
(C) Rearrange some devices
(D) Ask for approval from a manager

화자들은 다음에 무엇을 하겠는가?

(A) 웹사이트의 정보 검토
(B) 발표 준비
(C) 일부 기기 재배치
(D) 관리자 승인 요청

어휘　review 검토하다　prepare 준비하다　rearrange 재배치하다
　　　device 기기[장치]　approval 승인

해설　세부 사항 관련 – 화자들이 다음에 할 일
남자가 두 번째 대사에서 그들의 웹사이트는 B-and-R.com(Their Web site is B-and-R.com)이라고 알려주자, 여자가 지금 살펴보자(Let's take a look now)면서 그들의 서비스 옵션을 전부 검토해보자(we can go over all their service options)고 했으므로 정답은 (A)이다.

▶▶ **Paraphrasing**　대화의 go over all their service options
　　　　　　　　　→ 정답의 review information

35-37

W-Am　Hi, Mr. Jones? This is a courtesy call from Southern Asian Airways. **35There's been a change in the itinerary for your flight to Mumbai on November nineteenth. That flight will leave from New York, not Washington, D.C.**

M-Au　**36Right. I got an update e-mail on Friday explaining that.**

W-Am　Oh good, you're all confirmed then. Is there anything else I can help you with?

M-Au　Yes, actually. **37How can I ask for all vegetarian options for the in-flight meals?**

W-Am　On our Web site, go to "My Flight" and then follow the instructions for "tailoring food options."

M-Au　Terrific. Thank you for the call.

여 　안녕하십니까, 존스 씨? 서던 아시안 항공의 안내 전화입니다. 11월 19일 뭄바이행 항공편의 여행 일정에 변경 사항이 있습니다. 그 비행기는 워싱턴 D.C.가 아니라 뉴욕에서 출발할 거예요.

남 　네. 금요일에 그걸 설명하는 이메일을 받았습니다.

여 　아, 다행이네요. 그때 다 확인하셨군요. 제가 도와드릴 다른 일이 뭐 있을까요?

남 　네, 사실 있어요. 완전 채식 기내식 옵션을 어떻게 요청하면 되죠?

여 　저희 웹사이트에서 "내 항공편"으로 가서서 "맞춤 식사 옵션"을 위한 지침을 따르십시오.

남 　좋아요. 전화해주셔서 고마워요.

Test 8

어휘	courtesy call 고객 관리 전화 itinerary 여행 일정 flight 항공편 explain 설명하다 confirm 확인하다 vegetarian 채식주의(자) option 선택(권) in-flight meal 기내식 instruction 지침 tailoring 맞춤 terrific 멋진

35
According to the woman, what has changed about a trip itinerary?

(A) The operator of a flight
(B) The departure point
(C) The duration
(D) The number of connecting flights

여자에 따르면, 여행 일정에 대해 무엇이 바뀌었는가?
(A) 비행기 조종사
(B) 출발지
(C) 기간
(D) 연결 항공편 수

어휘 operator 조작(운전)하는 사람 departure 출발 duration 기간 connecting 연결하는

해설 세부 사항 관련 – 여자가 말하는 여행 일정상 변경 사항
여자가 첫 대사에서 11월 19일 뭄바이행 항공편의 여행 일정에 변경 사항이 있다(There's been a change in the itinerary for your flight to Mumbai on November nineteenth)고 했고, 그 비행기는 워싱턴 D.C.가 아니라 뉴욕에서 출발할 것(That flight will leave from New York, not Washington, D.C.)이라고 안내하고 있는 것으로 보아 정답은 (B)이다.

▶▶ Paraphrasing 대화의 leave → 정답의 departure

36
What does the man say happened on Friday?

(A) He received a notification message.
(B) He canceled a previous booking.
(C) He changed the date of a trip.
(D) He was given a ticket discount.

남자는 금요일에 무슨 일이 있었다고 말하는가?
(A) 알림 메시지를 받았다.
(B) 이전 예약을 취소했다.
(C) 여행 날짜를 바꿨다.
(D) 티켓 할인을 받았다.

어휘 receive 받다 notification 알림 cancel 취소하다 previous 이전의 booking 예약

해설 세부 사항 관련 – 남자가 금요일에 있었다고 말하는 일
남자가 첫 대사에서 금요일에 그걸 설명하는 이메일을 받았다(I got an update e-mail on Friday explaining that)고 했으므로 정답은 (A)이다.

▶▶ Paraphrasing 대화의 got an update e-mail
→ 정답의 received a notification message

37
What does the man want to know about?

(A) Choosing a seating option
(B) Checking in large baggage
(C) Requesting special meals
(D) Using an airport lounge

남자는 무엇에 대해 알고 싶어 하는가?
(A) 좌석 옵션 선택
(B) 대형 수하물 수속
(C) 특별식 요청
(D) 공항 라운지 이용

어휘 seating 좌석 baggage 수하물 request 요청하다

해설 세부 사항 관련 – 남자가 알고 싶어 하는 것
남자가 두 번째 대사에서 완전 채식 기내식 옵션을 어떻게 요청하면 되는지(How can I ask for all vegetarian options for the in-flight meals?)를 묻고 있는 것으로 보아 정답은 (C)이다.

▶▶ Paraphrasing 대화의 ask for all vegetarian options for the ~ meals
→ 정답의 requesting special meals

38-40

M-Cn Hi, I'm Fred Mason. I have a two o'clock dental appointment to see Dr. Evans. **38I was told to be here fifteen minutes ahead of time.** It's my first visit to the clinic.

W-Br Oh yes, normally you can download and print out our patient information forms. But we're updating our Web site. **39So... please fill out these forms here—only the parts that are circled or highlighted.**

M-Cn No problem.

W-Br Just bring them back to me when you're done. **40Plus, here are notepads and a calendar with dental care tips printed on them—it's a gift packet for new patients.**

M-Cn Great, thank you.

남 안녕하세요, 저는 프레드 메이슨입니다. 2시에 에반스 선생님을 뵙기로 치과 진료가 잡혀 있어요. 15분 일찍 여기 와 있으라고 들었어요. 이 병원에는 처음입니다.

여 아, 네, 보통은 저희 환자 정보 양식을 다운로드해서 출력하실 수 있는데요. 하지만 저희가 웹사이트를 업데이트 중이거든요. 그러니… 여기 이 양식들을 작성해주세요. 동그라미 치거나 강조 표시된 부분만요.

남 문제없어요.

여 다 하시면 그냥 저한테 가져다주세요. 그리고 여기 메모지와 치아 관리 팁이 인쇄되어 있는 달력이 있어요. 새로 오신 환자분들을 위한 증정 세트예요.

남 좋네요, 고마워요.

dental 치과의 appointment 예약 ahead of ~보다
빨리 clinic 병원 normally 보통 patient 환자 form
양식 fill out 작성하다 circle 동그라미를 그리다 highlight
강조하다 calendar 달력 packet 꾸러미, 소포

38

What was the man previously instructed to do?

(A) Bring his old dental records
(B) Enter through a side door
(C) Arrive early for an appointment
(D) Refer acquaintances to a clinic

남자는 이전에 무엇을 하라고 지시받았는가?
(A) 그의 예전 치과 기록을 가져올 것
(B) 옆문으로 들어올 것
(C) 예약에 일찍 도착할 것
(D) 지인을 병원에 소개할 것

어휘 enter 들어오다 early 일찍 refer (사람을 …에게) 보내다
acquaintance 지인

해설 세부 사항 관련 – 남자가 이전에 지시받은 사항
남자가 첫 대사에서 15분 일찍 여기 와 있으라고 들었다(I was told to be
here fifteen minutes ahead of time)고 한 것으로 보아 정답은 (C)이다.

▸▸ Paraphrasing 대화의 ahead of time → 정답의 early

39

[고난도]

What does the woman say about some paperwork?

(A) It had already been filled out electronically.
(B) It has marked sections for completion.
(C) It contains some printing errors.
(D) It was recently revised.

여자는 서류 작업에 대해 무엇을 말하는가?
(A) 이미 전자상으로 작성되었다.
(B) 작성을 위해 표시된 부분이 있다.
(C) 일부 인쇄 오류가 있다.
(D) 최근에 수정되었다.

어휘 electronically 전자상으로 mark 표시하다 section 부분
completion 완성 contain ~이 들어 있다 error 오류 revise
수정하다

해설 세부 사항 관련 – 여자가 서류 작업에 대해 말하는 것
여자가 첫 대사에서 여기 이 양식들을 작성해달라(please fill out these
forms here)고 요청하면서, 동그라미 치거나 강조 표시된 부분만(only the
parts that are circled or highlighted)이라고 했으므로 정답은 (B)이다.

▸▸ Paraphrasing 대화의 the parts that are circled or
highlighted → 정답의 marked sections

40

What does the woman give the man?

(A) Some tooth care tools
(B) Some customized stationery
(C) Some coupons for future visits
(D) Some bottled water

여자는 남자에게 무엇을 주는가?
(A) 치아 관리 도구
(B) 주문 제작한 문구류
(C) 향후 방문을 위한 쿠폰
(D) 생수 몇 병

어휘 tool 도구 customized 주문 제작한, 맞춤형 stationery 문구류
bottled 병에 든

해설 세부 사항 관련 – 여자가 남자에게 주는 것
여자가 마지막 대사에서 여기 메모지와 치아 관리 팁이 인쇄되어 있는 달력
이 있다(here are notepads and a calendar with dental care tips
printed on them)며, 새로 온 환자들을 위한 증정 세트(it's a gift packet
for new patients)라고 설명하며 남자에게 물건을 건네고 있으므로 정답은
(B)이다.

41-43

M-Au	Good news, Ah-Reum. **41 Our latest mobile phone app for language learning got a positive review from Nancy Batra—you know, the technology columnist for *The Watmon Times*.**
W-Am	Yes, I just read it. That'll help boost its sales, for sure. **42 I'm wondering if we should proceed with developing a mobile phone app for self-study in mathematics. There could be strong demand…**
M-Au	**42 It's worth considering,** and, well… many students are learning from home.
W-Am	OK. **43 I'll go ahead and e-mail Greg, our expert advisor on mobile apps, and set up a time to discuss our plans.**

남	좋은 소식이 있어요, 아름. 언어 학습을 위한 우리의 최신 휴대전화 앱이 〈왓몬 타임즈〉의 기술 칼럼니스트인 낸시 바트라로부터 긍정적인 평가를 받았어요.
여	네, 저도 방금 읽었어요. 판매 증진에 확실히 도움이 될 거예요. 전 수학 자율 학습용 휴대전화 앱의 개발을 추진해야 할지를 생각 중이에요. 수요가 많을 수 있어요….
남	고려해볼 가치가 있어요. 그리고, 음… 많은 학생들이 집에서 학습하고 있잖아요.
여	좋아요. 제가 그럼 휴대폰 앱 전문 고문인 그렉에게 이메일을 보내서 우리의 계획에 대해 논의할 시간을 잡을게요.

어휘 latest 최신의 language 언어 positive 긍정적인
columnist 칼럼니스트, 정기 기고가 boost 신장시키다
wonder 궁금해하다 proceed with ~을 추진하다
demand 수요 worth ~할 가치가 있는 consider 고려하다
expert 전문적인 advisor 고문

Test 8

41

Who most likely is Nancy Batra?

(A) A visiting professor
(B) An in-house translator
(C) A departmental intern
(D) A newspaper journalist

낸시 바트라는 누구일 것 같은가?

(A) 초빙 교수
(B) 사내 번역가
(C) 부서 인턴
(D) 신문 기자

해설 세부 사항 관련 - 낸시 바트라의 직업

남자가 첫 대사에서 언어 학습을 위한 우리의 최신 휴대전화 앱이 〈왓몬 타임즈〉의 기술 칼럼니스트인 낸시 바트라로부터 긍정적인 평가를 받았다 (Our latest mobile phone app for language learning got a positive review from Nancy Batra—you know, the technology columnist for *The Watmon Times*)고 했으므로 정답은 (D)이다.

▶▶ **Paraphrasing** 대화의 columnist → 정답의 journalist

42

고난도

Why does the man say, "many students are learning from home"?

(A) To decline an assignment
(B) To suggest delaying a product release
(C) To express agreement with the woman
(D) To admit that he is concerned about market competition

남자가 "많은 학생들이 집에서 학습하고 있잖아요"라고 말하는 이유는 무엇인가?

(A) 임무를 거절하려고
(B) 제품 출시의 연기를 제안하려고
(C) 여자에게 동의한다고 표현하려고
(D) 시장 경쟁에 대해 걱정하고 있음을 인정하려고

어휘 decline 거절하다 assignment 임무 suggest 제안하다 delay 연기하다 release 출시 express 표현하다 agreement 동의 admit 인정하다 concerned 걱정하는 competition 경쟁

해설 화자의 의도 파악 - 많은 학생들이 집에서 학습하고 있다는 말의 의도

여자가 첫 대사에서 수학 자율 학습용 휴대전화 앱의 개발을 추진해야 할지를 생각 중(I'm wondering if we should proceed with developing a mobile phone app for self-study in mathematics)이고 수요가 많을 수 있다(There could be strong demand)고 의견을 제시하자 남자가 고려해 볼 가치가 있다(It's worth considering)고 동의하면서 인용문을 언급했으므로 남자는 여자의 생각을 뒷받침하는 이유를 들어가며 동의한다는 것을 표현하려는 의도로 말한 것임을 알 수 있다. 따라서 정답은 (C)이다.

43

What will the woman probably do next?

(A) Contact a consultant
(B) Make a delivery
(C) Proofread a report
(D) Set up some equipment

여자는 다음에 무엇을 하겠는가?

(A) 자문 위원에게 연락
(B) 배송
(C) 보고서 교정
(D) 장비 설치

어휘 contact 연락하다 consultant 자문 위원 proofread 교정하다 equipment 장비

해설 세부 사항 관련 - 여자가 다음에 할 일

여자가 마지막 대사에서 제가 그럼 휴대폰 앱 전문 고문인 그렉에게 이메일을 보내서 우리의 계획에 대해 논의할 시간을 잡겠다(I'll go ahead and e-mail Greg, our expert advisor on mobile apps, and set up a time to discuss our plans)고 했으므로 정답은 (A)이다.

▶▶ **Paraphrasing** 대화의 e-mail our expert advisor
→ 정답의 contact a consultant

44-46 3인 대화

M-Cn	Ms. Jacobs? The desktop computer in the side office is working again.
W-Br	That was fast. Was it a problem with the electrical outlet in the wall?
M-Cn	No, **44actually one monitor cable wasn't secured tightly enough, so I just needed to plug it in again.** It was an easy fix.
W-Br	Ah, I see. Oh, **45hi, Stan. The computer's been fixed.**
M-Au	**45Great. I'll have the intern I'm overseeing get back to her digital art project.**
W-Br	Excellent, we're all set.
M-Cn	**46And Ms. Jacobs... if you have time, please leave a client review on the Web site for my repair business.** I would really appreciate it.

남1	제이콥스 씨? 옆 사무실의 데스크톱 컴퓨터가 다시 작동되고 있어요.
여	빠르네요. 벽에 있는 전기 콘센트에 문제가 있었나요?
남1	아니요, 사실 모니터 전선 하나가 충분히 꽉 고정되어 있지 않아서 다시 꽂기만 하면 됐어요. 쉽게 해결되었어요.
여	아, 그렇군요. 오, 안녕하세요, 스탠. 컴퓨터가 수리되었어요.
남2	잘됐네요. 제가 감독하고 있는 인턴이 다시 디지털 아트 작업을 하도록 해야 하겠네요.
여	훌륭해요. 준비 다 됐어요.
남1	그리고 제이콥스 씨… 시간이 있으시면 제 수리 사업 웹사이트에 고객 평가를 남겨주세요. 그럼 정말 감사하겠습니다.

어휘 electrical outlet 전기 콘센트 secure 고정시키다 tightly 꽉, 단단히 plug in 전원을 연결하다 fix 해결책; 수리하다 oversee 감독하다 excellent 훌륭한 set 준비가 된 review 평가 repair 수리; 수리하다 appreciate 고마워하다

44

What has caused a problem?

(A) An outdated software program
(B) A malfunctioning monitor
(C) A loose cable connection
(D) A faulty electrical outlet

무엇이 문제를 일으켰는가?

(A) 구식 소프트웨어 프로그램
(B) 오작동 모니터
(C) 느슨한 전선 연결
(D) 결함이 있는 전기 콘센트

어휘 outdated 구식인 malfunctioning 오작동하는 loose 느슨한
connection 연결 faulty 결함이 있는

해설 세부 사항 관련 – 문제의 원인

남자가 두 번째 대사에서 사실 모니터 전선 하나가 충분히 꽉 고정되어 있지 않아서 다시 꽂기만 하면 됐다(actually one monitor cable wasn't secured tightly enough, so I just needed to plug it in again)고 했으므로 정답은 (C)이다.

▸▸ Paraphrasing 대화의 **wasn't secured tightly enough**
→ 정답의 **loose**

45

What does Stan mention about himself?

(A) He supervises an intern.
(B) He has a project due soon.
(C) He previously tried to fix a computer.
(D) He referred Ms. Jacobs to a service.

스탠은 자신에 대해 무엇을 언급하는가?

(A) 인턴을 감독한다.
(B) 곧 프로젝트가 예정되어 있다.
(C) 전에 컴퓨터를 고치려고 노력했다.
(D) 제이콥스 씨를 서비스에 소개했다.

어휘 supervise 감독하다 due ~하기로 예정된 previously 이전에
refer (사람을 ~에게) 보내다

해설 세부 사항 관련 – 스탠이 자신에 대해 언급한 사항

여자가 두 번째 대사에서 스탠에게 인사를 하며(hi, Stan) 컴퓨터가 수리되었다(The computer's been fixed)고 알리자, 두 번째 남자가 잘됐다(Great)고 답한 것으로 보아 이 남자가 스탠이고, 자신이 감독하고 있는 인턴이 다시 디지털 아트 작업을 하도록 해야겠다(I'll have the intern I'm overseeing get back to her digital art project)고 했으므로 정답은 (A)이다.

▸▸ Paraphrasing 대화의 **overseeing** → 정답의 **supervise**

46

What is the woman asked to do?

(A) Distribute his business card
(B) Provide online feedback
(C) Present a warranty document
(D) Review an installation procedure

어자는 무엇을 하라는 요청을 받는가?

(A) 남자의 명함 배포
(B) 온라인 피드백 제공
(C) 보증서 제시
(D) 설치 절차 검토

어휘 distribute 배포하다 business card 명함 provide 제공하다
present 제시하다 warranty 보증서 installation 설치
procedure 절차

해설 세부 사항 관련 – 여자가 부탁 받은 일

첫 번째 남자가 마지막 대사에서 여자에게 제이콥스 씨, 시간이 있으시면 제 수리 사업 웹사이트에 고객 평가를 남겨주세요(Ms. Jacobs... if you have time, please leave a client review on the Web site for my repair business)라고 부탁하고 있으므로 정답은 (B)이다.

▸▸ Paraphrasing 대화의 **leave a client review on the Web site** → 정답의 **provide online feedback**

47-49

M-Cn	Hi, I'm Kevin. I'm here for my training to be a historical tour guide.
W-Am	Yes, I'm your trainer. [47]**I heard you got a high score on your written exam on the city's historical facts.** Congratulations!
M-Cn	Oh, thank you! I studied hard for it.
W-Am	OK. Well, today [48]**I'll show you around the city's history museum. It's important because every walking tour of the city originates from its lobby.** It's a great introduction to our past.
M-Cn	I see. [49]**Should I be taking notes on what we talk about?**
W-Am	That would be a great idea, if it will help you remember.

남	안녕하세요, 저는 케빈입니다. 역사 관광 가이드가 되기 위한 교육을 받으러 여기 왔어요.
여	네, 제가 당신의 강사입니다. **시의 역사적 사실에 대한 필기 시험에서 높은 점수를 받았다고 들었어요.** 축하합니다!
남	아, 고맙습니다! 열심히 공부했거든요.
여	좋아요. 자, 오늘은 **시의 역사 박물관을 구경시켜줄 거예요. 도시의 모든 도보 관광이 이 로비에서 시작하기 때문에 중요해요.** 우리의 과거에 대한 훌륭한 입문이죠.
남	그렇군요. 우리가 나누는 이야기에 대해 메모를 해야 할까요?
여	기억하는 데 도움이 된다면 좋은 생각인 것 같네요.

어휘 written exam 필기 시험 show somebody around
누군가를 둘러보도록 구경시켜주다 originate 시작하다
introduction 입문, 소개 take notes 메모하다

Test 8

47

According to the woman, what did the man do recently?

(A) Took a knowledge test
(B) Opened a souvenir shop
(C) Published a guidebook
(D) Trained a tour leader

여자에 따르면, 남자는 최근에 무엇을 했는가?

(A) 지식 시험을 보았다.
(B) 기념품 가게를 열었다.
(C) 가이드북을 출판했다.
(D) 관광 지도자를 교육시켰다.

어휘 knowledge 지식 souvenir 기념품 publish 출판하다

해설 세부 사항 관련 – 여자가 최근에 남자가 했다고 말하는 일
여자가 첫 대사에서 남자에게 시의 역사적 사실에 대한 필기 시험에서 높은 점수를 받았다고 들었다(I heard you got a high score on your written exam on the city's historical facts)고 한 것으로 보아 남자는 최근에 시의 역사에 관한 시험을 보았음을 알 수 있다. 따라서 정답은 (A)이다.

▸▸ Paraphrasing   대화의 exam → 정답의 test

48   고난도

Why does the woman say the city's history museum is important?

(A) It is the city's oldest tourist attraction.
(B) It is larger than other museums.
(C) It has new interactive exhibits.
(D) It is the starting point for walking tours.

여자는 왜 도시의 역사 박물관이 중요하다고 말하는가?

(A) 도시에서 가장 오래된 관광 명소이다.
(B) 다른 박물관들보다 크다.
(C) 새로운 쌍방향 전시품을 갖추고 있다.
(D) 도보 관광의 출발점이다.

어휘 tourist attraction 관광 명소 interactive 상호적인, 쌍방향의 exhibit 전시품

해설 세부 사항 관련 – 여자가 도시의 역사 박물관이 중요하다고 말하는 이유
여자가 두 번째 대사에서 시의 역사 박물관을 구경시켜주겠다(I'll show you around the city's history museum)며, 도시의 모든 도보 관광이 이 로비에서 시작하기 때문에 중요하다(It's important because every walking tour of the city originates from its lobby)고 했으므로 정답은 (D)이다.

▸▸ Paraphrasing   대화의 originates → 정답의 starting

49

What does the man ask the woman about?

(A) Taking special transportation to a venue
(B) Introducing himself to a group of people
(C) Earning a professional qualification
(D) Keeping a record of a conversation

남자는 여자에게 무엇에 대해 묻는가?

(A) 행사장까지 특별 교통수단을 이용하는 것
(B) 한 무리의 사람들에게 자신을 소개하는 것
(C) 전문 자격을 취득하는 것
(D) 대화를 기록하는 것

어휘 transportation 교통수단 venue (행사 등의) 장소 introduce 소개하다 earn 얻다 professional 전문적인 qualification 자격 conversation 대화

해설 세부 사항 관련 – 남자가 여자에게 묻는 것
남자가 마지막 대사에서 우리가 나누는 이야기에 대해 메모를 해야 할지(Should I be taking notes on what we talk about?)를 묻고 있으므로 정답은 (D)이다.

▸▸ Paraphrasing   대화의 taking notes on what we talk about → 정답의 keeping a record of a conversation

50-52

W-Br	Hi, I read about the rain garden at Cailson City Park—you know, ⁵⁰that sunken garden that collects rainwater so plants can absorb it. I'm a homeowner and would like to build one.
M-Au	⁵⁰Well, we have all the soil and plants you would need here at this store. ⁵¹For a rain garden project, I would recommend selecting plants that are native to this area. They're best adapted to our local weather patterns.
W-Br	I see.
M-Au	⁵²To help you choose, here on this tablet is a Web site called www.rain-resources.com. It tells all about rain gardens. You can look at it as you browse around.

여 안녕하세요. 케일슨 시티 공원에 있는 빗물 정원에 대해 읽었어요. 아시겠지만, 식물이 빗물을 흡수할 수 있도록 빗물을 모으는 낮은 정원 말이에요. 저는 집주인인데 그런 정원을 하나 가꾸고 싶어요.

남 음, 여기 이 상점에 당신이 필요한 흙과 식물이 모두 있어요. 빗물 정원 작업에는 이 지역의 토착 식물을 고르는 것을 추천드립니다. 그 식물들이 우리 지역의 날씨 패턴에 가장 잘 적응되어 있어요.

여 그렇군요.

남 선택하시는 걸 돕기 위해 여기 이 태블릿에 www.rain-resources.com이라는 웹사이트가 있어요. 빗물 정원에 관한 모든 것을 알려준답니다. 둘러보시면서 생각해보시죠.

어휘 sunken (주변 지역보다) 가라앉은[낮은] collect 모으다 absorb 흡수하다 homeowner 집주인 soil 토양 native 토종의 adapt 적응하다 browse 둘러보다

50

고난도

Where most likely is the conversation taking place?

(A) At a city park
(B) At a garden supply shop
(C) At an organic farm
(D) At a natural history museum

대화가 이루어지는 장소는 어디이겠는가?

(A) 도시 공원
(B) 정원 용품점
(C) 유기농 농장
(D) 자연사 박물관

해설 전체 내용 관련 – 대화의 장소
여자가 첫 대사에서 식물이 빗물을 흡수할 수 있도록 빗물을 모으는 낮은 정원(that sunken garden that collects rainwater so plants can absorb it)에 대해 언급하며, 자신은 집주인인데 그런 정원을 하나 가꾸고 싶다(I'm a homeowner and would like to build one)고 하자, 남자가 여기 이 상점에 당신이 필요한 흙과 식물이 모두 있다(we have all the soil and plants you would need here at this store)고 한 것으로 보아 정원 용품 판매점에서 대화가 이루어지고 있음을 알 수 있다. 따라서 정답은 (B)이다.

51

고난도

What does the man suggest doing for a project?

(A) Placing some plants in an indoor area
(B) Checking a local weather forecast daily
(C) Choosing plants that normally grow in a region
(D) Starting it during a warmer season

남자는 작업을 위해 무엇을 하라고 제안하는가?

(A) 일부 식물의 실내에 배치할 것
(B) 현지 일기 예보를 매일 확인할 것
(C) 지역에서 일반적으로 자라는 식물을 고를 것
(D) 더 따뜻한 계절에 시작할 것

어휘 place 배치하다 indoor 실내의 weather forecast 일기 예보
normally 일반적으로, 보통

해설 세부 사항 관련 – 남자가 작업을 위해 하라고 제안한 것
남자가 첫 대사에서 빗물 정원 작업에는 이 지역의 토착 식물을 고르는 것을 추천드린다(For a rain garden project, I would recommend selecting plants that are native to this area)고 했으므로 정답은 (C)이다.

▸▸ Paraphrasing 대화의 selecting plants that are native to this area → 정답의 choosing plants that normally grow in a region

52

What does the man show the woman?

(A) A directional sign
(B) An informational Web site
(C) An artificial body of water
(D) A price list for services

남자는 여자에게 무엇을 보여주는가?

(A) 방향 표지판
(B) 정보 웹사이트
(C) 인공 수역
(D) 서비스의 가격표

어휘 directional 방향의 artificial 인공의

해설 세부 사항 관련 – 남자가 여자에게 보여주는 것
남자가 마지막 대사에서 선택하는 걸 돕기 위해, 여기 이 태블릿에 www.rain-resources.com이라는 웹사이트가 있다(To help you choose, here on this tablet is a Web site called www.rain-resources.com)고 보여주며 빗물 정원에 관한 모든 것을 알려준다(It tells all about rain gardens)고 했으므로 정답은 (B)이다.

53-55 3인 대화

M-Cn	Thank you for giving me the chance to tell you about my company's products. **53At Carelli Graphics, our sole focus is producing high-quality posters to inspire and encourage workers.** This one, called "Success," is our top seller.
W-Am	Very nice!
M-Cn	**54What's more, our company only uses recycled or sustainably-sourced wood and paper in our products.**
W-Am	**54I like that. 55Sandra?**
W-Br	**54Yes, I like that too. 55Uh, and I wanted to say that my department is having a day of activities to improve our teamwork soon.** This one, with the title "Collaboration", would be great for us.
M-Cn	I'll set it aside.

남	저희 회사 제품에 대해 말씀드릴 기회를 주셔서 감사합니다. 카렐리 그래픽스의 유일한 주안점은 직원들을 격려하고 영감을 주기 위한 고품질 포스터를 제작하는 것입니다. "성공"이라고 불리는 이것이 우리의 가장 잘 팔리는 제품입니다.
여1	아주 멋지네요!
남	더구나 저희 회사는 재활용되거나 환경적으로 지속 가능하도록 조달된 원목과 종이만을 제품에 사용합니다.
여1	마음에 드는군요. 산드라?
여2	네, 저도 그 점이 좋네요. 어, 그리고 우리 부서가 곧 팀워크를 향상시키기 위한 행사일을 가질 거라는 점도 말하고 싶었는데요. "협력"이라는 제목이 붙은 이 포스터가 우리에게 좋겠어요.
남	따로 챙겨두겠습니다.

어휘	sole 유일한 produce 제작하다 inspire 영감을 주다 encourage 격려[고무]하다 recycle 재활용하다 sustainably (환경 파괴 없이) 지속 가능하게 source 얻다, 공급자를 찾다 improve 향상시키다 collaboration 협력 set aside 챙겨두다

Test 8

53

What kind of products does the man's company sell?

(A) Adjustable desks
(B) Instructional books
(C) Business software
(D) Motivational posters

남자의 회사는 어떤 종류의 제품을 판매하는가?

(A) 조절 가능한 책상
(B) 지침서
(C) 비즈니스 소프트웨어
(D) 동기 부여 포스터

어휘 adjustable 조절 가능한 instructional 교육용의 motivational
동기를 주는

해설 세부 사항 관련 – 남자의 회사가 판매하는 제품의 종류

남자가 첫 대사에서 카렐리 그래픽스의 유일한 주안점은 직원들을 격려하고 영감을 주기 위한 고품질 포스터를 제작하는 것이다(At Carelli Graphics, our sole focus is producing high-quality posters to inspire and encourage workers)고 했으므로 정답은 (D)이다.

▸▸ Paraphrasing 대화의 posters to inspire and encourage workers → 정답의 motivational posters

54 [고난도]

What do the women say they like about the man's company?

(A) It provides a fast delivery service.
(B) It uses environmentally-friendly materials.
(C) It participates in community fundraisers.
(D) It has a wide selection of products.

여자들은 남자의 회사에 대해 무엇이 마음에 든다고 말하는가?

(A) 빠른 배송 서비스를 제공한다.
(B) 친환경 소재를 사용한다.
(C) 지역 사회 모금 행사에 참여한다.
(D) 다양한 상품을 갖추고 있다.

어휘 provide 제공하다 delivery 배송 environmentally-friendly
친환경적인 material 재료 participate 참여하다 community
지역 사회 fundraiser 모금 행사 a selection of 다양한

해설 세부 사항 관련 – 여자들이 남자의 회사에 대해 좋다고 말한 것

남자가 두 번째 대사에서 저희 회사는 재활용되거나 환경적으로 지속 가능하도록 조달된 원목과 종이만을 제품에 사용한다(our company only uses recycled or sustainably-sourced wood and paper in our products)고 말하자 첫 번째 여자가 마음에 든다(I like that)고 했고, 두 번째 여자도 자신도 그 점이 좋다(I like that too)고 했으므로 정답은 (B)이다.

▸▸ Paraphrasing 대화의 recycled or sustainably-sourced wood and paper → 정답의 environmentally-friendly materials

55

What does Sandra say about her department?

(A) It will sponsor a running race.
(B) It will be given a different name.
(C) It will have team-building day.
(D) It will merge with another department.

산드라는 자신의 부서에 대해 무엇을 말하는가?

(A) 달리기 경주를 후원할 것이다.
(B) 다른 명칭이 주어질 것이다.
(C) 팀워크를 쌓는 날을 가질 것이다.
(D) 다른 부서와 합칠 것이다.

어휘 sponsor 후원하다 race 경주 merge 합치다

해설 세부 사항 관련 – 산드라가 자신의 부서에 대해 말하는 것

첫 번째 여자가 두 번째 대사에서 산드라(Sandra)를 부르자 두 번째 여자가 답했으므로 두 번째 여자가 산드라임을 알 수 있고, 여자가 우리 부서가 곧 팀워크를 향상시키기 위한 행사일을 가질 거라는 점도 말하고 싶었다(I wanted to say that my department is having a day of activities to improve our teamwork soon)고 한 것으로 보아 정답은 (C)이다.

▸▸ Paraphrasing 대화의 a day of activities to improve our teamwork → 정답의 team-building day

56-58

M-Au	Hi, thanks for calling Darvi's Restaurant. How may I help you?
W-Am	Hi. **56 I'm making plans to have an outdoor meal to celebrate our company's tenth year in business.** We'd like to have it on Sunday evening, but—would you be able to cater it in that case? I know that you're closed then...
M-Au	**57 Don't worry—we can schedule catering for any time, even before we open and after we close our dining room to customers.**
W-Am	Oh, that's good news. And could we substitute some ingredients in the meals?
M-Au	Absolutely. **58 For that, I'd recommend calling the owner, Mr. Darvi, on his mobile and speaking with him. His number is on our Web site.**

남	여보세요. 다비 식당에 전화 주셔서 감사합니다. 무엇을 도와드릴까요?
여	안녕하세요. 우리 회사 창립 10주년을 기념하여 야외에서 식사를 할 계획을 세우고 있는데요. 일요일 저녁에 하고 싶은데, 이 경우에 음식을 공급해줄 수 있으실까요? 그때쯤 식당이 문을 닫는 건 알아요….
남	걱정 마세요. 식당을 열기 전이나 손님들에게 식당 문을 닫은 후에도 언제든지 음식 공급 일정을 잡을 수 있어요.
여	아, 좋은 소식이네요. 그리고 식사의 일부 재료를 대체할 수 있을까요?
남	당연하죠. 그러려면 사장님인 다비 씨에게 휴대폰으로 전화를 걸어 통화하시는 것을 권해드릴게요. 그의 번호는 저희 웹사이트에 있습니다.

어휘 outdoor 야외의 celebrate 기념하다 cater 음식을 공급하다 schedule 일정을 잡다 dining room 식당 substitute 대체하다 ingredient 재료 absolutely 전적으로; 물론이죠

56

What kind of event is the woman planning?

(A) An awards banquet
(B) A birthday party
(C) An anniversary celebration
(D) A cooking contest

여자는 어떤 종류의 행사를 계획하고 있는가?
(A) 시상식 연회
(B) 생일 파티
(C) 기념일 축하
(D) 요리 경연 대회

해설 세부 사항 관련 – 여자가 계획하고 있는 행사

여자가 첫 대사에서 우리 회사 창립 10주년을 기념하여 야외에서 식사를 할 계획을 세우고 있다(I'm making plans to have an outdoor meal to celebrate our company's tenth year in business)고 했으므로 정답은 (C)이다.

57

고난도

What does the man say to reassure the woman about a catering service?

(A) It has won recognition from publications.
(B) It is used by the area's biggest companies.
(C) It can be provided in a range of venues.
(D) It is available outside of regular business hours.

남자는 여자에게 음식 제공 서비스에 대해 안심시키기 위해 무엇을 말하는가?
(A) 출판물로부터 인정을 받았다.
(B) 지역 최대 기업들에 의해 이용되고 있다.
(C) 다양한 장소에서 제공될 수 있다.
(D) 정규 영업시간 외에도 이용 가능하다.

어휘 reassure 안심시키다 recognition 인정 publication 출판물 provide 제공하다 a range of 다양한 venue 행사 available 이용 가능한 regular 정규적인

해설 세부 사항 관련 – 남자가 여자에게 음식 제공 서비스에 대해 안심시키려고 한 말

남자가 두 번째 대사에서 여자에게 걱정 말라(Don't worry)고 안심시키면서, 식당을 열기 전이나 손님들에게 식당 문을 닫은 후에도 언제든지 음식 공급 일정을 잡을 수 있다(we can schedule catering for any time, even before we open and after we close our dining room to customers)고 했으므로 정답은 (D)이다.

▸▸ **Paraphrasing** 대화의 before we open and after we close our dining room to customers → 정답의 outside of regular business hours

58

What does the man suggest doing?

(A) Requesting a discount for a large group
(B) Reserving a particular banquet room
(C) Phoning a business proprietor directly
(D) Ordering meals from an online menu

남자는 무엇을 하라고 제안하는가?
(A) 대규모 단체에 대한 할인 요청
(B) 특정 연회실 예약
(C) 사업주에게 직접 전화
(D) 온라인 메뉴에서 식사 주문

어휘 request 요청하다 reserve 예약하다 particular 특정한 banquet 연회 phone 전화를 걸다 proprietor 소유자 directly 직접적으로 order 주문하다

해설 세부 사항 관련 – 남자의 제안 사항

남자가 마지막 대사에서 사장인 다비 씨에게 휴대폰으로 전화를 걸어 통화하는 것을 권한다(I'd recommend calling the owner, Mr. Darvi, on his mobile and speaking with him)며, 그의 번호는 저희 웹사이트에 있다(His number is on our Web site)고 알려주고 있으므로 정답은 (C)이다.

▸▸ **Paraphrasing** 대화의 calling the owner → 정답의 Phoning a ~ proprietor

59-61

W-Br	Welcome to Marino's Farmer's Market. Oh, hi, Mr. Blakely.
M-Au	Hi. I placed an order online for two pounds of yellow corn, for pick-up.
W-Br	Yes, my assistant will be right out with your order.
M-Au	Great. **59 Hey, I like your new Web site—it's really easy to order from.**
W-Br	Thank you. **59 I designed it myself, and supplied all the photos.**
M-Au	Wow! **60 And I have to say that your corn is the best I've ever tasted**—and I grew up on a farm.
W-Br	So glad to hear that! **61 Now, while you're waiting, why don't you explore our new floral section? We have some beautiful bouquets of fresh-cut tulips and roses.**

여 마리노의 농산물 시장에 오신 것을 환영합니다. 안녕하세요, 블레이클리 씨.
남 안녕하세요. 온라인으로 2파운드의 황색 옥수수를 주문했는데, 가져가려고요.
여 네, 저희 점원이 바로 당신의 주문을 가지고 나올 거예요.
남 좋아요. 당신의 새로운 웹사이트가 좋던데요. 주문하기가 정말 쉬워요.
여 고마워요. 제가 직접 디자인하고 모든 사진을 공급했어요.
남 와! 그리고 당신의 옥수수는 제가 맛본 것 중 단연 최고예요. 참고로 저는 농장에서 자랐어요.

여 그 말을 들으니 정말 기분 좋네요! 자, 기다리시는 동안 우리의 새로운 꽃 구역을 둘러보시는 게 어떨까요? 싱싱한 튤립과 장미 꽃으로 만든 아름다운 꽃다발들이 있습니다.

어휘 place an order 주문하다 assistant 보조, 점원 supply 공급하다 taste 맛보다 explore 답사하다 section 부분

59

`고난도`

What does the woman say she did?

(A) Uploaded some images to the Internet
(B) Repaired some harvesting equipment
(C) Packed a box of produce for pick-up
(D) Submitted an order form to a manufacturer

여자는 무엇을 했다고 말하는가?

(A) 인터넷에 일부 이미지를 업로드했다.
(B) 일부 수확 장비를 수리했다.
(C) 픽업용 농산물 박스를 포장했다.
(D) 제조업체에 주문서를 제출했다.

어휘 upload 업로드하다 repair 수리하다 harvesting 수확 equipment 장비 pack 포장하다 produce 농산물 submit 제출하다 manufacturer 제조업체

해설 세부 사항 관련 – 여자가 자신이 했다고 말하는 것
남자가 두 번째 대사에서 당신의 새로운 웹사이트가 좋다(I like your new Web site)며 주문하기가 정말 쉽다(it's really easy to order from)고 하자, 여자가 자신이 직접 디자인하고 모든 사진을 공급했다(I designed it myself, and supplied all the photos)고 한 것으로 보아 정답은 (A)이다.

▸▸ Paraphrasing 대화의 supplied all the photos
→ 정답의 uploaded some images

60

`고난도`

Why most likely does the man say, "I grew up on a farm"?

(A) To support an opinion
(B) To explain a misunderstanding
(C) To offer assistance
(D) To show curiosity

남자가 "저는 농장에서 자랐어요"라고 말하는 이유는 무엇일 것 같은가?

(A) 의견을 뒷받침하기 위해
(B) 오해를 해명하기 위해
(C) 지원을 제공하기 위해
(D) 호기심을 보이기 위해

어휘 support 지지하다 opinion 의견 explain 설명하다 misunderstanding 오해 offer 제공하다 assistance 지원 curiosity 호기심

해설 화자의 의도 파악 – 나는 농장에서 자랐다는 말의 의도
앞에서 당신의 옥수수는 제가 맛본 것 중 단연 최고이다(I have to say that your corn is the best I've ever tasted)라고 한 뒤 인용문을 언급했으므로, 여자의 옥수수가 최고라고 말한 데 대해 설득력을 좀 더 부여하기 위해 한 말임을 알 수 있다. 따라서 정답은 (A)이다.

61

What does the woman suggest the man do?

(A) Feed some farm animals
(B) Park closer to an entrance
(C) Read over a promotional flyer
(D) Look at some flower arrangements

여자는 남자에게 무엇을 하라고 제안하는가?

(A) 농장 동물들에게 먹이 주기
(B) 입구 가까이에 주차하기
(C) 홍보 전단을 읽어 보기
(D) 꽃꽂이를 둘러보기

어휘 feed 먹이를 주다 park 주차하다 entrance 입구 promotional 홍보의 flyer 전단 flower arrangement 꽃꽂이

해설 세부 사항 관련 – 여자가 남자에게 제안한 일
여자가 마지막 대사에서 기다리는 동안 우리의 새로운 꽃 구역을 둘러보는 게 어떨지(while you're waiting, why don't you explore our new floral section?)를 제안하며, 싱싱한 튤립과 장미 꽃으로 만든 아름다운 꽃다발들이 있다(We have some beautiful bouquets of fresh-cut tulips and roses)고 했으므로 정답은 (D)이다.

62-64 대화 + 도표

M-Cn Hi, Leilani. Well, [62] **our initiative to move into new markets has succeeded. Our drinks are being sold in more places than ever before, and sales are strong overall.**

W-Br Excellent! How are sales for our Tropical Sun drink?

M-Cn They're up. [63] **Surveyed consumers say they like its blend of mango and strawberry flavors.** Here's a sales chart broken down by size of container.

W-Br I see... It seems our most popular container size historically is still our best seller.

M-Cn Yes. [64] **But I was surprised to see that this one is our second-best seller. So let's look at its sales figures in more depth.** I'll bring up more charts.

남 안녕하세요, 레일라니. 음, 새로운 시장으로 진출하려는 우리의 계획이 성공했어요. 우리 음료가 그 어느 때보다 더 많은 곳에서 판매되고 있고 판매량도 전반적으로 강세를 보이고 있어요.
여 훌륭해요! 트로피컬 선 음료 판매는 어떤가요?
남 상승했어요. 조사 대상 소비자들이 망고와 딸기 맛 혼합이 좋다고 하네요. 여기 용기 크기에 따라 분류된 판매 차트예요.
여 그렇군요… 역대 가장 인기 있는 용기 사이즈가 여전히 베스트 셀러인 것 같네요.
남 네. 그런데 이 제품이 우리의 두 번째 베스트셀러인 것을 보고 깜짝 놀랐어요. 그러니 이 판매 수치를 좀 더 심층적으로 살펴봅시다. 차트를 더 가져올게요.

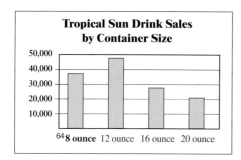

Tropical Sun Drink Sales by Container Size

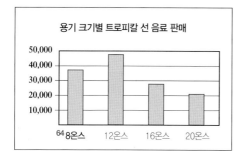

용기 크기별 트로피칼 선 음료 판매

62

According to the speakers, what has the company done?

(A) Relocated its head office
(B) Expanded its sales territory
(C) Created a new corporate logo
(D) Replaced a celebrity spokesperson

고난도

화자에 따르면, 회사는 무엇을 했는가?
(A) 본사 이전
(B) 판매 영역 확대
(C) 새 기업 로고 제작
(D) 유명 인사 대변인 교체

어휘 relocate 이전하다 head office 본사 expand 확대하다 territory 영역 create 만들다 corporate 기업의 replace 교체하다 celebrity 유명 인사 spokesperson 대변인

해설 세부 사항 관련 – 회사가 한 일
남자가 첫 대사에서 새로운 시장으로 진출하려는 우리의 계획이 성공했다(our initiative to move into new markets has succeeded)고 했고, 우리 음료가 그 어느 때보다 더 많은 곳에서 판매되고 있고 판매량도 전반적으로 강세를 보이고 있다(Our drinks are being sold in more places than ever before, and sales are strong overall)고 했으므로 정답은 (B)이다.

▸▸ Paraphrasing 대화의 move into new markets
→ 정답의 expanded its sales territory

63

What is mentioned about the Tropical Sun drink?

(A) It is stocked mostly in restaurants.
(B) It has a combination of flavors.
(C) It will soon be sold at discounts.
(D) It comes in glass bottles.

고난도

트로피칼 선 음료에 대해 언급된 것은 무엇인가?
(A) 주로 식당에 재고로 비축되어 있다.
(B) 조합된 맛이 있다.
(C) 곧 할인 판매된다.
(D) 유리병에 담겨 나온다.

어휘 stock (재고로) 비축하다 mostly 주로 combination 조합 come in (물품·상품 등이) ~로 나오다

해설 세부 사항 관련 – 트로피칼 선 음료에 대해 언급된 사항
남자가 두 번째 대사에서 조사 대상 소비자들이 망고와 딸기 맛 혼합이 좋다고 한다(Surveyed consumers say they like its blend of mango and strawberry flavors)고 한 것으로 보아 정답은 (B)이다.

▸▸ Paraphrasing 대화의 its blend of ~ flavors
→ 정답의 a combination of flavors

64

Look at the graphic. Which size of drink's sales data will the speakers focus on?

(A) 8 ounce
(B) 12 ounce
(C) 16 ounce
(D) 20 ounce

시각 정보에 의하면, 화자들은 어느 크기의 음료 판매 데이터에 초점을 둘 것인가?
(A) 8온스
(B) 12온스
(C) 16온스
(D) 20온스

해설 시각 정보 연계 – 화자들이 초점을 둘 판매 데이터의 음료 크기
남자가 마지막 대사에서 이 제품이 우리의 두 번째 베스트셀러인 것을 보고 깜짝 놀랐다(I was surprised to see that this one is our second-best seller)면서, 그러니 이 판매 수치를 좀 더 심층적으로 살펴보자(So let's look at its sales figures in more depth)고 했고, 도표에 따르면 두 번째로 많이 팔린 제품은 8온스 용량의 음료이므로 정답은 (A)이다.

65-67 대화 + 메뉴

W-Am Well, it sure has been quiet here.

M-Au I'll say. 65 Some of our hardware engineers don't have much to do these days. But we'll be busier when we start working on product updates.

W-Am	True. Oh, that reminds me—**⁶⁶you know Enzio's Café? They've just streamlined the way you order for delivery—now it's only two steps.** You click the menu item on the Web site and then click "order." I'll show you.
M-Au	Oh, that's nice. So, **⁶⁷do you want to order today's special?**
W-Am	**⁶⁷Well, it is the cheapest one. But it's on the light side. Why don't we order the special tomorrow?** It'll be more filling.
M-Au	Good plan.

여	음, 여긴 정말 한가했어요.
남	맞아요. 요즘 우리 하드웨어 엔지니어 중 몇몇은 별로 할 일이 많지 않거든요. 하지만 제품 업데이트 작업을 시작하면 더 바빠질 겁니다.
여	맞아요. 아, 생각나는 게 있어요. **엔지오 카페 알죠? 얼마 전 배달 주문하는 방법을 간소화했어요. 이제 딱 두 단계뿐이에요.** 웹사이트의 메뉴 항목을 누른 다음 "주문"을 누르면 돼요. 제가 보여줄게요.
남	오, 좋은데요. 그래서 **오늘의 특선을 주문할 건가요?**
여	음, 그게 가장 싼 거네요. 하지만 좀 가벼운 편이네요. 내일 특선을 주문하는 게 어때요? 그건 좀 더 배가 부르겠어요.
남	좋은 계획이에요.

어휘	I'll say (동의하며) 맞아요 remind 상기시키다 streamline 간소화하다 step 단계 light 가벼운 filling 배부른

```
╔═══════════════════════════════════════╗
        Enzio's Cafe—Daily Specials

     Monday        Chicken curry  $13
     Tuesday       Vegetable pasta $10
  ⁶⁷Wednesday      Cheese pizza   $12
     Thursday      Grilled salmon $14
╚═══════════════════════════════════════╝
```

```
╔═══════════════════════════════════════╗
          엔지오 카페—요일별 특선

     월요일         치킨 커리    13달러
     화요일         채소 파스타   10달러
  ⁶⁷수요일          치즈 피자    12달러
     목요일         구운 연어    14달러
╚═══════════════════════════════════════╝
```

65

What does the man say about some employees?

(A) They have been telecommuting.
(B) They will transfer to overseas offices.
(C) Their workloads have been reduced.
(D) They are attending a product launch.

남자는 일부 직원들에 대해 무엇을 말하는가?

(A) 재택근무를 해왔다.
(B) 해외 지사로 이전할 것이다.
(C) 업무량이 감소했다.
(D) 제품 출시 행사에 참석하고 있다.

어휘	telecommute 재택근무하다 transfer 이전하다 overseas 해외의 workload 업무량 reduce 줄이다 attend 참석하다 launch 출시(행사)

해설 세부 사항 관련 – 남자가 일부 직원들에 대해 말하는 것

남자가 첫 대사에서 요즘 우리 하드웨어 엔지니어 중 몇몇은 별로 할 일이 많지 않다(Some of our hardware engineers don't have much to do these days)고 한 것으로 보아 정답은 (C)이다.

> ▸▸ Paraphrasing 대화의 don't have much to do
> → 정답의 workloads have been reduced

66   고난도

According to the woman, what has Enzio's Café recently done?

(A) Raised its food prices
(B) Renovated its dining room
(C) Opened an additional location
(D) Simplified an ordering process

여자에 따르면, 엔지오 카페는 최근에 무엇을 했는가?

(A) 음식 가격 인상
(B) 식당 개조
(C) 추가 지점 개설
(D) 주문 절차 간소화

어휘	raise 올리다 renovate 개조하다 dining room 식당 additional 추가 location 장소, 위치 simplify 간소화하다 process 절차

해설 세부 사항 관련 – 여자가 말하는 엔지오 카페가 최근에 한 일

여자가 두 번째 대사에서 엔지오 카페(you know Enzio's Café?)를 언급하며 얼마 전 배달 주문하는 방법을 간소화했(They've just streamlined the way you order for delivery)며 이제 딱 두 단계뿐(now it's only two steps)이라고 했으므로 정답은 (D)이다.

> ▸▸ Paraphrasing 대화의 streamlined the way you order
> → 정답의 simplified an ordering process

67   고난도

Look at the graphic. What special will the speakers probably order for delivery?

(A) Chicken curry
(B) Vegetable pasta
(C) Cheese pizza
(D) Grilled salmon

시각 정보에 의하면, 화자들은 어떤 특선을 배송 주문하겠는가?

(A) 치킨 커리
(B) 채소 파스타
(C) 치즈 피자
(D) 구운 연어

반품 코드	반품 사유
01	배송 중 파손
69 02	**불량—오작동**
03	오배송
04	변심—원하지 않음

해설 시각 정보 연계 – 화자들이 배송 주문할 특선

남자가 두 번째 대사에서 오늘의 특선을 주문할지(do you want to order today's special?)를 묻자 여자가 그게 가장 싼 것(it is the cheapest one)이지만 좀 가벼운 편(But it's on the light side)이라면서 내일 특선을 주문하는 게 어떨지(Why don't we order the special tomorrow?) 제안했고, 도표에 따르면 가장 싼 것은 10달러짜리 채소 파스타이고 여자가 제안한 내일 즉 그 다음날의 특선은 치즈 피자이므로 정답은 (C)이다.

68-70 대화 + 목록

> M-Cn Hi, Judy. **68 Well, it's only your first week here on the job, but it looks like you're learning quickly.** Is there anything I can help you with?
>
> W-Am Actually, yes. **69 I'm processing a returned headset, and the purchaser said he returned it because it's a faulty product. There's sound only on one side.** Uh, no return code appears on the computer.
>
> M-Cn Oh, you have to enter it manually. **69 Here's a list of the codes.**
>
> W-Am Ah, thank you.
>
> M-Cn No problem. If you have any questions later, just ask another associate. **70 I'm headed to the back of the warehouse now to see if the picking crew needs help.**

> 남 안녕하세요, 주디. 음, 여기 근무한 지 일주일밖에 안 됐는데, 빨리 배우고 있는 것 같네요. 내가 뭐 도울 일이 있을까요?
>
> 여 사실, 네. 반품된 헤드셋을 처리하고 있는데, 구매자가 불량품이라서 반품했다고 했어요. 한쪽에서만 소리가 나요. 어, 컴퓨터에 반품 코드는 나오지 않고요.
>
> 남 아, 그건 수동으로 입력해야 해요. 여기 코드 목록이 있어요.
>
> 여 아, 고맙습니다.
>
> 남 뭘요. 나중에 궁금한 게 있으면 그냥 다른 동료에게 물어봐요. 전 지금 물품 수거팀에서 도움이 필요한지 보려고 창고 뒤편으로 가고 있거든요.

어휘 process 처리하다 return 반납하다; 반납 purchaser 구매자 faulty 결함이 있는 appear 나타나다 enter 입력하다 manually 수동으로 associate 동료 head 향하다 warehouse 창고 picking 수거, 채집

Return code	Reason for return
01	Damaged in shipping
69 02	**Defective—does not work properly**
03	Wrong item shipped
04	Changed mind—do not want

68

What does the man mention about the woman?

(A) She is working overtime.

(B) She is a new employee.

(C) She will soon go on vacation.

(D) She is handling a colleague's responsibilities.

남자는 여자에 대해 무엇을 언급하는가?

(A) 야근을 하고 있다.

(B) 신입 사원이다.

(C) 곧 휴가를 떠날 것이다.

(D) 동료의 업무를 처리하고 있다.

어휘 handle 처리하다 colleague 동료 responsibility 책무, 임무

해설 세부 사항 관련 – 남자가 여자에 대해 언급한 사항

남자가 첫 대사에서 여자에게 여기 근무한 지 일주일밖에 안 됐는데 빨리 배우고 있는 것 같다(it's only your first week here on the job, but it looks like you're learning quickly)고 한 것으로 보아 정답은 (B)이다.

69

Look at the graphic. Which return code will most likely be entered?

(A) Code 01

(B) Code 02

(C) Code 03

(D) Code 04

시각 정보에 의하면, 어느 반품 코드가 입력될 것 같은가?

(A) 코드 01

(B) 코드 02

(C) 코드 03

(D) 코드 04

해설 시각 정보 연계 – 입력될 것 같은 반품 코드

여자가 첫 대사에서 반품된 헤드셋을 처리하고 있는데 구매자가 불량품이라서 반품했다고 했다(I'm processing a returned headset, and the purchaser said he returned it because it's a faulty product)며 한쪽에서만 소리가 난다(There's sound only on one side)고 했고 컴퓨터에 반품 코드가 나오지 않는다(no return code appears on the computer)고 한 것으로 보아 기기가 제대로 작동하지 않아 반품된 것임을 알 수 있다. 목록에 의하면, 불량으로 오작동일 경우의 반품 코드는 02이므로 정답은 (B)이다.

70

What will the man probably do next?

(A) Go to a different part of a building

(B) Use a loudspeaker to ask for assistance

(C) Write down some questions

(D) Restart a handheld device

남자는 다음에 무엇을 하겠는가?

(A) 건물의 다른 부분으로 이동한다
(B) 도움을 요청하기 위해 확성기를 사용한다.
(C) 질문 몇 가지를 적는다.
(D) 휴대용 장치를 다시 시작한다.

어휘 different 다른 loudspeaker 확성기 assistance 도움
handheld 휴대용의, 손에 들고 쓰는 device 장치

해설 세부 사항 관련 - 남자가 다음에 할 일
남자가 마지막 대사에서 지금 물품 수거팀에서 도움이 필요한지 보려고 창고 뒤편으로 가고 있다(I'm headed to the back of the warehouse now to see if the picking crew needs help)고 했으므로 정답은 (A)이다.

PART 4

71-73 광고

M-Cn For everything you need to live and work smartly at home, ^{71}visit Caldarr Center. We guarantee the lowest everyday prices on all the TVs, laptops, and mobile phones that we sell. ^{72}And, for your convenience, we've just started a new curbside pickup option. Simply select the items you want from our Web site, then schedule a pick-up time, and a store associate will bring your goods to your car. ^{73}And for help in choosing the right product, we invite all our shoppers to look over our customer reviews Web page—read their honest opinions about the products they bought here at Caldarr Center.

집에서 스마트하게 생활하고 일하기 위해 필요한 모든 것을 위해, **칼다르 센터를 방문하십시오.** 우리가 판매하는 모든 TV, 노트북, 휴대전화의 상시 최저가를 보장해드립니다. 그리고 당신의 편의를 위해 우리는 최근에 새로운 길가 픽업 옵션을 시작했습니다. 우리 웹사이트에서 당신이 원하는 상품을 간단히 선택한 다음 픽업 시간을 정하면, 가게 직원이 당신의 제품을 당신의 차로 가져다드릴 것입니다. 그리고 알맞은 상품을 고르는 데 도움을 드리기 위해 우리는 모든 쇼핑객들에게 우리의 고객 평가 웹페이지를 살펴보시도록 청합니다. 이곳 칼다르 센터에서 구입한 제품에 대한 그들의 솔직한 의견을 읽어보십시오.

어휘 smartly 현명하게 guarantee 보장하다 convenience 편의 curbside 차도 가장자리 associate 동료 goods 제품

71

What kind of business most likely is Caldarr Center?

(A) A home furnishings retailer
(B) An electronics store
(C) A telecommunications service
(D) A maker of office supplies

칼다르 센터는 어떤 종류의 업체일 것 같은가?

(A) 가정용 가구 소매점
(B) 전자제품 매장
(C) 통신 서비스
(D) 사무용품 제조업체

해설 세부 사항 관련 - 칼다르 센터의 업종
화자가 초반부에 칼다르 센터를 방문하라(visit Caldarr Center)면서 우리가 판매하는 모든 TV, 노트북, 휴대전화의 상시 최저가를 보장한다(We guarantee the lowest everyday prices on all the TVs, laptops, and mobile phones that we sell)고 한 것으로 보아 칼다르 센터는 전자제품을 취급하는 곳임을 알 수 있다. 따라서 정답은 (B)이다.

▸▸ Paraphrasing 담화의 the TVs, laptops, mobile phones
→ 정답의 electronics

72   고난도

According to the advertisement, what has Caldarr Center done recently?

(A) Added a new way to shop
(B) Launched a loyalty program
(C) Expanded its range of products
(D) Hired new staff members

광고에 따르면, 칼다르 센터는 최근에 무엇을 했는가?

(A) 새로운 쇼핑 방법 추가
(B) 고객 보상제 실시
(C) 제품군 확대
(D) 신규 직원 채용

어휘 add 추가하다 launch 시작하다 loyalty program 고객 보상제 expand 확대하다 range 범위 hire 채용하다

해설 세부 사항 관련 - 칼다르 센터가 최근에 한 일
화자가 중반부에 당신의 편의를 위해 우리는 최근에 새로운 길가 픽업 옵션을 시작했다(for your convenience, we've just started a new curbside pickup option)고 했으므로 정답은 (A)이다.

73

What does the speaker encourage listeners to do?

(A) Browse a customer feedback page
(B) Upgrade some warranty coverage
(C) Purchase special gift cards
(D) Vote on a potential improvement

화자는 청자들에게 무엇을 하라고 권하는가?

(A) 고객 피드백 페이지를 둘러볼 것
(B) 보증 범위를 확대할 것
(C) 특별 상품권을 구입할 것
(D) 잠재 개선사항에 투표할 것

어휘 browse 둘러보다 warranty 보증 coverage 범위 purchase 구입하다 vote 투표하다 potential 잠재적인 improvement 개선

해설 세부 사항 관련 - 화자가 청자들에게 권하는 사항
화자가 마지막에 알맞은 상품을 고르는 데 도움을 드리기 위해 우리는 모든 쇼핑객들에게 우리의 고객 평가 웹페이지를 살펴보시도록 청한다(for help in choosing the right product, we invite all our shoppers to look over

our customer reviews Web page)며, 이곳 칼다르 센터에서 구입한 제품에 대한 그들의 솔직한 의견을 읽어보라(read their honest opinions about the products they bought here at Caldarr Center)고 했으므로 정답은 (A)이다.

> ▸▸ Paraphrasing　담화의 look over our customer reviews Web page → 정답의 browse a customer feedback page

74-76 공지

M-Au　**74 Welcome aboard the Northern Express train,** offering service to Portland Station with intermediate stops in Dover and Cumberland. **74 The first car of this train is for passengers seated in Business Class, and the remaining cars are for passengers seated in Coach Class. 75 Car Four is the train's Quiet Car, where passengers are asked to maintain a library-like atmosphere. Please refrain from making any mobile phone calls while riding in this car. 76 In just a few moments, we will open our café car, where passengers may purchase a variety of light snacks.** Please watch your step as you pass between the cars of the moving train. Thank you, and enjoy your trip.

도버와 컴벌랜드에서 중간 정차하며 포틀랜드 역으로 가는 서비스를 제공하는 노던 익스프레스 열차에 탑승하신 것을 환영합니다. 이 열차의 첫 번째 차량은 비즈니스석 승객을 위한 것이고, 나머지 차량들은 일반석 승객을 위한 것입니다. 4번 차량은 열차의 조용한 차 칸으로서, 승객들은 도서관 같은 분위기를 유지할 것이 요구됩니다. 이 차량에 타고 계신 동안 휴대전화 통화는 삼가십시오. 잠시 후 승객들이 다양한 가벼운 간식을 구입할 수 있는 카페 차량을 오픈합니다. 움직이는 열차의 차량 사이를 지나실 때 발걸음을 조심하십시오. 감사합니다. 즐거운 여행 되시기 바랍니다.

어휘　aboard 탑승한　intermediate 중간의　passenger 승객　seated 착석한　remaining 남아 있는　coach class 일반석　maintain 유지하다　atmosphere 분위기　refrain 자제하다　purchase 구입하다　a variety of 다양한　pass 지나가다

74
고난도

What is mentioned about the Northern Express Train?

(A) It costs more than ordinary trains.
(B) It operates several times each day.
(C) It makes no stops en route to its destination.
(D) It is divided into two seating classes.

노던 익스프레스 열차에 대해 언급된 것은 무엇인가?
(A) 일반 열차보다 가격이 더 높다.
(B) 매일 여러 번 운행한다.
(C) 목적지까지 가는 도중에 정차하지 않는다.
(D) 두 개의 좌석 등급으로 나뉜다.

어휘　cost 비용이 들다　ordinary 보통의　operate 운영하다　en route 도중에　destination 목적지　divide 나누다

해설　세부 사항 관련 – 노던 익스프레스 열차에 대해 언급된 것
화자가 도입부에 노던 익스프레스 열차에 탑승하신 것을 환영한다(Welcome aboard the Northern Express train)고 했고, 뒤이어 이 열차의 첫 번째 차량은 비즈니스석 승객을 위한 것이고, 나머지 차량들은 일반석 승객을 위한 것(The first car of this train is for passengers seated in Business Class, and the remaining cars are for passengers seated in Coach Class)이라고 했으므로 정답은 (D)이다.

75

What are passengers in Car Four of the train asked to do?

(A) Present photo identification
(B) Store luggage between cars
(C) Avoid mobile phone conversations
(D) Move forward to the next car

열차의 4번 차량에 탑승한 승객들은 무엇을 요구받는가?
(A) 사진 신분증을 제시할 것
(B) 차량 사이에 짐을 보관할 것
(C) 휴대전화 통화를 피할 것
(D) 다음 차량으로 이동할 것

어휘　present 제시하다　identification 신분증　store 보관하다　luggage 짐　avoid 피하다　conversation 대화　forward 앞으로

해설　세부 사항 관련 – 열차의 4번 차량에 탑승한 승객들이 요구받은 일
화자가 중반부에 4번 차량은 열차의 조용한 차 칸으로서, 승객들은 도서관 같은 분위기를 유지할 것이 요구된다(Car Four is the train's Quiet Car, where passengers are asked to maintain a library-like atmosphere)며 이 차량에 타고 계신 동안 휴대전화 통화는 삼가라(Please refrain from taking any mobile phone calls while riding in this car)고 했으므로 정답은 (C)이다.

> ▸▸ Paraphrasing　담화의 refrain from taking any mobile phone calls
> → 정답의 avoid mobile phone conversations

76

According to the announcement, what will happen shortly?

(A) Tickets will be inspected.
(B) A video will be shown.
(C) Boarding will be completed.
(D) Refreshments will be available.

공지에 따르면, 곧 무슨 일이 일어날 것인가?
(A) 표를 검사할 것이다.
(B) 영상이 상영될 것이다.
(C) 탑승이 완료될 것이다.
(D) 다과가 이용 가능해질 것이다.

Test 8

어휘 inspect 검사하다 boarding 탑승 complete 완료하다
refreshment 다과

해설 세부 사항 관련 – 공지에서 곧 일어난다고 말하는 일

화자가 후반부에 잠시 후 승객들이 다양한 가벼운 간식을 구입할 수 있는 카페 차량을 오픈한다(In just a few moments, we will open our café car, where passengers may purchase a variety of light snacks)고 했으므로 정답은 (D)이다.

▸▸ **Paraphrasing**   담화의 **snacks** → 정답의 **refreshments**

77-79 음성 메시지

> W-Br Thank you for calling Worldways Health.
> [77]**We are the area's best-known clinic offering
> health care services and advice for people who
> travel internationally.** [78]**Due to the high volume
> of calls in anticipation of the holiday period, our
> wait times are longer than usual. We apologize
> and ask that you please stay on the line.** The
> next available representative will be with you
> as soon as possible. [79]**Please take this time to
> ensure that you have any relevant travel and
> health insurance paperwork at hand.** This will
> enable your call to proceed smoothly.

> 월드웨이즈 헬스에 전화해주셔서 감사합니다. 우리는 이 지역에서 가장 잘 알려진 병원으로 해외로 이동 하는 사람들을 위한 건강 관리 서비스와 조언을 제공하고 있습니다. 휴가 기간을 앞두고 통화량이 많아 대기 시간이 평소보다 깁니다. 이 점을 사과드리며 끊지 말고 기다리시기를 부탁드립니다. 다음으로 가능한 담당자가 곧 연결될 것입니다. 대기 시간 동안 관련 여행 및 건강 보험 서류 작업이 준비되어 있는지 확인하십시오. 이렇게 하면 전화 통화가 순조롭게 진행될 수 있습니다.

> 어휘 clinic 병원 internationally 국제적으로 volume (~의)
> 양 in anticipation of ~을 예상하고 holiday 휴가 period 기간
> apologize 사과하다 available 가능한 representative 대리인,
> 대표 ensure 반드시 ~하게 하다 relevant 관련된 insurance
> 보험 paperwork 서류작업 at hand 준비된, 가까운 enable
> 가능하게 하다 proceed 진행하다 smoothly 순조롭게

77

What kind of business recorded the message?

(A) A real estate firm
(B) A travel agency
(C) A medical clinic
(D) A mobile app developer

어떤 업체에서 이 메시지를 녹음했는가?

(A) 부동산 회사
(B) 여행사
(C) 병원
(D) 휴대폰 앱 개발자

해설 전체 내용 관련 – 메시지를 녹음한 업체

화자가 초반부에 우리는 이 지역에서 가장 잘 알려진 병원으로 해외로 이동 하는 사람들을 위한 건강 관리 서비스와 조언을 제공하고 있다(We are the area's best-known clinic offering health care services and advice for people who travel internationally)고 했으므로 정답은 (C)이다.

78

What does the speaker apologize for?

(A) A recent price increase
(B) An upcoming holiday closure
(C) Extended holding times
(D) Possible audio problems

화자는 무엇에 대해 사과하는가?

(A) 최근의 가격 인상
(B) 곧 있을 휴일 휴업
(C) 늘어난 대기 시간
(D) 오디오 문제 발생 가능성

어휘 recent 최근의 increase 인상 upcoming 곧 있을 closure
휴업, 폐쇄 extended 늘어난 holding time 대기 시간

해설 세부 사항 관련 – 화자가 사과한 점

화자가 중반부에 휴가 기간을 앞두고 통화량이 많아 대기 시간이 평소보다 길다(Due to the high volume of calls in anticipation of the holiday period, our wait times are longer than usual)고 했고, 이 점을 사과드리며 끊지 말고 기다리시기를 부탁드린다(We apologize and ask that you please stay on the line)고 했으므로 정답은 (C)이다.

▸▸ **Paraphrasing**   담화의 **our wait times are longer than
usual** → 정답의 **extended holding times**

79

What is the listener encouraged to do?

(A) Meet a representative in person
(B) Prepare some documentation
(C) Use a business's other locations
(D) Try calling on another day

청자는 무엇을 하도록 권장되는가?

(A) 직접 담당자를 만날 것
(B) 서류를 준비할 것
(C) 업체의 다른 지점을 이용할 것
(D) 다른 날에 전화해볼 것

어휘 in person 직접 prepare 준비하다 documentation 서류
location 지점

해설 세부 사항 관련 – 청자가 권장 받은 일

화자가 후반부에 대기 시간 동안 관련 여행 및 건강 보험 서류 작업이 준비되어 있는지 확인하라(Please take this time to ensure that you have any relevant travel and health insurance paperwork at hand)고 했으므로 정답은 (B)이다.

▸▸ **Paraphrasing**   담화의 **have any ~ paperwork at hand**
→ 정답의 **prepare some documentation**

80-82 전화 메시지

> W-Am Hi, Mr. Martino? It's Sheila calling from 10 Westmont Street. ⁸⁰**You're probably on your way to my home to install new water pipes in the basement.** I had scheduled the two P.M. service visit on your Web site. ⁸¹**In the section for driving directions, I typed "white house on the right," and...** there are a lot of white houses in the area. ⁸¹**So I wanted to let you know my house has a large number "10" on the mailbox.** You'll see it. ⁸²**I'll move my car out of the driveway now so you can park your truck close to the house.** OK, see you soon.

> 안녕하세요, 마르티노 씨? 웨스트몬트 가 10번지에서 전화드리는 쉴라입니다. **아마 지하에 새 수도관을 설치하러 우리 집으로 오시는 길일텐데요.** 당신의 웹 사이트에서 오후 2시 서비스 방문으로 일정을 잡았거든요. **운전 길 안내 부분에 "오른쪽의 하얀 집"이라고 입력했는데…** 이 지역에는 하얀 집이 많이 있어요. 그 **래서 우리 집은 우편함에 "10"이라는 숫자가 크게 써 있다고 알려드리고 싶었어요.** 보이실 거예요. **지금 제 차를 진입로 밖으로 옮겨서 당신이 트럭을 집 가까이 에 주차할 수 있도록 할게요.** 그럼, 곧 뵙겠습니다.

> 어휘 install 설치하다 basement 지하 schedule 일정을 잡다 section 부분 type 입력하다 mailbox 우편함 driveway 진입로[차도]

80

Who most likely is the listener?

(A) A neighbor
(B) A plumber
(C) A house painter
(D) A delivery person

청자는 누구이겠는가?

(A) 이웃
(B) 배관공
(C) 주택 도장공
(D) 배달원

해설 전체 내용 관련 – 청자의 직업
화자가 전반부에 청자에게 아마 지하에 새 수도관을 설치하러 우리 집으로 오 시는 길일 것(You're probably on your way to my home to install new water pipes in the basement)이라고 한 것으로 보아 정답은 (B)이다.

81

고난도

What most likely does the speaker mean when she says, "there are a lot of white houses in the area"?

(A) A maintenance service could become popular.
(B) A neighborhood has few nearby businesses.
(C) Some renovations will make a home stand out.
(D) Some instructions may have been unclear.

화자가 "이 지역에는 하얀 집이 많이 있어요"라고 말하는 의도는 무엇일 것 같은가?

(A) 정비 서비스의 인기가 높아질 수 있다.
(B) 동네에 가까운 사업체가 거의 없다.
(C) 약간의 보수는 집을 돋보이게 할 것이다.
(D) 일부 설명이 명확하지 않았을 수 있다.

어휘 maintenance 유지 보수 neighborhood 동네 nearby 가까운 renovation 보수[개조] stand out 돋보이다 instruction 설명 unclear 분명하지 않은

해설 화자의 의도 파악 – 이 지역에는 하얀 집이 많이 있다는 말의 의도
앞에서 화자가 운전 길 안내 부분에 "오른쪽의 하얀 집"이라고 입력했다(In the section for driving directions, I typed "white house on the right,") 고 말한 뒤 인용문을 언급하고 나서 그래서 우리 집은 우편함에 "10"이라는 숫 자가 크게 써 있다고 알려드리고 싶었다(So I wanted to let you know my house has a large number "10" on the mailbox)고 집을 찾는 데 도움 이 될 수 있는 부연 설명을 덧붙인 것으로 보아 길 안내가 명확하지 않아 헷갈 릴 수 있음을 설명하려는 의도로 한 말임을 알 수 있다. 따라서 정답은 (D)이다.

82

What does the speaker say she will do next?

(A) Add her signature to an agreement
(B) Make a space available for parking
(C) Take some letters to a post office
(D) Put up some signs outside a structure

화자는 다음에 무엇을 할 것이라고 말하는가?

(A) 계약서에 서명 추가하기
(B) 주차할 수 있는 공간 만들기
(C) 우체국에 편지 몇 통 가져가기
(D) 구조물 바깥에 표지판 걸기

어휘 signature 서명 agreement 계약서, 동의 space 공간 available 가능한 post office 우체국 put up 내걸다 sign 표지판 structure 구조물

해설 세부 사항 관련 – 화자가 다음에 할 일
화자가 후반부에 지금 차를 진입로 밖으로 옮겨서 당신이 트럭을 집 가까이에 주 차할 수 있도록 하겠다(I'll move my car out of the driveway now so you can park your truck close to the house)고 했으므로 정답은 (B)이다.

83-85 뉴스 보도

> M-Au In local news, the long-awaited Shorepoint Shopping Mall will open to the public this Friday, after nearly three years of construction. ⁸³**Work on the mall fell behind schedule after adjustments were made to the layout of the indoor food court section to allow for more space separating its fifteen restaurants.** ⁸⁴**The mall, located alongside Highway 4, can be reached by City Bus Number 62, which stops in front of its main entrance.** ⁸⁵**The mall's management will broadcast its Grand**

Opening Day ceremony online via social media platforms. **Members of the public who won't be able to attend in person are invited to watch the live video from nine-thirty to ten A.M. on Friday.** Those who do will be rewarded with access to many of the same special discounts as in-person visitors.

지역 뉴스입니다. 오래 기다려온 쇼어포인트 쇼핑몰이 거의 3년의 공사 끝에 이번 주 금요일 오픈합니다. 15개의 식당을 분리할 수 있는 추가 공간을 확보하기 위해 실내 푸드코트 구역의 배치를 조정하고 나서 쇼핑몰 공사가 예정보다 늦어졌습니다. 4번 고속도로 옆에 위치한 이 쇼핑몰은 62번 시내버스로 갈 수 있으며, 버스는 정문 앞에 정차합니다. 쇼핑몰 운영진은 소셜미디어 플랫폼을 통해 개점 행사를 온라인으로 중계할 예정입니다. 직접 참석할 수 없는 분들은 금요일 오전 9시 30분부터 10시까지 라이브 영상을 시청하시기 바랍니다. 시청자들에게는 방문 고객들과 똑같은 여러 특별 할인을 받을 수 있는 권한이 주어질 것입니다.

어휘 long-awaited 오래 기다려온 public 대중 construction 공사 adjustment 조정 layout 배치 indoor 실내의 section 구역 separate 분리하다 located 위치한 alongside ~ 옆에 entrance 입구 management 경영진 broadcast 방송하다 ceremony 기념 행사 via ~을 통해 in person 직접 reward 보상하다 access 이용[참가]할 권리

83 [고난도]

According to the report, what delayed the mall's completion?

(A) Changes to its floor plan
(B) Difficulty receiving some permits
(C) A shortage of construction workers
(D) The hiring of a new contractor

보도에 따르면, 무엇이 쇼핑몰의 완공을 지연시켰는가?

(A) 평면도 변경
(B) 일부 허가를 받는 데 어려움
(C) 건설 인력의 부족
(D) 신규 도급업자의 고용

어휘 completion 완성[완공] floor plan 평면도 permit 허가 shortage 부족 contractor 도급업자, 계약자

해설 세부 사항 관련 - 보도에서 쇼핑몰 완공이 지연된 이유라고 말하는 것
화자가 전반부에 15개의 식당을 분리할 수 있는 추가 공간을 확보하기 위해 실내 푸드코트 구역의 배치를 조정하고 나서 쇼핑몰 공사가 예정보다 늦어졌다(Work on the mall fell behind schedule after adjustments were made to the layout of the indoor food court section to allow for more space separating its fifteen restaurants)고 했으므로 정답은 (A)이다.

▸▸ Paraphrasing 담화의 **adjustments were made to the layout** → 정답의 **changes to its floor plan**

84

What does the speaker say is a feature of the mall?

(A) A performance space
(B) An indoor garden
(C) A large entrance hall
(D) A public transportation stop

화자는 쇼핑몰의 특징이 무엇이라고 말하는가?

(A) 공연 공간
(B) 실내 정원
(C) 넓은 입구 로비
(D) 대중교통 정거장

해설 세부 사항 관련 - 화자가 말하는 쇼핑몰의 특징
화자가 중반부에 4번 고속도로 옆에 위치한 이 쇼핑몰은 62번 시내버스로 갈 수 있으며, 버스는 정문 앞에 정차한다(The mall, located alongside Highway 4, can be reached by City Bus Number 62, which stops in front of its main entrance)고 대중교통인 버스가 쇼핑몰 바로 앞에서 정차한다고 했으므로 정답은 (D)이다.

▸▸ Paraphrasing 담화의 **City Bus** → 정답의 **public transportation**

85 [고난도]

What are listeners invited to do?

(A) Stream footage of an opening-day event
(B) Submit feedback surveys to mall management
(C) Register for an e-mail update program
(D) Participate in a phone-in talk show

청자들은 무엇을 하라고 요청되는가?

(A) 개점 행사 영상 스트림
(B) 쇼핑몰 운영진에 피드백 설문지 제출
(C) 이메일 업데이트 프로그램 등록
(D) 전화 토크쇼 참여

어휘 stream 데이터 전송을 연속적으로 이어서 하다 footage 화면[장면] submit 제출하다 survey 설문 조사 register 등록하다

해설 세부 사항 관련 - 청자들이 하도록 요청받은 일
화자가 후반부에 쇼핑몰 운영진은 소셜미디어 플랫폼을 통해 개점 행사를 온라인으로 중계할 예정(The mall's management will broadcast its Grand Opening Day ceremony online via social media platforms)이라며, 직접 참석할 수 없는 사람들은 금요일 오전 9시 30분부터 10시까지 라이브 영상을 시청하기 바란다(Members of the public who won't be able to attend in person are invited to watch the live video from nine-thirty to ten A.M. on Friday)고 했으므로 정답은 (A)이다.

86-88 회의 발췌

W-Br **86 Finally, I'd like to review the brochure we're creating for Revdecc Plus. As a high-end health club, they focus on providing a comfortable workout environment for their members.** The brochure's front page shows people running near a tall building, and… it doesn't capture their brand image. We'll need to revise it. Now, we've had design challenges before. [87]The changes shouldn't be hard to make, and I'm confident we can give it more impact. Let's work on that now. [88]Then, at four this afternoon, let's get together again as a team, and discuss what we've done.

마지막으로, 리브덱 플러스를 위해 우리가 만들고 있는 책자를 검토하고 싶습니다. 고급 헬스클럽으로서 그들은 회원들에게 편안한 운동 환경을 제공하는 데 주력하고 있습니다. 이 책자의 1면은 높은 건물 근처에서 뛰고 있는 사람들의 모습을 보여주고 있는데… 그들의 브랜드 이미지를 포착하지 못하고 있습니다. 이 부분을 수정해야 할 것입니다. 자, 우리는 전에도 디자인 도전 과제가 있었던 적이 있습니다. 변화를 만드는 것은 어렵지 않을 것이고, 좀 더 강한 효과를 부여할 수 있을 것이라고 확신합니다. 지금 그것을 해봅시다. 그러고 나서 오늘 오후 4시에 팀으로 다시 한번 모여서 우리가 한 일을 논의합시다.

어휘 brochure 책자 comfortable 편안한 workout 운동
environment 환경 capture 포착하다 revise 수정하다
challenge 도전 (과제) confident 확신하는 impact 효과, 영향

86

What kind of business most likely is Revdecc Plus?

(A) A publishing company
(B) A real estate developer
(C) A fitness center
(D) An advertising agency

리브덱 플러스는 어떤 종류의 업체일 것 같은가?
(A) 출판사
(B) 부동산 개발업자
(C) 피트니스 센터
(D) 광고 대행사

해설 세부 사항 관련 – 리브덱 플러스의 업종
화자가 초반부에 리브덱 플러스를 위해 우리가 만들고 있는 책자를 검토하고 싶다(I'd like to review the brochure we're creating for Revdecc Plus)며, 고급 헬스클럽으로서 그들은 회원들에게 편안한 운동 환경을 제공하는 데 주력하고 있다(As a high-end health club, they focus on providing a comfortable workout environment for their members)고 설명했으므로 정답은 (C)이다.

▸▸ Paraphrasing   담화의 a health club
→ 정답의 a fitness center

87   고난도

Why most likely does the speaker say, "we've had design challenges before"?

(A) To suggest buying new design software
(B) To emphasize the need to recruit more staff
(C) To reassure the listeners about a task
(D) To praise the listeners for an accomplishment

화자가 "우리는 전에도 디자인 도전 과제가 있었던 적이 있습니다"라고 말하는 이유는 무엇일 것 같은가?
(A) 새로운 디자인 소프트웨어의 구입을 제안하려고
(B) 추가 직원 채용의 필요성을 강조하려고
(C) 업무에 대해 청자들을 안심시키려고
(D) 업적에 대해 청자들을 칭찬하려고

어휘 suggest 제안하다 emphasize 강조하다 recruit 채용하다
reassure 안심시키다 task 일 praise 칭찬하다
accomplishment 업적, 성취

해설 화자의 의도 파악 – 우리는 전에도 디자인 도전 과제가 어려움이 있었던 적이 있다는 말의 의도
화자가 인용문 뒤에서 변화를 만드는 것은 어렵지 않을 것이고, 좀 더 강한 효과를 부여할 수 있을 것이라고 확신한다(The changes shouldn't be hard to make, and I'm confident we can give it more impact)고 팀원들을 격려하고 있는 것으로 보아 청자들이 맞닥뜨린 과제를 수행해낼 수 있을 것이라고 안심시키려는 의도로 한 말임을 알 수 있다. 따라서 정답은 (C)이다.

88

What does the speaker recommend doing in the afternoon?

(A) Distributing some brochures
(B) Holding a team meeting
(C) Working past the end of a shift
(D) Visiting a client together

화자는 오후에 무엇을 하자고 권하는가?
(A) 일부 책자의 배포
(B) 팀 회의 개최
(C) 근무 시간 종료 후 작업
(D) 동반 고객 방문

어휘 distribute 배포하다 shift 근무 시간, 근무조 client 고객

해설 세부 사항 관련 – 화자가 오후에 하자고 권하는 일
화자가 마지막에 오늘 오후 4시에 팀으로 다시 한번 모여서 우리가 한 일을 논의하자(at four this afternoon, let's get together again as a team, and discuss what we've done)고 했으므로 정답은 (B)이다.

▸▸ Paraphrasing   담화의 let's get together again as a team, and discuss ~
→ 정답의 holding a team meeting

89-91 워크숍 발췌

M-Cn Hello, everyone. I'm Ed Tanaka, your instructor for this three-day workshop. [89]As we put our brushes to the canvas and try to create beautiful works of art, I will teach you various techniques for coloring and shading your works. [90]What makes this workshop unique is that it takes place entirely in an open-air setting, surrounded by the beautiful nature we're aiming to capture in our creations. [91]Now, as we move

to this park's rose garden, please mind your footing, as there is some uneven ground and loose gravel. Follow me this way.

여러분, 안녕하세요. 저는 이번 3일간의 워크숍 강사 에드 다나카입니다. 우리가 붓을 캔버스에 놓고 아름다운 예술 작품을 창조하려고 애쓰는 동안 저는 여러분의 작품을 채색하고 음영을 넣는 다양한 기법을 가르쳐드리겠습니다. 이 워크숍을 특별하게 만드는 것은 우리가 창작물에 담아내고자 하는 이 아름다운 자연에 둘러싸여 완전히 탁 트인 장소에서 워크샵이 열린다는 것입니다. 자, 이제 이 공원의 장미 정원으로 이동하는 동안 고르지 않은 땅과 헐거운 자갈이 있으니 발 딛는 것에 주의해주십시오. 이쪽으로 저를 따라오십시오.

어휘 instructor 강사 brush 붓 various 다양한 technique 기법 color 색칠하다 shade 음영을 넣다 entirely 전적으로 setting 환경[장소] surrounded 둘러싸인 aim 목표하다 capture 포착하다 creation 창작물 uneven 고르지 않은 loose 헐거운 gravel 자갈

89

What most likely is being taught in the workshop?

(A) Hiking for fitness
(B) Growing plants
(C) Writing journals
(D) Painting pictures

워크숍에서 무엇을 가르치고 있는 것 같은가?
(A) 체력 단련을 위한 하이킹
(B) 식물 재배
(C) 저널 작성
(D) 그림 그리기

해설 세부 사항 관련 – 워크숍에서 가르치고 있는 것
화자가 초반부에 우리가 붓을 캔버스에 놓고 아름다운 예술 작품을 창조하려고 애쓰는 동안 여러분의 작품을 채색하고 음영을 넣는 다양한 기법을 가르쳐드리겠다(As we put our brushes to the canvas and try to create beautiful works of art, I will teach you various techniques for coloring and shading your works)고 한 것으로 보아 정답은 (D)이다.

90

According to the speaker, what is special about the workshop?

(A) It has a high enrollment.
(B) It is being held outdoors.
(C) It is taught by two instructors.
(D) It takes place over multiple days.

화자에 따르면, 워크숍은 무엇이 특별한가?
(A) 등록률이 높다.
(B) 야외에서 개최되고 있다.
(C) 두 명의 강사가 가르친다.
(D) 며칠에 걸쳐 열린다.

어휘 enrollment 등록 outdoors 야외에서 multiple 다수의

해설 세부 사항 관련 – 화자가 말하는 워크숍의 특별한 점
화자가 중반부에 이 워크숍을 특별하게 만드는 것은 우리가 창작물에 담아내고자 하는 이 아름다운 자연에 둘러싸여 완전히 탁 트인 장소에서 워크샵이 열린다는 것(What makes this workshop unique is that it takes place entirely in an open-air setting, surrounded by the beautiful nature we're aiming to capture in our creations)이라고 했으므로 정답은 (B)이다.

▸▸ Paraphrasing 담화의 takes place ~ in an open-air setting → 정답의 is being held outdoors

91 　　　　　　　　　　　　　　　고난도

What are listeners advised to do?

(A) Obtain parking permits
(B) Carry minimal belongings
(C) Avoid picking flowers
(D) Walk carefully

청자들은 무엇을 하라고 권고되는가?
(A) 주차권을 받을 것
(B) 최소한의 소지품을 휴대할 것
(C) 꽃을 꺾지 말 것
(D) 조심해서 걸을 것

어휘 obtain 얻다 permit 허가증 carry 가지고 다니다 belongings 소지품 avoid 피하다

해설 세부 사항 관련 – 청자들이 권고 받은 일
화자가 후반부에 이 공원의 장미 정원으로 이동하는 동안 고르지 않은 땅과 헐거운 자갈이 있으니 발 딛는 것에 주의하라(as we move to this park's rose garden, please mind your footing, as there is some uneven ground and loose gravel)고 했으므로 정답은 (D)이다.

▸▸ Paraphrasing 담화의 mind your footing → 정답의 walk carefully

92-94 공지

M-Au OK, important announcement. **⁹²The new office on Taylor Street passed its safety inspection and is now ready for us to move into.** Isn't that exciting? We'll finally have space to grow. Now, we're going to try to finish the moving process over the first three days of next week. **⁹³This means that we need to have all office supplies packed and ready to move by Monday morning.** So, there's work to do, and... it's Thursday afternoon. **⁹⁴For now, I'll get a plastic bin for you to throw away unwanted items and place it right here by the entrance.** Please use it freely. We don't want to pack and move things that you won't actually need.

자, 중요한 발표가 있습니다. 테일러 가의 새 사무실이 안전 검사를 통과해서 이제 우리가 입주할 준비가 되었습니다. 흥분되지 않나요? 우리는 드디어 성장할 수 있는 공간을 갖게 될 것입니다. 이제 다음 주 초 3일에 걸쳐 이사 절차를 끝내도록 노력할 것입니다. 이는 즉 월요일 아침까지 모든 사무용품을 챙겨 이사할 준비를 해야 한다는 뜻입니다. 그래서 할 일이 생겼네요. 그리고… **지금은 목요일 오후이고요.** 일단 여러분이 원하지 않는 물건을 버릴 수 있게 플라스틱 통을 사서 바로 여기 입구 옆에 놓아두도록 하겠습니다. 자유롭게 쓰세요. 우리는 여러분이 실제로 필요하지 않은 물건들을 싸서 옮기기를 원하지 않습니다.

어휘 announcement 발표 pass 통과하다 safety 안전 inspection 검사 process 절차 office supply 사무용품 pack 포장하다 bin 통, 쓰레기통 throw away 버리다 entrance 입구 freely 자유롭게

92

What will the speaker's company do soon?

(A) Relocate to a different office
(B) Host a visit from potential clients
(C) Rearrange its current workspace
(D) Undergo a safety inspection

화자의 회사는 곧 무엇을 할 예정인가?

(A) 다른 사무실로의 이전
(B) 잠재 고객의 방문 접대
(C) 현재 작업 공간의 재배치
(D) 안전 점검 받기

어휘 relocate 이전하다 host 주최[접대]하다 potential 잠재적인 rearrange 재배치하다 undergo 받다[겪다]

해설 세부 사항 관련 – 화자의 회사가 곧 할 일
화자가 초반부에 테일러 가의 새 사무실이 안전 검사를 통과해서 이제 우리가 입주할 준비가 되었다(The new office on Taylor Street passed its safety inspection and is now ready for us to move into)고 한 것으로 보아 정답은 (A)이다.

▸▸ **Paraphrasing** 담화의 move → 정답의 relocate

93
고난도

What does the speaker imply when he says, "it's Thursday afternoon"?

(A) An executive is probably busy.
(B) A deadline is approaching.
(C) A previously stated date is incorrect.
(D) A meeting will be postponed.

화자가 "지금은 목요일 오후이고요"라고 말한 의미는 무엇인가?

(A) 임원이 아마 바쁠 것이다.
(B) 마감일이 다가오고 있다.
(C) 이전에 언급된 날짜는 부정확하다.
(D) 회의가 연기될 것이다.

어휘 executive 임원 deadline 마감일 approach 다가오다 previously 이전에 state 언급하다 incorrect 부정확한 postpone 연기하다

해설 화자의 의도 파악 – 지금은 목요일 오후라고 말한 의도
앞에서 화자가 월요일 아침까지 모든 사무용품을 챙겨 이사할 준비를 해야 한다(This means that we need to have all office supplies packed and ready to move by Monday morning)라며 해야 할 일과 마감 시한을 알려 주고 난 뒤 인용문을 언급한 것으로 보아 마감 시한까지 얼마 남지 않았음을 상기시키려 한 말임을 알 수 있다. 따라서 정답은 (B)이다.

94

What does the speaker say he will do next?

(A) Clean a work station
(B) Wait next to an external door
(C) Organize a supply closet
(D) Set up a waste container

화자는 다음에 무엇을 할 것이라고 말하는가?

(A) 작업장 청소
(B) 외부 출입구 옆에서 대기
(C) 물품 보관함 정리
(D) **폐기물 용기 설치**

어휘 work station 작업장 external 외부의 organize 정리하다 supply closet 물품 보관함 container 용기

해설 세부 사항 관련 – 화자가 다음에 하겠다고 한 일
화자가 후반부에 여러분이 원하지 않는 물건을 버릴 수 있게 플라스틱 통을 사서 바로 여기 입구 옆에 놓아두도록 하겠다(I'll get a plastic bin for you to throw away unwanted items and place it right here by the entrance)고 했으므로 정답은 (D)이다.

▸▸ **Paraphrasing** 담화의 a ~ bin for you to throw away → 정답의 a waste container

95-97 회의 발췌 + 도표

W-Am OK, now I'd like to mention our display counter at the front of the supermarket, by the café. **95 This is exclusively for products that the manufacturer has stopped making, and all the featured items are priced thirty percent off.** Now, your shelf diagram for our imported items is no longer accurate. **96 Trevoli Foods announced it will stop producing its sauces in bottles, so I took those items off the shelf and moved them to the promotional display.** I also posted a sign directing shoppers to that area. **97 Please do stress to our customers there's no need to present any coupons—they simply pay the marked prices.**

자, 이제 슈퍼마켓 앞, 카페 옆에 있는 우리 진열대에 대해 언급하고 싶어요. **이 진열대는 제조업체가 생산을 중단한 제품만을 위한 것으로, 해당되는 전품목은 30퍼센트 할인됩니다.** 자, 여러분이 갖고 있는 우리 수입품 선반 도표는 더 이상

정확하지 않습니다. 트레볼리 식품이 병에 담긴 소스 생산을 중단할 예정이라고 발표했기 때문에, 제가 그 제품들을 선반에서 꺼내 판촉 진열대로 옮겼어요. 또 쇼핑객들을 그 구역으로 안내하는 표지판도 게시했어요. 우리 고객들에게 쿠폰을 제시할 필요가 없다는 점을 강조해주세요. 그들은 단지 표시된 가격을 지불하면 됩니다.

Imported Items

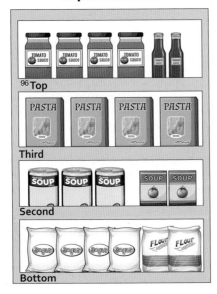

수입품

95 [고난도]

According to the speaker, what is being sold at reduced prices?

(A) Health foods
(B) Cooking tools
(C) Products sold in bulk
(D) Discontinued merchandise

화자에 따르면, 무엇이 할인된 가격에 판매되고 있는가?
(A) 건강식품
(B) 조리 도구
(C) 대용량 판매 제품
(D) 단종 상품

어휘 in bulk 대량으로 discontinue 중단하다

해설 세부 사항 관련 - 화자가 할인 가격에 판매된다고 말하는 제품

화자가 초반부에 진열대는 제조업체가 생산을 중단한 제품만을 위한 것으로, 해당되는 전품목은 30퍼센트 할인된다(This is exclusively for products that the manufacturer has stopped making, and all the featured items are priced thirty percent off)고 했으므로 정답은 (D)이다.

▶▶ Paraphrasing 담화의 **products that the manufacturer has stopped making**
→ 정답의 **discontinued merchandise**

96

Look at the graphic. Which shelf did the speaker remove items from?

(A) The top shelf
(B) The third shelf
(C) The second shelf
(D) The bottom shelf

시각 정보에 의하면, 화자는 어느 선반에서 제품을 치웠는가?
(A) 맨 위 선반
(B) 세 번째 선반
(C) 두 번째 선반
(D) 맨 아래 선반

해설 시각 정보 연계 - 화자가 제품을 치운 선반

화자가 중반부에 트레볼리 식품이 병에 담긴 소스 생산을 중단할 예정이라고 발표했기 때문에, 그 제품들을 선반에서 꺼내 판촉 진열대로 옮겼다(Trevoli Foods announced it will stop producing its sauces in bottles, so I took those items off the shelf and moved them to the promotional display)고 했고, 도표에 따르면 병으로 된 소스는 맨 위 선반에 배치되어 있으므로 화자는 맨 위 선반에 있던 소스병을 옮겼음을 알 수 있다. 따라서 정답은 (A)이다.

97

What are listeners asked to emphasize about a sale?

(A) It applies mostly to high priced items.
(B) It involves a mobile app.
(C) It will last for only one day.
(D) It does not require coupons.

청자들은 할인 판매에 대해 무엇을 강조하라고 요청받는가?
(A) 고가 품목에 주로 적용된다.
(B) 모바일 앱을 필요로 한다.
(C) 하루만 지속될 것이다.
(D) 쿠폰이 필요 없다.

어휘 apply 적용되다 mostly 주로 involve (부수적으로) ~을 필요로 하다
last 지속되다 require 필요로 하다

해설 세부 사항 관련 – 청자들이 할인 판매에 대해 강조하라고 요청받은 것
화자가 마지막에 우리 고객들에게 쿠폰을 제시할 필요가 없다는 점을 강조하라
(Please do stress to our customers there's no need to present any
coupons)면서, 그들은 단지 표시된 가격을 지불하면 된다(they simply pay
the marked prices)고 했으므로 정답은 (D)이다.

98-100 소개 + 일정표

W-Br Hi, I'm Jessica, and I'll be your trainer
today. **98 You've already been introduced
to the high-quality travel bags and rolling
suitcases that we produce here at Bocavian,
Incorporated.** Now, each of our afternoon
training modules will last one hour, with just one
adjustment. I'll spend more time focusing on
presentations, as you will present quite often in
your career here. **99 That means we'll spend less
time on software training, but it's OK because
you learned its main functions yesterday.** All
right, let's begin. **100 First, the policy guide runs
to fourteen pages, so please take a moment to
make sure your copy has every page.**

안녕하세요, 저는 제시카이고 오늘 여러분의 교육 담당입니다. 여러분은 이
미 이곳 보카비안 주식회사에서 우리가 생산하는 고급 여행 가방과 캐리어에 대
해 소개를 받으셨습니다. 이제 오후 교육 과정은 각각 한 시간씩 지속되는데 한
가지만 조정될 겁니다. 이곳에서는 여러분이 업무상 자주 발표하게 되므로 저
는 프레젠테이션에 더 많은 시간을 할애할 겁니다. 그 말은 즉 소프트웨어 교육
에 더 적은 시간을 들인다는 뜻이지만 어제 주요 기능을 익혔으니 괜찮을 겁니다.
자, 시작해봅시다. 먼저 정책 안내는 14페이지까지 이어지므로 잠깐 시간을 내어
복사본에 모든 페이지가 있는지 확인해주세요.

어휘 introduce 소개하다 rolling suitcase 바퀴 달린 여행 가방
module 교과목 단위 adjustment 조정 present 발표하다

Day 2 training
1:00 P.M. to 5:00 P.M.

Module 1	Company policies
Module 2	Making presentations
99 Module 3	Software training
Module 4	Customer relations

2일째 교육 오후 1시부터 5시까지	
과정 1	회사 규정
과정 2	프레젠테이션 하기
99 과정 3	소프트웨어 교육
과정 4	고객 관리

98

Where most likely is the introduction taking place?

(A) At a luggage manufacturer
(B) At a graphic design firm
(C) At a jewelry seller
(D) At a software developer

소개는 어디에서 이루어지고 있는 것 같은가?

(A) 짐가방 제조업체
(B) 그래픽 디자인 회사
(C) 보석상
(D) 소프트웨어 개발업체

해설 전체 내용 관련 – 담화의 장소
화자가 초반부에 여러분은 이미 이곳 보카비안 주식회사에서 우리가 생산하
는 고급 여행 가방과 캐리어에 대해 소개를 받았다(You've already been
introduced to the high-quality travel bags and rolling suitcases
that we produce here at Bocavian, Incorporated)고 한 것으로 보아 정
답은 (A)이다.

▶▶ Paraphrasing 담화의 the ~ travel bags and rolling
suitcases → 정답의 luggage

99

Look at the graphic. Which module most likely will be
shortened?

(A) Module 1
(B) Module 2
(C) Module 3
(D) Module 4

시각 정보에 의하면, 어느 교육 과정이 단축될 것 같은가?
(A) 과정 1
(B) 과정 2
(C) 과정 3
(D) 과정 4

해설 시각 정보 연계 – 단축될 것 같은 교육 과정
화자가 중반부에 그 말은 즉 소프트웨어 교육에 더 적은 시간을 들인다는 뜻이
지만 어제 주요 기능을 익혔으니 괜찮을 것(That means we'll spend less
time on software training, but it's OK because you learned its main
functions yesterday)이라고 했으므로 소프트웨어 교육 과정의 시간이 단축
된다는 것을 알 수 있고, 일정표에 따르면 소프트웨어 교육은 과정 3이므로 정
답은 (C)이다.

100

What does the speaker tell the listeners to do?

(A) Look at some product samples
(B) Share materials with a partner
(C) Ensure that a booklet is complete
(D) Turn off any personal electronics

화자는 청자들에게 무엇을 하라고 말하는가?

(A) 제품 샘플을 볼 것
(B) 파트너와 자료를 공유할 것
(C) 책자가 완전한지 확인할 것
(D) 개인용 전자제품을 끌 것

어휘 share 공유하다 material 자료 ensure 확실히 하다 booklet
소책자 complete 완전한 electronics 전자제품

해설 세부 사항 관련 – 화자가 청자들에게 요구한 일

화자가 마지막에 정책 안내는 14페이지까지 이어지므로 잠깐 시간을 내어 복
사본에 모든 페이지가 있는지 확인할 것(the policy guide runs to fourteen
pages, so please take a moment to make sure your copy has every
page)을 요구했으므로 정답은 (C)이다.

TEST 9

1 (D)	**2** (D)	**3** (C)	**4** (A)	**5** (B)
6 (D)	**7** (C)	**8** (B)	**9** (A)	**10** (B)
11 (A)	**12** (B)	**13** (A)	**14** (C)	**15** (B)
16 (B)	**17** (C)	**18** (A)	**19** (A)	**20** (C)
21 (A)	**22** (B)	**23** (C)	**24** (C)	**25** (C)
26 (B)	**27** (A)	**28** (C)	**29** (B)	**30** (A)
31 (B)	**32** (A)	**33** (B)	**34** (D)	**35** (D)
36 (C)	**37** (B)	**38** (C)	**39** (A)	**40** (C)
41 (D)	**42** (B)	**43** (C)	**44** (C)	**45** (B)
46 (D)	**47** (D)	**48** (A)	**49** (B)	**50** (B)
51 (D)	**52** (A)	**53** (D)	**54** (D)	**55** (B)
56 (B)	**57** (C)	**58** (C)	**59** (D)	**60** (C)
61 (D)	**62** (A)	**63** (C)	**64** (D)	**65** (B)
66 (B)	**67** (A)	**68** (B)	**69** (A)	**70** (D)
71 (D)	**72** (A)	**73** (B)	**74** (D)	**75** (C)
76 (B)	**77** (A)	**78** (B)	**79** (D)	**80** (B)
81 (B)	**82** (A)	**83** (C)	**84** (B)	**85** (C)
86 (C)	**87** (A)	**88** (C)	**89** (C)	**90** (B)
91 (A)	**92** (C)	**93** (B)	**94** (A)	**95** (B)
96 (D)	**97** (C)	**98** (A)	**99** (D)	**100** (B)

PART 1

1 M-Au

(A) She's opening a storage container.
(B) She's repairing some office equipment.
(C) She's cleaning a whiteboard.
(D) She's making a copy of a document.

(A) 여자는 보관 용기를 열고 있다.
(B) 여자는 사무기기를 수리하고 있다.
(C) 여자는 화이트보드를 닦고 있다.
(D) 여자는 문서를 복사하고 있다.

어휘 storage 보관 container 용기 repair 수리하다 equipment
장비 whiteboard 화이트보드, 칠판

해설 1인 등장 사진 – 인물의 동작 묘사
(C) 사진에 없는 명사를 이용한 오답. 사진에 보관 용기(a storage container)
의 모습이 보이지 않으므로 오답.
(B) 동사 오답. 여자가 사무기기를 수리하고 있는(is repairing some office
equipment) 모습이 아니므로 오답.
(C) 사진에 없는 명사를 이용한 오답. 사진에 화이트보드(a whiteboard)의 모
습이 보이지 않으므로 오답.
(D) 정답. 여자가 문서를 복사하고 있는(is making a copy of a document)
모습이므로 정답.

2 W-Br

(A) They're carrying safety helmets.
(B) They're parking next to some trees.
(C) They're pushing some bicycles.
(D) They're riding side by side.

(A) 사람들은 안전모를 들고 있다.
(B) 사람들은 나무 옆에 주차하고 있다.
(C) 사람들은 자전거를 밀고 있다.
(D) 사람들은 나란히 자전거를 타고 있다.

어휘 safety helmet 안전모 bicycle 자전거 ride (자전거 등을) 타다
side by side 나란히

해설 2인 이상 등장 사진 – 인물의 동작 묘사
(A) 동사 오답. 사람들이 안전모를 들고 있는(are carrying safety helmets)
모습이 아니라 착용하고 있는(are wearing safety helmets) 모습이므로
오답.
(B) 동사 오답. 사람들이 나무 옆에 주차하고 있는(are parking next to
some trees) 모습이 아니므로 오답.
(C) 동사 오답. 사람들이 자전거를 밀고 있는(are pushing some bicycles)
모습이 아니므로 오답.
(D) 정답. 사람들이 나란히 자전거를 타고 있는(are riding side by side) 모
습이므로 정답.

3 M-Cn

(A) Garden waste is being put into a bag.
(B) A man is holding the handle of a wooden gate.
(C) The lids of some bins have been raised.
(D) A man is organizing bottles on a shelf.

(A) 정원 쓰레기가 봉투에 담기고 있다.
(B) 남자는 나무 문의 손잡이를 잡고 있다.
(C) 통들의 뚜껑이 열려 있다.
(D) 남자는 선반 위에 병을 정리하고 있다.

어휘 lid 뚜껑 bin (쓰레기)통 raise 들어올리다 organize 정리하다
shelf 선반

해설 혼합 사진 – 사람 또는 사물 묘사
(A) 동사 오답. 정원 쓰레기(garden waste)가 가방에 넣어지고 있는(is
being put into a bag) 모습이 아니므로 오답.
(B) 동사 오답. 남자가 나무 문의 손잡이를 잡고 있는(is holding the handle
of a wooden gate) 모습이 아니므로 오답.

(C) 정답. 통들의 뚜껑(lids of some bins)이 열려 있는(have been raised) 모습이므로 정답.

(D) 사진에 없는 명사를 이용한 오답. 사진에 선반(shelf)의 모습이 보이지 않으므로 오답.

---

4 W-Am

(A) Newspapers have been folded to fit in a display.
(B) Racks have been positioned in front of a window.
(C) Merchandise is being removed from boxes.
(D) A magazine has been left on a store counter.

(A) 신문이 진열대에 맞게 접혀 있다.
(B) 선반들이 창문 앞에 배치되어 있다.
(C) 상품이 상자에서 꺼내어지고 있다.
(D) 잡지가 상점 카운터에 놓여 있다.

어휘 fold 접다 fit 맞다 rack 선반 position 배치하다
merchandise 상품 remove 치우다

해설 배경 사진 – 실내 사물의 상태 묘사

(A) 정답. 신문(newspapers)이 진열대에 맞게 접혀 있는(have been folded to fit in a display) 모습이므로 정답.

(B) 사진에 없는 명사를 이용한 오답. 사진에 창문(a window)의 모습이 보이지 않으므로 오답.

(C) 사진에 없는 명사를 이용한 오답. 사진에 상자(boxes)의 모습이 보이지 않으므로 오답.

(D) 동사 오답. 잡지가 카운터에 놓여 있는(has been left on a store counter) 모습이 아니므로 오답.

---

5 M-Au [고난도]

(A) Some people are boarding a public bus.
(B) There is a basket in the corner of a shelter.
(C) A woman has set her backpack down on a bench.
(D) A map has been attached to a standing sign.

(A) 사람들이 버스를 타고 있다.
(B) 정류소 구석에 통이 있다.
(C) 여자가 배낭을 벤치에 놓아뒀다.
(D) 지도가 입간판에 붙어 있다.

어휘 board 탑승하다 basket 바구니, 통 shelter (지붕이 달린) 정류소
attach 붙이다

해설 혼합 사진 – 사람 또는 사물 묘사

(A) 동사 오답. 사람들이 버스를 타고 있는(are boarding) 모습이 아니므로 오답.

(B) 정답. 정류소 구석(in the corner of a shelter)에 통이 있는(There is a basket) 모습이므로 정답.

(C) 위치 오답. 여자가 배낭을 벤치에 둔(set her backpack down on a bench) 모습이 아니라 손에 들고 있으므로 오답.

(D) 사진에 없는 명사를 이용한 오답. 사진에 입간판(a standing sign)의 모습이 보이지 않으므로 오답.

---

6 W-Br [고난도]

(A) A large group of people is waiting in a line.
(B) A podium has been placed on a raised stage.
(C) A speaker is gesturing toward the back of a room.
(D) A graph is being projected onto a screen.

(A) 한 무리의 사람들이 줄을 서서 기다리고 있다.
(B) 단상이 높은 무대 위에 놓여 있다.
(C) 발표자가 강의실 뒤쪽을 향해 손짓하고 있다.
(D) 그래프가 화면에 비춰지고 있다.

어휘 podium 단상 place 놓다 raised 높은 gesture 손짓하다
project 비추다

해설 혼합 사진 – 사람 또는 사물 묘사

(A) 동사 오답. 한 무리의 사람들(a large group of people)이 줄을 서서 기다리고 있는(is waiting in a line) 모습이 아니므로 오답.

(B) 사진에 없는 명사를 이용한 오답. 사진에 높은 무대(a raised stage)의 모습이 보이지 않으므로 오답.

(C) 동사 오답. 발표자(a speaker)가 강의실 뒤쪽을 향해 손짓하고 있는(is gesturing toward the back of a room) 모습이 아니므로 오답.

(D) 정답. 그래프(a graph)가 화면에 비춰지고 있는(is being projected onto a screen) 모습이므로 정답.

PART 2

7

W-Br Did you see the basketball game last night?

M-Cn (A) A big group of fans.
(B) The company sponsors a basketball team.
(C) Yes, I watched it on television.

어젯밤에 농구 경기를 보셨나요?
(A) 대규모의 팬들이요.
(B) 그 회사는 농구팀을 후원해요.
(C) 네, 텔레비전으로 봤어요.

어휘 sponsor 후원하다

해설 농구 경기를 봤는지 묻는 조동사(Did) 의문문
(A) 연상 단어 오답. 질문의 basketball game에서 연상 가능한 fans를 이용한 오답.
(B) 단어 반복 오답. 질문의 basketball을 반복 이용한 오답.
(C) 정답. 어젯밤에 농구 경기를 봤는지 묻는 질문에 자신은 네(Yes)라고 대답한 뒤, 텔레비전으로 봤다며 긍정 답변과 일관된 내용을 덧붙이고 있으므로 정답.

8

M-Au How would you like me to return the key?

W-Am (A) Use your key card.

(B) You can give it to the receptionist.

(C) That would be great.

열쇠를 어떻게 돌려드리면 될까요?
(A) 키카드를 사용하세요.
(B) 데스크 직원에게 주시면 됩니다.
(C) 그러면 좋겠네요.

어휘 return 돌려주다 receptionist 접수원

해설 열쇠를 돌려줄 방법을 묻는 How 의문문
(A) 단어 반복 오답. 질문의 key를 반복 이용한 오답.
(B) 정답. 열쇠를 돌려줄 방법을 묻는 질문에 데스크 직원에게 주면 된다고 알려주고 있으므로 정답.
(C) 질문과 상관없는 오답. 제안문에 대한 응답이므로 오답.

9

M-Cn Where can I find the notes from the departmental meeting?

W-Br (A) In the shared folder on the network.

(B) To the director of marketing.

(C) Make sure they're less than two pages long.

부서 회의 기록을 어디서 찾을 수 있나요?
(A) 네트워크의 공유 폴더에서요.
(B) 마케팅 이사님께요.
(C) 두 페이지를 넘기지 않도록 하세요.

어휘 note 기록 departmental 부서의 shared 공유의 director 이사

해설 회의 기록이 있는 장소를 묻는 Where 의문문
(A) 정답. 부서 회의 기록을 찾을 수 있는 장소를 묻는 질문에 네트워크의 공유 폴더라고 알려주고 있으므로 정답.
(B) 질문과 상관없는 오답. Who 의문문에 대한 응답이므로 오답.
(C) 연상 단어 오답. 질문의 note에서 연상 가능한 pages를 이용한 오답.

10

M-Au The computer won't accept my password.

W-Br (A) Our newest desktop model.

(B) Ah, I know what the problem is.

(C) No, they're mine.

컴퓨터가 제 암호를 받아들이지 않아요.
(A) 우리의 최신 데스크탑 모델입니다.
(B) 아, 무엇이 문제인지 알아요.
(C) 아니요, 그것들은 제 겁니다.

어휘 accept 인정하다[받아들이다] newest 최신의

해설 정보 전달의 평서문
(A) 연상 단어 오답. 평서문의 computer에서 연상 가능한 desktop model을 이용한 오답.
(B) 정답. 컴퓨터가 암호를 받아들이지 않는다는 평서문에 무엇이 문제인지 안다며 해결책을 알려주려 하고 있으므로 정답.
(C) 파생어 오답. 평서문의 my와 파생어 관계인 mine을 이용한 오답.

11 [고난도]

W-Am Do you know who left this cake on the table?

M-Au (A) I thought you did.

(B) It used to be Sophie's.

(C) For our tenth anniversary.

누가 이 케이크를 탁자에 두었는지 아세요?
(A) 당신이 그런 줄 알았어요.
(B) 그것은 소피의 것이었어요.
(C) 10주년 기념일을 위한 거예요.

어휘 anniversary 기념일

해설 케이크를 탁자에 둔 사람을 아는지 묻는 간접의문문
(A) 정답. 누가 케이크를 탁자에 두었는지 아는지 묻는 질문에 당신이 그런 줄 알았다며 자신도 알지 못함을 우회적으로 응답하고 있으므로 정답.
(B) 연상 단어 오답. 질문의 who에서 연상 가능한 사람 이름을 이용한 오답.
(C) 질문과 상관없는 오답. Why 의문문에 대한 응답이므로 오답.

12

W-Br When is the Wexler Film Festival held?

M-Cn (A) At the city's convention center.

(B) I don't think it's a regular event.

(C) Holova makes high-quality film, too.

웩슬러 영화제는 언제 열립니까?
(A) 시의 컨벤션 센터에서요.
(B) 정기 행사는 아닌 것 같아요.
(C) 홀로바는 고품질 영화도 만들어요.

어휘 regular 정기적인 high-quality 고급의

해설 영화제의 개최 시점을 묻는 When 의문문
(A) 질문과 상관없는 오답. Where 의문문에 대한 응답이므로 오답.
(B) 정답. 웩슬러 영화제의 개최 시점을 묻는 질문에 정기 행사는 아닌 것 같다며 시기를 정확히 알지 못함을 우회적으로 응답하고 있으므로 정답.
(C) 단어 반복 오답. 질문의 film을 반복 이용한 오답.

13

W-Br Why do we have to take our food out of the break room fridge?

W-Am (A) The cleaning crew is coming by.

(B) Anything without a label on it.

(C) We can also buy snacks on-site.

왜 휴게실 냉장고에서 음식을 꺼내야 하죠?

(A) **청소팀이 올 거예요.**

(B) 상표가 없는 것은 어떤 것이든요.

(C) 현장에서 간식도 살 수 있어요.

어휘 break room 휴게실 fridge 냉장고 crew (함께 일하는) 팀, 반 label 상표 on-site 현장에서

해설 냉장고에서 음식을 꺼내야 하는 이유를 묻는 Why 의문문

(A) 정답. 휴게실 냉장고에서 음식을 꺼내야 하는 이유를 묻는 질문에 청소팀이 올 거라며 내부 청소를 위해 냉장고를 비워야 한다는 이유를 제시하고 있으므로 정답.

(B) 질문과 상관없는 오답. Which 의문문에 대한 응답이므로 오답.

(C) 연상 단어 오답. 질문의 food에서 연상 가능한 snacks를 이용한 오답.

14

M-Au Isn't Austin Station your stop?

W-Am (A) As soon as the bus comes.

(B) There's no stop sign here.

(C) No, I get off at Cook Street.

오스틴 역에서 내리시지 않나요?

(A) 버스가 오자마자요.

(B) 여기에는 정지 표시가 없네요.

(C) **아니요, 쿡 가에서 내려요.**

해설 오스틴 역에서 내리는지 여부를 확인하는 부정의문문

(A) 연상 단어 오답. 질문의 station에서 연상 가능한 bus를 이용한 오답.

(B) 단어 반복 오답. 질문의 stop을 반복 이용한 오답.

(C) 정답. 오스틴 역에서 내리는지 묻는 질문에 아니요(No)라고 대답한 뒤, 쿡 가에서 내린다고 자신이 내릴 역을 알려주며 부정 답변과 일관된 내용을 덧붙이고 있으므로 정답.

15

M-Cn Should we staple these documents or just attach them with paperclips?

W-Br (A) They're attached to my most recent e-mail.

(B) Let's just use paperclips for now.

(C) So that we can hand them out at the workshop.

이 서류들을 스테이플러로 찍을까요, 아니면 그냥 클립으로 첨부할까요?

(A) 제 최근 이메일 대부분에 첨부되어 있어요.

(B) **일단 그냥 클립을 사용합시다.**

(C) 워크숍에서 나눠줄 수 있도록요.

어휘 staple 스테이플러로 고정하다 attach 붙이다, 첨부하다 hand out 나눠주다

해설 서류를 처리할 방법을 묻는 선택의문문

(A) 단어 반복 오답. 질문의 attach를 반복 이용한 오답.

(B) 정답. 서류를 처리할 방법을 묻는 선택의문문에서 일단 그냥 종이클립을 사용하자며 두 가지의 선택안 중에서 하나를 선택하여 응답하고 있으므로 정답.

(C) 연상 단어 오답. 질문의 documents에서 연상 가능한 hand out을 이용한 오답.

16 [고난도]

W-Am I'm working the Saturday morning shift this week.

M-Au (A) Could you send it to my apartment?

(B) That's my day to relax.

(C) No, mine starts this evening.

저는 이번 주에 토요일 오전 근무조로 일해요.

(A) 제 아파트로 그것을 보내주시겠습니까?

(B) **그날은 제가 쉬는 날이에요.**

(C) 아니요, 제 건 오늘 저녁에 시작해요.

어휘 shift 근무조, 근무 시간 relax 쉬다

해설 정보 전달의 평서문

(A) 연상 단어 오답. 평서문의 shift가 '옮기다'로 쓰였을 경우 연상 가능한 send를 이용한 오답.

(B) 정답. 이번 주에 토요일 오전 근무조로 일한다는 평서문에 그날은 본인이 쉬는 날이라며 관련 정보로 응답하고 있으므로 정답.

(C) 연상 단어 오답. 평서문의 Saturday morning에서 연상 가능한 this evening을 이용한 오답.

17

W-Br Will I have to set up the projector for the presentation?

M-Cn (A) A conference table and some chairs.

(B) I found it quite informative.

(C) We have an IT specialist for that.

프레젠테이션을 위해 프로젝터를 설치해야 할까요?

(A) 회의 탁자 하나와 의자 몇 개요.

(B) 그것이 꽤 유익하다고 생각했어요.

(C) **그 일을 위한 IT 전문가가 있어요.**

어휘 conference 회의 informative 유익한 specialist 전문가

해설 프로젝터의 설치 여부를 묻는 조동사(Will) 의문문

(A) 연상 단어 오답. 질문의 presentation에서 연상 가능한 conference를 이용한 오답.

(B) 연상 단어 오답. 질문의 presentation에서 연상 가능한 informative를 이용한 오답.

(C) 정답. 프레젠테이션을 위해 프로젝터를 설치해야 할지 묻는 질문에 그 일을 위한 IT 전문가가 있다며 직접 설치할 필요가 없음을 우회적으로 알려주고 있으므로 정답.

18

고난도

M-Au　We're going to take the executives on a tour of our office, aren't we?

W-Br　(A) Will there be enough time for that?

　　　(B) The new chief financial officer.

　　　(C) Oh, I already have one.

임원들을 모시고 우리 사무실을 둘러볼 예정이죠, 그렇죠?

(A) 그럴 시간이 충분히 있을까요?

(B) 신임 최고 재무 책임자예요.

(C) 아, 이미 하나 있어요.

어휘　executive 임원　chief 최고 권위의　financial 재무[금융]의

해설　임원들과 함께 사무실을 둘러볼지 여부를 확인하는 부가의문문

(A) 정답. 임원들을 모시고 사무실을 둘러볼 예정인지 묻는 질문에 그럴 시간이 충분히 있을지 되물으며 관련 사항을 확인하고 있으므로 정답.

(B) 연상 단어 오답. 질문의 executives에서 연상 가능한 chief financial officer를 이용한 오답.

(C) 질문과 상관없는 오답.

19

W-Am　How far in advance can we make the pasta sauce?

M-Cn　(A) No more than a day.

　　　(B) First, wash the tomatoes.

　　　(C) There's one a few miles from here.

얼마나 미리 파스타 소스를 만들 수 있을까요?

(A) 하루 이상은 안 돼요.

(B) 먼저, 토마토를 씻어요.

(C) 여기서 몇 마일 떨어진 곳에 하나 있어요.

해설　준비 시작점을 묻는 How far 의문문

(A) 정답. 얼마나 미리 파스타 소스를 만들 수 있을지 묻는 질문에 하루 이상은 안 된다고 구체적으로 응답하고 있으므로 정답.

(B) 연상 단어 오답. 질문의 pasta sauce에서 연상 가능한 tomatoes를 이용한 오답.

(C) 연상 단어 오답. 질문의 how far에서 연상 가능한 거리 표현(a few miles)을 이용한 오답.

20

W-Am　Why has the Henderson's Candy display been moved?

M-Cn　(A) Do you have a location in mind?

　　　(B) Thanks, but I don't really like candy.

　　　(C) The aisle was becoming too crowded.

핸더슨의 캔디 진열대는 왜 옮겨졌나요?

(A) 마음에 두고 있는 장소가 있으신가요?

(B) 고맙습니다만, 저는 사탕을 그다지 좋아하지 않습니다.

(C) 그 통로가 너무 붐비게 되었어요.

어휘　in mind 염두에 둔　aisle 통로　crowded 붐비는

해설　캔디 진열대가 옮겨진 이유를 묻는 Why 의문문

(A) 연상 단어 오답. 질문의 moved에서 연상 가능한 location을 이용한 오답.

(B) 단어 반복 오답. 질문의 candy를 반복 이용한 오답.

(C) 정답. 핸더슨의 캔디 진열대가 옮겨진 이유를 묻는 질문에 그 통로가 너무 붐비게 되었다며 이유를 구체적으로 제시하고 있으므로 정답.

21

고난도

W-Br　Where's the session on contract negotiation being held?

M-Au　(A) Here's the conference program.

　　　(B) Mr. Nakano has finally agreed to sign.

　　　(C) It was shipped from London on Thursday.

계약 협상에 관한 회의는 어디에서 열리고 있나요?

(A) 여기 회의 프로그램이 있습니다.

(B) 나카노 씨가 마침내 서명하기로 동의했습니다.

(C) 목요일에 런던에서 발송되었습니다.

어휘　session 회의[회기]　contract 계약　negotiation 협상　agree 동의하다　ship 수송[발송]하다

해설　회의 장소를 묻는 Where 의문문

(A) 정답. 계약 협상에 관한 회의가 열리고 있는 장소를 묻는 질문에 여기 회의 프로그램이 있다며 우회적으로 알려주고 있으므로 정답.

(B) 연상 단어 오답. 질문의 negotiation에서 연상 가능한 agreed를 이용한 오답.

(C) 연상 단어 오답. 질문의 Where에서 연상 가능한 London을 이용한 오답.

22

고난도

M-Cn　What are we doing to celebrate Ms. Lopez's retirement next month?

W-Am　(A) Coffee can help when you're feeling tired.

　　　(B) The events committee is meeting this week.

　　　(C) Yeah, she's a local celebrity.

다음 달 로페즈 씨의 은퇴를 축하하기 위해 무엇을 할까요?

(A) 피곤할 때는 커피가 도움이 될 수 있어요.

(B) 행사 위원회가 이번 주에 모여요.

(C) 네, 그녀는 지역 명사예요.

어휘　celebrate 축하하다　retirement 은퇴　committee 위원회　celebrity 유명 인사

해설　로페즈 씨의 은퇴를 축하하기 위해 무엇을 할지 묻는 What 의문문

(A) 유사 발음 오답. 질문의 retirement와 부분적으로 발음이 유사한 tired를 이용한 오답.

(B) 정답. 다음 달 로페즈 씨의 은퇴를 축하하기 위해 무엇을 할지 묻는 질문에 행사 위원회가 이번 주에 모인다며 아직 결정되지 않았음을 우회적으로 알려주고 있으므로 정답.

(C) Yes/No 불가 오답. What 의문문에는 Yes/No 응답이 불가능하므로 오답.

Test 9

23

M-Au Would you mind writing a post for the company blog?

W-Br (A) Yes, it got many comments from readers.
(B) A pencil and some paper.
(C) What would you like it to be about?

회사 블로그를 위해 글을 써주시겠습니까?
(A) 네, 독자들로부터 많은 평을 받았어요.
(B) 연필 한 자루와 종이요.
(C) 무엇에 관한 내용이 좋을까요?

어휘 post 게시물 comment 논평, 언급

해설 부탁/요청의 의문문
(A) 연상 단어 오답. 질문의 post에서 연상 가능한 comments를 이용한 오답.
(B) 연상 단어 오답. 질문의 writing에서 연상 가능한 pencil과 paper를 이용한 오답.
(C) 정답. 회사 블로그를 위해 글을 써달라고 부탁하는 질문에 무엇에 관한 내용이 좋을지 관련 사항을 확인하며 되묻고 있으므로 정답.

24

M-Cn Don't you think the administrators' workload is too heavy?

W-Br (A) It's under twenty kilograms.
(B) My computer uploads quickly.
(C) Only during our busy season.

행정 관리자들의 업무량이 너무 많다고 생각하지 않으세요?
(A) 20킬로그램 미만입니다.
(B) 제 컴퓨터는 업로드가 빨라요.
(C) 성수기 동안에만요.

어휘 administrator 관리자 workload 업무량 heavy (양, 정도 등이) 많은[심한]

해설 관리자들의 업무량 과중 여부를 확인하는 부정의문문
(A) 연상 단어 오답. 질문의 heavy에서 연상 가능한 twenty kilograms를 이용한 오답.
(B) 유사 발음 오답. 질문의 workload와 부분적으로 발음이 유사한 uploads를 이용한 오답.
(C) 정답. 관리자들의 업무량이 너무 많다고 생각하는지 여부를 묻는 질문에 성수기 동안에만 그렇다며 부분적인 동의를 하고 있으므로 정답.

25 고난도

W-Am Are we allowed to wear headphones while we work?

M-Au (A) I mostly wear casual clothing.
(B) You'll need a phone for client calls.
(C) It's not a very noisy office.

일하는 동안 헤드폰을 착용해도 되나요?
(A) 전 주로 캐주얼한 옷을 입어요.
(B) 고객 전화용 전화기가 필요할 거예요.
(C) 그렇게 시끄러운 사무실은 아니에요.

어휘 allowed 허용된 mostly 주로 noisy 시끄러운

해설 일하는 동안 헤드폰을 착용해도 되는지 여부를 묻는 Be동사 의문문
(A) 단어 반복 오답. 질문의 wear를 반복 이용한 오답.
(B) 단어 반복 오답. 질문의 headphones에서 phone을 반복 이용한 오답.
(C) 정답. 일하는 동안 헤드폰을 착용해도 되는지 여부를 묻는 질문에 그렇게 시끄러운 사무실은 아니라며 헤드폰 착용에 대한 부정적인 입장을 우회적으로 나타내고 있으므로 정답.

26 고난도

M-Cn We should print out the booking confirmation.

M-Au (A) To my work e-mail address, please.
(B) They usually just ask for identification.
(C) I packed some books to read on the train.

예약 확인서를 출력해야 해요.
(A) 제 직장 이메일 주소로요.
(B) 그들은 보통 신분증만 요구해요.
(C) 기차에서 읽을 책을 몇 권 챙겼어요.

어휘 booking 예약 confirmation 확인(서) address 주소 identification 신분증 pack 챙기다

해설 제안/권유의 평서문
(A) 평서문과 상관없는 오답. Where 의문문에 대한 응답이므로 오답.
(B) 정답. 예약 확인서를 출력해야 한다는 제안에 대해 그들은 보통 신분증만 요구한다며 예약 확인서를 출력할 필요가 없음을 우회적으로 나타내고 있으므로 정답.
(C) 유사 발음 오답. 평서문의 booking과 부분적으로 발음이 유사한 books를 이용한 오답.

27 고난도

W-Am Which one of these trees did you want us to trim?

M-Cn (A) We made an appointment for lawn care, actually.
(B) Because their leaves are falling in the swimming pool.
(C) Is that the longest term you have available?

이 나무들 중 어느 것을 다듬어드리길 원하셨나요?
(A) 사실 잔디 관리 예약을 잡았었어요.
(B) 그 잎들이 수영장에 떨어지고 있어서요.
(C) 그게 이용 가능한 가장 긴 기간인가요?

어휘 trim 다듬다 appointment 예약 lawn 잔디 care 관리 actually 사실 term 기간 available 이용 가능한

해설 다듬기를 원하는 나무를 묻는 Which 의문문

(A) 정답. 나무들 중 어느 것을 다듬기를 원하는지 묻는 질문에 사실 잔디 관리 예약을 잡았었다며 나무 다듬기를 원하는 것이 아님을 우회적으로 알려주고 있으므로 정답.

(B) 연상 단어 오답. 질문의 trees에서 연상 가능한 leaves를 이용한 오답.

(C) 질문과 상관없는 오답.

28

M-Au Shall we put up the holiday decorations today or tomorrow?

W-Br (A) I made a banner for the reception desk.
　　 (B) Plus the first two days of next week.
　　 (C) My schedule is completely open.

기념일 장식을 오늘 달까요, 아니면 내일 달까요?
(A) 제가 접수처용 현수막을 만들었어요.
(B) 추가로 다음 주 첫 이틀요.
(C) 제 일정은 완전히 비어 있어요.

어휘 decoration 장식 banner 현수막 reception 접수처 completely 완전히

해설 기념일 장식을 달 시기를 묻는 선택의문문

(A) 연상 단어 오답. 질문의 decorations에서 연상 가능한 banner를 이용한 오답.

(B) 유사 발음 오답. 질문의 today와 부분적으로 발음이 유사한 two days를 이용한 오답.

(C) 정답. 기념일 장식을 달 시기를 묻는 선택의문문에서 일정이 안전히 비어 있다며 두 날 중 아무 때나 상관없음을 우회적으로 나타내고 있으므로 정답.

29
[고난도]

W-Am This is the most up-to-date version of the spreadsheet, isn't it?

M-Au (A) The number in the bottom right corner.
　　 (B) I haven't made any changes lately.
　　 (C) There are a few dates that would work for me.

이게 가장 최신 버전의 데이터 문서죠, 그렇죠?
(A) 오른쪽 하단 구석에 있는 숫자요.
(B) 최근에 아무런 수정도 하지 않았어요.
(C) 제가 가능한 날짜가 며칠 있어요.

어휘 up-to-date 최신의 spreadsheet 데이터 문서 bottom 바닥

해설 해당 데이터 문서가 가장 최신 버전인지 여부를 확인하는 부가의문문

(A) 연상 단어 오답. 질문의 spreadsheet에서 연상 가능한 number를 이용한 오답.

(B) 정답. 해당 데이터 문서가 가장 최신 버전인지 확인하는 질문에 최근에 아무런 수정도 하지 않았다며 가장 최신 버전임을 우회적으로 확인해주고 있으므로 정답.

(C) 유사 발음 오답. 질문의 up-to-date와 부분적으로 발음이 유사한 a few dates를 이용한 오답.

30

M-Cn Can I get a copy of my medical records from this clinic?

W-Am (A) You'll have to fill out some forms first.
　　 (B) Well, that's not what our records show.
　　 (C) We keep medications in the back room.

이 병원의 제 의료 기록 사본을 좀 받을 수 있을까요?
(A) 먼저 몇 가지 양식을 작성하셔야 합니다.
(B) 글쎄요, 저희 기록에는 그렇게 나와 있지 않은데요.
(C) 우리는 안쪽 사무실에 약을 보관합니다.

어휘 medical 의료의 clinic 병원 fill out 작성하다 medication 약

해설 부탁/요청의 의문문

(A) 정답. 병원에 있는 자신의 의료 기록 사본을 받을 수 있는지 부탁하는 질문에 먼저 몇 가지 양식을 작성해야 한다며 요청 사항을 이행하는 데 필요한 조건을 알려주고 있으므로 정답.

(B) 단어 반복 오답. 질문의 records를 반복 이용한 오답.

(C) 파생어 오답. 질문의 medical과 파생어 관계인 medications를 이용한 오답.

31
[고난도]

W-Br Who's responsible for approving purchasing requests when Nick is away?

M-Au (A) That's an excellent idea.
　　 (B) But he'll be back this afternoon.
　　 (C) It's for a filing cabinet for the sales department.

닉이 없을 때는 누가 구매 요청 승인을 책임지나요?
(A) 그거 좋은 생각이네요.
(B) 하지만 그가 오늘 오후에 돌아올 거예요.
(C) 그것은 영업부의 서류 캐비닛용이에요.

어휘 responsible 책임지는 approve 승인하다 purchasing 구매 request 요청

해설 닉의 부재 시 구매 요청 승인 책임자를 묻는 Who 의문문

(A) 질문과 상관없는 오답. 제안문에 대한 응답이므로 오답.

(B) 정답. 닉이 없을 때 구매 요청 승인을 책임지는 사람을 묻는 질문에 그가 오늘 오후에 돌아올 것이라며 다른 구매 요청 승인 책임자를 알 필요가 없음을 우회적으로 나타내고 있으므로 정답.

(C) 연상 단어 오답. 질문의 purchasing에서 연상 가능한 sales를 이용한 오답.

Test 9

PART 3

32-34

M-Au Lynette, while you were at your meeting, I took a call from Carla Burns at Snadler Associates. ³²**She has that law conference in Sydney next month.** She said she asked you to plan her trip by today, and she's worried that she hasn't heard back from you.

W-Am ³³**Oh, I took care of all of her flight and hotel bookings this morning.** I just didn't have time to tell her before my meeting.

M-Au OK. ³⁴**Well, please send her a confirmation e-mail right now.** I want her to know that everything has been arranged.

남 리넷, 당신이 회의에 참석하고 있는 동안 스내들러 어소시에이츠의 칼라 번즈에게서 전화를 받았어요. 그녀는 다음 달에 시드니에서 법률 회의가 있어요. 오늘까지 여행 계획을 짜달라고 했는데 연락을 받지 못했다며 걱정된다고 했어요.

여 아, 오늘 아침에 그녀의 비행기와 호텔 예약을 모두 처리했어요. 단지 회의 전에 그녀에게 말할 시간이 없었네요.

남 알겠어요. 그럼 지금 바로 그녀에게 확인 이메일을 보내주세요. 그녀가 모든 것이 준비되었다는 것을 알았으면 합니다.

어휘 conference 회의 take care of ~을 처리하다 booking 예약 confirmation 확인 arrange 마련하다, 처리하다

32

What does the man say will happen next month?

(A) A conference will take place.
(B) A new law will go into effect.
(C) A tour will be given.
(D) A staff member will retire.

남자는 다음 달에 무슨 일이 일어날 것이라고 말하는가?

(A) 회의가 열릴 것이다.
(B) 새로운 법이 시행될 것이다.
(C) 견학을 시켜줄 것이다.
(D) 직원이 퇴직할 것이다.

어휘 take place 열리다 go into effect 시행되다 retire 퇴직하다

해설 세부 사항 관련 – 남자가 다음 달에 일어날 것이라고 말한 일
남자가 첫 대사에서 그녀(Carla Burns)는 다음 달에 시드니에서 법률 회의가 있다(She has that law conference in Sydney next month)고 했으므로 정답은 (A)이다.

33

What does the woman say she did?

(A) Picked up some materials
(B) Made some reservations
(C) Had lunch with a client
(D) Posted a job listing

여자는 무엇을 했다고 말하는가?

(A) 몇 가지 재료를 가져왔다.
(B) 몇 가지 예약을 했다.
(C) 고객과 점심식사를 했다.
(D) 구인 목록을 게시했다.

어휘 material 재료 reservation 예약 post 게시하다 listing 목록

해설 세부 사항 관련 – 여자가 했다고 말하는 일
여자가 첫 대사에서 오늘 아침에 그녀의 비행기와 호텔 예약을 모두 처리했다(I took care of all of her flight and hotel bookings this morning)고 했으므로 정답은 (B)이다.

▸▸ Paraphrasing   대화의 took care of all of her flight and hotel bookings
→ 정답의 made some reservations

34

What does the man ask the woman to do immediately?

(A) Listen to a telephone message
(B) Make copies of a file
(C) Correct a mistake
(D) Send a notification

남자는 여자에게 무엇을 즉시 하라고 요청하는가?

(A) 전화 메시지 듣기
(B) 파일의 사본 만들기
(C) 실수 정정하기
(D) 알림 메시지 보내기

어휘 correct 정정하다 notification 알림

해설 세부 사항 관련 – 남자가 여자에게 즉시 하라고 요청한 일
남자가 마지막 대사에서 지금 바로 그녀에게 확인 이메일을 보내라(please send her a confirmation e-mail right now)고 요청했으므로 정답은 (D)이다.

▸▸ Paraphrasing   대화의 a confirmation e-mail
→ 정답의 a notification

35-37 3인 대화

M-Cn Welcome to Riverside Coffee. What can I get for you?

W-Br ³⁵**I'd like a latte, but do you have almond milk? I'd like that instead of regular milk, please.**

M-Cn Oh, I'm sorry, but we don't have that.

M-Au Excuse me, ³⁶**Carl.** We actually started carrying almond milk last week because customers kept asking for it.

M-Cn Oh, I had no idea. ³⁶**Thanks for the correction, Bill.** OK ma'am, it looks like we'll be able to accommodate you. There's a fifty-cent additional charge for substitutions, though. Is that OK?

W-Br	That's no problem. ³⁷**Oh, I have this coupon for a free drink for frequent customers, too.** Can I use it to pay for this drink?
M-Au	Sure.

남1	리버사이드 커피에 오신 것을 환영합니다. 무엇을 드릴까요?
여	라떼를 먹고 싶은데 아몬드 우유 있으세요? 일반 우유 대신에 그것을 원해요.
남1	아, 죄송하지만 그건 없는데요.
남2	잠시만요, 칼. 손님들이 계속 요청하셔서 우리는 사실 지난주부터 아몬드 우유를 취급하기 시작했어요.
남1	아, 몰랐어요. **정정해줘서 고마워요, 빌.** 알겠습니다, 고객님, 저희가 손님의 요구를 수용할 수 있을 것 같네요. 그런데 대체하시면 50센트의 추가 요금이 있습니다. 괜찮으시겠어요?
여	문제없어요. **아, 저한테 단골 손님을 위한 무료 음료 쿠폰이 있어요.** 이 음료 값을 지불하는 데 사용할 수 있을까요?
남2	물론이죠.

어휘	carry 취급하다 correction 정정 accommodate 수용하다, (요구에) 부응하다 charge 요금 substitution 대체(품) frequent 빈번한

35

What does the woman ask for?

(A) A take-away cup
(B) A sales receipt
(C) A gift certificate
(D) An ingredient replacement

여자는 무엇을 요구하는가?
(A) 테이크어웨이 컵
(B) 판매 영수증
(C) 상품권
(D) 재료 교체

어휘 take-away (음식을 먹지 않고) 가지고 가다

해설 세부 사항 관련 – 여자의 요구사항
여자가 첫 대사에서 라떼를 먹고 싶은데 아몬드 우유가 있는지(I'd like a latte, but do you have almond milk?)를 물으며 일반 우유 대신에 그것을 원한다(I'd like that instead of regular milk, please)고 했으므로 정답은 (D)이다.

▶▶ Paraphrasing 대화의 **would like that instead of regular milk** → 정답의 **an ingredient replacement**

36 [고난도]

What does Bill correct Carl about?

(A) The name of a drink
(B) The operating hours of a café
(C) The availability of an item
(D) The cost of a change

빌은 무엇에 대해 칼을 정정해주는가?
(A) 음료의 이름
(B) 카페의 영업시간
(C) 제품의 이용 가능성
(D) 변경 비용

어휘 operating hour 영업시간 availability 이용 가능성

해설 세부 사항 관련 – 빌이 칼에게 정정해준 사항
두 번째 남자가 첫 대사에서 칼을 호명하며 손님들이 계속 요청해서 우리는 사실 지난주부터 아몬드 우유를 취급하기 시작했다(We actually started carrying almond milk last week because customers kept asking for it)고 했고, 뒤이어 첫 번째 남자가 정정해줘서 고마워요, 빌(Thanks for the correction, Bill)이라고 한 것으로 보아 두 번째 남자인 빌이 첫 번째 남자인 칼에게 아몬드 우유가 판매를 위해 구비되어 있다고 정정해주고 있으므로 정답은 (C)이다.

37

How does the woman want to pay for her order?

(A) With cash
(B) With a voucher
(C) With a credit card
(D) With a mobile app

여자는 주문에 대해 어떻게 지불하기를 원하는가?
(A) 현금으로
(B) 쿠폰으로
(C) 신용카드로
(D) 휴대전화 앱으로

어휘 voucher 쿠폰, 할인권

해설 세부 사항 관련 – 여자가 주문에 대해 원하는 지불 방법
여자가 마지막 대사에서 단골 손님을 위한 무료 음료 쿠폰이 있다(I have this coupon for a free drink for frequent customers, too)고 한 것으로 보아 정답은 (B)이다.

▶▶ Paraphrasing 대화의 **coupon** → 정답의 **voucher**

38-40

W-Br	All right, now let's talk about who to cast in the side parts. First up is "the character of the uncle." ³⁸**Uh, I liked Simon Witherspoon—I think he'd give the play a lively energy.**
M-Cn	It's true that he's quite a dynamic performer. ³⁹**But the character really needs to be able to sing, and the music part of Simon's audition was not impressive.**
W-Br	Well, then let's get him a singing coach! I think it's worth the investment.
M-Cn	I'm not convinced. ⁴⁰**Let's move on to another character for now, and talk about casting the uncle again later.**

여	자, 이제 조연들에 누구를 캐스팅할지에 대해 이야기해봅시다. 먼저 삼촌 배역부터요. 어, 저는 사이먼 위더스푼이 좋았어요. 그가 연극에 활기 넘치는 에너지를 줄 것 같아요.
남	그가 꽤 역동적인 연기자인 것은 사실이에요. 하지만 그 캐릭터는 정말 노래를 부를 수 있어야 하는데 사이먼의 음악 부분 오디션은 인상적이지 않았어요.
여	그럼, 그에게 노래 코치를 구해줍시다! 투자할 가치가 있다고 생각해요.
남	저는 확신이 서질 않네요. 일단 다른 캐릭터로 넘어가고 나중에 삼촌 역 캐스팅에 대해 다시 이야기합시다.

어휘	cast 캐스팅하다 paly 연극 lively 활기 넘치는 dynamic 역동적인 performer 연기자[연주자] impressive 인상적인 worth ~할 가치가 있는 investment 투자 convinced 확신하는

38

What are the speakers most likely choosing cast members for?

(A) A television program
(B) A feature film
(C) A stage show
(D) An online advertisement

화자들은 무엇을 위해 출연진을 선택하고 있을 것 같은가?
(A) 텔레비전 프로그램
(B) 장편 영화
(C) 무대 공연
(D) 온라인 광고

해설 세부 사항 관련 – 화자들이 출연진을 선택하고 있는 목적
여자가 첫 대사에서 자신은 사이먼 위더스푼이 좋았고(I liked Simon Witherspoon), 그가 연극에 활기 넘치는 에너지를 줄 것 같다(I think he'd give the play a lively energy)고 한 것으로 보아 정답은 (C)이다.

▶▶ Paraphrasing   대화의 the play → 정답의 a stage show

39

What does the man say about Mr. Witherspoon?

(A) He does not have a necessary skill.
(B) He should play another character.
(C) He will have to audition again.
(D) He has a scheduling conflict.

남자는 위더스푼 씨에 대해 무엇을 말하는가?
(A) 필요한 기술이 없다.
(B) 다른 캐릭터를 연기해야 한다.
(C) 다시 오디션을 봐야 할 것이다.
(D) 일정이 겹친다.

어휘 scheduling conflict 일정 겹침

해설 세부 사항 관련 – 남자가 위더스푼 씨에 대해 말하는 것
남자가 첫 대사에서 그 캐릭터는 정말 노래를 부를 수 있어야 하는데 사이먼의 음악 부분 오디션은 인상적이지 않았다(the character really needs to be able to sing, and the music part of Simon's audition was not impressive)고 했으므로 정답은 (A)이다.

40

What does the man decide to do?

(A) Speak with an investor
(B) Rewatch a performance
(C) Postpone a discussion
(D) Move a location

남자는 무엇을 하기로 결정하는가?
(A) 투자자와 대화
(B) 공연 다시보기
(C) 토론 연기
(D) 장소 이동

어휘 investor 투자자 performance 공연 postpone 연기하다

해설 세부 사항 관련 – 남자가 하기로 결정한 것
남자는 두 번째 대사에서 일단 다른 캐릭터로 넘어가고 나중에 삼촌 역 캐스팅에 대해 다시 이야기하자(Let's move on to another character for now, and talk about casting the uncle again later)고 했으므로 정답은 (C)이다.

▶▶ Paraphrasing   대화의 talk about ~ again later
                  → 정답의 postpone a discussion

41-43

W-Am	Good morning. **41 I'd like to check out. Here's my room key.**
M-Au	Thank you. Just a moment... OK, Ms. Suzuki, here's the bill for your stay.
W-Am	**42 Oh, this is charging me for two nights, but** I arrived yesterday morning. I'm attending the engineering convention.
M-Au	Hmm... I'm not sure why, but our system has you listed for July first and second in Room 407.
W-Am	Well, I did originally book two nights, but I changed my reservation about a week ago. Oh! **43 Would you like to see my confirmation e-mail? I think I have the printout here in my purse.**
M-Au	That would be very helpful.

여	좋은 아침입니다. 체크아웃하고 싶어요. 여기 제 방 열쇠요.
남	감사합니다. 잠시만요… 스즈키 씨, 여기 숙박 청구서입니다.
여	아, 이건 이틀 밤 요금을 청구하고 있는데 전 어제 아침에 도착했어요. 저는 엔지니어링 회의에 참석하고 있어요.
남	음… 이유는 모르겠지만 우리 시스템에는 당신이 407호실에 7월 1일과 2일로 등록이 되어 있어요.
여	음, 제가 원래 이틀 밤을 예약했는데 일주일 전에 예약을 바꿨어요. 아! 제 확인 이메일을 보시겠어요? 여기 제 지갑에 인쇄한 게 있는 것 같아요.
남	그러면 정말 도움이 되겠네요.

어휘	bill 청구서 stay 숙박 charge (요금을) 청구하다 convention 회의 list (목록, 명단 등에) 포함시키다 originally 원래 reservation 예약 confirmation 확인 purse 지갑

41

Where most likely is the conversation taking place?

(A) In a parking garage
(B) In a banquet hall
(C) In a seminar room
(D) In a hotel lobby

대화는 어디에서 이루어지고 있는 것 같은가?
(A) 주차장
(B) 연회장
(C) 세미나실
(D) **호텔 로비**

해설 전체 내용 관련 – 대화의 장소

여자가 첫 대사에서 체크아웃하고 싶다(I'd like to check out)며, 여기 제 방 열쇠가 있다(Here's my room key)고 한 것으로 보아 정답은 (D)이다.

42

What does the woman imply when she says, "I arrived yesterday morning"?

(A) She was not present for a talk.
(B) There is an error on an invoice.
(C) She did not have time for a social activity.
(D) There was strong competition for an opportunity.

여자가 "전 어제 아침에 도착했어요"라고 말하는 의미는 무엇인가?
(A) 회담에 참석하지 않았다.
(B) **청구서에 오류가 있다.**
(C) 사교 활동을 할 시간이 없었다.
(D) 기회를 놓고 경쟁이 치열했다.

어휘 present 참석한 invoice 청구서, 송장 competition 경쟁 opportunity 기회

해설 화자의 의도 파악 – 어제 아침에 도착했다는 말의 의도

앞에서 이건 이틀 밤 요금을 청구하고 있다(this is charging me for two nights)고 한 뒤 인용문을 언급했으므로 자신은 하룻밤만 숙박했는데 청구서의 내용이 사실과 다르다는 점을 알리려는 의도로 한 말임을 알 수 있다. 따라서 정답은 (B)이다.

43

고난도

What will the woman most likely do next?

(A) Look over a timetable
(B) Make a call to a colleague
(C) Search through her handbag
(D) E-mail the man from a device

여자는 다음에 무엇을 할 것 같은가?
(A) 시간표를 살펴본다.
(B) 동료에게 전화한다.
(C) **핸드백을 뒤져본다.**
(D) 장치에서 남자에게 이메일을 보낸다.

어휘 colleague 동료 device 장치

해설 세부 사항 관련 – 여자가 다음에 할 일

여자가 마지막 대사에서 자신의 확인 이메일을 보겠냐(Would you like to see my confirmation e-mail?)고 물으며, 자신의 지갑에 인쇄한 게 있는 것 같다(I think I have the printout here in my purse)고 한 것으로 보아 정답은 (C)이다.

▸▸ **Paraphrasing** 대화의 purse → 정답의 handbag

44-46

> W-Br **44 Delmer, I've finished loading the products onto the truck for the eleven o'clock shipment. It just left. I'm going to take my break now.**
>
> M-Au Sure, Megan. But can I talk to you for a minute first? **45 I noticed you rubbing your back earlier. Are you having back pain?**
>
> W-Br A little bit, actually. But I'm sure that it will go away once I get the chance to relax this weekend.
>
> M-Au I hope so. If it doesn't, come and see me. **46 I can recommend a massage therapist who specializes in treating lower back pain.** Several other workers have gone to see her, and they say she's great.

여 델머, 11시 배송을 위해 제품을 트럭에 싣는 것을 끝냈어요. 트럭이 방금 떠났어요. 저는 이제 쉬어야겠어요.

남 그래야죠, 메건. 그런데 먼저 잠깐 얘기 좀 할 수 있을까요? 아까 등을 문지르고 있는 걸 봤어요. 허리 통증이 있나요?

여 사실, 조금요. 하지만 이번 주말에 휴식을 취할 기회를 가지면 분명 사라질 거예요.

남 그러면 좋겠네요. 그렇지 않으면 저를 보러오세요. 하부 요통 치료를 전문으로 하는 마사지 치료사를 추천해드릴 수 있어요. 다른 직원들 몇 분도 그녀를 보러 갔는데 그녀가 훌륭하다고 하더라고요.

어휘 load (짐 등을) 싣다 shipment 수송 notice 알아차리다 rub 문지르다 back pain 요통 massage therapist 마사지 치료사 specialize in ~을 전문으로 하다 treat 치료하다

44

Who most likely is the woman?

(A) An assembly line manager
(B) A truck driver
(C) A warehouse worker
(D) A sales clerk

여자는 누구일 것 같은가?
(A) 조립 라인 관리자
(B) 트럭 기사
(C) **창고 직원**
(D) 판매 사원

Test 9

여자가 첫 대사에서 남자의 이름(Delmer)을 부르며 11시 배송을 위해 제품을 트럭에 싣는 것을 끝냈다(I've finished loading the products onto the truck for the eleven o'clock shipment)고 했고, 트럭이 방금 떠났다(It just left)며 자신은 이제 쉬어야겠다(I'm going to take my break now)고 한 것으로 보아 정답은 (C)이나.

45

What is the man concerned about?

(A) The status of a shipment
(B) The woman's health
(C) The opinion of an executive
(D) The woman's job satisfaction

남자는 무엇에 대해 걱정하는가?
(A) 배송 상태
(B) 여자의 건강
(C) 임원의 의견
(D) 여자의 직업 만족도

어휘 status 상태 executive 임원 satisfaction 만족

해설 세부 사항 관련 – 남자가 걱정하는 것

남자가 첫 대사에서 아까 등을 문지르고 있는 걸 봤다(I noticed you rubbing your back earlier)면서, 허리 통증이 있는지(Are you having back pain?)를 묻고 있는 것으로 보아 정답은 (B)이다.

46

고난도

What does the man offer the woman?

(A) Help from another staff member
(B) Use of a special piece of equipment
(C) A career development opportunity
(D) A referral to a service provider

남자는 여자에게 무엇을 제공하는가?
(A) 다른 직원의 도움
(B) 특수 장비의 사용
(C) 경력 개발 기회
(D) 서비스 제공업자 소개

어휘 equipment 장비 referral 소개, 보내기 provider 제공업자

해설 세부 사항 관련 – 남자가 여자에게 제안하는 것

남자가 마지막 대사에서 여자에게 하부 요통 치료를 전문으로 하는 마사지 치료사를 추천해드릴 수 있다(I can recommend a massage therapist who specializes in treating lower back pain)고 했으므로 정답은 (D)이다.

▶▶ Paraphrasing 대화의 recommend a massage therapist
→ 정답의 a referral to a service provider

47-49

M-Cn Hi, Jody. It's Randall Fisher. Did you get the draft lease I sent you for legal review? **47If everything looks good, I'd like to move my music shop into the space as soon as possible.**

W-Am I was planning to e-mail you about that. **48As your business lawyer, I'm concerned that the agreement doesn't allow you to transfer the lease or sublet the space. You'd be stuck there for the entire lease period. That's not very advantageous to you.**

M-Cn Oh, I see.

W-Am **49Of course, you could ask the landlord to revise that part of the lease, but you might have to give him something in return—higher rental fees, for example. Would you consider that?**

남 안녕하세요, 조디. 랜달 피셔예요. 법률 검토를 위해 제가 보내드린 임대차 계약서 초안을 받으셨나요? 다 괜찮아 보이면 제 악기점을 가능한 빨리 그 공간으로 옮기고 싶어요.

여 그 건에 대해서 이메일을 보낼 계획이었어요. 당신의 사업 변호사로서 계약상 임대차 계약을 양도하거나 공간을 전대하는 것이 허용되지 않는 점이 걱정돼요. 임대 기간 내내 거기에 묶여 있어야 될 거예요. 그것은 당신에게 그다지 유리하지 않아요.

남 아, 그렇군요.

여 물론 건물주에게 임대차 계약의 그 부분을 수정해달라고 요청할 수도 있지만 그 대가로 그에게 뭔가를 줘야 할 수도 있어요. 예를 들면, 더 높은 임대료라든지요. 이것을 고려해보시겠어요?

어휘 draft 초안 lease 임대차 계약 legal 법률과 관련된 lawyer 변호사 concerned 걱정하는 agreement 계약 transfer 양도하다 sublet 전대하다 stuck 갇힌, 묶인 entire 전체의 advantageous 유리한 landlord 집주인 revise 수정하다 in return 대가로 rental fee 임대료

47

What does the man hope to do?

(A) Release some music
(B) Rent some machinery
(C) Sell a piece of property
(D) Relocate a retail store

남자는 무엇을 하기를 바라는가?
(A) 음반 발매
(B) 기계 대여
(C) 재산 매각
(D) 소매점 이전

어휘 release 공개[발간]하다 property 재산, 부동산 relocate 이전하다 retail store 소매점

해설 세부 사항 관련 – 남자가 하기를 바라는 것

남자가 첫 대사에서 모든 게 좋아 보이면 제 악기점을 가능한 빨리 그 공간으로 옮기고 싶다(If everything looks good, I'd like to move my music shop into the space as soon as possible)고 했으므로 정답은 (D)이다.

▶▶ Paraphrasing 대화의 move my music shop
→ 정답의 relocate a retail store

48

고난도

What problem does the woman mention?

(A) A contract's terms are unfavorable.
(B) A space has some security issues.
(C) A local regulation is complicated.
(D) A certification has expired.

여자는 무슨 문제를 언급하는가?

(A) 계약 조건이 불리하다.
(B) 공간에 몇 가지 보안 문제가 있다.
(C) 지역 규정이 복잡하다.
(D) 인증이 만료되었다.

어휘 term 조건 unfavorable 불리한 security 보안 regulation 규정 complicated 복잡한 certification 인증(서) expire 만료되다

해설 세부 사항 관련 – 여자가 언급한 문제

여자가 첫 대사에서 당신의 사업 변호사로서 계약상 임대차 계약을 양도하거나 공간을 전대하는 것이 허용되지 않는 점이 걱정된다(As your business lawyer, I'm concerned that the agreement doesn't allow you to transfer the lease or sublet the space)며, 임대 기간 내내 거기에 묶여 있어야 될 것(You'd be stuck there for the entire lease period)이고, 그것은 당신에게 그다지 유리하지 않다(That's not very advantageous to you)고 했으므로 정답은 (A)이다.

▸ Paraphrasing 대화의 not very advantageous
→ 정답의 unfavorable

49

고난도

What does the woman ask the man about?

(A) His familiarity with a process
(B) His willingness to negotiate
(C) His ability to prove a claim
(D) His access to a resource

여자는 남자에게 무엇에 대해 물어보는가?

(A) 절차에 대한 친숙도
(B) 협상 의지
(C) 권리에 대한 입증 능력
(D) 자원에 대한 접근 권한

어휘 familiarity 익숙함, 친숙도 process 절차 willingness 의지 negotiate 협상하다 prove 입증하다 claim (재산 등에 대한) 권리 access 접근(권) resource 자원

해설 세부 사항 관련 – 여자가 남자에게 묻는 것

여자가 마지막 대사에서 물론 건물주에게 임대차 계약의 그 부분을 수정해달라고 요청할 수도 있지만 그 대가로 그에게 뭔가를 줘야 할 수도 있다(Of course, you could ask the landlord to revise that part of the lease, but you might have to give him something in return)고 했고, 예를 들면 더 높은 임대료가 있다(higher rental fees, for example)며 이것을 고려해보겠는지(Would you consider that?)를 묻고 있으므로 정답은 (B)이다.

50-52 3인 대화

M-Cn	Hi, Heather. **50 I'm glad you could join us for this meeting even though you're working from home today.** Can you see and hear us alright?
W-Am	Hi, Simon and Donna. Yes, the video and audio seem to be working just fine.
M-Cn	Great. Let's get started, then. Donna?
W-Br	All right. **51 As you both know, we'll be talking today about our proposed revisions to the employee handbook.** Heather, do you have your materials at hand?
W-Am	Yep.
W-Br	Great. **52 Then let's begin by discussing how each of our assigned sections is coming along.**

남	안녕하세요, 헤더. 오늘 재택근무임에도 불구하고 이 회의에 우리와 함께할 수 있어서 기쁘네요. 우리가 잘 보이고 들리시나요?
여1	안녕하세요, 사이먼 그리고 도나. 네, 영상과 오디오가 잘 작동하는 것 같네요.
남	좋아요. 그럼 시작해봅시다. 도나?
여2	네. 두 분 다 아시다시피, 오늘 직원 안내서에 대한 수정안에 대해 이야기할 거예요. 헤더, 자료가 준비되어 있으신가요?
여1	네.
여2	좋아요. 그럼 각각 배정받은 부분이 어떻게 되어가고 있는지 논의하는 것부터 시작해보죠.

어휘 proposed 제안된 revision 수정 at hand 가까이에 (있는), 준비된 discuss 논의하다 assigned 배정된 section 부분 come along 되어가다

50

고난도

What does the man mention about the meeting?

(A) It was not originally scheduled for today.
(B) It includes a remote participant.
(C) It is being recorded.
(D) It might last past closing time.

남자는 회의에 대해 무엇을 언급하는가?

(A) 원래 오늘 예정되어 있지 않았다.
(B) 원격 참석자를 포함한다.
(C) 기록되고 있다.
(D) 마감 시간 이후에도 지속될 수 있다.

어휘 originally 원래 scheduled 예정된 include 포함하다 remote 원격의 last 지속되다 past ~을 지나서

해설 세부 사항 관련 – 남자가 회의에 대해 언급한 사항

남자가 첫 대사에서 오늘 재택근무임에도 불구하고 이 회의에 우리와 함께할 수 있어서 기쁘다(I'm glad you could join us for this meeting even though you're working from home today)고 한 것으로 보아 정답은 (B)이다.

Test 9

51
고난도

What kind of project are the speakers working on?

(A) Recruiting for staff openings
(B) Developing a questionnaire
(C) Organizing a training program
(D) Rewriting a set of policies

화자들은 어떤 종류의 프로젝트에 관해 일하고 있는가?

(A) 직원 채용
(B) 설문지 개발
(C) 교육 프로그램 편성
(D) 정책 재작성

어휘 recruit 채용하다 opening 빈 자리 questionnaire 설문지
organize 조직하다 policy 정책

해설 세부 사항 관련 – 화자들이 진행 중인 프로젝트

두 번째 여자가 첫 대사에서 두 분 다 아시다시피 오늘 직원 안내서에 대한 수정안에 대해 이야기할 것(As you both know, we'll be talking today about our proposed revisions to the employee handbook)이라고 했으므로 정답은 (D)이다.

▶▶ Paraphrasing 대화의 **revisions to the employee handbook** → 정답의 **rewriting a set of policies**

52
고난도

What will the speakers do next?

(A) Give individual progress updates
(B) Read the minutes of a previous meeting
(C) Choose their preferred assignments
(D) Wait for an additional attendee

화자들은 다음에 무엇을 할 것인가?

(A) 개별 진행 상황 업데이트 제공
(B) 이전 회의록 읽기
(C) 선호하는 업무 선택
(D) 추가 참석자 기다리기

어휘 individual 개인의 progress 진척[진행] minutes 회의록
previous 이전의 preferred 선호하는 assignment 임무

해설 세부 사항 관련 – 화자들이 다음에 할 일

두 번째 여자가 마지막 대사에서 그럼 각각 배정받은 부분이 어떻게 되어가고 있는지 논의하는 것부터 시작해보자(Then let's begin by discussing how each of our assigned sections is coming along)고 했으므로 정답은 (A)이다.

▶▶ Paraphrasing 대화의 **how each of our assigned sections is coming along** → 정답의 **individual progress**

53-55

W-Br Good evening, sir. Is Ireland your final destination?

M-Au 53 **Yes, I'm visiting Dublin for a few days on business.**

W-Br All right. Then you'll need to fill out this landing card and submit it to Immigration when the plane lands.

M-Au Oh, OK. 54 **Do you have a pen I can borrow?**

W-Br 54 **Sure.** Here you are.

M-Au Thanks. Oh, this card is asking for my passport number, but I don't have it memorized. And my passport is in my bag in the overhead compartment.

W-Br 55 **Well, the "Fasten Seatbelts" sign is off, so you can open up the compartment now if you'd like.** Just make sure to close it when you're finished.

여	좋은 저녁입니다, 선생님. 아일랜드가 최종 목적지이십니까?
남	네, 업무차 며칠간 더블린을 방문할 거예요.
여	네. 그러면 이 착륙 카드를 작성하셔서 비행기가 착륙하면 출입국 관리소에 제출하셔야 할 거예요.
남	아, 알겠습니다. 펜을 빌릴 수 있을까요?
여	물론이죠. 여기 있습니다.
남	고마워요. 아, 이 카드에서 제 여권 번호를 묻고 있는데 외우고 있지를 않아요. 제 여권은 머리 위 짐칸에 있는 가방에 있어요.
여	음, "벨트 착용" 신호가 꺼졌으니 원하시면 지금 짐칸을 여실 수 있으세요. 다 끝나시면 꼭 닫아주십시오.

어휘 destination 목적지 fill out 작성하다 landing 착륙
submit 제출하다 immigration 출입국 관리소 land
착륙하다 passport 여권 memorize 외우다 overhead
머리 위의 compartment 짐칸 fasten 매다

53

What does the man say about his trip?

(A) He plans to visit a friend.
(B) It will be one week long.
(C) It has been enjoyable.
(D) He is traveling for work.

남자는 여행에 대해 무엇을 말하는가?

(A) 친구를 방문할 계획이다.
(B) 기간은 일주일이 될 것이다.
(C) 즐거웠다.
(D) 일 때문에 여행을 하고 있다.

해설 세부 사항 관련 – 남자가 여행에 대해 말하는 것

남자가 첫 대사에서 업무차 며칠간 더블린을 방문한다(I'm visiting Dublin for a few days on business)고 했으므로 정답은 (D)이다.

▶▶ Paraphrasing 대화의 **visiting ~ on business** → 정답의 **traveling for work**

54

How does the woman assist the man?

(A) By giving him an extra cushion
(B) By agreeing to talk to another passenger
(C) By accepting a container for disposal
(D) By lending him a writing tool

여자는 남자를 어떻게 돕는가?

(A) 여분의 쿠션을 줌으로써
(B) 다른 승객과 대화하는 것에 동의함으로써
(C) 용기를 폐기하도록 수락함으로써
(D) 필기 도구를 빌려줌으로써

어휘 container 용기 disposal 폐기

해설 세부 사항 관련 – 여자가 남자를 돕는 방법

남자가 두 번째 대사에서 빌릴 수 있는 펜이 있는지(Do you have a pen I can borrow?)를 묻자 여자가 물론이죠(Sure)라고 답한 것으로 보아 여자는 남자에게 펜을 빌려줄 것임을 알 수 있다. 따라서 정답은 (D)이다.

▸▸ **Paraphrasing**   대화의 **a pen** → 정답의 **a writing tool**

55

고난도

According to the woman, what can the man do?

(A) Lean his seat back
(B) Access a storage area
(C) Leave part of a form blank
(D) Turn off an overhead light

여자에 따르면, 남자는 무엇을 할 수 있는가?

(A) 좌석을 뒤로 젖히는 것
(B) 보관 구역을 이용하는 것
(C) 양식의 일부를 빈칸으로 두는 것
(D) 머리 위쪽 조명을 끄는 것

어휘 lean back 젖히다 access 접근[이용]하다 storage 보관

해설 세부 사항 관련 – 여자가 말하는 남자가 할 수 있는 일

여자가 마지막 대사에서 "벨트 착용" 신호가 꺼졌으니 원하면 지금 짐칸을 열 수 있다(the "Fasten Seatbelts" sign is off, so you can open up the compartment now if you'd like)고 했으므로 정답은 (B)이다.

▸▸ **Paraphrasing**   대화의 **open up the compartment** → 정답의 **access a storage area**

56-58

M-Cn Hey, Krista. ⁵⁶**How's your design for the concert hall coming along?**

W-Am It's going well, Curtis. How are you doing?

M-Cn I'm busy! ⁵⁷**I don't know if you've heard, but we're going to choose three students from the local university to do internships here this summer.** I'm in charge of the program.

W-Am No, I hadn't heard that! Is there anything I can do to help?

M-Cn Definitely! ⁵⁸**As a senior employee, it'd be great if you could give a talk to the students about your work and the skills it requires.** Would you be willing to do that sometime in July?

W-Am ⁵⁸**Sure.** I'd be happy to.

남 안녕하세요, 크리스타. 콘서트홀 설계는 어떻게 되어가고 있나요?
여 잘되고 있어요, 커티스. 어떻게 지내세요?
남 바빠요! 들으셨는지 모르겠지만 올여름 이곳에서 인턴십을 할 지역 대학생 3명을 뽑을 예정이에요. 제가 그 프로그램을 맡고 있어요.
여 아니요, 못 들었어요! 제가 도울 수 있는 일이 있을까요?
남 당연하죠! 선배 직원으로서 업무와 업무에 필요한 기술에 대해 학생들에게 강연을 해주시면 좋을 것 같아요. 7월 중에 그렇게 해주실 의향이 있으세요?
여 물론이죠. 기꺼이 할게요.

어휘 come along 되어가다 in charge of ~을 담당하는 senior 상급의 willing 기꺼이 하는 sometime 언젠가

56

Where do the speakers most likely work?

(A) At a public relations agency
(B) At an architectural firm
(C) At a recording studio
(D) At an art museum

화자들은 어디에서 일할 것 같은가?

(A) 홍보 대행사
(B) 건축 설계 회사
(C) 녹음실
(D) 미술관

해설 전체 내용 관련 – 화자들의 근무지

남자가 첫 대사에서 여자에게 콘서트홀 설계는 어떻게 되어가고 있는지(How's your design for the concert hall coming along?)를 묻고 있는 것으로 보아 정답은 (B)이다.

▸▸ **Paraphrasing**   대화의 **design** → 정답의 **architectural**

57

What does the man say will happen soon?

(A) A computer program will be upgraded.
(B) A building will be remodeled.
(C) Some interns will be selected.
(D) Business hours will change temporarily.

남자는 곧 무슨 일이 일어날 것이라고 말하는가?

(A) 컴퓨터 프로그램이 업그레이드될 것이다.
(B) 건물이 개조될 것이다.
(C) 인턴 몇 명이 선발될 것이다.
(D) 영업시간이 일시적으로 변경될 것이다.

어휘 remodel 개조하다 temporarily 일시적으로

해설 세부 사항 관련 – 남자가 곧 일어날 것이라고 말하는 일

남자가 두 번째 대사에서 들으셨는지 모르겠지만 올여름 이곳에서 인턴십을 할 지역 대학생 3명을 뽑을 예정(I don't know if you've heard, but we're going to choose three students from the local university to do internships here this summer)이라고 했으므로 정답은 (C)이다.

> ▸▸ Paraphrasing 대화의 choose three students from the local university to do internships → 정답의 Some interns will be selected

58

What does the woman agree to do?

(A) Calculate a budgetary requirement
(B) Telecommute for a short period
(C) Deliver a speech to a group
(D) Conduct some phone interviews

여자는 무엇을 하기로 동의하는가?

(A) 예산 소요액 추산
(B) 단기 재택근무
(C) **단체 대상 연설**
(D) 전화면접 실시

어휘 calculate 추산하다 budgetary 예산의 requirement 필요한 것 telecommute 재택근무하다 deliver a speech 연설하다 conduct 실시[수행]하다

해설 세부 사항 관련 – 여자가 하기로 동의한 일

남자가 마지막 대사에서 여자에게 선배 직원으로서 업무와 업무에 필요한 기술에 대해 학생들에게 강연을 해주면 좋을 것 같다(As a senior employee, it'd be great if you could give a talk to the students about your work and the skills it requires)고 제안하자 여자가 물론이죠(Sure)라고 답했으므로 정답은 (C)이다.

> ▸▸ Paraphrasing 대화의 give a talk → 정답의 deliver a speech

59-61

W-Br	Hi, Marcus. Where are you right now?
M-Cn	59 I'm on the fourth floor, putting up a wall fan for the accountants.
W-Br	Oh, OK. I'm back from my trip to the hardware store, and I was wondering where you'd gone.
M-Cn	Yeah, the fan was delivered after you left, and they asked me to put it up right away. 60 It's getting warm up here because of the sunlight bouncing off the new skyscraper across the street.
W-Br	Really? That's too bad. 61 Well, let me know if you need anything.

M-Cn	Oh, actually—I left my blue screwdriver on my desk.
W-Br	Uh... yes, I see it. I'll be there in a minute.

여	안녕하세요, 마커스. 지금 어디세요?
남	**4층에서 회계사들을 위해 벽걸이 선풍기를 달고 있어요.**
여	아, 알겠어요. 철물점에 다녀왔는데 당신이 어디에 갔는지 궁금했어요.
남	그랬군요, 당신이 나간 뒤에 선풍기가 배달됐는데 당장 설치해달라고 요청하더라고요. 길 건너편에 새로 지은 고층 건물에서 반사되는 햇살 때문에 여기가 점점 더워지고 있어요.
여	정말요? 그것 참 유감이네요. 뭐 필요한 거 있으면 알려주세요.
남	아, 사실은 **제 책상 위에 파란색 드라이버를 놓고 왔어요.**
여	어… 네, 보이네요. 금방 그리로 갈게요.

어휘 fan 선풍기 accountant 회계사 hardware store 철물점 wonder 궁금해하다 right away 곧바로 bounce (빛·소리가) 반사하다, 튀다 skyscraper 고층 건물 screwdriver 드라이버

59

What does the man say he is currently doing?

(A) Repairing some electronics
(B) Assembling some furniture
(C) Packing a moving crate
(D) Installing an appliance

남자는 현재 무엇을 하고 있다고 말하는가?

(A) 전자제품 수리
(B) 몇몇 가구 조립
(C) 이사 상자 포장
(D) **가전제품 설치**

어휘 repair 수리하다 electronics 전자제품 assemble 조립하다 crate 상자 install 설치하다 appliance 가전제품

해설 세부 사항 관련 – 남자가 현재 하고 있다고 말하는 일

남자가 첫 대사에서 4층에서 회계사들을 위해 벽걸이 선풍기를 달고 있다(I'm on the fourth floor, putting up a wall fan for the accountants)고 했으므로 정답은 (D)이다.

> ▸▸ Paraphrasing 대화의 putting up a wall fan → 정답의 installing an appliance

60   고난도

What is the problem with a nearby building?

(A) It is blocking some light.
(B) It is increasing noise levels.
(C) It is reflecting some heat.
(D) It is causing higher winds.

인근 건물의 문제는 무엇인가?

(A) 빛을 차단하고 있다.
(B) 소음 수준을 높이고 있다.
(C) **열을 반사하고 있다.**
(D) 더 강한 바람을 일으키고 있다.

어휘 block 차단하다 increase 높이다 reflect 반사하다 cause 초래하다

해설 세부 사항 관련 – 인근 건물의 문제

남자가 두 번째 대사에서 길 건너편에 새로 지은 고층 건물에서 반사되는 햇살 때문에 여기가 점점 더워지고 있다(It's getting warm up here because of the sunlight bouncing off the new skyscraper across the street)고 했으므로 정답은 (C)이다.

▶▶ Paraphrasing 대화의 the sunlight bouncing off ~
→ 정답의 It is reflecting some heat

61 [고난도]

What does the man mean when he says, "I left my blue screwdriver on my desk"?

(A) He is willing to lend his belongings to the woman.
(B) He will not be able to complete his task right away.
(C) He does not mind returning to his work station.
(D) He would like the woman to bring a tool to him.

남자가 "제 책상 위에 파란색 드라이버를 놓고 왔어요"라고 말하는 의도는 무엇인가?
(A) 여자에게 기꺼이 자신의 소지품을 빌려줄 의향이 있다.
(B) 즉시 임무를 완수할 수 없을 것이다.
(C) 자신의 작업장으로 돌아오는 것을 개의치 않는다.
(D) 여자가 도구를 가져다주기를 원한다.

어휘 willing 기꺼이 하는 belongings 소유물 complete 완수하다 task 일 mind 꺼리다 work station 작업장 tool 도구

해설 화자의 의도 파악 – 책상 위에 파란색 드라이버를 놓고 왔다는 말의 의도 앞에서 여자가 남자에게 뭐 필요한 거 있으면 알려주라(let me know if you need anything)고 제안하자 남자가 인용문을 언급했으므로 여자가 파란색 드라이버를 가져다주기를 바라 한 말임을 알 수 있다. 따라서 정답은 (D)이다.

62-64 대화 + 일기 예보

W-Am Kendrick, I'm concerned about the weather this week. 62We should probably schedule a few extra employees to repair potential damage to the power lines.

M-Au Why? What's going on?

W-Am 63Well, as you can see on this forecast I printed out, there's going to be one day of high winds. We'll want at least one extra crew per district on standby that day, I think.

M-Au Hmm. This forecast is from the Clancy Weather Service, though, isn't it? They're not always reliable, in my experience. 64Why don't you see what a few other meteorological services are predicting? If it's similar, then I'll approve your suggestion.

여 켄드릭, 이번 주 날씨가 걱정돼요. 아마도 직원 몇 명을 추가로 송전선의 잠재적 손상을 복구하도록 일정을 잡아야 할 것 같아요.
남 왜요? 무슨 일이요?
여 글쎄, 제가 출력한 이 예보에서 보시다시피, 하루 동안 강한 바람이 불 겁니다. 그날 적어도 구역당 한 명은 추가로 대기해야 할 듯해요.
남 흠. 그런데 이 일기 예보는 클랜시 기상 서비스에서 나온 거네요, 그렇죠? 제 경험상 그들은 항상 믿을 만하지는 못해요. 다른 기상 서비스 기관에서 예측하는 것을 확인하는 것이 어떨까요? 비슷하다면 당신의 제안을 승인할게요.

어휘 concerned 걱정하는 schedule 일정을 잡다 potential 잠재적인 power line 송전선 forecast 예보 crew (함께 일하는) 팀, 반 per ~당 district 구역 on standby 대기하고 있는 reliable 믿을 만한 meteorological 기상의 predict 예측하다 similar 비슷한 approve 승인하다 suggestion 제안

18°C / 24°C	15°C / 21°C	16°C / 21°C	17°C / 26°C
Tuesday	Wednesday	63 Thursday	Friday

18°C / 24°C	15°C / 21°C	16°C / 21°C	17°C / 26°C
화요일	수요일	63 목요일	금요일

62

What industry do the speakers most likely work in?

(A) Energy utilities
(B) Rail transportation
(C) Road construction
(D) Groundskeeping

화자들은 어떤 산업에 종사하고 있을 것 같은가?
(A) 에너지 설비
(B) 철도 운송
(C) 도로 공사
(D) 공원 관리

어휘 utilities (수도, 전기, 가스 등의) 공익사업 transportation 운송 construction 공사, 건설

해설 전체 내용 관련 – 화자들의 직업

여자가 첫 대사에서 아마도 직원 몇 명을 추가로 송전선의 잠재적 손상을 복구하도록 일정을 잡아야 할 것 같다(We should probably schedule a few extra employees to repair potential damage to the power lines)고 남자에게 전력과 관련된 업무 이야기를 꺼내고 있는 것으로 보아 정답은 (A)이다.

▶▶ Paraphrasing 대화의 the power lines
→ 정답의 energy utilities

63

Look at the graphic. Which day does the woman suggest scheduling extra workers for?

(A) Tuesday
(B) Wednesday
(C) Thursday
(D) Friday

시각 정보에 의하면, 여자는 어느 요일에 추가 직원의 일정을 잡아달라고 제안하는가?

(A) 화요일
(B) 수요일
(C) **목요일**
(D) 금요일

해설 **시각 정보 연계 – 여자가 추가 직원의 일정을 잡아달라고 제안하는 요일**
여자가 두 번째 대사에서 제가 출력한 이 예보에서 보시다시피, 하루 동안 강한 바람이 불 것(as you can see on this forecast I printed out, there's going to be one day of high winds)이라면서, 그날 적어도 구역당 한 명은 추가로 대기해야 할 듯하다(We'll want at least one extra crew per district on standby that day, I think)고 했고, 일기 예보에 따르면 바람이 부는 날은 목요일이므로 정답은 (C)이다.

---

64 고난도

What does the man recommend doing first?

(A) Asking a supervisor for approval
(B) Giving workers a chance to volunteer
(C) Determining some crews' responsibilities
(D) Checking some different forecasts

남자는 먼저 무엇을 하라고 권하는가?

(A) 관리자에게 승인을 요청할 것
(B) 직원들에게 자원할 기회를 줄 것
(C) 일부 팀원의 책무를 결정할 것
(D) **몇몇 다른 예보를 확인할 것**

어휘 supervisor 관리자 approval 승인 chance 기회 volunteer 자원[자진]하다 determine 결정하다 responsibility 책무, 책임

해설 **세부 사항 관련 – 남자가 먼저 하라고 권하는 일**
남자가 두 번째 대사에서 다른 기상 서비스 기관에서 예측하는 것을 확인하는 것이 어떨지(Why don't you see what a few other meteorological services are predicting?)를 권유하고 있으므로 정답은 (D)이다.

> ▶▶ Paraphrasing 대화의 see what a few other meteorological services are predicting → 정답의 checking some different forecasts

---

65-67 대화 + 문 디자인

M-Cn Hi Sonya, it's Kwang-Min Cho. I've picked the new gate for my yard.

W-Br Great! Let me just get your file out. OK, which one do you want?

M-Cn ⁶⁵**I like the one you showed me that is curved at the top and closed at the bottom.**

W-Br Good choice! It has an appealing mix of style and functionality.

M-Cn That's what I thought. ⁶⁶**I want a gate that will make the yard look nice, but that will also keep animals out of the vegetable garden I'm planning.**

W-Br Absolutely. ⁶⁷**Now, I'll call to make sure the wholesaler has it in stock.** If it is, the landscaping crew will be able to finish the fencing as scheduled.

남 안녕하세요 소냐, 조광민입니다. 제 마당을 위한 새 문을 골랐어요.
여 잘됐네요! 당신의 파일을 좀 꺼내올게요. 자, 어떤 걸 원하세요?
남 **당신이 보여줬던 위쪽은 곡선이고 아래쪽은 닫힌 것이 좋아요.**
여 좋은 선택이에요! 그것은 스타일과 기능성이 매력적인 조화를 이루고 있죠.
남 저도 그렇게 생각했어요. **마당을 멋져 보이게 할 수 있는 문을 원하지만, 제가 계획하고 있는 채소밭에 동물들이 들어가지 못하게도 해야 하니까요.**
여 물론이죠. **일단 도매업자에게 전화해서 재고를 가지고 있는지 확인할게요.** 재고가 있으면 조경팀이 예정대로 울타리 작업을 마칠 수 있을 거예요.

어휘 pick 고르다 gate 문 yard 마당 curved 곡선의
bottom 아래 (부분) appealing 매력적인 functionality
기능성 wholesaler 도매업자 in stock 재고로, 비축되어
landscaping 조경 crew (함께 일하는) 팀, 반 fencing
울타리

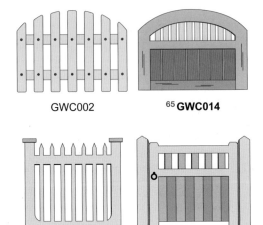

GWC002   ⁶⁵**GWC014**

GSC001   GSC009

65

Look at the graphic. Which gate does the man choose?

(A) GWC002
(B) GWC014
(C) GSC001
(D) GSC009

시각 정보에 의하면, 남자는 어느 문을 선택하는가?

(A) GWC002
(B) GWC014
(C) GSC001
(D) GSC009

해설 **시각 정보 연계 – 남자가 선택한 문**

남자가 두 번째 대사에서 당신이 보여줬던 위쪽이 곡선이고 아래쪽은 닫힌 것이 좋다(I like the one you showed me that is curved at the top and closed at the bottom)고 했고, 문 디자인에 따르면 위쪽이 곡선이고 아래쪽은 닫힌 것은 GWC014이므로 정답은 (B)이다.

66

고난도

What does the man say about his yard?

(A) He will keep a pet there.
(B) He will grow produce there.
(C) He plans to have parties there.
(D) He will put in a swimming pool there.

남자는 자신의 마당에 대해 무엇을 말하는가?

(A) 그곳에서 애완동물을 기를 것이다.
(B) 그곳에서 농산물을 기를 것이다.
(C) 그곳에서 파티를 열 계획이다.
(D) 그곳에 수영장을 설치할 계획이다.

어휘 pet 애완동물 produce 농산물

해설 **세부 사항 관련 – 남자가 마당에 대해 말하는 것**

남자가 세 번째 대사에서 마당을 멋져 보이게 할 수 있는 문을 원하지만, 자신이 계획하고 있는 채소밭에 동물들이 들어가지 못하게도 해야 한다(I want a gate that will make the yard look nice, but that will also keep animals out of the vegetable garden I'm planning)고 한 것으로 보아 정답은 (B)이다.

▸▸ **Paraphrasing** 대화의 **vegetable** → 정답의 **produce**

67

Who will the woman most likely call next?

(A) A supplier
(B) An employee
(C) Another client
(D) An inspector

여자는 다음에 누구에게 전화할 것 같은가?

(A) 공급업자
(B) 직원
(C) 다른 고객
(D) 검사관

해설 **세부 사항 관련 – 여자가 다음에 전화할 사람**

여자가 마지막 대사에서 도매업자에게 전화해서 재고를 가지고 있는지 확인하겠다(I'll call to make sure the wholesaler has it in stock)고 했으므로 정답은 (A)이다.

▸▸ **Paraphrasing** 대화의 **wholesaler** → 정답의 **supplier**

68-70 대화 + 에피소드 목록

M-Cn	**68All right, we now have a full tank of gas. We shouldn't have to stop again unless we want some snacks.**
W-Am	Great! Well, since there're a few more hours of highway ahead of us, why don't you find something for us to listen to?
M-Cn	Sure. **69I just subscribed to a new podcast for this trip, actually. It's a series of interviews with successful entrepreneurs.**
W-Am	That sounds good. Maybe we'll get some ideas that we can apply at the trade show tomorrow.
M-Cn	Exactly. OK, let's see, I'm most interested in the third episode here… **70but since we have enough time to listen to all of them, I'll just start with the oldest one.**

남	자, 이제 기름 탱크를 가득 채웠어요. 간식을 원하는 게 아니면 다시 멈출 필요가 없겠네요.
여	좋아요! 음, 앞으로 고속도로를 몇 시간 더 달려야 하니까, 우리가 들을 만한 것을 찾아보는 게 어때요?
남	좋아요. 실은 이번 여행을 위해 새 팟캐스트에 구독 신청을 했어요. 성공한 기업가들과의 인터뷰 연재예요.
여	좋은데요. 어쩌면 내일 무역 박람회에서 우리가 적용할 수 있는 아이디어를 얻을 수 있을지도 몰라요.
남	맞아요. 자, 봅시다. 여기 3회가 가장 끌리는데… 하지만 다 들을 시간은 충분하니까 그냥 가장 오래된 것부터 시작할게요.

어휘 full 가득한 highway 고속도로 ahead of ~ 앞에 subscribe 구독하다, 가입하다 actually 사실 a series of 일련의 successful 성공한 entrepreneur 기업가 apply 적용하다

Showing: Newest first ▾

"Amita Mittal" June 23	40 minutes
"Mateo Lozano" June 16	39 minutes
"Josh Dennis" June 9	42 minutes
70**"Verna Armstrong"** June 2	**44 minutes**

Test 9

방송: 최신순 ▼	
"아미타 미탈" 6월 23일	40분
"마테오 로차노" 6월 16일	39분
"조쉬 데니스" 6월 9일	42분
70 "베르나 암스트롱" 6월 2일	44분

68

What most likely has the man just finished doing?

(A) Buying food at a roadside store
(B) Putting fuel in a vehicle
(C) Arranging some baggage
(D) Receiving advice about a route

남자는 방금 무엇을 끝냈을 것 같은가?

(A) 길가 상점에서 식품 구입
(B) 차량에 연료 주입
(C) 수하물 정리
(D) 경로에 대한 조언 받기

어휘 roadside 길가 fuel 연료 vehicle 차량 arrange 정리하다
baggage 수하물 route 경로

해설 세부 사항 관련 – 남자가 방금 끝낸 일
남자가 첫 대사에서 이제 기름 탱크를 가득 채웠다(we now have a full tank of gas)고 한 것으로 보아 정답은 (B)이다.

▸▸ Paraphrasing 대화의 **now have a full tank of gas**
→ 정답의 **putting fuel in a vehicle**

69

`고난도`

What is mentioned about the people featured on the podcast?

(A) They founded their own businesses.
(B) They have spoken at a famous event.
(C) They are in the same industry.
(D) They conducted interesting research.

팟캐스트에 출연한 사람들에 대해 언급된 것은 무엇인가?

(A) 자신의 사업을 창립했다.
(B) 유명한 행사에서 연설한 적이 있다.
(C) 동종 업계에 종사한다.
(D) 흥미로운 연구를 수행했다.

어휘 feature 특별히 포함하다 found 창립하다 conduct 실시[수행]하다

해설 세부 사항 관련 – 팟캐스트에 출연한 사람들에 대해 언급된 사항
남자가 두 번째 대사에서 실은 이번 여행을 위해 새 팟캐스트에 구독 신청을 했다(I just subscribed to a new podcast for this trip, actually)며, 성공한 기업가들과의 인터뷰 연재(It's a series of interviews with successful entrepreneurs)라고 팟캐스트에 대해 소개한 것으로 보아 팟캐스트에는 기업가들이 출연했음을 알 수 있다. 따라서 정답은 (A)이다.

▸▸ Paraphrasing 대화의 **entrepreneurs**
→ 정답의 **founded their own businesses**

70

Look at the graphic. Which episode will the man play first?

(A) "Amita Mittal"
(B) "Mateo Lozano"
(C) "Josh Dennis"
(D) "Verna Armstrong"

시각 정보에 의하면, 남자는 어느 에피소드를 먼저 재생할 것인가?

(A) 아미타 미탈
(B) 마테오 로차노
(C) 조쉬 데니스
(D) 베르나 암스트롱

해설 시각 정보 연계 – 남자가 먼저 재생할 에피소드
남자가 마지막 대사에서 다 들을 시간은 충분하니까 그냥 가장 오래된 것부터 시작하겠다(since we have enough time to listen to all of them, I'll just start with the oldest one)고 했고, 에피소드 목록에 따르면 가장 오래된 것은 6월 2일에 방송된 베르나 암스트롱이므로 정답은 (D)이다.

PART 4

71-73 전화 메시지

W-Br Hi. 71**My name is Sally Fuller, and I'd like to use your overnight delivery service to send a package.** But I'm having a problem—I can't seem to find your storefront. 72**My map app says that it's at 650 Jackson Avenue—is that right?** Because I'm parked in front of that building now, and I don't see your sign anywhere. 73**Um, I know that I need to drop this package off by eleven in order for it to ship overnight, so please call me back at this number as soon as you get this message.** Thanks.

안녕하세요. 제 이름은 샐리 풀러입니다. 당신의 익일 배송 서비스를 이용해서 소포를 보내고 싶어요. 그런데 문제가 있습니다. 당신의 가게 앞을 못 찾겠어요. 제 지도 앱에 잭슨 가 650번지라고 나와 있는데 맞나요? 제가 지금 그 건물 앞에 주차해 있는데 당신의 간판이 어디에도 보이지 않아요. 음, 이 소포를 하룻밤 사이에 배송하기 위해서는 11시까지 가져다놓아야 한다고 알고 있으니 이 메시지를 받으시는 대로 이 번호로 다시 전화해주세요. 고맙습니다.

어휘 해설 overnight 하룻밤 동안의 package 소포 sign 간판
drop off 갖다주다 ship 운송하다

71

What kind of business is the speaker calling?

(A) A fitness center
(B) A hardware store
(C) An employment agency
(D) A shipping company

화자는 어떤 종류의 업체에 전화하고 있는가?
(A) 피트니스 센터
(B) 철물점
(C) 고용 대행사
(D) 배송 회사

해설 전체 내용 관련 - 화자가 전화한 업체의 종류
화자가 초반부에 자신의 이름은 샐리 풀러이고 당신의 익일 배송 서비스를 이용해서 소포를 보내고 싶다(My name is Sally Fuller, and I'd like to use your overnight delivery service to send a package)고 한 것으로 보아 정답은 (D)이다.

▸▸ Paraphrasing 담화의 delivery → 정답의 shipping

72

What is the purpose of the call?

(A) To confirm an address
(B) To make an appointment
(C) To ask about parking options
(D) To learn about a pricing system

전화의 목적은 무엇인가?
(A) 주소 확인
(B) 약속 잡기
(C) 주차 선택 사항 문의
(D) 가격 정책 알아보기

어휘 confirm 확인하다 pricing 가격 책정

해설 전체 내용 관련 - 전화의 목적
화자가 중반부에 자신의 지도 앱에 잭슨 가 650번지라고 나와 있는데 맞는지(My map app says that it's at 650 Jackson Avenue—is that right?)를 묻고 있으므로 정답은 (A)이다.

73

What is the speaker concerned about? 고난도

(A) An additional fee
(B) A limited amount of time
(C) An identification requirement
(D) A large number of customers

화자는 무엇에 대해 걱정하는가?
(A) 추가 수수료
(B) 한정된 시간
(C) 신원 확인 요구 사항
(D) 많은 고객

어휘 fee 수수료 limited 한정된 identification 신원 확인 requirement 요건

해설 세부 사항 관련 - 화자의 우려 사항
화자가 후반부에 이 소포를 하룻밤 사이에 배송하기 위해서는 11시까지 가져다놓아야 한다고 알고 있으니, 이 메시지를 받는 대로 이 번호로 다시 전화해달라(I know that I need to drop this package off by eleven in order for it to ship overnight, so please call me back at this number as soon as you get this message)고 한 것으로 보아 정답은 (B)이다.

74-76 뉴스 보도

M-Cn This is Terrence Barnes from KTQN News with an announcement regarding traffic in Thornlin. **74The substantial number of citizens and visitors driving to the Wilvard Center for tonight's sold-out charity concert is causing serious congestion downtown.** Traffic has slowed to a standstill on some streets. **75In response, officials from the Thornlin Department of Transportation have issued a statement on its Web site. 76It asks those without urgent business downtown to keep away from the area in order to prevent the situation from growing worse. KTQN urges our listeners to do the same.**

KTQN 뉴스의 테런스 반즈가 손린 지역 교통 소식을 전해드립니다. 오늘밤 매진된 자선 콘서트를 위해 차를 몰고 윌버드 센터로 가는 상당수의 시민과 방문객들로 인해 도심이 심각한 혼잡 상태입니다. 일부 거리에서는 교통이 정체 수준으로 더딥니다. 이에 대응하여 손린 교통부 관계자들은 웹사이트에 성명을 발표했습니다. 도심에서의 긴급한 용무가 없는 사람들은 상황이 악화되는 것을 막기 위해 이 지역을 피하라고 합니다. KTQN도 청취자 분들께 동일한 내용을 권해드립니다.

어휘 announcement 소식 regarding ~에 관하여 traffic 교통 substantial 상당한 citizen 시민 charity 자선 cause 초래하다 serious 심각한 congestion 혼잡 standstill 멈춤 in response 이에 대응하여 official 공무원 transportation 운송, 교통 issue 발표[공표]하다 statement 성명 urgent 긴급한 prevent 막다 grow worse 악화되다 situation 상황 urge 권하다

74

What has caused traffic problems?

(A) Bad weather
(B) A street closure
(C) Holiday travel
(D) A major event

무엇이 교통 문제를 초래했는가?
(A) 악천후
(B) 도로 폐쇄
(C) 휴가 여행
(D) 주요 행사

해설 세부 사항 관련 – 교통 문제의 원인
화자가 초반부에 오늘 밤 매진된 자선 콘서트를 위해 차를 몰고 윌버드 센터로 가는 상당수의 시민과 방문객들로 인해 도심이 심각한 혼잡 상태(The substantial number of citizens and visitors driving to the Wilvard Center for tonight's sold-out charity concert is causing serious congestion downtown)라고 했으므로 정답은 (D)이다.

> ▸▸ Paraphrasing   담화의 charity concert
> → 정답의 a major event

75

According to the speaker, what has a government department done?

(A) Issued a mass text message
(B) Sent personnel to an area
(C) Posted a statement online
(D) Suspended a transportation service

화자에 따르면, 정부 부처는 무엇을 했는가?
(A) 대량 문자 메시지 발송
(B) 지역으로 담당자 파견
(C) 온라인에 성명서 게시
(D) 교통 서비스 중단

어휘 mass 대량의 personnel 직원들 post 게시하다 suspend
중단하다

해설 세부 사항 관련 – 화자가 말하는 정부 부처가 한 일
화자가 중반부에 이에 대응하여 손린 교통부 관계자들은 웹사이트에 성명을 발표했다(In response, officials from the Thornlin Department of Transportation have issued a statement on its Web site)고 했으므로 정답은 (C)이다.

> ▸▸ Paraphrasing   담화의 issued a statement on its Web
> site → 정답의 posted a statement online

76

What are the listeners asked to do?

(A) Visit a city Web site
(B) Avoid a neighborhood
(C) Drive more slowly than usual
(D) Await a second radio announcement

청자들은 무엇을 하도록 요청되는가?
(A) 시 웹사이트 방문하기
(B) 인근 지역 피하기
(C) 평소보다 서행 운전하기
(D) 두 번째 라디오 방송 기다리기

어휘 avoid 피하다 neighborhood (특정) 지역, 인근 await 기다리다

해설 세부 사항 관련 – 청자들이 요청받은 일
화자가 후반부에 도심에서의 긴급한 용무가 없는 사람들은 상황이 악화되는 것을 막기 위해 이 지역을 피하라고 한다(It asks those without urgent business downtown to keep away from the area in order to prevent the situation from growing worse)며, KTQN도 청취자 분들께 동일한 내용을 권해드린다(KTQN urges our listeners to do the same)고 했으므로 정답은 (B)이다.

> ▸▸ Paraphrasing   담화의 keep away from the area
> → 정답의 avoid a neighborhood

77-79 회의 발췌

W-Am All right, we're here to discuss the results of last week's focus group testing our new hand lotion. **77 Jeremy has kindly organized the data into these charts—thanks, Jeremy. 78 Now, this lotion was developed to provide long-lasting moisturizing, so we had assumed that the advertising would focus on that. But really, we need to reflect consumers' actual experience with the product**—and as you can see, the 'scent' category received the highest approval rating, at 74%. I know that this change would mean that marketing team might not have its materials ready by September twenty-fifth as planned. **79 But I don't see a problem with moving that due date back a few weeks. What do you all think?**

자, 우리는 지난주 포커스 그룹이 우리의 새로운 핸드 로션을 테스트한 결과를 논의하기 위해 여기에 모였습니다. 제레미가 친절하게 데이터를 이 차트에 정리했습니다. 고마워요, 제레미. 이 로션은 오래 지속되는 보습을 제공하기 위해 개발되었고, 따라서 우리는 광고가 그 점을 부각해야 할 것이라고 짐작했습니다. 그러나 우리는 제품에 대한 소비자의 실제 경험을 반영할 필요가 있습니다. 그리고 보시다시피, 향기 카테고리가 74퍼센트로 가장 높은 지지율을 받았어요. 이 변화가 마케팅 팀이 계획대로 9월 25일까지 자료를 준비하지 못할 수도 있다는 것을 의미한다는 걸 알고 있습니다. 그렇지만 저는 마감일을 몇 주 뒤로 옮기는 것에 문제가 있다고 보지 않는데요. 다들 어떻게 생각하십니까?

어휘 focus group 포커스 그룹 (조사나 실험을 위해 각 계층을 대표하도록 뽑은 소수의 사람들로 구성된 그룹) organize 정리하다 long-lasting 오래 지속되는 moisturizing 보습 assume 추정하다 advertising 광고 reflect 반영하다 scent 향기 approval 찬성, 인정 rating 순위[평가] material 자료 due date 마감일

77   고난도

What does the speaker thank Jeremy for?

(A) Creating some visual aids
(B) Leading a discussion group
(C) Organizing the current meeting
(D) Preparing some lotion samples

화자는 제레미에게 무엇에 대해 감사하는가?
(A) 몇몇 시각 보조 자료를 만든 일
(B) 토론 그룹을 주도한 일
(C) 현재 회의를 준비한 일
(D) 몇몇 로션 샘플을 준비한 일

어휘 visual aid 시각 보조 자료

해설 세부 사항 관련 – 화자가 제레미에게 감사한 일

화자가 초반부에 제레미가 친절하게 데이터를 이 차트에 정리했다(Jeremy has kindly organized the data into these charts)면서 고마워요, 제레미(thanks, Jeremy)라고 했으므로 정답은 (A)이다.

> ▸ Paraphrasing   담화의 organized the data into these charts → 정답의 creating some visual aids

78

고난도

Why does the speaker say, "the 'scent' category received the highest approval rating, at 74%"?

(A) To show disappointment with all of the results
(B) To indicate a new direction for a marketing campaign
(C) To congratulate some of the listeners on an achievement
(D) To request that the listeners ignore some design flaws

화자가 "'향기' 카테고리가 74퍼센트로 가장 높은 지지율을 받았어요"라고 말하는 이유는 무엇인가?

(A) 모든 결과에 실망을 나타내기 위해
(B) 마케팅 캠페인를 위한 새로운 방향을 제시하기 위해
(C) 일부 청자들의 성과를 축하하기 위해
(D) 청자들에게 일부 설계 결함을 무시할 것을 요청하기 위해

어휘   disappointment 실망   indicate 내비치다   direction 방향   achievement 업적, 성취   ignore 무시하다   flaw 결함

해설   화자의 의도 파악 – '향기' 카테고리가 74퍼센트로 가장 높은 지지율을 받았다는 말의 의도

앞에서 이 로션은 오래 지속되는 보습을 제공하기 위해 개발되었고, 따라서 우리는 광고가 그 점을 부각해야 할 것이라고 짐작했다(this lotion was developed to provide long-lasting moisturizing, so we had assumed that the advertising would focus on that)고 하면서, 그러나 우리는 제품에 대한 소비자의 실제 경험을 반영할 필요가 있다(But really, we need to reflect consumers' actual experience with the product)라고 한 뒤, 인용문에서 보습보다는 향기가 호평을 받았다는 소비자의 실제 테스트 결과를 제시한 것으로 보아 마케팅의 방향을 수정해야 한다는 것을 설득하기 위한 의도로 한 말임을 알 수 있다. 따라서 정답은 (B)이다.

79

What does the speaker ask for the listeners' opinions on?

(A) Performing more market research
(B) Contacting a manufacturer
(C) Forming a special team
(D) Extending a deadline

화자는 무엇에 대해 청자들의 의견을 묻는가?

(A) 더 많은 시장 조사 실시
(B) 제조사 연락
(C) 특별팀 구성
(D) 마감 기한 연장

어휘   manufacturer 제조사   form 구성하다   extend 연장하다

해설 세부 사항 관련 – 화자가 청자들의 의견을 묻는 사항

화자가 마지막에 자신은 마감일을 몇 주 뒤로 옮기는 것에 문제가 있다고 보지 않는다(But I don't see a problem with moving that due date back a few weeks)며, 다들 어떻게 생각하는지(What do you all think?)를 묻고 있으므로 정답은 (D)이다.

> ▸ Paraphrasing   담화의 moving that due date back a few weeks → 정답의 extending a deadline

80-82 광고

M-Au   As the summer heat rises, you may find that your shirts, dresses, and suits become dirty and wrinkled more quickly. [80]**If you don't have hours to spend in the laundry room, try Zantrey Cleaners.** We'll wash or dry clean your apparel carefully to ensure that colors stay bright and fabrics stay strong. [81]**And for even more convenience, you can now have your items picked up and dropped off right at your door!** Customers can try this great new service once for free as part of a special offer. [82]**Simply download ZantryGo, our convenient app for smartphones, and the offer will be automatically applied to your first order.** Do it today to stay fresh throughout the summer!

여름 더위가 기승을 부릴수록 셔츠, 드레스, 정장이 더러워지고 구김이 더 빨리 가는 것을 발견할지도 모릅니다. 세탁실에서 보낼 시간이 없다면 잰트레이 클리너스를 한번 이용해보세요. 색상은 밝고 옷감은 튼튼하게 유지되도록 당신의 옷을 세심하게 세탁하거나 드라이클리닝을 해드리겠습니다. 그리고 훨씬 더 편리하게 이제 세탁물을 바로 문 앞에서 가져가고 가져다놓도록 하실 수 있습니다! 고객은 이 훌륭한 새로운 서비스를 특별 제공의 일환으로 무료로 한 번 체험하실 수 있습니다. 스마트폰에 우리의 편리한 앱 ZantryGo를 다운로드하기만 하시면 이 제공이 첫 주문에 자동으로 적용됩니다. 여름 내내 상쾌함을 유지하기 위해 오늘 시작하세요!

어휘   heat 더위   wrinkle 주름 지다   laundry room 세탁실   apparel 의류   ensure 반드시 ~이게 하다   fabric 옷감   convenience 편의   drop off 갖다주다   convenient 편리한   automatically 자동으로   apply 적용하다

80

What type of service is being advertised?

(A) Sign printing
(B) Clothes cleaning
(C) Automobile repair
(D) Air conditioner maintenance

어떤 종류의 서비스가 광고되고 있는가?

(A) 표지판 인쇄
(B) 옷 세탁
(C) 자동차 정비
(D) 에어컨 정비

Test 9

해설 전체 내용 관련 – 광고되고 있는 서비스

화자가 초반부에 세탁실에서 보낼 시간이 없다면 잰트레이 클리너스를 한번 이용해보라(If you don't have hours to spend in the laundry room, try Zantrey Cleaners)고 했으므로 정답은 (B)이다.

81

What does the speaker say is available for free?

(A) A care product
(B) Delivery service
(C) An initial inspection
(D) An extended warranty

화자는 무엇이 무료로 이용 가능하다고 말하는가?
(A) 관리 제품
(B) 배송 서비스
(C) 초기 점검
(D) 보증 연장

해설 세부 사항 관련 – 화자가 무료로 이용 가능하다고 말하는 것

화자가 중반부에 훨씬 더 편리하게 이제 세탁물을 바로 문 앞에서 가져가고 가져다놓도록 할 수 있다(for even more convenience, you can now have your items picked up and dropped off right at your door!)며 고객은 이 훌륭한 새로운 서비스를 특별 제공의 일환으로 무료로 한 번 체험할 수 있다(Customers can try this great new service once for free as part of a special offer)고 했으므로 정답은 (B)이다.

▸▸ **Paraphrasing** 담화의 have your items picked up and dropped off right at your door → 정답의 delivery service

82

How can listeners receive the offer?

(A) By installing a mobile app
(B) By mentioning the advertisement to a clerk
(C) By spending a certain amount of money
(D) By joining a mailing list

청자들은 어떻게 제공을 받을 수 있는가?
(A) 모바일 앱을 설치함으로써
(B) 점원에게 광고를 언급함으로써
(C) 특정 금액을 지출함으로써
(D) 우편물 수신자 명단에 등록함으로써

어휘 install 설치하다 certain 특정한 mailing 우편

해설 세부 사항 관련 – 청자들이 제공을 받을 수 있는 방법

화자가 후반부에 스마트폰에 우리의 편리한 앱 ZantryGo를 다운로드하기만 하면 이 제공이 첫 주문에 자동으로 적용된다(Simply download ZantryGo, our convenient app for smartphones, and the offer will be automatically applied to your first order)고 했으므로 정답은 (A)이다.

▸▸ **Paraphrasing** 담화의 download our convenient app for smartphones → 정답의 installing a mobile app

83-85 방송

W-Br Welcome back to "Everyday Parenting" on WTUY Radio. **83Before the break, I was talking to Byron Young about his popular blog, "While We're Young", which is full of humorous and heartfelt writings about his children.** Now, it's your turn to talk to Mr. Young. **84, 85Call us now at 555-0139 with your burning questions about parenting.** Remember, he's a full-time parent to three kids, **85so you can ask him about anything.** Sleep issues, fights between siblings, problems adjusting to school—he's dealt with it all.

WTUY 라디오의 "매일 육아"를 다시 찾아주신 것을 환영합니다. 광고 전에 바이런 영과 그의 인기 블로그 "우리가 어릴 때"에 대해 이야기를 나눴습니다. 자녀들에 대한 재미있고 진심 어린 글로 가득한 블로그죠. 자, 이제 여러분이 영 씨에게 이야기할 차례입니다. 육아에 관한 여러분의 절실한 질문과 함께 지금 555-0139번으로 전화 주십시오. 기억하세요, 그는 세 아이의 전업 부모입니다. 따라서 그에게 무엇이든 물어보실 수 있습니다. 수면 문제, 형제자매간의 싸움, 학교 적응 문제 등 그는 모든 것을 다 다뤄봤습니다.

어휘 parenting 육아 humorous 재미있는 heartfelt 진심 어린 burning 간절한 sibling 형제자매 adjust 적응하다

83

What did the speaker interview Mr. Young about?

(A) An award he won
(B) A structure he built
(C) His personal Web site
(D) His new book

화자는 무엇에 관해 영 씨를 인터뷰했는가?
(A) 그가 받은 상
(B) 그가 지은 건축물
(C) 그의 개인 웹사이트
(D) 그의 신간 도서

해설 세부 사항 관련 – 화자가 영 씨를 인터뷰한 사안

화자가 초반부에 광고 전에 바이런 영과 그의 인기 블로그 "우리가 어릴 때"에 대해 이야기를 나눴다(Before the break, I was talking to Byron Young about his popular blog, "While We're Young")라며, 자녀들에 대한 재미있고 진심 어린 글로 가득한 블로그이다(which is full of humorous and heartfelt writings about his children)라고 했으므로 정답은 (C)이다.

▸▸ **Paraphrasing** 담화의 blog → 정답의 personal Web site

84

What does the speaker encourage listeners to do?

(A) Attend a celebration
(B) Phone the radio station
(C) Make an online purchase
(D) Write down some information

화자는 청자들에게 무엇을 하라고 권하는가?

(A) 기념 행사 참석하기
(B) 라디오 방송국에 전화하기
(C) 온라인 구매하기
(D) 몇 가지 정보 작성하기

어휘 attend 참석하다 celebration 기념 행사 phone 전화 걸다
purchase 구매

해설 세부 사항 관련 – 화자가 청자들에게 하라고 권하는 일
화자가 중반부에 육아에 관한 여러분의 절실한 질문과 함께 지금 555-0139번으로 전화하라(Call us now at 555-0139 with your burning questions about parenting)고 했으므로 정답은 (B)이다.

▶▶ **Paraphrasing** 담화의 call → 정답의 phone

85
고난도

What does the speaker imply when she says, "he's a full-time parent to three kids"?

(A) Mr. Young does not have much time to talk.
(B) Mr. Young's productivity is impressive.
(C) Mr. Young is an expert on a topic.
(D) Mr. Young often engages in an activity.

화자가 "그는 세 아이의 전업 부모입니다"라고 말하는 의미는 무엇인가?
(A) 영 씨는 이야기할 시간이 많지 않다.
(B) 영 씨의 생산성이 인상 깊다.
(C) 영 씨는 주제에 관한 전문가이다.
(D) 영 씨는 활동에 자주 참여한다.

어휘 productivity 생산성 impressive 인상적인 engage in ~에
참여[관여]하다

해설 화자의 의도 파악 – 그는 세 아이의 전업 부모라는 말의 의도
앞에서 육아에 관한 여러분의 절실한 질문과 함께 지금 555-0139번으로 전화하라(Call us now at 555-0139 with your burning questions about parenting)면서, 인용문을 언급하며 그에게 무엇이든 물어볼 수 있다(you can ask him about anything)이라고 한 것으로 보아 영 씨는 아이를 셋이나 키운 경험이 있어 육아라는 주제에 관해 전문가라는 점을 강조하려는 의도로 한 말임을 알 수 있다. 따라서 정답은 (C)이다.

86-88 설명

M-Cn **86Thank you for watching this tutorial on Londa, the mobile app that helps you track your spending and balance your personal budget.** Let's start with the basics. When you open up Londa for the first time, you'll need to create your user account by linking accounts, cards, and so on from any banks you use. **87This may sound complicated, but—Londa is designed to be simple.** Just enter the requested information like this, and you can complete set-up pretty quickly. One clear advantage of Londa that you can see at this stage is that it supports a long

list of banks. **88Londa can collect and organize details about funds and transactions from all of these institutions.**

여러분의 지출을 기록하고 개인 예산의 균형 유지를 돕는 모바일 앱 론다에 관한 이 교육 과정을 시청해주셔서 감사합니다. 기초부터 시작해봅시다. 론다를 처음 시작하실 때는 사용하고 계신 은행으로부터 계좌, 카드 등을 연결하여 사용자 계정을 만드셔야 합니다. 이것은 복잡하게 들릴 수는 있지만, 론다는 단순하게 설계되어 있습니다. 이렇게 요청된 정보를 입력하기만 하면 설치를 꽤 빨리 완료하실 수 있습니다. 현 단계에서 보실 수 있는 론다의 한 가지 분명한 장점은 지원 은행이 많다는 점입니다. 론다는 이 모든 기관들로부터 자금과 거래에 관한 정보를 수집하고 정리할 수 있습니다.

어휘 tutorial 개별 지도시간 track 추적하다 spending 지출
balance 균형을 유지하다 budget 예산 account 계정
complicated 복잡한 enter 입력하다 complete 완료하다
set-up 설치 advantage 장점 stage 단계 collect 수집하다
organize 정리하다 transaction 거래 institution 기관

86

What does Londa help users do?

(A) Learn a foreign language
(B) Improve their physical fitness
(C) Manage their finances
(D) Follow current affairs

론다는 사용자들이 무엇을 하도록 돕는가?
(A) 외국어 학습
(B) 체력 향상
(C) 재무 관리
(D) 시사 따라잡기

어휘 improve 향상시키다 physical 신체의 manage 관리하다
finance 재무 current affairs 시사

해설 세부 사항 관련 – 론다가 사용자들이 하도록 돕는 것
화자가 도입부에 여러분의 지출을 기록하고 개인 예산의 균형 유지를 돕는 모바일 앱 론다에 관한 이 교육 과정을 시청해주셔서 감사합니다(Thank you for watching this tutorial on Londa, the mobile app that helps you track your spending and balance your personal budget)라고 한 것으로 보아 정답은 (C)이다.

▶▶ **Paraphrasing** 담화의 track your spending and balance
your personal budget
→ 정답의 manage their finances

87

Why does the speaker say, "Londa is designed to be simple"?

(A) To provide reassurance about user-friendliness
(B) To justify a lack of sophisticated features
(C) To explain why an optional service is not necessary
(D) To express confusion about some advertising claims

화자가 "론다는 단순하게 설계되어 있습니다"라고 말하는 이유는 무엇인가?

(A) 사용자 친화성에 대해 안심시키기 위해
(B) 정교한 기능의 부족을 합리화하기 위해
(C) 선택적 서비스가 필요하지 않은 이유를 설명하기 위해
(D) 일부 광고의 주장에 대해 혼동을 표현하기 위해

어휘 reassurance 안심 user-friendliness 사용자 친화성 justify 합리화하다 lack 부족 sophisticated 정교한 feature 기능 confusion 혼동 claim 주장

해설 화자의 의도 파악 – 론다는 단순하게 설계되었다는 말의 의도
앞에서 이것은 복잡하게 들릴 수는 있지만(This may sound complicated, but)이라고 한 뒤, 인용문을 언급한 것으로 보아 론다가 복잡해 보이는 것과는 달리 단순하게 설계되어 사용하기 쉽다는 점을 강조하기 위해 한 말임을 알 수 있다. 따라서 정답은 (A)이다.

88 [고난도]

According to the speaker, what is an advantage of Londa?

(A) It can be downloaded for free.
(B) It offers excellent customer support.
(C) It can retrieve data from many sources.
(D) It does not require much storage space.

화자에 따르면, 론다의 장점은 무엇인가?
(A) 무료로 다운로드 받을 수 있다.
(B) 뛰어난 고객 지원을 제공한다.
(C) 여러 출처에서 데이터를 가져올 수 있다.
(D) 많은 저장 공간이 필요하지 않다.

어휘 retrieve 되찾다, 가져오다 source 출처 storage 저장

해설 세부 사항 관련 – 화자가 말하는 론다의 장점
화자가 마지막에 론다는 이 모든 기관들로부터 자금과 거래에 관한 정보를 수집하고 정리할 수 있다(Londa can collect and organize details about funds and transactions from all of these institutions)고 했으므로 정답은 (C)이다.

▶▶ Paraphrasing 담화의 collect and organize details ~ from all of these institutions → 정답의 retrieve data from many sources

89-91 전화 메시지

W-Am Hi, Ms. Stephens? My name is Valerie Fleming. I saw your Internet ad for your used car. I just moved into town, and [89]**I'm having trouble getting around just by bus. It's like the times on the bus schedules are just suggestions!** Anyway, so I'm interested in buying your car. [90]**But I have a question about it—can the seats be adjusted electronically?** I've found that that tends to allow a much more comfortable ride. Uh, so please call me back and let me know. [91]**I'm going to be trying out**

another car around seven this evening, but otherwise I should be able to answer the phone immediately. Thanks.

안녕하세요, 스티븐스 씨? 제 이름은 발레리 플레밍입니다. 당신의 중고차에 대한 인터넷 광고를 봤어요. 얼마 전 마을로 이사 왔는데 버스로만 다니기가 힘들더군요. 버스 시간표에 나오는 시간들은 그냥 제안 사항일 뿐인 것 같아요! 어쨌든, 그래서 당신의 차를 사는 데 관심이 있어요. 그런데 질문이 하나 있어요. 좌석이 전동으로 조정될 수 있나요? 그것이 훨씬 더 편안한 승차감을 주는 경향이 있더라고요. 어, 그럼 다시 전화해서 알려주세요. 오늘 저녁 7시쯤에 다른 차를 타 보려고 하는데 그 외에는 바로 전화를 받을 수 있을 거예요. 고맙습니다.

어휘 ad 광고 used 중고의 adjust 조정하다 electronically 전자적으로 tend (~하는) 경향이 있다 comfortable 편안한 otherwise 그 외에는, 그렇지 않으면 immediately 즉시

89 [고난도]

Why is the speaker interested in buying a car?

(A) She often has to move large items.
(B) She wants to go on unplanned trips out of town.
(C) She lives in an area with unreliable public transportation.
(D) She likes to have privacy when going on journeys.

화자는 왜 차를 사는 데 관심이 있는가?
(A) 종종 큰 물품들을 옮겨야 한다.
(B) 시외로 계획되지 않은 여행을 떠나길 원한다.
(C) 신뢰할 수 없는 대중교통이 있는 지역에 산다.
(D) 여행을 갈 때 혼자 있는 시간을 갖고자 한다.

어휘 unreliable 신뢰할 수 없는 public transportation 대중교통

해설 세부 사항 관련 – 화자가 차를 사는 데 관심이 있는 이유
화자가 초반부에 버스로만 다니기가 힘들다(I'm having trouble getting around just by bus)면서, 버스 시간표에 나오는 시간들은 그냥 제안 사항일 뿐인 것 같다(It's like the times on the bus schedules are just suggestions!)고 한 것으로 보아 정답은 (C)이다.

90

What feature does the speaker ask about?

(A) Electronic door locks
(B) Power seats
(C) Darkened windows
(D) Temperature control systems

화자는 무슨 특징에 대해 묻는가?
(A) 전자식 문 잠금장치
(B) 파워 시트
(C) 어둡게 한 창
(D) 온도 제어 시스템

어휘 darkened 어둡게 한 temperature 온도

해설 세부 사항 관련 – 화자가 묻는 특징
화자가 중반부에 그런데 질문이 하나 있다(But I have a question about it)면서, 좌석이 전동으로 조정될 수 있는지(can the seats be adjusted electronically?)를 묻고 있으므로 정답은 (B)이다.

91

What does the speaker say she will do in the evening?

(A) Go for a test drive
(B) Attend a job interview
(C) Have dinner with friends
(D) Suggest a sale price

화자는 저녁에 무엇을 할 것이라고 말하는가?

(A) 시승
(B) 구직 면접 참석
(C) 친구들과 저녁식사
(D) 판매가 제안

해설 세부 사항 관련 – 화자가 저녁에 할 일

화자가 후반부에 오늘 저녁 7시쯤에 다른 차를 타 보려고 한다(I'm going to be trying out another car around seven this evening)고 했으므로 정답은 (A)이다.

▸▸ Paraphrasing   담화의 trying out another car
→ 정답의 go for a test drive

92-94 연설

M-Au Thank you for the warm welcome. [92]**I am honored to be taking over as interim CEO until a permanent replacement for Ms. Riley can be found.** Now, given the circumstances of my appointment, I want to assure you that I will not be making any major changes to our overall direction and practices. [93]**However, I will make an effort to facilitate the exchange of information and ideas between staff in different areas of the company.** This will give us a solid basis of trust as we enter the next era of Shorman Industries. All right. Now it's time to hear from you. [94]**Please ask me anything you'd like to know about my or the company's plans.**

따뜻한 환영에 감사드립니다. **라일리 씨의 정식 후임자를 찾을 때까지 임시 CEO를 맡게 되어 영광입니다.** 자, 제가 임명된 상황을 감안하여, 저는 우리의 전반적인 방향과 관행에 큰 변화를 주지 않을 것을 약속드리고 싶습니다. **하지만 저는 회사의 다른 분야에 있는 직원들 간의 정보 및 아이디어 교환이 원활히 이루어질 수 있도록 노력을 기울일 것입니다.** 이는 쇼먼 인더스트리즈가 다음 시대로 접어드는 동안 우리에게 견고한 신뢰의 기반을 마련해줄 것입니다. 자, 이제 여러분의 목소리를 들을 시간입니다. 저와 회사의 계획에 대해 알고 싶은 것이 있으면 무엇이든 질문해주십시오.

어휘 honored 영광스러운 take over 인계 받다, 맡다 interim 중간임시의 CEO 최고 경영자 permanent 영구적인, 정규직의 replacement 후임자 circumstance 상황 appointment 임명 assure 보장하다, 확약하다 major 중대한 overall 전반적인 direction 방향 practice 관행, 업무 facilitate 용이하게 하다 exchange 교환 solid 견고한 basis 기반 trust 신뢰 era 시대

92

What does the speaker mention about his appointment to CEO?

(A) It has not been officially announced.
(B) It has caused controversy.
(C) It will be temporary.
(D) It was unexpected.

화자는 최고 경영자로 임명된 데 대해 무엇을 언급하는가?

(A) 공식적으로 발표되지 않았다.
(B) 논란을 야기시켰다.
(C) 임시적일 것이다.
(D) 예상 밖이었다.

어휘 officially 공식적으로 announce 발표하다 cause 야기하다 controversy 논란 temporary 임시의, 일시적인 unexpected 예상 밖의

해설 세부 사항 관련 – 화자가 최고 경영자로 임명된 데 대해 언급한 사항

화자가 초반부에 라일리 씨의 정식 후임자를 찾을 때까지 임시 CEO를 맡게 되어 영광이다(I am honored to be taking over as interim CEO until a permanent replacement for Ms. Riley can be found)라고 했으므로 정답은 (C)이다.

▸▸ Paraphrasing   담화의 interim → 정답의 temporary

93   고난도

What does the speaker say he will try to do?

(A) Expand a training initiative
(B) Improve internal communication
(C) Upgrade the safety of a facility
(D) Increase employee benefits

화자는 무엇을 하려고 노력하겠다고 말하는가?

(A) 교육 목표 확대
(B) 내부 소통 증진
(C) 시설 안전 개선
(D) 직원 복지 신장

어휘 expand 확대하다 initiative 계획 internal 내부의 facility 시설 benefit 복지, 혜택

해설 세부 사항 관련 – 화자가 노력하겠다고 말한 것

화자가 중반부에 저는 회사의 다른 분야에 있는 직원들 간의 정보 및 아이디어 교환이 원활히 이루어질 수 있도록 노력을 기울일 것(I will make an effort to facilitate the exchange of information and ideas between staff in different areas of the company)이라고 했으므로 정답은 (B)이다.

▸▸ Paraphrasing   담화의 facilitate the exchange of information and ideas between staff in different areas of the company
→ 정답의 improve internal communication

Test 9

94

What most likely will take place next?

(A) A question-and-answer session
(B) A welcome reception
(C) A slide presentation
(D) A photo shoot

다음에 무슨 일이 일어날 것 같은가?

(A) 질의응답 시간
(B) 환영회
(C) 슬라이드 프레젠테이션
(D) 사진 촬영

해설　세부 사항 관련 – 다음에 일어날 일
화자가 마지막에 본인과 회사의 계획에 대해 알고 싶은 것이 있으면 무엇이든 질문하라(Please ask me anything you'd like to know about my or the company's plans)고 했으므로 정답은 (A)이다.

95-97 담화 + 표

> W-Br I appreciate your letting me speak to you about the advantages of choosing Vallond for your video hosting needs. ⁹⁵I know that you have been making videos on how to care for the trees, bushes, and flowers that you sell. Well, you won't find a better way to make those videos available on the Web than Vallond. Our platform is straightforward, fast, and reliable, and ⁹⁶all of our service packages allow you to include links to other pages in your videos. That's a great way to engage viewers. ⁹⁷Now, since you've already made over a hundred videos, I want to recommend our package that has a five-hundred-video limit. It even gives you special access to viewing statistics!

동영상 호스팅 목적을 위해 발론드를 선택할 때의 장점에 대해 말할 기회를 주셔서 감사합니다. 여러분이 판매하시는 나무와 관목, 꽃들을 돌보는 방법에 대한 동영상을 만들어오셨다는 것을 알고 있습니다. 음, 웹에서 그 동영상을 볼 수 있도록 하는 데 발론드보다 더 좋은 방법은 찾기 힘드실 겁니다. 저희 플랫폼은 간단하고 빠르고 신뢰할 수 있으며, 저희의 모든 서비스 패키지는 여러분이 다른 페이지에 대한 링크를 동영상에 포함시킬 수 있도록 해줍니다. 시청자들을 사로잡는 훌륭한 방법이죠. 여러분이 이미 100개 이상의 동영상을 만드셨기 때문에 동영상 한도가 500개인 저희 패키지를 추천해드리고 싶습니다. 이 패키지는 심지어 시청 통계 자료에 대한 특별 이용권도 줍니다!

어휘　appreciate 고마워하다　advantage 장점　care for ~을 돌보다　bush 관목, 덤불　available 이용 가능한　straightforward 간단한　reliable 신뢰할 수 있는　allow 가능하게 하다　engage 사로잡다[끌다]　access 이용(권)　viewing 시청　statistics 통계 (자료)

Vallond Video Hosting Packages

Package	Features	Monthly Cost
Package A	20 videos	Free
Package B	100 videos	$25
⁹⁷Package C	500 videos + viewing statistics	$100
Package D	Unlimited videos + viewing statistics	$300

발론드 동영상 호스팅 패키지

패키지	특징	월간 비용
패키지 A	동영상 20개	무료
패키지 B	동영상 100개	25달러
⁹⁷패키지 C	동영상 500개 + 시청 통계 자료	100달러
패키지 D	무제한 동영상 + 시청 통계 자료	300달러

95 고난도

Where most likely do the listeners work?

(A) At a commercial farm
(B) At a plant shop
(C) At a public park
(D) At a landscaping firm

청자들은 어디에서 일할 것 같은가?

(A) 상업 농장
(B) 식물 가게
(C) 공원
(D) 조경 회사

해설　전체 내용 관련 – 청자들의 근무지
화자가 초반부에 여러분이 판매하시는 나무와 관목, 꽃들을 돌보는 방법에 대한 동영상을 만들어오셨다는 것을 알고 있다(I know that you have been making videos on how to care for the trees, bushes, and flowers that you sell)고 한 것으로 보아 청자는 식물을 판매하는 일을 하고 있음을 알 수 있다. 따라서 정답은 (B)이다.

> ▸▸ Paraphrasing　담화의 trees, bushes, and flowers
> → 정답의 plant

96 고난도

What does the speaker say all packages allow customers to do?

(A) Customize the video player's appearance
(B) Place regional restrictions on videos
(C) Enable viewers to share videos
(D) Display a Web link in a video

화자는 모든 패키지가 고객들에게 무엇을 허용한다고 말하는가?

(A) 동영상 플레이어 외관의 개인 설정
(B) 동영상에 대한 지역 제한 설정
(C) 시청자의 동영상 공유 지원
(D) 동영상에 웹 링크 표시

어휘 customize 원하는 대로 바꾸다 appearance 외관 place 두다,
설정하다 regional 지역의 restriction 제한 enable 가능하게
하다 share 공유하다

해설 세부 사항 관련 – 화자가 모든 패키지에서 고객에게 허용한다고 말하는
사항

화자가 중반부에 저희의 모든 서비스 패키지는 여러분이 다른 페이지에 대한
링크를 동영상에 포함시킬 수 있도록 해준다(all of our service packages
allow you to include links to other pages in your videos)고 했으므로
정답은 (D)이다.

▸▸ **Paraphrasing** 담화의 **include links to other pages**
→ 정답의 **display a Web link**

97

Look at the graphic. Which package does the speaker
recommend?

(A) Package A
(B) Package B
(C) Package C
(D) Package D

시각 정보에 의하면, 화자는 어느 패키지를 추천하는가?

(A) 패키지 A
(B) 패키지 B
(C) 패키지 C
(D) 패키지 D

해설 시각 정보 연계 – 화자가 추천하는 패키지

화자가 후반부에 여러분이 이미 100개 이상의 동영상을 만드셨기 때문에 동
영상 한도가 500개인 저희 패키지를 추천하고 싶다(since you've already
made over a hundred videos, I want to recommend our package
that has a five-hundred-video limit)고 했고, 표에 따르면 동영상 한도가
500개인 패키지는 패키지 C이므로 정답은 (C)이다.

98-100 전화 메시지 + 문자 메시지

M-Cn Hi, this is Jake Coleman. You sent me a
text message today about my appointment on
October seventeenth. ⁹⁸**I'm sorry I didn't call
earlier—I was in the middle of a tennis match
when the text arrived, and I didn't see it until
after your closing time.** ⁹⁹**Anyway, I'll need
to move my appointment to a little later that
day.** Does Greg have any openings around four
P.M.? ¹⁰⁰**Also, I was wondering—do you sell the
shampoo that you use?** I really liked the way it
made my hair feel last time. Call me back and let
me know.

안녕하세요, 제이크 콜맨입니다. 10월 17일 제 예약에 대해 문자 메시지를 오늘
보내셨더군요. 좀 더 일찍 전화하지 못해서 죄송해요. 문자가 왔을 때 테니스 경
기 중이었는데 당신의 폐점 시간이 지나고서야 봤어요. 어쨌든 제가 그날 예약 시
간을 조금 늦춰야겠어요. 그렉에게 오후 4시쯤 빈 시간이 있을까요? 또 궁금한
게 있는데, 당신이 사용하는 샴푸를 판매하시나요? 지난번 머리 감촉이 너무 좋
았어요. 다시 전화해서 알려주세요.

어휘 appointment 예약 in the middle of ~의 도중에 text
문자 opening 빈 자리 wonder 궁금하다

Appointment Confirmation
Line 2 ······ Steele Salon
Line 3 ······ Stylist Greg Byrd
Line 4 ······ Saturday, October 17
⁹⁸ Line 5 ······ **1:30 P.M.**
Text "Yes" to confirm or
call 555-0148 to change.

예약 확인
2번 줄 ······ 스틸 살롱
3번 줄 ······ 스타일리스트 그렉 버드
4번 줄 ······ 토요일, 10월 17일
⁹⁹ 5번 줄 ······ **오후 1:30**
확정 시 "네"라고 문자 주시고 변경 시
555-0148로 전화 주세요.

98

What does the speaker say he was doing when the text
message arrived?

(A) Playing a sport
(B) Making a call
(C) Seeing a movie
(D) Boarding a flight

화자는 문자 메시지가 도착했을 때 무엇을 하고 있었다고 말하는가?

(A) 운동
(B) 전화 통화
(C) 영화 관람
(D) 비행기 탑승

해설 세부 사항 관련 – 화자가 문자 메시지가 왔을 때 하고 있었다고 말한 일

화자가 초반부에 좀 더 일찍 전화하지 못해서 죄송하다(I'm sorry I didn't
call earlier)면서, 문자가 왔을 때 테니스 경기 중이었는데 당신의 폐점 시간이
지나고서야 봤다(I was in the middle of a tennis match when the text
arrived, and I didn't see it until after your closing time)고 했으므로 정
답은 (A)이다.

▸▸ **Paraphrasing** 담화의 **in the middle of a tennis match**
→ 정답의 **playing a sport**

Test 9

99

Look at the graphic. Which line includes information that the speaker would like to change?

(A) Line 2
(B) Line 3
(C) Line 4
(D) Line 5

시각 정보에 의하면, 어느 줄에 화자가 바꾸고 싶어 하는 정보가 있는가?

(A) 2번 줄
(B) 3번 줄
(C) 4번 줄
(D) 5번 줄

해설　시각 정보 연계 – 화자가 바꾸고 싶어하는 정보가 있는 줄

화자가 중반부에 제가 그날 예약 시간을 조금 늦춰야겠다(I'll need to move my appointment to a little later that day)고 했으므로 화자는 시간을 바꾸기를 원하고 있고, 문자 메시지에 따르면 시간 정보는 5번 줄에 나와 있으므로 정답은 (D)이다.

100

What does the speaker want to know about the salon?

(A) Whether its shampoos contain certain chemicals
(B) Whether it offers a product for purchase
(C) How much it charges for a hair treatment
(D) How long the effects of one of its services will last

화자는 미용실에 대해 무엇을 알기를 원하는가?

(A) 샴푸에 특정 화학 물질이 들어 있는지 여부
(B) 제품을 구매용으로 제공하는지 여부
(C) 헤어 트리트먼트에 청구하는 금액
(D) 서비스 중 하나의 효과가 지속되는 기간

어휘　contain ~이 들어 있다　certain 특정한　chemical 화학 물질　charge 청구하다　effect 효과　last 지속되다

해설　세부 사항 관련 – 화자가 미용실에 대해 알기를 원하는 것

화자가 후반부에 궁금한 게 있다(I was wondering)며 청자가 사용하는 샴푸를 판매하는지(do you sell the shampoo that you use?) 여부를 묻고 있으므로 정답은 (B)이다.

▸▸ **Paraphrasing**　담화의 **sell the shampoo**
→ 정답의 **offers a product for purchase**

TEST 10

1 (B)	**2** (A)	**3** (C)	**4** (C)	**5** (D)
6 (B)	**7** (C)	**8** (B)	**9** (B)	**10** (C)
11 (A)	**12** (B)	**13** (C)	**14** (A)	**15** (B)
16 (A)	**17** (C)	**18** (C)	**19** (A)	**20** (B)
21 (B)	**22** (A)	**23** (C)	**24** (B)	**25** (C)
26 (A)	**27** (A)	**28** (C)	**29** (B)	**30** (A)
31 (C)	**32** (D)	**33** (A)	**34** (B)	**35** (B)
36 (D)	**37** (C)	**38** (A)	**39** (B)	**40** (D)
41 (C)	**42** (B)	**43** (A)	**44** (D)	**45** (A)
46 (C)	**47** (C)	**48** (D)	**49** (B)	**50** (A)
51 (D)	**52** (A)	**53** (D)	**54** (B)	**55** (D)
56 (D)	**57** (A)	**58** (B)	**59** (C)	**60** (D)
61 (B)	**62** (B)	**63** (C)	**64** (A)	**65** (B)
66 (A)	**67** (B)	**68** (A)	**69** (C)	**70** (C)
71 (D)	**72** (B)	**73** (D)	**74** (C)	**75** (B)
76 (D)	**77** (B)	**78** (A)	**79** (B)	**80** (C)
81 (A)	**82** (D)	**83** (A)	**84** (C)	**85** (C)
86 (B)	**87** (D)	**88** (C)	**89** (A)	**90** (C)
91 (D)	**92** (B)	**93** (C)	**94** (A)	**95** (C)
96 (A)	**97** (B)	**98** (C)	**99** (D)	**100** (A)

PART 1

1　W-Am

(A) He's pulling a bottle from a bag.
(B) He's tying one of his shoes.
(C) He's jogging on a paved path.
(D) He's relaxing on a park bench.

(A) 남자는 가방에서 병을 꺼내고 있다.
(B) 남자는 신발 한 짝을 묶고 있다.
(C) 남자는 포장된 길에서 조깅을 하고 있다.
(D) 남자는 공원 벤치에서 쉬고 있다.

어휘　pull 꺼내다　tie 묶다　paved 포장된　path 길

해설　1인 등장 사진 – 인물의 동작 묘사

(A) 동사 오답. 남자가 가방에서 병을 꺼내고 있는(is pulling a bottle from a bag) 모습이 아니므로 오답.
(B) 정답. 남자가 신발 한 짝을 묶고 있는(is tying one of his shoes) 모습이므로 정답.
(C) 동사 오답. 남자가 포장된 길에서 조깅을 하고 있는(is jogging on a paved path) 모습이 아니므로 오답.
(D) 동사 오답. 남자가 공원 벤치에서 쉬고 있는(is relaxing on a park bench) 모습이 아니므로 오답.

2　M-Au

(A) She's standing in front of a bookcase.
(B) She's climbing a staircase in a library.
(C) She's carrying a stack of books.
(D) She's resting one arm on a counter.

(A) 여자는 책장 앞에 서 있다.
(B) 여자는 도서관에서 계단을 오르고 있다.
(C) 여자는 책더미를 나르고 있다.
(D) 여자는 카운터에 한쪽 팔을 얹고 있다.

어휘　bookcase 책장　climb 오르다　staircase 계단　stack 더미
　　　rest (어떤 것에) 기대다[받치다]

해설　1인 등장 사진 – 인물의 동작 묘사

(A) 정답. 여자가 책장 앞에 서 있는(is standing in front of a bookcase) 모습이므로 정답.
(B) 사진에 없는 명사를 이용한 오답. 사진에 계단(a staircase)의 모습이 보이지 않으므로 오답.
(C) 동사 오답. 여자가 책더미를 나르고 있는(is carrying a stack of books) 모습이 아니므로 오답.
(D) 사진에 없는 명사를 이용한 오답. 사진에 카운터(a counter)의 모습이 보이지 않으므로 오답.

3　W-Br

(A) They are having coffee inside a café.
(B) They are looking at the screen of a mobile device.
(C) One of the men is reaching for something on the table.
(D) One of the men is adjusting some sliding windows.

(A) 사람들은 카페 안에서 커피를 마시고 있다.
(B) 사람들은 모바일 장치의 화면을 보고 있다.
(C) 남자들 중 한 명이 탁자 위의 무언가에 손을 뻗고 있다.
(D) 남자들 중 한 명이 미닫이창을 조정하고 있다.

어휘　device 장치　reach for ~에 손을 뻗다　adjust 조정하다　sliding
　　　미끄러져 움직이는

해설　2인 이상 등장 사진 – 인물의 동작 묘사

(A) 동사 오답. 사람들이 카페 안에서 커피를 마시고 있는(are having coffee inside a café) 모습이 아니라 카페 밖에 있는(outside a café) 모습이므로 오답.
(B) 동사 오답. 사람들이 모바일 장치의 화면을 보고 있는(are looking at the screen of a mobile device) 모습이 아니므로 오답.

(C) 정답. 남자들 중 한 명이 탁자 위의 무언가에 손을 뻗고 있는(is reaching for something on the table) 모습이므로 정답.

(D) 동사 오답. 남자들 중 한 명이 미닫이창을 조정하고 있는(is adjusting some sliding windows) 모습이 아니므로 오답.

---

4 M-Cn

(A) Some people are posing for a photograph.
(B) A walking tour is taking place in a forest.
(C) A boat is being rowed down a river.
(D) Leaves are being removed from the water.

(A) 몇몇 사람들이 사진을 찍으려고 포즈를 취하고 있다.
(B) 도보 여행이 숲에서 행해지고 있다.
(C) 보트가 강을 따라 노 저어지고 있다.
(D) 나뭇잎들이 물에서 치워지고 있다.

어휘 pose 포즈를 취하다 take place 개최되다[일어나다] forest 숲
row (노로) 배를 젓다 remove 치우다

해설 혼합 사진 - 사람 또는 사물 묘사

(A) 동사 오답. 사진을 찍으려고 포즈를 취하고 있는(are posing for a photograph) 사람들의 모습이 보이지 않으므로 오답.

(B) 동사 오답. 도보 여행(a walking tour)이 숲에서 행해지고 있는(is taking place in a forest) 모습이 아니므로 오답.

(C) 정답. 보트(a boat)가 강을 따라 노 저어지고 있는(is being rowed down a river) 모습이므로 정답.

(D) 동사 오답. 나뭇잎들(leaves)이 물에서 치워지고 있는(are being removed from the water) 모습이 아니므로 오답.

---

5 M-Au

(A) Papers have been attached to a bulletin board.
(B) Chairs have been left in a conference room.
(C) A small trash bin is being emptied.
(D) Cords have been connected to a computer.

(A) 종이들이 게시판에 붙여져 있다.
(B) 의자들이 회의실에 놓여 있다.
(C) 작은 쓰레기통이 비워지고 있다.
(D) 코드가 컴퓨터에 연결되어 있다.

어휘 attach 붙이다 bulletin board 게시판 trash bin 쓰레기통
empty 비우다; 비어 있는 connect 연결하다

해설 배경 사진 - 실내 사물의 상태 묘사

(A) 동사 오답. 종이들(papers)이 게시판에 붙여져 있는(have been attached to a bulletin board) 모습이 아니므로 오답.

(B) 동사 오답. 의자들(chairs)이 회의실에 놓여 있는(have been left in a conference room) 모습이 아니므로 오답.

(C) 동사 오답. 작은 쓰레기통(a small trash bin)이 비워지고 있는(is being emptied) 모습이 아니므로 오답.

(D) 정답. 코드(cords)가 컴퓨터에 연결되어 있는(have been connected to a computer) 모습이므로 정답.

---

6 W-Am   고난도

(A) A plastic container holds a set of tools.
(B) A piece of pottery is being shaped.
(C) Some artwork is being displayed on walls.
(D) A woman is picking up an apron.

(A) 플라스틱 용기에 공구 세트가 들어 있다.
(B) 도자기가 빚어지고 있다.
(C) 예술 작품이 벽에 전시되어 있다.
(D) 여자가 앞치마를 주워 들고 있다.

어휘 container 용기 hold 수용하다[담다] pottery 도자기 shape
(어떤) 모양으로 빚다[만들다] artwork 예술 작품 display 전시하다
apron 앞치마

해설 혼합 사진 - 사람 또는 사물 묘사

(A) 사진에 없는 명사를 이용한 오답. 사진에 공구 세트(a set of tools)의 모습이 보이지 않으므로 오답.

(B) 정답. 도자기(a piece of pottery)가 빚어지고 있는(is being shaped) 모습이므로 정답.

(C) 동사 오답. 예술 작품(some artwork)이 벽에 전시되어 있는(is being displayed on walls) 모습이 아니므로 오답.

(D) 동사 오답. 여자가 앞치마를 주워 들고 있는(is picking up an apron) 모습이 아니므로 오답.

PART 2

7

M-Cn Who discovered the water leak?

W-Br (A) Our insurance covered most of it.

(B) No, I heard about it this morning.

(C) The tenant in Apartment 3A.

누가 물이 새는 것을 발견했나요?
(A) 우리 보험은 그 대부분을 보상했어요.
(B) 아니요, 오늘 아침에 들었어요.
(C) 3A 아파트의 입주민이요.

어휘 discover 발견하다 leak 누수 insurance 보험 cover 보장[보상]히디 tenant 세입자

해설 물이 새는 것을 발견한 사람을 묻는 Who 의문문
(A) 유사 발음 오답. 질문의 discovered와 부분적으로 발음이 유사한 covered를 이용한 오답.
(B) Yes/No 불가 오답. Who 의문문에는 Yes/No 응답이 불가능하므로 오답.
(C) 정답. 물이 새는 것을 발견한 사람을 묻는 질문에 3A 아파트의 입주민이라고 구체적으로 응답하고 있으므로 정답.

8 고난도

W-Am If we decide to hire you, when will you be able to start?
M-Cn (A) Excellent—I look forward to it.
(B) My current employer requires two weeks' notice.
(C) As long as we can agree on the contract terms.

만약 우리가 당신을 고용하기로 결정한다면, 언제 일을 시작할 수 있나요?
(A) 훌륭해요. 기대하겠습니다.
(B) 제 현재 고용주는 2주 전 통지를 요구합니다.
(C) 계약 조건에 합의할 수만 있다면요.

어휘 look forward to ~을 기대하다 current 현재의 require 요구하다 notice 통지 contract 계약 term 조건

해설 근무 시작 가능 시점을 묻는 When 의문문
(A) 질문과 상관없는 오답.
(B) 정답. 일을 시작할 수 있는 시점을 묻는 질문에 현재 고용주가 2주 전 통지를 요구한다며 최소 2주가 지나야 일을 시작할 수 있음을 우회적으로 나타내고 있으므로 정답.
(C) 연상 단어 오답. 질문의 hire에서 연상 가능한 contract를 이용한 오답.

9 고난도

M-Au How much space will we need for the new sofa?
W-Am (A) All employees will be allowed to use it.
(B) Its measurements are in the catalog.
(C) Wherever there's empty space.

새 소파를 위해 얼마나 많은 공간이 필요할까요?
(A) 전직원이 사용할 수 있게 될 겁니다.
(B) 치수가 카탈로그에 나와 있어요.
(C) 빈 공간이 있는 곳이면 어디든지요.

어휘 measurement 치수[크기]

해설 새 소파에 필요한 공간의 크기를 묻는 How much 의문문
(A) 질문과 상관없는 오답.
(B) 정답. 새 소파를 위해 얼마나 많은 공간이 필요한지 묻는 질문에 치수가 카탈로그에 나와 있다며 필요한 정보가 있는 곳을 알려주고 있으므로 정답.
(C) 단어 반복 오답. 질문의 space를 반복 이용한 오답.

10

M-Au Can you show me how to use the library's scanner?
W-Br (A) Yes, just a few minutes ago.
(B) It creates digital images of documents.
(C) Did you try reading the posted instructions?

도서관 스캐너를 어떻게 사용하는지 좀 알려주시겠어요?
(A) 네, 바로 몇 분 전에요.
(B) 그것은 문서의 디지털 이미지를 생성합니다.
(C) 게시된 설명문을 읽어보셨나요?

어휘 post 게시하다 instruction 설명문

해설 부탁/요청의 의문문
(A) 질문과 상관없는 오답.
(B) 연상 단어 오답. 질문의 scanner에서 연상 가능한 digital images를 이용한 오답.
(C) 정답. 도서관 스캐너를 어떻게 사용하는지 알려달라고 부탁하는 질문에 게시된 설명문을 읽어봤는지 되물으며 사용법을 익힐 수 있는 방법을 우회적으로 알려주고 있으므로 정답.

11

M-Cn Why do I have to provide a note from my doctor?
W-Br (A) It's company policy.
(B) Once you return to work.
(C) Oh, are you feeling unwell?

왜 주치의로부터 받은 기록을 제공해야 합니까?
(A) 회사 방침입니다.
(B) 일단 직장에 복귀하면요.
(C) 아, 몸이 안 좋으세요?

어휘 note 메모, 기록 policy 방침 unwell 몸이 편치 않은

해설 주치의로부터 받은 메모를 제공해야 하는 이유를 묻는 Why 의문문
(A) 정답. 주치의로부터 받은 메모를 제공해야 하는 이유를 묻는 질문에 회사 방침이라고 이유를 제시하고 있으므로 정답.
(B) 질문과 상관없는 오답. When 의문문에 대한 응답이므로 오답.
(C) 연상 단어 오답. 질문의 doctor에서 연상 가능한 unwell을 이용한 오답.

12 고난도

W-Am There's a package for you at Reception.
M-Au (A) I'm sorry, but I won't have time to attend.
(B) That must be my new business cards.
(C) Melissa is going to the post office later.

프런트에 당신에게 온 소포가 있습니다.
(A) 죄송하지만, 참석할 시간이 없을 겁니다.
(B) 제 새 명함일 겁니다.
(C) 멜리사가 나중에 우체국에 갈 겁니다.

어휘 package 소포 reception 접수처[프런트] business card 명함

해설 정보 전달의 평서문

(A) 연상 단어 오답. 질문의 reception이 '환영회'로 쓰였을 경우 연상 가능한 attend를 이용한 오답.

(B) 정답. 프런트에 소포가 와 있다는 평서문에 자신의 새 명함일 거라며 관련 사항을 추측하고 있으므로 정답.

(C) 연상 단어 오답. 질문의 package에서 연상 가능한 post office를 이용한 오답.

13

M-Cn What are these buttons on the steering wheel for?

W-Am (A) The premium model is two thousand dollars more.

(B) I often drive on mountain roads.

(C) Controlling the car's audio system.

자동차 핸들의 이 버튼들은 뭘 위한 거죠?
(A) 고급 사양은 2천 달러 더 비쌉니다.
(B) 저는 종종 산길을 운전합니다.
(C) 차의 오디오 시스템 조작이요.

어휘 steering wheel (자동차의) 핸들 premium 고급의

해설 자동차 핸들 버튼의 용도를 묻는 What 의문문

(A) 질문과 상관없는 오답.

(B) 연상 단어 오답. 질문의 steering wheel에서 연상 가능한 drive를 이용한 오답.

(C) 정답. 자동차 핸들의 버튼들이 무엇을 위한 것인지 묻는 질문에 차의 오디오 시스템을 조작하는 것이라고 구체적으로 응답하고 있으므로 정답.

14　고난도

W-Br Is Lewis Hardware a chain store?

M-Au (A) I'm only aware of the Greenley location.

(B) Most hardware stores sell chains.

(C) Monday through Saturday.

루이스 철물점은 체인점입니까?
(A) 저는 그린리 지점만 알고 있어요.
(B) 대부분의 철물점은 사슬을 팔아요.
(C) 월요일부터 토요일까지요.

어휘 chain store 체인점　aware 아는　location 장소　hardware store 철물점　chain 사슬

해설 루이스 철물점이 체인점인지 여부를 묻는 Be동사 의문문

(A) 정답. 루이스 철물점이 체인점인지 여부를 묻는 질문에 자신은 그린리 지점만 알고 있다며 확실한 답을 알지 못함을 우회적으로 응답하고 있으므로 정답.

(B) 단어 반복 오답. 질문의 hardware를 반복 이용한 오답.

(C) 질문과 상관없는 오답. When 의문문에 대한 응답이므로 오답.

15　고난도

W-Br Where did this box of donuts come from?

M-Cn (A) Brumfield Bakery makes great donuts.

(B) There was a meeting in here earlier.

(C) I like the plain ones best.

이 도넛 상자는 어디서 왔죠?
(A) 브룸필드 베이커리는 훌륭한 도넛을 만들어요.
(B) 아까 여기에서 회의가 있었어요.
(C) 저는 오리지널이 가장 좋아요.

어휘 plain 있는 그대로의, (맛이) 담백한

해설 도넛 상자의 출처를 묻는 Where 의문문

(A) 단어 반복 오답. 질문의 donuts를 반복 이용한 오답.

(B) 정답. 도넛 상자가 어디서 왔는지 묻는 질문에 아까 여기에서 회의가 있었다고 우회적으로 알려주고 있으므로 정답.

(C) 연상 단어 오답. 질문의 donuts에서 연상 가능한 plain을 이용한 오답.

16

M-Au Is your jacket the black one or the tan one?

M-Cn (A) I didn't bring a jacket.

(B) On the coat rack is fine.

(C) Do you have the same style in red?

당신의 재킷은 검정색입니까, 아니면 황갈색입니까?
(A) 저는 재킷을 가져오지 않았어요.
(B) 외투 걸이에 두면 돼요.
(C) 같은 스타일로 빨간색이 있나요?

어휘 tan 황갈색　coat rack 외투 걸이

해설 재킷이 무슨 색인지 묻는 선택의문문

(A) 정답. 재킷이 무슨 색인지 묻는 선택의문문에서 자신은 재킷을 가져오지 않았다며 둘 다 자신의 것이 아님을 우회적으로 밝히고 있으므로 정답.

(B) 질문과 상관없는 오답. Where 의문문에 대한 응답이므로 오답.

(C) 연상 단어 오답. 질문의 jacket에서 연상 가능한 style을 이용한 오답.

17

W-Am You got my e-mail about the project delay, right?

M-Au (A) Let's call the projector technician.

(B) Sure—here's my e-mail address.

(C) Such a frustrating situation.

프로젝트 지연에 대한 제 이메일을 받으셨죠, 그렇죠?
(A) 프로젝터 기술자를 부릅시다.
(B) 물론이죠. 여기 제 이메일 주소요.
(C) 정말 답답한 상황이에요.

어휘 delay 지연　technician 기술자　such 너무나 ~한　frustrating 불만스러운

해설 이메일을 받았는지 여부를 확인하는 부가의문문

(A) 파생어 오답. 질문의 project와 파생어 관계인 projector를 이용한 오답.

(B) 단어 반복 오답. 질문의 e-mail을 반복 이용한 오답.

(C) 정답. 프로젝트 지연에 대한 자신의 이메일을 받았는지 여부를 확인하는 질문에 정말 답답한 상황이라며 이메일의 내용을 확인했음을 우회적으로 나타내고 있으므로 정답.

18

W-Br When did you last check our social media page?

W-Am (A) Online businesses don't usually take checks.

(B) A few inquiries from customers.

(C) Nick has taken over that responsibility.

언제 마지막으로 우리 소셜 미디어 페이지를 확인하셨나요?

(A) 온라인 업체들은 보통 수표를 받지 않습니다.

(B) 고객들로부터 받은 몇 가지 문의요.

(C) 닉이 그 임무를 넘겨받았습니다.

어휘 last 마지막으로 check 확인하다; 수표 inquiry 문의 take over 넘겨받다 responsibility 임무, 책임

해설 마지막으로 소셜 미디어 페이지를 확인한 시점을 묻는 When 의문문

(A) 단어 반복 오답. 질문의 check를 반복 이용한 오답.

(B) 질문과 상관없는 오답. What 의문문에 대한 응답이므로 오답.

(C) 정답. 마지막으로 우리의 소셜 미디어 페이지를 확인한 시점을 묻는 질문에 닉이 그 임무를 넘겨받았다며 자신은 더 이상 관련 업무를 하지 않는다는 것을 우회적으로 밝히고 있으므로 정답.

19

M-Cn Has the afternoon session on management started?

W-Br (A) It's not even one-fifteen yet.

(B) Thanks for letting me know!

(C) Industry trends, I think.

경영에 관한 오후 회의가 시작했나요?

(A) 아직 1시 15분도 안 됐어요.

(B) 알려주셔서 고맙습니다!

(C) 업계 동향인 것 같아요.

어휘 session (특정 활동을 위한) 시간, 회기[회의] management 경영, 관리 industry 산업

해설 경영에 관한 오후 회의가 시작했는지 여부를 묻는 조동사(Has) 의문문

(A) 정답. 경영에 관한 오후 회의가 시작했는지 묻는 질문에 아직 1시 15분도 안 됐다며 시작하지 않았음을 우회적으로 알려주고 있으므로 정답.

(B) 질문과 상관없는 오답.

(C) 질문과 상관없는 오답. What 의문문에 대한 응답이므로 오답.

20

W-Am Let's send everyone home while the labeling machine is being repaired.

M-Cn (A) OK—I'll buy some additional envelopes.

(B) We'll need them to work overtime tomorrow.

(C) It's not attaching the labels correctly.

상표 부착 기계가 수리되는 동안 전원 귀가시킵시다.

(A) 좋아요. 전 봉투를 몇 장 더 살게요.

(B) 그들은 내일 초과 근무를 해야 할 겁니다.

(C) 상표를 제대로 부착하지 못하고 있어요.

어휘 label 상표를 붙이다; 상표 repair 수리하다 additional 추가의 envelope 봉투 overtime 초과 근무, 야근 attach 붙이다 correctly 바르게

해설 제안/권유의 평서문

(A) 평서문과 상관없는 오답.

(B) 정답. 상표 부착 기계가 수리되는 동안 전원 귀가시키자는 제안에 그들은 내일 초과 근무를 해야 할 것이라며 제안대로 하는 경우 발생할 수 있는 결과를 알려주고 있으므로 정답.

(C) 파생어 오답. 평서문의 labeling과 파생어 관계인 labels를 이용한 오답.

21

M-Au Which platform is our train leaving from?

W-Am (A) He's a personal trainer.

(B) Just follow me this way.

(C) That's why we'd better hurry.

우리 기차는 어느 플랫폼에서 출발합니까?

(A) 그는 개인 트레이너예요.

(B) 이쪽으로 저를 따라오시기만 해요.

(C) 그러니 서두르는 게 좋겠어요.

어휘 had better ~하는 것이 좋다

해설 기차가 출발하는 플랫폼을 묻는 Which 의문문

(A) 유사 발음 오답. 질문의 train과 부분적으로 발음이 유사한 trainer를 이용한 오답.

(B) 정답. 기차가 어느 플랫폼에서 출발하는지 묻는 질문에 따라오라며 직접 안내하겠다는 의사를 우회적으로 밝히고 있으므로 정답.

(C) 연상 단어 오답. 질문의 leaving에서 연상 가능한 hurry를 이용한 오답.

22

W-Br Who gave Isabelle that bouquet of flowers?

M-Au (A) Her team loves to celebrate work anniversaries.

(B) You can set them on the table for now.

(C) There was some extra flour in the kitchen.

누가 이사벨에게 그 꽃다발을 주었나요?

(A) 그녀의 팀은 근무 기념일을 축하하는 것을 좋아해요.

(B) 우선 탁자 위에 올려놓으면 돼요.

(C) 부엌에 여분의 밀가루가 있었어요.

어휘 bouquet 꽃다발 celebrate 축하하다 anniversary 기념일 for now 우선 flour 밀가루

해설 이사벨에게 꽃다발을 준 사람을 묻는 Who 의문문

(A) 정답. 이사벨에게 꽃다발을 준 사람을 묻는 질문에 그녀의 팀은 근무 기념일을 축하하는 것을 좋아한다며 꽃을 준 것이 그녀의 팀임을 우회적으로 밝히고 있으므로 정답.

(B) 질문과 상관없는 오답.

(C) 유사 발음 오답. 질문의 flowers와 부분적으로 발음이 유사한 flour를 이용한 오답.

23

W-Br Where should I put the chart comparing our sales with competitors'?

M-Cn (A) Only for the northeastern market.
(B) They're serious competition, actually.
(C) Make a separate slide.

우리 매출을 경쟁사 매출과 비교한 차트를 어디에 넣어야 할까요?
(A) 북동부 시장에만 해당됩니다.
(B) 그들은 사실 만만찮은 경쟁 상대예요.
(C) 별도의 슬라이드를 만드세요.

어휘 competitor 경쟁사 northeastern 북동부의 competition 경쟁, 경쟁 상대 separate 별개의

해설 차트를 삽입할 위치를 묻는 Where 의문문
(A) 연상 단어 오답. 질문의 sales에서 연상 가능한 market을 이용한 오답.
(B) 파생어 오답. 질문의 competitors와 파생어 관계인 competition을 이용한 오답.
(C) 정답. 우리 매출을 경쟁사 매출과 비교한 차트를 어디에 넣어야 할지 묻는 질문에 별도의 슬라이드를 만들 것을 구체적으로 지시하고 있으므로 정답.

24

W-Am It may be time for us to get a staff accountant.

M-Au (A) Tuesday at nine A.M.
(B) Can we afford one?
(C) We can place orders without an account.

회계사 직원을 구해야 할 때인지도 모르겠습니다.
(A) 화요일 오전 9시요.
(B) 우리가 그럴 형편이 될까요?
(C) 계정 없이 주문할 수 있습니다.

어휘 accountant 회계사 afford 형편[여유]이 되다 account 계정, 계좌

해설 제안/권유의 평서문
(A) 연상 단어 오답. 평서문의 time에서 연상 가능한 nine A.M.을 이용한 오답.
(B) 정답. 회계사 직원을 구해야 할 때인지도 모르겠다는 제안에 대해 우리가 그럴 형편이 될지 되물으며 제안에 대해 회의적임을 우회적으로 나타내고 있으므로 정답.
(C) 파생어 오답. 평서문의 accountant와 파생어 관계인 account를 이용한 오답.

25

M-Cn Didn't you want to share a pizza?

W-Am (A) This restaurant is famous online.
(B) Because it's too big for one person.
(C) That was before I saw they have lasagna.

피자를 나눠 먹고 싶어 하지 않았나요?
(A) 이 식당은 온라인에서 유명해요.
(B) 1인분으로는 너무 크니까요.
(C) 그건 라자냐가 있는 걸 보기 전이었어요.

해설 피자를 나눠 먹고 싶어 하지 않았는지 여부를 확인하는 부정의문문
(A) 연상 단어 오답. 질문의 pizza에서 연상 가능한 restaurant을 이용한 오답.
(B) 질문과 상관없는 오답. Why 의문문에 대한 응답이므로 오답.
(C) 정답. 피자를 나눠 먹고 싶어 하지 않았는지 묻는 질문에 그건 라자냐가 있는 걸 보기 전이었다며 더 이상 원치 않음을 우회적으로 밝히고 있으므로 정답.

26

W-Br Why was my expense reimbursement request denied?

M-Au (A) Mine have always been approved.
(B) After the finance director reviewed it.
(C) No, it wasn't that expensive.

왜 제 경비 환급 신청이 반려되었나요?
(A) 제 것은 항상 승인되었어요.
(B) 재무 이사님이 검토하신 후에요.
(C) 아니요, 그렇게 비싸진 않았어요.

어휘 expense 경비 reimbursement 환급 deny 거부하다 approve 승인하다 finance 재무 director 이사

해설 신청이 반려된 이유를 묻는 Why 의문문
(A) 정답. 경비 환급 신청이 반려된 이유를 묻는 질문에 자신의 것은 항상 승인이 되었다며 이유를 알지 못함을 우회적으로 나타내고 있으므로 정답.
(B) 질문과 상관없는 오답. When 의문문에 대한 응답이므로 오답.
(C) Yes/No 불가 오답. Why 의문문에는 Yes/No 응답이 불가능하므로 오답.

27

W-Br Those bookshelves aren't being moved to the new office, are they?

M-Cn (A) Don't worry—that truck is going to the used furniture store.
(B) A replacement set of shelves made of dark wood.
(C) Dave and John are, but they'll take the subway there.

저 책꽂이들은 새 사무실로 옮겨지지 않을 거죠, 그렇죠?
(A) 걱정 마세요. 저 트럭은 중고 가구점으로 갈 거예요.
(B) 짙은 색 나무로 만들어진 교체 선반 세트예요.
(C) 데이브와 존이 있지만, 그들은 거기서 지하철을 탈 거예요.

어휘 bookshelves bookshelf(책꽂이)의 복수 used 중고의 replacement 교체

해설 책꽂이가 새 사무실로 옮겨지지 여부를 확인하는 부가의문문
(A) 정답. 책꽂이들이 새 사무실로 옮겨지지 여부를 확인하는 질문에 트럭이 중고 가구점으로 갈 것이라며 새 사무실로 운반되지 않음을 우회적으로 밝히고 있으므로 정답.
(B) 파생어 오답. 질문의 bookshelves와 파생어 관계인 shelves를 이용한 오답.
(C) 질문과 상관없는 오답.

28 [고난도]

M-Au Should the next team-building event be a day hike or a bike ride?

W-Am (A) To improve relationships among team members.

(B) A weekend afternoon would be better.

(C) Not everyone likes outdoor activities.

다음 팀워크 강화 행사는 당일 하이킹으로 할까요, 자전거 타기로 할까요?
(A) 팀원들 간의 관계를 개선하기 위해서요.
(B) 주말 오후가 좋겠어요.
(C) 모두가 야외 활동을 좋아하는 건 아니에요.

어휘 team-building 팀워크 구축 hike 도보 여행

해설 팀워크 강화 행사에서 할 활동에 대해 묻는 선택의문문
(A) 단어 반복 오답. 질문의 team을 반복 이용한 오답.
(B) 질문과 상관없는 오답. When 의문문에 대한 응답이므로 오답.
(C) 정답. 팀워크 강화 행사에서 할 활동을 묻는 선택의문문에서 모두가 야외 활동을 좋아하는 건 아니라며 두 선택안에 대한 부정적인 의사를 우회적으로 밝히고 있으므로 정답.

29

M-Cn Do you work at one of the businesses in this building?

W-Br (A) The travel agency is closing soon.

(B) Here's my identification badge.

(C) Some discounts at the first-floor café.

이 건물의 업체들 중 한 곳에서 일하세요?
(A) 여행사는 곧 문을 닫습니다.
(B) 여기 제 신분증 배지입니다.
(C) 1층 카페 할인이요.

어휘 identification 신분증

해설 해당 건물의 입주 업체에서 일하는지 여부를 묻는 조동사(Do) 의문문
(A) 질문과 상관없는 오답.
(B) 정답. 해당 건물의 업체들 중 한 곳에서 일하는지 묻는 질문에 신분증을 제시하며 입주 업체에서 근무하고 있음을 우회적으로 밝히고 있으므로 정답.
(C) 연상 단어 오답. 질문의 building에서 연상 가능한 first-floor를 이용한 오답.

30 [고난도]

W-Am Aren't we supposed to be paid for participating in this focus group?

M-Cn (A) The money will be sent electronically.

(B) Testing a video game for Hanjoon Entertainment.

(C) Well, the participants meet all the qualifications.

이 포커스 그룹에 참여하는 데 대해 돈을 받기로 되어 있지 않나요?
(A) 돈은 전자상으로 보내질 것입니다.
(B) 한준 엔터테인먼트의 비디오 게임을 테스트하는 거요.
(C) 참가자들은 모든 자격 요건에 충족됩니다.

어휘 be supposed to ~하기로 되어 있다 electronically 전자상으로 meet 충족시키다 qualification 자격, 조건

해설 포커스 그룹 참여에 대한 보수 지급 여부를 확인하는 부정의문문
(A) 정답. 포커스 그룹에 참여하는 데 대해 돈을 받기로 되어 있는지 묻는 질문에 네(Yes)를 생략한 채 돈은 온라인으로 송금될 것이라며 보수가 지급될 것임을 알려주고 있으므로 정답.
(B) 질문과 상관없는 오답. What 의문문에 대한 응답이므로 오답.
(C) 파생어 오답. 질문의 participating과 파생어 관계인 participants를 이용한 오답.

31 [고난도]

M-Au We offer reduced-price admission for university students.

W-Br (A) But your Web site says you do.

(B) Some of the museums downtown.

(C) I graduated last year, unfortunately.

우리는 대학생들을 위해 할인 가격 입장을 제공합니다.
(A) 하지만 웹사이트에는 그렇게 한다고 나와 있어요.
(B) 시내에 있는 일부 박물관들이요.
(C) 전 아쉽게도 작년에 졸업했습니다.

어휘 reduced 할인된 admission 입장

해설 정보 전달의 평서문
(A) 평서문과 상관없는 오답. 제공하지 않는다고 할 때 할 수 있는 응답이므로 오답.
(B) 연상 단어 오답. 평서문의 admission에서 연상 가능한 museums를 이용한 오답.
(C) 정답. 대학생들을 위해 할인 가격 입장을 제공한다는 평서문에 자신은 아쉽게도 작년에 졸업했다며 할인을 받을 자격이 되지 않는다는 것을 우회적으로 알려주고 있으므로 정답.

PART 3

32-34

W-Am Oh, hello, Mr. Quinn. It's good to see you again. How are your new glasses working out?

M-Cn The prescription lenses are great, but it turns out that the frames are a little tight. That's why I'm here. **32 Could you widen these parts that go over my ears?**

W-Am Absolutely. It will take just a few minutes. **33 Why don't you have a seat in our waiting area? 33, 34 We just got some new magazines.**

M-Cn **34 Well, I can't read comfortably without my glasses.** I'll just listen to music on my phone.

여	안녕하십니까, 퀸 씨. 다시 뵙게 되어 반갑습니다. 새 안경은 잘 맞으세요?
남	처방 렌즈는 훌륭한데, 테가 좀 꽉 조이는 것 같아요. 그래서 여기 온 거예요. 귀 위로 넘어가는 이 부분을 넓혀주실 수 있을까요?
여	당연하죠. 단 몇 분이면 될 겁니다. 우리 대기실에 앉아 계시는 게 어떠세요? 막 새 잡지를 몇 권 샀어요.
남	음, 안경 없이는 편하게 읽지 못해요. 그냥 제 핸드폰으로 음악이나 들을게요.

어휘	work out 잘 풀리다, 좋게 진행되다　prescription 처방 turn out 나타나다, 드러나다　frame 틀, 뼈대　tight 꽉 조이는　widen 넓히다

32

What is the purpose of the man's visit?

(A) To inquire about a bill
(B) To pick up an order
(C) To renew a prescription
(D) To request a fit adjustment

남자가 방문한 목적은 무엇인가?

(A) 청구서에 대해 문의하려고
(B) 주문품을 가져가려고
(C) 처방전을 갱신하려고
(D) **맞음새 조정을 요청하려고**

어휘　inquire 문의하다　bill 청구서　renew 갱신하다　prescription 처방전　adjustment 조정

해설　세부 사항 관련 - 남자의 방문 목적

남자가 첫 대사에서 귀 위로 넘어가는 이 부분을 넓혀줄 수 있는지(Could you widen these parts that go over my ears?) 묻고 있는 것으로 보아 정답은 (D)이다.

33

What does the woman say is available?

(A) Some publications
(B) Some beverages
(C) Internet access
(D) Charging stations

여자는 무엇이 이용 가능하다고 말하는가?

(A) **간행물**
(B) 음료
(C) 인터넷 접속
(D) 충전소

해설　세부 사항 관련 - 여자가 이용 가능하다고 말하는 것

여자가 두 번째 대사에서 우리 대기실에 앉아 계시는 게 어떨지(Why don't you have a seat in our waiting area?) 물었고, 막 새 잡지를 몇 권 샀다 (We just got some new magazines)며 대기실에 앉아 새로 산 잡지를 읽을 것을 권하고 있으므로 정답은 (A)이다.

▸▸ **Paraphrasing**　대화의 magazines → 정답의 publications

34

What problem does the man mention?

(A) He did not bring a required item.
(B) He is unable to use an amenity.
(C) He can only wait a short duration.
(D) His contact information has changed.

남자는 무슨 문제를 언급하는가?

(A) 필요한 물품을 가져오지 않았다.
(B) **서비스 용품을 이용할 수 없다.**
(C) 짧은 기간만 기다릴 수 있다.
(D) 연락처가 바뀌었다.

어휘　amenity 편의시설, 서비스 용품　duration 기간

해설　세부 사항 관련 - 남자가 언급한 문제

여자가 두 번째 대사에서 막 새 잡지를 몇 권 샀다(We just got some new magazines)며 잡지를 읽으라고 권하자, 남자가 안경 없이는 편하게 읽지 못한 다(I can't read comfortably without my glasses)고 했으므로 정답은 (B) 이다.

▸▸ **Paraphrasing**　대화의 magazines → 정답의 an amenity

35-37

W-Br	Good afternoon, Mr. Morgan. ³⁵ **This is Chelsea Vasquez calling from Habernathy Credit Union. I've got some good news about your request for a business loan. You've been approved.**
M-Cn	That's fantastic! ³⁶ **Our community will really benefit from the bicycle shop I'm going to open.** I know there are a lot of people who will be happy to buy their bikes locally.
W-Br	We agree, Mr. Morgan. ³⁷ **Now, there are a few documents we need to go over together before we can release the money. When can you come into the office?**
M-Cn	I'm free tomorrow morning.

여	좋은 오후입니다, 모건 씨. 해버나시 신용 조합에서 전화드리는 첼시 바스케스입니다. 사업 대출을 신청하신 건에 대해 좋은 소식이 있습니다. 승인을 받으셨네요.
남	정말 잘됐네요! 우리 주민들도 제가 개업하려는 자전거 가게로부터 확실히 혜택을 받을 거예요. 많은 사람들이 자전거를 가까이에서 구입하게 되어 기쁠 것이라는 걸 알아요.
여	동의합니다, 모건 씨. 일단, 돈을 보내드리기 전에 함께 검토해야 할 서류가 몇 가지 있어요. 언제 사무실에 오실 수 있을까요?
남	내일 아침에 시간이 됩니다.

어휘	loan 대출　approve 승인하다　benefit 득을 보다　go over 검토하다　release 풀다, 방출하다

35

Where does the woman work?

(A) At a city department
(B) At a financial institution
(C) At a news outlet
(D) At a law office

여자는 어디에서 일하는가?

(A) 시 부서
(B) 금융 기관
(C) 뉴스 매체
(D) 법률 사무소

해설 전체 내용 관련 – 여자의 근무지

여자가 첫 대사에서 해버나시 신용 조합에서 전화드리는 첼시 바스케스(This is Chelsea Vasquez calling from Habernathy Credit Union)라고 자신을 소개했고, 사업 대출을 신청하신 건에 대해 좋은 소식이 있다(I've got some good news about your request for a business loan)면서 승인을 받으셨다(You've been approved)고 한 것으로 보아 여자는 금융 기관에서 일하고 있음을 알 수 있다. 따라서 정답은 (B)이다.

36

What does the man plan to do?

(A) Donate money to a charity
(B) Bid for a government contract
(C) Organize a community activity
(D) Launch a retail business

남자는 무엇을 할 계획인가?

(A) 자선 단체에 기부
(B) 정부 계약 입찰
(C) 지역 사회 활동 조직
(D) 소매 창업

어휘 donate 기부하다 charity 자선 단체 bid 입찰하다 organize 조직하다 launch 시작하다 retail 소매

해설 세부 사항 관련 – 남자가 계획한 일

남자가 첫 대사에서 우리 주민들도 제가 개업하려는 자전거 가게로부터 확실히 혜택을 받을 것(Our community will really benefit from the bicycle shop I'm going to open)이라고 했으므로 정답은 (D)이다.

▸▸ **Paraphrasing** 대화의 **open the bicycle shop**
→ 정답의 **launch a retail business**

37

Why does the woman ask the man to visit her office?

(A) To discuss an idea
(B) To submit a payment
(C) To review some paperwork
(D) To meet a manager

여자는 왜 남자에게 사무실을 방문해달라고 요청하는가?

(A) 아이디어를 논의하려고
(B) 지급을 제출하려고
(C) 서류를 검토하려고
(D) 관리자를 만나려고

어휘 discuss 논의하다 submit 제출하다 payment 지급[지불] review 검토하다

해설 세부 사항 관련 – 여자가 남자에게 사무실 방문을 요청한 이유

여자가 두 번째 대사에서 돈을 보내기 전에 함께 검토해야 할 서류가 몇 가지 있다(there are a few documents we need to go over together before we can release the money)면서, 언제 사무실에 올 수 있는지(When can you come into the office?)를 묻고 있으므로 정답은 (C)이다.

▸▸ **Paraphrasing** 대화의 **go over** → 정답의 **review**

38-40

W-Br	Hi, Lorenzo. It's good to see you. Are you enjoying the conference so far?
M-Au	Yes, very much. **38 Before lunch, I attended a session on using the advanced functions of the Medina Laboratory Automation System.** That's the system my lab has.
W-Br	**39 Oh, that must have been very useful, then.**
M-Au	**39 Yes, I took detailed notes.** I can't wait to go back and tell my lab manager about it. Anyway, how has the conference been for you?
W-Br	**40 Fine, but—I'm a bit nervous for this afternoon. I'm going to present on my current research.**
M-Au	Right, I saw that in the program. Good luck! I'm sure you'll do fine.

여	안녕하세요, 로렌조. 만나서 반가워요. 지금까지 컨퍼런스는 재미있으시고요?
남	네, 아주 많이요. 점심 식사 전에 메디나 실험실 자동화 시스템의 고급 기능 사용에 관한 회의에 참석했어요. 저희 연구실이 갖고 있는 시스템이거든요.
여	아, 그렇다면 아주 유용했겠네요.
남	네, 상세히 메모했어요. 빨리 돌아가서 저희 연구실 관리자에게 그것에 대해 이야기하고 싶어요. 그나저나, 회의는 어떠셨어요?
여	괜찮긴 한데, 오늘 오후 일로 좀 긴장되네요. 제가 지금 하고 있는 연구에 대해 발표를 하거든요.
남	그러네요, 프로그램에서 봤어요. 행운을 빌어요! 잘 하시리라 믿어요.

어휘 session (특정 활동을 위한) 시간, 회의 advanced 고급의 function 기능 automation 자동화 lab 실험실 detailed 상세한 nervous 긴장되는 present 발표하다 current 현재의

38

According to the man, what took place in the morning?

(A) A training workshop
(B) A laboratory meeting
(C) A university class
(D) An inventory check

남자에 따르면, 아침에 무슨 일이 일어났는가?

(A) 교육 워크숍
(B) 실험실 회의
(C) 대학 수업
(D) 재고 확인

해설 세부 사항 관련 – 남자가 아침에 일어났다고 말하는 일

남자가 첫 대사에서 점심식사 전에 메디나 실험실 자동화 시스템의 고급 기능 사용에 관한 회의에 참석했다(Before lunch, I attended a session on using the advanced functions of the Medina Laboratory Automation System)고 했으므로 정답은 (A)이다.

39

고난도

Why does the man say, "I took detailed notes"?

(A) To explain why he could not be contacted
(B) To emphasize the value of some information
(C) To show willingness to share a resource with the woman
(D) To decline the woman's offer of assistance

남자가 "상세히 메모했어요"라고 말하는 이유는 무엇인가?

(A) 연락이 되지 않았던 이유를 설명하려고
(B) 어떤 정보의 가치를 강조하려고
(C) 여자와 정보를 공유하고자 하는 의지를 보여주려고
(D) 여자의 지원 제의를 거절하려고

어휘 emphasize 강조하다 value 가치 willingness 기꺼이 하는 마음 resource 자원 decline 거절하다 assistance 지원, 도움

해설 화자의 의도 파악 – 상세히 메모했다는 말의 의도

앞에서 여자가 아주 유용했겠다(that must have been very useful)라고 한데 대해 남자가 네(Yes)라고 대답하며 인용문을 언급했으므로, 꼼꼼히 기록할 만큼 유용한 정보였다는 것을 강조하려는 의도로 한 말임을 알 수 있다. 따라서 정답은 (B)이다.

40

What is the woman nervous about?

(A) Leading a research project
(B) Interviewing for a job opening
(C) Learning the result of an application
(D) Giving a conference presentation

여자는 무엇에 대해 긴장하는가?

(A) 연구 프로젝트 주도
(B) 일자리 면접
(C) 지원 결과 알기
(D) 컨퍼런스 발표

어휘 application 지원 presentation 발표

해설 세부 사항 관련 – 여자가 긴장하는 것

여자가 마지막 대사에서 오늘 오후 일로 좀 긴장된다(I'm a bit nervous for this afternoon)면서, 자신의 지금 하고 있는 연구에 대해 발표를 할 것(I'm going to present on my current research)이라고 했으므로 정답은 (D)이다.

> ▸▸ **Paraphrasing** 대화의 **present**
> → 정답의 **giving a ~ presentation**

41-43 3인 대화

W-Am	Hi. You're the site supervisor, right? **41We're the crew from Soto Contractors, and we're here to put in the countertops.**
M-Au	Uh, hi... I think there's been a mistake. You're not scheduled to work today.
W-Am	Really? This is when the project manager told us to come.
M-Au	Well, luckily he's on site today. **42Eric,** could you come over here? This woman is from Soto Contractors.
M-Cn	Uh-oh—didn't you get my voice mail? **42The kitchen blueprints were changed suddenly last week.**
W-Am	Oh, no, I missed that. **43Does that mean you're canceling our contract?**
M-Cn	**43No, the material is still granite, so we'll need your specialized skills.** But now we're behind schedule. Could you come in next Monday?
W-Am	I'll check and let you know.

여	안녕하세요. 현장 감독관 맞으시죠? 저희는 소토 컨트랙터에서 온 작업반인데 작업대를 설치하려고 여기 왔습니다.
남1	어, 안녕하세요… 뭔가 착오가 있었던 것 같네요. 오늘 일하기로 일정이 잡혀 있지 않아요.
여	정말요? 지금이 프로젝트 담당자께서 우리에게 오라고 말씀하신 때인데요.
남1	다행히 그분이 오늘 현장에 계시네요. 에릭, 이쪽으로 와주시겠어요? 이 여자분은 소토 컨트랙터에서 오셨어요.
남2	오, 이런. 제 음성 메일 못 받았나요? 지난주에 부엌 설계도가 갑자기 바뀌었어요.
여	아, 이런, 그걸 놓쳤네요. 그럼 저희 계약을 취소하신다는 뜻인가요?
남2	아니요, 자재는 여전히 화강암이라서 당신의 전문적인 기술이 필요할 거예요. 하지만 지금 우리는 예정보다 늦어지고 있네요. 다음 주 월요일에 오시겠어요?
여	확인해서 알려드릴게요.

어휘 site 현장, 장소 supervisor 감독관 crew (함께 일하는) 팀, 반 countertop 작업대 blueprint 설계도 miss 놓치다 material 자재 granite 화강암 specialized 전문적인

41

고난도

What has the woman's crew come to do?

(A) Connect power wiring
(B) Modify an outdoor space
(C) Install some interior surfaces
(D) Set up temperature control systems

여자의 작업반은 무엇을 하러 왔는가?

(A) 전원 배선 연결
(B) 야외 공간 변경
(C) 내부 작업대 설치
(D) 온도 제어 시스템 설정

어휘 wiring 배선 modify 변경하다 install 설치하다 surface 작업대(의 표면), 표면 temperature 온도

해설 세부 사항 관련 – 여자의 작업반이 하러 온 일

여자가 첫 대사에서 우리는 소토 컨트랙터에서 온 작업반이고 작업대를 설치하려 여기 왔다(We're the crew from Soto Contractors, and we're here to put in the countertops)고 했으므로 정답은 (C)이다.

▶▶ Paraphrasing 대화의 put in the countertops
→ 정답의 install some interior surfaces

42

What problem does Eric report?

(A) A budget limit has been reached.
(B) Some design plans have been revised.
(C) Some construction materials have flaws.
(D) The weather has been unfavorable.

에릭은 어떤 문제를 보고하는가?

(A) 예산 한도에 도달했다.
(B) **일부 설계안이 수정되었다.**
(C) 일부 건축 자재에 결함이 있다.
(D) 날씨가 좋지 않았다.

어휘 budget 예산 limit 한도 revise 수정하다 construction 건축 flaw 결함 unfavorable 좋지 않은

해설 세부 사항 관련 – 에릭이 보고한 문제

첫 번째 남자가 두 번째 대사에서 에릭(Eric)을 부르며 말을 걸자, 두 번째 남자가 대답한 것으로 보아 두 번째 남자가 에릭이고, 지난주에 부엌 설계도가 갑자기 바뀌었다(The kitchen blueprints were changed suddenly last week)고 말했으므로 정답은 (B)이다.

▶▶ Paraphrasing 대화의 blueprints were changed
→ 정답의 Some design plans have been revised

43

고난도

What does Eric say to reassure the woman?

(A) Her company's expertise will still be necessary.
(B) Her company can probably complete a job swiftly.
(C) Her company will not be blamed for an issue.
(D) Her company will receive a cancelation fee.

에릭은 여자를 안심시키기 위해 무엇을 말하는가?

(A) **그녀 회사의 전문성이 여전히 필요할 것이다.**
(B) 그녀의 회사는 아마 작업을 신속하게 완료할 수 있을 것이다.
(C) 그녀의 회사는 문제에 대해 비난받지 않을 것이다.
(D) 그녀의 회사는 취소 수수료를 받을 것이다.

어휘 expertise 전문성 necessary 필요한 complete 완료하다 swiftly 신속하게 blame 비난하다 cancelation fee 취소 수수료

해설 세부 사항 관련 – 에릭이 여자를 안심시키려 한 말

여자가 세 번째 대사에서 그럼 계약을 취소한다는 뜻인지(Does that mean you're canceling our contract?)를 묻자 두 번째 남자인 에릭이 뒤이어 아니(No)라며 자재가 여전히 화강암이라서 당신의 전문적인 기술이 필요할 것

(the material is still granite, so we'll need your specialized skills)이라고 안심시키고 있으므로 정답은 (A)이다.

▶▶ Paraphrasing 대화의 specialized skills
→ 정답의 expertise

44-46

M-Cn **44 Thanks for coming to this exit interview,** Ichika. So, let's start with the most important question—**44 why did you decide to leave?**

W-Br It's for the usual reason—I got a better job at another company.

M-Cn Could you tell me more about that? What makes that job more attractive?

W-Br Well, to be honest, I'll be doing the same work for more pay. **45 Our pay here is below market rate, you know.**

M-Cn **46 Yes, we've heard this comment from other departing employees.** I'll be sure to pass it on to management again, though. Now, tell me your impression of your supervisor.

남 **퇴사자 면접에 와주셔서 고마워요,** 이치카. 자, 가장 중요한 질문부터 시작합시다. **왜 떠나기로 결심했나요?**

여 흔한 이유 때문이에요. 다른 회사에서 더 좋은 직장을 구했거든요.

남 그것에 대해 더 말해줄 수 있나요? 그 직장을 더 매력적으로 만드는 게 무엇인가요?

여 음, 솔직히 말해서, 같은 일을 더 많은 보수를 받고 하게 될 거예요. **여기 우리의 보수는 시장 시세보다 낮아요.**

남 **네, 퇴사하는 다른 직원들로부터 이런 언급을 들은 적이 있어요.** 그래도 경영진에게 꼭 다시 전달할게요. 이제 당신의 상관에 대한 인상을 이야기해주세요.

어휘 exit interview 퇴사자 면접 leave 떠나다 attractive 매력적인 honest 솔직한 market rate 시세 comment 언급 depart 떠나다 pass 전하다 management 경영진 impression 인상 supervisor 감독관

44

What has the woman decided to do?

(A) Ask for a pay raise
(B) Suspend a subscription
(C) Obtain an academic degree
(D) Resign from her position

여자는 무엇을 하기로 결심했는가?

(A) 임금 인상 요청
(B) 구독 중단
(C) 학위 취득
(D) **직책 사임**

어휘 raise 인상 suspend 중단하다 subscription 구독 obtain 얻다 academic degree 학위 resign 사임하다

남자가 첫 대사에서 여자에게 퇴사자 면접에 와줘서 고맙다(Thanks for coming to this exit interview)면서, 왜 떠나기로 결심했는지(why did you decide to leave?)를 묻고 있는 것으로 보아 여자는 퇴사하기로 결심했다는 것을 알 수 있다. 따라서 정답은 (D)이다.

▸▸ **Paraphrasing** 대화의 leave → 정답의 resign

45

What problem does the woman mention?

(A) Her compensation is unusually small.
(B) The market for a service is shrinking.
(C) A required task is unpleasant.
(D) Her workload has increased.

여자는 무슨 문제를 언급하는가?

(A) 보수가 몹시 적다.
(B) 서비스 시장이 위축되고 있다.
(C) 필수 업무가 불편하다.
(D) 그녀의 업무량이 증가했다.

어휘 compensation 보수, 보상 unusually 몹시 shrink 줄어들다 unpleasant 불편한 workload 업무량

해설 세부 사항 관련 – 여자가 언급한 문제

여자가 두 번째 대사에서 여기 우리의 보수는 시장 시세보다 낮다(Our pay here is below market rate, you know)고 했으므로 정답은 (A)이다.

▸▸ **Paraphrasing** 대화의 pay → 정답의 **compensation**

46

What does the man promise to do?

(A) Consider a request
(B) Supervise a transition
(C) Deliver some feedback
(D) Make an introduction

남자는 무엇을 하겠다고 약속하는가?

(A) 요청에 대해 고려하기
(B) 이동 과정 감독하기
(C) 일부 피드백 전달하기
(D) 소개하기

어휘 consider 고려하다 request 요청 supervise 감독하다 transition 변화, 전환 deliver 전하다 introduction 소개

해설 세부 사항 관련 – 남자가 약속한 일

남자가 마지막 대사에서 퇴사하는 다른 직원들로부터 이런 언급을 들은 적이 있다(we've heard this comment from other departing employees)며, 그래도 경영진에게 꼭 다시 전달하겠다(I'll be sure to pass it on to management again, though)고 했으므로 정답은 (C)이다.

47-49 3인 대화

W-Br Hi, Mr. Semwal. My name's Andrea, and this is my friend Tracy. ⁴⁷**We really**

enjoyed your talk on the process of launching your startup.

M-Au Oh, thank you. Are you two students here?

W-Am Yes, we're business majors. Uh, Mr. Semwal, I have a question that I didn't get to ask during the Q&A. Could I ask it now?

M-Au Sure, Tracy, go ahead.

W-Am So, ⁴⁸you're an inspiration to us, but—when you were young, who inspired you?

M-Au Well, I wouldn't be here without Deborah Gold, who was my professor during my senior year in university. She was a mentor to me.

W-Br ⁴⁹She wrote *A History of Innovation*, right?

M-Au ⁴⁹Yes, and I'd recommend that to both of you. It's a bestseller for a reason.

여1 안녕하세요, 셈왈 씨. 저는 안드레아입니다. 이쪽은 제 친구 트레이시예요. 당신이 스타트업을 시작한 과정에 관한 이야기를 정말 잘 들었습니다.

남 아, 감사합니다. 두 분은 여기 학생이신가요?

여2 네, 경영 전공이요. 음, 셈왈 씨. 질의응답 시간에 하지 못했던 질문이 있는데요. 지금 여쭤도 괜찮을까요?

남 물론이죠, 트레이시. 하세요.

여2 음, 당신은 저희에게 영감이 됩니다. 근데 셈왈 씨가 젊으셨을 때는 누가 영감을 주셨나요?

남 음, 대학 졸업반 때 제 교수님이셨던 데보라 골드가 안 계셨다면 저는 이 자리에 없을 거예요. 그녀는 제 멘토이셨습니다.

여1 그녀가 〈혁신의 역사〉를 쓰셨죠?

남 맞아요, 두 분에게 그 책을 추천합니다. 그것이 베스트셀러인 데는 이유가 있답니다.

어휘 process 과정 launch 시작하다 startup 스타트업, 신생기업 major 전공(자) inspiration 영감 inspire 영감을 주다 professor 교수 senior 졸업반의 innovation 혁신

47 　　　　　　　　　　　　　　　　　고난도

Who is the man?

(A) An author
(B) A musician
(C) An entrepreneur
(D) A politician

남자는 누구인가?

(A) 작가
(B) 음악가
(C) 기업가
(D) 정치인

해설 전체 내용 관련 – 남자의 직업

첫 번째 여자가 첫 대사에서 셈왈 씨(Mr. Semwal)라고 남자를 부르며, 당신이 스타트업을 시작한 과정에 관한 이야기를 정말 잘 들었다(We really enjoyed your talk on the process of launching your startup)고 했으므로 정답은 (C)이다.

48

What does Tracy ask the man about?

(A) Challenges he faced
(B) His advice for youth
(C) His hopes for the future
(D) People who influenced him

트레이시는 남자에게 무엇에 관해 묻는가?

(A) 그가 직면한 도전들
(B) 청년들을 위한 조언
(C) 미래에 대한 희망
(D) **그에게 영향을 준 사람들**

어휘   challenge 도전   face 직면하다   youth 청년   influence 영향을 주다

해설   세부 사항 관련 – 트레이시가 남자에게 질문한 것

트레이시가 남자에게 당신은 저희에게 영감이 됩니다(you're an inspiration to us)라고 말하며, 젊으셨을 때 누가 당신에게 영감을 주었나요(When you were young, who inspired you?)라고 묻고 있으므로 정답은 (D)이다.

▸▸ **Paraphrasing**   대화의 inspired → 정답의 influenced

49

What does the man recommend doing?

(A) Seeking a mentor relationship
(B) Reading a certain book
(C) Traveling to other countries
(D) Choosing a small university

남자는 무엇을 하라고 추천하는가?

(A) 멘토 관계 모색
(B) **특정 도서 읽기**
(C) 다른 나라 여행
(D) 작은 대학 선택

어휘   seek 구하다   relationship 관계   certain 특정한, 어떤

해설   세부 사항 관련 – 남자의 권고 사항

첫 번째 여자가 마지막 대사에서 남자의 멘토를 지칭하며 〈혁신의 역사〉를 쓰신 분이 맞는지(She wrote *A History of Innovation*, right?) 묻자, 남자가 맞다고 확인해주며 두 분에게 그 책을 추천한다(Yes, and I'd recommend that to both of you)고 했으므로 정답은 (B)이다.

50-52

W-Am	Noah, I was just checking our page on City-Consumers.com, and I noticed that **⁵⁰we got a two-star rating for Ashley's work on the Loper Incorporated photos. The review said she was too hurried and made the subjects feel nervous.**
M-Au	That's not good. **⁵¹I'll talk to her about how to make customers comfortable.** She has such a great eye for composition. If she can learn how to handle people better, she'll be a real asset.
W-Am	I hope so, because right now she's costing us money. **⁵²We'll have to give Loper Incorporated some of their fee back in order to save our relationship with them.**

여	노아, 방금 시티-컨슈머 닷컴에서 우리 페이지를 확인하던 중 에슐리의 로퍼 주식회사 사진 작업이 별 2개 등급을 받은 것을 알게 되었어요. 평가에 그녀가 너무 서둘러서 촬영 대상들을 불안하게 만들었다고 언급돼 있어요.
남	그건 좋지 않은데요. 손님들을 편하게 해주는 방법에 대해 그녀에게 얘기해볼게요. 그녀는 작품 구성에 대해 뛰어난 안목을 갖고 있어요. 만약 그녀가 사람들을 더 잘 다루는 방법을 배울 수 있다면, 그녀는 진정한 자산이 될 거예요.
여	그러길 바라요. 지금 상당은 그녀로 인해 돈이 들고 있으니까요. 로퍼 주식회사와 우리의 관계를 살리기 위해 그들의 수수료 일부를 돌려줘야 하겠어요.

어휘	notice 알아차리다 rating 등급 hurried 서둘러 하는 subject (사진 등의) 대상 nervous 불안해하는 comfortable 편안한 composition 구성, 작품 handle 다루다 asset 자산

50

What does the woman tell the man about?

(A) A negative review
(B) A broken Web link
(C) A scheduling error
(D) A security risk

여자는 남자에게 무엇에 대해 말하는가?

(A) **부정적인 평가**
(B) 손상된 웹 링크
(C) 일정상 착오
(D) 보안 위험

해설   세부 사항 관련 – 여자가 남자에게 말하는 것

여자가 첫 대사에서 동료의 사진 작업이 별 2개 등급을 받았다(we got a two-star rating for Ashley's work on the Loper Incorporated photos)라며, 평가에 그녀가 너무 서둘러서 촬영 대상들을 불안하게 만들었다고 언급돼 있다(The review said she was too hurried and made the subjects feel nervous)고 했으므로 정답은 (A)이다.

51

Why will the man speak to Ashley?

(A) To ask for her help
(B) To give her some news
(C) To express his gratitude
(D) To provide some guidance

남자는 왜 애슐리에게 말을 할 것인가?

(A) 도움을 요청하려고
(B) 소식을 전하려고
(C) 감사의 뜻을 표하려고
(D) **몇몇 지침을 제공하려고**

어휘 express 표현하다 gratitude 감사 provide 제공하다
guidance 지침[안내]

해설 세부 사항 관련 – 남자가 애슐리에게 말하려는 이유

남자가 첫 대사에서 손님들을 편하게 해주는 방법에 대해 그녀에게 얘기해보겠다(I'll talk to her about how to make customers comfortable)고 한 것으로 보아 정답은 (D)이다.

52

According to the woman, what must the speakers' company do?

(A) Issue a partial refund
(B) Save copies of some images
(C) Replace a software program
(D) Make an official announcement

여자에 따르면, 화자들의 회사는 무엇을 해야 하는가?

(A) 부분 환불 처리
(B) 일부 이미지의 사본 저장
(C) 소프트웨어 프로그램 교체
(D) 공식 발표

어휘 issue 발급하다 partial 부분적인 refund 환불 replace
교체하다 official 공식의

해설 세부 사항 관련 – 여자가 말하는 화자들의 회사가 해야 할 일

여자가 마지막 대사에서 로퍼 주식회사와 우리의 관계를 살리기 위해 그들의 수수료 일부를 돌려줘야 하겠다(We'll have to give Loper Incorporated some of their fee back in order to save our relationship with them)고 했으므로 정답은 (A)이다.

▸▸ Paraphrasing 대화의 give ~ some of their fee back
→ 정답의 issue a partial refund

53-55

M-Cn I can ring up your purchase over here, ma'am. So, did you find everything you were looking for today?

W-Br Yes, and more! 53 **I just came to get some holiday greeting cards, but then I saw that you have these Cantling journals.**

M-Cn Oh, yes, we just got them last month. Have you seen them before?

W-Br I bought one when I visited London, and I really like it. 54 **Since Cantling is a British company, it was a surprise to see its journals here.**

M-Cn I'm glad you like them. 55 **We try to stock a variety of interesting products.**

W-Br Well, I'll be back soon, then!

M-Cn Excellent. OK, your total is twenty-four dollars and thirty-eight cents. How would you like to pay?

남 구매하신 물품은 이쪽에서 결제해드리겠습니다, 사모님. 오늘 찾고 계시던 건 다 찾으셨나요?

여 네, 그리고 더 많이요! 명절 연하장만 좀 사러 왔는데, 보니까 캔틀링 일지가 있더라구요.

남 아, 네, 지난달에 들어 놨어요. 전에 보신 적 있으세요?

여 런던에 갔을 때 하나 샀는데 정말 마음에 들어요. 캔틀링은 영국 회사라서 여기서 그 일지를 보게 되어 깜짝 놀랐어요.

남 마음에 드셨다니 다행이에요. 다양한 흥미로운 상품들을 갖추려고 노력하고 있거든요.

여 그럼, 곧 또 올게요!

남 좋습니다. 자, 총 24달러 38센트입니다. 결제는 어떻게 하시겠습 l 까?

어휘 ring up (금전 등록기로) 입력하다 purchase 구매(품)
holiday greeting 휴가[명절] 안부 인사 journal 저널, 일기
stock (재고로) 비축하다 a variety of 다양한

53

What does the man's store mainly sell?

(A) Cosmetics
(B) Health food
(C) Housewares
(D) Stationery

남자의 가게는 주로 무엇을 판매하는가?

(A) 화장품
(B) 건강식품
(C) 가정용품
(D) 문구류

해설 세부 사항 관련 – 남자의 가게의 주요 판매 제품

여자가 첫 대사에서 남자에게 명절 연하장만 좀 사러 왔는데, 보니까 캔틀링 일지가 있다(I just came to get some holiday greeting cards, but then I saw that you have these Cantling journals)고 한 것으로 보아 남자의 가게는 문구류를 취급하는 곳임을 알 수 있다. 따라서 정답은 (D)이다.

▸▸ Paraphrasing 대화의 greeting cards, journals
→ 정답의 stationery

54   고난도

What does the woman mention about the Cantling product?

(A) It was recently released.
(B) It is imported from abroad.
(C) It is not often sold at a discount.
(D) It has been discontinued.

여자는 캔틀링 제품에 대해 무엇을 언급하는가?

(A) 최근에 출시되었다.
(B) 해외에서 수입되었다.
(C) 할인 가격에 자주 판매되지 않는다.
(D) 단종되었다.

어휘 release 출시하다 import 수입하다 abroad 해외에
discontinue (생산을) 중단하다

286

해설 세부 사항 관련 - 여자가 캔틀링 제품에 대해 언급한 것

여자가 두 번째 대사에서 캔틀링은 영국 회사라서 여기서 그 일지를 보게 되어 깜짝 놀랐다(Since Cantling is a British company, it was a surprise to see its journals here)고 한 것으로 보아 정답은 (B)이다.

55
고난도

What does the woman most likely mean when she says, "I'll be back soon"?

(A) She expects to use up a purchase quickly.
(B) She hopes that the man will do a favor for her.
(C) She parked close to the store's entrance.
(D) She intends to become a regular customer.

여자가 "곧 또 올게요"라고 말한 의도는 무엇일 것 같은가?

(A) 구입품을 빠르게 다 써버릴 것으로 예상한다.
(B) 남자가 자신에게 친절을 베풀기를 바란다.
(C) 가게 입구 가까이에 주차했다.
(D) 단골 고객이 되고자 한다.

어휘 expect 예상하다 use up 다 써버리다 favor 친절 entrance 입구 intend 의도하다 regular 정기적인

해설 화자의 의도 파악 - 곧 또 오겠다는 말의 의도

앞에서 남자가 다양한 흥미로운 상품들을 갖추려고 노력하고 있다(We try to stock a variety of interesting products)고 하자 여자가 인용문을 언급했으므로 다양하고 흥미로운 상품들을 보러 남자의 가게에 재방문하려는 의사를 표현한 말임을 알 수 있다. 따라서 정답은 (D)이다.

56-58

M-Cn Noland Airport customer service. How can I help you?

W-Am Hi, I'm calling from Clementas Company. ⁵⁶**One of our executives is flying into your airport next month, and he'll be on a tight schedule, so his arrival has to go smoothly.** Do you have any services you can offer?

M-Cn Yes—I'd recommend "Airport Concierge". An attendant would greet your executive at the disembarking gate and assist him through the arrival process. ⁵⁷**They could even have a private car service take him wherever he needs to go from the airport.**

W-Am ⁵⁷**Oh, a local contact is going to pick him up.** But otherwise, that sounds great. ⁵⁸**How do I reserve it?**

M-Cn It's operated by a separate company. ⁵⁸**I'll give you its number.**

남 놀랜드 공항 고객 서비스입니다. 어떻게 도와드릴까요?
여 안녕하세요, 클레멘타스 컴퍼니에서 전화드립니다. **다음 달에 저희 임원 한 분이 그쪽 공항에 비행기를 타고 가시는데, 일정이 빠듯해서 도착이 순조롭게 진행되어야 합니다.** 제공할 수 있는 서비스가 있습니까?

남 네—"공항 컨시어지"를 추천드립니다. 안내원이 착륙 게이트에서 임원을 맞이하고 입국 절차 동안 도와드릴 겁니다. **공항에서 가셔야 하는 곳이라면 어디든 개인 차량 서비스로 모실 수도 있습니다.**
여 아, 현지 연락책이 마중 나올 거예요. 하지만 그 외에는 괜찮겠네요. **예약은 어떻게 하죠?**
남 그건 별도의 회사에 의해서 운영되고 있습니다. **번호를 알려드릴게요.**

어휘 executive 임원 tight 빡빡한 smoothly 순조롭게 recommend 추천하다 concierge 안내 서비스 attendant 안내원[종업원] greet 맞이하다 disembark (비행기에서) 내리다 process 절차 private 개인 전용의 contact 연락책 otherwise 그 외에는, 그렇지 않으면 reserve 예약하다 separate 별도의

56

What does the woman say about a company executive?

(A) He does not speak a local language.
(B) He will bring a lot of luggage.
(C) He has a minor injury.
(D) He will not have much time.

여자는 회사 임원에 대해 무엇을 말하는가?

(A) 현지어를 하지 않는다.
(B) 많은 짐을 가져올 것이다.
(C) 경미한 부상을 입었다.
(D) 시간이 많지 않을 것이다.

어휘 luggage 짐 minor 작은 injury 부상

해설 세부 사항 관련 - 여자가 회사 임원에 대해 말하는 것

여자가 첫 대사에서 다음 달에 저희 임원 한 분이 그쪽 공항에 비행기를 타고 가시는데, 일정이 빠듯해서 도착이 순조롭게 진행되어야 한다(One of our executives is flying into your airport next month, and he'll be on a tight schedule, so his arrival has to go smoothly)고 했으므로 정답은 (D)이다.

▶ Paraphrasing 대화의 be on a tight schedule
→ 정답의 not have much time

57
고난도

According to the woman, what will not be necessary?

(A) Arranging ground transportation
(B) Giving a special greeting
(C) Reserving a private rest space
(D) Sending electronic flight updates

여자에 따르면, 무엇이 필요 없을 것인가?

(A) 지상 교통수단 준비
(B) 특별한 인사말 하기
(C) 개인 휴식 공간 예약
(D) 항공편 업데이트 전자 발송

어휘 arrange 준비하다 transportation 교통수단 rest 휴식 space 공간 electronic 전자의

해설 세부 사항 관련 - 여자가 필요하지 않다고 말하는 것

남자가 두 번째 대사에서 공항에서 가셔야 하는 곳이라면 어디든 개인 차량 서비스로 모실 수도 있다(They could even have a private car service take him wherever he needs to go from the airport)고 하자, 여자가 현지 연락책이 마중 나올 것(a local contact is going to pick him up)이라고 했으므로 차량 서비스는 따로 준비할 필요가 없음을 알 수 있다. 따라서 정답은 (A)이다.

| 어휘 | concerned 걱정하는 go ahead 진행하다 schedule 일정을 잡다 quality 품질 hazard 위험 worth ~할 가치가 있는 rest 나머지 |

58

What will the woman most likely do after the conversation?

(A) Forward a confirmation e-mail
(B) Make another phone call
(C) Begin a car journey
(D) Visit a travel Web site

여자는 대화 후에 무엇을 할 것 같은가?
(A) 확인 이메일 전달
(B) **다른 전화 걸기**
(C) 자동차 여행 시작
(D) 여행 웹사이트 방문

어휘 forward 전달하다 confirmation 확인 journey 여행

해설 세부 사항 관련 – 여자가 대화 후에 할 것 같은 일
여자가 두 번째 대사에서 예약을 어떻게 하는지(How do I reserve it?) 묻자, 남자가 번호를 알려주겠다(I'll give you its number)고 했으므로 여자는 남자에게 받은 번호로 전화를 할 것임을 알 수 있다. 따라서 정답은 (B)이다.

59-61

M-Au	59 **Mona, remember how you said the building's windows were getting dirty, but you were concerned about the cost of having them washed?** Well, I found a company that does it for much cheaper than others, so I went ahead and scheduled a service visit.
W-Am	That's great, but... why are they so much cheaper than other companies?
M-Au	It's interesting, actually. 60 **They use robots to do the work.** They say the quality is the same and there's less of a safety hazard.
W-Am	Wow! That sounds like it's worth a try. 61 **OK, I'll let the rest of our team know about the service visit.** Oh, wait—when are they coming?
M-Au	Next Thursday morning.

남	모나, 건물의 유리창이 더러워지고 있다고 말씀하셨잖아요. 그런데 그것을 청소하는 데 드는 비용에 대해 걱정했었죠? 음, 다른 곳들보다 훨씬 싸게 하는 회사를 발견해서 그냥 서비스 방문 일정을 잡았어요.
여	잘 했어요, 그런데… 왜 그곳이 다른 회사들보다 훨씬 저렴한 거죠?
남	그게 사실 재미있어요. **그들은 그 일을 하는 데 로봇을 사용해요.** 품질도 같고 안전 위험이 더 적다고 하네요.
여	왜! 한번 시도해볼 만할 것 같네요. **좋아요, 나머지 팀원들에게 서비스 방문에 대해 알릴게요.** 아, 잠시만요. 그들이 언제 오나요?
남	다음 주 목요일 아침에요.

59

What service does the man say he has scheduled?

(A) Plant care
(B) Appliance repair
(C) Window cleaning
(D) Furniture removal

남자는 무슨 서비스 일정을 잡았다고 말하는가?
(A) 식물 관리
(B) 기기 수리
(C) **창문 청소**
(D) 가구 제거

해설 세부 사항 관련 – 남자가 일정을 잡은 서비스
남자가 첫 대사에서 건물의 유리창이 더러워지고 있다고 여자가 말했던 것을 상기시키며(remember how you said the building's windows were getting dirty) 여자가 비용을 걱정했는데 다른 곳들보다 훨씬 싸게 하는 회사를 발견해서 서비스 방문 일정을 잡았다(but you were concerned ~ I found a company that does it for much cheaper than others, so I went ahead and scheduled a service visit)고 했으므로 정답은 (C)이다.

60

According to the man, what is special about the service?

(A) It is done outside of business hours.
(B) It does not involve hazardous chemicals.
(C) It is not available in all seasons.
(D) It is performed by machines.

남자에 따르면, 서비스에서 무엇이 특별한가?
(A) 영업시간 외에 행해진다.
(B) 유해 화학 물질을 포함하지 않는다.
(C) 모든 계절에 이용 가능한 것은 아니다.
(D) **기계에 의해 수행된다.**

어휘 involve 포함하다 hazardous 유해한 chemical 화학 물질 available 이용 가능한 season 계절 perform 수행하다

해설 세부 사항 관련 – 남자가 말하는 서비스의 특별한 점
남자가 두 번째 대사에서 그들은 그 일을 하는 데 로봇을 사용한다(They use robots to do the work)고 했으므로 정답은 (D)이다.

▸▸ Paraphrasing 대화의 use robots to do the work → 정답의 performed by machines

61

What does the woman say she will do?

(A) Watch a demonstration
(B) Inform some colleagues
(C) Permit an inconvenience
(D) Take the rest of the day off

여자는 무엇을 하겠다고 말하는가?

(A) 시연을 관람한다.
(B) 몇몇 동료들에게 알린다
(C) 불편함을 허용한다.
(D) 조퇴한다.

어휘   demonstration 시연 inform 알리다 colleague 동료
      permit 허용하다 inconvenience 불편 take ~ off ~ (동안) 쉬다

해설   세부 사항 관련 – 여자가 하겠다고 말한 일

여자가 마지막 대사에서 나머지 팀원들에게 서비스 방문에 대해 알리겠다(I'll let the rest of our team know about the service visit)고 했으므로 정답은 (B)이다.

▸▸ **Paraphrasing**   대화의 **let the rest of our team know**
                     → 정답의 **inform some colleagues**

62-64 대화 + 티켓

M-Au	Caroline, where are you? The concert's about to start!
W-Br	Yes, 62 **sorry that I'm running late! I didn't know that the stadium doesn't allow backpacks. I had to run back to the parking area to put mine in my car.**
M-Au	That's too bad. Well, are you almost here now?
W-Br	Yeah. Our area is near Flash Burgers, right?
M-Au	No, I don't think so. I didn't see that on my way in.
W-Br	Hmm. Oh, I made a mistake! 63 **I confused the "section" and "row" numbers on my ticket.** I'll be there in a minute.
M-Au	Great. 64 **But wait—since you're right by Flash Burgers, could you pick me up a Flash Meal?** I'm really hungry.

남	캐롤라인, 어디에요? 콘서트가 막 시작하려고 해요!
여	네, 늦어서 미안해요! 경기장에서 배낭을 허용하지 않는 줄 몰랐어요. 차에 배낭을 두려고 주차장으로 다시 뛰어가야 했어요.
남	저런, 그럼 이제 거의 다 온 거예요?
여	네. 우리 구역은 플래시 버거 근처가 맞죠?
남	아니요, 그런 것 같지 않은데요. 들어오는 길에 못 봤어요.
여	흠. 아, 제가 실수했어요! 표에 있는 "구역"과 "줄" 번호를 헷갈렸어요. 금방 갈게요.
남	좋아요. 그런데 잠깐만요. 플래시 버거 바로 옆에 있는 김에 플래시 밀 좀 사다 주시겠어요? 제가 정말 배가 고프네요.

어휘   be about to 막 ~하려고 하다 stadium 경기장 confuse
      혼동하다 section 구역 row 줄

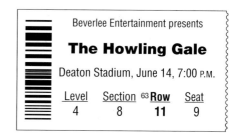

Beverlee Entertainment presents
The Howling Gale
Deaton Stadium, June 14, 7:00 P.M.

Level	Section	63 **Row**	Seat
4	8	**11**	9

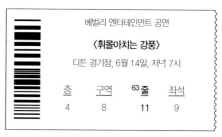

베벌리 엔터테인먼트 공연
〈휘몰아치는 강풍〉
디튼 경기장, 6월 14일, 저녁 7시

층	구역	63줄	좌석
4	8	11	9

62

Why is the woman late?

(A) It took her a long time to find parking.
(B) She was unaware of an admission policy.
(C) She misunderstood a spoken invitation.
(D) There was traffic around the stadium.

여자는 왜 늦었는가?
(A) 주차 공간을 찾는 데 오랜 시간이 걸렸다.
(B) 입장 규정을 알지 못했다.
(C) 구두 초대를 오해했다.
(D) 경기장 주변에 교통이 혼잡했다.

어휘   unaware 알지 못하는 admission 입장 policy 방침
      misunderstand 오해하다 invitation 초대 traffic 교통(량)

해설   세부 사항 관련 – 여자가 늦은 이유

여자가 첫 대사에서 늦어서 미안하다(sorry that I'm running late!)고 사과하며, 경기장에서 배낭을 허용하지 않는 줄 몰랐다(I didn't know that the stadium doesn't allow backpacks)면서, 차에 배낭을 두려고 주차장으로 다시 뛰어가야 했다(I had to run back to the parking area to put mine in my car)고 했으므로 정답은 (B)이다.

▸▸ **Paraphrasing**   대화의 **didn't know**
                     → 정답의 **was unaware of**

63   고난도

Look at the graphic. What section did the woman go to by mistake?

(A) 4
(B) 8
(C) 11
(D) 9

시각 정보에 의하면, 여자는 실수로 어느 구역으로 갔는가?
(A) 4
(B) 8
(C) 11
(D) 9

여자가 세 번째 대사에서 표에 있는 "구역"과 "줄" 번호를 헷갈렸다(I confused the "section" and "row" numbers on my ticket)고 했고, 티켓에 줄 번호는 11로 나와 있으므로 여자는 8번 구역 대신 11번 구역에 잘못 가 있음을 알 수 있다. 따라서 정답은 (C)이다.

64

What does the man ask the woman to do?

(A) Bring him some refreshments
(B) Send him a photograph
(C) Look for concert staff
(D) Wait by a landmark

남자는 여자에게 무엇을 해달라고 부탁하는가?

(A) 가벼운 식사를 가져다줄 것
(B) 사진을 보내줄 것
(C) 콘서트 직원을 찾을 것
(D) 주요 지형물 옆에서 기다릴 것

어휘　refreshment 가벼운 식사　landmark 주요 지형지물, 랜드마크

해설　세부 사항 관련 – 남자가 여자에게 부탁한 일

남자가 마지막 대사에서 플래시 버거 바로 옆에 있는 김에 플래시 밀 좀 사다줄 수 있는지(since you're right by Flash Burgers, could you pick me up a Flash Meal?)를 묻고 있으므로 정답은 (A)이다.

▸▸ Paraphrasing　대화의 **pick me up a ~ Meal**
　　　　　　　　　　→ 정답의 **bring him some refreshments**

65-67 대화 + 공지

W-Br	Otto, do you have a moment? **65 I'd like to pitch an article series for our Saturday edition.**
M-Cn	Sure, Bridget. What is it?
W-Br	**66 I want to interview each of the winners of the Jasper Environmental Awards. It's a great program, and it should get more attention.** We only ran a short news piece on it after they were announced.
M-Cn	Tell me about the winners.
W-Br	**67 Well, I would start with the winner of the "Waste Management" category.** She leads a group that collects the healthy but unattractive produce that local supermarkets throw away, and then distributes it to people who need it.
M-Cn	OK. That does sound like a good fit for the weekend. **67 Ask her if she's interested.**

여	오토, 시간 좀 있으세요? 우리 토요일 간행물에 연재 기사를 제안하고 싶어요.
남	물론이죠, 브리짓. 뭔데요?
여	재스퍼 환경상 수상자들을 각각 인터뷰하고 싶어요. 그건 훌륭한 프로그램이고 더 많은 관심을 받아야 해요. 그들이 발표된 후에 우리는 단지 짧은 뉴스 기사를 실었을 뿐이에요.
남	수상자들에 대해 얘기 좀 해주세요.
여	음, "쓰레기 관리" 부문의 수상자부터 시작할게요. 그녀는 지역 슈퍼마켓에서 버리는 상하지 않았지만 겉보기엔 좋지 않은 농산물을 모아 필요한 사람들에게 나눠주는 그룹을 이끌고 있어요.
남	좋아요. 주말에 딱 어울리는 것 같네요. **그녀에게 관심이 있는지 물어보세요.**

어휘　pitch 권유하다, 제안하다　edition (출판물의) 판, 호　winner 수상자　environmental 환경의　award 상　attention 관심　announce 발표하다　waste 쓰레기　management 관리　category 부문　lead 이끌다　unattractive 보기 좋지 않은　produce 농산물　throw away 버리다　distribute 나눠주다　fit 어울림

2nd Annual Jasper Environmental Awards Winners

| *Conservation*
Jamie Wright | 67 *Waste Management*
Taylor Bowers |
| *Technology*
Hyun-Jin Wi | *Communications*
Cameron Kennedy |

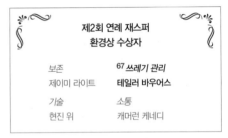

제2회 연례 재스퍼 환경상 수상자

| 보존
제이미 라이트 | 67 쓰레기 관리
테일러 바우어스 |
| 기술
현진 위 | 소통
캐머런 케네디 |

65

Who most likely is the woman?

(A) A city official
(B) A reporter
(C) A nonprofit executive
(D) A marketing consultant

여자는 누구일 것 같은가?

(A) 시 공무원
(B) 기자
(C) 비영리 임원
(D) 마케팅 컨설턴트

해설　전체 내용 관련 – 여자의 직업

여자가 첫 대사에서 우리 토요일 간행물에 연재 기사를 제안하고 싶다(I'd like to pitch an article series for our Saturday edition)고 한 것으로 보아 정답은 (B)이다.

66

고난도

What does the woman say about the awards program?

(A) It deserves more publicity.
(B) It selects surprising winners.
(C) It added a new category this year.
(D) Its ceremony can be viewed online.

여자는 시상 프로그램에 대해 무엇을 말하는가?

(A) 더 많은 인지도를 누릴 만하다.
(B) 놀라운 수상자들을 선정한다.
(C) 올해 새로운 부문을 추가했다.
(D) 온라인으로 시상식을 볼 수 있다.

어휘 deserve ~을 받을 만하다 publicity 인지도, 언론의 관심 select 선정하다 surprising 놀라운 ceremony 기념행사 view 보다

해설 세부 사항 관련 – 여자가 시상 프로그램에 대해 말하는 것

여자가 두 번째 대사에서 재스퍼 환경상의 수상자들을 각각 인터뷰하고 싶다(I want to interview each of the winners of the Jasper Environmental Awards)고 시상 프로그램에 대해 언급하며, 그건 훌륭한 프로그램이고 더 많은 관심을 받아야 한다(It's a great program, and it should get more attention)고 했으므로 정답은 (A)이다.

▸▸ **Paraphrasing** 대화의 more attention
→ 정답의 more publicity

67

Look at the graphic. Whom will the woman most likely contact?

(A) Jamie Wright
(B) Taylor Bowers
(C) Hyun-Jin Wi
(D) Cameron Kennedy

시각 정보에 의하면, 여자는 누구에게 연락할 것 같은가?

(A) 제이미 라이트
(B) 테일러 바우어스
(C) 현진 위
(D) 캐머런 케네디

해설 시각 정보 연계 – 여자가 연락할 것 같은 사람

여자가 세 번째 대사에서 "쓰레기 관리" 부문의 수상자부터 시작하겠다(I would start with the winner of the "Waste Management" category)며 수상자에 대해 소개하자 남자가 뒤이어 그녀에게 관심이 있는지 물어보라(Ask her if she's interested)고 했으므로 여자는 쓰레기 관리 부문의 수상자에게 연락할 것임을 알 수 있다. 공지문에 따르면 쓰레기 관리 부문의 수상자는 테일러 바우어스이므로 정답은 (B)이다.

68-70 대화 + 경비 코드 목록

M-Cn Hi, Ms. Diaz, it's your bookkeeper. **68I'm entering your salon's operating expenses now, and—there's an invoice from a company called "Baxell" for a few dozen**

manicure kits. Can you confirm that you placed that order?

W-Am Yes, I did. Why? Is there a problem with the invoice?

M-Cn **69Well, I hadn't heard of Baxell, and your invoices for this kind of expense usually come from Reidmont.** So I thought I should check.

W-Am I see. **70Yes, I learned about Baxell at a trade show last month and decided to try them out.** You might see more invoices from them in the future.

남 안녕하세요, 디아즈 씨, 당신의 회계 담당입니다. 지금 당신의 **살롱 운영비를 입력하고 있는데, 수십 개의 매니큐어 키트에 대해 "백셀"이라는 회사에서 보낸 청구서가 있어요.** 당신이 그 주문을 했는지 확인해주시겠습니까?

여 네, 제가 했어요. 왜요? 그 청구서에 문제가 있나요?

남 음, 나는 벡셀에 대해 들어본 적이 없고, 이런 종류의 비용에 대한 당신의 청구서는 보통 리드몬트에서 온 것이라서요. 그래서 확인해야겠다고 생각했어요.

여 그렇군요. 맞아요. 지난달 무역 박람회에서 백셀에 대해 알게 돼서 한번 써 보기로 결정했어요. 앞으로 그들로부터 온 청구서를 더 많이 보시게 될 거예요.

어휘 bookkeeper 회계 장부 담당자 enter 입력하다 operating expense 운영비 invoice 청구서 a few dozen 수십 개의 confirm 확인하다 expense 경비[비용] trade 무역

Operating Expenses	
68520	Business Supplies
530	Utilities
540	Telecommunications
550	Repair and Maintenance

운영비	
68520	사업 보급품
530	공과금
540	통신
550	보수 및 유지

68

고난도

Look at the graphic. Which code will the expense most likely be entered under?

(A) 520
(B) 530
(C) 540
(D) 550

Test 10

시각 정보에 의하면, 비용은 어느 코드 하에 입력될 것 같은가?

(A) 520
(B) 530
(C) 540
(D) 550

해설 **시각 정보 연계 – 비용이 입력될 코드**
남자가 첫 대사에서 지금 당신의 살롱 운영비를 입력하고 있는데, 수십 개의 매니큐어 키트에 대해 "백셀"이라는 회사에서 보낸 청구서가 있다(I'm entering your salon's operating expenses now, and—there's an invoice from a company called "Baxell" for a few dozen manicure kits)고 했고, 경비 코드 목록에 따르면 매니큐어 키트가 속하는 사업 보급품은 520번으로 나와 있으므로 정답은 (A)이다.

69
[고난도]

Why is the man concerned about the invoice?

(A) Its due date has already passed.
(B) It does not include some details.
(C) It is from an unfamiliar company.
(D) It requests an unusual amount of money.

남자는 왜 청구서에 대해 걱정하는가?
(A) 만기일이 이미 지났다.
(B) 일부 세부사항이 포함되지 않았다.
(C) 생소한 회사에서 온 것이다.
(D) 흔치 않은 금액을 요구한다.

어휘 due date 만기일 include 포함하다 detail 세부 사항
unfamiliar 생소한 unusual 흔치 않은 amount 액수

해설 **세부 사항 관련 – 남자가 송장에 대해 걱정하는 이유**
남자가 두 번째 대사에서 백셀에 대해 들어본 적이 없고 이런 종류의 비용에 대한 당신의 청구서는 보통 리드몬트에서 온 것이었다(I hadn't heard of Baxell, and your invoices for this kind of expense usually come from Reidmont)고 했으므로 정답은 (C)이다.

▸▸ **Paraphrasing** 대화의 **hadn't heard of**
→ 정답의 **unfamiliar**

70

What did the woman most likely do recently?

(A) Watched a television news show
(B) Cleared out a storage area
(C) Attended an industry event
(D) Delegated a task to an employee

여자는 최근에 무엇을 했을 것 같은가?
(A) 텔레비전 뉴스 프로그램 시청
(B) 보관 장소 정리
(C) 업계 행사 참석
(D) 직원에게 업무 위임

어휘 storage 보관 clear out 정리[처분]하다 industry 업계
delegate 위임하다 task 업무

해설 **세부 사항 관련 – 여자가 최근에 했을 것 같은 일**
여자가 마지막 대사에서 지난달 무역 박람회에서 백셀에 대해 알게 돼서 한번 써 보기로 결정했다(I learned about Baxell at a trade show last month and decided to try them out)고 한 것으로 보아 여자는 최근에 무역 박람회에 참석했음을 알 수 있다. 따라서 정답은 (C)이다.

▸▸ **Paraphrasing** 대화의 **a trade show**
→ 정답의 **an industry event**

PART 4

71-73 회의 발췌

M-Au All right, everyone, it's 11:01, so we'd better get started. **71Remember, it's now company policy that meetings can't go over thirty minutes.** I'm sure that will help our productivity overall, but it does mean that we need to really focus right now. **72I've made a list of everything we're going to talk about today. Please take a look at it now.** **73As you can see, we've got to decide on the venue, program, and food for our yearly holiday party.** I have a few suggestions for the first of these.

자, 여러분, 11시 1분이니까 시작하는 게 좋겠습니다. 이제 회의가 30분을 넘길 수 없다는 것이 회사 방침임을 명심하십시오. 이것이 전반적으로 생산성에 도움이 되리라 확신하지만, 지금 당장 정말 집중해야 한다는 것을 의미합니다. 오늘 우리가 이야기할 모든 것에 대한 목록을 만들었습니다. 지금 한번 살펴보십시오. 보시다시피, 매년 열리는 휴가 파티를 위한 장소와 프로그램, 음식을 결정해야 합니다. 저에게 이것들 중 첫 번째 것에 대해 몇 가지 제안이 있습니다.

어휘 policy 방침 productivity 생산성 overall 전반적으로
focus 집중하다 venue 장소 yearly 해마다의 suggestion 제안

71

What did the company recently adopt a policy on?

(A) How meeting notifications are sent out
(B) How many people must attend a meeting
(C) How meeting spaces can be used
(D) How long meetings can last

회사는 최근에 무엇에 관한 방침을 채택했는가?
(A) 회의 통지 발송 방법
(B) 회의에 참석해야 하는 사람의 수
(C) 회의 공간 이용 방법
(D) 회의가 지속될 수 있는 시간

어휘 adopt (정책 등을) 채택하다 notification 통지 last 지속하다

해설 세부 사항 관련 – 회사가 최근에 채택한 방침
화자가 초반부에 이제 회의가 30분을 넘길 수 없다는 것이 회사 방침임을 명심하라(Remember, it's now company policy that meetings can't go over thirty minutes)고 했으므로 정답은 (D)이다.

72
What does the speaker ask the listeners to do first?
(A) Put away some snacks
(B) Examine an agenda
(C) Prepare to take notes
(D) Write their names on a form

화자는 청자들에게 먼저 무엇을 하라고 요청하는가?
(A) 간식을 치울 것
(B) 안건을 검토할 것
(C) 메모할 준비를 할 것
(D) 양식에 이름을 쓸 것

어휘 put away 치우다 examine 검토[조사]하다 agenda 안건 take notes 메모하다 form 양식

해설 세부 사항 관련 – 화자가 청자들에게 먼저 하라고 요청한 일
화자가 중반부에 오늘 우리가 이야기할 모든 것에 대한 목록을 만들었다(I've made a list of everything we're going to talk about today)며, 지금 한번 살펴보라(Please take a look at it now)고 요청했으므로 정답은 (B)이다.

▸▸ Paraphrasing 담화의 **a list of everything we're going to talk about** → 정답의 **an agenda**

73
What is the purpose of the meeting?
(A) To discuss a safety issue
(B) To choose a new employee
(C) To evaluate a training program
(D) To plan an annual gathering

회의의 목적은 무엇인가?
(A) 안전 문제 논의
(B) 신입 사원 선발
(C) 교육 프로그램 평가
(D) 연례 모임 계획

어휘 evaluate 평가하다 annual 연례의 gathering 모임

해설 세부 사항 관련 – 회의의 목적
화자가 후반부에 매년 열리는 휴가 파티를 위한 장소와 프로그램, 음식을 결정해야 한다(we've got to decide on the venue, program, and food for our yearly holiday party)고 했으므로 정답은 (D)이다.

▸▸ Paraphrasing 담화의 **our yearly ~ party** → 정답의 **an annual gathering**

74-76 전화 메시지

W-Br Hi, Mr. Price. This is Julie at Stonebend Furniture. **74I received the delivery of the Muldock chair prototype this morning. Your craftmanship is excellent, but... the wood has water damage. 75So I looked at the packaging, and it's the wrong choice for that type of wood. Hickory is quite sensitive to moisture, and I assumed you knew that...** but I guess it's not native to your area. Anyway, I'll need to know that you can ship the product safely before I make a larger production order. **76Could you look into the matter until you find a more suitable packaging method?** Thanks.

안녕하십니까, 프라이스 씨. 스톤벤드 가구의 줄리입니다. 오늘 아침에 멀독 의자 시제품의 배달을 받았습니다. 당신의 솜씨는 훌륭하지만… 나무에 물에 의한 손상이 있습니다. 그래서 포장을 봤는데 그런 종류의 나무에는 잘못된 선택이었습니다. 히코리는 습기에 꽤 민감한데 알고 계셨을 거라 생각했지만… 당신 지역의 토착 식물은 아닌가 보네요. 어쨌든 제가 더 큰 생산 주문을 하기 전에 제품을 안전하게 운송할 수 있다는 것을 알아야 하겠습니다. 좀 더 적절한 포장 방법을 찾으실 때까지 이 문제를 조사해주시겠습니까? 감사합니다.

어휘 prototype 시제품 craftmanship 솜씨 excellent 훌륭한 damage 손상 packaging 포장 Hickory 히코리(북미산의 단단한 나무) sensitive 민감한 moisture 습기 assume 추정하다 native ~원산[토종]의 ship 운송하다 production 생산 suitable 적절한 method 방법

74
고난도

What did the speaker do in the morning?
(A) Finalized a digital drawing
(B) Browsed a furniture catalog
(C) Checked a sample item
(D) Received a sales proposal

화자는 아침에 무엇을 했는가?
(A) 디지털 도면 마무리
(B) 가구 카탈로그 검색
(C) 샘플 제품 점검
(D) 판매 제안서 수령

어휘 finalize 마무리 짓다 browse 검색하다 proposal 제안(서)

해설 세부 사항 관련 – 화자가 아침에 한 일
화자가 초반부에 오늘 아침에 멀독 의자 시제품의 배달을 받았다(I received the delivery of the Muldock chair prototype this morning)며 당신의 솜씨는 훌륭하지만 나무에 물에 의한 손상이 있다(Your craftmanship is excellent, but... the wood has water damage)고 했으므로 정답은 (C)이다.

▸▸ Paraphrasing 담화의 **prototype** → 정답의 **a sample item**

Test 10

75

고난도

What does the speaker imply when she says, "I guess it's not native to your area"?

(A) She knows why a cost might be high.
(B) She understands how a mistake happened.
(C) She is suggesting entering a new market.
(D) She is doubtful about a product's authenticity.

여자가 "당신 지역의 토착 식물은 아닌가 보네요"라고 말하는 의미는 무엇인가?
(A) 비용이 많이 들 수도 있는 이유를 안다.
(B) 어떻게 실수가 발생했는지 이해한다.
(C) 새로운 시장에 진입할 것을 제안하고 있다.
(D) 제품의 진위 여부에 대해 의심한다.

어휘 doubtful 의심을 품은 authenticity 진위

해설 화자의 의도 파악 – 당신 지역의 토착 식물은 아닌가 보다라는 말의 의도
앞에서 포장을 봤는데 그런 종류의 나무에는 잘못된 선택이었다(I looked at the packaging, and it's the wrong choice for that type of wood)고 지적하며, 히코리는 습기에 꽤 민감한데 알고 계셨을 거라 생각했지만(Hickory is quite sensitive to moisture, and I assumed you knew that... but I guess)이라고 말한 뒤 인용문을 언급한 것으로 보아, 지역에서 나지 않는 나무라 잘 알지 못해서 적합하지 않은 포장 방법을 선택해 실수가 생겼을 거라고 짐작하는 말임을 알 수 있다. 따라서 정답은 (B)이다.

76

What does the speaker ask the listener to do?

(A) Give his opinion
(B) Expedite an order
(C) Update some machinery
(D) Search for an alternative

화자는 청자에게 무엇을 하라고 요청하는가?
(A) 의견을 낼 것
(B) 주문을 신속히 처리할 것
(C) 일부 기계를 업데이트할 것
(D) 대안을 찾아볼 것

어휘 opinion 의견 expedite 신속히 처리하다 machinery 기계(류)
search 찾아보다 alternative 대안

해설 세부 사항 관련 – 화자가 청자에게 요청한 일
화자가 후반부에 좀 더 적절한 포장 방법을 찾을 때까지 이 문제를 조사해줄 수 있는지(Could you look into the matter until you find a more suitable packaging method?) 묻고 있으므로 정답은 (D)이다.

▸▸ Paraphrasing   담화의 **find a more suitable ~ method**
   → 정답의 **search for an alternative**

77-79 여행 정보

> W-Am Attention, passengers. **77Thank you for joining us for this cruise around the coast of Mapsalak National Park. 78In case you haven't noticed already, there are two whales passing**

by on our left. We can tell from the large bumps on their backs that they are humpback whales. Oh, one of them just jumped out of the water! It seems like they're putting on a show for us. I hope you all saw that. **79If not, or if you'd like to see more, I recommend buying a "Whales of Mapsalak" DVD from our gift shop when we return to land.** It's full of really amazing footage.

승객 여러분, 주목해주세요. 맵살락 국립 공원의 해안을 도는 이 유람선에 함께해주셔서 감사합니다. 혹시 이미 알아채지 못하셨다면, 우리 왼쪽으로 고래 두 마리가 지나가고 있습니다. 우리는 그들의 등에 있는 커다란 혹으로부터 그들이 혹등고래라는 것을 알 수 있습니다. 오, 그들 중 한 마리가 방금 물 밖으로 뛰어올랐어요! 우리를 위해 쇼를 하는 것 같네요. 여러분 모두 보셨기를 바랍니다. 그렇지 않다면, 혹은 더 보고 싶으시다면, 육지로 돌아갔을 때 저희 선물 가게에서 "맵살락의 고래들" DVD를 구입하시라고 권해드립니다. 정말 놀라운 장면들로 가득하답니다.

어휘 cruise 유람선 coast 해안 national park 국립 공원
in case (~할) 경우에 대비해서 notice 알아차리다 whale 고래
bump 혹 humpback whale 혹등고래 amazing 놀라운
footage 장면

77

Where most likely are the listeners?

(A) On a bus
(B) On a boat
(C) On a footpath
(D) On an aircraft

청자들은 어디에 있을 것 같은가?
(A) 버스
(B) 배
(C) 오솔길
(D) 비행기

해설 전체 내용 관련 – 청자들이 있는 장소
화자가 초반부에 맵살락 국립공원의 해안을 도는 이 유람선에 함께해주셔서 감사하다(Thank you for joining us for this cruise around the coast of Mapsalak National Park)고 한 것으로 보아 정답은 (B)이다.

▸▸ Paraphrasing   담화의 **cruise** → 정답의 **boat**

78

What does the speaker point out to the listeners?

(A) Some wild animals
(B) Some rare plants
(C) A famous building
(D) A large body of water

화자는 청자들에게 무엇을 언급하는가?
(A) 야생 동물
(B) 희귀 식물
(C) 유명한 건물
(D) 큰 수역

해설 세부 사항 관련 – 화자가 청자들에게 언급하는 것

화자가 초반부에 혹시 이미 알아채지 못했다면 우리 왼쪽으로 고래 두 마리가 지나가고 있다(In case you haven't noticed already, there are two whales passing by on our left)고 했으므로 정답은 (A)이다.

79

What does the speaker encourage listeners to do later?

(A) Return some rental gear
(B) Purchase a video souvenir
(C) Post their photographs online
(D) Recommend the tour to others

화자는 청자들에게 나중에 무엇을 하라고 권하는가?

(A) 대여 장비 반납
(B) 비디오 기념품 구입
(C) 온라인에 사진 게시
(D) 타인에게 투어 추천

어휘 return 반납하다 rental 대여 gear 장비 purchase 구입하다 souvenir 기념품 post 게시하다 photograph 사진

해설 세부 사항 관련 – 화자가 청자들에게 하라고 권하는 일

화자가 후반부에 그렇지 않다면, 혹은 더 보고 싶으시다면, 육지로 돌아갔을 때 저희 선물가게에서 "맵살락의 고래들" DVD를 구입하시라고 권해드린다(If not, or if you'd like to see more, I recommend buying a "Whales of Mapsalak" DVD from our gift shop when we return to land)고 했으므로 정답은 (B)이다.

80-82 공지

M-Cn Managers, thank you for joining me today. **80 I wanted to let you know that Arvina Software is going to restructure.** Instead of employees being grouped by function, such as sales or finance, we're going to be divided into business units that each focus on customers in a particular industry, such as transportation or retail. I believe this will improve our service and lead to higher revenues. Obviously, this will be a major change. **81 But don't worry—from now on, you'll be involved in every step of the process.** Your input will be crucial. **82 I only ask that you keep this information to yourselves until the plans are finalized.** Telling employees now would only cause unnecessary worries about the transition.

관리자 여러분, 오늘 함께해주셔서 감사합니다. **아르비나 소프트웨어가 조직 개편을 한다는 것을 알려드리고 싶었습니다.** 직원들은 영업이나 금융처럼 기능별로 묶이는 대신, 운송이나 소매와 같이 특정 산업의 고객에게 각각 집중하는 사업 단위로 나뉘어질 것입니다. 저는 이것이 우리의 서비스를 향상시키고 더 많은 수입으로 이어질 것이라고 믿습니다. 분명히, **이것은 중대한 변화가 될 것**

입니다. 하지만 걱정하지 마십시오. 이제부터, 여러분은 그 과정의 모든 단계에 관여하게 될 겁니다. 당신의 의견은 매우 중요할 것입니다. 계획이 마무리될 때까지 이 정보는 여러분만 알고 계실 것을 당부드립니다. 직원들에게 지금 말하는 것은 전환에 대한 불필요한 걱정만 불러일으킬 뿐입니다.

어휘 restructure 구조를 조정하다[개편하다] instead of ~ 대신에 function 기능 divide 나누다 unit 구성 단위, 단체 focus 집중하다 particular 특정한 industry 산업 transportation 운송 retail 소매 improve 향상시키다 lead ~에 이르다 revenue 수입 obviously 분명히 involve 관련시키다 process 과정 input 의견, 조언 crucial 중요한 finalize 마무리 짓다 cause 야기하다 unnecessary 불필요한 transition 이행, 전환

80

What is the speaker announcing?

(A) The revision of a document
(B) The relocation of a workplace
(C) The reorganization of a company
(D) The retirement of an executive

화자는 무엇을 발표하고 있는가?

(A) 문서의 수정
(B) 사업장의 이전
(C) 회사의 조직 개편
(D) 임원의 퇴직

어휘 revision 수정 relocation 이전 workplace 업무 현장 reorganization 재편성 retirement 퇴직 executive 임원

해설 전체 내용 관련 – 발표의 주제

화자가 초반부에 아르비나 소프트웨어가 조직 개편을 한다는 것을 알려드리고 싶었다(I wanted to let you know that Arvina Software is going to restructure)고 했으므로 정답은 (C)이다.

▸▸ Paraphrasing 담화의 restructure
→ 정답의 reorganization

81 고난도

What does the speaker imply when he says, "this will be a major change"?

(A) The listeners might be feeling concerned.
(B) A process will take place over a long period.
(C) He is optimistic about an outcome.
(D) A previous project had a limited impact.

화자가 "이것은 중대한 변화가 될 것입니다"라고 말하는 의미는 무엇인가?

(A) 청자들이 걱정하고 있을지도 모른다.
(B) 오랜 기간에 걸쳐 절차가 진행될 것이다.
(C) 결과에 대해 낙관적이다.
(D) 이전 프로젝트는 효과에 한계가 있었다.

어휘 concerned 걱정하는 period 기간 optimistic 낙관적인 outcome 결과 previous 이전의 impact 영향(력), 효과

해설 화자의 의도 파악 – 이것은 중대한 변화가 될 것이라는 말의 의도

인용문을 언급한 뒤 곧바로 하지만 걱정하지 말라(But don't worry)며, 이제부터 여러분은 그 과정의 모든 단계에 관여하게 될 것(from now on, you'll be involved in every step of the process)이라고 청자들을 안심시키고 있

는 것으로 보아 청자들이 변화에 대해 걱정할 수도 있다는 것을 인지하고 있음을 알리려는 의도로 한 말임을 알 수 있다. 따라서 정답은 (A)이다.

82
고난도

What are the listeners asked to do?
(A) Schedule regular planning sessions
(B) Conserve some office supplies
(C) Monitor the results of a transition
(D) Avoid disclosing some information

청자들은 무엇을 하도록 요청되는가?
(A) 정기적인 기획 회의 일정을 잡을 것
(B) 일부 사무용품을 아껴 쓸 것
(C) 전환 결과를 관찰할 것
(D) 일부 정보의 공개를 피할 것

어휘 schedule 일정을 잡다 regular 정기적인 planning 기획
session (특정 활동을 위한) 시간, 회의 conserve 아껴 쓰다 office
supplies 사무용품 monitor 추적 관찰하다 result 결과 avoid
피하다 disclose 공개하다

해설 세부 사항 관련 – 청자들이 요청받은 일
화자가 후반부에 계획이 마무리될 때까지 이 정보는 여러분만 알고 계실 것을
당부드린다(I only ask that you keep this information to yourselves
until the plans are finalized)고 했으므로 정답은 (D)이다.

▸▸ Paraphrasing 담화의 keep this information to
yourselves → 정답의 avoid disclosing
some information

83-85 전화 메시지

W-Br ⁸³Hello, this is Joo-Hee from Regency
Comfort Suites calling for Desmond Smith
regarding your reservation for March fourth. It
turns out that on that day, we're washing all the
hallway carpets on the fourth floor, where your
room is located. ⁸⁴But rest assured that, as a
member of our loyalty program, your comfort
and convenience are extremely important to
us. ⁸⁵We'd like to offer you one of our executive
suites on the fifth floor at no extra charge. Uh, if
you'd like to take advantage of this offer, call me
back at (513) 555-0106. Have a nice day.

여보세요, 데스몬드 스미스 씨께 3월 4일 예약 건으로 전화드리는 리젠시 컴포
트 스위트의 주희입니다. 알고 보니 그날은 귀하의 객실이 위치한 4층의 복도
카펫을 모두 세척하기로 되어 있습니다. 그러나 저희 고객 보상제의 회원이신 귀
하의 편안함과 편리함은 저희에게 대단히 중요하므로 안심하십시오. 저희는 귀
하께 5층의 고급 특실 중 하나를 추가 요금 없이 제공해드리고 싶습니다. 음, 이
혜택을 누리시려면 (513) 555-0106번으로 다시 전화 주십시오. 좋은 하루
보내십시오.

어휘 regarding ~에 관하여 reservation 예약 turn out
나타나다, 드러나다 hallway 복도 rest assured 안심하세요
loyalty program 고객 보상제 comfort 편안 convenience
편리 extremely 극히 executive suite (호텔의) 고급 특실
charge 요금 take advantage of ~을 이용하다

83
Where does the speaker work?
(A) At a hotel
(B) At a travel agency
(C) At an architectural firm
(D) At a cleaning company

화자는 어디에서 일하는가?
(A) 호텔
(B) 여행사
(C) 건축 설계 사무소
(D) 청소 업체

해설 전체 내용 관련 – 화자의 근무지
화자가 초반부에 데스몬드 스미스 씨께 3월 4일 예약 건으로 전화드리는 리젠
시 컴포트 스위트의 주희(this is Joo-Hee from Regency Comfort Suites
calling for Desmond Smith regarding your reservation for March
fourth)라고 했고, 알고 보니 그날은 귀하의 객실이 위치한 4층의 복도 카펫을
모두 세척하기로 되어 있다(It turns out that on that day, we're washing
all the hallway carpets on the fourth floor, where your room is
located)고 객실에 대해 언급하고 있는 것으로 보아 정답은 (A)이다. 참고로,
suite는 고급 객실을 뜻하며 호텔 이름에 자주 사용된다는 것을 알고 있으면 첫
문장만 듣고도 바로 정답을 알 수 있다.

84
고난도

What does the speaker indicate about the listener?
(A) He has recently been hired.
(B) He has won a competition.
(C) He is a member of a rewards club.
(D) He is a professional public speaker.

화자는 청자에 대해 무엇을 암시하는가?
(A) 최근에 고용되었다.
(B) 대회에서 우승했다.
(C) 보상 클럽의 회원이다.
(D) 전문적인 대중 연설가다.

어휘 competition 대회 reward 보상 professional 전문적인

해설 세부 사항 관련 – 화자가 청자에 대해 암시하는 점
화자가 중반부에 저희 고객 보상제의 회원이신 귀하의 편안함과 편리함은 저
희에게 대단히 중요하므로 안심하십시오(But rest assured that, as a
member of our loyalty program, your comfort and convenience are
extremely important to us)라고 한 것으로 보아 정답은 (C)이다.

▸▸ Paraphrasing 담화의 our loyalty program
→ 정답의 a rewards club

85

고난도

What does the speaker say the listener can do?

(A) Try out a new offering
(B) Submit a form electronically
(C) Enjoy upgraded accommodations
(D) Participate in a celebration remotely

화자는 청자가 무엇을 할 수 있다고 말하는가?
(A) 새로운 제품 사용해보기
(B) 온라인으로 양식 제출하기
(C) 업그레이드된 숙박시설 누리기
(D) 원격으로 기념 행사 참가하기

어휘 offering 제공된 것 submit 제출하다 form 양식
electronically 온라인으로 accommodation 숙박 시설
participate in ~에 참가하다 celebration 기념 행사 remotely
원격으로

해설 세부 사항 관련 – 화자가 청자가 할 수 있다고 말하는 것
화자가 후반부에 귀하께 5층의 고급 특실 중 하나를 추가 요금 없이 제공해드
리고 싶다(We'd like to offer you one of our executive suites on the
fifth floor at no extra charge)고 했으므로 정답은 (C)이다.

▸▸ **Paraphrasing** 담화의 **suites** → 정답의 **accommodations**

86-88 안내

M-Au Thank you all for coming to the McAllister
Convention Center's open house. **86I hope
you've enjoyed the tour of our facilities, and
that you might decide to host your next
conference or employee retreat here.** We are
completely booked up for the next six months,
so remember to contact us well in advance.
**87Let me also remind you that our largest
conference room is fully equipped with the
latest audio-visual equipment, so we're the
ideal venue for any events that rely on the use
of advanced technology.** **88We also contract
with the full-service event-planning agency, A
Perfect Night,** so we can help your occasion be
a huge success.

맥알리스터 컨벤션 센터의 오픈 하우스 행사에 와주셔서 감사합니다. **저희 시설
의 견학이 즐거우셨기를 바라며, 다음 회의나 직원 수련회를 이곳에서 주최하기
로 결정하시기를 바랍니다.** 앞으로 6개월 동안 예약이 꽉 찼으니 저희에게 미리
연락을 주시도록 기억해주세요. **저희의 가장 큰 회의실은 최신 시청각 장비가 완
비되어 있어서, 첨단 기술의 활용에 의존하는 어떤 행사에도 이상적인 장소라는
점도 상기시켜드립니다. 저희는 또한 풀서비스 행사 기획사인 퍼펙트 나이트와도
계약을 맺고 있어서** 여러분의 행사가 큰 성공을 거두도록 도울 수 있습니다.

어휘 facility 시설 host 주최하다 conference 회의 retreat
수련회 in advance 미리 remind 상기시키다 equip 장비를
갖추다 latest 최신 equipment 장비 venue 장소 rely on
의존하다 advanced 선진의 contract 계약하다 agency 대행사
occasion 행사 huge 큰

86

고난도

Who most likely are the listeners?

(A) Company shareholders
(B) Potential clients
(C) Volunteer workers
(D) Safety inspectors

청자는 누구일 것 같은가?
(A) 회사 주주
(B) 잠재 고객
(C) 자원봉사 근로자
(D) 안전 검사관

해설 전체 내용 관련 – 청자의 직업
화자가 초반부에 청자들을 향해 저희 시설의 견학이 즐거우셨기를 바라며 다음
회의나 직원 수련회를 이곳에서 주최하기로 결정하시기를 바란다(I hope you've
enjoyed the tour of our facilities, and that you might decide to host
your next conference or employee retreat here)고 한 것으로 보아 정
답은 (B)이다.

87

What does the speaker mention about the convention
center?

(A) It is the largest venue in the region.
(B) It will be renovated soon.
(C) It is affordable to rent.
(D) It uses modern technology.

화자는 컨벤션 센터에 대해 무엇을 언급하는가?
(A) 지역에서 가장 큰 행사장이다.
(B) 곧 개조될 것이다.
(C) 대여하기에 가격이 적당하다.
(D) 현대 기술을 사용한다.

어휘 region 지역 renovate 개조하다 affordable (가격이) 적당한
rent 대여하다 modern 현대의

해설 세부 사항 관련 – 화자가 컨벤션 센터에 대해 언급하는 것
화자가 중반부에 저희의 가장 큰 회의실은 최신 시청각 장비가 완비되어 있어
서, 첨단 기술의 활용에 의존하는 어떤 행사에도 이상적인 장소라는 점도 상
기시켜드린다(Let me also remind you that our largest conference
room is fully equipped with the latest audio-visual equipment,
so we're the ideal venue for any events that rely on the use of
advanced technology)고 했으므로 정답은 (D)이다.

▸▸ **Paraphrasing** 담화의 **latest** → 정답의 **modern**

88

What type of company is A Perfect Night?

(A) A prepared-meal delivery provider
(B) A chauffeur service
(C) An event organizer
(D) An employment agency

퍼펙트 나이트는 어떤 종류의 회사인가?
(A) 미리 조리된 식사 배달 제공업체
(B) 대리운전 서비스
(C) 행사 기획업체
(D) 고용 대행사

어휘 meal 식사 provider 제공업자 chauffeur 운전기사 organizer 조직자 employment 고용

해설 세부 사항 관련 – 퍼펙트 나이트의 업종

화자가 마지막에 저희는 또한 풀서비스 행사 기획사인 퍼펙트 나이트와도 계약을 맺고 있어서 여러분의 행사가 큰 성공을 거두도록 도울 수 있다(We also contract with the full-service event-planning agency, A Perfect Night, so we can help your occasion be a huge success)고 한 것으로 보아 정답은 (C)이다.

▸▸ Paraphrasing 담화의 event-planning agency → 정답의 event organizer

89-91 워크숍 발췌

W-Am All right, let's move on to a particularly difficult area—handling customer complaints. **89On the screen, you can see the four-step process you should follow when you get a complaint.** First, stay calm, even if the customer is upset. Second, listen well and make sure you understand the problem. Ask questions if needed, but not in a challenging way. Third, acknowledge the problem. **90Don't say, "That doesn't sound so bad."** Would you like to hear that? Finally, provide a resolution, such as an apology or refund. **91Now, these are skills that are best learned by doing, so let's partner up and act out sample situations.** Take one of these papers with scenario suggestions.

자, 특히 어려운 분야인 고객 불만 처리로 넘어갑시다. **화면에서 불만이 접수되었을 때 따라야 할 4단계 절차를 볼 수 있습니다.** 첫째, 고객이 화를 내더라도 침착하라. 둘째, 잘 듣고 문제를 확실히 이해하라. 필요한 경우 질문을 하되, 항의하는 방식으로 하지 말라. 셋째, 문제를 인정하라. **"그렇게 나쁜 것 같지 않다"고 말하지 마라.** 여러분은 그 말을 듣고 싶으세요? 마지막으로, 사과나 환불과 같은 해결책을 제공하라. **자, 이러한 것들은 해봄으로써 가장 잘 학습되는 기술이므로 짝을 지어서 샘플 상황을 제연해봅시다.** 시나리오 제안이 나와 있는 이 서류들 중 하나를 가져가세요.

어휘 particularly 특히 handle 다루다 complaint 불만 process 절차 challenging 도전적인, 항의하는 acknowledge 인정하다 resolution 해결책 apology 사과 partner up 짝을 짓다 act out 실연[연출]하다 situation 상황 scenario 시나리오, 기본 suggestion 제안

89

What does the speaker show on a screen?

(A) A list of actions
(B) A customer profile
(C) A set of statistics
(D) A Web page

화자는 화면에서 무엇을 보여주는가?
(A) 행동 목록
(B) 고객 프로필
(C) 일련의 통계
(D) 웹페이지

해설 세부 사항 관련 – 화자가 화면에서 보여주는 것

화자가 초반부에 화면에서 불만이 접수되었을 때 따라야 할 4단계 절차를 볼 수 있다(On the screen, you can see the four-step process you should follow when you get a complaint)고 했으므로 정답은 (A)이다.

90 고난도

Why does the speaker say, "Would you like to hear that"?

(A) To confirm that she should set up some audio equipment
(B) To express surprise at the listeners' interest in a story
(C) To make the listeners consider another person's perspective
(D) To indicate that a certain part of the workshop is unpopular

화자가 "여러분은 그 말을 듣고 싶으세요"라고 말하는 이유는 무엇인가?
(A) 일부 오디오 장비를 설치해야 하는지 확인하려고
(B) 이야기에 대한 청자들의 관심에 놀라움을 표현하려고
(C) 청자들이 다른 사람의 관점을 고려하도록 하려고
(D) 워크숍 특정 부분이 인기 없다는 것을 보여주려고

어휘 confirm 확인하다 set up 설치하다 equipment 장비 express 표현하다 surprise 놀라움 interest 관심 consider 고려하다 perspective 관점 indicate 보여주다 certain 특정한 unpopular 인기 없는

해설 화자의 의도 파악 – 여러분은 그 말을 듣고 싶냐는 말의 의도

앞에서 "그렇게 나쁜 것 같지 않다"고 말하지 마라(Don't say, "That doesn't sound so bad.")고 한 뒤, 인용문을 언급했으므로 그 말을 들었을 때 기분이 어떨지 상대방의 입장에서 생각해보라는 의도로 한 말임을 알 수 있다. 따라서 정답은 (C)이다.

91

What will the listeners most likely do next?

(A) Take a short break
(B) Vote on a suggestion
(C) Open some packages
(D) Engage in role plays

청자들은 다음에 무엇을 할 것 같은가?

(A) 짧은 휴식을 취한다.
(B) 제안에 대해 투표한다.
(C) 일부 패키지를 열어본다.
(D) 역할극에 참여한다.

어휘 break 휴식 vote 투표하다 engage in 참여하다 role 역할
play 연극

해설 세부 사항 관련 – 청자들이 다음에 할 일

화자가 후반부에 이러한 것들은 해봄으로써 가장 잘 학습되는 기술이므로, 짝을 지어서 샘플 상황을 재연해보자(these are skills that are best learned by doing, so let's partner up and act out sample situations)고 권했으므로 정답은 (D)이다.

▸▸ Paraphrasing 담화의 **partner up and act out sample
situations** → 정답의 **engage in role plays**

92-94 뉴스 보도

M-Cn Now, on to our top story in local news. **⁹²This is the first day that vehicles will not be allowed to use Fourth Street between Scott Street and Sutter Avenue.** Brilson city council decided to turn that section of the roadway into a pedestrian zone in order to create a pleasant shopping and leisure destination. **⁹³If the zone is a success, its northern boundary may eventually be extended up to Bailey Street.** **⁹⁴To prepare citizens for the zone's implementation, the city government erected signs on neighboring streets and hung notices in the affected public buses last month.** For the next few days, however, drivers and bus passengers in the area should expect some difficulties and delays.

이제, 지역 뉴스의 톱 스토리로 넘어가봅시다. 오늘은 차량들이 스콧 가와 서터 가 사이의 4번 가를 이용할 수 없게 되는 첫날입니다. 브릴슨 시 의회는 쾌적한 쇼핑과 레저 장소를 조성하기 위해 그 구간의 도로를 보행자 구역으로 바꾸기로 결정했습니다. 이 구역이 성공한다면 종국에는 북쪽 경계선이 베일리 가까지 확장될 수도 있습니다. 구역의 시행에 시민들을 대비시키기 위해, 시 당국은 지난달 인접한 거리에 표지판을 세우고 영향을 받는 대중 버스들에 안내문을 걸었습니다. 그러나 앞으로 며칠 동안 이 지역의 운전자와 버스 승객들은 약간의 어려움과 지연을 예상해야 할 것입니다.

어휘 city council 시의회 section 구역, 부분 roadway 도로
pedestrian 보행자 zone 구역 pleasant 쾌적한 leisure
레저, 여가 destination 목적지 northern 북쪽의 boundary
경계(선) eventually 결국 extend 확장하다 citizen 시민
implementation 실행 erect 세우다 neighboring 인접한
notice 안내문 affect 영향을 미치다 passenger 승객 expect
예상하다 difficulty 어려움 delay 지연

92   고난도

What is the news report mainly about?

(A) A forthcoming mode of transportation
(B) The banning of automobiles from a street
(C) Some work to improve the quality of a road
(D) The creation of additional parking facilities

뉴스 보도는 주로 무엇에 관한 것인가?

(A) 앞으로 다가오는 교통수단의 유형
(B) 거리에서의 자동차 금지
(C) 도로의 질을 개선하기 위한 일부 작업
(D) 추가 주차 시설의 조성

어휘 forthcoming 다가오는 mode 유형, 모드 banning 금지
automobile 자동차 improve 개선하다 quality 질 creation
설립, 조성 facility 시설

해설 전체 내용 관련 – 뉴스 보도의 주제

화자가 초반부에 오늘은 차량들이 스콧 가와 서터 가 사이의 4번 가를 이용할 수 없게 되는 첫날(This is the first day that vehicles will not be allowed to use Fourth Street between Scott Street and Sutter Avenue)이라고 한 뒤 관련 소식에 대해 계속 전하고 있으므로 정답은 (B)이다.

▸▸ Paraphrasing 담화의 **vehicles will not be allowed**
→ 정답의 **the banning of automobiles**

93   고난도

What does the speaker indicate about a project?

(A) It is intended to reduce environmental damage.
(B) It is opposed by a merchants' association.
(C) Its scope might expand in the future.
(D) It was carried out successfully in other cities.

화자는 프로젝트에 대해 무엇을 암시하는가?

(A) 환경 피해를 줄이기 위한 것이다.
(B) 상인 협회에서 반대한다.
(C) 향후 범위가 확대될 수도 있다.
(D) 다른 도시들에서 성공적으로 실행되었다.

어휘 intend 의도하다 reduce 줄이다 environmental 환경의
oppose 반대하다 merchant 상인 association 협회 scope
범위 expand 확대하다 carry out 실행하다

해설 세부 사항 관련 – 화자가 프로젝트에 대해 암시한 것

화자가 중반부에 이 구역이 성공한다면 종국에는 북쪽 경계선이 베일리 가까지 확장될 수도 있다(If the zone is a success, its northern boundary may eventually be extended up to Bailey Street)고 했으므로 정답은 (C)이다.

94 　　고난도

What did the city government do for citizens in the past month?

(A) Notified them of an upcoming change
(B) Surveyed them about a proposal
(C) Relaxed a local regulation
(D) Held a special public event

시 당국은 지난달에 시민들을 위해 무엇을 했는가?
(A) 곧 있을 변화에 대한 알림
(B) 제안에 대한 설문 조사
(C) 지역 규제 완화
(D) 특별 공공 행사 개최

어휘　notify 알리다　upcoming 곧 있을　survey 설문 조사하다
proposal 제안　relax 완화하다　regulation 규제

해설　세부 사항 관련 – 시 당국에서 시민들을 위해 지난달에 한 일
화자가 후반부에 구역의 시행에 시민들을 대비시키기 위해 시 당국이 지난달 인접한 거리에 표지판을 세우고 영향을 받는 대중 버스들에 안내문을 걸었다(To prepare citizens for the zone's implementation, the city government erected signs on neighboring streets and hung notices in the affected public buses last month)고 했으므로 정답은 (A)이다.

95-97 전화 메시지 + 카페 배치도

M-Au　Hi, my name is Silvio Esposito. **95I was at your café this afternoon to network with a professional contact, and I think I left my umbrella behind.** I didn't notice until later because the rain had stopped by the time we left. Did you happen to find it? It's a black umbrella with white trim around the edges, and **96I was sitting in the booth closest to the window,** in case that helps. If you do find it, please set it aside behind your counter and let me know. **97It was a present from my daughter, so I'd really like to get it back.** My number is 555-0196. Thank you.

안녕하세요, 제 이름은 실비오 에스포지토입니다. **오늘 오후에 직업상 지인과 교류하기 위해 당신의 카페에 있었는데 제 우산을 두고 온 것 같아요.** 우리가 떠날 때쯤 비가 그쳐서 나중에야 알았어요. 혹시라도 찾으셨나요? 가장자리 둘레에 흰 장식이 달린 검정색 우산이고, 혹시 도움이 될까 해서 말씀드리면, **저는 창문에서 가장 가까운 칸막이 공간에 앉아 있었어요.** 만약 찾으시면 카운터 뒤쪽에 챙겨두시고 제게 알려주세요. **딸이 준 선물이어서 정말 되찾고 싶어요.** 제 번호는 555-0196입니다. 고맙습니다.

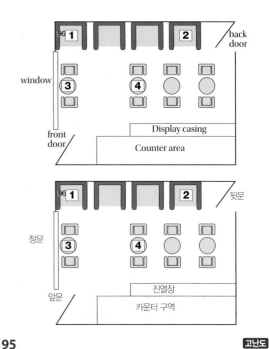

95 　　고난도

What was the speaker mainly doing at the café?

(A) Engaging in a leisure activity
(B) Completing some freelance work
(C) Speaking with a business associate
(D) Studying for a professional exam

화자는 카페에서 주로 무엇을 하고 있었는가?
(A) 여가 활동 참여
(B) 자유 계약 업무 완수
(C) 사업 관계자와 대화
(D) 전문 시험 공부

어휘　engage in ~에 참여하다　leisure 여가　activity 활동
complete 완수하다　associate 동료, 제휴자　exam 시험

해설　세부 사항 관련 – 화자가 카페에서 주로 하던 일
화자가 초반부에 오늘 오후에 직업상 지인과 교류하기 위해 당신의 카페에 있었는데, 우산을 두고 온 것 같다(I was at your café this afternoon to network with a professional contact, and I think I left my umbrella behind)고 했으므로 정답은 (C)이다.

96

Look at the graphic. At which location was the speaker sitting?

(A) 1
(B) 2
(C) 3
(D) 4

시각 정보에 의하면, 화자는 어느 위치에 앉아 있었는가?

(A) 1
(B) 2
(C) 3
(D) 4

해설　시각 정보 연계 – 화자가 앉아 있던 위치

화자가 중반부에 창문에서 가장 가까운 칸막이 공간에 앉아 있었다(I was sitting in the booth closest to the window)고 했고, 카페 배치도에 따르면 창문에서 가장 가까운 칸막이 공간 자리는 1번이므로 정답은 (A)이다.

97

What does the speaker say about the umbrella?

(A) It was expensive.
(B) It was a gift.
(C) Its design is unique.
(D) It belongs to a relative.

화자는 우산에 대해 무엇을 말하는가?

(A) 비쌌다.
(B) 선물이었다.
(C) 디자인이 독특하다.
(D) 가족의 것이다.

어휘　expensive 비싼　unique 독특한　belong to ~ 소유다

해설　세부 사항 관련 – 화자가 우산에 대해 말한 것

화자가 후반부에 딸이 준 선물이어서 정말 되찾고 싶다(It was a present from my daughter, so I'd really like to get it back)고 했으므로 정답은 (B)이다.

▸▸ **Paraphrasing**　담화의 **a present** → 정답의 **a gift**

98-100 회의 발췌 + 도표

W-Br All right, it's been a month since we released the Little Artist painting set, and it hasn't been the success that we'd hoped. It's the lowest-selling new art product on Hall's Market's Web site, and the figures from Success Arts are only a little better. However, we've received great customer reviews from the people who do buy it. **⁹⁸In fact, Little Artist is the second highest rated product in Delta Mall Online's art department, and third on Creative Ideas. So clearly it has the potential to be popular. ⁹⁹I believe we should expand our advertising campaign for it. ¹⁰⁰Jenny, how much money do we have available to put towards that?** You know our budget the best.

자, 우리가 리틀 아티스트 그림 세트를 발매한 지 한 달이 지났는데, 우리가 바라던 성공은 아니었습니다. 이것은 홀스 마켓의 웹사이트에서 가장 적게 팔리는 미술 신제품이며, 석세스 아트의 수치는 조금 더 나을 뿐입니다. 하지만 우리는 그것을 구매한 사람들로부터 훌륭한 고객 평가를 받았습니다. 사실, 리틀 아티스트는 델타몰 온라인 미술 부문에서 두 번째로 높은 등급을 받은 제품이고, 크리에이티브 아이디어에서는 세 번째입니다. 그러니 분명히 인기를 끌 수 있는 잠재력이 있습니다. 저는 우리의 광고 캠페인을 확대해야 한다고 믿습니다. 제니, 그쪽으로 투입 가능한 돈이 얼마나 있죠? 우리 예산은 당신이 가장 잘 알잖아요.

어휘　release 공개[발표]하다　success 성공　figure 수치　in fact 사실　rated ~ 등급의　department 부서　clearly 분명히　potential 잠재력　expand 확대하다　advertising campaign 광고 캠페인　available 이용 가능한　budget 예산

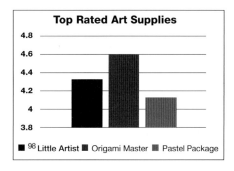

Top Rated Art Supplies

■ ⁹⁸Little Artist　■ Origami Master　■ Pastel Package

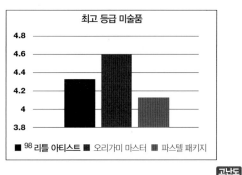

최고 등급 미술품

■ ⁹⁸리틀 아티스트　■ 오리가미 마스터　■ 파스텔 패키지

98　고난도

Look at the graphic. What Web site is the chart for?

(A) Hall's Market
(B) Success Arts
(C) Delta Mall Online
(D) Creative Ideas

시각 정보에 의하면, 이 차트는 어느 웹사이트의 것인가?

(A) 홀스 마켓
(B) 석세스 아트
(C) 델타몰 온라인
(D) 크리에이티브 아이디어

화자가 중반부에 리틀 아티스트는 델타몰 온라인 미술 부문에서 두 번째로 높은 등급을 받은 제품이고, 크리에이티브 아이디어에서는 세 번째(Little Artist is the second highest rated product in Delta Mall Online's art department, and third on Creative Ideas)라고 했고, 도표에 따르면 리틀 아티스트는 두 번째로 높은 등급을 받았으므로 해당 도표는 델타몰 온라인의 것임을 알 수 있다. 따라서 정답은 (C)이다.

99　[고난도]

What does the speaker propose doing?

(A) Hiring a consulting firm
(B) Expanding a product line
(C) Renegotiating a contract
(D) Increasing a promotional effort

화자는 무엇을 하자고 제안하는가?
(A) 컨설팅 회사 고용
(B) 제품군 확대
(C) 계약 재협상
(D) 판촉 활동 증대

어휘 consulting 자문 firm 회사 renegotiate 재협상하다
increase 늘리다 promotional 판촉의 effort 노력, 활동

해설 세부 사항 관련 – 화자의 제안 사항
화자가 후반부에 자신은 우리의 광고 캠페인을 확대해야 한다고 믿는다(I believe we should expand our advertising campaign for it)고 했으므로 정답은 (D)이다.

> ▸▸ Paraphrasing　담화의 **expand our advertising campaign**
> → 정답의 **increasing a promotional effort**

100

What does the speaker ask Jenny about?

(A) Some financial resources
(B) Some employees' availability
(C) A manufacturing process
(D) A competitor's practices

화자는 제니에게 무엇에 대해 묻는가?
(A) 일부 금융 자원
(B) 일부 직원의 참석 가능성
(C) 제조 공정
(D) 경쟁사의 관행

어휘 financial 금융의 resource 자원 availability 이용 가능성
manufacturing 제조 process 과정 competitor 경쟁자
practice 관행, 실무

해설 세부 사항 관련 – 화자가 제니에게 묻는 것
화자가 후반부에 제니(Jenny)를 부르며 그쪽으로 투입 가능한 돈이 얼마나 있는지(how much money do we have available to put towards that?)를 묻고 있으므로 정답은 (A)이다.

> ▸▸ Paraphrasing　담화의 **money**
> → 정답의 **some financial resources**